THE
PROCESS OF
SOCIAL
INFLUENCE

Edited by

THOMAS D. BEISECKER

DONN W. PARSON

University of Kansas

THE
PROCESS OF
SOCIAL
INFLUENCE

Readings in Persuasion

ABBOT MEMORIAL LIBRARY
EMERSON COLLEGE

Prentice-Hall, Inc., Englewood Cliffs, New Jersey

HM
291
B384

© 1972 by Prentice-Hall, Inc., Englewood Cliffs, N. J.

All rights reserved. No part of this book may be
reproduced in any form or by any means without
permission in writing from the publisher.

Library of Congress Catalog Card Number: 77–164923

Printed in the United States of America

C 13–723312–4
P 13–723304–3

Current Printing (last digit):
10 9 8 7 6 5 4 3 2 1

PRENTICE-HALL INTERNATIONAL, INC., London
PRENTICE-HALL OF AUSTRALIA, PTY. LTD., Sydney
PRENTICE-HALL OF CANADA, LTD., Toronto
PRENTICE-HALL OF INDIA PRIVATE LIMITED, New Delhi
PRENTICE-HALL OF JAPAN, INC., Tokyo

PREFACE

This book is an attempt to synthesize primarily experimental studies of the process of social influence. The importance of persuasion as a method for social influence can hardly be underestimated, but a clear understanding of this process is difficult to obtain since investigations of relevant variables have been scattered across numerous disciplines. In this book we attempt to pull together material from several disciplines to provide a more cohesive picture of factors involved in persuasion. We have attempted to do this by choosing selections which draw together and organize significant bodies of research. We have normally given preference to reviews and critical analyses of research areas over reports of individual experiments. In addition we have attempted to include selections by individuals who represent diverse orientations to the study of persuasion and who have made significant contributions to the field.

Several persons have contributed to the development and evaluation of this book. We are indebted to David Swanson and Jesse Delia for their suggestions of organizational patterns and material to be included. Students in a graduate seminar in persuasion also contributed to the evaluation of potential selections. B. L. Ware, Jr. and Steve Hunt assisted with the preparation of the manuscript. Finally, we are indebted to our wives, Analee and Andrea, for their evaluation and criticism of the manuscript, their assistance with proofreading, and above all their extreme patience throughout the two years of this project.

CONTENTS

SECTION III
CHARACTERISTICS OF THE MESSAGE   **271**

SECTION IV
THE EFFECTS OF PERSUASION   **371**

THE
PROCESS OF
SOCIAL
INFLUENCE

INTRODUCTION

The question of how one individual or group influences the attitudes or behavior of others recurs throughout our lives. Each of us is involved in the process of social influence, both because we often attempt to influence someone else, and because we are constantly targets for attempts at social influence. We want others to vote for our favorite political candidate, to stop misusing insecticides, to quit smoking, or to prefer baseball to football. On the other hand, we receive appeals to donate money and time to various causes, to purchase specific brands of products, to support or oppose the United Nations.

Given the importance of social influence, it should not be surprising that the process by which individuals go about forming, maintaining and changing attitudes has attracted considerable research attention. In the last eighteen years, for example, over fifteen hundred articles which discuss some aspect of this process have appeared in professional journals alone. The research reported in these articles has come from many academic disciplines, among them psychology, sociology, speech, business, journalism, and communications. The basic approaches employed have varied, and the results have not always been consistent.

For the student who is just becoming acquainted with this area, or one who wishes only an overview of the activity within it, this voluminous amount of material presents a mixed blessing. On one hand, he has available a wealth of material on almost any aspect of the process of persuasion or attitude change. On the other hand, the mass of information available may be so great or widely scattered that he is unable to obtain an adequate perspective. We attempt to cope with this problem. The primary purpose of this book is to survey and synthesize current experimental research central to important variables in the process of persuasion. Its secondary purpose is to introduce the reader to the positions and orientations of several authors who have provided major contributions to the field.

The general focus of the book is psychological. That is, it emphasizes the role

1

played by individuals in the persuasive process rather than influence through mass communication. Certainly many of the principles treated in these essays have relevance to the process of mass influence; however, a direct discussion of their relevance is beyond the scope of this book.

Various authors have suggested alternate—occasionally incompatible—frameworks for approaching attitude change and persuasion. Each author has then interpreted experimental data in terms of his particular orientation. As a result, no one comprehensive theory capable of accounting for all, or even most, experimental findings currently exists. What does exist is a group of less comprehensive theories, each capable of explaining relevant data in more specialized areas. For this reason, we have avoided adopting one theoretical orientation. Rather, we have attempted to present a number of theoretical orientations where they best explain aspects of the persuasive process.

THE RELATIONSHIP BETWEEN ATTITUDES AND PERSUASION

Despite the fact that the study of attitude formation, attitude change, and persuasion has accounted for a substantial body of literature, the relationship between the concepts of attitude and persuasion remains relatively ambiguous. One underlying assumption of this book is that these two concepts are closely interrelated. We shall identify the nature of this relationship shortly, after we define the concepts themselves.

Currently there exists no universally accepted definition for the concept of attitude. Recent definitions have ranged from treating an attitude as an entirely mental process to defining it as a behavioral response syndrome. For example, Osgood and Tannenbaum state that "the *meaning* of a concept is its location in a space defined by some number of factors or dimensions, and *attitude* toward a concept is its projection onto one of these dimensions defined as 'evaluative'" (16, p. 42). Similarly, Insko summarizes his discussion of the concept of attitude by contending:

> ... more recent definitions focus on the affective tendency to favorably or unfavorably evaluate objects and entirely discard the notion that any overt behavior is implied. The most common contemporary usage seems to follow this example, thus regarding the evaluative dimension as the single defining dimension for attitude (11, p. 2).

In contrast, DeFleur and Westie suggest that "attitude is equated with the probability of recurrence of behavior forms of a given type or direction," (8, p. 21) and Cronkhite concurs, calling it "a cluster of evaluative or approach-avoidance behavior" (7, p. 12).

It seems likely that no single definitional approach to the concept of attitude will prove uniquely best suited for all investigative frameworks. McGuire comments:

> It is unlikely that any one approach to defining attitudes will be superior to the others in all regards. There are numerous desiderata for such definitions—testability, parsimony, heuristic constructs, generality, etc.—and it is unlikely that one choice of definition will optimize all of them (14, p. 149).

Nevertheless, for the term to have any significant meaning there must exist some attributes of the concept common to at least most of the definitions. The late Arthur R. Cohen implied that such a commonality exists when he circumvented the task of defining attitude and attitude change with the comment:

> This book does not take up the definition and conceptualization of attitude, but instead assumes that there is a commonly accepted core of meaning for the term 'attitude change' which can serve as a working basis in the present review (6, p. xi).

Since it is the purpose of this volume to present material drawn from investigators who have operated under various, and at times diverse, definitions of attitude, we shall not attempt to develop or impose an overall definition which reflects the sentiments of the material included. Rather we shall indicate five attributes of the concept of attitude which tend to recur in current definitions. These are (1) an attitude has an object or focus, (2) it has an evaluative dimension, (3) it is learned, (4) it is enduring, and (5) it results in (or is related to) characteristic and consistent behavior.

Roger Brown comments that "An attitude has always a focus; it may be a person, a group, a nation, a product, anything whatever really" (4, p. 420). Thus, an attitude is pointed toward that which Krech, Crutchfield and Ballachey call a "social object" (13, p. 177).

Second, attitudes possess an evaluative dimension. They reflect an affective relationship between the individual and the social object which can be measured on a like-dislike continuum. As mentioned earlier, Insko contends that this attribute is the single essential attribute in most contemporary definitions.

Third, an attitude is learned. Allport in his pioneering definition suggests that attitudes are "organized through experience" (1, p. 810). More recently Sherif and Sherif have echoed this statement:

> When we talk about attitudes, we are talking about what a person has *learned* in the process of becoming a member of a family, a member of a group, and of society that makes him react to his social work in a *consistent* and *characteristic* way, instead of a transitory and haphazard way (17, p. 2).

McGuire comments that agreement on this attribute is widespread, so much so that "we worry lest the issue may have escaped examination" (14, p. 147).

Fourth, an attitude is "an enduring system" (13, p. 177). It affects an individual over a period of time rather than for just a brief moment. It is something which enables him to exhibit "a syndrome of response consistency with regard to social objects" (5, p. 31).

Finally, an attitude results in (or is related to) overt action and observed behavior. The precise relationship between attitudes and behavior is one which has attracted much recent controversy, and McGuire has identified five distinct positions which have been taken (14, pp. 144-47). We shall examine the issue in greater detail in Section IV. It is sufficient at this point merely to indicate that virtually all who are interested in the phenomena of attitudes and attitude change postulate some relationship between attitudes and behavior. As Kiesler points out, "Thus social philosophers and action-oriented pragmatists have used the concept of attitude because it offered a theoretical explanation for socially significant *behaviors*" (12, p. 8). It is the nature of this relationship which is at issue.

Each of these attributes has been used to generate definitions of attitude. Differences among the definitions derived result from choices of which attribute or attributes to emphasize and the position taken on them. Our goal at this point is not to arbitrarily designate a single definition for attitude, but to indicate the variety of definitions which underlie the material found in this volume.

Like attitude, persuasion has been defined in various ways. As far back as 1952, Brembeck and Howell defined it as "the conscious attempt to modify thought and action by manipulating the motives of men toward predetermined ends" (3, p. 24). English and English, in their *Comprehensive Dictionary of Psychological and Psychoanalytical Terms,* viewed persuasion as "the process of obtaining another's adoption of a course of action, or his assent to a proposition, by an appeal to both feeling and intellect" (9, p. 385). Minnick spoke of persuasion as "discourse, written or oral, in which the author controls all appropriate communication variables in an attempt to determine the response of the receiver toward a particular choice of belief or conduct" (15, p. 6).

For Fotheringham, "Persuasion is conceived as that body of effects in receivers, relevant and instrumental to source-desired goals, brought about by a process in which messages have been a major determinant of those effects" (10, p. 7). Similarly, Cronkhite contends that persuasion refers to "the evaluative or approach-avoidance behavior of those who interpret the symbols" (7, p. 15). Finally, Bettinghaus argues that in order to be persuasive, a communication must involve a "conscious attempt by one individual to change the behavior of another individual or group of individuals through the transmission of some message" (2, p. 13).

Several attributes can be observed in these definitions, although no single definition need include all of them. First, the process of persuasion involves a conscious attempt by one individual to modify the thought or behavior of others. Persuasion is thus related to intent. Second, for some authors the effects produced are central to the persuasive process. The definitions by Fotheringham and Cronkhite most clearly take this position. Third, the persuasive process involves the production and transmission of a message. All definitions included here suggest that the message plays an important role in persuasion. Thus one might view the persuasive message and the process by which it comes to the attention of receivers as central to the concept of persuasion, regardless of whether or not the message succeeds in eliciting a desired response.

If we accept the idea that the existence of a message is central to the concept of persuasion, then the relationship between attitudes and persuasion can be specified. Each individual possesses a "psychological space"—some would term it a response syndrome—which determines his affective relationship with objects. This attitude universe can be modified by many factors: the individual's perceptions, his behavior and how it is rewarded, his felt inconsistencies among cognitions, or conscious attempts to introduce information designed to change his response syndrome (persuasion). Thus persuasion is one process—and perhaps the primary process—by which attitudes are modified, but it is by no means the only process resulting in attitude change.

Persuasion inherently has attitude change as its goal. This rather strong assertion incorporates the assumptions that attitude change is a principal determinant of behavioral change, and that all definitions of persuasion suggest attitude or behavioral change as its goal. There are situations where a persuasive message induces behavioral change without producing immediate corresponding attitude change (forced compliance situations, for example). Such situations, however, do not invalidate the claim that persuasion aims at attitude change. They merely determine the type of persuasive impact produced by a message.

However, while persuasion is a primary factor in attitude change, it is by no means the only vehicle for such change. An individual's opinions may be modified by the social context in which he finds himself. Being caught in a riot may polarize one's opinions much more quickly than being exposed to numerous, well-constructed persuasive messages. It is for these reasons that we contend persuasion usually— but not always—results in attitude change; attitude change often—but not always —is the result of an attempt to persuade.

THE ORGANIZATION OF THE BOOK

The book is divided into four sections: The Psychological Context, The Source: Properties of Speaker Credibility, Characteristics of the Message, and Effects. Our focus in Section I is on characteristics of individual participants in the process of persuasion, whether they be the sender or receiver of the persuasive message. We are interested in the manner in which they maintain or modify initially-held attitudes. This section contains material quite often included under the heading of "receiver." We have relabeled this body of material "Psychological Context" to emphasize that the same psychological processes impinge on the initiator of a persuasive message as well as on the receiver. Often the labeling of one participant as "source" and the other as "receiver" results in the impression that each is subjected to different psychological forces. Such an impression is misleading in most situations, and even designating one participant as "source" (persuader) and the other as "receiver" (persuadee) is impossible to maintain in interpersonal interactions. These roles are continually being interchanged.

Although both the source and receiver of a persuasive message are subject to similar psychological pressures, characteristics of the source often provide additional influence on the effectiveness of the message. Research relevant to this phenomenon is treated in Section II.

Section III deals with factors of message construction which influence the persuasiveness of the message. The material in this section focuses more on the structural aspects of a persuasive message, the types of appeals used, the use of evidence, and the order of arguments.

Section IV focuses on the residual effects of the persuasive message. The research presented here deals with the amount of change produced by a message, the likelihood that any attitude change produced will be retained and under what conditions, the relationship between the attitudes and behaviors of individuals, and the persuasive effect on the source of the message himself (self-persuasion).

REFERENCES

1. ALLPORT, G. W. "Attitudes." *Handbook of Social Psychology,* C. Murchison, Ed. New York: Russell & Russell, 1967, v. II, pp. 798–844.
2. BETTINGHAUS, E. P. *Persuasive Communication.* New York: Holt, Rinehart and Winston, 1968.
3. BREMBECK, W. L., and W. S. HOWELL. *Persuasion, A Means of Social Control.* New York: Prentice-Hall, 1952.
4. BROWN, R. *Social Psychology.* New York: Free Press, 1965.
5. CAMPBELL, D. T. "The Indirect Assessment of Social Attitudes," *Psychological Bulletin,* 47 (1950), 15–38.
6. COHEN, A. R. *Attitude Change and Social Influence.* New York: Basic Books, 1964.
7. CRONKHITE, G. *Persuasion: Speech and Behavioral Change.* New York: Bobbs-Merrill, 1969.
8. DeFLEUR, M. L., and F. R. WESTIE. "Attitude as a Scientific Concept," *Social Forces,* 42 (1963), 17–31.
9. ENGLISH, H. B., and A. C. ENGLISH. *A Comprehensive Dictionary of Psychological and Psychoanalytical Terms.* New York: Longmans, Green and Co., 1958.
10. FOTHERINGHAM, W. C. *Perspectives on Persuasion.* Boston: Allyn and Bacon, 1966.
11. INSKO, C. A. *Theories of Attitude Change.* New York: Appleton-Century-Crofts, 1967.
12. KIESLER, C. A., B. E. COLLINS, and N. MILLER. *Attitude Change: A Critical Analysis of Theoretical Approaches.* New York: Wiley, 1969.
13. KRECH, D., R. S. CRUTCHFIELD, and E. L. BALLACHEY. *Individual in Society.* New York: McGraw-Hill, 1962.
14. McGUIRE, W. J. "The Nature of Attitudes and Attitude Change," in *The Handbook of Social Psychology,* 2nd Edition, G. Lindzey and E. Aronson, Eds. Reading, Mass.: Addison-Wesley, 1969, v. III, pp. 136–314.
15. MINNICK, W. C. *The Art of Persuasion.* Boston: Houghton-Mifflin, 1957.
16. OSGOOD, C. E., and P. H. TANNENBAUM. "The Principle of Congruity in the Prediction of Attitude Change," *Psychological Review,* 62 (1955), 42–55.
17. SHERIF, C. W., and M. SHERIF, Eds. *Attitude, Ego-Involvement and Change.* New York: Wiley, 1967.

SECTION I

THE PSYCHOLOGICAL CONTEXT

OVERVIEW

It may seem paradoxical to begin our consideration of the persuasive process by focusing on the psychological context. In one sense, the persuader has the least control over those factors involved in the psychological make-up of the receiver. Yet on the other hand, the psychological context is crucial to the process of persuasion, since any persuasive effect is inevitably linked to the psychological make-up of the receiver.

Our consideration in Section I is divided into two parts: The Principles of Attitude Change and Other Psychological Factors. In Part I we deal with commonalities—those psychological operations which are supposedly the same for all people. In Part II we look at individual differences which partially account for the variations among responses to a persuasive attempt.

PART I: BASIC PRINCIPLES OF ATTITUDE CHANGE

In this part we consider several different attempts to identify psychological operations which act as common denominators in the attitude change process. The identification of such common denominators has attracted considerable attention. Proposals have been advanced from a variety of theoretical perspectives, with the result that there exist a number of distinct theories, each purporting to explain some facet of the attitude change process. Insko (11), for example, identifies and elaborates thirteen different theoretical approaches. Although we can distinguish a number of distinct theories, these theories can be grouped into four broad orientations according to their central assumptions. These four categories include (1) Functional Theories, (2) Consistency Theories, (3) Learning Theories, and (4) The Social Judgment-Involvement Approach.

As the name implies, functional theories are characterized by the assumption that an individual's attitudes are determined by the functions that they serve for him. Consistency theories all share the assumption that an individual strives for internal harmony in his belief system, and between his beliefs and overt behavior. Learning theories assume that attitudes—like other forms of behavior—can be acquired and modified through reinforcement. The Social Judgment-Involvement approach focuses on the influence that an individual's perception of an object or message has on his response to it. Each of these four perspectives will be discussed separately in some detail. However, one issue relating to all four deserves prior consideration.

One assumption commonly made is that an individual's attitudes and motives are related. That is, a person's attitude toward the construction of a Country Fried Chicken franchise across the street from his house is influenced, to some extent, by his having a perpetual craving for country fried chicken. Or, if someone holds positive attitudes toward two contradictory types of behavior—for example, good grades and no studying, this disparity will result in some kind of seemingly appropriate behavior—such as enrolling in courses requiring little effort. In the first case, the person's motives influenced his attitudes toward an object. In the second, his attitudes influenced his motivational state. But to say that an individual's attitudes and motives are related is at best a general statement. If we want to infer an individual's attitudes from his motives (or vice-versa) we must further specify the nature of the relationship by examining the characteristics of a motive state and then suggesting the role played by attitudes.

The concept of a motive state involves two dimensions, energy and direction. When a motive is aroused, the individual initiates and continues behavior until that motive is satisfied. The behavior is not random. It is directed toward achieving specific ends—ends which are perceived as satisfying the motive state.

The arousal and maintenance of a motive state involve (1) two or more psychological processes somehow associated and hence mutually activating, (2) which are seen as disparate—that is, in some sense incompatible, (3) and which arouse in the individual forces for assimilation or isolation. As long as these forces are in equilibrium the motive state will remain aroused; when either assimilation or isolation predominates, the motivation will cease.[1] Thus the lazy student is motivated. His desire for good grades is disparate with his attitude toward study. Since grades and study are associated, and hence the attitudes associated are mutually self-activating, they create a tension-producing situation. This motive state will exist and produce activity until the student satisfies himself that good grades are no longer desirable, that studying is rewarding, or that good grades can be obtained without study.

Attitudes influence motives, and motives affect attitudes. Attitudes toward two or more separate but related concepts create a disparity relationship, and hence bring about the arousal of a motive state. Attitudes are a function of an individual's prior motivational states in the sense that an individual's affective relationship with

[1] The principles discussed here have been adapted from an article by Helen Peak (16).

concepts is determined by how those concepts assist or hinder his efforts to obtain desired goals.

It may appear that the task of identifying the basic principles of attitude change is relatively simple. Identify an individual's motives and you will be able to infer his attitudes and their influence. Unfortunately this task is not simple, for motives have proved difficult to isolate. Katz comments:

> Attempts at such typologies [of human needs and their characteristic properties] however, have produced little agreement and it is not difficult to understand why. Even the simplest biological drives become so intertwined with social motives that they are difficult if not impossible to unscramble. People seek gratification of hunger, sex, and shelter in ways which accord with their self-esteem. Moreover, the nature of ego needs and the direction they assume is so complex as to defy classificatory analysis. The difficulties with motivational analysis in fact constitute one of the reasons for the increasing interest in cognitive theory (12, pp. 179–80).

A. Functional Theories

Katz does suggest one way to circumvent the problem of specifying individual needs, by considering "broad motivational patterns of differing characteristics" (12, p. 180). This consideration is essentially the focus of functional theories. The functional approach to the study of attitudes stresses classifying the characteristics of observable behavior rather than speculating about unobservable needs. Functional theorists assume that behavior can be classified, and that attitudes will relate to the various classes of behavior in different ways. Because of this, the emphasis of the functionalist approach is on the manner in which an individual's attitudes serve him in achieving his basic goals, and little emphasis is placed on his perception of, knowledge of, or even behavior toward concepts. "Hence, attitude change is achieved not so much by changing the person's information about, perception of, or behavior toward the object, but rather by changing the believer's underlying motivational and personality needs" (14, p. 270).

The two illustrations of functional theories which are included here, those by Katz and Kelman, share these central assumptions. They differ, however, on the criteria used to classify behavior. For Katz, behavior is classified in terms of how it relates to individual needs. In this sense, Katz's position is perhaps most typical of the functionalist approach. According to him, all human behavior can be classified as either instrumental, ego-defensive, value-expressive, or knowledge-seeking. Thus, as his essay suggests, all attitudes function relative to one or more of these four classes.

Kelman, on the other hand, classifies human behavior in terms of how it relates to external sources of influence. "Specific needs are not described but it is assumed that the change process will be differentially related to the power of the influencing agent, his attractiveness, and his credibility" (12, p. 180). The Kelman essay develops and interrelates three different processes of social influence: compliance, identification, and internalization.

Because Katz and Kelman use different criteria to classify human behavior, it is difficult to compare directly the systems they develop. Moreover, by employing other sets of criteria, still different classification systems for attitudes can be devised. For example, Smith, Bruner, and White (19) argue that attitudes can be classified into those which assist an individual either in his appraisal of objects, his social adjustment, or as externalizations of his internal tension.

The validity of each functional approach rests on the justification of the criteria for classification. One argument raised concerning these approaches is that criteria have been developed from empirical rather than theoretical grounds, and therefore many functional systems possess no prior logical claim. In other words, why is one method of classifying attitudes better than another? If this question cannot be answered, why should any functional system be preferred to another, or, indeed, why should any functional system be preferred at all? Insko (11) suggests that a partial answer to this question may be provided by factor analysis studies of individuals' attitude clusters.

B. Consistency Theories

One of the behavioral functions identified by Katz is the knowledge, or cognitive function. According to Katz, individuals "seek knowledge to give meaning to what would otherwise be an unorganized chaotic universe" (13, p. 175). Consistency theories focus on this function and attempt to describe the rules and procedures involved.

Consistency theories include a number of specific theories, each of which makes the assumption that an individual attempts to avoid psychologically inconsistent cognitions. These theories fall under the general headings of balance, congruity, and dissonance. Within each of these headings, numerous formulations exist. For example, Heider (8), Newcomb (15), Abelson and Rosenberg (1), Cartwright and Harary (3), and Feather (6) all provide different formulations of balance theory.

The term "consistency" implies that these authors presume a form of "rational" behavior. However this rationality must not be confused with the rules of formal logic. Abelson and Rosenberg (1) argue that an individual's behavior conforms to a set of "psychological" rules. These rules define a consistent yet perhaps not formally valid inference-making structure. For example, suppose you are a Republican. Chances are you do not like socialists. In addition, you probably do not like communists. But you probably believe that socialists like communists. Obviously inference patterns such as this one are not "logical" in a formal sense. Nevertheless, they are intuitively satisfying. That is, they conform to a type of "psycho-logic." While the terminology of "psycho-logic" is not found in the writings of many consistency theorists, the concept expressed is implicit in their theories.

We have included two selections indicative of consistency theory approaches. The article by Zajonc provides an exceptionally clear and concise summary of the theories of balance, congruity and dissonance. In addition it suggests the basic interrelationships and commonalities among these three versions of consistency theory.

The selection by Abelson focuses on one issue central to the predictive capabilities of consistency theory. Since consistency theory postulates a system of cognitions and their relationships, any unbalanced system may be balanced in a number of ways. For example, you and one of your friends disagree on the merits of a certain rock band. This disagreement defines an unbalanced cognitive system. There are a number of ways in which you can restore balance. You can persuade your friend to change his evaluation of the group, or you in turn can be persuaded by him. You can consciously or unconsciously misperceive his evaluation of the group. You can differentiate the concept of the group into two or more new concepts in such a way that the two of you agree on both newly defined concepts.[2] You can tacitly refuse to continue the discussion, thus achieving balance by isolating the inconsistent components. Finally, you can decide you no longer like your friend.

Although in this situation you have a number of choices available, some may be more likely to occur. In other words, the alternatives may form a hierarchy in which some are more frequent. This is the thesis of the Abelson article.

C. Learning Theories

How are attitudes created? The answer most commonly given is that they are learned. People associate concepts such as liberal, Republican, professor, or military with whether or not the concepts affect them favorably. Based on these associations they assign evaluative connotations (that is, attitudes) to the concepts. For example, a small boy becomes aware that frequently when he practices his violin, he cannot play ball with his friends. Since he enjoys playing ball, his violin sessions are paired with an unfavorable outcome and hence he acquires a negative attitude toward practicing.

Attitudes are learned through association. The manner in which attitudes are associated with concepts can either take the form of classical conditioning or instrumental learning. In the process of classical conditioning, concepts with already developed attitudes are paired with concepts without strong evaluative valences. As a result of this pairing, the previously more neutral concept acquires similar evaluative dimensions to those associated with the other concept. Thus, for our young J. Heifitz, the fact that he cannot play ball is paired with his music practice, and eventually the negative attitude he holds toward being absent from the baseball diamond becomes associated with his violin. Staats (20) provided evidence of this process when they demonstrated that if a neutral word (Dutch) is paired with evaluative words (sacred, happy, bitter, or ugly) the neutral word takes on the evaluative meaning of the words with which it is paired.

Attitudes can also be formed and modified through instrumental learning. In this process an individual first reacts evaluatively to a concept (that is, expressing an attitude). This reaction is subsequently reinforced. If the reinforcement is positive, then the attitude expressed is strengthened. If the reinforcement is negative, then the expressed attitude is weakened and may ultimately be extinguished or replaced by another attitude. Thus, if our frustrated ballplayer comments to a friend that he thinks practicing the violin is worthless and his friend agrees, his negative attitude toward violin practicing will be strengthened. If he makes a similar statement to his mother, her reinforcement is likely to be negative and *theoretically* his negative attitude toward practicing should be weakened.

[2] Perhaps your friend dislikes the lead vocalist, and you agree that the lead vocalist is poor but that the rest of the group is good.

The overall relation between attitudes and learning is explored in the selection by Doob. He defines the concept of attitude in terms of learning principles and argues that research concerning attitudes and attitude change can be subsumed under research on learning behavior. His conclusion is that behavior associated with attitudes is governed by the same principles that govern other forms of behavior and hence is not conceptually unique. Attitudes, according to Doob, are just another form of learned human behavior.

While Doob considers the general relationship between attitudes and behavior, there is one aspect of this relationship which deserves additional attention—the learning and modifying of attitudes as the result of persuasive messages. According to Weiss (22) the persuasive message can be conceptualized as a vehicle for either classical conditioning or instrumental learning. When used as a medium for classical conditioning, the message first presents some concept which serves as a cue statement. This concept is then paired with an opinion-eliciting argument. If the pairing is repeated, then the opinion elicited becomes associated with the concept. When cast in the framework of instrumental learning, the persuasive message contains both an opinion to be learned and some form of reinforcement. The precise nature of the reinforcement depends on the message source, the context within which the message is presented, or the verbal argument presented by the message.

The selection by Hovland, Janis, and Kelley focuses on the relationship between the persuasive situation and the learning process. It is included primarily because it provides an overview of the assumptions of the Yale group of attitude researchers. The impact of this group on the direction of attitude change research has been enduring.

D. The Social Judgment-Involvement Approach

One basic psychological process is that of comparative judgment—the process through which people evaluate attributes of objects and concepts. For example, we judge an object as heavy by comparing its weight to that of a similar object. We judge one pan of water to be hot by comparing its temperature to that of another pan. Or, we judge someone to be tall by comparing his height to that of other people. The process of comparative judgment also applies to an individual's system of attitudes. Over forty years ago Thurstone (21) postulated that individuals could compare two statements about an issue and judge which of the statements was more favorable or unfavorable to that issue. But does an individual's opinion on an issue influence his ability to judge the position of statements made about that issue? Thurstone assumed that it did not: "If the scale is to be regarded as valid, the scale values of the statements should not be affected by the opinions of the people who help to construct it" (21, p. 92).

More recently this position has been challenged. Hovland and Sherif (10), for example, found that subjects who held extreme views on an issue tended not to discriminate among statements contradictory to their position. For example, when pro-Negro subjects evaluated attitude statements concerning Negroes, they tended to group together both neutral and anti-Negro statements. What this evidence suggested was that the position held by an individual on an issue influenced the manner in which he discriminated among statements made about that issue. His own position provided him with an "anchor"—a reference point from which to judge other positions.

This finding forms the basis of the Social Judgment-Involvement approach to attitude change. The key assumption of this approach is that the manner in which an individual perceives and classifies a message determines the influence the message has on him. Attitude statements about an issue can be ordered on a continuum ranging from those completely favorable to those totally opposed. Some place on this continuum an individual identifies that point which most closely approximates his own opinion (his anchor) and a surrounding area of statements which he finds acceptable. He also identifies areas of statements which are unacceptable. If he classifies a persuasive communication within the area of acceptable statements (his latitude of acceptance), then he will assimilate the position presented by the communication toward his own. If he classifies a persuasive communication within an area of unacceptable statements (his latitude of rejection), then he will contrast the position presented away from his own. The influence provided by the persuasive message, therefore, depends on the initial message classification.

The size of an individual's latitudes of acceptance and rejection is determined primarily by his ego-involvement with the issue. As an individual's ego-involvement increases, the proportional size of his latitude of rejection to his latitude of acceptance increases. The most complete statement of the Social Judgment-Involvement approach is contained in *Attitude and Attitude Change,* by Sherif, Sherif, and Nebergall. The selection included here is taken from their summary statement.

PART II:
OTHER PSYCHOLOGICAL FACTORS

Thus far in this section we have discussed principles of attitude change which affect individual recipients of a persuasive message similarly. However, when a persuasive message is presented to an audience, wide variations in the response of individual members usually occur. Some audience members are completely persuaded by the message. Others remain unconvinced or become increasingly opposed to the position advocated. That is, there exist substantial individual variations in message responses.

Furthermore, individual variations in responses to persuasive messages usually are not randomly distributed across audience members. Some audience members are convinced by persuasive messages regardless of the topic. Some are susceptible to influence only on particular types of topics. Still others react negatively to any attempt at influence. The individual differences in responses to persuasive messages are somewhat consistent within each audience member.

This part focuses on psychological factors which account, at least partially, for these individual differences and their consistencies. We divide our consideration into three aspects. First, we examine differences in effects which result from the personality characteristics of the receiver. Second, we consider those factors which prompt individuals to avail themselves of information or isolate themselves from it. Finally, we examine the effect of preparing an individual for a persuasive message, either by warning him about the impending message or by inoculating him against its effects.

A. Personality Characteristics

An individual's personality influences his response to a persuasive message. This is hardly a startling statement, and it is one which is well supported by experimental evidence. However, the functional relationships between specific personality factors and an individual's susceptibility to influence have proved difficult to isolate. Initially, investigators sought to establish monotonic (ever-increasing or ever-decreasing) relationships between levels of personality variables and an individual's persuasibility. One prediction, for example, was that persuasibility is a monotonically decreasing function of intelligence. That is, as an individual's intelligence increases, his susceptibility to influence becomes smaller. Support for this relationship can be found in the results of an experiment conducted by Crutchfield (4). However, support for a monotonically increasing relationship (as intelligence increases, susceptibility to influence also increases) can be attributed to the results of a study by Hovland, Lumsdaine, and Sheffield (9). Furthermore, numerous other investigators have reported no significant relationship between intelligence and influence susceptibility. Based on these results, it seems unlikely that intelligence and persuasibility form a monotonic relationship, whether it be increasing or decreasing.

This pattern of results is not unique. Similar, seemingly inconsistent findings have been reported in research relating persuasibility to level of self-esteem, chronic anxiety, aggressiveness, and dogmatism. Appley and Moeller (2) found that only five out of thirty-eight personality variables tested exhibited monotonic relationships with persuasibility.

The selection included by McGuire represents one attempt to account for this pattern of nonmonotonic relationships. McGuire contends that changing the level of a personality factor has implications for both 1) how effectively an individual comprehends a message and 2) how likely he is to yield to it. Furthermore, these two implications usually work at cross purposes. For example, as the persuader confronts increasingly intelligent audiences, his audiences become better equipped to comprehend the message, but less likely to yield to its demands. The result is that intelligence and susceptibility to influence exhibit a nonmonotonic relationship with the greatest amount of susceptibility occurring at some middle range of intelligence.

B. Selective Exposure

One critical feature of most experiments focusing on the persuasive process is that after subjects have agreed to participate, they have little choice whether or not to be exposed to a persuasive message. This decision is made by the experimenter and all the subject can do is listen and respond. Such a situation, however, is not indicative of most "real life" conditions. People normally choose whether they wish to be exposed to persuasive messages and what types they wish to hear.

They voluntarily go to political rallies—the rally is not forced upon them. They turn on their television set to listen to a Presidential news conference rather than reading a book or newspaper. In other words, people constantly choose the sources and types of influence to which they attend.

An interesting question arises from this fact. Does an individual's attitude on an issue influence his willingness to expose himself to material about that issue? Stated another way, does an individual selectively expose himself to material in a consistent fashion? Dissonance theory provides one theoretical answer. If an individual has chosen a position on an issue from several attractive positions, this stand should produce some degree of dissonance. To reduce this dissonance he should seek out consonant information (hence adding supportive cognitions) and avoid discrepant information. This prediction was first investigated by Ehrlich, Guttmann, Schonbach, and Mills (5). In this investigation the authors interviewed two groups of people. The first group consisted of people who recently had purchased a new automobile. The second was composed of people who owned an automobile at least three years old. The authors hypothesized that the new car owners would read more advertisements for the car they purchased than advertisements either for cars they considered but did not buy or for makes of cars they did not consider. They further hypothesized that new car owners would read advertisements for makes of cars that they considered but did not buy less frequently than advertisements for car makes not considered (hence avoiding discrepant information). Finally, they hypothesized that since dissonance dissipates over time, these differences would not be present for the old car owners.

The results of this investigation strongly support the prediction that people seek out consonant information. New car owners read a significantly greater percentage of advertisements for the car they bought as opposed either to other makes considered or not considered. These differences were not found for the old car owners. However, no support was found for the prediction that new car owners avoid exposure to advertisements for other car makes considered but rejected. Thus, the results suggest that individuals seek out consonant information but do not necessarily avoid discrepant information.

A number of later investigations have focused on the phenomenon of selective exposure. Their results have not served to clarify whether the phenomenon exists, and if so, under what conditions it operates. Rosen (17), Freedman (7), and Sears (18), for example, report evidence that individuals still in the process of forming an opinion prefer dissonant to consonant information. Sears argues that this preference may result from an individual's desire to obtain information on both sides of an issue before committing himself to a stand. In any event, the process of selective exposure appears not nearly as universal as originally believed. The selection by Sears and Freedman presents a review of recent research and attempts to reconcile the findings.

C. The Effects of Warning

Most people undoubtedly have been subjected to magazine or encyclopedia salesmen who concealed their true persuasive intent until they were well into their sales pitch. Although the analogy may not be too flattering, most experiments about persuasion have operated similarly. Subjects have been deceived about the true purpose of the experiment. They are told that its purpose is to rate the quality of an educational film, to evaluate the effectiveness of a public speaker, to determine the relative desirability of several small appliances, or any of a number of plausible but unrelated tasks.

The reason for these deceptions—both by the magazine salesman and the social scientist—is quite explicit. Both operate under the assumption that warning the potential client or subject that he is to be exposed to a persuasive message will increase his resistance to any such message. The likelihood that attitude change will result is reduced.

But does warning an individual that he is to be exposed to a persuasive message influence his responsiveness to the message? This is the central question considered by Papageorgis. He suggests that we need to distinguish between two types of warning: warning the individual that some unspecified persuasive attempt is forthcoming and warning the individual that he is to be subjected to a persuasive message advocating a specific position on an issue. He also suggests that we need to distinguish between effects produced by the warning itself and effects produced by the influence of the warning on the individual's acceptance of subsequent messages. In this selection he relates relevant research to each of these issues.

The selection by McGuire deals with an issue closely related to the effects of forewarning. McGuire is concerned with how individuals can be made resistant to persuasive attacks. The process which he explores involves warning individuals of an impending persuasive attack and then "inoculating" them against this attack. Factors relevant to the inoculation process which he considers include the type of defense employed (supportive or refutational), the effectiveness of refutational defenses in building resistance to the same or different counterarguments, the degree of active participation in the defense, and the persistence of the induced resistance.

One feature of McGuire's approach which must be kept in mind (our attempt at forewarning) is that he has applied the inoculation process only to "cultural truisms"—attitudes which are shared by a large majority of a culture and hence have not been subjected to previous attack. How well the inoculation process generalizes to attitudes which have previously been attacked must still be established.

REFERENCES

1. ABELSON, R., and M. ROSENBERG. "Symbolic Psycho-logic: A Model of Attitudinal Cognition," *Behavioral Science,* 3(1958), 1–13.
2. APPLEY, M. H., and G. MOELLER. "Conforming Behavior and Personality Variables in College Women," *Journal of Abnormal and Social Psychology,* 66(1963), 284–90.
3. CARTWRIGHT, D., and F. HARARY. "Structural Balance: A Generalization of Heider's Theory," *Psychological Review,* 63(1956), 277–93.
4. CRUTCHFIELD, R. S. "Conformity and Character," *American Psychologist,* 10(1955), 191–98.
5. EHRLICH, D., I. GUTTMANN, P. SCHONBACH, and J. MILLS. "Post-Decision Exposure to Relevant Information," *Journal of Abnormal and Social Psychology,* 54(1957), 98–102.

6. FEATHER, N. "A Structural Balance Model of Communication Effects," *Psychological Review,* 71(1964), 291–313.

7. FREEDMAN, J. L. "Preference for Dissonant Information," *Journal of Personality and Social Psychology,* 2 (1965), 287–89.

8. HEIDER, F. *The Psychology of Interpersonal Relations.* New York: Wiley, 1958.

9. HOVLAND, C. I., A. A. LUMSDAINE, and F. D. SHEFFIELD. *Experiments on Mass Communications.* Princeton, N. J.: Princeton University Press, 1949.

10. HOVLAND, C. I., and M. SHERIF. "Judgmental Phenomena and Scales of Attitude Measurement: Item Displacement in Thurstone Scales," *Journal of Abnormal and Social Psychology,* 47 (1952), 822–32.

11. INSKO, C. A. *Theories of Attitude Change.* New York: Appleton-Century-Crofts, 1967.

12. KATZ, D. "Consistency for What? The Functional Approach," *Theories of Cognitive Consistency: A Sourcebook,* R. P. Abelson, *et al.,* Eds. Chicago: Rand McNally and Co., 1968, pp. 179–91.

13. KATZ, D. "The Functional Approach to the Study of Attitudes," *Public Opinion Quarterly,* 24 (1960), 163–204.

14. McGUIRE, W. J. "The Nature of Attitudes and Attitude Change," *The Handbook of Social Psychology,* 2nd Edition, G. Lindzey and E. Aronson, Eds. Reading, Mass.: Addison-Wesley, 1969, v. III, pp. 136–314.

15. NEWCOMB, T. N. "An Approach to the Study of Communicative Acts," *Psychological Review,* 60 (1953), 393–404.

16. PEAK, H. "Attitude and Motivation," *Nebraska Symposium on Motivation, 1955,* M. R. Jones, Ed. Lincoln: University of Nebraska Press, 1955, pp. 149–88.

17. ROSEN, S. "Post-Decision Affinity for Incompatible Information," *Journal of Abnormal and Social Psychology,* 63 (1961), 188–90.

18. SEARS, D. O. "Opinion Formation and Information Preferences in Adversary Situations," *Journal of Experimental Social Psychology,* 2 (1966), 130–42.

19. SMITH, M. B., J. S. BRUNER, and R. W. WHITE. *Opinions and Personality.* New York: Wiley, 1956.

20. STAATS, A. W., and C. K. STAATS. "Attitudes Established by Classical Conditioning," *Journal of Abnormal and Social Psychology,* 57 (1958), 37–40.

21. THURSTONE, L. L., and E. J. CHAVE. *The Measurement of Attitude.* Chicago: University of Chicago Press, 1929.

22. WEISS, R. F. "Persuasion and Acquisition of Attitudes: Models from Conditioning and Selective Learning," *Psychological Reports,* 11 (1962), 709–32.

Daniel Katz

THE FUNCTIONAL
APPROACH
TO THE STUDY
OF ATTITUDES

NATURE OF ATTITUDES:
THEIR DIMENSIONS

Attitude is the predisposition of the individual to evaluate some symbol or object or aspect of his world in a favorable or unfavorable manner. Opinion is the verbal expression of an attitude, but attitudes can also be expressed in nonverbal behavior. Attitudes include both the affective, or feeling core of liking or disliking, and the cognitive, or belief, elements which describe the object of the attitude, its characteristics, and its relations to other objects. All attitudes thus include beliefs, but not all beliefs are attitudes. When specific attitudes are organized into a hierarchical structure, they comprise *value systems*. Thus a person may not only hold specific attitudes against deficit spending and unbalanced budgets but may also have a systematic organization of such beliefs and attitudes in the form of a value system of economic conservatism.

The dimensions of attitudes can be stated more precisely if the above distinctions between beliefs and feelings and attitudes and value systems are kept in mind. The *intensity* of an attitude refers to the strength of the *affective* component. In fact, rating scales and even Thurstone scales deal primarily with the intensity of feeling of the individual for or against some social object.

Excerpted from the *Public Opinion Quarterly*, 24 (1960), 163–204, with permission of the author and the Public Opinion Quarterly.

The cognitive, or belief, component suggests two additional dimensions, the *specificity* or *generality* of the attitude and the *degree of differentiation* of the beliefs. Differentiation refers to the number of beliefs or cognitive items contained in the attitude, and the general assumption is that the simpler the attitude in cognitive structure the easier it is to change.[1] For simple structures there is no defense in depth, and once a single item of belief has been changed the attitude will change. A rather different dimension of attitude is the *number and strength of its linkages to a related value system*. If an attitude favoring budget balancing by the Federal government is tied in strongly with a value system of economic conservatism, it will be more difficult to change than if it were a fairly isolated attitude of the person. Finally, the relation of the value system to the personality is a consideration of first importance. If an attitude is tied to a value system which is closely related to, or which consists of, the individual's conception of himself, then the appropriate change procedures become more complex. The *centrality* of an attitude refers to its role as part of a value system which is closely related to the individual's self-concept.

An additional aspect of attitudes is not clearly described in most theories, namely, their relation to action or overt behavior. Though behavior related to the attitude has other determinants than the attitude itself, it is also true that some attitudes in themselves have more of what Cartwright calls an action structure than do others.[2] Brewster Smith refers to this dimension as policy orientation[3] and Katz and Stotland speak of it as the action component.[4] For example, while many people have attitudes of approval toward one or the other of the two political parties, these attitudes will differ in their structure with respect to relevant action. One man may be prepared to vote on election day and will know where and when he should vote and will go to the polls no matter what the weather or how great the inconvenience. Another man will only vote if a party worker calls for him in a car. Himmelstrand's work is concerned with all aspects of the relationship between attitude and behavior, but he deals with the action structure of the attitude itself by distinguishing between attitudes where the affect is tied to verbal expression and attitudes where the affect is tied to behavior concerned with more objective referents of the attitude.[5] In the first case an individual derives satisfaction from talking

[1] David Krech and Richard S. Crutchfield, *Theory and Problems of Social Psychology.* (New York: McGraw-Hill, 1948), pp. 160–63.

[2] Dorwin Cartwright, "Some Principles of Mass Persuasion," *Human Relations,* Vol. 2 (1949), pp. 253–67.

[3] M. Brewster Smith, "The Personal Setting of Public Opinions: A Study of Attitudes toward Russia," *Public Opinion Quarterly,* Vol. 11 (1947), pp. 507–23.

[4] Daniel Katz and Ezra Stotland, "A Preliminary Statement to a Theory of Attitude Structure and Change," in *Psychology: A Study of a Science,* Vol. 3, ed. Sigmund Koch (New York: McGraw-Hill, 1959), pp. 423–75.

[5] See Ulf Himmelstrand, "Verbal Attitudes and Behavior: A Paradigm for the Study of Message Transmission and Transformation," *Public Opinion Quarterly,* Vol. 24 (1960), pp. 224–50.

about a problem; in the second case he derives satisfaction from taking some form of concrete action.

Attempts to change attitudes can be directed primarily at the belief component or at the feeling, or affective, component. Rosenberg theorizes that an effective change in one component will result in changes in the other component and presents experimental evidence to confirm this hypothesis.[6] For example, a political candidate will often attempt to win people by making them like him and dislike his opponent, and thus communicate affect rather than ideas. If he is successful, people will not only like him but entertain favorable beliefs about him. Another candidate may deal primarily with ideas and hope that, if he can change people's beliefs about an issue, their feelings will also change.

FOUR FUNCTIONS WHICH ATTITUDES PERFORM FOR THE INDIVIDUAL

The major functions which attitudes perform for the personality can be grouped according to their motivational basis as follows:

1. *The instrumental, adjustive, or utilitarian function* upon which Jeremy Bentham and the utilitarians constructed their model of man. A modern expression of this approach can be found in behavioristic learning theory.
2. *The ego-defensive function* in which the person protects himself from acknowledging the basic truths about himself or the harsh realities in his external world. Freudian psychology and neo-Freudian thinking have been preoccupied with this type of motivation and its outcomes.
3. *The value-expressive function* in which the individual derives satisfactions from expressing attitudes appropriate to his personal values and to his concept of himself. This function is central to doctrines of ego psychology which stress the importance of self-expression, self-development, and self-realization.
4. *The knowledge function* based upon the individual's need to give adequate structure to his universe. The search for meaning, the need to understand, the trend toward better organization of perceptions and beliefs to provide clarity and consistency for the individual, are other descriptions of this function. The development of principles about perceptual and cognitive structure have been the contribution of Gestalt psychology.

Stated simply, the functional approach is the attempt to understand the reasons people hold the attitudes they do. The reasons, however, are at the level of psychological motivations and not of the accidents of external events and circumstances. Unless we know the psychological need which is met by the hold-

---

[6] Milton J. Rosenberg, "A Structural Theory of Attitude Dynamics," *Public Opinion Quarterly*, Vol. 24 (1960), pp. 319–40.

ing of an attitude we are in a poor position to predict when and how it will change. Moreover, the same attitude expressed toward a political candidate may not perform the same function for all the people who express it. And while many attitudes are predominantly in the service of a single type of motivational process, as described above, other attitudes may serve more than one purpose for the individual. A fuller discussion of how attitudes serve the above four functions is in order.

1. The Adjustment Function. Essentially this function is a recognition of the fact that people strive to maximize the rewards in their external environment and to minimize the penalties. The child develops favorable attitudes toward the objects in his world which are associated with the satisfactions of his needs and unfavorable attitudes toward objects which thwart him or punish him. Attitudes acquired in the service of the adjustment function are either the means for reaching the desired goal or avoiding the undesirable one, or are affective associations based upon experiences in attaining motive satisfactions.[7] The attitudes of the worker favoring a political party which will advance his economic lot are an example of the first type of utilitarian attitude. The pleasant image one has of one's favorite food is an example of the second type of utilitarian attitude.

In general, then, the dynamics of attitude formation with respect to the adjustment function are dependent upon present or past perceptions of the utility of the attitudinal object for the individual. The clarity, consistency, and nearness of rewards and punishments, as they relate to the individual's activities and goals, are important factors in the acquisition of such attitudes.

. . . .

2. The Ego-Defensive Function. People not only seek to make the most of their external world and what it offers, but they also expend a great deal of their energy on living with themselves. The mechanisms by which the individual protects his ego from his own unacceptable impulses and from the knowledge of threatening forces from without, and the methods by which he reduces his anxieties created by such problems, are known as mechanisms of ego defense. A more complete account of their origin and nature will be found in Sarnoff's article in this issue.[8] They include the devices by which the individual avoids facing either the inner reality of the kind of person he is, or the outer reality of the dangers the world holds for him. They stem basically from internal conflict with its resulting insecurities. In one sense the mechanisms of defense are adaptive in temporarily removing the sharp edges of conflict and in saving the individual from complete disaster. In another sense they are not adaptive in that they handicap the individual in his social adjustments and in obtaining the maximum satisfactions available to him from the world in which

[7] Katz and Stotland, *op. cit.*, pp. 434–43.
[8] Irving Sarnoff, "Psychoanalytic Theory and Social Attitudes," *Public Opinion Quarterly*, Vol. 24 (1960), pp. 251–79.

he lives. The worker who persistently quarrels with his boss and with his fellow workers, because he is acting out some of his own internal conflicts, may in this manner relieve himself of some of the emotional tensions which beset him. He is not, however, solving his problem of adjusting to his work situation and thus may deprive himself of advancement or even of steady employment.

. . . .

Many of our attitudes have the function of defending our self-image. When we cannot admit to ourselves that we have deep feelings of inferiority we may project those feelings onto some convenient minority group and bolster our egos by attitudes of superiority toward this underprivileged group. The formation of such defensive attitudes differs in essential ways from the formation of attitudes which serve the adjustment function. They proceed from within the person, and the objects and situation to which they are attached are merely convenient outlets for their expression. Not all targets are equally satisfactory for a given defense mechanism, but the point is that the attitude is not created by the target but by the individual's emotional conflicts. And when no convenient target exists the individual will create one. Utilitarian attitudes, on the other hand, are formed with specific reference to the nature of the attitudinal object. They are thus appropriate to the nature of the social world to which they are geared. The high school student who values high grades because he wants to be admitted to a good college has a utilitarian attitude appropriate to the situation to which it is related.

All people employ defense mechanisms, but they differ with respect to the extent that they use them and some of their attitudes may be more defensive in function than others. It follows that the techniques and conditions for attitude change will not be the same for ego-defensive as for utilitarian attitudes.

. . . .

3. *The Value-Expressive Function.*   While many attitudes have the function of preventing the individual from revealing to himself and others his true nature, other attitudes have the function of giving positive expression to his central values and to the type of person he conceives himself to be. A man may consider himself to be an enlightened conservative or an internationalist or a liberal, and will hold attitudes which are the appropriate indication of his central values. Thus we need to take account of the fact that not all behavior has the negative function of reducing the tensions of biological drives or of internal conflicts. Satisfactions also accrue to the person from the expression of attitudes which reflect his cherished beliefs and his self-image. The reward to the person in these instances is not so much a matter of gaining social recognition or monetary rewards as of establishing his self-identity and confirming his notion of the sort of person he sees himself to be. The gratifications obtained from value expression may go beyond the confirmation of self-identity. Just as we find satisfaction in the exercise of our talents and abilities, so we find reward in the expression of any attributes associated with our egos.

Value-expressive attitudes not only give clarity to the self-image but also mold that self-image closer to the heart's desire. The teenager who by dress and speech establishes his identity as similar to his own peer group may appear to the outsider a weakling and a craven conformer. To himself he is asserting his independence of the adult world to which he has rendered childlike subservience and conformity all his life. Very early in the development of the personality the need for clarity of self-image is important—the need to know "who I am." Later it may be even more important to know that in some measure I am the type of person I want to be. Even as adults, however, the clarity and stability of the self-image is of primary significance. Just as the kind, considerate person will cover over his acts of selfishness, so too will the ruthless individualist become confused and embarrassed by his acts of sympathetic compassion. One reason it is difficult to change the character of the adult is that he is not comfortable with the new "me." Group support for such personality change is almost a necessity, as in Alcoholics Anonymous, so that the individual is aware of approval of his new self by people who are like him.

4. The Knowledge Function.   Individuals not only acquire beliefs in the interest of satisfying various specific needs, they also seek knowledge to give meaning to what would otherwise be an unorganized chaotic universe. People need standards or frames of reference for understanding their world, and attitudes help to supply such standards. The problem of understanding, as John Dewey made clear years ago, is one "of introducing (1) *definiteness and distinction* and (2) *consistency and stability* of meaning into what is otherwise vague and wavering."[9] The definiteness and stability are provided in good measure by the norms of our culture, which give the otherwise perplexed individual ready-made attitudes for comprehending his universe. Walter Lippmann's classical contribution to the study of opinions and attitudes was his description of stereotypes and the way they provided order and clarity for a bewildering set of complexities.[10] The most interesting finding in Herzog's familiar study of the gratifications obtained by housewives in listening to daytime serials was the unsuspected role of information and advice.[11] The stories were liked "because they explained things to the inarticulate listener."

The need to know does not of course imply that people are driven by a thirst for universal knowledge. The American public's appalling lack of political information has been documented many times. In 1956, for example, only 13 per cent of the people in Detroit could correctly name the two United States Senators from the state of Michigan and only 18 per cent knew the name

[9] John Dewey, *How We Think* (New York: The Macmillan Company, 1910).

[10] Walter Lippmann, *Public Opinion* (New York: The Macmillan Company, 1922).

[11] Herta Herzog, "What Do We Really Know about Daytime Serial Listeners?" in *Radio Research* 1942–1943, Paul F. Lazarsfeld and Frank N. Stanton, eds. (New York: Duell, Sloan & Pearce, 1944), pp. 3–33.

of their own Congressman.[12] People are not avid seekers after knowledge as judged by what the educator or social reformer would desire. But they do want to understand the events which impinge directly on their own life. Moreover, many of the attitudes they have already acquired give them sufficient basis for interpreting much of what they perceive to be important for them. Our already existing stereotypes, in Lippmann's language, "are an ordered, more or less consistent picture of the world, to which our habits, our tastes, our capacities, our comforts and our hopes have adjusted themselves. They may not be a complete picture of the world, but they are a picture of a possible world to which we are adapted."[13] It follows that new information will not modify old attitudes unless there is some inadequacy or incompleteness or inconsistency in the existing attitudinal structure as it relates to the perceptions of new situations.

. . . .

DETERMINANTS OF ATTITUDE AROUSAL AND ATTITUDE CHANGE

The problems of attitude arousal and of attitude change are separate problems. The first has to do with the fact that the individual has many predispositions to act and many influences playing upon him. Hence we need a more precise description of the appropriate conditions which will evoke a given attitude. The second problem is that of specifying the factors which will help to predict the modification of different types of attitude.

The most general statement that can be made concerning attitude arousal is that it is dependent upon the excitation of some need in the individual, or some relevant cue in the environment. When a man grows hungry, he talks of food. Even when not hungry he may express favorable attitudes toward a preferred food if an external stimulus cues him. The ego-defensive person who hates foreigners will express such attitudes under conditions of increased anxiety or threat or when a foreigner is perceived to be getting out of place.

The most general statement that can be made about the conditions conducive to attitude change is that the expression of the old attitude or its anticipated expression no longer gives satisfaction to its related need state. In other words, it no longer serves its function and the individual feels blocked or frustrated. Modifying an old attitude or replacing it with a new one is a process of learning, and learning always starts with a problem, or being thwarted in coping with a situation. Being blocked is a necessary, but not a sufficient,

---

[12] From a study of the impact of party organization on political behavior in the Detroit area, by Daniel Katz & Samuel Eldersveld, in manuscript.

[13] Lippmann, *op. cit.*, p. 95.

condition for attitude change. Other factors must be operative and will vary in effectiveness depending upon the function involved.

AROUSING AND CHANGING
UTILITARIAN ATTITUDES

Political parties have both the problem of converting people with antago-nistic attitudes (attitude change) and the problem of mobilizing the support of their own followers (attitude arousal). To accomplish the latter they attempt to revive the needs basic to old attitudes. For example, the Democrats still utilize the appeals of the New Deal and the Republicans still talk of the bal-anced budget. The assumption is that many people still hold attitudes acquired in earlier circumstances and that appropriate communication can reinstate the old needs. For most people, however, utilitarian needs are reinforced by experience and not by verbal appeals. Hence invoking the symbols of the New Deal will be relatively ineffective with respect to adjustive attitudes unless there are corresponding experiences with unemployment, decreased income, and so forth. Though the need state may not be under the control of the propagandist, he can exaggerate or minimize its importance. In addition to playing upon states of need, the propagandist can make perceptible the old cues associated with the attitude he is trying to elicit. These cues may have associated with them favorable affect, or feeling, though the related needs are inactive. For example, the fighters for old causes can be paraded across the political platform in an attempt to arouse the attitudes of the past.

The two basic conditions, then, for the arousal of existing attitudes are the activation of their relevant need states and the perception of the appropriate cues associated with the content of the attitude.

To change attitudes which serve a utilitarian function, one of two con-ditions must prevail: (1) the attitude and the activities related to it no longer provide the satisfactions they once did, or (2) the individual's level of aspiration has been raised. The Chevrolet owner who had positive attitudes toward his old car may now want a more expensive car commensurate with his new status.

. . . .

The area of freedom for changing utilitarian attitudes is of course much greater in dealing with methods of satisfying needs than with needs themselves. Needs change more slowly than the means for gratifying them, even though one role of the advertiser is to create new needs. Change in attitudes occurs more readily when people perceive that they can accomplish their objectives through revising existing attitudes. Integration of white and Negro personnel in the armed forces came to pass partly because political leaders and military leaders perceived that such a move would strengthen our fighting forces. And one of the powerful arguments for changing our attitudes toward Negroes is that in the struggle for world democracy we need to put our own house in order to present a more convincing picture of our own society to other countries. Carlson has experimentally demonstrated that discriminatory attitudes toward minority groups can be altered by showing the relevance of more positive beliefs to such individual goals and values as American international prestige and democratic equalitarianism.[14]

. . . .

The use of negative sanctions and of punishment to change utilitarian attitudes is more complex than the use of rewards. To be successful in changing attitudes and behavior, punishment should be used only when there is clearly available a course of action that will save the individual from the undesirable consequences. To arouse fear among the enemy in time of war does not necessarily result in desertion, surrender, or a disruption of the enemy war effort. Such channels of action may not be available to the people whose fears are aroused. The experiment of Janis and Feshbach in using fear appeals to coerce children into good habits of dental hygiene had the interesting outcome of a negative relationship between the amount of fear and the degree of change. Lurid pictures of the gangrene jaws of old people who had not observed good dental habits were not effective.[15] Moreover, the group exposed to the strongest fear appeal was the most susceptible to counterpropaganda. One factor which helps to account for the results of this investigation was the lack of a clear-cut relation in the minds of the children between failure to brush their teeth in the prescribed manner and the pictures of the gangrene jaws of the aged.

. . . .

AROUSAL AND CHANGE OF
EGO-DEFENSIVE ATTITUDES

Attitudes which help to protect the individual from internally induced anxieties or from facing up to external dangers are readily elicited by any form of threat to the ego. The threat may be external, as in the case of a highly competitive situation, or a failure experience, or a derogatory remark. It is the stock in trade of demagogues to exaggerate the dangers confronting the people, for instance, Joe McCarthy's tactics with respect to Communists in the State Department. Many people have existing attitudes of withdrawal or of aggres-

[14] Earl R. Carlson, "Attitude Change through Modification of Attitude Structure," *Journal of Abnormal and Social Psychology*, Vol. 52 (1956), pp. 256–61.

[15] Irving L. Janis and Seymour Feshbach, "Effects of Fear-arousing Communications," *Journal of Abnormal and Social Psychology*, Vol. 48 (1953), pp. 78–92.

sion toward deviants or out-groups based upon their ego-defensive needs. When threatened, these attitudes come into play, and defensive people either avoid the unpleasant situation entirely, as is common in the desegregation controversy, or exhibit hostility.

Another condition for eliciting the ego-defensive attitude is the encouragement given to its expression by some form of social support. The agitator may appeal to repressed hatred by providing moral justification for its expression. A mob leader before an audience with emotionally held attitudes toward Negroes may call out these attitudes in the most violent form by invoking the good of the community or the honor of white womanhood.

A third condition for the arousal of ego-defensive attitudes is the appeal to authority. The insecurity of the defensive person makes him particularly susceptible to authoritarian suggestion. When this type of authoritarian command is in the direction already indicated by his attitudes of antipathy toward other people, he responds quickly and joyously. It is no accident that movements of hate and aggression such as the Ku Klux Klan or the Nazi Party are authoritarian in their organized structure. Wagman, in an experimental investigation of the uses of authoritarian suggestion, found that students high in ego-defensiveness as measured by the F-scale were much more responsive to directives from military leaders than were less defensive students.[16] In fact, the subjects low in defensiveness were not affected at all by authoritarian suggestion when this influence ran counter to their own attitudes. The subjects high in F-scores could be moved in either direction, although they moved more readily in the direction of their own beliefs.

A fourth condition for defensive arousal is the building up over time of inhibited drives in the individual, for example, repressed sex impulses. As the drive strength of forbidden impulses increases, anxiety mounts and release from tension is found in the expression of defensive attitudes. The deprivations of prison life, for example, build up tensions which can find expression in riots against the hated prison officials.

In other words, the drive strength for defensive reactions can be increased by situation frustration. Though the basic source is the long-standing internal conflict of the person, he can encounter additional frustration in immediate circumstances.

. . . .

The usual procedures for changing attitudes and behavior have little positive effect upon attitudes geared into our ego defenses. In fact they may have a boomerang effect of making the individual cling more tenaciously to his emotionally held beliefs. In the category of usual procedures should be included

---

[16] Morton Wagman, "Attitude Change and the Authoritarian Personality," *Journal of Psychology*, Vol. 40 (1955), pp. 3–24. The F-scale is a measure of authoritarianism comprising items indicative of both defensiveness and ideology.

increasing the flow of information, promising and bestowing rewards, and invoking penalties.

. . . .

Three basic factors, however, can help change ego-defensive attitudes. In the first place,   the removal of threat is a necessary though not a sufficient condition. The permissive and even supportive atmosphere which the therapist attempts to create for his patients is a special instance of the removal of threat . . . .

In the second place, catharsis or the ventilation of feelings can help to set the stage for attitude change. Mention has already been made of the building up of tension owing to the lack of discharge of inhibited impulses. When emotional tension is at a high level the individual will respond defensively and resist attempts to change him. Hence, providing him with opportunities to blow off steam may often be necessary before attempting a serious discussion of new possibilities of behavior. Again, humor can serve this purpose.

. . . .

In the third place, ego-defensive behavior can be altered as the individual acquires insight into his own mechanisms of defense. Information about the nature of the problem in the external world will not affect him. Information about his own functioning may have an influence, if presented without threat, and if the defenses do not go too deep into the personality . . . .

CONDITIONS FOR AROUSING AND CHANGING VALUE-EXPRESSIVE ATTITUDES

Two conditions for the arousal of value-expressive attitudes can be specified. The first is the occurrence of the cue in the stimulus situation which has been associated with the attitude. The liberal Democrat, as a liberal Democrat, has always believed in principle that an income tax is more just than a sales tax. Now the issue has arisen in his state, and the group in which he happens to be at the moment are discussing an increase in sales tax. This will be sufficient to cue off his opposition to the proposal without consideration of the specific local aspects of the tax problem. The second condition for the arousal of this type of attitude is some degree of thwarting of the individual's expressive behavior in the immediate past. The housewife occupied with the routine care of the home and the children during the day may seek opportunities to express her views to other women at the first social gathering she attends.

We have referred to voters backing their party for bread and butter reasons. Perhaps the bulk of voting behavior, however, is the elicitation of value-expressive attitudes. Voting is a symbolic expression of being a Republican or a Democrat. Party identification accounts for more variance in voting behavior than any other single factor.[17] Though there is a minority who consider themselves independent and though there are minor shifts in political allegiance, the great majority of the people identify themselves as the supporters of a political party. Their voting behavior is an expression of this self-concept, and it takes a major event such as a depression to affect their voting habits seriously.

Identification with party is in good measure a function of the political socialization of the child, as Hyman has shown.[18] An analysis of a national sample of the electorate in 1952 by Campbell, Gurin, and Miller revealed that of voters both of whose parents were Democrats, 76 per cent identified themselves as Democrats, another 10 per cent as independent Democrats, and 12 per cent as Republicans.[19] Similarly, of those with Republican parents 63 per cent considered themselves Republican and another 10 per cent as independent Republicans. Attachment to party, Hyman suggests, furnishes an organizing principle for the individual and gives stability to his political orientation in the confusion of changing issues.

. . . .

Again, two conditions are relevant in changing value-expressive attitudes:

1. Some degree of dissatisfaction with one's self-concept or its associated values is the opening wedge for fundamental change. The complacent person, smugly satisfied with all aspects of himself, is immune to attempts to change his values. Dissatisfaction with the self can result from failures or from the inadequacy of one's values in preserving a favorable image of oneself in a changing world. The man with pacifist values may have become dissatisfied with himself during a period of fascist expansion and terror. Once there is a crack in the individual's central belief systems, it can be exploited by appropriately directed influences. The techniques of brain washing employed by the Chinese Communists both on prisoners of war in Korea and in the thought reform of Chinese intellectuals were essentially procedures for changing value systems.

. . . .

2. Dissatisfaction with old attitudes as inappropriate to one's values can also lead to change. In fact, people are much less likely to find their values uncongenial than they are to find some of their attitudes inappropriate to their values. The discomfort with one's old attitudes may stem from new experiences or from the suggestions of other people. Senator Vandenburg, as an enlightened conservative, changed his attitudes on foreign relations from an isolationist to an internationalist position when critical events in our history suggested change.

. . . .

---

[17] Angus A. Campbell, Philip Converse, Warren Miller, and Donald Stokes, *The American Voter* (New York: Wiley, 1960).

[18] Herbert H. Hyman, *Political Socialization* (Glencoe, Ill.: Free Press, 1959).

[19] Angus A. Campbell, Gerald Gurin, and Warren Miller, *The Voter Decides* (Evanston, Ill.: Row, Peterson, 1954).

AROUSING AND CHANGING
ATTITUDES WHICH SERVE
THE KNOWLEDGE FUNCTION

Attitudes acquired in the interests of the need to know are elicited by a stimulus associated with the attitude. The child who learns from his reading and from his parents that Orientals are treacherous will not have the attitude aroused unless some appropriate cue concerning the cognitive object is presented. He may even meet and interact with Orientals without identifying them as such and with no corresponding arousal of his attitude. Considerable prejudice in this sense is race-name prejudice and is only aroused when a premium is placed upon social identification. Since members of a minority group have many other memberships in common with a majority group, the latent prejudiced attitude may not necessarily be activated. Prejudice based upon ego-defensiveness, however, will result in ready identification of the disliked group.

The factors which are productive of change of attitudes of this character are inadequacies of the existing attitudes to deal with new and changing situations. The person who has been taught that Orientals are treacherous may read extended accounts of the honesty of the Chinese or may have favorable interactions with Japanese. He finds his old attitudes in conflict with new information and new experience, and proceeds to modify his beliefs. In this instance we are dealing with fictitious stereotypes which never corresponded to reality. In other cases the beliefs may have been adequate to the situation but the world has changed. Thus, some British military men formerly in favor of armaments have changed their attitude toward disarmament because of the character of nuclear weapons. The theory of cognitive consistency later elaborated in this issue can draw its best examples from attitudes related to the knowledge function.

Any situation, then, which is ambiguous for the individual is likely to produce attitude change. His need for cognitive structure is such that he will either modify his beliefs to impose structure or accept some new formula presented by others. He seeks a meaningful picture of his universe, and when there is ambiguity he will reach for a ready solution. Rumors abound when information is unavailable.

GLOBAL INFLUENCES
AND ATTITUDE CHANGE

In the foregoing analysis we have attempted to clarify the functions which attitudes perform and to give some psychological specifications of the conditions under which they are formed, elicited, and changed. This material is summarized in the table on page 32. We must recognize, however, that the influences in the real world are not as a rule directed toward a single type of motivation. Contact with other peoples, experience in foreign cultures, group pressures, group discussion and decision, the impact of legislation, and the techniques of brain washing are all global variables. They represent combinations of forces. To predict their effectiveness in any given situation it is necessary to analyze their components in relation to the conditions of administration and the type of population toward which they are directed.

DETERMINANTS OF ATTITUDE FORMATION, AROUSAL, AND CHANGE
IN RELATION TO TYPE OF FUNCTION

Function	Origin and Dynamics	Arousal Conditions	Change Conditions
Adjustment	Utility of attitudinal object in need satisfaction. Maximizing external rewards and minimizing punishments	1. Activation of needs 2. Salience of cues associated with need satisfaction	1. Need deprivation 2. Creation of new needs and new levels of aspiration 3. Shifting rewards and punishments 4. Emphasis on new and better paths for need satisfaction
Ego defense	Protecting against internal conflicts and external dangers	1. Posing of threats 2. Appeals to hatred and repressed impulses 3. Rise in frustrations 4. Use of authoritarian suggestion	1. Removal of threats 2. Catharsis 3. Development of self-insight
Value expression	Maintaining self identity; enhancing favorable self-image; self-expression and self-determination	1. Salience of cues associated with values 2. Appeals to individual to reassert self-image 3. Ambiguities which threaten self-concept	1. Some degree of dissatisfaction with self 2. Greater appropriateness of new attitude for the self 3. Control of all environmental supports to undermine old values
Knowledge	Need for understanding, for meaningful cognitive organization, for consistency and clarity	1. Reinstatement of cues associated with old problem or of old problem itself	1. Ambiguity created by new information or change in environment 2. More meaningful information about problems

SUMMARY

The purpose of this paper was to provide a psychological framework for the systematic consideration of the dynamics of public and private attitudes. Four functions which attitudes perform for the personality were identified: the *adjustive function* of satisfying utilitarian needs, the *ego-defensive function* of handling internal conflicts, the *value-expressive function* of maintaining self-identity and of enhancing the self-image, and the *knowledge function* of giving understanding and meaning to the ambiguities of the world about us. The role of these functions in attitude formation was described. Their relevance for the conditions determining attitude arousal and attitude change were analyzed. Finally, constellations of variables such as group contact and legislative control of behavior were considered in terms of their motivational impact.

Herbert C. Kelman

PROCESSES OF
OPINION CHANGE

THE STUDY OF SOCIAL INFLUENCE

Social influence has been a central area of concern for experimental social psychology almost since its beginnings. Three general research traditions in this area can be distinguished: (1) the study of social influences on judgments, stemming from the earlier work on prestige suggestion;[1] (2) the study of social influences arising from small-group interaction;[2] and (3) the study of social influences arising from persuasive communications.[3] In recent years, there has been a considerable convergence between these three traditions, going hand in hand with an increased interest in developing general principles of social influence and socially induced behavior change.

One result of these developments has been that many investigators found it necessary to make qualitative distinctions between different types of influence. In some cases, these distinctions arose primarily out of the observation that social influence may have qualitatively different effects, that it may produce different kinds of change. For example, under some conditions it may result in mere public conformity—in superficial changes on a verbal or overt level without accompanying changes in belief; in other situations it may result in private acceptance—in a change that is more general, more durable, more

[1] See, for example, S. E. Asch, *Social Psychology*, New York, Prentice-Hall, 1952.
[2] See, for example, D. Cartwright and A. Zander, editors, *Group Dynamics*, Evanston, Ill., Row, Peterson, 1953.
[3] See, for example, C. I. Hovland, I. L. Janis, and H. H. Kelley, *Communication and Persuasion*, New Haven, Yale University Press, 1953.

Excerpted from the *Public Opinion Quarterly,* 25 (1961), 58–78, with permission of the author and the Public Opinion Quarterly.

integrated with the person's own values.[4] Other investigators found it necessary to make distinctions because they observed that influence may occur for different reasons, that it may arise out of different motivations and orientations. For example, under some conditions influence may be primarily informational —the subject may conform to the influencing person or group because he views him as a source of valid information; in other situations influence may be primarily normative—the subject may conform in order to meet the positive expectations of the influencing person or group.[5]

My own work can be viewed in the general context that I have outlined here. I started out with the distinction between public conformity and private acceptance, and tried to establish some of the distinct determinants of each. I became dissatisfied with this dichotomy as I began to look at important examples of social influence that could not be encompassed by it. I was especially impressed with the accounts of ideological conversion of the "true believer" variety, and with the recent accounts of "brainwashing," particularly the Chinese Communist methods of "thought reform."[6] It is apparent that these experiences do not simply involve public conformity, but that indeed they produce a change in underlying beliefs. But it is equally apparent that they do not produce what we would usually consider private acceptance—changes that are in some sense integrated with the person's own value system and that have become independent of the external source. Rather, they seem to produce new beliefs that are isolated from the rest of the person's values and that are highly dependent on external support.

These considerations eventually led me to distinguish three processes of social influence, each characterized by a distinct set of antecedent and a distinct set of consequent conditions. I have called these processes *compliance*, *identification*, and *internalization*.[7]

[4] See, for example, L. Festinger, "An Analysis of Compliant Behavior," in M. Sherif and M. O. Wilson, editors, *Group Relations at the Crossroads*, New York, Harper, 1953, pp. 232–256; H. C. Kelman, "Attitude Change as a Function of Response Restriction," *Human Relations*, Vol. 6, 1953, pp. 185–214; J. R. P. French, Jr., and B. Raven, "The Bases of Social Power," in D. Cartwright, editor, *Studies in Social Power*, Ann Arbor, Mich., Institute for Social Research, 1959, pp. 150–167; and Marie Jahoda, "Conformity and Independence," *Human Relations*, Vol. 12, 1959, pp. 99–120.

[5] See, for example, M. Deutsch and H. B. Gerard, "A Study of Normative and Informational Social Influence upon Individual Judgment," *Journal of Abnormal and Social Psychology*, Vol. 51, 1955, pp. 629–636; J. W. Thibaut and L. Strickland, "Psychological Set and Social Conformity," *Journal of Personality*, Vol. 25, 1956, pp. 115–129; and J. M. Jackson and H. D. Saltzstein, "The Effect of Person-Group Relationships on Conformity Processes," *Journal of Abnormal and Social Psychology*, Vol. 57, 1958, pp. 17–24.

[6] For instance, R. J. Lifton, " 'Thought Reform' of Western Civilians in Chinese Communist Prisons," *Psychiatry*, Vol. 19, 1956, pp. 173–195.

[7] A detailed description of these processes and the experimental work based on them will be contained in a forthcoming book, *Social Influence and Personal Belief: A Theoretical and Experimental Approach to the Study of Behavior Change*, to be published by John Wiley & Sons.

THREE PROCESSES OF SOCIAL
INFLUENCE

Compliance can be said to occur when an individual accepts influence from another person or from a group because he hopes to achieve a favorable reaction from the other. He may be interested in attaining certain specific rewards or in avoiding certain specific punishments that the influencing agent controls. For example, an individual may make a special effort to express only "correct" opinions in order to gain admission into a particular group or social set, or in order to avoid being fired from his government job. Or, the individual may be concerned with gaining approval or avoiding disapproval from the influencing agent in a more general way. For example, some individuals may compulsively try to say the expected thing in all situations and please everyone with whom they come in contact, out of a disproportionate need for favorable responses from others of a direct and immediate kind. In any event, when the individual complies, he does what the agent wants him to do—or what he thinks the agent wants him to do—because he sees this as a way of achieving a desired response from him. He does not adopt the induced behavior—for example, a particular opinion response—because he believes in its content, but because it is instrumental in the production of a satisfying social effect. What the individual learns, essentially, is to say or do the expected thing in special situations, regardless of what his private beliefs may be. Opinions adopted through compliance should be expressed only when the person's behavior is observable by the influencing agent.

Identification can be said to occur when an individual adopts behavior derived from another person or a group because this behavior is associated with a satisfying self-defining relationship to this person or group. By a self-defining relationship I mean a role relationship that forms a part of the person's self-image. Accepting influence through identification, then, is a way of establishing or maintaining the desired relationship to the other, and the self-definition that is anchored in this relationship.

The relationship that an individual tries to establish or maintain through identification may take different forms. It may take the form of classical identification, that is, of a relationship in which the individual takes over all or part of the role of the influencing agent. To the extent to which such a relationship exists, the individual defines his own role in terms of the role of the other. He attempts to be like or actually to *be* the other person. By saying what the other says, doing what he does, believing what he believes, the individual maintains this relationship and the satisfying self-definition that it provides him. An influencing agent who is likely to be an attractive object for such a relationship is one who occupies a role desired by the individual—who possesses those characteristics that the individual himself lacks—such as control in a situation in which the individual is helpless, direction in a situation in which he is disoriented, or belongingness in a situation in which he is isolated.

The behavior of the brainwashed prisoner in Communist China provides one example of this type of identification. By adopting the attitudes and beliefs of the prison authorities—including *their* evaluation of *him*—he attempts to regain his identity, which has been subjected to severe threats. But this kind of identification does not occur only in such severe crisis situations. It can also be observed, for example, in the context of socialization of children, where the taking over of parental attitudes and actions is a normal, and probably essential, part of personality development. The more or less conscious efforts involved when an individual learns to play a desired occupational role and imitates an appropriate role model would also exemplify this process. Here, of course, the individual is much more selective in the attitudes and actions he takes over from the other person. What is at stake is not his basic sense of identity or the stability of his self-concept, but rather his more limited "professional identity."

The self-defining relationship that an individual tries to establish or maintain through identification may also take the form of a reciprocal role relationship—that is, of a relationship in which the roles of the two parties are defined with reference to one another. An individual may be involved in a reciprocal relationship with another specific individual, as in a friendship relationship between two people. Or he may enact a social role which is defined with reference to another (reciprocal) role, as in the relationship between patient and doctor. A reciprocal-role relationship can be maintained only if the participants have mutually shared expectations of one another's behavior. Thus, if an individual finds a particular relationship satisfying, he will tend to behave in such a way as to meet the expectations of the other. In other words, he will tend to behave in line with the requirements of this particular relationship. This should be true regardless of whether the other is watching or not: quite apart from the reactions of the other, it is important to the individual's own self-concept to meet the expectations of his friendship role, for example, or those of his occupational role.

Thus, the acceptance of influence through identification should take place when the person sees the induced behavior as relevant to and required by a reciprocal-role relationship in which he is a participant. Acceptance of influence based on a reciprocal-role relationship is similar to that involved in classical identification in that it is a way of establishing or maintaining a satisfying self-defining relationship to another. The nature of the relationship differs, of course. In one case it is a relationship of identity; in the other, one of reciprocity. In the case of reciprocal-role relationships, the individual is not identifying with the other in the sense of taking over *his* identity, but in the sense of empathically reacting in terms of the other person's expectations, feelings, or needs.

Identification may also serve to maintain an individual's relationship to a group in which his self-definition is anchored. Such a relationship may have elements of classical identification as well as of reciprocal roles: to maintain his self-definition as a group member an individual, typically, has to model his behavior along particular lines and has to meet the expectations of his fellow members. An example of identification with a group would be the member of the Communist Party who derives strength and a sense of identity from his self-definition as part of the vanguard of the proletarian revolution and as an agent of historical destiny. A similar process, but at a low degree of intensity, is probably involved in many of the conventions that people acquire as part of their socialization into a particular group.

Identification is similar to compliance in that the individual does not adopt the induced behavior because its content per se is intrinsically satisfying. Identification differs from compliance, however, in that the individual actually believes in the opinions and actions that he adopts. The behavior is accepted both publicly and privately, and its manifestation does not depend on observability by the influencing agent. It does depend, however, on the role that an individual takes at any given moment in time. Only when the appropriate role is activated—only when the individual is acting within the relationship upon which the identification is based—will the induced opinions be expressed. The individual is not primarily concerned with pleasing the other, with giving him what he wants (as in compliance), but he is concerned with meeting the other's expectations for his own role performance. Thus, opinions adopted through identification do remain tied to the external source and dependent on social support. They are not integrated with the individual's value system, but rather tend to be isolated from the rest of his values—to remain encapsulated.

Finally, *internalization* can be said to occur when an individual accepts influence because the induced behavior is congruent with his value system. It is the content of the induced behavior that is intrinsically rewarding here. The individual adopts it because he finds it useful for the solution of a problem, or because it is congenial to his own orientation, or because it is demanded by his own values—in short, because he perceives it as inherently conducive to the maximization of his values. The characteristics of the influencing agent do play an important role in internalization, but the crucial dimension here— as we shall see below—is the agent's credibility, that is, his relation to the content.

The most obvious examples of internalization are those that involve the evaluation and acceptance of induced behavior on rational grounds. A person may adopt the recommendations of an expert, for example, because he finds them relevant to his own problems and congruent with his own values. Typically, when internalization is involved, he will not accept these recommendations *in toto* but modify them to some degree so that they will fit his own unique situation. Or a visitor to a foreign country may be challenged by the different patterns of behavior to which he is exposed, and he may decide to adopt them (again, selectively and in modified form) because he finds them more in keeping with his own values than the patterns in his home country. I am not implying, of course, that internalization is always involved in the situations mentioned. One would speak of internalization only if acceptance of influence took the particular form that I described.

Internalization, however, does not necessarily involve the adoption of induced behavior on rational grounds. I would not want to equate internalization with rationality, even though the description of the process has decidedly rationalist overtones. For example, I would characterize as internalization the adoption of beliefs because of their congruence with a value system that is basically *irrational*. Thus, an authoritarian individual may adopt certain racist attitudes because they fit into his paranoid, irrational view of the world. Presumably, what is involved here is internalization, since it is the content of the induced behavior and its relation to the person's value system that is satisfying. Similarly, it should be noted that congruence with a person's value system does not necessarily imply logical consistency. Behavior would be congruent if, in some way or other, it fit into the person's value system, if it seemed to belong there and be demanded by it.

It follows from this conception that behavior adopted through internalization is in some way—rational or otherwise—integrated with the individual's existing values. It becomes part of a personal system, as distinguished from a system of social-role expectations. Such behavior gradually becomes independent of the external source. Its manifestation depends neither on observability by the influencing agent nor on the activation of the relevant role, but on the extent to which the underlying values have been made relevant by the issues under consideration. This does not mean that the individual will invariably express internalized opinions, regardless of the social situation. In any specific situation, he has to choose among competing values in the face of a variety of situational requirements. It does mean, however, that these opinions will at least enter into competition with other alternatives whenever they are relevant in content.

It should be stressed that the three processes are not mutually exclusive. While they have been defined in terms of pure cases, they do not generally occur in pure form in real-life situations. The examples that have been given are, at best, situations in which a particular process predominates and determines the central features of the interaction.

ANTECEDENTS AND CONSEQUENTS OF THE THREE PROCESSES

For each of the three processes, a distinct set of antecedents and a distinct set of consequents have been proposed. These are summarized in the table below. First, with respect to the antecedents of the three processes, it should be noted that no systematic quantitative differences between them are hypothe-

SUMMARY OF THE DISTINCTIONS BETWEEN THE THREE PROCESSES

	Compliance	Identification	Internalization
Antecedents:			
1. Basis for the *importance of the induction*	Concern with social effect of behavior	Concern with social anchorage of behavior	Concern with value congruence of behavior
2. Source of *power of the influencing agent*	Means control	Attractiveness	Credibility
3. Manner of achieving *prepotency of the induced response*	Limitation of choice behavior	Delineation of role requirements	Reorganization of means-ends framework
Consequents:			
1. Conditions of performance of induced response	Surveillance by influencing agent	Salience of relationship to agent	Relevance of values to issue
2. Conditions of change and extinction of induced response	Changed perception of conditions for social rewards	Changed perception of conditions for satisfying self-defining relationships	Changed perception of conditions for value maximization
3. Type of behavior system in which induced response is embedded	External demands of a specific setting	Expectations defining a specific role	Person's value system

sized. The probability of each process is presented as a function of the same three determinants: the importance of the induction for the individual's goal achievement, the power of the influencing agent, and the prepotency of the induced response. For each process, the magnitude of these determinants may vary over the entire range: each may be based on an induction with varying degrees of importance, on an influencing agent with varying degrees of power, and so on. The processes differ only in terms of the *qualitative* form that these determinants take. They differ, as can be seen in the table, in terms of the *basis* for the importance of the induction, the *source* of the influencing agent's power, and the *manner* of achieving prepotency of the induced response.

1. The processes can be distinguished in terms of the basis for the importance of the induction, that is, in terms of the nature of the motivational system that is activated in the influence situation. What is it about the influence situation that makes it important, that makes it relevant to the individual's goals? What are the primary concerns that the individual brings to the situation or that are aroused by it? The differences between the three processes in this respect are implicit in the descriptions of the processes given above: (a) To the extent that the individual is concerned—for whatever reason—with the

social effect of his behavior, influence will tend to take the form of compliance. (b) To the extent that he is concerned with the *social anchorage* of his behavior, influence will tend to take the form of identification. (c) To the extent that he is concerned with the *value congruence* of his behavior (rational or otherwise), influence will tend to take the form of internalization.

2. A difference between the three processes in terms of the source of the influencing agent's power is hypothesized. (a) To the extent that the agent's power is based on his *means control*, influence will tend to take the form of compliance. An agent possesses means control if he is in a position to supply or withhold means needed by the individual for the achievement of his goals. The perception of means control may depend on the agent's *actual* control over specific rewards and punishments, or on his *potential* control, which would be related to his position in the social structure (his status, authority, or general prestige). (b) To the extent that the agent's power is based on his *attractiveness*, influence will tend to take the form of identification. An agent is attractive if he occupies a role which the individual himself desires[8] or if he occupies a role reciprocal to one the individual wants to establish or maintain. The term "attractiveness," as used here, does not refer to the possession of qualities that make a person likable, but rather to the possession of qualities on the part of the agent that make a continued relationship to him particularly desirable. In other words, an agent is attractive when the individual is able to derive satisfaction from a self-definition with reference to him. (c) To the extent that the agent's power is based on his *credibility*, influence will tend to take the form of internalization. An agent possesses credibility if his statements are considered truthful and valid, and hence worthy of serious consideration. Hovland, Janis, and Kelley[9] distinguish two bases for credibility: expertness and trustworthiness. In other words, an agent may be perceived as possessing credibility because he is likely to *know* the truth, or because he is likely to *tell* the truth. Trustworthiness, in turn, may be related to over-all respect, likemindedness, and lack of vested interest.

3. It is proposed that the three processes differ in terms of the way in which prepotency is achieved. (a) To the extent that the induced response becomes prepotent—that is, becomes a "distinguished path" relative to alternative response possibilities—because the individual's choice behavior is limited, influence will tend to take the form of compliance. This may happen if the individual is pressured into the induced response, or if alternative responses are blocked. The induced response thus becomes prepotent because it is, essentially, the only response permitted: the individual sees himself as having no choice and as being restricted to this particular alternative. (b) To the extent that the

---

[8] This is similar to John Whiting's conception of "Status Envy" as a basis for identification. See J. W. M. Whiting, "Sorcery, Sin, and the Superego," in M. R. Jones, editor, *Nebraska Symposium on Motivation*, Lincoln, University of Nebraska Press, 1959, pp. 174–195.

[9] *Op. cit.*, p. 21.

induced response becomes prepotent because the requirements of a particular role are delineated, influence will tend to take the form of identification. This may happen if the situation is defined in terms of a particular role relationship and the demands of that role are more or less clearly specified; for instance, if this role is made especially salient and the expectations deriving from it dominate the field. Or it may happen if alternative roles are made ineffective because the situation is ambiguous and consensual validation is lacking. The induced response thus becomes prepotent because it is one of the few alternatives available to the individual: his choice behavior may be unrestricted, but his opportunity for selecting alternative responses is limited by the fact that he is operating exclusively from the point of view of a particular role system. (c) Finally, to the extent that the induced response becomes prepotent because there has been a reorganization in the individual's conception of means-ends relationships, influence will tend to take the form of internalization. This may happen if the implications of the induced response for certain important values —implications of which the individual had been unaware heretofore—are brought out, or if the advantages of the induced response as a path to the individual's goals, compared to the various alternatives that are available, are made apparent. The induced response thus becomes prepotent because it has taken on a new meaning: as the relationships between various means and ends become restructured, it emerges as the preferred course of action in terms of the person's own values.

Depending, then, on the nature of these three antecedents, the influence process will take the form of compliance, identification, or internalization. Each of these corresponds to a characteristic pattern of internal responses— thoughts and feelings—in which the individual engages as he accepts influence. The resulting changes will, in turn, be different for the three processes, as indicated in the second half of the table. Here, again, it is assumed that there are no systematic quantitative differences between the processes, but rather qualitative variations in the subsequent histories of behavior adopted through each process.

1. It is proposed that the processes differ in terms of the subsequent conditions under which the induced response will be performed or expressed. (a) When an individual adopts an induced response through compliance, he tends to perform it only under conditions of *surveillance* by the influencing agent. These conditions are met if the agent is physically present, or if he is likely to find out about the individual's actions. (b) When an individual adopts an induced response through identification, he tends to perform it only under conditions of *salience* of his relationship to the agent. That is, the occurrence of the behavior will depend on the extent to which the person's relationship to the agent has been engaged in the situation. Somehow this relationship has to be brought into focus and the individual has to be acting within the particular role that is involved in the identification. This does not necessarily mean, however,

that he is consciously aware of the relationship; the role can be activated without such awareness. (c) When an individual adopts an induced response through internalization, he tends to perform it under conditions of *relevance of the values* that were initially involved in the influence situation. The behavior will tend to occur whenever these values are activated by the issues under consideration in a given situation, quite regardless of surveillance or salience of the influencing agent. This does not mean, of course, that the behavior will occur every time it becomes relevant. It may be out-competed by other responses in certain situations. The probability of occurrence with a given degree of issue relevance will depend on the strength of the internalized behavior.

2. It is hypothesized that responses adopted through the three processes will differ in terms of the conditions under which they will subsequently be abandoned or changed. (a) A response adopted through compliance will be abandoned if it is no longer perceived as the best path toward the attainment of social rewards. (b) A response adopted through identification will be abandoned if it is no longer perceived as the best path toward the maintenance or establishment of satisfying self-defining relationships. (c) A response adopted through internalization will be abandoned if it is no longer perceived as the best path toward the maximization of the individual's values.

3. Finally, it is hypothesized that responses adopted through the three processes will differ from each other along certain qualitative dimensions. These can best be summarized, perhaps, by referring to the type of behavior system in which the induced response is embedded. (a) Behavior adopted through compliance is part of a system of external demands that characterize a specific setting. In other words, it is part of the rules of conduct that an individual learns in order to get along in a particular situation or series of situations. The behavior tends to be related to the person's values only in an instrumental rather than an intrinsic way. As long as opinions, for example, remain at that level, the individual will tend to regard them as not really representative of his true beliefs. (b) Behavior adopted through identification is part of a system of expectations defining a particular role—whether this is the role of the other which he is taking over, or a role reciprocal to the other's. This behavior will be regarded by the person as representing himself, and may in fact form an important aspect of himself. It will tend to be isolated, however, from the rest of the person's values—to have little interplay with them. In extreme cases, the system in which the induced response is embedded may be encapsulated and function almost like a foreign body within the person. The induced responses here will be relatively inflexible and stereotyped. (c) Behavior adopted through internalization is part of an internal system. It is fitted into the person's basic framework of values and is congruent with it. This does not imply complete consistency: the degree of consistency can vary for different individuals and different areas of behavior. It does mean, however, that there is some interplay between the new beliefs and the rest of the person's

values. The new behavior can serve to modify existing beliefs and can in turn be modified by them. As a result of this interaction, behavior adopted through internalization will tend to be relatively idiosyncratic, flexible, complex, and differentiated.

Robert B. Zajonc

THE CONCEPTS OF
BALANCE, CONGRUITY,
AND DISSONANCE

The concept of consistency in man, a special case of a
concept of universal consistency, has in recent years been
productive of systematic theories and programs of research.
Attitude change has been a focal area in this theoretical
development. Consistency doctrines, however, lack
specification of the conditions under which their predictions
will hold. People like to make sense of their world, but they
also seek out the magician to be entertained by incongruity.
Historically the concept of consistency resembles the
concept of vacuum in physics—a useful doctrine for
organizing knowledge, although full of exceptions and
contradictions.

The author is an Assistant Program Director at the
Research Center for Group Dynamics, an Assistant
Professor of Psychology at the University of Michigan,
and a member of the Editorial Board of *Contemporary
Psychology* and of *Human Relations*.

Common to the concepts of balance, congruity, and dissonance is the
notion that thoughts, beliefs, attitudes, and behavior tend to organize themselves in meaningful and sensible ways.[1] Members of the White Citizens

[1] The concepts of balance, congruity, and dissonance are due to Heider, Osgood and
Tannenbaum, and Festinger, respectively. (F. Heider, "Attitudes and Cognitive Organization,"
Journal of Psychology, Vol. 21, 1946, pp. 107–112. C. E. Osgood and P. H. Tannenbaum, "The
Principle of Congruity in the Prediction of Attitude Change," *Psychological Review*, Vol. 62,
1955, pp. 42–55. L. Festinger, *A Theory of Cognitive Dissonance*, Evanston, Ill., Row, Peterson,
1957.) For purposes of simplicity we will subsume these concepts under the label of consistency.

Reprinted from the *Public Opinion Quarterly*, 24 (1960), 280–96, with permission of the
author and the Public Opinion Quarterly.

Council do not ordinarily contribute to NAACP. Adherents of the New Deal seldom support Republican candidates. Christian Scientists do not enroll in medical schools. And people who live in glass houses apparently do not throw stones. In this respect the concept of consistency underscores and presumes human *rationality*. It holds that behavior and attitudes are not only consistent to the objective observer, but that individuals try to appear consistent to themselves. It assumes that inconsistency is a noxious state setting up pressures to eliminate it or reduce it. But in the *ways* that consistency in human behavior and attitudes is achieved we see rather often a striking lack of rationality. A heavy smoker cannot readily accept evidence relating cancer to smoking;[2] a socialist, told that Hoover's endorsement of certain political slogans agreed perfectly with his own, calls him a "typical hypocrite and a liar."[3] Allport illustrates this irrationality in the following conversation:

MR. X: The trouble with Jews is that they only take care of their own group.

MR. Y: But the record of the Community Chest shows that they give more generously than non-Jews.

MR. X: That shows that they are always trying to buy favor and intrude in Christian affairs. They think of nothing but money; that is why there are so many Jewish bankers.

MR. Y: But a recent study shows that the per cent of Jews in banking is proportionally much smaller than the per cent of non-Jews.

MR. X: That's just it. They don't go in for respectable business. They would rather run night clubs.[4]

Thus, while the concept of consistency acknowledges man's rationality, observation of the means of its achievement simultaneously unveils his irrationality. The psychoanalytic notion of rationalization is a literal example of a concept which assumes both rationality and irrationality—it holds, namely, that man strives to understand and justify painful experiences and to make them sensible and rational, but he employs completely irrational methods to achieve this end.

The concepts of consistency are not novel. Nor are they indigenous to the study of attitudes, behavior, or personality. These concepts have appeared in various forms in almost all sciences. It has been argued by some that it is the existence of consistencies in the universe that made science possible, and by others that consistencies in the universe are a proof of divine power.[5] There

[2] Festinger, *op. cit.*, pp. 153–156,

[3] H. B. Lewis, "Studies in the Principles of Judgments and Attitudes: IV, The Operation of 'Prestige Suggestion'," *Journal of Social Psychology*, Vol. 14, 1941, pp. 229–256.

[4] G. W. Allport, *The Nature of Prejudice*, Cambridge, Mass., Addison-Wesley, 1954.

[5] W. P. Montague, *Belief Unbound*, New Haven, Conn., Yale University Press, 1930, pp. 70–73.

is, of course, a question of whether consistencies are "real" or mere products of ingenious abstraction and conceptualization. For it would be entirely possible to categorize natural phenomena in such a haphazard way that instead of order, unity, and consistency, one would see a picture of utter chaos. If we were to eliminate one of the spatial dimensions from the conception of the physical world, the consistencies we now know and the consistencies which allow us to make reliable predictions would be vastly depleted.

The concept of consistency in man is, then, a special case of the concept of universal consistency. The fascination with this concept led some psychologists to rather extreme positions. Franke, for instance, wrote, ". . . the unity of a person can be traced in each instant of his life. There is nothing in character that contradicts itself. If a person who is known to us seems to be incongruous with himself that is only an indication of the inadequacy and superficiality of our previous observations."[6] This sort of hypothesis is, of course, incapable of either verification or disproof and therefore has no significant consequences.

Empirical investigations employing the concepts of consistency have been carried out for many years. Not until recently, however, has there been a programmatic and systematic effort to explore with precision and detail their particular consequences for behavior and attitudes. The greatest impetus to the study of attitudinal consistency was given recently by Festinger and his students. In addition to those already named, other related contributions in this area are those of Newcomb, who introduced the concept of "strain toward symmetry,"[7] and of Cartwright and Harary, who expressed the notions of balance and symmetry in a mathematical form.[8] These notions all assume inconsistency to be a painful or at least psychologically uncomfortable state, but they differ in the generality of application. The most restrictive and specific is the principle of congruity, since it restricts itself to the problems of the effects of information about objects and events on the attitudes toward the source of information. The most general is the notion of cognitive dissonance, since it considers consistency among any cognitions. In between are the notions of balance and symmetry, which consider attitudes toward people and objects in relation to one another, either within one person's cognitive structure, as in the case of Heider's theory of balance, or among a given group of individuals, as in the case of Newcomb's strain toward symmetry. It is the purpose of this paper to survey these concepts and to consider their implications for theory and research on attitudes.

[6] R. Franke, "Gang und Character," *Beihefte, Zeitschrift für angewandte Psychologie*, No. 58, 1931, p. 45.

[7] T. M. Newcomb, "An Approach to the Study of Communicative Acts," *Psychological Review*, Vol. 60, 1953, pp. 393–404.

[8] D. Cartwright and F. Harary, "Structural Balance: A Generalization of Heider's Theory," *Psychological Review*, Vol. 63, 1956, pp. 277–293.

THE CONCEPTS OF BALANCE
AND STRAIN TOWARD SYMMETRY

The earliest formalization of consistency is attributed to Heider,[9] who was concerned with the way relations among persons involving some impersonal entity are cognitively experienced by the individual. The consistencies in which Heider was interested were those to be found in the ways people view their relations with other people and with the environment. The analysis was limited to two persons, labeled P and O, with P as the focus of the analysis and with O representing some other person, and to one impersonal entity, which could be a physical object, an idea, an event, or the like, labeled X. The object of Heider's inquiry was to discover how relations among P, O, and X are organized in P's cognitive structure, and whether there exist recurrent and systematic tendencies in the way these relations are experienced. Two types of relation, liking (L) and so-called U, or unit, relations (such as possession, cause, similarity, and the like) were distinguished. On the basis of incidental observations and intuitive judgment, probably, Heider proposed that the person's (P's) cognitive structure representing relations among P, O, and X are either what he termed "balanced" or "unbalanced." In particular, he proposed, "In the case of three entities, a balanced state exists if all three relations are positive in all respects or if two are negative and one positive." Thus a balanced state is obtained when, for instance, P likes O, P likes X, and O likes X; or when P likes O, P dislikes X, and O dislikes X; or when P dislikes O, P likes X, and O dislikes X (see Figure 1). It should be noted that within Heider's conception a relation may be either positive or negative; degrees of liking cannot be rep-

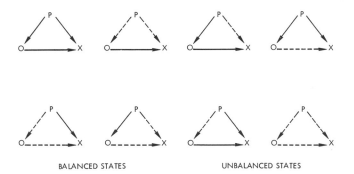

BALANCED STATES   UNBALANCED STATES

FIGURE 1.   *Examples of balanced and unbalanced states according to Heider's definition of balance. Solid lines represent positive, and broken lines negative, relations.*

[9] Heider, *op. cit.*

resented. The fundamental assumption of balance theory is that an unbalanced state produces tension and generates forces to restore balance. This hypothesis was tested by Jordan.[10] He presented subjects with hypothetical situations involving two persons and an impersonal entity to rate for "pleasantness." Half the situations were by Heider's definition balanced and half unbalanced. Jordan's data showed somewhat higher unpleasantness ratings for the unbalanced than the balanced situations.

Cartwright and Harary[11] have cast Heider's formulation in graph-theoretical terms and derived some interesting consequences beyond those stated by Heider. Heider's concept allows either a balanced or an unbalanced state. Cartwright and Harary have constructed a more general definition of balance, with balance treated as a matter of degree, ranging from 0 to 1. Furthermore, their formulation of balance theory extended the notion to any number of entities, and an experiment by Morrissette[12] similar in design to that of Jordan obtained evidence for Cartwright and Harary's derivations.

A notion very similar to balance was advanced by Newcomb in 1953.[13] In addition to substituting A for P, and B for O, Newcomb took Heider's notion of balance out of one person's head and applied it to communication among people. Newcomb postulates a "strain toward symmetry" which leads to a communality of attitudes of two people (A and B) oriented toward an object (X). The strain toward symmetry influences communication between A and B so as to bring their attitudes toward X into congruence. Newcomb cites a study in which a questionnaire was administered to college students in 1951 following the dismissal of General MacArthur by President Truman. Data were obtained on students' attitudes toward Truman's decision and their perception of the attitudes of their closest friends. Of the pro-Truman subjects 48 said that their closest friends favored Truman and none that their closest friends were opposed to his decision. Of the anti-Truman subjects only 2 said that their friends were generally pro-Truman and 34 that they were anti-Truman. In a longitudinal study, considerably more convincing evidence was obtained in support of the strain-toward-symmetry hypothesis. In 1954 Newcomb set up a house at the University of Michigan which offered free rent for one semester for seventeen students who would serve as subjects. The residents of the house were observed, questioned, and rated for four to five hours a week during the entire semester. The study was then repeated with another set of seventeen students. The findings revealed a tendency for those who were attracted to one another to agree on many matters, including the way they perceived their own selves

[10] N. Jordan, "Behavioral Forces That Are a Function of Attitudes and of Cognitive Organization," *Human Relations*, Vol. 6, 1953, pp. 273–287.

[11] Cartwright and Harary, *op. cit.*

[12] J. Morrissette, "An Experimental Study of the Theory of Structural Balance," *Human Relations*, Vol. 11, 1958, pp. 239–254.

[13] Newcomb, *op. cit.*

and their ideal selves, and their attractions for other group members. Moreover, in line with the prediction, these similarities, real as well as perceived, seemed to increase over time.[14]

Newcomb also cites the work of Festinger and his associates on social communication[15] in support of this hypothesis. Festinger's studies on communication have clearly shown that the tendency to influence other group members toward one's own opinion increases with the degree of attraction. More recently Burdick and Burnes reported two experiments in which measures of skin resistance (GSR) were obtained as an index of emotional reaction in the presence of balanced and unbalanced situations.[16] They observed significant differences in skin resistance depending on whether the subjects agreed or disagreed with a "well-liked experimenter." In the second experiment Burdick and Burnes found that subjects who liked the experimenter tended to change their opinions toward greater agreement with his, and those who disliked him, toward greater disagreement. There are, of course, many other studies to show that the attitude toward the communicator determines his persuasive effectiveness. Hovland and his co-workers have demonstrated these effects in several studies.[17] They have also shown, however, that these effects are fleeting; that is, the attitude change produced by the communication seems to dissipate over time. Their interpretation is that over time subjects tend to dissociate the source from the message and are therefore subsequently less influenced by the prestige of the communicator. This proposition was substantiated by Kelman and Hovland,[18] who produced attitude changes with a prestigeful communicator and retested subjects after a four-week interval with and without reminding the subjects about the communicator. The results showed that the permanence of the attitude change depended on the association with the source.

In general, the consequences of balance theories have up to now been rather limited. Except for Newcomb's longitudinal study, the experimental situations dealt mostly with subjects who responded to hypothetical situations, and direct evidence is scarce. The Burdick and Burnes experiment is the only one bearing more directly on the assumption that imbalance or asymmetry produces tension. Cartwright and Harary's mathematization of the concept

[14] T. M. Newcomb, "The Prediction of Interpersonal Attraction," *American Psychologist*, Vol. 11, 1956, pp. 575–586.

[15] L. Festinger, K. Back, S. Schachter, H. H. Kelley, and J. Thibaut, *Theory and Experiment in Social Communication*, Ann Arbor, Mich., University of Michigan, Institute for Social Research, 1950.

[16] H. A. Burdick and A. J. Burnes, "A Test of 'Strain toward Symmetry' Theories," *Journal of Abnormal and Social Psychology*, Vol. 57, 1958, pp. 367–369.

[17] C. I. Hovland, I. L. Janis, and H. H. Kelley, *Communication and Persuasion: Psychological Studies of Opinion Change*, New Haven, Conn., Yale University Press, 1953.

[18] H. C. Kelman and C. I. Hovland, "'Reinstatement' of the Communicator in Delayed Measurement of Opinion Change," *Journal of Abnormal and Social Psychology*, Vol. 48, 1953, pp. 327–335.

of balance should, however, lead to important empirical and theoretical developments. One difficulty is that there really has not been a serious experimental attempt to *disprove* the theory. It is conceivable that some situations defined by the theory as unbalanced may in fact remain stable and produce no significant pressures toward balance. Festinger once inquired in a jocular mood if it followed from balance theory that since he likes chicken, and since chickens like chicken feed, he must also like chicken feed or else experience the tension of imbalance. While this counterexample is, of course, not to be taken seriously, it does point to some difficulties in the concepts of balance. It is not clear from Heider's theory of balance and Newcomb's theory of symmetry what predictions are to be made when attraction of both P and O toward X exists but when the origin and nature of these attractions are different. In other words, suppose both P and O like X but for different reasons and in entirely different ways, as was the case with Festinger and the chickens. Are the consequences of balance theory the same then as in the case where P and O like X for the same reasons and in the same way? It is also not clear, incidentally, what the consequences are when the relation between P and O is cooperative and when it is competitive. Two men vying for the hand of the same fair maiden might experience tesnion whether they are close friends or deadly enemies.

In a yet unpublished study conducted by Harburg and Price at the University of Michigan, students were asked to name two of their best friends. When those named were of opposite sexes, subjects reported they would feel uneasy if the two friends liked one another. In a subsequent experiment subjects were asked whether they desired their good friend to like, be neutral to, or dislike one of their strongly disliked acquaintances, and whether they desired the disliked acquaintance to like or dislike the friend. It will be recalled that in either case a balanced state obtains only if the two persons are negatively related to one another. However, Harburg and Price found that 39 per cent desired their friend to be liked by the disliked acquaintance, and only 24 per cent to be disliked. Moreover, faced with the alternative that the disliked acquaintance dislikes their friend, 55 per cent as opposed to 25 per cent expressed uneasiness. These results are quite inconsistent with balance theory. Although one may want one's friends to dislike one's enemies, one may not want the enemies to dislike one's friends. The reason for the latter may be simply a concern for the friends' welfare.

OSGOOD AND TANNENBAUM'S PRINCIPLE OF CONGRUITY

The principle of congruity, which is in fact a special case of balance, was advanced by Osgood and Tannenbaum in 1955.[19] It deals specifically with the problem of *direction* of attitude change. The authors assume that

[19] Osgood and Tannenbaum, *op. cit.*

"judgmental frames of reference tend toward maximal simplicity." Thus, since extreme "black-and-white," "all-or-nothing," judgments are simpler than refined ones, valuations tend to move toward extremes or, in the words of the authors, there is "a continuing pressure toward polarization." Together with the notion of maximization of simplicity is the assumption of identity as being less complex than the discrimination of fine differences. Therefore, related "concepts" will tend to be evaluated in a similar manner. Given these assumptions, the principle of congruity holds that when change in evaluation or attitude occurs it always occurs in the direction of increased congruity with the prevailing frame of reference. The paradigm of congruity is that of an individual who is confronted with an assertion regarding a particular matter about which he believes and feels in a certain way, made by a person toward whom he also has some attitude. Given that Eisenhower is evaluated positively and freedom of the press also positively, and given that Eisenhower (+) comes out in favor of freedom of the press (+), congruity is said to exist. But given that the *Daily Worker* is evaluated negatively, and given that the *Daily Worker* (−) comes out in favor of freedom of the press (+), incongruity is said to exist. Examples of congruity and incongruity are shown in Figure 2. The diagram shows the attitudes of a given individual toward the source and the object of the assertion. The assertions represented by heavy lines imply either positive or negative attitudes of the source toward the object. It is clear from a comparison of Figures 1 and 2 that in terms of their formal properties, the defini-

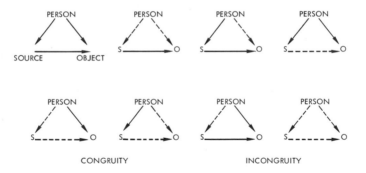

FIGURE 2. *Examples of congruity and incongruity. Heavy lines represent assertions, light lines attitudes. Solid heavy lines represent assertions which imply a positive attitude on the part of the source, and broken heavy lines negative attitudes. Solid light lines represent positive, and broken light lines negative, attitudes.*

tions of balance and congruity are identical. Thus, incongruity is said to exist when the attitudes toward the source and the object are similar and the assertion is negative, or when they are dissimilar and the assertion is positive. In comparison, unbalanced states are defined as having either one or all negative relations, which is of course equivalent to the above. To the extent that

the person's attitudes are congruent with those implied in the assertion, a stable state exists. When the attitudes toward the person and the assertion are incongruent, there will be a tendency to change the attitudes toward the person and the object of the assertion in the direction of increased congruity. Tannenbaum obtained measures on 405 college students regarding their attitudes toward labor leaders, the *Chicago Tribune*, and Senator Robert Taft as sources, and toward legalized gambling, abstract art, and accelerated college programs as objects. Some time after the attitude scores were obtained, the subjects were presented with "highly realistic" newspaper clippings involving assertions made by the various sources regarding the concepts. In general, when the original attitudes toward the source and the concept were both positive and the assertion presented in the newspaper clippings was also positive, no significant attitude changes were observed in the results. When the original attitudes toward the source and the concept were negative and the assertion was positive, again no changes were obtained. As predicted, however, when a positively valued source was seen as making a positive assertion about a negatively valued concept, the attitude toward the source became less favorable, and toward the concept more favorable. Conversely, when a negatively valued source was seen as making a positive assertion about a positively valued concept, attitudes toward the source became more favorable and toward the concept less favorable. The entire gamut of predicted changes was confirmed in Tannenbaum's data; it is summarized in the accompanying table, in which the direction of change is represented by either a plus or a minus sign, and the extent of change by either one or two such signs.

CHANGE OF ATTITUDE TOWARD THE SOURCE AND THE OBJECT
WHEN POSITIVE AND NEGATIVE ASSERTIONS ARE
MADE BY THE SOURCE

Original Attitude toward the Source	Positive Assertion about an Object toward Which the Attitude Is		Negative Assertion about an Object toward Which the Attitude Is	
	Positive	*Negative*	*Positive*	*Negative*
	CHANGE OF ATTITUDE TOWARD THE SOURCE			
Positive	+	— —	— —	+
Negative	+ +	--	—	+ +
	CHANGE OF ATTITUDE TOWARD THE OBJECT			
Positive	+	+ +	— —	—
Negative	— —	—	+	+ +

A further derivation of the congruity principle is that incongruity do not invariably produce attitude change, but that it may at times lead incredulity on the part of the individual. When confronted by an assertion whi stands in an incongruous relation to the person who made it, there will be

tendency not to believe that the person made the assertion, thus reducing incongruity.

There is a good deal of evidence supporting Osgood and Tannenbaum's principle of congruity. As early as 1921, H. T. Moore had subjects judge statements for their grammar, ethical infringements for their seriousness, and resolutions of the dominant seventh chord for their dissonance.[20] After two and one-half months the subjects returned and were presented with judgments of "experts." This experimental manipulation resulted in 62 per cent reversals of judgments on grammar, 50 per cent of ethical judgments, and 43 per cent of musical judgments. And in 1935 in a study on a similar problem of prestige suggestion, Sherif let subjects rank sixteen authors for their literary merit.[21] Subsequently, the subjects were given sixteen passages presumably written by the various authors previously ranked. The subjects were asked to rank-order the passages for literary merit. Although in actuality *all* the passages were written by Robert Louis Stevenson, the subjects were able to rank the passages. Moreover, the correlations between the merit of the author and the merit of the passage ranged from between .33 to .53. These correlations are not very dramatic, yet they do represent some impact of attitude toward the source on attitude toward the passage.

With respect to incredulity, an interesting experiment was conducted recently by Jones and Kohler in which subjects learned statements which either supported their attitudes or were in disagreement with them.[22] Some of the statements were plausible and some implausible. The results were rather striking. Subjects whose attitudes favored segregation learned plausible pro-segregation statements and implausible anti-segregation statements much more rapidly than plausible anti-segregation and implausible pro-segregation statements. The reverse was of course true for subjects whose attitudes favored desegregation.

While the principle of congruity presents no new ideas, it has a great advantage over the earlier attempts in its precision. Osgood and Tannenbaum have formulated the principle of congruity in quantitative terms allowing for precise predictions regarding the extent and direction of attitude change— predictions which in their studies were fairly well confirmed. While balance theory allows merely a dichotomy of attitudes, either positive or negative, the principle of congruity allows refined measurements using Osgood's method of the semantic differential.[23] Moreover, while it is not clear from Heider's

[20] H. T. Moore, "The Comparative Influence of Majority and Expert Opinion," *American Journal of Psychology*, Vol. 32, 1921, pp. 16–20.

[21] M. Sherif, "An Experimental Study of Stereotypes," *Journal of Abnormal and Social Psychology*, Vol. 29, 1935, pp. 371–375.

[22] E. E. Jones and R. Kohler, "The Effects of Plausibility on the Learning of Controversial Statements," *Journal of Abnormal and Social Psychology*, Vol. 57, 1958, pp. 315–320.

[23] C. E. Osgood, "The Nature and Measurement of Meaning," *Psychological Bulletin*, Vol. 49, 1952, pp. 197–237.

statement of balance in just what direction changes will occur when an unbalanced state exists, such predictions can be made on the basis of the congruity principle.

FESTINGER'S THEORY OF COGNITIVE DISSONANCE

Perhaps the largest systematic body of data is that collected in the realm of Festinger's dissonance theory. The statement of the dissonance principle is simple. It holds that two elements of knowledge ". . . are in dissonant relation if, considering these two alone, the obverse of one element would follow from the other."[24] It further holds that dissonance ". . . being psychologically uncomfortable, will motivate the person to try to reduce dissonance and achieve consonance" and ". . . in addition to trying to reduce it, the person will actively avoid situations and information which would likely increase the dissonance."[25] A number of rather interesting and provocative consequences follow from Festinger's dissonance hypothesis.

First, it is predicted that all decisions or choices result in dissonance to the extent that the alternative not chosen contains positive features which make it attractive also, and the alternative chosen contains features which might have resulted in rejecting it. Hence after making a choice people seek evidence to confirm their decision and so reduce dissonance. In the Ehrlich experiment cited by Cohen in this issue the finding was that new car owners noticed and read ads about the cars they had recently purchased more than ads about other cars.[26]

Post-decision dissonance was also shown to result in a change of attractiveness of the alternative involved in a decision. Brehm had female subjects rate eight appliances for desirability.[27] Subsequently, the subjects were given a choice between two of the eight products, given the chosen product, and after some interpolated activity (consisting of reading research reports about four of the appliances) were asked to rate the products again. Half the subjects were given a choice between products which they rated in a similar manner, and half between products on which the ratings differed. Thus in the first case higher dissonance was to be expected than in the second. The prediction from dissonance theory that there should be an increase in the attractiveness of the chosen alternative and decrease in the attractiveness of the rejected alternative was on the whole confirmed. Moreover, the further implication was also

[24] Festinger, *op. cit.*, p. 13.

[25] *Ibid.*, p. 3.

[26] D. Ehrlich, I. Guttman, P. Schönbach, and J. Mills, "Post-decision Exposure to Relevant Information," *Journal of Abnormal and Social Psychology*, Vol. 54, 1957, pp. 98–102.

[27] J. Brehm, "Post-decision Changes in the Desirability of Alternatives," *Journal of Abnormal and Social Psychology*, Vol. 52, 1956, pp. 384–389.

confirmed that the pressure to reduce dissonance (which was accomplished in the above experiment by changes in attractiveness of the alternatives) varies directly with the extent of dissonance.

Another body of data accounted for by the dissonance hypothesis deals with situations in which the person is forced (either by reward or punishment) to express an opinion publicly or make a public judgment or statement which is contrary to his own opinions and beliefs. In cases where the person actually makes such a judgment or expresses an opinion contrary to his own as a result of a promised reward or threat, dissonance exists between the knowledge of the overt behavior of the person and his privately held beliefs. Festinger also argues that in the case of noncompliance dissonance will exist between the knowledge of overt behavior and the anticipation of reward and punishment.

An example of how dissonance theory accounts for forced-compliance data is given by Brehm.[28] Brehm offered prizes to eighth-graders for eating disliked vegetables and obtained measures of how well the children liked the vegetables. Children who ate the vegetables increased their liking for them. Of course, one might argue that a simpler explanation of the results is that the attractiveness of the prize generalized to the vegetable, or that, even more simply, the vegetables increased in utility because a reward came with them. However, this argument would also lead one to predict that the increment in attraction under such conditions is a *direct* function of the magnitude of the reward. Dissonance theory makes the opposite prediction, and therefore a test of the validity of the two explanations is possible. Data collected by Festinger and Carlsmith[29] and by Aronson and Mills[30] support the dissonance point of view. In Festinger and Carlsmith's experiment subjects were offered either $20 or $1 for telling someone that an experience which had actually been quite boring had been rather enjoyable and interesting. When measures of the subjects' private opinions about their actual enjoyment of the task were taken, those who were to be paid only $1 for the false testimony showed considerably higher scores than those who were to be paid $20. Aronson and Mills, on the other hand, tested the effects of negative incentive. They invited college women to join a group requiring them to go through a process of initiation. For some women the initiation was quite severe, for others it was mild. The prediction from dissonance theory that those who had to undergo severe initiation would increase their attraction for the group more than those having no initiation or mild initiation was borne out.

A third set of consequences of the theory of dissonance deals with exposure to information. Since dissonance occurs between cognitive elements, and since

[28] J. Brehm, "Increasing Cognitive Dissonance by a *Fait Accompli*," *Journal of Abnormal and Social Psychology*, Vol. 58, 1959, pp. 379–382.

[29] L. Festinger and J. M. Carlsmith, "Cognitive Consequences of Forced Compliance," *Journal of Abnormal and Social Psychology*, Vol. 58, 1959, pp. 203–210.

[30] E. Aronson and J. Mills, "The Effect of Severity of Initiation on Liking for a Group," *Journal of Abnormal and Social Psychology*, Vol. 59, 1959, pp. 177–181.

information may lead to change in these elements, the principle of dissonance should have a close bearing on the individual's commerce with information. In particular, the assumption that dissonance is a psychologically uncomfortable state leads to the prediction that individuals will seek out information reducing dissonance and avoid information increasing it. The study on automobile-advertising readership described above is a demonstration of this hypothesis.[31] In another study Mills, Aronson, and Robinson gave college students a choice between an objective and an essay examination.[32] Following the decision, the subjects were given articles about examinations presumably written by experts, and they were asked if they would like to read them. In addition, in order to vary the intensity of dissonance, half the subjects were told that the examination counted 70 per cent toward the final grade, and half that it counted only 5 per cent. The data were obtained in the form of rankings of the articles for preference. While there was a clear preference for reading articles containing positive information about the alternative chosen, no significant selective effects were found when the articles presented arguments against the given type of examination. Also, the authors failed to demonstrate effects relating selectivity in exposure to information to the magnitude of dissonance, in that no significant differences were found between subjects for whom the examination was quite important (70 per cent of the final grade) and those for whom it was relatively unimportant (5 per cent of the final grade).

Festinger was able to account for many other results by means of the dissonance principle, and in general his theory is rather successful in organizing a diverse body of empirical knowledge by means of a limited number of fairly reasonable assumptions. Moreover, from these reasonable assumptions dissonance theory generated several nontrivial and nonobvious consequences. The negative relationship between the magnitude of incentive and attraction of the object of false testimony is not at all obvious. Also not obvious is the prediction of an increase in proselytizing for a mystical belief following an event that clearly contradicts it. Festinger, Riecken, and Schachter studied a group of "Seekers"—people who presumably received a message from outer space informing them of an incipient major flood.[33] When the flood failed to materialize on the critical date, instead of quietly withdrawing from the public scene, as one would expect, the "Seekers" summoned press representatives, gave extended interviews, and invited the public to visit them and be informed of the details of the whole affair. In a very recent study by Brehm, a "nonobvious" derivation from dissonance theory was tested.[34] Brehm predicted that when

---

[31] Ehrlich *et al., op.cit.*

[32] J. Mills, E. Aronson, and H. Robinson, "Selectivity in Exposure to Information," *Journal of Abnormal and Social Psychology,* Vol. 59, 1959, pp. 250–253.

[33] L. Festinger, J. Riecken, and S. Schachter, *When Prophecy Fails,* Minneapolis, University of Minnesota Press, 1956.

[34] J. W. Brehm, "Attitudinal Consequences of Commitment to Unpleasant Behavior," *Journal of Abnormal and Social Psychology,* Vol. 60, 1960, pp. 379–383.

forced to engage in an unpleasant activity, an individual's liking for this activity will increase more when he receives information essentially berating the activity than when he receives information promoting it. The results tended to support Brehm's prediction. Since negative information is said to increase dissonance, and since increased dissonance leads to an increased tendency to reduce it, and since the only means of dissonance reduction was increasing the attractiveness of the activity, such an increase would in fact be expected.

CONCLUSIONS

The theories and empirical work dealing with consistencies are mainly concerned with intra-individual phenomena, be it with relationships between one attitude and another, between attitudes and values, or information, or perception, or behavior, or the like. One exception is Newcomb's concept of "strain toward symmetry." Here the concern is primarily with the interplay of forces among individuals which results in uniformities or consistencies among them. There is no question that the concepts of consistency, and especially the theory of cognitive dissonance, account for many varied attitudinal phenomena. Of course, the various formulations of consistency do not pretend, nor are they able, to account completely for the phenomena they examine. Principles of consistency, like all other principles, are prefaced by the *ceteris paribus* preamble. Thus, when other factors are held constant, then the principles of consistency should be able to explain behavior and attitudes completely. But the question to be raised here is just what factors must be held constant and how important and significant, relative to consistency, are they.

Suppose a man feels hostile toward the British and also dislikes cricket. One might be tempted to conclude that if one of his attitudes were different he would experience the discomfort of incongruity. But there are probably many people whose attitudes toward the British and cricket are incongruent, although the exact proportions are not known and are hardly worth serious inquiry. But if such an inquiry were undertaken it would probably disclose that attitudes depend largely on the conditions under which they have been acquired. For one thing, it would show that the attitudes depend at least to some extent on the relationship of the attitude object to the individual's needs and fears, and that these may be stronger than forces toward balance. There are in this world things to be avoided and feared. A child bitten by a dog will not develop favorable attitudes toward dogs. And no matter how much he likes Popeye you can't make him like spinach, although according to balance theory he should.

The relationship between attitudes and values or needs has been explored, for instance, in *The Authoritarian Personality*, which appeared in 1950.[35] The

---

[35] T. W. Adorno, E. Frenkel-Brunswik, D. J. Levinson, and R. N. Sanford, *The Authoritarian Personality*, New York, Harper, 1950.

authors of this work hypothesized a close relationship between attitudes and values on the one hand and personality on the other. They assumed that the ". . . convictions of an individual often form a broad and coherent pattern, as if bound together by a mentality or spirit." They further assumed that ". . . opinions, attitudes, and values depend on human needs and since personality is essentially an organization of needs, then personality may be regarded as a determinant of ideological preference." Thus the *Authoritarian Personality* approach also stresses consistency, but while the concepts of congruity, balance, and dissonance are satisfied with assuming a general tendency toward consistency, the *Authoritarian Personality* theory goes further in that it holds that the dynamic of consistency is to be found in personality, and it is personality which gives consistency meaning and direction. Attitudes and values are thus seen to be consistent among themselves and with one another because they are both consistent with the basic personality needs, and they are consistent with needs because they are determined by them.

The very ambitious research deriving from the *Authoritarian Personality* formulation encountered many difficulties and, mainly because of serious methodological and theoretical shortcomings, has gradually lost its popularity. However, some aspects of this general approach have been salvaged by others. Rosenberg, for instance, has shown that attitudes are intimately related to the capacity of the attitude object to be instrumental to the attainment of the individual's values.[36] Carlson went a step further and has shown that, if the perceived instrumentality of the object with respect to a person's values and needs is changed, the attitude itself may be modified.[37] These studies, while not assuming a general consistency principle, illustrate a special instance of consistency, namely that between attitudes and utility, or instrumentality of attitude objects, with respect to the person's values and needs.

The concepts of consistency bear a striking historical similarity to the concept of vacuum. According to an excellent account by Conant,[38] for centuries the principle that nature abhors a vacuum served to account for various phenomena, such as the action of pumps, behavior of liquids in joined vessels, suction, and the like. The strength of everyday evidence was so overwhelming that the principle was seldom questioned. However, it was known that one cannot draw water to a height of more than 34 feet. The simplest solution of this problem was to reformulate the principle to read that "nature abhors a vacuum below 34 feet." This modified version of *horror vacui* again was satisfactory for the phenomena it dealt with, until it was discovered that "nature abhors a vacuum below 34 feet only when we deal with water." As

[36] M. J. Rosenberg, "Cognitive Structure and Attitudinal Affect," *Journal of Abnormal and Social Psychology*, Vol. 53, 1956, pp. 367–372.

[37] E. R. Carlson, "Attitude Change through Modification of Attitude Structure," *Journal of Abnormal and Social Psychology*, Vol. 52, 1956, pp. 256–261.

[38] James B. Conant, *On Understanding Science*, New Haven, Conn., Yale University Press, 1947.

Torricelli has shown, when it comes to mercury "nature abhors a vacuum below 30 inches." Displeased with the crudity of a principle which must accommodate numerous exceptions, Torricelli formulated the notion that it was the pressure of air acting upon the surface of the liquid which was responsible for the height to which one could draw liquid by the action of pumps. The 34-foot limit represented the weight of water which the air pressure on the surface of earth could maintain, and the 30-inch limit represented the weight of mercury that air pressure could maintain. This was an entirely different and revolutionary concept, and its consequences had drastic impact on physics. Human nature, on the other hand, is said to abhor inconsistency. For the time being the principle is quite adequate, since it accounts systematically for many phenomena, some of which have never been explained and all of which have never been explained by one principle. But already today there are exceptions to consistency and balance. Some people who spend a good portion of their earnings on insurance also gamble. The first action presumably is intended to protect them from risks, the other to expose them to risks. Almost everybody enjoys a magician. And the magician only creates dissonance—you see before you an event which you know to be impossible on the basis of previous knowledge—the obverse of what you see follows from what you know. If the art of magic is essentially the art of producing dissonance, and if human nature abhors dissonance, why is the art of magic still flourishing? If decisions are necessarily followed by dissonance, and if nature abhors dissonance, why are decisions ever made? Although it is true that those decisions which would ordinarily lead to great dissonance take a very long time to make, they are made anyway. And it is also true that human nature does not abhor dissonance absolutely, as nature abhors a vacuum. Human nature merely avoids dissonance, and it would follow from dissonance theory that decisions whose instrumental consequences would not be worth the dissonance to follow would never be made. There are thus far no data to support this hypothesis, nor data to disprove it.

According to Conant, *horror vacui* served an important purpose besides explaining and organizing some aspects of physical knowledge. Without it the discomfort of "exceptions to the rule" would never have been felt, and the important developments in theory might have been delayed considerably. If a formulation has then a virtue in being wrong, the theories of consistency do have this virtue. They do organize a large body of knowledge. Also, they point out exceptions, and thereby they demand a new formulation. It will not suffice simply to reformulate them so as to accommodate the exceptions. I doubt if Festinger would be satisfied with a modification of his dissonance principle which would read that dissonance, being psychologically uncomfortable, leads a person to actively avoid situations and information which would be likely to increase the dissonance, except when there is an opportunity to watch a magician. Also, simply to disprove the theories by counterexamples would not in itself constitute an important contribution. We would merely lose explanations of phenomena which had been explained. And it is doubtful that the theories of consistency could be rejected simply *because* of counterexamples. Only a theory which accounts for all the data that the consistency principles now account for, for all the exceptions to those principles, and for all the phenomena which these principles should now but do not consider, is capable of replacing them. It is only a matter of time until such a development takes place.

Robert P. Abelson

MODES
OF RESOLUTION
OF BELIEF
DILEMMAS

INTRODUCTION

This is a paper about intrapersonal conflict resolution.[1] We first identify the kind of conflict to be considered.

There are two levels of analysis of intrapersonal conflict: the action level and the belief level, the former dealing with external motor responses and the latter with internal affective and cognitive processes. Particular instances of conflict may, for theoretical convenience, be localized at one or another of these levels. For example, one may ask how a person acts when simultaneously motivated to approach and to avoid an external object (3, 9, 10). Or one may ask instead what happens to the cognitive representation of an external object when the object simultaneously incurs favorable and unfavorable cognitions (12). The present paper is addressed to the latter type of question. We shall not consider the problem of whether and how the action level is to be reduced to the belief level or vice versa. We only consider conflicts between one belief and another or, more generally, conflicts within a belief structure. The term "belief dilemma" is intended to enforce the distinction between the variety of conflict here considered and conflict in general.

[1] This paper was written at the Center for Advanced Study in the Behavioral Sciences, Yale University.

Reprinted from the *Journal of Conflict Resolution,* 3 (1959), 343–52, with permission of the Journal of Conflict Resolution.

BELIEF DILEMMAS

The model of cognitive structure to be described is similar at various points to other recent models (6, 8, 13).

First, we imagine a cognitive representation, a "cognitive element," corresponding to any attitude object. Associated with such a cognitive element is a numerical value, positive if the object is liked, negative if the object is disliked. Next, we suppose that between each pair of cognitive elements there may exist some kind of perceived relation. Assigned to each relation is another numerical value, positive if the relation is "associative," negative if the relation is "dissociative" (11). Examples of associative relations are: is, has, includes, likes, helps, produces, implies. Examples of disssociative relations are: avoids, hates, hinders, defeats, destroys, is incompatible with. A zero value indicates a null, or irrelevant, relation.

Given an attitude issue or "conceptual arena" (1), a certain set of cognitive elements would be relevant for a given individual. The set of relevant elements and the particular relations among them define the *content* of the individual's belief system on the issue. The form, or *structure*, of belief may be expressed independently of the content according to the array of numerical affect values and relation values defined above.

A belief structure may or may not contain inconsistencies. By inconsistency is meant not logical inconsistency but psychological inconsistency, or, as it has been variously referred to, imbalance (7), incongruity (12, 13), or dissonance (5). We shall use the term "imbalance."

Heider (7), Festinger (5), and Osgood and Tannenbaum (12) have all postulated a motivation for the reduction of imbalance. There is said to be a tendency, a pressure, toward the attainment of cognitive balance. An essential qualification to this postulate has been pointed out by Abelson and Rosenberg (1). There are innumerable inconsistencies in anyone's belief system which may lie dormant and unthought about. Pressure toward cognitive balance, if always operative on all cognitive elements, would produce much more balance in belief systems than one finds empirically. It is much more plausible to assume that this pressure operates only when the issue is salient; that is, when the issue is being "thought about," or, if this is too rational a terminology, when "cognitive work" is applied on the issue. General methods for identifying the presence of imbalance in a structure of any size have been given elsewhere (1, 4). Here we confine our analysis to a simple case of imbalance: two elements and the relation between them.

There are six possible cases to be considered: two positively valued objects, related associatively or related dissociatively; one positively valued object and one negatively valued object, related dissociatively or related associatively; and two negatively valued objects, related associatively or related dissociatively. In each of these three pairs of cases, the first possibility is bal-

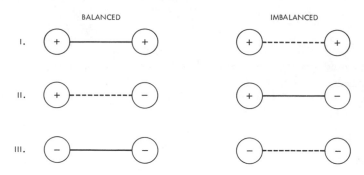

FIGURE 1.   *Cognitive structures with two elements and one relation. An unbroken line symbolizes an associative (positive) relation; a broken line a dissociative (negative) relation.*

The mechanism of denial aims toward the conversion of a structure on the right into one on the left, either through change of affect toward the element ("denial of the element") or change in the sign of the relation ("denial of the relation").

anced, the second one is imbalanced. This may be clarified by reference to Figure 1.

An imbalanced dyad will be said to constitute a belief dilemma when the intensity of affect toward the objects is strong and when the dyad is often salient (i.e., often present in thought).

MODES OF RESOLUTION

Four possible modes of resolution are specified below. Each can manifest itself in several ways. The modes are labeled: (a) denial, (b) bolstering, (c) differentiation, and (d) transcendence.

Denial refers to a direct attack upon one or both of the cognitive elements or the relation between them. The value felt toward the object, whether positive or negative, is denied, or the opposite is asserted; or the sign of the relation between the elements is explained away, or the opposite is asserted. Examples are: the man on a diet professing that he never liked rich foods anyway, the groom convincing himself of his avid belief in his bride's religion, John Calvin interpreting the scriptures to show that Christ never really condemned usury. If an attempt at denial is successful, it will convert an imbalanced structure into a balanced one. However, denial attempts may run into various difficulties, as, for example, when the denial is too great a distortion of reality or conflicts with other elements in the larger belief system. For example, the Boston colonists faced in 1773 with the odious taxation on tea went so far as to vote that "it is the sense of this Body that the use of tea is improper and pernicious." It is unlikely that this denial of the desirability of tea, albeit effective in encouraging group action, was effective in suppressing the taste for tea of the individuals concerned.

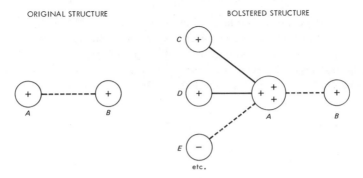

ORIGINAL STRUCTURE   BOLSTERED STRUCTURE

FIGURE 2. *The mechanism of bolstering in reducing cognitive imbalance. In the bolstered structure* (right) *the units AC, AD, . . . are all balanced. The relative effect of the imbalanced unit AB is thus reduced.*

The mechanism called "bolstering" consists of relating one or the other of the two cognitive objects in a balanced way to other valued objects (Fig. 2), thereby minimizing the relative imbalance in the structure. This mechanism plays an important part in Festinger's theory of cognitive dissonance (5). He points out many situations in which the introduction of new cognitive elements is useful in reducing dissonance. This is a mechanism not for eliminating imbalance entirely but only for drowning it out, so to speak. Examples are: the smoker who is worried about lung cancer telling himself that smoking is extremely enjoyable, good for his nerves, and socially necessary; and the proponent of a large standing army, unwelcome in peacetime, claiming that it is good character training for the nation's youth. The mechanism of bolstering may be used in conjunction with the mechanism of denial. For example, in the example of the large standing army the advocate might also say that the large standing army was not contrary to peaceful purposes; in fact, it aided the cause of peace to have a large standing army.

The two mechanisms listed thus far have the property that they preserve the identity of the cognitive elements. The meaning of the attitude objects remains the same even though attitude toward the objects may be weakened by denial or strengthened by bolstering. Another mode of resolution arises if we consider the possibility of differentiation of the cognitive elements. An element may be split into two parts with a strong dissociative relation between the parts. To see how this mechanism might restore cognitive balance, consider the issue of hydrogen-bomb testing. For many people, continued hydrogen-bomb testing is positively valued, but poisoning of the atmosphere is negatively valued. These two cognitive objects are associatively related—there is a causal connection of some degree. This dyad is therefore imbalanced. But there is bomb testing and there is bomb testing: one might differentiate this attitude object into two—testing "dirty bombs" and testing "clean bombs." It is only the testing of dirty bombs that contributes to poisoning of the atmosphere; the testing of clean bombs presumably does not. Thus the imbalance is resolved.

To take another example, the facts of evolution, positively valued, are contradictory to the Bible which is also positively valued. But there are two Bibles: the Bible as literally interpreted and the Bible as figuratively interpreted. The Bible as figuratively interpreted is not contradictory to the facts of evolution but may be seen as concordant with them. In a third example, from an ex-

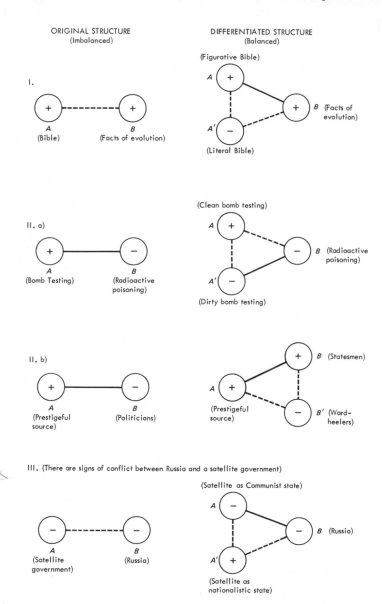

FIGURE 3.   *The mechanism of differentiation in restoring cognitive balance.*

periment by Asch (2), subjects who feel unfavorable toward "politicians" are confronted with a highly prestigeful source who glorifies the political profession. Many subjects get off the hook by differentiating statesmen (good politicians) from wardheelers (bad politicians). In these examples one element is differentiated into two parts, a new part and an old part. The old part retains the relation with the other element in the structure, but the affect toward it is changed. The new part, on the other hand, retains the old affect toward the differentiated element, but the sign of the relation with the other element is changed. These changes are reviewed in Figure 3.

It is interesting to note the large number of dimensions along which objects can be differentiated. They may be differentiated according to the internal content of the object, the object as viewed in a social context versus a personal context, the object as it is versus as it should be, the object as it is versus the object as it will be, etc.

The mechanism of transcendence is in a sense obverse to the mechanism of differentiation. Elements, instead of being split down, are built up and combined into larger units organized on a superordinate level, as indicated in Figure 4. For example, the dilemma pitting science against religion is transcended by the consideration that both the rational man and the spiritual man must be jointly cultivated to reach a fuller life or a better society or a deeper understanding of the universe. Thus the dilemma is transcended by imbedding the conflicting parts in a new concept instrumental to some higher purpose.

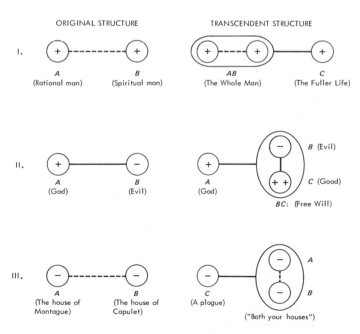

FIGURE 4.   *The mechanism of transcendence in restoring cognitive balance.*

The theosophical dilemma of God's presumed permissiveness toward evil is sometimes resolved by appeal to transcendent concepts. In the intriguing case study (6) of a group of individuals who prepared for a cataclysm that never occurred, it is reported that the group leader offered a transcendent resolution for the belief crisis: the cataclysm was said to have been stayed by God because of the group's devotion.

CHOICE AMONG THE MODES
OF RESOLUTION

Presumably, the individual with an imbalanced cognition will strive to choose among the various modes of resolution. Imbalanced structure would then be under a variety of pressures to change. The theoretical specification of which particular changes are likely to take place is a complex problem. Several working propositions are sketched here. A more rigorous theory is in the process of development.

Proposition 1.—There will be a hierarchy of resolution attempts in general proceeding in the following order: denial, bolstering, denial, differentiation, and transcendence.

The hierarchy of resolution attempts is based upon the relative ease of achieving success with each of the methods. The reason denial appears twice in the listing is that there are usually two points in the process at which denial may enter. If we consider the situation in which imbalance is introduced by forced or accidental exposure to propaganda or opinions seeking to establish new cognitive relations or to contradict previously held affect values, a first opportunity for denial may arise by a rejection of the relevance of the new material. If the initial denial fails, bolstering will be attempted and then another attempt at denial, this time buttressed by further thought about the issue. The presumption here is that denial and bolstering are simpler cognitive mechanisms than differentiation and transcendence, although they are not necessarily more effective in reducing cognitive imbalance. Differentiation is difficult because it requires intellectual ability, flexibility, and because, when there is strong affect toward a cognitive object, it is not easily split apart. Transcendence is presumably still more difficult, for it requires the existence of a compelling superordinate structure in which a given imbalance may be imbedded.

Proposition 2.—When two cognitive elements stand in imbalanced relation to each other and the affect toward one is more intense than toward the other, the tendency will be to apply bolstering toward the more intensely affected element and/or denial toward (*a*) the less intensely affected element and/or (*b*) the relation between the elements.

Proposition 2a.—The probability that an attempt will be made to bolster an element is high if other elements relevant to it are strong and stand in balanced relation to it (Fig. 2) and is low if other relevant elements are weak or stand in imbalanced relation to it.

Corollary.—Elements for which the individual's affect is intensely socially supported are readily subject to bolstering attempts when caught in a strong dilemma.

Proposition 2b.—The probability that an attempt will be made to deny an element is high if other relevant elements are strong and stand in imbalanced relation to it and is low if other relevant elements are weak or stand in balanced relation to it.

Corollary.—Elements with which considerable shame or guilt is associated (e.g., elements connoting the overindulgence of appetites) are readily subject to denial attempts when caught in a strong dilemma (i.e., when firmly related in imbalanced fashion to a strongly affected element). See Example 1.

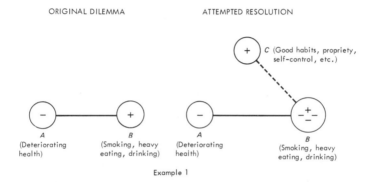

Example 1

NOTE.   *The element C must be compelling for the resolution to be stable. If original positive affect toward B is strong, the stability of the attempted resolution is jeopardized.*

Proposition 2c.—Relations between cognitive elements are readily denied when the external evidence for the relation is remote, ambiguous, under suspicion of bias, or dependent upon specific circumstances which can readily be perceived as inapplicable in general.

Proposition 2d.—A relation between cognitive elements A and B is readily subject to denial attempts when there is available an element A', formally similar to A and standing in associative relation with it, such that *the relation between* A' *and* B *is of opposite sign as between* A *and* B, *and is stronger.*

Proposition 2e.—A relation between cognitive elements A and B is readily subject to denial attempts when there is available an element A', formally similar to A, yet standing psychologically in dissociative relation to A, such that *the relation between* A' *and* B *is of the same sign as between* A *and* B, *but stronger* (the "mote-beam" technique).

See Example 2 (from the point of view of a liberal but very proud southerner).

ORIGINAL DILEMMA   INTERMEDIATE STAGE   NET RESULT

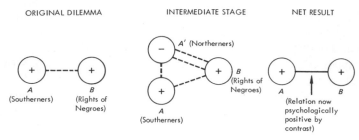

Example 2

Proposition 3.—If the affects toward two cognitive elements which stand in imbalanced relation to each other are nearly equal and the resolutions suggested in Proposition 2 fail, the converse resolutions will be attempted; that is, there will be attempts to bolster the less intense element and/or to deny the more intense element.

Proposition 4.—The classical relationship between the intensity and extremity of attitude may be explained in terms of a succession of dilemma resolutions in individual histories with the attitude object.

Explanation: The mechanism of bolstering used in the service of dilemma resolution increases the intensity of affect toward the object. An object which has been repeatedly bolstered is therefore the object of an intense attitude. But repeated bolstering also increases the extremity of attitude. In bolstering, the attitude object is connected with other objects. New reasons and supports are given for it; it is seen to be instrumental to other values; it is seen to be supported by various people and groups. In short, it is imbedded in a cognitive system of ever widening circumference. If scope of cognitive support is equated with extremity of attitude, then the relationship between extremity and intensity follows.

Those individuals who do not invoke bolstering will in general be the ones with moderate attitudes of low intensity.

Proposition 5.—If, in the search for new elements to bolster an original element in imbalance, further imbalance is created (usually because the new elements are imbalanced with each other), differentiation of the original element is encouraged.

See Example 3 (it is pointed out to an individual that universal public school education, by being compulsory, violates the democratic ideal of individual free choice—some parents might want to keep children out of school).

Proposition 6.—When an element is differentiated it is crucial to the maintenance of the resolution that the old part and the new part of the element be strongly dissociated.

Proposition 7.—Transcendent resolutions are likely to be invoked only in the case of chronically insoluble dilemmas. However, once a transcendent resolution is achieved, it may be found applicable to a variety of dilemmas.

IMBALANCED STRUCTURE

BOLSTERING ATTEMPT

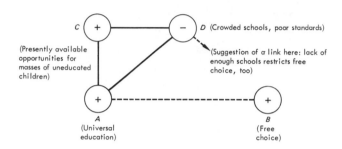

DIFFERENTIATED STRUCTURE

(Elements A and D have been differentiated)

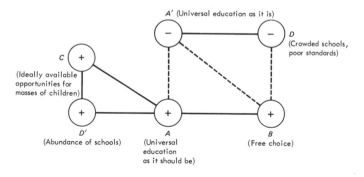

Example 3

Proposition 8.—Mass propaganda efforts seek dilemma resolutions effective for a large number of people simultaneously.

See Example 4 (a nation in a period of hard times).

Revolutionary propaganda aims to bolster *A* and differentiate *B* along

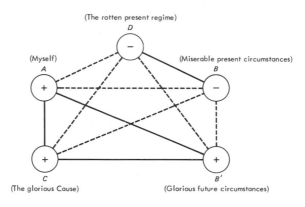

Example 4

a time dimension. The dissociated parts of *B* are each doubly bolstered, as follows:

> (*English translation:* "You are now part of the glorious Cause. Reject with us your miserable present circumstances. Look forward to the glorious future when all will be different. The rotten present regime despises you and is responsible for your misery. The Cause will attack the regime and lead you to the glorious future. The regime will try to prevent this but we shall triumph.")

Explicit in this analysis is the reason revolutionists should be so concerned over public apathy. Those "Indifferents" who are not dissatisfied with their present circumstances have no dilemma to resolve, and consequently the propaganda does not "take" (unless the Indifferents can be convinced that their situation is indeed grim).

REFERENCES

1. ABELSON, R. P., and ROSENBERG, M. J. "Symbolic Psychologic: A Model of Attitudinal Cognition." *Behavioral Science*, III (1958), 1–13.
2. ASCH, S. E. "Studies in the Principles of Judgments and Attitudes: II. Determination of Judgments by Group and Ego Standards." *Journal of Social Psychology*, XII (1940), 433–65.
3. BROWN, J. S. "Principles of Intrapersonal Conflict." *Conflict Resolution*, I (1957), 135–54.

4. CARTWRIGHT, D., and HARARY, F. "Structural Balance: A Generalization of Heider's Theory." *Psychological Review*, LXIII (1956), 277–93.
5. FESTINGER, L. *Theory of Cognitive Dissonance.* Evanston, Ill.: Row, Peterson & Co., 1957.
6. FESTINGER, L., RIECKEN, H., and SCHACHTER, S. *When Prophecy Fails.* Minneapolis: University of Minnesota Press, 1956.
7. HEIDER, F. "Attitudes and Cognitive Organization." *Journal of Psychology*, XXI (1946), 107–12.
8. ———. *The Psychology of Interpersonal Relations.* New York: John Wiley & Sons, 1958.
9. LEWIN, K. "Environmental Forces in Child Behavior and Development." In C. MURCHISON (ed.), *A Handbook of Child Psychology.* Worcester, Mass.: Clark University Press, 1931.
10. MILLER, N. "Experimental Studies of Conflict." In J. McV. HUNT, (ed.), *Personality and the Behavior Disorders.* New York: Ronald Press Co., 1944.
11. OSGOOD, C. E., SAPORTA, S., and NUNNALLY, J. C. "Evaluative Assertion Analysis." *Litera*, III (1956), 47–102.
12. OSGOOD, C. E., and TANNENBAUM, P. H. "The Principle of Congruity in the Prediction of Attitude Change." *Psychological Review*, LXII (1955), 42–55.
13. OSGOOD, C. E., SUCI, G. T., and TANNENBAUM, P. H. *The Measurement of Meaning.* Urbana: University of Illinois Press, 1957.

Leonard W. Doob*

THE BEHAVIOR
OF ATTITUDES

There is no question that the subject of attitude and attitude measurements is important in sociology and social psychology. Social scientists continue
to discuss the nature of attitudes in articles like this, to conduct experiments
which show that behavior is affected by attitude, and to measure attitudes for
theoretical or practical purposes. The problem of what an attitude is and how
it functions, nevertheless, persists and—as many writers on attitudes likewise
point out in their introductory paragraph—little explicit agreement is apparent in the published literature.

The purpose of this paper is not to criticize other definitions or usages of
the term but systematically, if partially, to relate the concept of attitude to
what is known as behavior theory (17).[1] Almost all writers, no matter what their
bias, agree that attitudes are learned. If this is so, then the learning, retention,
and decline of an attitude are no different from the learning of a skill, a piece
of prose, or a set of nonsense syllables; and they must also involve the problems
of perception and motivation.

Immediately it is necessary to raise and answer the question as to why a
simple, commonsense, ubiquitous concept like attitude should be translated
into semi-technical jargon. There are at least two answers to the question.
The first and less important answer involves scientific methodology: it is
thought desirable to bring as many terms as possible relating to a field of
research (in this instance, human behavior) within one universe of discourse.

*Yale University.

[1] The writer is deeply grateful especially to Neal E. Miller as well as to Irvin L. Child,
John Dollard, and Mark A. May for their constructive criticisms. He has promiscuously and
deliberately borrowed some of their ideas and, as an insignificant token of his gratitude, here-
with absolves them of any responsibility for the final product.

Reprinted from the *Psychological Review,* 54 (1947), 135–56, with permission of the
author and the American Psychological Association.

Misunderstandings result from using one set of concepts to describe perception, learning, and motivation on one level and another set on a different level. Even if some sociologists who use the concept 'attitude' are not attracted by the terminology of behavior theory and if they remain inclined merely to assume perception, learning, and motivation without inquiring into the details of the processes, unified knowledge concerning human behavior requires that there be a connection between what the sociologist studies or measures and what the psychologist studies or measures. Secondly and of crucial importance, a tentative translation of a term from one level to another and into an already and perhaps better developed theoretical system is fully justified if thereby inadequacies on the higher level can be pointed out. Murray and Morgan (27), for example, have recently shed new light on the nature of attitude by incorporating the closely related concept of sentiment into the former's previous conceptualization of personality.

The procedure to be followed in this paper is as follows:

1. A definition of attitude in behavioral terms will be given. It is felt that such a definition represents an advance beyond the stage of defining an attitude as the subjective counterpart of something in the environment, as a predisposition within the organism, or as being what the attitude scale measures. The psychological implications of the definition will be made clear.

2. The consequences of this definition and the theoretical structure it assumes will then be summarized briefly by calling attention to the factors which should be known to make a completely adequate analysis of attitudes.

3. Illustrative research employing the concept of attitude will be critically examined in terms of these factors. Such a detailed examination seems preferable to surveying the attitude literature in general terms.

DEFINITION OF ATTITUDE

Attitude is defined as *an implicit, drive-producing response considered socially significant in the individual's society.* This definition states, in effect, that from the psychological point of view attitude is an implicit reponse with drive strength which occurs within the individual as a reaction to stimulus patterns and which affects subsequent overt responses. Since psychologists and other social scientists sometimes disagree concerning the nature and attributes of an implicit response of this type, the definition is therefore elaborated and broken down typographically into the phrases and clauses requiring further definition, elaboration, and discussion:

"An attitude is:

(1) "an implicit response

(2) "which is both (a) anticipatory and (b) mediating in reference to patterns of overt responses,

(3) "which is evoked (a) by a variety of stimulus patterns (b) as a result of previous learning or of gradients of generalization and discrimination,

(4) "which is itself cue- and drive-producing,

(5) "and which is considered socially significant in the individual's society."

1. *"An attitude is an implicit response. . . ."* By an implicit response is meant a response occurring within the individual and not immediately observable to an outsider. Motor 'attitudes' like the physical set of the runner before the starter's gun is fired, therefore, are not included within the universe of discourse being analyzed because they are not entirely implicit and hence are instrumental rather than mediating acts. The semantic connection of such sets with the concept of attitude employed by social scientists is considered to be largely fortuitous from an historical standpoint.

Overt behavior that is observable to an outsider may be affected by the evoked attitude but is not here defined as the attitude itself. Attitude refers to the individual's immediate but implicit response to a stimulus pattern and his consequent tendency to respond still further as a result of that implicit response. Such an implicit response may be conscious or unconscious, distinctly verbal or vaguely proprioceptive. What is expressed results not from the attitude alone but represents, as will be indicated, another response in a behavior sequence—an overt one—which is a function of the attitude-response and other tendencies within the individual.

2(a). *"An attitude is an implicit response which is . . . anticipatory . . . in reference to patterns of overt responses. . . ."* An anticipatory response—called also an antedating response by Hull (17, p. 74)—is one which originally preceded another rewarded response and which, as a result of being associated with or producing this reward, has been reinforced so that it occurs before its "original time in the response series" (25, p. 49). If an individual, for example, dislikes a fruit or a person, he tends to avoid eating the fruit or meeting the person. Originally the avoidance occurred only after actual contact had been established and after that contact had proven to be punishing and the withdrawal to be rewarding. When a thorough investigation reveals no actual prior contact, some process of generalization or discrimination must have occurred since all behavior has antecedents. The possibility of exceptions under different psychological conditions must be noted, even in these trivial illustrations: the fruit may be eaten anyhow if the individual is very hungry and the person may be met and greeted if social circumstances so require.

The conditions under which a response moves up in the behavior sequence and becomes anticipatory have so far been determined concretely in relatively simple situations. It has been shown (25, p. 79), for example, that the closer the response is in the series leading to the reward, the more likely it is to be learned and then subsequently to antedate other responses not leading to the reward. This principle suggests why few objects or individuals in society fail to arouse attitudes. Originally the individual has had to react to them or has been taught to react to them in the course of being socialized. One of the responses leading to the goal response (which by definition involves reward or the avoidance of punishment) has implicit components, is reinforced, and is here called an attitude.

2(b). *"An attitude is an implicit response which is . . . mediating in reference to patterns of overt responses. . . ."* Whereas the anticipatory character of attitude indicates its temporal relation to a goal, its mediating attribute calls attention to its functional connection with that goal. A mediating response is made in an attempt to increase the likelihood of the occurrence of reward rather than punishment in connection with a goal response. In reasoning, for example, implicit responses intervene between the original stimulus pattern and the goal response and may assist the individual in achieving that goal. Attitudes can be evoked so easily because as mediating responses involving only language, imagery, or proprioceptive reactions they need not conflict with the overt behavior of the individual or with his environment.

The mediating function of attitude has led May to suggest that attitude is "a kind of substitute goal response" which "arises when the goal response cannot be immediately and easily made" (24). This attribute, which has also been suggested by other writers (*e.g.*, 3, pp. 425–6 and 28, pp. 28–9), does seem to characterize certain attitudes. The individual who dislikes another person is restrained or restrains himself from hurting his antagonist; instead he makes an implicit response involving aggression and feelings of avoidance or repulsion. It is felt, however, that all attitudes cannot be so characterized. The liked object, for example, evokes an implicit response which facilitates rather than acts as a substitute for overt behavior in reference to it. Overt behavior, in short, may be mediated by attitudes almost immediately and there need not necessarily be a conflict or a restraint before the attitude is evoked.

Three consequences arise immediately from this conceptualization of attitude. In the first place, it appears psychologically futile—as Sherif and Cantril have indicated (33, pp. 304–5)—to attempt to classify attitudes. Responses can be characterized in so many different ways that a simple dichotomy or trichotomy usually must be willfully stretched if it is to include all types of behavior. The response defined as attitude might be called positive or negative or be said to involve approach or withdrawal were it not for the fact that these terms then require further definition which cannot be consistently or usefully applied to all situations. Both approach and avoidance, for example, may be but are not necessarily involved in what has been called a neutral attitude or in any attitude for that matter. It seems better, in short, to apply *socially* useful labels to attitude as the need arises, in order to indicate the direction in which the individual thereby is oriented; but it should be clearly recognized that the labels have social and not psychological significance. A psychologically important distinction, however, is that between general and specific attitudes (5), a distinction which refers to the stimulus patterns evoking the response or to the evoked responses.

In the second place, reference is made in the definition to "patterns of overt responses." For reasons hereafter suggested, overt behavior can seldom be predicted from knowledge of attitude alone. Under varying conditions within the individual, a given attitude can mediate a repertoire of overt responses. A favorable attitude toward a social institution, for example, can mediate innumerable responses connected with what is considered to be the welfare of that institution.

Then, thirdly, this definition of attitude emphasizes its acquired or learned character. There are no psychic rays which enable the investigator, even though he be equipped with a poll or a scale, to determine the 'strength' of an attitude, the overt responses with which it has become associated, or its present functioning within the personality. Such knowledge can be obtained only from knowing approximately under what conditions the attitude was acquired in the first place and the extent to which it secures present and future reinforcement. The learning process, therefore, is crucial to an understanding of the behavior of attitudes.

The nature of that process cannot be ignored in a treatise on attitude as it has been by Sherif and Cantril: "Just what the psychological or physiological mechanisms of this learning may be are irrelevant to the present discussion," they write in their articles on "The Psychology of 'Attitudes'" (33, p. 302). It is difficult to see how psychologists can call these mechanisms 'irrelevant' and still contend, as the authors do in the introduction to the same articles, that the 'task' of the psychologist is to "give an adequate account of the psychological mechanisms involved in the formation of an attitude in any individual" (33, p. 295). The authors rest their case by stating that they "do not need to take sides in favor of any learning theory" (33, p. 307). Of course, as they write, "the primary stage in the formation of attitudes is a perceptual stage," which is merely saying that there must be a stimulus and that the stimulus must be perceived before there can be any kind of learning.

In contrast, Allport (1, pp. 810–2) has set the problem of the genesis of attitudes in terms which explicitly suggest the need for learning theory. His often quoted summary of the literature indicates that attitudes may be formed through "the integration of numerous specific responses of a similar type"; "individuation, differentiation, or segregation" of experiences; 'trauma'; and the adoption of 'ready-made' attitudes of others. The genesis of almost any attitude is undoubtedly more or less unique. Society sets the rewards and punishments regarding much of overt behavior; the individual being socialized then is forced into the learning situation; although he reacts to the situation uniquely, one of the end products—the attitude—he may share in large degree with others.

3(a). *"An attitude is an implicit response . . . which is evoked by a variety of stimulus patterns. . . ."* The stimuli evoking an attitude may be in the external world or within the individual. The latter range from a verbal response to an autonomic disturbance or a drive. The existing literature on attitudes testifies to the fact that the stimuli may be various. Such is the assumption behind any attitude scale in which a variety of situations is judged or behind a distinction like that between specific and general attitudes.

The arousal of an attitude involves two traditional problems in psychology, those of perception and learning. The two are interrelated and can be separated only for purposes of analysis. Perception indicates that the individual is responding because he has previously paid attention to or been oriented toward certain stimuli which then affect his sense organs and thus evoke his attitude. Learning in this connection emphasizes the reasons in the past history of the individual which have brought about the bond between the stimulus pattern and the attitude.

Gestalt psychologists especially point out that paying attention and then perceiving occur in many instances as a result of the individual's set to respond: letter boxes are not noticed unless the person has a letter to post, etc. Writers on attitude are fond of recalling that the tradition of set is somewhat hoary in academic psychology, in order to demonstrate their own respectability and their acquaintance with long German terms like *Bewusstseinslage*. In other words, perceiving depends upon drive or set (which orients the individual to respond to certain stimuli and then to respond to them in a particular way) as well as upon the arrangements of the external stimuli. Attitude may be included among the sets determining both the orientation of the individual as well as the kind of perceptual response he makes: The southerner notices incipient aggression in a Negro which a northerner will overlook.

It must be recognized, however, that in some situations the individual's attitude is not evoked until the stimulus has been actually perceived: It affects perception after its arousal but does not orient him originally in the direction of the stimuli involved. The southerner who has learned to discriminate incipient hostility from genuine docility among Negroes can make the discrimination when confronted with a Negro. It is on the basis of this discrimination that his attitude toward the Negro is or is not aroused. If he goes about the streets looking for hostility in Negroes, he may be set to make the discrimination not necessarily by his attitude toward Negroes or by his ability to detect such behavior but by some particular drive which has been previously aroused and which may or may not involve Negroes. To say that he searches for aggression solely because of his attitude toward Negroes is to fail to distinguish him from another southerner who has a more or less identical attitude (so far as content and even 'affect' are concerned) but who has no 'chip on his shoulder.' In this case the sensible problem remains of accounting for the 'chip.'

In controlled experimental situations dedicated to observing the behavior of attitudes, the attention of the subjects is secured by the experimenter not through arousing the attitude being studied but through the evocation of some other drive. Subjects perceived the autokinetic phenomenon of Sherif (30) or they looked at Seeleman's photographs of white and colored individuals (29) because they had agreed to cooperate with the experimenter. This was the drive which oriented them in the experimental situation. Then their attitudes were aroused and these attitudes affected both their perceptual responses and the reports they gave the experimenters. Later on in the experiments, their evoked attitudes may have had sufficient drive strength also to orient them selectively.

3(b). *"An attitude is an implicit response . . . which is evoked . . . as a result of previous learning or of gradients of generalization and discrimination. . . ."* The previous section has indicated the possible relation between perception and the evocation of an attitude and therein it was suggested that an attitude can almost always be aroused by a variety of stimuli. Here it is stated that previous learning determines whether or not particular stimulus patterns will evoke the attitude. Some stimuli come to arouse an attitude after a relatively simple process of conditioning has occurred. As a result of being originally present in the situation, for example, the wrapper of the disliked fruit or the signature of the disliked person may produce an anticipatory response which mediates the goal response of avoiding it or him. Other stimuli evoke or fail to evoke an attitude not because of their presence or absence in previous situations but because they fall along a stimulus gradient of generalization or discrimination. If an individual likes or dislikes one particular Negro, there is stimulus discrimination; if all Negroes are involved, there is stimulus generalization along a gradient, for example, of skin color; if only certain 'types' of Negroes arouse the attitude, there is generalization and discrimination.

Frequently attitudes are thought to be puzzling and mysterious because they can be aroused when the psychologist, the sociologist, the layman, and the individual least expect them to be. The stimulus pattern, for example, may be a word or a sentence, or some other symbol (like a flag, a face, or a gesture) which represents only a portion of the original stimulus pattern. The behavior of attitudes under these circumstances, however, becomes more intelligible when the implications of the "gradient of generalization and discrimination" are understood. This gradient is especially efficacious in the case of attitude since language can readily perform the function of mediating generalization and discrimination. Cofer and Foley (11), for example, are able *a priori* to list over fifty gradients along which generalization or discrimination from a single word can conceivably occur in purely formal (*i.e.*, in non-idiosyncratic) manner. The word 'Negro,' for example, through previous learning may become the one part of the original stimulus pattern which evokes an attitude regarding Negroes. Without any difficulty there can be a semantic gradient including words like 'colored,' 'African,' and the various epithets and appellations applied to this group. Through a slightly more complicated process, eventually 'zoot suit' may arouse the same attitude: if the individual has associated this type of clothing with Negroes, the response of seeing such clothing or hearing its name evokes the internal response of 'Negro' which in turn has the property of arousing the attitude. This phenomenon has been called secondary stimulus generalization or acquired cue value. Similarly, thinking can aid generalization and discrimination.

Cantril in his work on attitudes fails to comprehend this stimulus gradient involved in most if not all learning and conditioning. He states, for example, that what he calls "a standard of judgment" must not be "confused with a conditioned response" (8, p. 25). What he means by "a standard of judgment" or a "frame of reference" he never makes operationally clear, although they seem to be related to attitude since they are employed profusely in his two articles on the subject. It may be that terms like these—to use Cantril's own words in reference to 'conditioning'—are "so loosely employed" that they "explain nothing at all" (8, p. 55). His conception of a conditioned response is indeed narrow: "a specific reaction to a specific stimulus" (8, p. 25). In spite of a general, noncommittal reference in a footnote to a standard book on conditioning (that of Hilgard and Marquis) and an irrelevant quotation from A. N. Whitehead, this simplification of behavior theory leads him to conclude that such a theory is "by no means adequate to explain the apparent meaningfulness of man's experience" (8, p. 56). More specifically, for example, he maintains that the "analysis of the backgrounds of the people who became panicky listening to the Hallowe'en broadcast [of Orson Welles in 1938] clearly shows that in no way had they been specifically conditioned against Martian invaders' mowing down people on this planet" (8, p. 25). The point of Cantril's study (7), however, is to discover the previously existing attitudes and traits which made people prone to panic or sanity. After discovering many of them with admirable ingenuity, he gives a commonsense 'explanation' of the behavior; *i.e.*, he uses his particular vocabulary to describe what happened (7, pp. 190–201). His failure to apply Chapter 8 of Hilgard and Marquis (15) to his own data prevents him from realizing that at the time of the broadcast people had learned to respond with anxiety to various stimuli as a result, for example, of the 'war scare' associated with the Munich crisis (*cf.* 7, pp. 159–60). Certain Americans, some of whose socio-economic and psychological characteristics Cantril has indicated, apparently generalized from these stimuli to a broadcast which of course they had not previously experienced but which nevertheless was sufficiently similar to other stimulus patterns previously evoking the anxiety. Such individuals 'jumped the gun' by behaving—after their attitudes had been aroused by Mr. Welles and his associates—as they would have in the face of genuine catastrophe.

From experiments in other fields of behavior, Hull states that the amplitude of a response "diminishes steadily with the increase in the extent of deviation . . . of the evocation stimulus . . . from the stimulus originally conditoned . . ." (17, p. 185) and that "The strength of the connections at other points of the zone can be determined only from a knowledge of the strength of the receptor-effector connection . . . at the point of reinforcement and the extent of the difference . . . between the position of the conditioned stimulus . . . and that of the evocation stimulus . . . on the stimulus continuum connecting them" (17, p. 187). Whether or not the principle holds true of attitudes has not been tested, so far as this writer knows. To test it, it would be necessary to

ABBOT MEMORIAL LIBRARY
EMERSON COLLEGE

know "the stimulus originally conditioned," the gradient along which the various 'evocation stimuli' are located, and whether or not in fact these latter stimuli have never been previously reinforced or extinguished. This could be done only by means of a careful life history of various individuals and by some objective measurement of the strength of the attitude.

At any rate, this generalization of Hull has an important bearing on the strength of attitude. The 'strength' of an attitude is almost as ambiguous as the concept of attitude itself. One type of strength that seems important for predicting future behavior of the individual is the *afferent-habit strength* of the attitude, *i.e.*, the strength of the bond between the stimulus pattern and the response which is here defined as attitude. In these terms the afferent-habit strength of an attitude is a function of the number of previous reinforcements as well as the position along the gradient occupied by a particular stimulus pattern.

4. *"An attitude is an implicit response . . . which is itself cue-and drive-producing. . . ."* Like all implicit responses, attitudes can be said to have stimulus-value, *i.e.*, they arouse other responses. The responses they evoke may indeed be various. They may produce a perceiving response, as has been suggested, and in this sense determine to what other stimuli the individual subsequently responds. They may produce linguistic responses, thoughts, images, or stereotypes. They eventually have an effect upon overt behavior. Here again reference must be made to the habit strength of the attitude, only this time it is a bond between attitude as a stimulus and a response pattern (implicit or overt), rather than between a stimulus pattern and attitude as a response. This phenomenon will be called the *efferent-habit strength* and, like the afferent-habit strength, it too can be strengthened or weakened through learning. The stimulus-value of attitude suggests why investigators have discovered so many different phenomena—aside from overt behavior—associated with attitude.

The definition of attitude refers to the distinction made by Miller and Dollard (25, pp. 22-3) between the cue- and drive-producing characteristics of a stimulus. The numbers used in counting, they point out, have cue value: the number 'six' is a response to the cue of 'five' and in turn acts as a cue to elicit 'seven.' An attitude has cue-value in the sense that it acts as a stimulus to produce another response, but it also is a drive in the sense that its tension is reduced through subsequent behavior leading to a reward. It is proper, consequently, to refer to the *drive strength* of an attitude as well as to the strength of the bond between the attitude and the responses it evokes. An individual, for example, who has not been thinking of food is shown a picture of a type of food he likes. The picture may be said to evoke his favorable attitude toward the food which is a drive whose goal response is eating. If the secondarily evoked response pattern is only salivation and the thought or statement of how he likes the food, the drive may be considered relatively weak. But if he drops what he is doing and goes out to eat immediately after seeing the picture, the drive is relatively strong.

The strength of an attitude, therefore, may refer to its afferent-habit strength, its efferent-habit strength, or its drive strength. Knowledge of an attitude's direction or content is not equivalent to measuring its strength. The attitude possessed by two people, for example, may be more or less identical in formal content as measured by an attitude scale, but its role in determining overt behavior may be quite diverse. In one individual it may be evoked by a restricted stimulus pattern (specific attitude), it may not be frequently evoked (a weak afferent-habit), or the entire pattern of additional implicit and overt responses may be restricted (a weak drive). Any one or more of these conditions may be different in the second individual. Thus the role of the patriotic attitude in the average citizen is different from the way it functions within a professional patriot. Or within the same individual the patriotic attitude may be more easily and variously aroused and lead more certainly to a greater number of responses during a war than when there is peace.

The fate of an attitude over time—whether it persists or changes—is obviously a function of complicated processes within the individual. At least three factors are involved. The first is the reward or punishment associated with the goal response. An attitude will persist when it is constantly reinforced or it will change when it is partially or wholly extinguished. Its afferent- and efferent-habit strength is then increased or decreased. The efferent-habit strength is a direct function of the frequency with which the attitude has mediated rewarding or non-rewarding behavior as well as of the immediacy and amount of the reward or non-reward. Afferent-habit strength depends ultimately upon efferent-habit strength since reinforcement or non-reinforcement results not from the arousal of the attitude but from the behavior mediated by the attitude; it also depends on the frequency with which particular stimulus patterns have aroused the mediating attitude and the distinctiveness of those patterns. In Hull's words (16), attitudes have the property of 'pure stimulus acts' within a single individual: they are responses which are reinforced "because they, as stimuli, evoke *other* acts . . . which will bring about a reinforcing state of affairs. . . ."

Secondly, there is the factor of conflict with competing drives which may determine the fate of an attitude. The afferent- and efferent-habit strength of an attitude may be great, but its drive strength may be weak in comparison with other attitudes or drives aroused by the same or different stimulus patterns. The individual, for example, may not express his attitude in overt behavior because its expression would be contrary to his general philosophy; but his attitude persists. Finally, there is forgetting which may involve other psychological processes besides extinction through non-reinforcement.

It is possible, consequently, to have an attitude play a less significant role in a personality by diminishing the number of stimuli which evoke it, by having the attitude aroused less frequently, by weakening its drive strength, by setting up stronger competing drives, or by punishing the overt behavior which it mediates. Since the afferent-habit strength is affected by the final goal response, moreover, it follows that the attitude's strength in this respect can remain more or less constant even though its efferent-habit strength vis-à-vis a particular response pattern is weakened: it is only necessary that some reinforcement be obtained by having the attitude mediate other goal responses. The prejudiced individual, for example, can retain his prejudice not by always behaving identically in response to a given stimulus pattern in his society but by behaving differently and with more or less equal satisfaction.

There is a voluminous literature on the subject of attitude change, a good part of which is called experimental (*cf.* 26, pp. 946–80). In general, the approach has been to subject a group of individuals to a collection of stimuli (like a course in race relations, a motion picture, propaganda analysis, or a visit to an ethnic group in a large American city). Their changes in attitude (if any) are ascertained by comparing their scores on an attitude scale before and after being subjected to the stimuli. Sometimes the changes are compared with those of a control group which has not been so stimulated. It must be said that this type of approach is socially useful but psychologically sterile: it is important to know that lectures or visits do or do not affect students but, except for sporadic attempts to correlate attitude change with obvious factors like intelligence and 'intensity' of the attitude at the outset, no effort has been made to suggest precisely why the attitudes do or do not change. They change, it is said, 'because' the student heard the lecture or met a Negro or saw a motion picture. Obviously the word 'because' is misleading. All that has been demonstrated is a correlation, not a causal connection. Two people with approximately the same attitude and subject to approximately the same stimulus pattern, for example, will be affected differently because different responses, including or excluding the attitude, are evoked within them. Or the overt effect may be the same for different reasons: in one, the afferent strength of the attitude may be altered only in respect to particular stimulus patterns and not to others; whereas in another, the drive strength of the attitude may be reduced. To maintain, therefore, that a course or a contact produces attitude change in a group of individuals (with a large or small sigma) is to state an historically limited conclusion which certainly may be socially useful at a given moment. It is like indicating that the abolition of a slum area diminishes the delinquency rate; it does, but thereby little insight is gained into the nature of delinquency (*e.g.*, why there are delinquents from non-slum areas). Research on attitude change, consequently, is likely to produce superficial generalizations which, being derived so uniquely from particular phenomena, can be applied to future situations only with extreme difficulty.

The psychological aspects of this definition of attitude, finally, can shed some light on another traditional problem: the relation between attitude and stereotype. Numerous studies, especially those of Katz and Braly (18) and of Child and Doob (10), have demonstrated the close connection between the two. The term 'stereotype' is loosely employed. Like attitude, it seems to be an implicit response—this is what Lippmann (23) many years ago must have meant by defining it as "the picture in our heads." It becomes an attitude, however, only when it is also drive-producing. An individual, for example, has a favorable attitude toward Great Britain, it is said in oversimplified fashion, because he considers the British 'patriotic.' If the oversimplified explanation be accepted as valid, some learning process in the past must be presumed. A word like 'good' must first have produced a 'favorable' response since it was conditioned to a stimulus pattern like parent or food which for other reasons evoked that response. Then 'patriotic' became associated with 'good' for reasons to be found in the individual's milieu and also evoked that response. 'Great Britain' as a stimulus came to produce the response of 'patriotic' (the stereotype), a bit of learning doubtlessly also socially conditioned. 'Patriotic' thus is a stimulus-producing response which, finally, evokes the 'favorable' response to which it has been previously linked. In this instance, the stereotype evoked by 'Great Britain' is a mediating response in a long response sequence and does evoke a drive. In like manner, most people in our society reply to the question, "Is the earth round or flat?" by means of some stereotype which produces the word 'round.' The stereotype appears to have cue- but essentially no drive-value and hence is not an attitude, although the question itself may rouse another implicit response with drive-value (attitude): to reply incorrectly to a simple question is usually non-rewarding.

5. *"An attitude is an implicit response . . . which is considered socially significant in the individual's society."* If attitudes are defined as implicit, drive-producing responses, it is obvious that they thereby are placed within the psychological sub-class of such responses but that simultaneously they are not distinguished from other responses in this group. The other psychological qualifications which have been discussed—their anticipatory and mediating character, the variety of stimuli which evoke them, and the variety of responses they evoke—are also common to other responses which, according to conventional usage, may not be considered attitudes. The rat's aversion to a grid on which it has been shocked is doubtless implicit, it is anticipatory and mediating in avoiding the shock, it can be evoked by a gradient of stimuli, and it has drive value resulting in other responses which serve perhaps to allay its anxiety; but it is ordinarily not useful to call such a response an attitude. Similarly the human being's favorable disposition toward cream cheese or a style of hat may or may not be called an attitude. Psychologically, therefore, attitude is not and —it is deliberately maintained—should not be distinguished from the larger sub-class of responses to which it appears to belong.

The distinction between attitude and other types of responses can be made not on a psychological but on a social basis: its socially evaluated significance must be considered. The rat's aversion to the grid is not an attitude unless it plays an important part in its behavior in other situations involving rats; from the human standpoint, it is not at all socially significant. The liking of cream cheese or a hat may or may not be considered socially significant: from an overall point of view, it is doubtless trivial and hence not an attitude, although it undoubtedly is of importance to cheese producers and hat manufacturers as well as their clients. The words 'socially significant' must be left unspecific, since social values fluctuate from society to society and, within a particular society, over time and in various groups. Almost always the socially significant in a society is evaluated or, more simply, is called 'good' or 'bad' to indicate its actual or potential effect on people. A useful test to decide whether an implicit response with drive-value is an attitude is to discover whether that response is labelled desirable or undesirable by the individual's contemporaries. In any segment of society at a given moment, people are likely to acquire attitudes because they are subject to similar learning conditions.

ANALYSIS OF ATTITUDES

An ideally thorough analysis of an attitude requires knowledge (quantitative if possible) of the following factors, if its behavior and role in determining overt behavior in various situations are to be understood:

1. *Goal response:* the response pattern or patterns which the attitude anticipates and mediates and which determine its reinforcement or extinction.

2. *Perception:* the drive orienting the individual to pay attention to the stimulus pattern evoking the attitude.

3. *Afferent-habit strength:* the strength of the bond between the attitude and the evoking stimulus patterns, including the gradients of generalization and discrimination.

4. *Efferent-habit strength:* the strength of the bond between the attitude and the evoked responses, including overt ones.

5. *Drive strength:* the drive strength of the stimuli produced by the attitude.

6. *Interaction:* the strength of the other attitudes, drives, etc. with which the attitude interacts to evoke overt behavior.

7. *Social significance:* the evaluation in the society of the attitude and its direction (*e.g.*, whether positive, negative, or neutral; favorable, unfavorable, or ambivalent; friendly or unfriendly; desirable or undesirable; good or bad).

In the next section, references to these factors are placed in italics.

ILLUSTRATIVE RESEARCH ON ATTITUDES

1. *Measurement.* It has been said and perhaps demonstrated for a quarter of a century that attitudes can be measured. Frequently it has been declared that an opinion is an expression of an attitude and therefore that

attitude scales and polls secure a measure not of the attitude itself but of its expression in the form of an opinion. This is a simplified way of referring both to the *efferent-habit strength* of an attitude and its *interaction* with simultaneously evoked tendencies.

If the behavior of measured attitudes be analyzed, a picture like the following emerges:

a. Subjects or respondents must be motivated to cooperate. Frequently the coercive situation of the classroom provides the drive to obey the instructor, at other times there is a financial incentive, and in polling respondents may like to talk about themselves or feel flattered that their opinions are being probed. Some drive is aroused before the subject *perceives* the stimulus-pattern of the investigator and before the attitude itself is evoked.

b. Informants are then confronted with a complex arrangement of stimuli which are words on a piece of paper or from an interviewer's mouth. The perception of the stimuli elicits some kind of an implicit response: sentences, thoughts, images, stereotypes, or attitudes, all of which may not be completely conscious. One of these responses may be the attitude being investigated or may act as a stimulus to evoke it. Whether or not the attitude is evoked depends not only on whether the individual has previously learned that type of implicit response but also upon the extent to which previous stimulus patterns are similar to or different from the present pattern, *i.e.*, on earlier learning or on the gradient of generalization and discrimination (*afferent-habit strength*). Much of the research on the measurement of attitude, consequently, is an attempt to discover the various stimuli along the gradient or gradients arousing or not arousing the attitude in question. The respondent could be asked simply, "Do you like Turks?" were it not for the fact that he might falsify his reply, that he may not have previously considered all the implications of his attitude toward Turks, or that his reply could not be scaled. Instead the investigator raises questions which ask him what he has done or would do in relation to Turks. Tests involving 'social distance,' for example, suggest situations which some of the subjects probably have never seriously contemplated, like marrying a Turk or sharing a room with one: There has been no reinforcement one way or the other. The subject then generalizes from some other situation (like including a Turk or some vaguely differentiated and exotic foreigner in his club) with which he has had experience or which is meaningful to him. The gradient is from that situation to the word 'Turk.'

Guttman's (14) procedure of measuring attitudes by means of a short series of questions arranged along a continuum so that the individual's score indicates how he has answered all of them represents a very systematic attempt to determine the gradient of generalization and discrimination which a particular group reveals at a particular moment regarding a particular collection of stimulus patterns. Such a score is unambiguous only regarding the answers to the questions, but the genesis of the gradient for the individual remains unclear: The response to each question is not only a function of how closely the question approximates the original learning situation but also of the *afferent-habit strength* of the attitude, its *efferent-habit strength*, and the *interaction* occurring at the time the replies are given. The importance of previous learning and of interaction can be seen when some of the difficulties this technique encounters are considered. Replies to a series of questions which the investigator believes elicits a particular attitude do not always assume the form of a 'scalogram'; this suggests that for some attitudes there is no consistent gradient of generalization and discrimination in the society. Guttman, moreover, works with a so-called 'coefficient of reproducibility' of 85 per cent, which means that 15 per cent of the subjects' replies do not fall within the parallelogram. These deviants of course may have misinterpreted some of the questions or have been uncooperative, but many of them probably were responding to stimulus patterns arranged along different gradients.

c. After the investigator's words have been comprehended and after, perhaps, an attitude has been evoked, the subject knows—except in the case of an open-ended question—which type of further response he can make, *i.e.*, which alternatives he may check or what he can say. What he checks or says depends on the *interaction* among all the attitudes, stereotypes, drives, etc. evoked by the investigator's words and the entire social situation. Conflict, for example, may occur between what he 'really' feels (*i.e.*, the response symbolically or actually to approach or avoid the situation in question) and what he believes is 'respectable' or what he is 'required' to write or say (*i.e.*, another implicit, drive-producing response associated with conformity or prestige or face-saving or what not); thus arises the distinction between a public and private attitude, the former of which is frequently not an attitude as here defined but an overt response to competing drives and attitudes. This interaction creates another difficulty for the attitude scale or the poll: The *afferent-habit strength* of the attitude may be such that it can be aroused by the questions but its *efferent-habit strength* or its *drive strength* may not be sufficient to affect the overt response.

d. In like manner the discrepancy between the answers which the individual gives to a written or spoken question and his subsequent behavior in the future becomes intelligible. It has been frequently pointed out that polls now possess so much prestige in the United States principally because of their ability to predict a national election. Aside from a sound approach to the problem of sampling, such accurate prediction results from a number of factors peculiar to voting and therefore cannot be considered typical or indicative of other types of polls. Except in some instances, as studies employing a secret ballot have sometimes demonstrated (2), respondents around election time do not hesitate to express their political preference to the pollster; in different words, this means that the *drive strength* of the attitude in question is greater than other interacting or competing responses. The interview and the actual voting situations are so similar that the anticipatory response when polled is likely to be aroused and to be approximately the same one eventually evoked in the polling booth (*afferent-habit strength*); and the overt response of answering the question is also similar to the overt response of voting (*efferent-habit strength*). Previously many of the respondents have told other people how they intend to vote and thus the attitude has also been reinforced. The pollster, finally, usually takes out additional insurance by polling his sample right before the election, in order to be reasonably certain that psychological changes will not occur in the interim; thus approximately the same reinforcing state of affairs continues between interview and voting.

In almost all other polling or testing situations, there are additional complications which diminish the predictive value of the replies:

(1) The question may involve a cliché which evokes an attitude not directly related to the one being measured. Since there is an overt verbal response, however, it must be assumed that something is being measured; but that something may be a function of another attitude or drive, or of a combination of drives.

(2) The question may be answered 'superficially,' which means that the stimulus pattern in the question is so different from that in the real-life situation that different implicit responses and hence overt ones are evoked. The stimulus-value of the word 'Turk' on a paper-and-pencil social-distance test is not the same as that of a flesh-and-blood Turk, even though the person may arouse the word 'Turk' which will then elicit—along with the other response already elicited—an implicit response similar to that evoked on the test.

(3) The question may be answered genuinely and the response may be a function of innumerable attitudes and drives but—because the individual may change in the interim, because he does not think things through in advance, because some of his impulses are repressed, or because he simply cannot anticipate how he will react in a future situation that is unknown to him or out of his range of experience (*cf.* 12)—the future overt response will nevertheless be a function of other drives or attitudes that are not aroused by the question.

e. Students of attitude measurement and public opinion polls have amassed evidence which indicates certainly that the replies they obtain are consistent. The same question is repeated on the same people or another comparable sample, or a split-ballot technique is employed and the results frequently remain practically the same. It could be argued that these are measures of reliability and that reliability should not be confused with validity, were it not for the fact that this verbal distinction is somewhat meaningless when applied to the problem at hand. Such consistency does demonstrate that, when confronted with a set of nearly equivalent stimuli and when other attitudes and drives within the individual remain more or less equal (as required by this technique of measurement), the implicit response affects the overt response consistently under the given conditions. It seems operationally true that some kind of attitude is being measured, but its strength and its probable influence on the individual when other drives are aroused are not thereby indicated. It is also possible that the overt verbal response can remain consistent, although in different or the same individuals it results from different attitudes and different drives.

f. The apparent fluctuation of many attitudes, which are measured by large polls, with events and changes in society indicates how weak their habit and drive strengths are. Theoretically at least, the open-ended question has a better chance of giving insight into the importance and probable stability of the attitude being measured; but its disadvantages on technical grounds are also obvious (21). In like manner, the more alternatives offered an individual, the more likely additional and relevant attitudes and drives will be aroused and the more likely it is that his overt response be a reliable guide to his future conduct. Drive and other attitudes remaining equal, one discovers how people react to words like 'capitalism' and 'communism' when they are asked to choose between the two, but this knowledge of their attitude may not be helpful in understanding or predicting their behavior when confronted with a real-life situation involving capitalism or communism and not necessarily so labelled. It may be important to point out that people make such decisions on a superficial, semantic level. More insight would be obtained, however, concerning their actual choice in the future situation if they were made completely aware—by books, a course, motion pictures, or explicit and detailed alternatives and explanations—of what the political arrangements connoted by these terms would mean to them.

g. The principal psychological disadvantage under which attitude scales and polls labor is that, although they indirectly measure an implicit anticipatory response which is *socially significant*, they cannot determine what *goal response* the attitude now precedes. A respondent who signifies his intention to vote for a particular candidate, for example, can offer reasons for his choice and a poll can make note of these reasons. Presumably some prior contact with the candidate, his deeds, his party, or his promises (or generalization gradients therefrom, many of which are mediated by other verbal responses) has set up the anticipatory, mediating response which then is evoked literally before election time. It is the *efferent-habit strength* of the connection between those stimulus patterns and whatever the *goal response* in the individual was that is crucial and that has given rise to the attitude and hence the voting preference. Cantril and Fried (9, p. 19) make the same point when they indicate the meaninglessness of the response by people earning less than $1,000 a year to a question concerning the rate at which people earning $100,000 a year should be taxed. A crude measure of the intensity of feeling or of the importance to the respondents of the subject gives some insight, as shown by Katz (19) and by Doob (13), but this measure alone apparently does not increase predictive value in any useful way. It is a measure which does not differentiate between *afferent-habit strength* and *efferent-habit strength* nor between either of these and *drive strength*. Adequate measures of all three strengths as well as the various factors within a given personality and his society which continually reinforce or extinguish his attitude require an investigation of his life history, which scales and polls by their very nature cannot and should not be required to perform.

2. *Effect on judgment.* Social psychologists have shown experimentally that the arousal of an attitude or the interpretation of an event in one 'frame of reference' and not in another has a differential effect upon the overt behavior they call 'judgment.' This means no doubt that overt behavior is a function of *interacting* tendencies within the individual. The pioneering feeling pervading such experiments is somewhat surprising.

Over ten years ago, for example, Sherif found that judgments concerning the literary value of 16 samples of prose all taken from the same author were affected by the esteem in which the subjects held the 16 authors to whom the samples were *falsely* attributed; similar results were obtained from students in Turkey. He states that "the attitudes towards authors serve as reference points" (31, p. 374).

If the subject had seen the prose *without* the false labels, the situation might have been something like the following:

a. drive: to coöperate with the experimenter, *viz.*, to perceive the paper and to think and act.

b. stimulus pattern: the prose, the experimenter, co-acting subjects, etc.

c. implicit response sequence: verbal reactions, thoughts, attitudes, drives, and whatever it is from past experience and in terms of momentary appreciation which *interact* to determine literary judgment.

It may be argued that the above scheme is perhaps an oversimplification of what occurs, but Sherif presents no evidence one way or the other. It is certainly clear from his work, however, that the false label introduces more complications into the reaction. The overall drive is presumably the same, the stimulus pattern is altered to include the labels, and therefore—since the label-stimuli have been previously associated with some additional response—the implicit response-sequence is different. The responses evoked by the labels are the attitudes toward the authors. If the *direction* of that response is favorable or positive, the author must be liked because contact with his words in the past has been rewarding or because the individual knows that it is fashionable (and hence rewarding in a social sense) to like such a man. As a result of this previous reinforcement, the attitude in turn must have evoked responses like "this must be good," "I like this because so-and-so is such an excellent writer," "I don't like this but I know the man has written some good books," etc. These responses apparently helped determine the overt response, the rating of the prose.

Such responses, however, were not crucial for all the individuals: Sherif's subjects displayed individual differences and his results are expressed in statistical terms. They were only relatively important in this situation, moreover, because literary judgment is notoriously subjective, which means that it results from a variety of responses whose *efferent-habit strength* fluctuates from individual to individual and within the same individual. When Birch (4) used prose passages dealing with a well-structured social point of view, he found that the attitude evoked by a false label did not always compete successfully with other stronger responses; e.g., even though some of the subjects were anti-communist, many of them nevertheless agreed with statements falsely labeled 'communist' because they apparently were more strongly impressed with the arguments therein.

It is an interesting, empirical fact to know that literary judgments are affected by an author's reputation, but no more interesting nor scientifically important than the knowledge that most thirsty men want water. Sherif has noted the fact that some of his subjects deliberately weakened the drive strength of the response evoked by their attitude: in one experiment, some of them made "a special effort to overcome the influence of the authors' names" and hence their judgments were not correlated with their preferences for the authors (r. = − .03 for one group and + .04 for another). He has also pointed out that other subjects were unsuccessful in this attempt: in "written introspective records obtained right after the experiments several subjects *spontaneously* reported 'they wished that the names of the authors were not there' ..." (31, p. 375; italics his). Why and how did these subjects make such an attempt? In addition, the fact that none of the positive correlations between authors' ranks and preferences for the prose attributed to them was higher than .53 and that at least one was as low as .30 for those "subjects who did not make a consistent special effort to overcome the influence of the authors' names or to ignore them altogether" requires an explanation in terms of the unreliability of both sets of ratings or of the *interaction* within the subjects of competing attitudes and drives. No explanation is given in Sherif's treatment of the experiment in his book (32, pp. 122–3), nor in the work of Cantril (6).

In short, social psychologists no longer need to tax their ingenuity to devise new experiments merely to demonstrate that attitude affects judgment. This is truly an established fact, one indeed that was fairly well known even in psychophysics and before social psychologists felt impelled to blow the fresh air of what they call 'everyday life' into the laboratory. The time has come when it is possible and also necessary to relate the fact to systematic theory. Conclusions to additional experimentation should begin not with "attitude has been shown to affect judgment ..." but with "the effect of attitude upon judgments is a function of. . . ."

3. *Effects on memory.* One section of an experiment by Levine and Murphy (22) can serve as an illustration of this effect. It has been shown by them, for example, that students who are pro-communist tend to learn more rapidly and forget less readily a piece of pro-Soviet prose than does a group of anticommunists. The authors attribute the difference to the fact that for the first group the material was, and for the second it was not, congruent with 'social attitudes.'

Under ordinary laboratory conditions, the rate of memorizing and then forgetting sense material has been found to be a function of a variety of factors related to the difficulty of the material, the number of repetitions, the spacing of the repetitions, the familiarity of the subjects with the stimuli, etc. Drive and reward are frequently neglected as factors or at least assumed to be the general, convenient ones of cooperating with the experimenter and then securing his approval. In some experiments, the strength of drive has been varied, specific rewards have been offered, or successes or failures have served as rewards. Enough is certainly known, therefore, to state the flabby generalization that drive and reward affect learning and forgetting.

The subjects of Levine and Murphy agreed to cooperate: This is the drive which is so easily aroused among college students and others and which induces them to *perceive* a stimulus pattern and otherwise respond. The prose then evoked an attitude within them, that associated with communism, because it was deliberately selected by the experimenters to fall along the gradient of other stimuli to which the response involving communism had been previously made (*afferent-habit strength*). The attitude in turn had drive value which increased the motivation of the pro-communist students and decreased that of the anti-communist group. The former may have been pleased that the experimenter was 'liberal' enough to give them communist prose and they may have anticipated that the learning of another pro-Soviet argument would be rewarding. The latter, in contrast, may have been annoyed with the experimenter for exposing them to such arguments and they may have anticipated only grief from memorizing the passage. In terms of motivation alone, then, the differential result in this experiment may be only a variation of the principle that learning is a function of reward and punishment. Other factors may have been involved, but Levine and Murphy do not provide the necessary data. The pro-communists, for example, may have been more familiar with this type of material. Or the anti-communists may have been distracted by the communist arguments and have spent some time denying their validity or refuting them.

The demonstration by the investigators of *an* effect of attitude upon learning is just another fact, in the way Sherif's experiments produce another fact. If hunger makes a rat learn to run a maze faster than one which is not hungry, why should not a communist attitude which is drive-producing also affect the processes of learning and forgetting something about the Soviet Union? Important to note in this experiment, for example, is the fact that learning occurred regardless of attitude concerning communism and hence that the attitude affected only the rate of learning; apparently the overall drive to work with Levine and Murphy or some other drive involving individual prestige was sufficient. There were also the usual individual differences and apparently intra-individual variations.

The writers are well aware of the complexity of the problem when, in terms of what they call 'field theory,' they state:

"The particular attitude being studied; the number and kind of subjects; their motivation; the difficulty of the material; its affective tone; the degree of conflict between the material and the attitude; the external testing situation, which includes the relations of the experimenter and the subjects; changes in the broader field from which the attitude stems—these are some of the variables that would seem to affect the way in which material which supports or contradicts our social attitudes would be learned and forgotten" (22, p. 514).

Awareness of the complexity of the problem, however, is only a commendable first step. What is also needed is a systematic theory of behavior in which these various factors can be weighted and their effects ascertained. More carefully designed experiments, moreover, will enable investigators to measure such factors.

4. *Race prejudice.* Lasker, after surveying the genesis of race prejudice among children, comes to the conclusion that, "while it would not be safe at this stage of our knowledge to attribute a relative weight to different kinds of influences, the evidence makes it probable that the attitudes unconsciously transmitted are much more effective than those deliberately taught" (20, p. 371). The kind of evidence submitted by him is illustrated by the following incident:

"Walking across the playground, a settlement worker found a little Italian boy crying bitterly. She asked him what was the matter. 'Hit by Polish boy,' the little man repeated several times. Inquiry among the bystanders showed that the offender was not Polish at all. Turning again to her little friend, she said, 'You mean, hit by a big, naughty boy.' But he would not have it thus and went on repeating that he had been hit by a Polish boy. This struck the worker as so curious that she made inquiries about the little fellow's family. She learned that it lived in the same house with a Polish family and that the Italian mother, by constantly quarreling with her Polish neighbor, had put into the heads of her children the notion that Polish and bad were synonymous terms" (20, p. 98).

No additional data are submitted to explain this prejudice. In their absence, it must be assumed that the learning process prior to this incident involved the following steps:

a. The child overheard his mother many times describing Poles in unflattering terms and he must have seen her grow irritated by people she called 'Poles.' Gradually he learned a sentence or thought like "Poles are bad" from these stimuli. He learned the sentence or thought, as Miller and Dollard point out (25), because he wished to please his mother and to win her approval and/or because he knew from past experience that imitating her proved more often to be rewarding than punishing. At this point, he could merely respond, "Poles are bad," in response to a stimulus like "Do you like Poles?" The drive remained associated with his mother; the reward was her approval; the response to Poles was not anticipatory or drive-producing; the child, consequently, had not yet acquired an attitude involving race prejudice.

b. It is being presumed that the child did not know the meaning of 'badness.' Gradually, as he acquired experience and more language, he learned that people and objects called 'bad' are punishing and not rewarding. This is a process of further conditioning and generalization; as a result, a response pattern of withdrawing occurred to a variety of stimuli which the child was able to label 'bad.'

c. When the child had learned that "Poles are bad" and that people called 'bad' punished him, the withdrawal response pattern previously evoked by 'bad' then could be elicited by 'Poles.' The category of Poles, in short, had become part of the secondary generalization gradient of badness to which appropriate responses were made prior to actual punishment (*afferent-habit strength*). Thereafter the sentence or person thought to be Polish produced the responses before contact had been established; and these responses in turn eventually led to overt responses relating to Poles (*effect-habit strength*). If the child already possessed an attitude regarding people and objects called 'bad' *before* he heard his mother cast aspersions on Poles, the learning process would have been slightly different: he would again have accepted her characterization of Poles in order to win her approval and/or imitate her, but he then would immediately—without the mediating responses indicated above—have responded negatively regarding Poles even as he had been responding to all stimuli labelled 'bad.'

d. In the absence of any data from Lasker, it must be added that the acquiring of the prejudice concerning Poles might have occurred in still a different way. The generalization might not have involved the stimulus 'bad'; instead the mediating stimuli may have been those associated with anger or anxiety. The child perceived anger or anxiety in his mother whenever she mentioned 'Poles.' The sight of her reactions produced equivalent responses within him, since—again an assumption—similar behavior on her part in the past has eventually led to some kind of punishment for him. Through simple conditioning, then, the word 'Pole' came to evoke this previously acquired response pattern in him which, since it also had *social significance*, can be called an attitude.

e. This particular child for understandable reasons had difficulty in perceiving Poles. If his prejudice had been directed by his mother against Negroes or Orientals, groups with so-called 'high visibility,' his learning would have been facilitated because such groups can be discriminated on the basis of color which can be easily perceived. If his attitude toward Poles is not extinguished, he undoubtedly will gradually learn to perceive Poles as he matures; he may be able to do so on the basis of their names, the place where they live, the physical characteristics which he will come to believe they possess, the way they pronounce English, etc.

Lasker also does not indicate whether any incident similar to the one he reports had previously occurred in the life of the child. Even without this important information, however, it is possible to attempt an analysis of what must have taken place:

(1) The child was punished by another boy. This was a frustration and he felt aggressive toward the cause of his pain.

(2) The pain, aggression, anger, anxiety or whatever it was which welled up within him was a cue-producing response that mediated the response 'bad.' The 'bad' response in turn mediated 'Pole' since it is presumed he knew a sentence like 'All Poles are bad'—the conversion of the proposition may have been a logical fallacy on his part but it was psychologically sound since the latter word fell along his gradient of generalization. Or the cue-producing response might have mediated directly the response of 'Pole' because in the past such a response within him, evoked by the sight of similar behavior on the part of his mother, had been followed or accompanied by his own response of 'Pole' (as provided by his mother or—perhaps in a sub-vocal form or as a fleeting thought—by himself). Probably there were also other implicit responses mediated by the pain, some of which—if expressed—were unsuited for the ears of the social worker. It is important to note that the child did not perceive his antagonist as a 'Pole' until he was hurt and that it was the hurting which mediated the response he gave.

(3) The social worker attempted to convince him that the boy was not a Pole but a human being who happened to be 'big' and 'naughty.' She wished to prevent the pain from mediating the response of 'Pole' and thus for the future weaken the efferent-habit strength of his attitude. Evidently the child was unable to make the discrimination for at least two reasons. In the past, firstly, both the *afferent-* and the *efferent-habit strengths* of his attitude had been heavily reinforced in his home and perhaps elsewhere; they could not be weakened by a single admonition. Then, secondly, the aggressive tendencies of the hurt child were so strong that he was in no mood to make a discrimination; *i.e.*, he sought immediate tension-reduction in a way that had brought him some relief in the past, in comparison with which drive any other drive evoked in him by the adult-status of the social worker was weaker.

(4) From a painful experience like this, it can be anticipated that the strength of the child's attitude toward Poles will be greater. He will avoid Poles or seek to hurt Poles not to please his mother—although conceivably this drive will still be aroused from time to time—but so that he himself can reduce his anxiety and avoid the punishment he might now more reasonably anticipate. The prejudice may be further reinforced by other incidents and its habit strength may be increased by the existence of similar prejudice in his milieu.

This incident has been analyzed in some detail to indicate the complex problems an apparently simple incident raises. Lasker has presented the bare externalities. Before this child's attitude toward the Poles can be changed and before race prejudice *en masse* can be tackled, the complicated factors that are present must be understood by collecting not more but the right kind of data and by analyzing them systematically.

CONCLUSION

Although tempting, it would be socially useless to conclude this analysis of the behavior of attitudes by proposing that the concept be dropped from social science. A popular word, no matter how ambiguous or unspecific, however, cannot be legislated out of existence because the fact of its popularity indicates that for the moment it is satisfying some kind of social (in this case, quasi-scientific) need. The concept of attitude is frequently accompanied by various not-too-well or clearly-formulated theories which inspire useful investigations to be conducted and thus it does discharge certain functions. In addition, it is a cozy word which laymen and social scientists think they have no difficulty in understanding: it is easier to 'intuit' the 'meaning' of a word than to search for its referents.

The telling question to ask concerning attitude is: Does the term belong in a set of systematic theories which together approximate something that might be called science? In this writer's opinion, the answer is no. Using attitude along with a few other terms does not make science but reveals polysyllabic commonsense. If the answer is no, then it follows that attitude is merely a makeshift concept which cannot stand on its own theoretical legs but requires bolstering on a more basic level and that any 'principles' pertaining to attitude are only special cases of psychological theory.

This paper has proposed that bolstering can come from general behavior theory as outlined here, and a preliminary effort has been made to relate attitude to that theory. In this way it has been possible to observe how inadequate research can be which employs the concept and to observe, too, why the research is inadequate. A theory in science, among other things, tells investigators what to look for, what to measure, and what to control. Calling an attitude "an implicit, drive-producing response" or identifying it with most of the internal responses which intervene between a stimulus pattern and a response pattern obviously does not change the phenomena to which the word refers, but it does call attention to the heterogeneous problems in human behavior. It specifies 'the other things' which the investigator of attitude has always been compelled to consider equal or has disregarded. It suggests the limited character of the results which necessarily must be anticipated when only a particular attitude—of all the tendencies affecting human beings—is studied at a given moment. It indicates, too, what the next step in attitude research might be: the application of basic psychological principles which have heretofore been derived from carefully controlled but socially limited situations.

Social scientists are interested in more than quantifying history (which is what their polls, scales, and experiments generally do accomplish). They presumably seek principles which transcend the historically limited example, not that the past or the present is unimportant but because a set of principles can set the problem for the future. Historically limited data, aside from their social utility, will always have to be collected, for only thereby can the variables affecting a given situation be weighted and predictions emerge. As behavior theory develops, it will inevitably absorb a word like attitude, perhaps in some such manner as has been indicated. Whether 'attitude' then will continue to be employed in social science is unimportant. The personal guess of the writer is that the demise of attitude in the far future will be a happy day for social science, since this event will signify the emergence of a more integrated and scientific system of human behavior.

REFERENCES

1. ALLPORT, G. W. Attitudes. In *A handbook of social psychology* (Murchison, C., Ed.). Worcester: Clark Univ. Press, 1935. Chap. 17.
2. BENSON, L. W. Studies in secret-ballot technique. *Publ. Opin. Quart.*, 1941, 5, 79–82.
3. BERNARD, L. L. *An introduction to social psychology.* New York: Henry Holt, 1926.
4. BIRCH, H. G. The effect of socially disapproved labeling upon a well-structured attitude. *J. abnorm. & soc. Psychol.*, 1945, 40, 301–310.
5. CANTRIL, H. General and specific attitudes, *Psychol. Monogr.*, 1932, no. 192.
6. ———. Experimental studies of prestige suggestion. *Psychol. Bull.*, 1937, 34, 528.
7. ———, GAUDET, H., and HERZOG, H. *The invasion from Mars.* Princeton: Princeton Univ. Press, 1940.
8. ———. *The psychology of social movements.* New York: Wiley, 1941.
9. ———, and FRIED, E. The meaning of questions. In *Gauging public opinion* (Cantril, H., Ed.). Princeton: Princeton Univ. Press, 1944. Chap. I.
10. CHILD, I. L., and DOOB, L. W. Factors determining national stereotypes. *J. soc. Psychol.*, 1943, 17, 203–219.
11. COFER, C. N., and FOLEY, J. P., JR. Mediated generalization and the interpretation of verbal behavior: I. prolegomena. PSYCHOL. REV., 1942, 49, 513–540.
12. DOLLARD, J. Under what conditions do opinions predict behavior? Unpublished paper delivered before Joint Meeting of the Washington Statistical Society and the Washington Chapter of the Institute of Mathematical Statistics, Washington, D. C., March 9–10, 1944.
13. DOOB, L. W. Some factors determining change in attitude. *J. abnorm. & soc. Psychol.*, 1940, 35, 549–565.
14. GUTTMAN, L. A basis for scaling qualitative data. *Amer. sociol. Rev.*, 1944, 9, 139–150.
15. HILGARD, E. R., and MARQUIS, D. G. *Conditioning and learning.* New York: Appleton-Century, 1940.
16. HULL, C. L. Fractional antedating goal reactions as pure stimulus acts. Paper delivered before Monday Night Meeting of the Institute of Human Relations, Oct. 24, 1941.

17. ———. *Principles of behavior.* New York: Appleton-Century, 1943.

18. KATZ, D., and BRALY, K. W. Racial prejudice and racial stereotypes. *J. abnorm. & soc. Psychol.*, 1935, 30, 175–193.

19. ———. The measurement of intensity. In *Gauging public opinion* (H. Cantril, Ed.). Princeton: Princeton Univ. Press, 1944. Chap. III.

20. LASKER, B. *Race attitudes in children.* New York: Holt, 1929.

21. LAZARSFELD, P. F. The controversy over detailed interviews—an offer for negotiations. *Publ. Opin. Quart.*, 1944, 8, 38–60.

22. LEVINE, J. M., and MURPHY, G. The learning and forgetting of controversial material. *J. abnorm. & soc. Psychol.*, 1943, 38, 507–517.

23. LIPPMANN, W. *Public opinion.* New York: Macmillan, 1922.

24. MAY, M. A. A stimulus-response interpretation of "attitudes." Unpublished paper.

25. MILLER, N. E., and DOLLARD, J. *Social learning and imitation.* New Haven: Yale Univ. Press, 1941.

26. MURPHY, G., MURPHY, L. B., and NEWCOMB, T. B. *Experimental social psychology.* New York: Harpers, 1937.

27. MURRAY, H. A., and MORGAN, C. D. A clinical study of sentiments. *Genet. psychol. Monogr.*, 1945, no. 32.

28. RICHARDS, I. A. *Science and poetry.* New York: Norton, 1926.

29. SEELEMAN, V. The influence of attitude upon the remembering of pictorial material. *Arch. Psychol.*, 1940, no. 258.

30. SHERIF, M. A. A study of some social factors in perception. *Arch. Psychol*, 1935, no. 187.

31. ———. An experimental study of stereotypes. *J. abnorm. & soc. Psychol.*, 1935, 29, 371–375.

32. ———. *The psychology of social norms.* New York: Harpers, 1936.

33. ———, and CANTRIL, H. The psychology of 'attitudes.' *Psychol. Rev.*, 1945, 52, 295–319; 1946, 53, 1–24.

C. I. Hovland / I. L. Janis / H. H. Kelley

COMMUNICATION
AND PERSUASION

NATURE OF PERSUASIVE COMMUNICATION

We assume that opinions, like other habits, will tend to persist unless the individual undergoes some new learning experiences. Exposure to a persuasive communication which successfully induces the individual to accept a new opinion constitutes a learning experience in which a new verbal habit is acquired. That is to say, when presented with a given question, the individual now thinks of and prefers the new answer suggested by the communication to the old one held prior to exposure to the communication.

What are the factors in the communication situation responsible for this change and how do they operate so as to replace the original verbal response by a new one? Without attempting to give a full theoretical account of this learning process, we shall present a tentative summary of the main factors in communication situations which are assumed to be responsible for producing opinion changes.

One key element in the persuasion situation is, of course, the "recommended opinion" presented in the communication. This element may be conceptualized as a compound stimulus which raises the critical question and gives a new answer. For example, imagine the communicator's conclusion to be that "It will be at least ten years before the United States will engage in a war with Russia." We assume that in presenting this idea the communication contains words which operate as effective stimuli in posing the question, "How long before the United States will be at war with Russia?" At the same time

Excerpted from *Communication and Persuasion,* pp. 10–12, 15–17, with permission of Yale University Press. Copyright © 1953 by Yale University Press.

the conclusion states a specific answer, "At least ten years." In the course of a lengthy communication this conclusion may be asserted dozens of times or perhaps only once. Even when a communicator does not give an explicit statement of his conclusion, the indirect verbal statements he presents must operate implicitly to pose a question and suggest an answer; otherwise we would not regard the communication as capable of inducing a new opinion.

When exposed to the recommended opinion, a member of the audience is assumed to react with at least two distinct responses. He thinks of his own answer to the question, and also of the answer suggested by the communicator. The first response results from the previously established verbal habit constituting the individual's original opinion; the second response is assumed to result from a general aspect of verbal behavior, namely, the acquired tendency to repeat to oneself communications to which one is attending. Hence, a major effect of persuasive communication lies in stimulating the individual to think both of his initial opinion and of the new opinion recommended in the communication.

Merely thinking about the new opinion along with the old would not, in itself, lead to opinion change. The individual could *memorize* the content of the conclusion while his opinion remained unchanged. Practice, which is so important for memorizing verbal material in educational or training situations, is not sufficient for bringing about the *acceptance* of a new opinion. We assume that acceptance is contingent upon *incentives*, and that in order to change an opinion it is necessary to create a greater incentive for making the new implicit response than for making the old one. A major basis for acceptance of a given opinion is provided by arguments or reasons which, according to the individual's own thinking habits, constitute "rational" or "logical" support for the conclusions. In addition to supporting reasons, there are likely to be other special incentives involving anticipated rewards and punishments which motivate the individual to accept or reject a given opinion. . . .

It is assumed that there are three main classes of stimuli present in the communication situation which are capable of producing the shifts in incentive described above. One set of stimuli has to do with the observable characteristics of the perceived source of the communication. Another involves the setting in which the person is exposed to the communication, including, for example, the way in which other members of the audience respond during the presentation. Communication stimuli also include important content elements, referred to as "arguments" and "appeals." Whether or not stimuli of these various types operate successfully as incentives depends upon the predispositions of the individual. A successful communication is one in which these various stimuli are both adapted to the level of verbal skill of the individual and capable of stimulating his motives so as to foster acceptance of the recommended opinion.

. . . .

CHARACTERISTICS OF
COMMUNICATION LEARNING

In the foregoing discussion, we have assumed that the effectiveness of persuasive communications is a matter of learning. To some extent, we would expect to find that there are common principles which apply equally to the learning of new opinions, of various verbal and motor skills, and of other habits. But it is necessary to recognize that the *type* of learning and the *conditions* of learning are ordinarily quite different in the case of producing opinion change through persuasive communication than in the case of other learning situations.

In his preface to Klapper's recent book Lazarsfeld has emphasized the difficulties involved in taking results from laboratory studies of human learning and applying them to the presentation of persuasive communications via mass media, where the audience may "leave the field" if uninterested. He characterizes the mass communication situation as one equivalent to "a learning experiment where people walk in and out as they please, where some of the most valuable effects are achieved with people who come in by mere accident, where the motivation to learn is often very low and where the possible rewards for learning are obvious neither to the experimenter nor to the subject . . ." (Klapper, Foreword, pp. 6 and 7).

The utilizer of mass communications often has an antecedent problem with which our research has not been concerned, that of attracting an audience in the first place. But even when persuasive arguments are presented to a relatively "captive" audience—for example, to delegates at a political convention—there are still a number of unique features which make the learning situation different from academic teaching or from skill instruction in which new verbal habits are acquired:

1. When formal instruction is given, the audience ordinarily is set to learn, and voluntarily accepts the status of students in relation to an instructor. This is generally not the case with persuasive communications in everyday life.

2. In many situations of verbal learning, as in courses on science, a major goal is to teach a large number of facts and propositions. In order to attain this objective, a great deal of practice is necessary before the individual can memorize and retain all of the information which he is expected to learn. In the case of persuasive communications, however, the recommended opinion generally consists of a single statement which is within the memory span of most individuals and in many instances a single communication is sufficient to induce opinion change. During exposure to the communication, the audience may rehearse the recommended opinion several times, but sometimes only once is sufficient for the simple task of memorizing the recommended conclusion. The main problem for the communicator, of course, is to induce the audience to accept. Thus, routine practice plays a smaller role in this type of learning. On the other hand, while one-trial learning may be within the repertoire of

the learner, the communicator must often provide the special kind of practice necessary for "transfer of training," so that the learner will apply the new opinion in the many different situations in which it is subsequently relevant.

3. The retention of verbally mediated skills or of memorized verbal material sometimes suffers interference from the subsequent practice of new responses to the same stimuli. Generally speaking, however, it seldom happens that, following formal instruction, the individual is exposed to competing instruction designed to break down the new verbal habits which he has just acquired. In the case of persuasive communications dealing with controversial opinions, on the other hand, this type of interference occurs fairly frequently. Shortly after being exposed to one communication, the audience is likely to be exposed to additional communications presenting completely different points of view and designed to create completely different opinions. Hence, the long-run effectiveness of a persuasive communication depends not only upon its success in inducing a momentary shift in opinion but also upon the sustained resistance it can create with respect to subsequent competing pressures.

. . . .

REFERENCE

KLAPPER, J. T. The effects of the mass media. New York, Columbia University Bureau of Applied Social Research, 1949.

C. W. Sherif / M. Sherif / R. E. Nebergall

ATTITUDE
AND ATTITUDE CHANGE:
THE SOCIAL JUDGMENT-
INVOLVEMENT
APPROACH

CONCEPTS, OPERATIONS,
AND FINDINGS

Stripped to its bare essential, the problem of attitude change is the problem of the degree of discrepancy from communication and the felt necessity of coping with the discrepancy. The discrepancy in question is the degree of divergence between the position advocated in a communication or message and the own position of the subject exposed to it. Of course, psychologically, the discrepancy in question is the divergence experienced or felt by the individual between the position he upholds and the position to which he is exposed.

One way or another, rival theories dealing with attempts to change attitudes on an issue are concerned with the discrepancy problem, specifically with explanation of the effects of a felt discrepancy and a person's attempt to cope with it through various measures at his command.

Since this is a core problem, an adequate theory should provide conceptual tools to assess, as validly and precisely as possible, the discrepancy between attitude and communication, in terms of the position of the individual, the

Reprinted from *Attitude and Attitude Change: The Social Judgment-Involvement Approach,* pp. 225–44, with permission of the authors and W. B. Saunders, Company.

104

position of communication, and the individual's appraisal of the position of communication (placement), specifying the stimulus conditions under which the discrepancy is experienced. Developing procedures and tools for this purpose means nothing more or less than developing the appropriate psychophysics for studying attitude and attitude change. Then, and only then, a theory can deal effectively with the alternative reactions or measures that the individual will use to deal with the discrepancy.

Because of concern over the needed concepts and associated research operations, we have been preoccupied in the present approach for years with developing appropriate units for assessing an attitude, as elaborated in Chapters 2 to 4. These will be summarized in the next section. Let us consider the task of developing operational procedures for indicators of felt discrepancy by looking into the nature of the discrepancy experienced by the individual.

Obviously, the term "discrepancy" implies at least two positions on a given issue that are close together or diverge from one another to some extent. What are the positions in question? One is a position upheld by the individual; another is the position of a communication or message presented to him. The felt discrepancy, therefore, implies an appraisal of the communication by the individual relative to his own position, whether he is conscious or not that he is comparing. This appraisal or evaluation is a judgment process, that is, a *placement* of the communication in question as close to or distant from his own position in some degree.

When the individual's reaction to a communication is thus formulated, as his placement or categorization of the communication relative to his own stand, we are moving to develop valid and precise measurement procedures to express the magnitude of the discrepancy. And this is the only way we can predict the individual's experience of discrepancies and his reactions to them.

Conceptualizing the discrepancy problem as a judgment process provides us with the essential principles derived from the psychology of judgment, which can be used to predict attitude change, resistance to change, or susceptibility to change. Here we will state only the overall approach, without specifying all the variables that may modify it.

Placement of Communication Is Basic in Predicting Reactions to It

The attitude of a person represents a range of acceptances and range of rejections for a class of objects or positions on an issue, and it may include positions toward which he is noncommittal (Chapter 2). If a message or communication does not fall appreciably beyond the range of acceptances, the discrepancy will be minimized in placing the communication. Hence, the communication is likely to be *assimilated* into his range of acceptances.

If the message falls well beyond the range of acceptances, the individual will appraise it as more discrepant than it actually is. Its position will be displaced away from his acceptable range, and the extent of the *contrast effect* will be in proportion to the divergence of the communication from his acceptable range.

The greater the commitment or dedication of an individual to his stand on an issue, the greater the displacement of a discrepant message away from the bounds of his acceptance. The technical details for assessing the range of assimilation and contrast effects with differing degrees of involvement in the issue are presented in Chapters 2, 5, and 6.

Whether there will be change in attitude *toward* the position advocated in communication or reaffirmation of the individual's stand *away* from communication is initially determined by the appraisal or placement of the advocated position relative to his own. In other words, attitude change or resistance to change is a function of individual categorization of communication. Placement of communication as within, near to, or far from the bounds of acceptability is the crucial process underlying attitude change including the direction and amount of change.

As change or no change is a function of placement of communication toward or away from the bounds of acceptance, so are associated affective and behavioral consequences of categorizing the communication relative to own stand. Change of attitude, resistance to change, debunking the communicator, attempts to persuade the communicator, seeking social support, and other measures, which have been proposed as *alternative* reactions to discrepant communication in Festinger's "dissonance" theory are all associated consequences of placement of communication at varying discrepancies from the person's own stand (Festinger, 1957, 1963; Brehm and Cohen, 1962). Although variations in situational opportunity for one or others of these measures were recognized in that approach, the option of one or another of the alternatives has been stated so generally otherwise as to become a matter of individual differences in psychodynamic mechanisms.

On the contrary, change, resistance to change, debunking the source or the communicator or both, are not isolated and optional alternatives, the selection of which depends merely on circumstantial possibility or individual differences in "coping mechanisms," even though both enter into any behavioral outcome. It is substantiated by findings in Chapter 5 that when a communication opposed to a subject's position is displaced away from his stand, it is dubbed *at the same time* as unreasonable, propagandistic, false, and even obnoxious, depending on the degree of displacement. Correspondingly, when a communication is assimilated closer to the bounds of acceptability, it is found more truthful, more factual, less biased, and tolerable. Evidence to this effect was presented from the studies of the 1956 and 1960 presidential elections, in the reactions of wets and drys during two referendums on the prohibition issue, and by persons favorable and unfavorable on a farm policy issue.

The predicament of being exposed to a message or exhortation advocating a stand diametrically opposite to the position to which we are wedded is not to be taken lightly. One does not accept this with the same good nature as when someone contradicts our opinion that a planet is 2 million miles away by saying it is 20 million miles away. Unless we are astronomers with personal claims and a professional stake, it may be more comfortable to change our guess tenfold than to appear a social bonehead, especially if we seem to be alone in our opinion.

In highly ego-involving issues (for example, when the religious beliefs of a devout person are at stake, when the honor of the good father's family is challenged, or when a person dedicated to democracy faces a debate on the democratic way of life versus the totalitarian), the individual's entrenched position is the weighty anchor that *overrides situational concerns* to be tolerant of contrary opinions or to be agreeable. The felt discrepancy in these highly involving issues is never resolved by moving toward the advocated position. The advocated position is invariably felt as an outrage, a violation of what is sacred, as a travesty of human decency in our eyes. In ego-involving issues, therefore, the present approach predicts further displacement of a discrepant position away from the subject's own, unless the exhortation to change is sufficiently camouflaged or otherwise unstructured. In addition, the present approach predicts denunciation and, if possible, attempts to eliminate the position advocated—contrary to statements of dissonance theory in regard to optional ways of reducing dissonance.

The recent moves by proponents of dissonance theory to include ego involvement in their theoretical scheme are steps in the positive direction. Otherwise, the very experience of dissonance remains axiomatic, its arousal depends on matters of logic, and ways of reducing dissonance appear to be optional mechanisms, the choice of which rests on individual differences.

The individual's commitments, dedications, and cherished positions in highly involving matters (matters related to family, sex role, religion, school, politics, or profession) are ingredients of his self picture, with all their affective-emotional overtones. These are ingredients of the individual's very self identity and its continuity from day to day. The psychological stability of his self identity consists of the stability and continuity of these ties and attitudes related to them. Exposure to communication aimed at disrupting or contradicting these ties and attitudes produces tension, or dissonance. The challenge to change or contradict ties and stands that constitute the self picture produces feelings of uncertainty or anxiety, which are conducive to the individual's efforts to restore the stability through all kinds of measures (*cf.* Sherif and Cantril, 1947; Sherif, 1948; Sherif and Harvey, 1952). The more the challenge in question touches upon ego attitudes higher in this scheme of personal priorities, the more relentless and persistent, even the more frantic, the measures he engages in to restore stability.

It is one thing to underscore the motivational urge to restore personal stability. It is altogether a different, and even a contradictory, emphasis to argue that the individual will restore his stability by giving up his positions near and dear to him as a family member, a member of a social group, an intellectual clique, or a religious sect, just because he feels situational discomfiture in the face of discrepant communication. Attitude change is not an option, psychologically, under these circumstances.

On the whole, there seems a tendency for theories of "imbalance," "equilibrium," "dissonance," "incongruence," and their variants to ignore the time dimension in the patterning of human behavior, which is necessary in the study of attitudes and behavior of men living in any cultural setting. By neglecting the time dimension, the basis for the psychological tensions dealt with in such theories is ignored, namely, the ego or self-formation. And predictions of behavior in specific cross sections of situations are liable to rest on sheerly logical grounds, with occasional psychological absurdities as the outcome.

Curtailing the scope of behavioral sequences to immediate situations and manifestations may be due to theory derived by analogy from the prestigeful physical models of equilibrium. With such models, there is less cause to consider the consequences of measures to restore stability. But consider how much more serious the reverberations will be in the individual if he copes with situationally induced dissonance or imbalance by giving up his religious faith, loyalty to his country, or loyalty to his professional code just because he is momentarily subjected to contrary points of view. The consequences of the momentary mode of coping with dissonance or imbalance may be much more serious than temporary disruption of psychological stability with accompanying feelings of guilt, shame, or disgrace.

It is emphasized that this statement holds in the case of change or resistance to change of highly ego-involving attitudes. When the individual is exposed to *less* ego-involving messages, situational considerations may very well outweigh the ego issues aroused by the message. For example, the concern not to be unpleasant or out of step in a social situation, or consideration for the prestige of the investigator, may outweigh any psychological tension a person might feel at a message that challenges his opinion on poetry, or the possibility of life on Mars, or social problems trivial in his personal scheme.

As elaborated in Chapter 6, the less ego-involving the issue is, the more important situational factors become, including the prestige of other persons and the order of arguments. To that extent, the likelihood of attitude change with greater discrepancies is increased. The range of assimilation and the individual's receptiveness to situational factors are in inverse relationship to his degree of ego involvement in his stand. The more ego-involved he is in his position, the narrower the range of assimilation, the wider the contrast range, and the greater the displacement of communication away from his own stand with increasing discrepancies. With greater ego involvement in his stand, the greater the likelihood of entrenchment in his position, with all the affective and motivational accompaniments (denunciation of the communication or the source, attribution of falsehood, propagandistic intent, maliciousness, etc.).

The conclusion that the evidence is contradictory on the question whether greater change results from greater or smaller attitude-communication discrepancies should be taken with a grain of salt (cf. Miller, 1963; Aronson *et al.*, 1963). It is true that data have been reported showing resistance to change with increased discrepancy and showing greater change with increased discrepancy. The data are only superficially contradictory. As seen in Chapter 6, a careful examination of the nature of issues utilized in the studies that yield different results goes a long way toward explaining the apparent contradiction. Those studies reporting greater change with greater discrepancy between attitude and communication utilized, on the whole, issues of little consequence to the subjects, so that it made little difference whether a favorable or unfavorable position was adopted, except in terms of the situational demands of the experiment.

Of course, ego attitudes may change, even highly involved ones. All attitudes are learned and are not, therefore, immutable; ego attitudes are no exception. But those high in the individual's scheme of personal priorities seldom are altered by temporary exposure to discrepant messages, even though the latter arouse ego tensions. A thorough grasp of the stability of the individual's ego ties, as well as changes in highly involved attitudes, requires inclusion of the individual's reference groups in the analytic framework.

"Social support" is not merely another option for resolving uncertainty or dissonance: it is a *sine qua non* for personal stability. Even if the individual does not actively search for social support, it is a psychological reality as long as he knows the persons and relationships in his reference groups. Conversely, changes in reference group values and ties, as seen in Chapter 6, are the context for the most striking alterations in ego attitudes.

The present approach detects susceptibility to change on ego-involving issues through the relative size of the latitude of noncommitment, as indicated in Chapters 2 and 6.

Latitudes of Acceptance, Rejection, and Noncommitment

The summary generalizations in the preceding section did not include the specifics on assessing discrepancies between a position advocated in communication and the individual's position on the issue in question. In the present approach, these specifics are more than mere procedural details. It is through these procedures that some crucial questions of theory can be brought into focus.

For example, how discrepant does a message have to be to arouse ego tension, or dissonance? How discrepant a message falls upon an open mind, and how discrepant a message finds that same mind closed? Why may two persons who choose the same position as most acceptable place the same message at different discrepancies from that position?

The specifics of these questions still remain unsolved by major theories applied to attitude and attitude change problems. Conditions for dissonance arousal were stated in logical terms as a position succeeded by its logical obverse. After excellent phenomenal description of open and closed minds, including the observation that a person may close his mind more quickly on one issue than another, Rokeach (1960) focused on the closed and open mind as global classifications for persons, even though he noted variations in level of rejection of disbelief systems according to group membership.

The questions cannot be answered by procedures and measurement techniques that yield an attitude indicator based on average responses nor those which assign arbitrary and invariant scale values to the positions. Were it not for these questions, the arbitrary scale values on the semantic differential, for example, and the degree of their polarity would be sufficient to define discrepancy or incongruence between attitude and communication (Osgood *et al.*, 1957). The reason that the arbitrary scale values on the semantic differential are not adequate for the purpose can be shown through example.

A rating of *zero*, the center of a linear rating scale, is arbitrarily defined as neutrality, favorable evaluations by the positive integers, and unfavorable ratings by the negative integers. Logically, a discrepancy between -1 and $+1$ is equivalent to a discrepancy between $+1$ and $+3$ except for the differences in sign. Our findings suggest that psychologically the discrepancy between $+1$ and $+3$ may be greater. If the person who checks $+3$ is highly involved in his stand, he may not only find a $+1$ position unacceptable; he may object strenuously to such a vacillating and "wishy-washy" position and displace it toward the opposing segment. The individual who checks a -1 position, on the other hand, may very well be somewhat indifferent to the entire matter, assimilate a $+1$ position toward his own, and regard the discrepancy between -1 and $+1$ as trivial.

The present approach started with the search for psychologically valid reference scales to assess discrepancies and to measure attitudes and their change. In keeping with the operational definition of attitude as a characteristic and consistent patterning of behavior, this search started in 1948 with study of the bounds of individual acceptances and rejections for the various positions on an issue. Individuals do vary in the patterning of their acceptances, rejections, and noncommitments, even when they agree on the single most acceptable position. Therefore, the structure of an attitude is not adequately represented by a single point, whether this point is a composite score, an average scale value of acceptances, or a cumulative rank of agreements for a restricted segment of positions on the issue. In the past, predictions about behavior from such punctiform measures have been far from satisfactory.

Operationally, an attitude is defined more accurately as a set of evaluative categories the individual has formed (or learned) during interaction with the persons and objects in his social world and which demarcate a *latitude of acceptance* (the positions he finds acceptable including the most acceptable single position) and the *latitude of rejection* (the positions he finds objectionable in varying degree, including the most objectionable position). Since the techniques for attitude assessment developed in the present approach do not arbitrarily force the individual to respond to every position (Chapters 2 and 4), there remains the possibility of *noncommitment* on certain positions.

In fact, research findings reported in this book require that *latitude of noncommitment* be included in an adequate characterization of attitude, defined as those positions the individual chooses neither to accept or to reject when he is not forced by the research procedures to evaluate every position. The heuristic value of the latitude of noncommitment will be made explicit.

Research into latitudes of acceptance, rejection, and noncommitment over the last 15 years permits certain generalizations about the structure of attitudes and suggests several paths for fruitful exploration. The following generalizations are based on studies of a variety of social issues reported in the present volume, including our studies of the 1956 and 1960 presidential elections in different regions of the country, the right-to-work study by Elbing, a farm policy issue studied by Whittaker, study of the segregation controversy by La Fave and Sherif, anti-Latin attitudes as studied by Vaughan, and the reapportionment issue studied by Reich and Sherif:

1. In proportion to the extremeness of an individual's stand on an issue, the latitude of rejection is greater than the latitude of acceptance and noncommitment approaches zero.

2. Proportional to the moderateness of the individual's position on an issue, the size of his latitudes of acceptance and rejection approaches equality.

3. As a result, the latitude of rejection of a person with an extreme stand is greater than that of a person taking a moderate position on the issue and his latitude of noncommitment is smaller.

We have presented considerable evidence that these characteristic patterns are not specific to particular issues nor determined by the particular procedures evolved for data collection. However, the research presented in this book contains strong evidence that the crucial determinant of the relationship between extremeness of stand and the pattern of evaluations is not extremeness *as such*, but rather the high probability that the individual extreme in his position will be highly involved in it. The evidence may be summarized as follows:

1. Persons selected for study on the basis of public commitment to support a favorable or unfavorable stand on a controversial issue have typically revealed the pattern of evaluations described above for extreme stands, even though many of them did not find the most extreme positions most acceptable.

2. Systematic variations are not found, on the average, in size of the latitude of acceptance according to extremeness of stand, even though other

evidence suggests such variation according to intense versus moderate involvement.

3. The variances in size of latitude of rejection (number of positions rejected) for persons finding extreme and moderate positions most acceptable do not differ significantly, except for persons endorsing *nonpartisanship* as most acceptable. In other words, for all but the latter subjects, individual differences in number of positions rejected occur to a similar extent but around averages that do differ systematically according to extremeness of stand. The variance in latitudes of rejection for the nonpartisan (those labeled "undecided" in a survey) is *greater* than that for others, owing to the presence of a substantial minority of persons who accept *only* nonpartisanship and who reject all the partisan alternatives offered them. When questioned, such persons report that they are highly involved in the issue. Their latitudes of rejection exceed their acceptances and noncommitments approach zero, exactly like the highly involved person who adopts an *extreme* stand.

4. The relationship between relative size of rejection range and extremeness of stand holds for a variety of issues, and noncommitment increases with moderateness on all of them, but the overall frequency of noncommitment for all subjects does vary strikingly from issue to issue. We found less noncommitment (refraining from accepting or rejecting one or more positions) on the issue of who should be elected president in the weeks preceding the 1956 and 1960 presidential elections than Elbing found on the right to work among business students or than Whittaker found among nonfarmers on a farm policy issue. Reich and Sherif reported that persons highly involved on reapportionment were noncommittal on only about 4 per cent of the statements on the issue, whereas less involved but otherwise comparable subjects were noncommittal on 21 per cent.

In short, we postulate on the basis of research findings that size of latitudes of rejection *increases* and size of latitudes of noncommitment *decreases* in proportion to degree of involvement in the issue, regardless of extremeness of the most acceptable position. On this basis, we have suggested the average frequency of noncommitment (failure to endorse or reject positions) as a general measure of involvement in an issue or lack of it. More frequent noncommitment would be expected on issues not high in the concerns of the persons and fewer noncommittal positions on issues more involving for them.

We have effectively used *size of latitude of rejection on a particular issue (the 1960 presidential election) as a measure of varying ego involvement on the part of persons upholding different stands from extreme to moderate positions.* The results in Chapter 5 on placement of communication indicate that highly involved and less-involved persons do appraise communications differently. The felt discrepancy of a communication from the individual's own stand is, on the whole, greater for highly involved persons. The discrepancy is experienced relative to the person's reference scale, composed of the latitudes of acceptance, rejection, and noncommitment, which differ characteristically according to degree of personal commitment to a stand. Reactions to communication in the way of change, reaffirmation of stand, or deprecation of the communicator become predictable in terms of the position of the communication on this reference scale.

Individual differences are to be found in latitudes of acceptance and rejection, as in any psychological phenomenon. But the regularities in their patterning according to the location of the bounds of acceptability and the degree of the individual's involvement in his stand permit more accurate prediction of his reaction to communication and his susceptibility or resistance to attitude change, than qualities of the person in the abstract, such as rigidity or flexibility assessed without regard to task or content. For future exploration of personal flexibility and rigidity, we propose that the person's latitudes of acceptance, rejection, and noncommitment be studied on a variety of issues of differing personal import to him.

Our hypothesis is that every individual possesses content areas or clusters in which he is open minded and others in which he is more closed. We would expect that these clusters are related to degree of personal involvement in the content areas. Thus, we predict that for matters high in the individual's scheme of ego-involved priorities, his latitude of rejection would be greater and latitude of noncommitment smaller than for matters lower in the hierarchy of ego values (Chapter 3). To a considerable extent, those high in the hierarchy should be predictable from the values of his reference groups.

If these expectations were supported by research findings, they could lead to variational analysis of individual differences in flexibility on the same and different matters, as well as overall comparisons between individuals in typical modes of functioning, specified through relationships among value dimensions that constitute their personal priority schemes.

Principles Governing Placement of Communication

The characteristic and consistent patterns of behavior from which an attitude is inferred reveal an underlying process of judgment—of evaluations of the persons, objects, groups, ideas, or events encompassed by the attitude. Like any judgment process whatsoever, the evaluative activities that reveal an attitude are *relational* affairs. Appraisal of a particular item is a joint product of the properties of that item relative to the immediate context in which it appears and to preceding stimulus contexts. For example, quite apart from personal attitudes on the issue, a statement that "We must keep the future interests of school children in mind" is appraised differently when it is preceded or surrounded by statements opposed to school desegregation, on the one hand, or favoring school desegregation, on the other.

Even in judging motivationally neutral stimuli, as in the psychophysical experiment, not all the stimuli present or just preceding a situation have equal weight in affecting the judgmental outcome. In orthodox methods, the standard presented with each new stimulus to be judged is more influential than others less frequently presented or not designated as a standard (Helson, 1959, p. 591). If certain stimulus values recur more frequently or are designated as standards, they too become anchors for the individual's judgments. Lacking an explicit standard, the individual uses the most extreme representatives (end stimuli) as anchors to size up the intermediate values; thus, the end stimuli contribute more than others to the judgmental outcome (Parducci, 1963).

Owing to their greater contribution to the outcome, anchoring stimuli are focal in several systematic variations in judgment. In this connection, it should be recognized that the emphasis on anchors as the salient reference points that produce variations in placing related stimuli, and especially the insistence on the greater functional contribution of the end stimuli in the series, owes much to the work of Volkmann and his associates since the 1930s (Volkmann, 1951).

Assimilation-contrast effects are governed primarily by relationships between anchors and the items being appraised. As correctly emphasized by Helson recently (1964), and in line with the Sherif-Hovland representation of assimilation-contrast ranges in psychophysical judgments (1961, Chapter 3), assimilation and contrast are not separate processes or mechanisms. They are phenomena governed by similarities and differences between anchors and the objects being appraised. In other words, the present approach considers them complementary. An anchor stimulus enhances accurate placement of objects that coincide with it in value but produces systematic shifts or displacements in judgments of objects differing from it.

An anchor that differs slightly from the object of judgment results in displacement *toward* the anchor—assimilation effect (cf. Sherif, Taub, and Hovland, 1958; Parducci and Marshall, 1962; Helson, 1964). With increasing discrepancies between the anchor and the object of judgment, assimilation ceases and displacement begins to occur *away* from the anchor; the difference between them is exaggerated—contrast effect.

After research into the characteristic patterns of acceptance and rejection began in 1948, a series of studies was initiated into the judgment processes underlying these patterns, ranging from experiments on lifted weights to studies of the scale values of verbal attitudinal statements on controversial issues, such as the social status of Negroes in the United States. By clarifying the empirical relationships involved in judging both neutral and socially relevant items, a conceptual approach was developed that accounts for the distinctive patterning of latitudes of acceptance and rejection and displacements in social judgment. It is based on the relationships governing assimilation-contrast effects, the following extensions of which are derived from the accumulating findings from research on social judgment:

1. If a person has an attitude toward the stimulus domain, he has a set of well-learned categories for evaluating it, including a range he accepts and

a range he rejects. Henceforth, his judgments of specific objects in that domain are to some extent relative to these categories, in addition to the context of immediate and preceding stimulation.

2. To the extent that the domain of objects is personally involving to the individual, that is, in proportion to its priority in his scheme of relatedness to his social world, the positions that he accepts as his own stand anchor his placement of other items in the domain.

3. To the extent that his own stand becomes the most salient anchor, the individual's *placement* of items is evaluation of them, even when he is instructed to heed only the stimulus (objective) attributes of the items and his assigned task is simply comparison of the items on an impersonal dimension (e.g., favorableness—unfavorableness toward the object or event).

4. When his own stand is the anchor, other items will be displaced toward (assimilation) or away (contrast) from it in proportion to their proximity or discrepancy from his own stand, provided only that the stimulus objects lack, in some degree, objective properties that are readily perceived as defining membership in the categories he is instructed to use.

The identification of an ego-involved stand as an *anchor* is advantageous in handling systematic variations in placement in that it becomes directly comparable to anchoring stimuli in its effects, without invoking special psychodynamic mechanisms usually thought necessary for motivational factors. Similarly, this designation seems preferable to interpreting the individual's own stand as his "adaptation level" (e.g., Helson, 1959, p. 568) or neutrality region. His own stand represents a segment of highly positive affectivity, and the adaptation levels of less-involved persons do not produce similar systematic displacements under the same stimulus conditions.

The present conceptual approach has been tested in a series of studies on placement when subjects were instructed to use a prescribed number of categories (as in the procedures for Thurstone's equal-appearing intervals method of scaling statements) and when they were instructed to use any number of categories that seemed appropriate (own-categories procedure). As summarized in Chapters 4 and 5, certain findings are common to either procedure, as stated in the following generalizations:

1. Extreme representatives of the domain (e.g., strongly worded, unequivocal statements of extreme positions on a social issue) are consistently and accurately placed in extreme categories with low variability, regardless of own stand.

2. Proportional to the individual's ego involvement in the issue, the distribution of his placements into the categories is *bimodal*, the greatest concentration of judgments being in the extreme category *opposite* to his own stand (whether favorable or unfavorable) and the second mode in the categories with which he agrees, with consequent neglect of intermediate categories.

3. Proportional to the individual's involvement, items intermediate to the most extreme representatives are subject to displacements toward his own

stand (assimilation) or away from it (contrast), depending on their proximity to or distance from it and also depending on the ambiguousness of the item.

4. The preceding systematic displacements do not occur in the judgments of less-involved persons, even though they endorse similar positions as most acceptable. Such persons use the categories with fair equality throughout the range of items judged, without such marked variations in placement.

These findings are predictable in terms of the conceptual scheme outlined earlier. Using his own stand as an anchor, the highly involved individual becomes choosy about items to be placed in categories acceptable to him. While items differing only slightly from his stand are assimilated into acceptable categories, the *threshold for acceptance* is high compared to the threshold for rejection. The range of positions subject to assimilation will be inversely proportional to the degree of involvement, but it increases to the extent that neighboring items are ambiguous.

Items differing in various degrees from his acceptable range are displaced away from his own stand in proportion to his involvement, that is, to the extent that his own stand is a salient anchor. The contrast effect is revealed in a *lower threshold for rejection*, with disproportionate bunching of judgments in categories furthest removed from his stand.

Own-Categories Procedure. The phenomena just described are revealed in more accentuated form by the findings on placements of highly involved and less-involved persons using any number of categories that seems appropriate to them and distributing their judgments without restrictions (Chapter 4). The displacements are accentuated because of the tendency of highly involved persons to use a restricted number of categories.

The findings may be summarized as follows:

1. The number of categories used in the own-categories procedure varies with the person's involvement: fewer categories are used by persons more strongly committed to a stand, and the same individuals use fewer categories for objects more ego-involving to them than for objects less involving.

2. The widths of categories used by highly involved persons vary systematically, whereas those for moderate or disinterested persons do not. Specifically, committed persons bunch large numbers of items into categories objectionable to them, neglecting intermediate categories, and using acceptable categories more sparingly than objectionable categories.

3. The variations in distribution of items into categories occur through assimilation-contrast effects relative to the person's own stand on items intermediate or moderate in rank position, especially those which are ambiguous (subject to considerable variation in placement even by uninvolved persons).

4. The phenomena are found for persons with both favorable and unfavorable stands toward the domain; their distributions of judgments into categories resemble mirror images.

Since the own-categories procedure is based on general principles of judgment, it may be applied, with appropriate content, in any culture where sorting of objects is not unfamiliar for the purpose of making *cross-cultural comparisons* of the ranges and/or discontinuities in reference scales. Since the task may be presented as an objective one, e.g., placing statements by their relative positions on an issue, it need not arouse the individual's awareness that his attitude is being studied, thus eliminating a bias toward socially desirable responses. In this sense, the own-categories procedure represents a broadly general method for *indirect assessment of attitudes and cultural reference scales*. Unlike most indirect or projective tests, however, the data obtained are quantitative: number of categories used and category width (relative frequencies of judgments in the categories). With additional instructions after the items are categorized, the range of the individual's acceptances, rejections, and non-commitments may also be obtained.

Variables Affecting
Assimilation-Contrast Ranges

Research findings on placement of verbal statements and longer, more complex communications show that systematic displacements vary according to several factors besides discrepancy from the individual's own stand.

Degree of Ego Involvement. As noted earlier, the individual's stand becomes an anchor for his placements when he is personally involved in that stand in some degree. When he is unconcerned with the issue, systematic variations relative to his own position are not found. Given some involvement in his stand, the range of positions assimilated toward it is inversely related to the degree of involvement. With high involvement, the range of assimilation is smaller. Conversely, the range of positions subject to contrast effects is greater with higher involvement.

In placements of communications on the 1960 presidential election, persons differentiated as less ego-involved on the basis of the size of their latitudes of rejection assimilated moderately partisan communications over a wide range of discrepancies from the limit of their acceptances. Highly involved persons, however, revealed a contrast effect, with smaller discrepancies; they saw the same communication as more discrepant from their own stands in proportion to the divergence of the communication from the nearest limit of the acceptable range. Study of degrees of involvement of the individual and measures to assess them will prove one of the most fruitful and clarifying efforts in the present stage of research into social judgment and attitude.

Properties of Communication. Clearcut statements of extreme positions and strongly partisan communications are not subject to assimilation-contrast effects to any appreciable extent. The possibility of systematic displacement presumes some measure of ambiguity, or of lack of identifying properties as to

position. In large pools of discrete statements on an issue, typically those intermediate in value are subject to systematic displacements; but not *all* intermediate statements are affected. As discussed in Chapter 4 and 5, the problem
of what constitutes ambiguity or lack of structure in verbal statements richly
deserves further exploration in research.

Nevertheless, it is clear from a number of laboratory studies that when
the object of judgment is unstructured in a relevant dimension, it is subject
to systematic displacements, whereas clearcut, unambiguous dimensions are
not. The *range of assimilation* is greater for judgments of communications that
provide equally weighted alternative arguments than for those that support
a single alternative, even a mild one. This was shown in the findings on the
fence-straddling communication speech on the 1960 election issue and on the
great debates on television by the two candidates (Chapter 5). The predominant
trend in placing these communications with equally weighted alternatives
was assimilation; the displacement was proportional to discrepancy between
the individual's stand and the nonpartisan (E) position (Chapter 5). The
assimilation trend was more pronounced for less-involved subjects.

Stimulus Arrangements and the Context of Placement. Aside from the immediate
statement or message being appraised, the extent of systematic displacements
depends on the context of the communication situation, particularly on the
availability or absence of explicit external standards for comparison. In laboratory research, the context is defined by the research methods, procedures, and
instructions to an important extent. Yet, it would be exceedingly short-sighted
to dismiss the problem as merely a matter of method.

For example, it is undeniably true that any research procedure that
provides the individual with an explicit external standard and requires him
to use it, or requires that he compare each item with another, *reduces* systematic
variations according to the individual's own stand. This fact is of too great
theoretical importance to be taken for granted or to be used to dismiss systematic
displacements as merely a question of methods and procedures. Researchers
are sometimes prone to glorify their methods and procedures, forgetting that
they are also patterns of stimulus arrangements and, as such, independent
variables with respect to behavior.

Instead, researchers on attitude and social judgment should regard their
methods as variations in *stimulus arrangements* to be studied and compared with
the contexts of behavior in real life (cf. Sherif and Hovland, 1961, Chapter 2).
In this perspective certain generalizations become possible:

To the extent that the stimulus context for placement provides explicit
external standards for comparison and requires, through verbal instruction
or timing, that the individual heed them, his placements will be largely the
outcome of comparisons with those standards. (This is the case, for example,
in the methods of paired comparisons and order of merit.)

To the extent that the stimulus context lacks explicit standards, owing either to their absence or to sequential presentation and timing, the individual's attitude will become a major anchor for his judgments.

It is obvious that both kinds of stimulus arrangements occur in real life outside the laboratory, but it is also apparent that the flow, sequence, and patterning of social life frequently present contexts for judgment that lack compelling external standards for the individual's evaluations. In such contexts, his placements will be relative to his own reference scale. Such stimulus arrangements are, therefore, suitable and representative for the study of attitudinal functioning and ensuing displacements in evaluation.

SUSCEPTIBILITY TO CHANGE OR TO REAFFIRM ONE'S ATTITUDE

We have asked the crucial question: What is it that is to be changed by communication aimed at attitude change? We have answered that what is to be changed is the individual's evaluative categories for appraising some class of persons, objects, ideas, or events and his own relationship to them. His attitudes thus are constituents of his self system, varying in their priority in his personal scheme. They are inferred from the characteristic and consistent patterns of his stated opinions, his expressions, and other behaviors.

A change in attitude, therefore, implies a change in his categories for evaluation, which amounts to changing a part of himself; and it implies manifest change in the patterned behaviors from which they are inferred. The frame of reference for studying attitude change, therefore, includes the individual's stand and his degree of involvement in it, which affects the extent to which it is the major anchor in a communication situation. It includes the communication itself, its form, and the order of arguments. It includes the communicator and the source, both of which affect the extent to which the position presented in communication anchors the individual's subsequent appraisals of the issue. Thus, a source and speaker with high standing or prestige in the person's eyes, in effect, enhances the anchoring function of the advocated position. Similarly, any event or procedure that successfully involves the individual in a position presented to him, such as the necessity of doing a good job of presenting it or defending it himself, increases the salience of that position as an anchor when he subsequently evaluates the issue.

The first and foremost implication of the present approach is that susceptibility to change decreases with increased ego involvement in own stand. Thus, persons who are noncommittal to few if any positions on an issue and have a very broad latitude of rejection at the outset are particularly likely to displace a discrepant communication away from their own stand and less likely to change toward the position presented. The typical person with an extreme stand on the presidential election, or right to work, or a farm policy issue is an example. In fact, the enhanced discrepancy felt from communication because of the contrast effect in placement is likely to lead to reaffirmation of his own stand and even change away from the communication, if the discrepancy is extreme and if there are available positions for the individual to endorse in that direction.

Susceptibility to change is initially greater on the part of less-involved persons, including the majority of those who endorse moderate points of view on an issue. With their broader latitudes of noncommitment, less-involved persons assimilate communications over a wider range and are more likely to change toward it, since their own stand is less salient as an anchor. Similarly, the effects of variations in the communication situation, such as primacy-recency effects, are greater for less-involved persons than for those strongly committed to a position.

It should be emphasized once more that the so-called contradiction in findings on discrepancy between attitude and communication as it relates to attitude change is only apparent. It stems from failure to take the following variables into account when assessing research findings:

1. The objective structure of the object (topic).

2. The degree of the individual's familiarity and involvement with the issue.

3. The standing of the communicator and source in the social scale of the individual's reference groups.

4. The relative size of the discrepancy.

The probability of change toward an advocated position is greater when the number of feasible alternative interpretations of the topic is great, when the individual is somewhat unfamiliar and is not highly involved with the topic, and when the source and communicator have high prestige. Investigations that have found increased attitude change with increasing discrepancies have typically used some combination of these conditions and have not used extreme discrepancies.

When the individual is familiar and ego-involved with the issue, attitude change toward communication increases within a smaller range of discrepancies, then decreases to no change, and with greatest discrepancies shifts to change away from the advocated position when this is possible. The assimilation range is smaller when the topic allows for few alternative interpretations and the communicator or source is not prestigious or is identified with a group unfriend-ly to one's own reference group. We mention the source as well as the communicator here, since they are not always identical and since the source in any laboratory experiment is ordinarily confounded by the aura of the sponsorship by "science."

The felt discrepancy from a communication is relative to the bounds of latitudes of acceptance, noncommitment, and rejection. Therefore, the key to more fruitful research on attitude-communication discrepancy lies in systematic variation in personal commitment, which is associated with differences in these bounds.

REFERENCES

ARONSON, E., JUDITH A. TURNER, and J. M. CARLSMITH. "Communicator Credibility and Communicator Discrepancy as Determinants of Opinion Change," *Journal of Abnormal and Social Psychology*, 67 (1963), 31–37.

BREHM, J. W., and A. R. COHEN. *Explorations in Cognitive Dissonance*. New York: Wiley, 1962.

FESTINGER, L. *A Theory of Cognitive Dissonance*. Evanston, Ill.: Row-Peterson, 1957.

———. "The Theory of Cognitive Dissonance," In *The Science of Human Communication*, W. Schramm. New York: Basic Books, 1963.

HELSON, H. "Current Trends and Issues in Adaptation-level Theory," *American Psychologist*, 19 (1964), 26–38.

MILLER, N. "Involvement and Dogmatism as Inhibitors of Attitude Change: Prepublication Report," Yale Studies in Attitude and Communication, Yale University, Mimeographed, 1963.

OSGOOD, C. E., G. J. SUCI, and P. H. TANNENBAUM. *The Measurement of Meaning*. Urbana: University of Illinois Press, 1957.

PARDUCCI, A. "Range-frequency Compromise in Judgment," *Psychological Monographs*, 77, 2, no. 565, 1963.

PARDUCCI, A., and L. M. MARSHALL. "Assimilation vs. Contrast in the Anchoring of Perceptual Judgments of Weight," *Journal of Experimental Psychology*, 63 (1962), 426–37.

ROKEACH, M. *The Open and Closed Mind*. New York: Basic Books, 1960.

SHERIF, M. *Outline of Social Psychology*. New York: Harper & Row, 1948.

SHERIF, M., and H. CANTRIL. *The Psychology of Ego Involvements*. New York: Wiley, 1947.

SHERIF, M., and O. J. HARVEY. "A Study in Ego Functioning: Elimination of Stable Anchorages in Individual and Group Situations," *Sociometry* 15, (1952), 272–305.

SHERIF, M., and C. I. HOVLAND. *Social Judgment: Assimilation and Contrast Effects in Communication and Attitude Change*. New Haven: Yale University Press, 1961.

SHERIF, M., D. TAUB, and C. I. HOVLAND. "Assimilation and Contrast Effects of Anchoring Stimuli on Judgments," *Journal of Experimental Psychology*, 55 (1958), 150–55.

VOLKMANN, J. "Scales of Judgment and their Implication for Social Psychology," In *Social Psychology at the Crossroads*, J. H. Rohrer and M. Sherif. New York: Harper & Row, 1951.

William J. McGuire*

PERSONALITY
AND SUSCEPTIBILITY
TO SOCIAL INFLUENCE[1]

INFLUENCEABILITY AS A
GENERAL TRAIT

To avoid from the outset misunderstandings as to the scope of this chapter, we should clarify that we are using "influenceability" in the very broad sense of covering any tendency of the person to change as a function of social pressure. We stress ideological change but not to the exclusion of other types of changes. Hence, we include changing one's opinion on a matter-of-fact or a matter-of-taste issue as a consequence of an argumentative message (rational or emotional) from some source. We also include changing one's judgment on an objective issue (like the relative lengths of lines) or on a subjective issue (the relative pleasantness of two paintings) after hearing the bare statement of a deviant judgment voiced by a peer or authority source. We include even movements (like body sway or eyelid closure) as a consequence of waking or hypnotic suggestion. Some will find this usage of "influenceability" objectionably over-inclusive of processes they like to distinguish under such labels as suggestibility, compliance, conformity, indoctrination, persuasibility, attitude change. On the verbal issue, we feel apologetic for this admittedly overinclusive usage. We choose "influenceability" for economy of expression, as the most inclusive

*University of California, SD, La Jolla, California.

[1] Preparation of this chapter was facilitated by grant G19799 received from the National Science Foundation, Division of Social Sciences.

Excerpted from "Personality and Susceptibility to Social Influence," by William J. McGuire in *Handbook of Personality Theory and Research,* pp. 1130–87, with permission of the author and Rand-McNally and Company.

one-word label to refer to the generic class. In any case, terminology in the field is very fluid (Allport, 1935; Campbell, 1963; De Fleur & Westie, 1963).

More serious than the nominal objection is the worry that we are throwing together behavioral outcomes that are the resultants of quite different psychological processes. It might be felt that the several forms of susceptibility to social influence are quite different in their relations to personality variables. In anticipation of the remainder of the chapter, we can say that both theory and the empirical data do indicate that the various forms of susceptibility to influence are different from one another in their relations to personality. Indeed, it is these very differences that have compelled us to include the various types of influence situations within this review chapter. Otherwise, selecting one type by fiat would have resulted in an imbalanced and misleading coverage. Moreover, the changes in these personality relationships as we go from one type of influence situation to another tend to clarify the processes in each situation and allow the building of a more inclusive theory. In a sense, the whole is greater than the sum of its parts as regards heuristic and testing dividends. By considering personality-influenceability relations not just in one susceptibility situation but across a wide range of situations, we obtain information not only on first-order effects but on interaction effects as well.

Our contention here is that the data indicate that susceptibility to social influence in its myriad forms is indeed a (weak) general trait. The person's standing as to relative persuasibility in one situation tends to have a significant positive relationship to his standings on persuasibility in a very wide range of other social influence situations. Until this minimum degree of interrelation can be demonstrated, it makes little sense to examine how susceptibility in general is related to other personality dimensions. In this section, we shall present the evidence that there is such an overall trend to positivity among the various indices of susceptibility. In later sections (particularly in discussing principles 3 and 5) we shall take the opposite tack and point out that the intercorrelations, while predominantly positive, are usually quite low. We shall be arguing, then, that while there is an underlying general trait of susceptibility-to-influence, there are group and specific factors as well, so that many specifiable situational factors operate as moderator variables on the relationship between influenceability and personality.

The number and range of social influence situations that have been used in research are formidable. We shall attempt to reduce the problem to manageable size, without obscuring the essential complexities of the problem, by considering three general classes of influence situations to which we shall give the names *suggestion, conformity,* and *persuasion* situations. Each is operationally definable and distinguishable; each has received a great amount of research attention; and together they cover a wide range of social influence situations. (To give this *ad hoc* trichotomy a vague aura of theoretical imprimatur, we can point out that these classes have a superficial correspondence to the three processes of opinion change singled out by Kelman (Kelman, 1958, 1961; Kelman & Eagly, 1965): compliance, identification, and internalization. The parallelism, however, breaks down when we bring to bear the full details of Kelman's analysis.) In the following section, we shall take up each of the three classes separately, operationally defining each and considering the homogeneity of influenceability tests falling within each class. Then we shall discuss the correlations of influenceability scores across classes.

SUGGESTIBILITY AS A GENERAL TRAIT

We feel that there is an underlying trait of general suggestibility, though all so-called suggestibility tests load on other factors as well. Hypnotizability and body-sway tests load heavily on this factor; progressive lines and heat illusion tests have lower loadings while other tests (false report) have very low loadings. In addition there are probably several other more specific dimensions, such as separate positive and negative hallucination factors and a "difficulty" factor, as suggested by Hilgard's (1965) Stanford group. The correlations tend to be predominantly positive, though their magnitudes are usually quite low, with a cluster of primary motor tests intercorrelating fairly highly, a cluster of secondary sensory tests with somewhat lower correlations and with even lower correlations between clusters (Stukát, 1958). The lowness of the between-test intercorrelations is partly ascribable to the discouraging low reliabilities of suggestibility tests. More reliable data are needed before the generality question can be answered with confidence. Such data probably await the development of longer tests, more precise scoring, and more standardized administration procedures (de Rivera, 1959) than hitherto, prescriptions which impose heavy burdens on subjects and experimenters alike. Hilgard's (1965) work shows what painstaking care can achieve.

CONFORMITY AS A GENERAL TRAIT

The second general type of social influence situation, which we call "conformity," also shows signs of a general factor, but again with considerable differences from situation to situation in loadings on other factors. By "conformity" situations here we mean those in which the individual is informed simply that a certain source (e.g., a peer participating in the study) holds a certain position on an issue. This source position is usually picked to be deliberately discrepant from the subject's as measured earlier (Zimbardo, 1960) or selected at an extremely unlikely erroneous position (Asch, 1956) or allowed to vary naturally (M. Sherif, 1935). The index of conformity is the extent to which the subject, after he hears the source's position, gives a similar position as his own judgment. For the situation to be called a "conformity" one in the present sense, it is required that the source give no arguments for his position and that he not give any explicit indication that he expects the subject to agree with him. Classic examples include the Sherif (M. Sherif, 1935) autokinetic studies and Asch's (1956) study on peer influence on the judgment of line lengths.

A number of investigators have demonstrated that "conformity" in one situation tends to be correlated with conformity in other situations. Rosner (1957) has shown that student nurses who conform to peers on one task tend to conform to other peers on other tasks at other times. Harper and Tuddenham (1964) show that conformity to strangers is much the same as conformity to acquaintances. Sears (1963) reports generality of various forms of dependency in children.

. . . .

Correlation, of course, does not indicate identity. There tends to be an underlying conformity factor on which our various conformity tests load, so that we usually find significant positive correlation between them. But rarely do these correlations attain a magnitude that indicates even as much as a 50 per cent covariance between the two tests. In part, the lowness of the typical correlations reflects the unreliability of the tests; but also it indicates that scores on our conformity tests reflect reliable variance other than that on a common conformity factor. . . .

PERSUASIBILITY AS A GENERAL TRAIT

The third area of social influence situations, which we here call "persuasibility," refers to situations in which a source gives his position on an issue and (unlike the conformity situation) presents various arguments, based on emotional or rational considerations, why this position is correct. The subject is then asked his position on the issue and his susceptibility is measured by the degree it agrees with the source's (as compared to the subject's "before" score, or the score of a no-communication control group).

We deal with such persuasibility situations in various laboratory situations (e.g., the face-to-face group interaction studies summarized by Kelley and Thibaut, 1954; and the persuasive communication studies summarized by Hovland, 1954) and in various naturalistic situations such as political, advertising, and indoctrination campaigns using mass media (Hovland, Lumsdaine, & Sheffield, 1949) or personal influence (E. Katz & Lazarsfeld, 1955).

There is abundant evidence that persuasibility on one issue is positively related to persuasibility by other messages on other issues. Indeed, the attitude-change researcher takes it for granted that he is involved in a correlated-measures design when he carries out an experiment in which one subject receives several persuasive treatments, each on a different issue. The experienced investigator routinely uses different error terms for the among-subject and the within-subject treatments. Usually he finds that he was wise in doing so, since the among-subject variance is typically several times the within-subject variance.

One study will suffice to illustrate the magnitude of the relationships. Janis and Field (1956, reprinted in Janis & Hovland, 1959) gave a set of ten persuasive messages to about 185 high school students. Each was purportedly from a different newspaper reporter and they included a wide range of topics, each with a pro and con form. Each person's persuasibility for each message was scored 0 or I on the basis of a median split with respect to amount of change. Tetrachoric correlations were calculated between the impacts of each pair of messages, yielding 45 correlations in all. Only 6 negative correlations emerged. Of the 39 positive correlations 25 are significant at the .05 level. Again, we must caution that while there was a predominance of significant positive correlations, suggesting an underlying general factor, these correlations were not high (the highest was $+.52$), indicating that scores on these persuasibility tests are affected by many things besides this general common factor.

BETWEEN-CLASS CORRELATIONS

The previous sections have shown that there is a singificant, though far from complete, overlap between susceptibility to social influence on one test and another when both fall within one of our three, somewhat arbitrary classes: suggestion, conformity, and persuasion. We now turn to the rather more demanding question of how highly the influenceability scores correlate when the tests come from different classes . . .

The general picture is much the same within class and across class: tests of susceptibility to social influence tend to show significant but low positive intercorrelations. Similar results could be cited with respect to other classifications of social influence situations, e.g., susceptibility on involving vs. noninvolving issues, on simple vs. complex issues, etc. The predominant positivity of the correlation matrix indicates that there is a detectible amount of communality underlying a wide range of tests of social influenceability, thus giving some support for the existence of a general persuasibility trait, such as the Yale group (Hovland, Janis, & Kelley, 1953; Hovland & Janis, 1959) has long sought to demonstrate. On the other hand, the intercorrelations between tests are sufficiently low (even allowing for the often low reliabilities of the individual test) to indicate a considerable degree of independence among the various forms of influenceability. It is quite possible that the relationship of a given personality variable to susceptibility will vary considerably among influence situations. A basic goal of this chapter is to present principles that will account for the situational variations in personality-influenceability relations.

. . . .

GENERAL PRINCIPLES UNDERLYING PERSONALITY-INFLUENCEABILITY RELATIONSHIPS

Six principles serve to summarize the considerations to which we wish to call attention in our analysis of obtained personality-influenceability interrelations. In outline they are as follows:

1. The Mediational Principle—opinion change is not a direct response but the net outcome of a chain of behavioral steps. As a minimum it requires (a) adequate reception (through attention and comprehension) of the persuasive message; and (b) yielding to what is comprehended. The mediational role of reception is often overlooked, while that of yielding is over-emphasized.

2. The Combinatory Principle—While each of the two behavioral steps (receptivity to the content of the persuasive message and tendency to yield to what is received) is positively related to influenceability, the relation of a given personality variable to one of these steps is often quite different from its relationship to the other. Hence its net relationship to the resultant influenceability can be complex and even nonmonotonic.

3. The Situational-Weighting Principle—The relative importance of receptivity and of yieldingness in determining net influenceability will vary from situation to situation. Consequently, the relationship between a personality characteristic and influenceability will vary from situation to situation in a predictable way in accordance with these relative weights.

4. The Confounded-Variable Principle—There tend to be cross-individual regularities in personality structure such that one trait tends to be associated with others. Hence an adequate prediction of how a personality variable will be related to influenceability requires that we consider its relation to other personality variables and the relations of these others to the two mediators of influenceability. It follows that influenceability may be differently related to a personality variable depending on whether the latter is varied by experimental manipulation to produce different acute levels or whether we take the subjects at their different chronic levels in a correlational study.

5. The Interaction Principle—In any social situation, personality factors are only one of several classes of relevant independent variables. It is highly likely that the personality factors will interact with variables of other classes (source, message, etc.) in affecting influenceability. Hence, although we should seek the most general relationships in mapping the domain of personality-influenceability interrelations, it is likely that these will tend to be interaction effects, rather than condition-free main effects of single personality variables. The relationship of a given personality characteristic to influenceability may change in size and even in direction as other aspects of the communication situation change.

6. *The Compensation Principle*—There is an optimal level of influenceability for adequate adaptation to the human environment. Hence, it is implied by an adaptivity approach that there will tend to be compensatory mechanisms, such that a characteristic which tends in some ways to make an individual extremely open (or opaque) to influence will tend in other ways to have the reverse effect, resulting in a dynamic equilibrium. The pervasiveness of nonmonotonic relationships between personality and influenceability is one of the results.

Each of these six principles is in accord with common sense as well as congruent with obtained experimental results in its derivations. Yet, while they are rather obvious when our attention is called to them, the principles themselves and particularly some of their implications have often been overlooked, with the result that the various experimental results regarding influenceability relationships often seem implausible or mutually contradictory. The implications of these principles will become clearer when we explicate them in more detail in the sections that follow.

PRINCIPLE 1:
PERSUASION AS A MEDIATED BEHAVIOR

Our first principle states that opinion change is not a simple direct response but the residual outcome of a series of behavioral steps. The Yale group (Hovland, Janis, & Kelley, 1953) has long advocated a three-step process analysis of the behavior leading to opinion change: (a) attention to the communication, (b) comprehension of its contents, and (c) yielding to what is comprehended. Two further steps might be added: (d) retention of the position agreed with, and (e) action in accordance with the retained agreement, constituting in all a five-step stochastic process.

Researchers frequently overlook the fact that a personality characteristic could have an effect on influenceability by affecting any of the five links in the chain. Probably the error most frequently committed in this regard is overemphasis on the third step of the chain. This overemphasis results in inferring erroneously that a given personality variable will be related to influenceability simply insofar as it involves a tendency to yield to perceived interpersonal pressure. Many empirically determined relationships remain incomprehensible when viewed from this narrow perspective. As we shall discuss later, a given personality variable may make the person influenceable by being associated with a tendency to yield; but it may all the same protect him from persuasion at some other point in the chain (for example, by making him inattentive to the influencing message). The resultant multiple-mediated relationship between the personality variable and influenceability may be quite complex, as is illustrated below in our discussion of the combinatory principle.

It will not be necessary to analyze personality-influenceability relations in terms of the full five-step behavioral chain in order to demonstrate the necessity and utility of the multiple-process principle. Our first simplification will be to disregard the last two steps, retention and action. Considerable work has been done recently on the fourth step, retention of induced opinion change (McGuire, 1962; Papageorgis, 1963; Watts & McGuire, 1964), revealing the operation of complex psychodynamics in addition to passive forgetting. It seems highly likely, therefore, that personality factors affect this link in the chain. Likewise, there has been a considerable resurgence recently of the theoretical interest in the fifth step, as it involves the relationship between verbalized opinion change and gross overt action (Fishbein, 1966; Festinger, 1964a). This interest has been stirred by dissonance theorists (Festinger, 1957, 1964b; Brehm & Cohen, 1962) and by those working in the marketing and advertising areas (Howard, 1963; Steward, 1964). But since space is limited and since the interest in these topics has as yet resulted in only a little empirical research on influenceability correlates (Cohen, 1957; Steiner & Johnson, 1963; Steiner, 1960; Aronson & Festinger, 1958), we shall forego further discussion of the last two steps in this chapter. We shall make a second simplification of the behavioral chain by combining the first two steps, attention and comprehension, into one general step which we shall call "reception." Perhaps it will eventually become convenient to distinguish between the attention and comprehension steps, but at present it seems more economical to combine the two into a composite reception step.

We are left here with an oversimplified, two-step analysis of the behavioral process in social influence: reception of the message content and yielding to what is comprehended. Impoverished as it is, this analysis suffices for the exposition of our first principle. Understanding the relationship between personality and influenceability requires that we analyze the personality variable's effect on receptivity as well as on yieldingness (Walters & Parke, 1964).

. . . .

PRINCIPLE 2:
THE COMBINATORY PRINCIPLE

The general theoretical situation that we are depicting is one common in the behavioral sciences: the independent variable (here, a personality characteristic) is related to the dependent variable (influenceability) through the mediation of two intervening variables (receptivity and yieldingness). Four primary relationships are therefore involved: the relationships of the personality variable to receptivity and yieldingness, and the relationships of receptivity and yieldingness to influenceability. The resultant relationship between personality and influenceability which we are trying to define is the outcome of these four. Our second principle, here under discussion, specifies what this resultant relationship will be in terms of the characteristics of the four mediating relationships.

The General Equation

We have already postulated in our first principle that opinion change is a positive function of reception and of yielding. The person changes insofar as he effectively receives the message and yields to the point received. The principle can be summed up in the following equation:

$$Pr(o) = Pr(R) \times Pr(Y) \times Pr(K)$$

where $Pr(o)$ represents the probability of opinion change; $Pr(R)$ the probability of effective reception; and $Pr(Y)$, the probability of yielding to what is received; and $Pr(K)$ a residual factor representing the probability of the other processes (retention, etc.) that effect opinion change but need not concern us in this exposition. In the subsequent discussion we shall ignore this residual factor on the assumption that it is not consistently related to the personality characteristic that serves as the independent variable in the given study and that we aspire only to predict variations in $Pr(o)$, rather than its absolute level. (This "everything else equal" assumption is, of course, always dangerous.)

. . . .

Empirical Evidence for
the Nonmonotonic Case

We have discussed the combinatory principle in terms of progressively more stringent assumptions, producing cases capable of increasingly simpler solutions but having more and more narrow applicability. In the discussion of the principles that follow we shall go back to a more general case. For example, in our discussion of the situational-weighting principle which is taken up in the next section, we shall deal with how certain definable aspects of the persuasion situation affect all of the parameters in equation 7. Throughout the chapter we shall, however, be retaining the assumption that the personality variable affects the two mediators in opposite directions, thus tending to yield nonmonotonic relations between the personality variable, considered over its full range, and influenceability. Some broad theoretical considerations that would lead us to expect the wide empirical validity of this case are discussed in later sections, particularly in connection with the sixth "dynamic equilibrium" principle.

Aside from this question of why it is so, there is widespread empirical evidence that personality variables do in fact tend to be nonmonotonically related to influenceability. Indeed, considering that in most studies the personality characteristic varies over a rather narrow range (e.g., within the range of natural variation among college sophomores or as manipulated by rather mild laboratory inductions), it is surprising that so many nonmonotonic relations have been detected in experiments, even granting that over the full range of variation found in the population the relationship is nonmonotonic. Nonmonotonic effects seem particularly ubiquitous if we allow either influenceability or the personality variable to be a function of the other. One illustrative study by Appley and Moeller (1963) illustrates the ubiquity of nonmonotonic relationships between personality characteristics and influenceability. They obtained conformity scores for 41 college women (freshmen) in terms of the number of times they were influenced by a unanimously wrong majority of peers in an Asch-type (1956) situation. Scores were obtained for all subjects on 38 personality characteristics from three standardized self-report inventories: the Edwards (1954) EPPS, Gough's (1957) CPI, and Gordon's (1956).

To measure the relationship between the personality variables and influenceability they partitioned their sample of 41 subjects into three groups: high, middle, and low conformers. They computed the mean scores of each of these three subgroups on each of the 38 personality variables. On only 5 of the 38 variables was a monotonic relation found. On 33 of the 38, the high and low subgroups lay on the same side of the middle personality group as regards conformity. These results do not, of course, constitute 38 independent tests, since the personality characteristics measured by these standardized inventories are far from orthogonal (Peterson, 1965). However, the results are impressive when we consider the overwhelming ratio of nonmonotonic effects despite the homogeneity of the sample.

These nonmonotonic effects are by no means confined to Appley and Moeller's female college students. Even confining ourselves to the single variable of self-esteem (which would operate much like the intelligence variable used as our example, above), recent studies can be cited showing nonmonotonic relationships between this personality variable and persuasibility in a wide variety of subjects and situations. Gelfand (1962) showed such a relationship in fifth-grade boys and girls; Harvey and Consalvi (1960) in delinquent boys in a state training school; Cox and Bauer (1964) in middle-aged women belonging to a Catholic ladies' sodality; Silverman (1964) in elderly male residents in a VA domiciliary. We may cite, as a final example, one that involves an extremely different population and situation from the above, namely the individual-difference correlates of compliance with their Chinese captors of American prisoners during the Korean War (Segal, 1956, 1957; Schein, Hill, Williams, & Lubin, 1957). The over 3,000 U.S. Army repatriates were divided into three groups in terms of resistance to their captors' demands: collaborators (15 per cent of total) who were judged to have yielded to a degree that warranted disciplinary action by the U.S. Army upon release; the "neutrals" (80 per cent) who yielded only slightly or on whom there was no strong evidence one way or the other; and the resisters (5 per cent) who resisted to a degree that called for U.S. Army commendation after their release. These three groups were compared on an exhaustive series of demographic, biographical, and test variables. Although the differences were small, with variable after variable (age, education, length of service, information, vocabulary, comprehension, psychopathy, anxiety, marriage rates, participation in sports, etc.) the small differences were such that the two extreme groups, collaborators and resisters, tended again and again to be both on the same side of the neutrals, so that the overall relationship was nonmonotonic.

One interim conclusion that may be drawn at this point is that forms of analysis which are insensitive to nonmonotonicity (e.g., Pearson correlations, two-group designs subjected to chi-square or analysis of variance) are likely to be misleading in this area of research. Proper experimental design calls for many levels spread over a wide range on the independent (personality) variable, and the inferential statistics should involve analyses that provide a check of higher order trend components. . . .

PRINCIPLE 3:
SITUATIONAL WEIGHTING

As was pointed out in the previous section, we frequently deal with personality variables whose relationship to influenceability is mediated by two processes that work in opposite directions. . . . Such a situation tends to result in a mutual cancellation. Hence, unless we make further specifications, no empirical outcome could refute the theoretical formulation. A finding of a positive, negative, or nonmonotonic relationship (or of no relationship at all) could be accounted for by the theory, provided that we are allowed complete freedom in choice of parameters.

The way out of this embarrassing richness of predictions—which tends to lose our theory its scientific status, since no empirical outcome could disconfirm it—is provided by the present principle. This situational-weighting principle specifies that we are not free to make any assumption we please about the importance of the mediators in a given situation. The weights of the mediators will tend to vary from situation to situation in predictable ways: different social influence situations vary greatly in the absolute and relative strains they put on reception and yielding. By specifying the weightings of these mediators, we can predict for a specific situation whether the resultant personality-influenceability relationship will be positive or negative. This predicted outcome depends on the relative contribution of the two mediators, reception and yielding, to the total opinion-change variance in the given situation. Where we cannot make absolute predictions about a given situation, it is often possible to make predictions about the difference between situations. To the extent that the situation allows considerable individual difference in attention and comprehension of the message, then the personality-receptivity relation is likely to be more important in mediating how the personality variable will be related to influenceability. To the extent that there is likely to be wide individual difference in yielding to whatever is comprehended, then the personality variable's relation to the yielding mediator is likely to be more important.

. . . .

Situational Differences in Receptivity Demands

Even before formal empirical analyses of social influence situations . . . have been carried out, it is possible to hazard an a priori ordering in regard to loadings on reception and yielding of some of the commonly studied situations. Concerning reception loadings, the influence messages used in some situations are so obvious (and in others, so subtle) that there would be little individual-difference variance in reception. Other influence situations involve an intermediate level of subtlety and thus would have a high loading on reception variance. At one low variance extreme are the typical suggestibility situations (e.g., the simple and repetitive communications used in body-sway or hypnosis inductions) which put so little strain on attention and comprehension that almost all subjects sufficiently functional to get along in the ordinary environment would be near the asymptote of complete receptivity. In these situations, the effect of the personality variable on receptivity would be of little importance in determining its relation to influenceability. For the normal range of subjects, reception would be practically complete whether the individual was relatively high or low on general attention and comprehension proclivity.

Other influence situations are intermediate in the strain they put on receptivity. For example, persuasion situations using meaningful rational or emotional arguments, such as the World War II indoctrination program of the U.S. Army (Hovland, Lumsdaine, & Sheffield, 1949), political campaign speeches, and much advertising, put a more appreciable demand on attention and comprehension. Hence a wide range of individual differences in reception scores would result. In these situations the effect of the personality variable on reception would be of considerable importance in determining its relation to influenceability.

As a general principle, then, if situations are extremely hard or easy in terms of their strain on the sample's capacity for attention and comprehension, a personality variable will tend to affect influenceability mainly via its relation to yielding. In situations of intermediate difficulty, where there will be a wide range of individual differences in attention and comprehension, the personality variable's effect on influenceability will be determined to a considerable extent by its relation to receptivity as well as to yielding.

These various situations can be illustrated for the case where self-esteem is the personality variable. Let us make the reasonable assumption that self-esteem is negatively related to yielding: the higher the individual's self-esteem, the less (due to self-confidence, etc.) he will yield to influence attempts that he has effectively received at a given level. Hence, considered only as regards its relation to yielding, self-esteem would tend to have a monotonically decreasing relation to influenceability. We shall also assume that self-esteem is positively related to attention and comprehension, since lack of self-esteem is usually associated with distractibility, lack of intelligence, and social withdrawal, all of which tend to insulate the person from being influenced. Hence, if receptivity alone were considered, self-esteem would have a monotonically increasing relation to opinion change. In situations where both receptivity and yielding must be considered, then self-esteem would be nonmonotonically related to opinion change. Influenceability would first increase and then decrease as our range of individuals varied from low to high in self-esteem.

These relationships are illustrated in Figure 2 for the three situations discussed above: where the reception is easy, moderate, or hard. The strains on yielding are assumed to be intermediate and constant across the three illustrative situations. In simple suggestibility situations (e.g., Stukát, 1958) there would be high overall compliance and it would show a continuously decreasing relationship to self-esteem. In persuasion situations using very subtle, complex appeals (McGuire, 1960b; Stotland, Katz, & Patchen, 1959), the immediate overall persuasive impact would be small, and such as it is, it also would show a continuous decrease as self-esteem increased. In the more typical mass media advertising and face-to-face personal influence persuasion situations (Hovland, Lumsdaine, & Sheffield, 1949; Klapper, 1961) which put an intermediate strain on attention and comprehension, there will be wide individual differences in reception and hence there will be an intermediate level of overall opinion change and the impact will have a nonmonotonic relation to self-esteem. Figure 2a shows the functions for the underlying mediators in the three situations; Figure 2b shows the resultant influenceability functions in the three situations.

The situations illustrated in Figure 2 are rather artificial ones for several reasons. First, the proviso that yielding be held constant across situations is a demanding one. Secondly, the assumption that in suggestibility situations, reception is practically complete for all individuals is not a safe generalization. We could, for example, dip into a range of subjects (such as psychotics or preschool children) where reception might be different even for the simple repetitive induction typically used in suggestion situations (Kramer & Brennan,

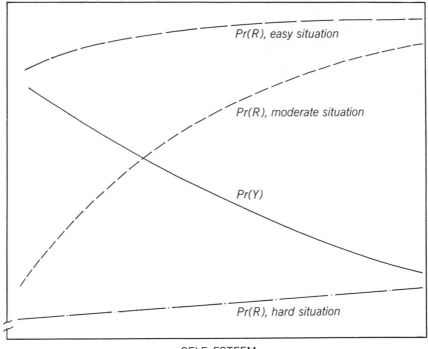

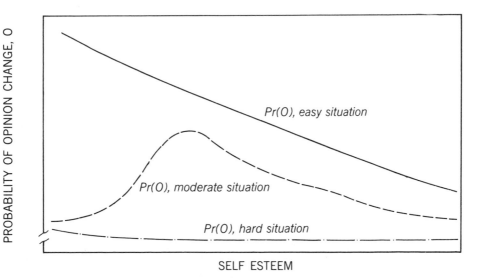

FIGURE 2. *Effects of situational differences in comprehension difficulty on the resultant personality-influenceability relationship.* FIGURE 2a: *Three levels of reception difficulty as they affect the mediators (reception and yielding).* FIGURE 2b: *The three levels as they affect the resultant influenceability measure (opinion change).*

1964; Abrams, 1964). Alternatively, we could use so brief an induction, or one sufficiently obscured by background noise, that even for the normal subject reception would be demanding. By so changing the usual suggestion situation, we could produce considerable individual differences in reception, and the relation of self-esteem to influenceability would approximate the nonmonotonic one shown for the moderate situation in Figure 2.

Thirdly, the assumption that usually there is negligible reception of obscure, subtle persuasive messages is likely to be valid only as regards immediate impact and for relatively unmotivated subjects. There is evidence that such indirect messages do seep in over time (Cohen, 1957; Stotland, Katz, & Patchen, 1959; McGuire, 1960b). Also, highly motivated patients undergoing nondirective therapy do seem to manage to draw conclusions from subtle messages. In such modifications of the "hard" situation, the relation of self-esteem to influenceability would also approximate the nonmonotonic one shown in the figure for the moderate situation. The three cases do serve, however, as ideal prototypes.

Situational Variations in Demands on Yieldingness

. . . . If the situation puts an intermediate level of strain on yieldingness (so that there result considerable individual differences in degree of yielding), then the personality variable's effect on the yielding mediator will be of considerable importance in determining its relationship to influenceability. If, on the other hand, the situation so compels yielding that virtually everyone is at the asymptote of complete yielding, or if it puts so little strain on yielding that hardly anyone shows any appreciable yielding, then the persons' individual proclivities toward yielding will be unimportant in determining the outcome. In these extreme situations, a personality variable's impact on the yielding mediator will have little effect on its relationship to influenceability. Rather, its impact on the reception mediator will be the commanding determinant. Only in the intermediate situation will the personality variable's impact on the yielding mediator be of major importance in determining its relation to influenceability.

Here again (as earlier with the reception mediator), commonplace illustrations for the two extreme and the intermediate yielding situations come readily to mind. Certain situations can be assumed to have very low loadings on the yielding factor because almost any normal subject will yield virtually completely to the message insofar as he receives it. Several components contribute to such a situation. Let the issue be a technical, matter-of-fact (rather than of-taste) one; let the source be expert and trustworthy; let the arguments be reasonable-sounding and dispassionate; and let the receiver have no strong preconception on the issue. Let us deal, in short, with the typical educational situation, such as is involved when a physics professor teaches the introductory course in his field. The question of the student's yielding to the teacher's position on the content he is trying to communicate hardly arises. We assume that insofar as the message is adequately attended to and comprehended, it will be accepted. In these educational situations, the personality variable's relation to opinion change will be determined almost entirely by its impact on the reception mediator, to the exclusion of its impact on yielding. . . .

At the opposite extreme is the situation where a prejudiced nonexpert source gives impassioned arguments regarding a matter of taste on which the receiver has strong initial opinions. In this case we might assume that there would be relatively little yielding by any normal subject. With such a lack of individual differences in yielding, the situational loading on this factor . . . would once again be negligible. Hence in both of these opposite situations, where the message is extremely compelling or extremely unconvincing, the personality variable's relation to influenceability is mediated almost entirely by the reception process, with the loading on the yielding factor of only negligible importance.

In situations intermediate or mixed as regards the characteristics cited, there would be a wider range of individual differences in yielding. For example, the situation might involve a low credible source using reasonable and dispassionate arguments; or might deal with a matter-of-taste issue but one on which the receiver has no initial opinion; or might use arguments of intermediate reasonableness.

. . . .

Propaganda vs. Education

This principle 3, dealing with situational weighting, offers a more precise basis for the frequently but vaguely made distinction between education and persuasion (or between information and propaganda). We say that a situation involves education or the communicating of information insofar as $a_{sr} > a_{sy}$, that is, insofar as the situation's loading on reception is large compared to its loading on yielding. Conversely, we say that the situation involves persuasion or propaganda to the extent that $a_{sy} > a_{sr}$. Hence, the relationship between the individual's personality and the amount of change produced in him by a message will vary considerably with the type of situation. In an "educational" situation, for example, self-esteem would tend to be related positively to the communication's impact; while in a "pure propaganda" situation, self-esteem will be negatively related to the impact. The point that is being stressed here is that most of the field and laboratory situations employed to study opinion change involve variance due to mediators, reception and yielding.

Hence, it would be very misleading to regard the relationship of the personality variable to influenceability in the typically studied situations as if it were determined solely by the personality variable's impact on yielding.

PRINCIPLE 4:
CONFOUNDED VARIABLES

Even when we consider the single personality variable's relation to influenceability in all the complexities introduced by the multiple mediators, we are still dangerously oversimplifying the situation. We must also consider the effects of other personality variables that are correlated with the one we are studying. Personality is more than a series of index numbers giving the individual's standing on orthogonal dimensions. It has a structure such that the personality dimensions we commonly deal with in psychological research (authoritarianism, anxiety, self-esteem, need for approval, etc.) tend to be intercorrelated. We recognize such confounding when the issue is explicitly raised, but all too frequently we try to test a hypothesized relationship between a specific personality variable and some dependent variable like influenceability, while ignoring the invalidity of the hypothesis' hidden assumption that "everything else is equal."

If among our subjects the given personality variable is correlated with other personality variables, then subgroups of subjects selected to represent different levels on the given variable will be contaminated in that the subgroups will tend to differ also with respect to the correlated variables. When the correlated personality variables are themselves related to influenceability (by having an impact on the mediating processes: attention, comprehension, yielding, etc.), any finding regarding our given variable's relations to influenceability must be re-examined in the light of the confounding. Any relationship found between the given variable and influenceability might be spurious, due to the correlated variable's producing the predicted effect on persuasibility; while if we found no relationship, there might actually have been one that was washed out by the correlated variables' having the opposite effect.

. . . .

Empirical Results Using
Chronic vs. Acute Levels

We can illustrate the consideration involved by examining the findings regarding self-esteem. In studies using acute levels of self-esteem, the subjects are typically manipulated as to an experimentally induced failure experience (e.g., the high self-esteem condition might consist of calling the subject "right" on 30 out of 35 trials during a prior test, and the low self-esteem condition might tell him he is right on only 5 of the 35 trials, as in Mausner and Block, 1957). Then all subjects are given a social influence induction, and the re-lationship of self-esteem to influenceability is ascertained by comparing the mean opinion-change scores in success vs. failure conditions. The success vs. failure manipulation varies self-esteem in isolation, as it would exist if the failure-prone person had no long experience adapting to his low self-esteem and hence had never learned to develop a set of rationalizations, evasive behaviors, and other defenses by which he would have adjusted to this chronic lack of self-esteem (Cohen, 1959). We would thus be manipulating a conceptually pure but "unnatural" variable of self-esteem. Not surprisingly, subjects put through the failure induction for which they are unprepared and to which they have no opportunity to adjust tend to be more susceptible to influence than groups of subjects given the success induction (Kelman, 1950; Mausner, 1954; Hochbaum, 1954; Samelson, 1957; Stukát, 1958). The increased susceptibility after failure tends to obtain even when the induced failure is given on a task irrelevant to the persuasion task (Gelfand, 1962). The opinion-change promot-ing effect of failure is augmented when the source of the influence attempt is shown himself to be successful (Mausner & Block, 1957).

Studies using the alternative, chronic-level approach measure the subjects as to pre-existing chronic level of self-esteem (by *ad hoc* or standardized self-report inventories or by self-ideal discrepancy). Then all subjects are put in a social influence situation, and the relation of self-esteem to influenceability is ascertained by correlating the self-esteem scores with the opinion change or by partitioning the subjects by a median split into low vs. high chronic self-esteem groups and comparing the mean opinion change scores of the two groups. (Actually, the nonmonotonic relationship suggested in our previous discussion of combinatory principle 2 makes these types of analysis ill advised, since they assume a monotonic and even rectilinear relationship between the personality variable and influenceability. But we will not labor this point here.) This chron-ic self-esteem variable is embedded in a whole syndrome of correlated variables (depression, withdrawal, intelligence, ability to cope, etc.) in contrast to the relatively pure and artificial acute variation of isolated self-esteem by experimen-tal manipulation. The effects of these correlated variables on the mediators of opinion change may result in obtaining a relationship of influenceability to chronic self-esteem that is considerably different from that of acute self-esteem.

Data on this question are still somewhat ambiguous. One chronic self-esteem study produced results similar to the acute self-esteem studies cited above. This was the Janis and Rife (1959) study that did find a strong negative relationship ($r = -.66$, $N = 56$) between influenceability and chronic self-esteem in institutionalized psychotics. Other chronic self-esteem studies have failed to show any significant relation, or have found a negative relationship that attains conventional significance levels only if we do a posteriori analyses of extreme cells (Janis & Field, 1959b; Lesser & Abelson, 1959, pp. 187–94;

Leventhal & Perloe, 1962). Still other chronic self-esteem studies find non-monotonic relationships (Linton & Graham, 1959; Appley & Moeller, 1963; Silverman, 1964; Cox & Bauer, 1964).

This chronic vs. acute level consideration becomes particularly interesting when the personality characteristic is varied by both approaches within the same experimental design. Several studies on self-esteem and influenceability have employed an approximation of an acute-chronic orthogonal design. One of these (Gelfand, 1962) is particularly interesting because it included in the design a third variable, subtlety of the influence induction, which is relevant to the previous principle involving situational weighting. Chronic self-esteem was measured by Sears' (1960) self-report inventory. Acute self-esteem was manipulated by pre-programmed success or failure experience on irrelevant tasks immediately before the social influence tests. (There was also a third, neither-success-nor-failure control group.) One influence score was from an Asch-type situation in which a peer gave preprogrammed deviant judgments prior to the subject's own judgment. In this conformity situation, the reception mediator is rather unimportant, since all Gelfand's subjects (normal fifth-graders) are likely with no difficulty to have comprehended the peer's choice. In this situation, the acute self-esteem level has a very strong negative relation to conformity ($p < .001$), while chronic self-esteem has no appreciable relation at all.

Her other social influence task follows the typical verbal conditioning technique (Taffel, 1955) with the experimenter's comment of "good" used to reinforce choice of certain pronouns in starting sentences. This is a much more subtle situation where there would be more individual differences in reception and where the social withdrawal tendencies associated with low self-esteem (Bennis & Peabody, 1962) would tend to furnish protection from influence. In this situation the most salient finding is a curvilinear relation ($p < .01$) such that those low on both chronic and acute self-esteem, as well as those high on both, show less compliance with the verbal reinforcement than do those on an intermediate level (the low-highs and the high-lows). A like result was obtained by Millman (1965) using anxiety as the personality variable and a rather subtle taped interview about China as the persuasion induction. She found that those high in both chronic and acute anxiety and those low in both were less persuasible than those in mixed conditions (low-highs and high-lows).

A third relevant study is that by Lesser and Abelson (1959) in which young children were given suggestions by teachers to make certain judgments. Influenceability was measured by degree of conformity to these suggestions. Chronic self-esteem was measured by the child's self-rating of his relative position in the class in terms of ability and popularity. Acute self-esteem was manipulated on a prior task where the teacher consistently agreed with the child's judgment or consistently disagreed with it. We are saying that this prior teacher behavior was perceived by the child as indicating his own success or failure, respectively. There were two replications of the study and both replications agreed on all the findings cited here. Lesser and Abelson found that there was more opinion change ($p < .05$) after the success experience than after failure. This is one of the few studies in which acute self-esteem was positively related to influenceability (the prior agreeing behavior of the teacher may have raised not only the child's self-esteem but his liking for the teacher, his interest in the tasks, etc.). Chronic self-esteem was related significantly negatively to influenceability. There were, however, interactions ($p < .05$) such that the effect of chronic self-esteem on influenceability was due entirely to the success condition. This interaction is in agreement with the results from the Gelfand (1962) study.

Perhaps reconciliation of the chronic and acute variation studies will be promoted by continuing the theoretical analysis of the Michigan group regarding preferences for the different defense mechanisms as a function of self-esteem (Cohen, 1959; Katz, 1960; Stotland & Hillmer, 1962). But these studies all agree in pointing up the implication of our principle 4 regarding confounding. Influenceability can differ greatly depending on whether we use acute or chronic variations in the characteristic. Furthermore, there tends to be an interaction effect on influenceability of the acute X chronic variables.

. . . .

PRINCIPLE 5:
SITUATIONAL INTERACTIONS

Our discussion of the previous principles stressed that the relationships between a personality variable and influenceability will tend to be specific and vary with other aspects of the communication situation. This stress might seem to be in conflict with one of the main streams of persuasibility research. The Yale group (Hovland, Janis, & Kelley, 1953; Janis & Hovland, 1959) devoted a great deal of conceptual and empirical activity to teasing out topic-free personality correlates of "general, unbounded persuasibility." This work contrasted with other research that was designed to find personality correlates of susceptibility to persuasion toward specific ideological positions, such as the work of Hartley (1946), Adorno *et al.* (1950), and Bettelheim and Janowitz (1950) on susceptibility to antiminority propaganda or of Smith, Bruner, and White (1956) on proneness to acquire anti-Soviet attitudes. Hovland and his colleagues sought to find broader relationships between personality and influenceability, relatively unbounded by the specifics of the communication situation.

The Yale program of seeking transcendental relationships between personality and influenceability is appealing in that a scientific principle is useful in proportion to its generality, assuming that validity remains constant. The problem lies in this final qualification. Janis and Hovland themselves (1959, p. 15) point out that "boundedness" is a matter of degree. There are probably few influenceability relationships that are absolutely unbounded by other classes of communication variables. At best one may hope to uncover relationships that do not appreciably interact with certain classes of variables, but one should always be alert to the likelihood that ultimately there will be discovered some class of variables that do interact with the given personality variable in affecting influenceability. In an early section of this chapter we reviewed the empirical evidence that a general trait of influenceability does exist, but to a very limited extent.

Some dimensions of boundedness being practically inevitable, we feel that it is better research strategy to seek out the classes of communication variables that may limit a given personality-influenceability relationship, rather than to try to circumvent such limitations in the quest for relatively unbounded generalizations. Indeed if, as we maintain, a valid mapping of the personality-influenceability domain requires interaction formulations, then such formulations yield wider (albeit, more complex) generalizations than would delusively simple and transcendental main-effect formulations.

This principle that a given personality-influenceability relationship will be limited in size and even direction by other, interacting variables in the communication situation becomes useful to the extent that we have at our disposal a manageable and heuristically provocative classification of these other communication variables. Hence, we shall consider seriatim the five broad classes into which communication variables can be conveniently divided: source, message, channel, receiver, and destination. As we mentioned at the outset of this chapter, this classification has received wide usage in the communication areas. (Other systems have been suggested by Holland, 1959, and by Doob, 1961. Any of these classifications would serve to provide the heuristics for uncovering interaction variables.) Examples will be given to show how variables from each of the five classes interact with personality variables in determining influenceability. It will be seen that the relationship between a specific personality dimension and influenceability may vary drastically depending on the levels of these other, interactional variables at which our experimental parameters have been set. It will also be seen that these interactions between personality characteristics and other situational variables are in keeping with the implications of the previous four principles.

Interactions with Source Factors

Many studies have shown that the opinion-change impact of a given communication varies with the characteristics of the attributed source of the message. Kelman (1961) has exhaustively analyzed how these source effects operate through various psychodynamics involving credibility, likability, or power. Interactions between source characteristics and receiver personality variables in determining influenceability are inevitable, since personality plays a part in determining one's reference groups and hence how credible, likable, or powerful one perceives a given source to be. Hence, a personality variable may be positively or negatively related to the persuasive impact of a given message, depending on the source to whom the message is attributed. To cite an obvious case of the reference group consideration, Catholics will turn out to be more or less persuasible than Protestants, depending on whether the message is attributed to a Catholic or to a Protestant spokesman.

Source-personality interactions can occur also because certain personality traits are associated with higher sensitivity to source differentials. A number of studies have shown that the lower the self-esteem of the receiver, the more susceptible he is to differences in source status in regard to changing his judgment to agree with that source. This effect of self-esteem has been demonstrated in studies that manipulated the acute level of self-esteem, e.g., by induced failure experiences (Kelman, 1950; Mausner, 1954) or by rejection experiences (Kelley & Shapiro, 1954; Dittes & Kelley, 1956). Whether chronic level of self-esteem likewise interacts by sensitizing the person to differences in source status has not yet been demonstrated, and as was pointed out in the discussion of the fourth principle, there is reason to be cautious in assuming that it does so interact in the same way as does acute self-esteem.

One personality variable that seems extremely likely to interact with source factors in determining the opinion-change impact of a given communication is authoritarianism as measured by the California *F* scale (Adorno *et al.*, 1950). A number of studies have been done on the relationship between authoritarianism and influenceability, continuing even into the recent past, after the peak of substantive interest in the *F* scale had passed (Wright & Harvey, 1965). The relevant aspect of the authoritarian syndrome, as originally described by Adorno *et al.* (1950), is a tendency toward oversimplified categorization of people on the evaluative dimension into a few extreme groups, so that people are seen as being either very good or very bad. Hence, there would be more difference in the opinion-change impact of a positively vs. negatively valenced source with increasing authoritarianism in the receiver. Restating this interacting effect, authoritarianism is positively correlated with influenceability when the message is from positive sources, and negatively when from negative sources.

At first glance, the description of the syndrome might seem to imply that high authoritarian subjects would be more susceptible than low to differences in source factors. A closer scrutiny shows that this view is oversimplified. The relationship would tend to reverse when we consider the source diffential where both sources have the same direction (sign) of evaluation but vary in degree: e.g., a mildly positive vs. a highly positive source. Authoritarians, seeing the world in blacks and whites, magnify differences between the good and the bad but overlook differences between gradations within goodness or badness. Hence, there would be less difference in opinion-change impact of moderately vs. strongly positive (or negative) sources with increasing authoritarianism in the receiver. Over the whole range of source valence we would expect a second-order personality-influenceability interaction effect, involving the authoritarianism of the receiver and the sign of and size of the source valence. This theoretical analysis is indicative of the need to consider complex interactions in mapping the domain of personality-influenceability relationships. A study by Berkowitz and Lundy (1957) and an unpublished study by the writer touch on aspects of the above predictions, but it must be admitted that the formulation presented here has not yet been fully tested.

Whether dogmatism as measured by Rokeach's (1956, 1960) scale would function in the manner hypothesized for authoritarianism is not completely clear to this writer. It might be that all source differentials would be enhanced by dogmatism, but on the other hand the syndrome seems to include the same black vs. white polarizing tendency as does authoritarianism. Powell (1962) did find an enhancement of source differential associated with dogmatism. He used perceptual D^2 scores, rather than opinion change, as the dependent variable, but Rokeach's (1960, p. 396) formulation seems to imply a like finding would hold for opinion change also.

Another personality variable of the cognitive style type that might function as hypothesized above for authoritarianism is what has been called "category width" (Pettigrew, 1958), "leveling-and-sharpening" (Klein, 1958; Gardner, Holzman, Klein, Linton, & Spence, 1959), and "latitude of acceptance" (Sherif & Hovland, 1961). The implication of these partially overlapping formulations is that receivers high on category width (e.g., tendency to perceive the world in terms of a few, broad categories) will tend to be less affected by small source differences and perhaps more affected by wide differences than would subjects scoring low on the category-width scale (Zimbardo, 1960; Bergin, 1962; Aronson, Turner, & Carlsmith, 1963; Steiner & Johnson, 1965).

Interactions with
Message Factors

The richest variety of independent variables in social influence research is found in this area of message factors. Included are (a) content variables, such as type of appeals, inclusions and omissions of material, amount of change advocated, etc.; and (b) structural variables, such as amount of material, order of presentation, etc. These subcategories themselves include many subdivisions of empirically investigated variables. Interactions of such a myriad of message factors with personality factors are so numerous that we can here only select rather arbitrarily a few to illustrate some general considerations. To promote at least geographical and theoretical diversity, we shall select one example from each of the two most active research centers, the Michigan and the Yale groups.

The functional approach (Katz, 1960) to attitude change advocated by the Michigan group (Katz, Sarnoff, McClintock, Stotland, etc.) directed the attention of these researchers to the role of ego-defensiveness as a personality variable related to susceptibility to influence inductions involving self-insight. In general, they expected a nonmonotonic relationship such that messages using self-insight appeals (attempting to reduce prejudice by depicting the unattractive psychodynamics underlying ethnic hostilities) would be more effective with subjects having intermediate levels of ego-defensiveness than with subjects either high or low on this variable. The empirical validity of this formulation is still unclear (Stotland & Patchen, 1961), but the point that concerns us here involves a peripheral issue. In one study in their series (Katz, Sarnoff, & McClintock, 1956) it was demonstrated that this personality variable, ego-defensiveness, was related to influenceability either positively or negatively, depending on the kind of appeal used in the message. With the self-insight appeal that showed the unattractive psychodynamics underlying prejudice, there was a nonmonotonic relationship between ego-defensiveness and favorable change toward Negroes; with an informational appeal that presented Negroes in a sympathetic light, there was a positive relationship between ego-defensiveness and favorable change toward Negroes.

A finding of the Yale group illustrating an interaction between individual-difference variables and message variables comes from their research on "one-sided" vs. "two-sided" messages (Hovland, Lumsdaine, & Sheffield, 1949, Ch. 8). Two forms of a recording arguing that the war with Japan would not be won for a long time after the defeat of Germany were presented to American soldiers in World War II. The "one-sided" form ignored any arguments against the position being defended; the "two-sided" form mentioned incidentally or with refutations some of the opposition arguments. The less intelligent soldiers (those not completing high school) were more influenced than the more intelligent by the one-sided recording, but this relationship between intelligence and persuasibility was reversed with the two-sided message.

On the other hand, the Yale group failed to find any interaction between the intelligence variable and the message variable of implicit vs. explicit conclusion (Hovland & Mandell, 1952), although it would be predicted on the same theoretical basis as would the intelligence-sidedness interaction. Other researchers have indeed found some evidence for an interaction between intelligence and implicit-explicit conclusion (Cooper & Dinerman, 1951; Thistlethwaite, de Haan, & Kamenetsky, 1955). Still other interactions between personality and message variables in determining influenceability have been shown by Cohen (1957) and Lana (1961, 1964), both of whom deal with ordering variables within the message. The reasons for such interactions become clearer in the light of the earlier principles. In most of those discussed here, the personality variable's effect on the reception mediator is the crucial consideration.

A final example that we shall use to illustrate personality-message interaction in affecting influenceability has to do with the receiver's chronic anxiety level and the amount of fear aroused within the message. An interaction in this case would be predicted from our discussion of principle 2 on the basis of which an overall nonmonotonic relation between anxiety and influenceability would be expected, with maximum susceptibility coming at intermediate levels of anxiety. Hence, if the person is chronically low in anxiety, raising it by a high fear appeal would tend to increase opinion change; while to the extent that the person is already chronically high, inducing further anxiety by a high fear appeal in the persuasive message should become detrimental to opinion change. This detrimental interaction from compounding chronic anxiety with high fear appeals should become more pronounced as the influence situation puts a progressively greater strain on reception by the person, e.g., as we go from suggestibility and conformity situations to persuasion situations.

Empirical results tend to confirm this expected interaction. Niles (1964) found that low fear appeals were more effective than high on the smoking-cancer issue when the subjects were already worried about health, but for those who felt relatively invulnerable about illness, the high fear appeal produced more change. Berkowitz and Cottingham (1960) found some suggestion, by an internal analysis, that as initial concern about the issue went up, the persuasive efficacy of adding threat to the message went down. Goldstein (1959) found that an added fear appeal had a detrimental effect on persuasive impact for those who chronically reacted to threat by "avoidance," but not for "copers."

.   .   .   .

Interactions with Receiver Factors: Sex as a Moderator Variable

Personality variables themselves constitute a large subclass of receiver factors, but what we wish to point out here is that these personality variables tend to interact with one another and with other kinds of receiver variables in determining influenceability. Studies abound which show that the relationship between a given personality variable and influenceability varies, depending on the individual's standing on some other personality variable. For example, the Berkowitz and Lundy (1957) study shows that the relationship between one personality variable and influenceability can vary in magnitude and even direction by varying the subjects' level on another personality dimension. Thus, the relationship between receivers' authoritarianism (California-F) and influenceability as measured by change toward a peer source is negative among persons with low self-esteem (or low interpersonal confidence) while the relationship becomes positive as the subsample changes to include those higher in self-esteem.

These interaction effects between one receiver factor and another are even more common when we consider individual-difference variables that interact simply to intensify rather than reverse a personality-influenceability relationship; that is, where one characteristic acts as a moderator variable to intensify the relationship between influenceability and another characteristic. One such case that has attracted a considerable amount of research attention involves sex acting as the moderator variable for personality-influenceability relations. We already referred to the general finding that women tend to be more susceptible to social influence than men. What we refer to here, however, is another general finding that the correlations between personality characteristics and influenceability tend to be higher in males than in females. This finding of lower correlations for women than for men is not peculiar to the personality-influenceability area. Part of the lore of laborers in the experimental-personality vineyard is that if one wants to find strong relationships between personality variables and behavioral measures in college sophomores, one is wise to use male rather than female students as subjects. Typical of the results in the influenceability area is the finding by Janis and Field (1959b) that the correlations between personality variables and persuasibility were higher in men than in women for eight of the nine personality variables studied. None of the correlations in females was significant at even the .25 level, while in men most of the correlations were, and four of the nine were significant at the conventional .05 level. Similar results with hypnotizability were obtained by Hilgard, Lauer, and Melei (1965).

. . . .

Evaluation

The moral is that we should not, in our quest for generality, seek absolute relationships between personality variables and influenceability. We may frequently find such relationships that are relatively source-free, or appeal-free, or issue-free, etc., but we should not hope to find relationships which are pervasive across all other aspects of the communication situation. Hence, we may generalize the personality-influenceability relationship found under a specific set of experimental conditions to other conditions only with fear and trembling. Obviously some generalization is necessary, since we are constructing a science. But it is to be expected that any simple relationship found will, if studied under a wide enough range of communication conditions, vanish and even reverse in some of the situations. What we have done here is to show a rough classification of the types of other variables with which generalization-limiting interactions might be sought.

. . . .

PRINCIPLE 6:
THE COMPENSATION OR
DYNAMIC-EQUILIBRIUM PRINCIPLE

In discussion of the previous five principles we have been repeatedly confronting, empirically and theoretically, the situations in which the relationship between the independent variable (some personality characteristic) and the dependent variable (susceptibility to social influence) is mediated by two opposing relationships, with the result that the overall personality-influenceability relationship is nonmonotonic. The actual occurrence of this case is quite widespread. We saw in the Appley and Moeller study, for example, that 33 of their 38 personality variables showed a nonmonotonic relation to conformity. We suspect this situation obtains fairly generally between personality characteristics and many other dependent variables besides influenceability. In this section we shall, however, restrict ourselves to the social influence area in trying to make explicit our thinking regarding why this situation is so general and explore the limits within which it obtains.

In general, our "explanation" of the prevalence of this situation is based on a functional analysis of the person's adaptation problem. In the case of susceptibility to social influence (as for many other behavioral dimensions, if we are to accept Aristotle's *Nicomachean Ethics*) there seems to be a golden middle range. The person should be open, but not too open, to outside influence if he is to thrive in the natural environment. It is intuitively plausible (and a common biological and engineering practice) that behavior can most satisfactorily be held at an optimal intermediate level by means of a dynamic equilibrium, i.e., in a steady state produced by the mutual cancellation of two opposing factors.

Maintaining behavior at a golden mean by a dynamic equilibrium situation has particularly obvious advantages for an organism adapting, ontogenetically and phylogenetically, to a complex and variable natural environment. It allows ready adjustment of fluctuations that occur in either direction. Variation thus becomes less costly, allowing for built-in trial-and-error oscillatory searchings that would permit readjustment to a changing environment. The dynamic equilibrium situation is also particularly apt for allowing a complex solution, in which the organism learns to switch its functioning to different optimal levels depending on the conditions.

Susceptibility to social influence is an area in which all of these circumstances obtain. An intermediate level seems optimal, since if the person were completely closed to influence from others, he would lose out on one of the most efficient sources of information about the environment and how to deal with it. On the other hand, if he were completely open to influence, he would hardly pursue any path to a goal before being diverted from it by some new social pressure. Hence, it is adaptive for him to be in a dynamic equilibrium where some of his personality proclivities make for openness, while others make him closed to social influence, resulting in his maintaining his influenceability within an intermediate range.

The easy fluctuation and return which are facilitated by the dynamic equilibrium adjustment are particularly adaptive with influenceability. We saw that such ease of fluctuations yielded two dividends: it permitted long-term secular trends to new levels of stabilization if environmental changes required it, and it permitted a complex solution where different equilibrium levels could be adopted under different sets of environmental conditions. As for openness to persuasion, an armchair ecological survey indicates a long-term ontogenetic trend, with the optimal level going downward over the lifespan, at least during the period from early childhood to maturity. The inexpensive searching fluctuations allowed by the dynamic equilibrium arrangement permit constant testing and a creeping readjustment downward with maturation, which is highly adaptive. The multilevel solution facilitiated by the dynamic equilibrium arrangement also has a special utility in the case of influenceability. Such a solution permits the personality variable to function in interactions with other aspects of the influence situation in determing the characteristic level of influenceability. The person can, for example, function at one level with a credible source and at a lower level with a less credible source; at a higher level on a matter-of-fact issue than a matter-of-test one; at one level in the classroom and at another in political disputation.

We are presenting this dynamic equilibrium principle not as a proof of (or even evidence for) the preceding principles, which must stand or fall on the degree to which the hypotheses derived from them are confirmed by experimental outcomes. The functional reasoning, on which the present principle is based, is always hazardous. It rests on the following argument: that behavior in accord with a certain model would be adaptive in the existing environment; organisms seem fairly well adapted; therefore organisms might well behave as depicted in the model. The argument hardly compels assent. Among the more obvious possibilities of error in this functional approach are the following: behavior in accord with the model might be adaptive in the present environment; however, the contemporary social environment (which is the one on which we performed our hopefully correct ecological analysis) might be radically different from that in which people evolved and to which they adapted. Furthermore, the organism is no doubt generally adapted but is perhaps not adapted regarding the behavior in question. Also, even though behavior in accord with the model might be adaptive, it is still possible that the organism might have adapted along the lines of another model.

Hence, we are not offering this dynamic equilibrium principle as evidence but merely as a high order generalization, hardly testable by empirical outcomes in view of its tenuous multistep logical relation to any testable derivations. The principle serves mainly as a heuristic device for guiding our thinking. The hypotheses it suggests gain only a measure of plausibility from their relation to the principle. Rather than supporting any hypothesis, this plausibility at most makes the hypothesis a nominee for empirical testing.

CONCLUSIONS BASED ON THE SIX PRINCIPLES

If it is safe to make any simple generalization about personality-influenceability relations, it is that no simple generalizations are valid. Our discussion of the preceding principles showed again and again that there are few, if any, simple personality-influenceability relations that are valid over a wide range of conditions. The compensation principle under discussion argues further that additional research is unlikely to "improve" this situation. As a golden-mean variable, influenceability is likely to be held at an optimal range by means of a dynamic equilibrium between opposing personality forces. Any valid theory of personality-influenceability relations must, therefore, hypothesize relations that are complex and situational-interacting or else must be of very narrow generalizability. The complexities are imposed on the theory, not by our failure to find the crucial key but by the complexities of the slice of reality we have chosen to describe.

REFERENCES

ABELSON, R. P. Modes of resolution of belief dilemmas. *J. Conflict Resolution*, 1959, 3, 343–352.

ABELSON, R. P., and LESSER, G. S. The measurement of persuasibility in children. In I. L. Janis and C. I. Hovland (Eds.), *Personality and persuasibility*. New Haven: Yale Univer. Press, 1959, pp. 141–166. (a)

———. A developmental theory of persuasibility. In I. L. Janis and C. I. Hovland (Eds.), *Personality and persuasibility*. New Haven: Yale Univer. Press, 1959, pp. 167–186. (b)

ABELSON, R. P., and ROSENBERG, M. J. Symbolic psycho-logic: a model of attitude cognition. *Behavioral Sci.*, 1958, 3, 1–13.

ABRAMS, S. The use of hypnotic techniques with psychotics. *Amer. J. Psychotherapy*, 1964, 18, 79–94.

ADORNO, T. W., FRENKEL-BRUNSWIK, ELSE, LEVINSON, D. J., and SANFORD, R. N. *The authoritarian personality*. New York: Harper, 1950.

ALLPORT, G. Attitudes. In C. Murchison (Ed.), *Handbook of social psychology*. Worcester, Mass.: Clark Univer. Press, 1935. pp. 798–844.

ANDERSON, N. H. Primacy effects in personality impression formation using a generalized order effect paradigm. *J. abnorm. soc. Psychol.*, 1965, 2, 1–9.

APPEL, V. An experimental test of the superiority and theory of forced-choice questionnaire construction. *Dissertation Abstr.*, 1959, 20, 1067.

APPLEY, M. H., and MOELLER, G. Conforming behavior and personality variables in college women. *J. abnorm. soc. Psychol.*, 1963, 66, 284–290.

ARONSON, E., and FESTINGER, L. Some attempts to measure tolerance for dissonance. USAF WADC Tech. Rep., 1958, No. 58–942.

ARONSON, E., TURNER, JUDITH, and CARLSMITH, J. M. Communicator credibility and communicator discrepancy as determinants of opinion change. *J. abnorm. soc. Psychol.*, 1963, 67, 31–36.

ASCH, S. E. *Social psychology*. Englewood Cliffs, N.J.: Prentice-Hall, 1952.

———. Studies of independence and conformity: a minority of one against a unanimous majority. *Psychol. Monogr.*, 1956, 70, No. 9 (Whole No. 416).

AVELING, F., and HARGREAVES, H. L. Suggestibility with and without prestige in children. *Brit. J. Psychol.*, 1921, 12, 53–75.

BAIN, R. Stability in questionnaire response. *Amer. J. Sociol.*, 1931, 37, 445–453.

BAKAN, D. A generalization of Sidman's results on group and individual functions and a criterion. *Psychol. Bull.*, 1954, 51, 63–67.

BARBER, T. X., and CALVERLEY, D. S. "Hypnotic-like" suggestibility in children and adults. *J. abnorm. soc. Psychol.*, 1963, 66, 589–597

BARRY, H., JR., MACKENNON, D. W., and MURRAY, H. A., JR. Studies in personality: A. Hypnotizability as a personality trait and its typological relations. *Hum. Biol.*, 1931, 13, 1–36.

BELOFF, H. Two forms of social conformity: acquiescence and conventionality. *J. abnorm. soc. Psychol.*, 1958, 56, 99–104.

BENNIS, W. G., and PEABODY, D. The conceptualization of two personality orientations and sociometric choice. *J. soc. Psychol.*, 1962, 57, 203–215.

BENTON, A. L., and BANDURA, A. "Primary" and "secondary" suggestibility. *J. abnorm. soc. Psychol.*, 1953, 48, 336–340.

BEREITER, C. Some persisting dilemmas in the measurement of change. In C. W. Harris (Ed.), *Problems in measuring change.* Madison: Univer. of Wisconsin Press, 1963. pp. 3–20.

BERGIN, A. E. The effect of dissonant persuasive communications on changes in a self-referring attitude. *J. Pers.*, 1962, 30, 423–438.

BERKOWITZ, L., and COTTINGHAM, D. R. The interest value and relevance of fear arousing communications. *J. abnorm. soc. Psychol.*, 1960, 60, 37–43.

BERKOWITZ, L., and LUNDY, R. M. Personality characteristics related to susceptibility to influence by peers or authority figures. *J. Pers.*, 1957, 25, 385–397.

BETTELHEIM, B., and JANOWITZ, M. *Dynamics of prejudice: a psychological and sociological study of veterans.* New York: Harper, 1950.

BINET, A. *La suggestibilité.* Paris: Scheicher Frères, 1900.

BLAKE, R. R., HELSON, H., and MOUTON, JANE S. The generality of conformity behavior as a function of factual anchor, difficulty of task, and amount of social pressure. *J. Pers.*, 1956, 25, 294–305.

BLOCK, J. The equivalence of measures and the correction for attenuation. *Psychol. Bull.*, 1963, 60, 152–156.

———. Recognizing attenuation effects in the strategy of research. *Psychol. Bull.*, 1964, 62, 214–216.

BORING, E. G. *History of experimental psychology.* (2nd ed.) New York: Appleton-Century, 1950.

BREHM, J. W., and COHEN, A. R. *Explorations in cognitive dissonance.* New York: Wiley, 1962.

BROWN, J. S. *The motivation of behavior.* New York: McGraw-Hill, 1961.

BUSH, R. R. Estimation and evaluation. In R. D. Luce, R. R. Bush, and E. Galanter (Eds.), *Handbook of mathematical psychology.* Vol. 1. New York: Wiley, 1963. pp. 429–469.

BUSS, A. H. Two anxiety factors in psychiatric patients. *J. abnorm. soc. Psychol.*, 1962, 65, 426–427.

BYRNE, D., and RHAMEY, R. Magnitude of positive and negative reinforcement as a determinant of attraction. *J. pers. soc. Psychol.*, 1965, 2, 884–889.

CAMPBELL, D. T. Factors relevant to the validity of experiments in social settings. *Psychol. Bull.*, 1957, 54, 297–312.

————. Social attitudes and other acquired behavioral dispositions. In S. Koch (Ed.), *Psychology: a study of a science*. Vol. 6. New York: McGraw-Hill, 1963. pp. 94–172.

CAMPBELL, D. T., and STANLEY, J. C. Experimental and quasi-experimental designs for research on teaching. In N. L. Gage (Ed.), *Handbook of research on teaching*. Chicago: Rand McNally, 1963. pp. 171–246.

CARTWRIGHT, D., and HARARY, F. Structural balance: a generalization of Heider's theory. *Psychol. Rev.*, 1956, 63, 277–293.

CATTELL, R. B., SAUNDERS, D. R., and STICE, G. *Handbook for the sixteen personality factor questionnaire*. Champaign, Ill.: Institute for Personality & Ability Testing, 1957.

CHRISTIE, R., and LINDAUER, FLORENCE. Personality structure. In P. R. Farnsworth (Ed.), *Annual review of psychology*. Vol. 14. Palo Alto, Calif.: Annual Reviews, 1963. pp. 201–230.

COFER, C., and APPLEY, M. *Motivation theory and research*. New York: Wiley, 1964.

COHEN, A. R. Need for cognition and order of communication as determinants of opinion change. In C. I. Hovland (Ed.), *The order of presentation in persuasion*. New Haven: Yale Univer. Press, 1957. pp. 79–97.

————. Some implications of self-esteem for social influence. In I. L. Janis and C. I. Hovland (Eds.), *Personality and persuasibility*. New Haven: Yale Univer. Press, 1959. pp. 102–120.

COOLEY, W. W., and LOHNES, P. R. *Multivariate procedures for the behavioral sciences*. New York: Wiley, 1962.

COOPER, EUNICE, and DINERMAN, HELEN. Analysis of the film "Don't Be a Sucker": a study of communication. *Publ. opin. Quart.*, 1951, 15, 243–264.

COUCH, A., and KENISTON, K. Yeasayers and naysayers: agreeing response set as a personality variable. *J. abnorm. soc. Psychol.*, 1960, 60, 151–174.

COX, D. F., and BAUER, R. A. Self-confidence and persuasibility in women. *Publ. opin. Quart.*, 1964, 28, 453–466.

CRONBACH, L. J. *Essentials of psychological testing*. (2nd ed.) New York: Harper, 1960.

CROWNE, D. P., and MARLOW, D. *The approval motive*. New York: Wiley, 1964.

CRUTCHFIELD, R. S. Conformity and character. *Amer. Psychol.*, 1955, 10, 191–198.

DE FLEUR, M. L., and WESTIE, F. R. Attitude as a scientific concept. *Soc. Forces*, 1963, 42, 17–31.

DE RIVERA, J. The postural sway test and its correlates. Pensacola, Fla.: U.S. Naval School of Aviation Medicine. Bureau of Medicine & Surgery, Res. Proj. MR005. 13-3001. Subtask 7, Rpt. No. 3. Nov. 12, 1959.

DE WOLFE, A. S., and GOVERNALE, C. N. Fear and attitude change. *J. abnorm. soc. Psychol.*, 1964, 69, 119–123.

DITTES, J. E., and KELLEY, H. H. Effects of different conditions of acceptance upon conformity to group norms. *J. abnorm. soc. Psychol.*, 1956, 53, 100–107.

DIVESTA, F. J., and MERWIN, J. C. Effects of need-oriented communication on attitude change. *J. abnorm. soc. Psychol.*, 1960, 60, 80–85.

DOHRENWEND, B., and DOHRENWEND, BARBARA. The problem of validity in field studies of psychological disorder. *J. abnorm. Psychol.*, 1965, 70, 52–69.

DOOB, L. W. *Communication in Africa*. New Haven: Yale Univer. Press, 1961.

EBBINGHAUS, H. *Abriss der Psychologie*. Leipzig: Veit, 1908.

EDWARDS, A. L. *Edwards Personal Preference Schedule (Manual)*. New York: Psychological Corp., 1954.

EDWARDS, A. L. *Experimental design in psychological research*. New York: Holt, Rinehart, and Winston, 1960.

EYSENCK, H. J., and FURNEAUX, W. D. Primary and secondary suggestibility: an experimental and statistical study. *J. exp. Psychol.*, 1945, 35, 485–503.

FERGUSON, L. W. An analysis of the generality of suggestibility to group opinion. *Charact. and Pers.*, 1944, 12, 237–243.

FESTINGER, L. *A theory of cognitive dissonance*. Stanford, Calif.: Stanford Univer. Press, 1957.

———. Behavioral support for opinion change. *Publ. opin. Quart.*, 1964, 28, 404–417. (a)

———. *Conflict, decision and dissonance*. Stanford, Calif.: Stanford Univer. Press, 1964. (b)

FISHBEIN, M. The relationship between beliefs, attitudes, and behavior. In S. Feldman (Ed.), *Cognitive consistency in relation to behavior*. New York: Academic Press, 1966.

FREEDMAN, J. L. Involvement, discrepancy, and opinion change. *J. abnorm. soc. Psychol.*, 1964, 69, 290–295.

FREUD, S. *The problem of anxiety*. New York: Horton, 1936.

FRYE, R., and BASS, B. M. Social acquiescence and behavior in groups. Paper read at Midwest Psychol. Assoc. Convention, Detroit, Mich., May 3, 1958.

GAITO, J. Unequal intervals and unequal n in trend analyses. *Psychol. Bull.*, 1965, 63, 125–127.

GAITO, J., and TURNER, E. Error terms in trend analysis. *Psychol. Bull.*, 1963, 60, 464–474.

GARDNER, R. W., HOLZMAN, P. S., KLEIN, G. S., LINTON, HARRIET B., and SPENCE, D. P. Cognitive control. *Psychol. Issues*, 1959, 1, No. 4.

GELFAND, D. M. The influence of self-esteem on the rate of verbal conditioning and social matching behavior. *J. abnorm. soc. Psychol.*, 1962, 65, 259–265.

GOLDSTEIN, M. J. The relationship between coping and avoiding behavior and response to fear-arousing propaganda. *J. abnorm. soc. Psychol.*, 1959, 58, 247–252.

GORDON, L. U. *Gordon personality profile (manual)*. New York: Harcourt, Brace, 1956.

GOUGH, H. G. *California personality inventory (manual)*. Palo Alto, Calif.: Consulting Psychologist Press, 1957.

GREENWALD, H. The involvement-discrepancy controversy in persuasion research. Unpublished doctoral dissertation, Columbia Univer., 1964.

GUILFORD, J. P., and ZIMMERMAN, W. S. *The Guilford-Zimmerman temperament survey (manual)*. Beverly Hills, Calif.: Sheridan Supply Co., 1949.

GUTTMAN, L. A general nonmetric technique for finding the smallest Euclidean space for a configuration of points. *Psychometrika*, in press.

———. Order analysis of correlation matrices. In R. B. Cattell (Ed.), *Handbook of multivariate experimental psychology*. Chicago: Rand McNally, 1966.

HAEFNER, D. P. Some effects of guilt-arousing and fear-arousing persuasive communications on opinion change. Unpublished doctoral dissertation, Univ. of Rochester, 1956.

HARMAN, H. *Modern factor analysis*. Chicago: Univer. of Chicago Press, 1960.

HARPER, B. W., and TUDDENHAM, R. D. The sociometric composition of the group as a determinant of yielding to a distorted norm. *J. Psychol.*, 1964, 58, 307–311.

HARRIS, C. W. *Problems in measuring change.* Madison: Univer. of Wisconsin Press, 1963.

HARTLEY, E. L. *Problems in prejudice.* New York: King's Crown Press, 1946.

HARVEY, O. J., and CONSALVI, C. Status and conformity to pressure in informal groups. *J. abnorm. soc. Psychol.*, 1960, 60, 182–187.

HARVEY, O. J., HUNT, D. E., and SCHRODER, H. M. *Conceptual systems and personality organization.* New York: Wiley, 1961.

HECHT, S. The nature of the photoreceptor process. In C. Murchison (Ed.), *Handbook of general experimental psychology.* Worcester, Mass.: Clark Univer. Press, 1934. pp. 704–828.

HEIDER, F. Attitudes and cognitive organization. *J. Psychol.*, 1946, 21, 107–112.

———. *The psychology of interpersonal relations.* New York: Wiley, 1958.

HELSON, H. *Adaptation-level theory.* New York: Harper & Row, 1964.

HILGARD, E. R. *Hypnotic susceptibility.* New York: Harcourt, Brace, 1965.

HILGARD, E. R., LAUER, LILLIAN W., and MELEI, JANET P. Acquiescence, hypnotic susceptibility & the MMPI. *J. consult. Psychol.*, in press.

HOCHBAUM, G. M. The relation between group members' self-confidence and their reactions to group pressure to uniformity. *Amer. sociol. Rev.*, 1954, 6, 678–687.

HOFFMAN, M. L. Some psychodynamic factors in compulsive conformity. *J. abnorm. soc. Psychol.*, 1953, 48, 383–393.

HOLLAND, L. V. *Counterpoint: Kenneth Burke and Aristotle's theory of rhetoric.* New York: Philosophical Library, 1959.

HOLLANDER, E. P. Reconsidering the issue of conformity in personality. In H. P. David & J. C. Brengelmann (Eds.), *Perspectives in personality research.* New York: Springer, 1960. pp. 210–225.

HOVLAND, C. I. Effects of the mass media of communication. In G. Lindzey (Ed.), *Handbook of social psychology.* Cambridge, Mass.: Addison-Wesley, 1954. pp. 1062–1103.

———. (Ed.) *Order of presentation in persuasion.* New Haven: Yale Univer. Press, 1957.

HOVLAND, C. I., and JANIS, I. L. Summary and implications for future research. In I. L. Janis & C. I. Hovland (Eds.), *Personality and persuasibility.* New Haven: Yale Univer. Press, 1959. pp. 225–254.

HOVLAND, C. I., JANIS, I. L., and KELLEY, H. H. *Communication and persuasion.* New Haven: Yale Univer. Press, 1953.

HOVLAND, C. I., LUMSDAINE, A. A., and SHEFFIELD, F. D. *Experiments on mass communications.* Princeton, N.J.: Princeton Univer. Press, 1949.

HOVLAND, C. I., and MANDELL, W. An experimental comparison of conclusion-drawing by the communicator and by the audience. *J. abnorm. soc. Psychol.*, 1952, 47, 581–588.

HOVLAND, C. I., and WEISS, W. The influence of source credibility on communication effectiveness. *Publ. opin. Quart.*, 1951, 15, 635–650.

HOWARD, J. A. *Marketing: executive and buyer behavior.* New York: Columbia Univer. Press, 1963.

HULL, C. L. *Hypnosis and suggestibility.* New York: Appleton-Century, 1933.

HULL, C. L., HOVLAND, C. I., ROSS, R. T., HALL, M., PERKINS, D. T. and FITCH, F. B. *Mathematico-deductive theory of rote learning.* New Haven: Yale Univer. Press, 1940.

INSKO, C. A. Primacy vs. recency in persuasion as a function of the timing of arguments and measures. *J. abnorm. soc. Psychol.*, 1964, 69, 381–391.

INSKO, C. A., ARKOFF, A., and INSKO, V. M. Effects of high and low fear-arousing communications upon opinions toward smoking. *J. exp. soc. Psychol.*, 1965, 1, 256–266.

JACKSON, D. N., and PACINE, L. Response styles and academic achievement. *Educ. psychol. Measmt.*, 1961, 21, 1015–1028.

JANIS, I. L. Personality correlates of susceptibility to persuasion. *J. Pers.*, 1954, 22, 504–518.

———. Anxiety indices related to susceptibility to persuasion. *J. abnorm. soc. Psychol.*, 1955, 51, 663–667.

JANIS, I. L., and FESHBACH, S. Effects of fear arousing communications. *J. abnorm. soc. Psychol.*, 1953, 48, 78–92.

JANIS, I. L., and FIELD, P. B. A behavioral assessment of persuasibility: consistency of individual differences. In I. L. Janis and C. I. Hovland (Eds.), *Personality and persuasibility*. New Haven: Yale Univer. Press, 1959. pp. 29–54. (a)

———. Sex differences and personality factors related to persuasibility. In I. L. Janis & C. I. Hovland (Eds.), *Personality and persuasibility*. New Haven: Yale Univer. Press, 1959. pp. 55–68. (b)

JANIS, I. L., and HOVLAND, C. I. (Eds.) *Personality and persuasibility*. New Haven: Yale Univer. Press, 1959.

JANIS, I. L., and RIFE, D. Persuasibility and emotional disorder. In I. L. Janis & C. I. Hovland (Eds.), *Personality and persuasibility*. New Haven: Yale Univer. Press, 1959.

JANIS, I. L., and TERWILLIGER, R. An experimental study of psychological resistance to fear-arousing communication. *J. abnorm. soc. Psychol.*, 1962, 65, 403–410.

JOHNSON, H. H., and STEINER, I. Effort and subjective probability. *J. pers. soc. Psychol.*, 1965, 1, 365–368.

KATZ, D. Functional approach to the study of attitude. *Publ. opin. Quart.*, 1960, 24, 163–204.

KATZ, D., SARNOFF, I., and McCLINTOCK, C. Ego-defense and attitude change. *Hum. Relat.*, 1956, 9, 27–45.

KATZ, D., and STOTLAND, E. A preliminary statement of a theory of attitude structure and change. In S. Koch (Ed.), *Psychology: Study of a science*. Vol. 3. New York: McGraw-Hill, 1959. pp. 423–475.

KATZ, E., and LAZARSFELD, P. F. *Personal influence*. Glencoe, Ill.: Free Press, 1955.

KEGELES, S. S. Some motives for seeking preventative dental care. *J. Amer. dental Assoc.*, 1963, 67, 110–118.

KELLEY, H. H., and SHAPIRO, M. M. An experiment on conformity to group norms where conformity is detrimental to group achievement. *Amer. sociol. Rev.*, 1954, 19, 667–677.

KELLEY, H. H., and THIBAUT, J. Experimental studies of group problem solving and process. In G. Lindzey (Ed.), *Handbook of social psychology*. Cambridge, Mass.: Addison-Wesley, 1954. pp. 735–785.

KELMAN, H. C. Effect of success and failure on "suggestibility" in the autokinetic situation. *J. abnorm. soc. Psychol.*, 1950, 45, 267–285.

———. Compliance, identification, and internalization: three processes of opinion change. *J. Conflict Resolution*, 1958, 2, 51–60.

———. Processes of opinion change. *Publ. opin. Quart.*, 1961, 25, 51–78.

KELMAN, H. C., and EAGLY, ALICE H. Attitude toward the communicator, perception of communication content, and attitude change. *J. abnorm. soc. Psychol.*, 1965, 1, 63–78.

KENDALL, PATRICIA L., and WOLF, KATHERINE M. The analysis of deviant cases in communications research. In P. F. Lazarsfeld and F. N. Stanton (Eds.), *Communication research, 1948–1949.* New York: Harper, 1949.

KING, B. T. Relationships between susceptibility to opinion change and child rearing practices. In I. L. Janis and C. I. Hovland (Eds.), *Personality and persuasibility.* New Haven: Yale Univer. Press, 1959. pp. 207–224.

KLAPPER, J. T. *Effects of mass communication.* Glencoe, Ill.: Free Press, 1961.

KLEIN, G. Cognitive control and motivation. In G. Lindzey (Ed.), *Assessment of human motives.* New York: Rinehart, 1958.

KNOWER, F. H. Experimental studies of changes in attitudes. I. A study of the effect of oral arguments on changes of attitudes. *J. soc. Psychol.*, 1935, 6, 315–347.

KRAMER, E., and BRENNAN, E. P. Hypnotic susceptibility of schizophrenic patients. *J. abnorm. soc. Psychol.*, 1964, 69, 657–659.

KRUSKAL, J. B. Multidimensional scaling by optimizing goodness of fit to a nonmetric hypothesis. *Psychometrika*, 1964, 29, 1–27.

LANA, R. E. Familiarity and the order of presentation in persuasive communications. *J. abnorm. soc. Psychol.*, 1961, 62, 573–577.

———. Three interpretations of order effects in persuasive communications. *Psychol. Bull.*, 1964, 61, 314–320.

LASSWELL, H. D. The structure and function of communication in society. In L. Bryson (Ed.), *Communication of ideas.* New York: Harper, 1948.

LAVER, LILLIAN W. Factorial components of hypnotic susceptibility. Ph. D. dissertation, Stanford Univer., 1965.

LAZARUS, R. S., DEESE, J., and OSLER, S. F. The effect of psychological stress upon performance. *Psychol. Bull.*, 1952, 49, 293–317.

LESSER, G. S., and ABELSON, R. P. Personality correlates of persuasibility in children. In I. L. Janis & C. I. Hovland (Eds.), *Personality and persuasibility.* New Haven: Yale Univer. Press, 1959. pp. 187–206.

LEVENTHAL, H., and NILES, PATRICIA. A field experiment on fear arousal with data on the validity of questionnaire measures. *J. Pers.*, 1964, 32, 459–479.

LEVENTHAL, H., and PERLOE, S. I. A relationship between self-esteem and persuasibility. *J. abnorm. soc. Psychol.*, 1962, 64, 385–388.

LEVENTHAL, H., SINGER, R. P., and JONES, S. H. The effects of fear and specificity of recommendation upon attitudes and behavior. *J. pers. soc. Psychol.*, 1965, 2, 20–29.

LINGOES, J. C. An IBM 7090 program for Guttman-Lingoes smallest space analysis. I. *Behav. Sci.*, 1965, 10, 183–184.

LINTON, HARRIET B. Autokinetic judgments as a measure of influence. *J. abnorm. soc. Psychol.*, 1954, 49, 464–466.

LINTON, HARRIET, and GRAHAM, ELAINE. Personality correlates of persuasibility. In I. L. Janis & C. I. Hovland (Eds.), *Personality and persuasibility.* New Haven: Yale Univer. Press, 1959. pp. 69–101.

MAHLER, I. Yeasayers and naysayers: a validity study. *J. abnorm. soc. Psychol.*, 1962, 64, 317–318.

MAUSNER, B. The effect of prior reinforcement on the interaction of observed pairs. *J. abnorm. soc. Psychol.*, 1954, 49, 65–68.

MAUSNER, B., and BLOCK, BARBARA L. A study of the additivity of variables affecting social interaction. *J. abnorm. soc. Psychol.*, 1957, 54, 250–256.

MCALLISTER, IRMA. Interference, immoderation, inconsistency, and dependency: differences in the behavior of mothers toward first and later-born children. Unpublished doctoral dissertation, Columbia Univer., 1965.

MCGUIRE, W. J. Cognitive consistency and attitude change. *J. abnorm. soc. Psychol.*, 1960, 60, 345–353. (a)

———. A syllogistic analysis of cognitive relationships. In M. J. Rosenberg & C. I. Hovland (Eds.), *Attitude organization and attitude change.* New Haven: Yale Univer. Press, 1960. pp. 65–111. (b)

———. A multiprocess model for paired-associate learning. *J. exp. Psychol.*, 1961, 62, 335–347.

———. Persistence of the resistance to persuasion induced by various types of prior belief defenses. *J. abnorm. soc. Psychol.*, 1962, 64, 241–248.

———. Attitudes and opinions. In P. R. Farnsworth (Ed.), *Annual review of psychology.* Vol. 17. Palo Alto, Calif.: Annual Reviews, 1966.

MCNEMAR, Q. *Psychological statistics.* (3rd ed.) New York: Wiley, 1962.

MENZEL, H., and KATZ, E. Social relations and innovations in the medical profession: the epidemiology of a new drug. *Publ. opin. Quart.*, 1956, 19, 337–352.

MILLER, N., and CAMPBELL, D. T. Recency and primacy in persuasion as a function of the timing of speeches and measurement. *J. abnorm. soc. Psychol.*, 1959, 59, 1–9.

MILLER, N. E., and DOLLARD, J. *Social learning and imitation.* New Haven: Yale Univer. Press, 1941.

MILLMAN, SUSAN. The relationship between anxiety, learning and opinion change. Unpublished doctoral dissertation, Columbia Univer., 1965.

MITRA, S. F., and FISKE, D. W. Intra-individual variability as related to test score and items. *Educ. psychol. Measmt*, 1956, 16, 3–12.

MOELLER, G., and APPLEZWEIG, M. H. A motivational factor in conformity. *J. abnorm. soc. Psychol.*, 1957, 55, 114–120.

MOLTZ, H., and THISTLETHWAITE, D. Attitude modification and anxiety reduction. *J. abnorm. soc. Psychol.*, 1955, 50, 231–237.

MOORE, ROSEMARIE K. Susceptibility to hypnosis and susceptibility to social influence. *J. abnorm. soc. Psychol.*, 1964, 68, 282–294.

MURPHY, G., MURPHY, LOIS B., and NEWCOMB, T. N. *Experimental social psychology.* (Rev. ed.) New York: Harper, 1937.

NEWCOMB, T. M. An approach to the study of communicative acts. *Psychol. Rev.*, 1953, 60, 393–404.

NILES, PATRICIA. The relationship of susceptibility and anxiety to acceptance of fear-arousing communications. Unpublished doctoral dissertation, Yale Univer., 1964.

OSGOOD, C. E., and TANNENBAUM, P. H. The principle of congruity in the prediction of attitude change. *Psychol. Rev.*, 1955, 62, 42–55.

OSTERWEIL, J., and FISKE, D. W. Intra-individual variability in sentence completion responses. *J. abnorm. soc. Psychol.*, 1956, 52, 195–199.

PAPAGEORGIS, D. Bartlett effect and the persistence of induced opinion change. *J. abnorm. soc. Psychol.*, 1963, 67, 61–67.

PEAK, HELEN. Attitude and motivation. In M. R. Jones (Ed.), *Nebraska symposium on motivation.* Lincoln, Nebr.: Univer. of Nebraska Press, 1955. pp. 149–188.

PETERSON, D. R. Scope and generality of verbally defined personality factors. *Psychol. Rev.*, 1965, 72, 48–59.

PETTIGREW, T. F. The measurement and correlates of category width as a cognitive variable. *J. Pers.*, 1958, 26, 532–544.

POWELL, F. A. Open- and closed-mindedness and the ability to differentiate source and message. *J. abnorm. soc. Psychol.*, 1962, 65, 61–63.

ROKEACH, M. Political and religious dogmatism: an alternative to the authoritarian personality. *Psychol. Monogr.*, 1956, 70, 18 (Whole No. 425).

———. *Open and closed mind.* New York: Basic Books, 1960.

RORER, L. G. The great response-style myth. *Psychol. Bull.*, 1965, 63, 129–156.

ROSENBERG, J. Persuasibility in personality and culture. Unpublished doctoral dissertation, Columbia Univer., 1962.

ROSNER, S. Consistency in response to group pressure. *J. abnorm. soc. Psychol.*, 1957, 55, 145–146.

RUNKEL, P. J. Some consistency effects. *Educ. psychol. Measmt*, 1958, 18, 527–541.

SAMELSON, F. Conforming behavior under two conditions of conflict in the cognitive field. *J. abnorm. soc. Psychol.*, 1957, 55, 181–187.

SARNOFF, I., and ZIMBARDO, P. G. Anxiety, fear, and social affiliations. *J. abnorm. soc. Psychol.*, 1961, 62, 356–363.

SCHEIN, E. H., HILL, W. F., WILLIAMS, H. L., and LUBIN, A. Distinguishing characteristics of collaborators and resistors among American prisoners of war. *J. abnorm. soc. Psychol.*, 1957, 55, 197–201.

SCHOFIELD, W. Changes in response to the MMPI following certain therapies. *Psychol. Monogr.*, 1950, 64, No. 5.

———. A further study of the effects of therapy on MMPI responses. *J. abnorm. soc. Psychol.*, 1953, 48, 66–77.

SCOTT, J. P., and FULLER, J. L. *Genetics and the social behavior of the dog.* Chicago: Univer. of Chicago Press, 1965.

SEARS, PAULINE S. The pursuit of self esteem: the middle childhood years. Paper read at annual Amer. Psychol. Assoc. convention, Chicago, Sept., 1960.

SEARS, R. R. Dependency motivation. In M. R. Jones (Ed.), *Nebraska symposium on motivation.* Lincoln: Univer. of Nebraska Press, 1963. pp. 25–64.

SEGAL, J. Factors related to the collaboration and resistance behavior of U.S. Army POWs in Korea. Tech. Rep. 33, Human Resources Research Office. Washington, D.C.: George Washington Univer., Dec., 1956.

———. Correlates of collaboration and resistance behavior among U.S. Army POWs in Korea. *J. soc. Issues*, 1957, 13, 31–40.

SHEPARD, R. N. The analysis of proximities: multidimensional scaling with an unknown distance function. I. *Psychometrika*, 1962, 27, 125–140. (a)

———. The analysis of proximities: multidimensional scaling with an unknown distance function. II. *Psychometrika*, 1962, 27, 219–246. (b)

———. Attention and the metric structure of the stimulus space. *J. math. Psychol.*, 1964, 1, 54–87.

SHERIF, CAROLYN W., SHERIF, M., and NEBERGALL, R. E. *Attitude and attitude change.* Philadelphia: Saunders, 1965.

SHERIF, M. A study of some social factors in perception. *Arch. Psychol.*, 1935, 27, No. 187. 60 pp.

SHERIF, M., and HOVLAND, C. I. *Social judgment.* New Haven: Yale Univer. Press, 1961.

SIDMAN, M. A note on functional relations obtained from group data. *Psychol. Bull.*, 1952, 49, 263–269.

SILVERMAN, I. Differential effects of ego threat upon persuasibility for high and low self-esteem subjects. *J. abnorm. soc. Psychol.*, 1964, 69, 567–572.

SMITH, M. A note on stability in questionnaire responses. *Amer. J. Sociol.*, 1933, 38, 713–720.

SMITH, M. B. Attitude change. In David L. Sills (Ed.), *International Encyclopedia of the Social Sciences.* New York: Macmillan, 1968, Vol. 1, 459–467.

SMITH, M. B., BRUNER, J. S., and WHITE, R. W. *Opinions and personality.* New York: Wiley, 1956.

SPENCE, K. W., FARBER, I. E., and TAYLOR, ELAINE. The relation of electric shock and anxiety to level of performance in eyelid conditioning. *J. exp. Psychol.*, 1954, 48, 404–408.

STEINER, I. D. Sex differences in the resolution of A-B-X conflicts. *J. Pers.*, 1960, 28, 118–128.

STEINER, I. D., and JOHNSON, H. H. Authoritarianism and "tolerance for trait inconsistency." *J. abnorm. soc. Psychol.*, 1963, 67, 388–391.

————. Category width and response to interpersonal disagreement. *J. pers. soc. Psychol.*, 1965, 2, 290–292.

STEPHENS, M. W., and CROWNE, D. P. Correction for attenuation and the equivalence of tests. *Psychol. Bull.*, 1964, 62, 210–213.

STERNLICHT, M., and WANDERER, Z. W. Hypnotic susceptibility and mental deficiency. *Int. J. clin. exp. Hypnosis*, 1963, 11, 104–111.

STEWARD, J. B. *Repetitive advertising in newspapers: a study in two new products.* Boston: Harvard Business School, 1964.

STOTLAND, E., and HILLMER, M. L., JR. Identification, authoritarian defensiveness and self-esteem. *J. abnorm. soc. Psychol.*, 1962, 64, 334–342.

STOTLAND, E., KATZ, D., and PATCHEN, M. The reduction of prejudice through the arousal of self-insight. *J. Pers.*, 1959, 27, 507–531.

STOTLAND, E., and PATCHEN, M. Identification and changes in prejudice and in authoritarianism. *J. abnorm. soc. Psychol.*, 1961, 62, 265–274.

STUKÁT, K. G. *Suggestibility: a factorial and experimental study.* Stockholm: Almquist & Wiksell, 1958.

TAFFEL, C. Anxiety and the conditioning of verbal behavior. *J. abnorm. soc. Psychol.*, 1955, 51, 496–501.

TAYLOR, JANET A. A personality scale of manifest anxiety. *J. abnorm. soc. Psychol.*, 1953, 48, 285–290.

THISTLETHWAITE, D. L., DE HANN, H., and KAMENETSKY, J. The effects of "directive" and "nondirective" communication procedures on attitudes. *J. abnorm. soc. Psychol.*, 1955, 51, 107–113.

TRIANDIS, H. C., and TRIANDIS, LEIGH M. A cross-cultural study of social distance. *Psychol. Monogr.*, 1962, 76, No. 21 (Whole No. 540).

TUDDENHAM, R. D. Correlates of yielding to a distorted group norm. *J. Pers.*, 1959, 27, 272–284.

WALTERS, R. H., and PARKE, R. D. Social motivation, dependency, and susceptibility to social influence. In L. Berkowitz (Ed.), *Advances in experimental social psychology*. Vol. 1. New York: Academic Press, 1964. pp. 232–277.

WATTS, W. A., and McGUIRE, W. J. Persistency of induced opinion change and retention of inducing message content. *J. abnorm. soc. Psychol.*, 1964, 68, 233–241.

WEISS, W., and FINE, B. J. The effect of induced aggressiveness on opinion change. *J. abnorm. soc. Psychol.*, 1956, 52, 109–114.

WEITZENHOFFER, A. M. *Hypnotism: an objective study in suggestibility.* New York: Wiley, 1953.

WHIPPLE, G. M. *Manual of mental and physical tests.* Baltimore: Warwick, 1910.

WINDLE, C. Test-retest effects on personality questionnaires. *Educ. psychol. Measmt,* 1954, 14, 617–633.

———. Further studies in test-retest effects on personality questionnaires. *Educ. psychol. Measmt,* 1955, 15, 246–253.

WINER, B. J. *Statistical principles in experimental design.* New York: McGraw-Hill, 1962.

WOLF, THETA. Alfred Binet: a time of crisis. *Amer. Psychol.*, 1964, 19, 762–771.

WOODRUFF, A. D., and DiVESTA, F. J. The relation between values, concepts and attitudes. *Educ. psychol. Measmt,* 1948, 8, 645–659.

WRIGHT, J. M., and HARVEY, O. J. Attitude changes as a function of authoritarianism and punitiveness. *J. pers. soc. Psychol.*, 1965, 1, 177–180.

ZAVALA, A. Development of the forced-choice rating scale technique. *Psychol. Bull.,* 1965, 63, 117–124.

ZIMBARDO, P. G. Involvement and communication discrepancy as determinants of opinion conformity. *J. abnorm. soc. Psychol.*, 1960, 60, 86–94.

David O. Sears / Jonathan L. Freedman

SELECTIVE EXPOSURE
TO INFORMATION:
A CRITICAL REVIEW*

This study reviews the literature on selective exposure to information and re-analyzes prevalent theories by pointing up existing knowledge regarding the extent to which communication bias and attitude bias actually correlate, and by considering other factors than attitude bias that might account for selectivity. If attitude bias is not a prime cause of selectivity, what about the desire for supportive information, for useful information, for relief from cognitive dissonance, and many other factors?
David O. Sears is Assistant Professor of Psychology at the University of California, Los Angeles. Jonathan L. Freedman is Associate Professor of Psychology at Stanford University.

One of the most widely accepted principles in sociology and social psychology is the principle of selective exposure. It is a basic fact in the thinking of many social scientists about communication effects. For example, Lazarsfeld, Berelson, and Gaudet find it an indispensable link in their explanation of why a political campaign mainly activates and reinforces pre-existing preferences or predispositions.[1] Hyman and Sheatsley[2] and Klapper[3] make the more

*Preparation of this manuscript was supported by NSF grants to the authors.

[1] P. F. Lazarsfeld, B. Berelson, and Hazel Gaudet, *The People's Choice*, 2nd ed., New York, Columbia University Press, 1948.

[2] H. H. Hyman and P. B. Sheatsley, "Some Reasons Why Information Campaigns Fail," *Public Opinion Quarterly*, Vol. 11, 1947, pp. 413–423.

[3] J. T. Klapper, *The Effects of Mass Communications*, Glencoe, Ill., Free Press, 1960.

Reprinted from the *Public Opinion Quarterly*, 31 (1967), 194–213, with permission of the authors and the Public Opinion Quarterly.

general point: information campaigns, and mass communications of any kind, rarely have important persuasive impact because, among other things, of selective exposure. In Festinger's very influential cognitive dissonance theory, selective exposure plays a central role as a prime mechanism for dissonance reduction.[4] McGuire based an extensive program of research on immunization against persuasion on the assumption that people are often quite unacquainted with counterpropaganda, because of selective exposure.[5] Experimental psychologists and survey researchers alike agree that laboratory and field studies of mass communications often come to quite different conclusions because, in large part, of selective exposure.[6] So the theme of selective exposure runs through much of the research on attitudes and communication of the past two decades.

Nevertheless, the empirical literature on selective exposure has been rather unsatisfying. Partly this is because the term itself has been used in a confusing way. The observation of an empirical correlation between attitudes and exposure has rarely been distinguished from an active psychological preference for supportive information, although they clearly may be quite different. Perhaps more important, a substantial amount of research has been done in the last decade relating to these two questions, and the results are not as unequivocal as one might expect.[7] Under these circumstances, a thorough review and assessment of this research would appear to be in order. The purpose of this paper is, therefore, first to clarify what is meant by "selective exposure," then to characterize the evidence leading to its use, and finally to evaluate the evidence regarding whether or not there is a psychological tendency to prefer supportive to nonsupportive information.

DEFINITION

First, what is meant by "selective exposure"? How is the term generally used?

Any Systematic Bias in Audience Composition. Sometimes it is used to describe any bias whatever in the composition of a communication audience, as long as

[4] L. Festinger, *A Theory of Cognitive Dissonance*, Evanston, Ill., Row, Peterson, 1957.

[5] W. J. McGuire, "Inducing Resistance to Persuasion: Some Contemporary Approaches," in L. Berkowitz, ed., *Advances in Experimental Social Psychology*, Vol. 1, New York, Academic Press, 1964.

[6] C. I. Hovland, "Reconciling Conflicting Results Derived from Experimental and Survey Studies of Attitude Change," *American Psychologist*, Vol. 14, 1959, pp. 8–17. S. M. Lipset, P. F. Lazarsfeld, A. Barton, and J. Linz, "The Psychology of Voting: An Analysis of Political Behavior," in G. Lindzey, ed., *Handbook of Social Psychology*, Vol. 2, Cambridge, Mass., Addison-Wesley, 1954.

[7] Several other writers have commented upon this in passing. See D. Papageorgis and W. J. McGuire, "The Generality of Immunity to Persuasion Produced by Pre-exposure to

the bias can be correlated with anything unusual in communication content. So, when the audience for educational broadcasts on the radio is disproportionately composed of highly educated persons, selective or "partisan" exposure is said to be present. The same is said when broadcasts about a particular ethnic group reach more members of that group than would be expected by chance.[8]

Perhaps the most general statement has been made by Berelson and Steiner in their redoubtable collection of propositions about human behavior: "People tend to see and hear communications that are favorable or congenial to their predispositions; they are more likely to see and hear congenial communications than neutral or hostile ones." The predispositions referred to include "sex role, educational status, interest and involvement, ethnic status, political attitude, aesthetic position, and, indeed, any way of characterising people that matters to them."[9] Expressed in this form, the selective exposure hypothesis offers no explanation for *why* audiences are biased. The only assertion is that they are biased, and are biased systematically along dimensions that parallel salient aspects of the communication or attributes of the communicator. In this form, the proposition is perhaps too general to be of much use.

Unusual Agreement about a Matter of Opinion. The most common, and perhaps most interesting, application of the previous definition has to do with matters of opinion. "Selectivity" describes audience bias in the direction of agreeing to an unusual extent with the communicator's stand on an issue relevant to the communication. Lazarsfeld *et al.* put it this way: "Exposure is always selective; in other words, a positive relationship exists between people's opinions and what they choose to listen to or read."[10] Lipset *et al.* later said that "most people expose themselves, most of the time, to the kind of propaganda with which they agree to begin with."[11] Klapper summarized the point this way: "By and large, people tend to expose themselves to those mass communications which are in accord with their existing attitudes."[12] Childs concludes: "Innumerable studies show that readers tend to read what they agree with, approve, or like."[13] These are simply descriptive statements: they only assert that communication audiences usually share, to an extraordinary degree, the view-

Weakened Counterarguments," *Journal of Abnormal and Social Psychology*, Vol. 62, 1961, pp. 475–481; I. D. Steiner, "Receptivity to Supportive versus Nonsupportive Communications," *Journal of Abnormal and Social Psychology*, Vol. 65, 1962, pp. 266–267; and J. W. Brehm and A. R. Cohen, *Explorations in Cognitive Dissonance*, New York, Wiley, 1962.

[8] Lazarsfeld *et al., op. cit.,* p. 166.

[9] B. Berelson and G. A. Steiner, *Human Behavior*, New York, Harcourt Brace & World, 1964, pp. 529–530.

[10] *Op. cit.,* p. 164.

[11] *Op. cit.,* p. 1158.

[12] *Op. cit.,* p. 19.

[13] H. L. Childs, *Public Opinion*, Princeton, N. J., Van Nostrand, 1965.

points of the communicator. These statements again are noncommittal with respect to the *cause* of this bias. For that reason, this form of the selective exposure hypothesis will be referred to below as *"de facto* selectivity."

Preference for Supportive, Rather than Nonsupportive, Information. The strongest form of the selective exposure proposition is that people prefer exposure to communications that agree with their pre-existing opinions. Hence, people are thought actively to seek out material that supports their opinions, and actively to avoid material that challenges them. Lazarsfeld *et al.* hypothesized: "It is likely that a desire for reinforcement of one's own point of view exists."[14] Two decades later, the hypothesis had been confirmed: "Although self-selection of exposure in line with predispositions is mainly conscious and deliberate, it can also operate nonconsciously as well."[15] And the Behavioral Sciences Subpanel of the President's Science Advisory Committee felt the proposition was sufficiently well-documented to be included in the corpus of established social science fact: ". . . individuals engage in selective exposure. . . . If a new piece of information would weaken the existing structure of their ideas and emotions, it will be shunned . . . if it reinforces the structure, it will be sought out. . . ."[16] In this form, then, the cause of *de facto* selectivity is quite explicit. People expose themselves to communications with which they already agree and do not expose themselves to those with which they disagree, because they actively seek the former and actively avoid the latter. Why? Presumably because of a general psychological preference for compatible information.

Since the focus of this paper is upon opinions and attitudes, the first and most general of these definitions will not be discussed. Let us then consider the evidence for selective exposure in these latter two senses. For consistency of usage, they will be referred to as *"de facto* selectivity" and "selective exposure," respectively, in the remainder of the paper.

DE FACTO SELECTIVITY

Biases in the composition of voluntary audiences to mass communications have been reported often in survey studies. Often these biases parallel the opinion dimension emphasized by the communicator, and are in the direction of unusual initial agreement between audience and communicator. A typical example is Senator William Knowland's telethon in the 1958 California gubernatorial election. Interviews with voters immediately after the election revealed that twice as many Republicans as Democrats (proportionately) had seen this Republican candidate's program. Thirty per cent more viewers

[14] *Loc. cit.*
[15] Berelson and Steiner, *op. cit.,* p. 530.
[16] Behavioral Sciences Subpanel, President's Science Advisory Committee, "Report to the President," *Behavioral Science,* Vol. 7, 1962, p. 277.

watched the program in Republican homes than in Democratic homes, and the average Republican viewer watched the program for about an hour longer than did the average Democratic viewer.[17]

Mass meetings also seem to attract biased audiences. A typical example is the audience of the Christian Anti-Communist Crusade School held in Oakland, California, in 1962. The Crusade is largely organized and run by white Protestants of a conservative political persuasion. And those who attended the school were over three times as likely to think the internal Communist threat to be "a very great danger" as a national sample of citizens asked the same question. Republicans were also heavily overrepresented: 66 per cent were Republicans and 8 per cent identified themselves as Democrats.[18]

Extended propaganda campaigns seem to elicit *de facto* selectivity as well. The classic finding is Lazarsfeld *et al.'s*: Of those respondents with constant voting intentions from May to October, about two-thirds were exposed predominantly to propaganda favoring their side, and less than one-fourth mainly to propaganda favoring the other side.[19] Similarly, in a study done on the University of California loyalty oath controversy, Lipset found newspaper-reading habits to be systematically related to general liberalism or conservatism, party preference, and attitudes toward the controversy. Students tended to read newspapers whose editorial policy was closest to their own opinions.[20] And in a somewhat different realm, Ehrlich *et al.* found that people, whether or not they had just bought new cars, had read a higher percentage of the available ads about their own makes than about any other make.[21]

Each of these demonstrations shares a common basis: the correlation of positions on an attitude dimension with an act, or a series of acts, of exposure to mass communications. A causal relationship has often been inferred from these correlations, although they do not permit it to be determined in any rigorous sense, of course. Data collected in experimental situations are more appropriate for that end, and will be discussed later. Yet, for it to be likely that attitudes are an important cause of selective exposure, two criteria must be met by correlational studies: (1) The correlation must be well documented. It should hold, fairly unequivocally, in most cases. (2) Attitudes should be better predictors of (i.e. correlate more highly with) exposure than other vari-

---

[17] W. Schramm and R. F. Carter, "Effectiveness of a Political Telethon," *Public Opinion Quarterly*, Vol. 23, 1959, pp. 121–126.

[18] R. E. Wolfinger, Barbara K. Wolfinger, K. Prewitt, and Sheilah Rosenhack, "The Clientele of the Christian Anti-Communism Crusade," in D. E. Apter, ed., *Ideology and Discontent*, Glencoe, Ill., Free Press, 1964. These authors do not discuss "selective exposure" per se, but the data are relevant in the present context.

[19] *Op. cit.*

[20] S. M. Lipset, "Opinion Formation in a Crisis Situation," *Public Opinion Quarterly*, Vol. 17, 1953, pp. 20–46.

[21] Danuta Ehrlich, I. Guttmann, P. Schonbach, and J. Mills, "Post-decision Exposure to Relevant Information," *Journal of Abnormal and Social Psychology*, Vol. 54, 1957, pp. 98–102.

ables. These studies should be evaluated with respect to these two criteria, for if they fall short, the causal role of attitudes seems likely to be modest.

Strength and Generality of the Effect. It is not appropriate to review all studies yielding *de facto* selectivity, since the only point here is to see whether or not it has been established beyond much doubt. Let us consider the strength of the effect as it appears in the classic study by Lazarsfeld, Berelson, and Gaudet, since it is almost always cited as representative. They indeed found that their respondents had been exposed predominantly to propaganda supporting their predispositions. A breakdown into parties, however, reveals the fact that this finding held only for persons with Republican predispositions. Far from being selectively exposed, those with Democratic predispositions were almost evenly divided, 50.4 per cent being exposed primarily to Democratic propaganda, and 49.6 per cent primarily to Republican propaganda.[22] Thus, only the Republicans appear actually to have been selective.

However, if one considers the relative availability of pro-Republican and pro-Democratic propaganda, the finding becomes even more paradoxical. Actually, 68.8 per cent of the available partisan propaganda in the campaign was pro-Republican.[23] It is thus hardly surprising that 69.7 per cent of those with Republican predispositions were exposed primarily to pro-Republican information, and 30.3 per cent primarily to pro-Democratic publicity.[24] The exposure of those with Republican predispositions almost exactly matched the partisan division of available information. In fact, looked at from this point of view, it was the Democrats who were selectively exposed, even though actually exposed to equal amounts of Democratic and Republican propaganda, since they were exposed to considerably more Democratic propaganda than might have been expected by chance. And in the later Elmira study one finds a similar pattern: the Republicans' exposure was only 54 per cent pro-Dewey, not up to the considerable pro-Republican margin in available information. The Democrats' exposure was 57 per cent pro-Truman, despite the rarity of pro-Democratic items in the media.[25] So it is obvious that even in these well-designed studies the effect does not clearly hold for both sets of partisans.

Measurement Problems. Even so, many reports of *de facto* selectivity may well overestimate the magnitude of the effect because of the kinds of measures used. Perhaps the most obvious problem is that only one interview has been used in most studies. If, in this interview, attitudes and exposure favor the same side

---

[22] *Op. cit.,* p. 96.

[23] *Ibid.,* p. 111.

[24] *Ibid.,* p. 96. The Republican "constant partisans" were slightly more selective than would be expected from availability alone, while late-deciding Republicans were slightly less so. Constant and late-deciding Democrats, alike, were exposed to more supportive propaganda than would be expected from availability (*ibid.,* pp. 82, 164). These percentages all exclude respondents exposed equally to both sides, and exclude neutral propaganda.

[25] B. R. Berelson, P. F. Lazarsfeld, and W. N. McPhee, *Voting: A Study of Opinion Formation in a Presidential Election,* Chicago, University of Chicago Press, 1954, p. 245.

of an issue, the interpretation is ambiguous: the congruence may reflect either attitude change or *de facto* selectivity.[26] It is not ambiguous, of course, when the attitude or preference has been unequivocally proven to antedate the opportunities for exposure, as, for instance, when the respondent is known to have bought a particular car before the specific ads in question appeared, or in panel studies. However, most studies do not allow this, and must simply hope the respondent is recalling accurately, ignore the possibility of attitude change altogether, or try to argue it away. None of these is a substitute for an advance measure, and each one maximizes the probability of obtaining *de facto* selectivity, since any attitude change is likely to reduce the discrepancy between communication and respondent's position, rather than increase it.

Second, almost all studies have depended upon retrospective self-reports of exposure, rather than direct and immediate observation of it. It is not possible to say with any certainty what kind of bias this may introduce (owing to selective memory, selective reporting, etc.), but it does seem highly likely to be a systematic bias in any given study. This shortcoming is, of course, a much more difficult one to remedy.

Alternative Predictors. Two general possibilities arise when we consider whether other variables are better predictors of selectivity than attitudes. One is relatively straightforward: sometimes other variables simply are more strongly correlated with selectivity than are political or social attitudes. This raises the question of which is the more likely causal agent. The second possibility is that other variables, themselves associated with differences in *absolute* rates of exposure, have artifactually produced *de facto* selectivity.

As an illustration of the first possibility, let us consider a case in which the communications are expressly ideological, and in which one would thus think exposure to be unequivocally determined by ideological preferences. Those attending the Christian Anti-Communist Crusade were indeed unrepresentative ideologically, but also, as it happened, religiously (only one-third as many Catholics as in the Bay Area generally), racially (no nonwhites in the sample at all, as opposed to 12 per cent in the Bay Area generally), educationally (52 per cent were college graduates, as opposed to 13 per cent in the Bay Area), and so on.[27] Clearly, the school was an upper-middle-class WASP affair. Political conservatism predicted attendance rather well, but then so did a variety of other background variables. In fact, a substantial number of Crusaders ascribed their own attendance to church influence. So it may be quite arbitrary to give ideology the major credit for exposure, even in this seemingly obvious case.

[26] Raymond and Alice Bauer take a strong position on this point. In the absence of any other information, they say, one must interpret any such correlations as "a result of *selective exposure*, rather than evidence for the effects of communications." See their "America, Mass Society, and Mass Media," *Journal of Social Issues*, Vol. 16, 1960, p. 29.

[27] Wolfinger *et al.*, *op. cit.*

To illustrate the second possibility, consider the variable that predicts differences in absolute rates of exposure to public affairs communications most powerfully, years of education. Now, clearly, *de facto* selectivity effects could be obtained with any issue about which highly educated people generally disagree with poorly educated people, if we consider only propaganda favorable to the former's position. There are numerous positions of this kind: pro-civil liberties, pro-civil rights, and internationalist positions are (at present) positively related to years of education. So, naturally, pro-civil liberties, pro-civil rights, and pro-internationalism propaganda reaches mainly those sympathetic to it. A typical example is the massive pro-UN campaign in Cincinnati in 1947-1948. As usual, those who had favored the UN at the beginning of the campaign turned out to have received most of the pro-UN propaganda. It was therefore concluded that, "if there was an increase in exposure [during the campaign], *it was their previous orientation* [i.e. attitude toward the UN] *which determined the extent to which people exposed themselves to further information about the United Nations*" (emphasis ours).[28] But the best way to be exposed to the campaign was to go to church, attend service club and PTA meetings, be a regular newspaper reader, have the radio on most of the time, and talk to one's children about what had happened in school. Thus, not surprisingly, college-educated persons were exposed to the campaign at a rate *four times* that of grammar-school-educated persons. These are all things that well-educated people are likely to do more than poorly educated people, regardless of how they feel about the United Nations. So exposure to the campaign is at least as well predicted by education as by internationalist attitudes, and education seems to be the more likely predictor.

Thus many reports of *de facto* selective exposure may represent little more than cases in which highly educated persons, who normally are over-represented in any audience for public affairs presentations, also share a common set of political, social, and/or economic attitudes. Star and Hughes are clearly on solid ground in recommending that information campaigns be directed especially at "women, the relatively uneducated, the elderly, and the poor," since they are normally least likely to be reached.[29] However, low rates of exposure of such population groups must be distinguished from alleged avoidance of information because of discrepant beliefs.[30]

[28] Shirley A. Star and Helen M. Hughes, "Report of an Educational Campaign: The Cincinnati Plan for the United Nations," *American Journal of Sociology*, Vol. 55, 1950, p. 398.

[29] *Ibid.*, p. 397.

[30] In fact, sometimes well-educated groups expose themselves to discrepant propaganda even more than groups who should agree with it. Lazarsfeld reports that the "high" socio-economic class listened to two of the most important New Deal speeches at a rate better than 50 per cent greater than the "low" class. It seems unlikely that this great interest among "high" class listeners arose because they generally agreed so much with the two speakers, Franklin Roosevelt and Hugo Black. P. F. Lazarsfeld, *Radio and the Printed Page*, New York, Duell, Sloan, and Pearce, 1940, pp. 26–28.

Conclusion.   So, on several grounds, published reports of *de facto* selectivity fall somewhat short of representing ideal proof that people do in fact "tend to expose themselves to those mass communications which are in accord with their existing attitudes." Often it has not been established that these attitudes actually did exist beforehand, and often it is not entirely clear what the pattern of exposure actually was. The magnitude of the effect seems rather small, or limited to one set of partisans in some cases. And allegedly selective information seekers often cannot be distinguished from promiscuous information gatherers, because it is not clear that they have both high rates of exposure to friendly propaganda and low rates of exposure to hostile propaganda. Finally, "existing attitudes" often represent only one of several variables that correlate highly with exposure, and their selection as the best predictor may be unnecessarily arbitrary.

Nevertheless, it still seems likely that *de facto* selectivity holds, as a descriptive generalization, on many occasions and for many people. Clearly, demonstrations of the effect have been considerably less conclusive than one might think. But even if it had been clearly demonstrated, it would not indicate that people prefer exposure to supportive information, although that would be a very natural implication. So the next step is to examine the evidence for selective exposure defined in the third sense cited above.

IS THERE A GENERAL PSYCHOLOGICAL PREFERENCE FOR SUPPORTIVE INFORMATION?

If a person is given a choice between supportive and nonsupportive information, will he prefer exposure to the former, all other things being equal? This is the crucial question, and there is a considerable amount of research bearing on it. The typical procedure has been to measure a subject's opinion on an issue and then determine which of several communications on the issue he would like to read or hear. The opinions have ranged from firmly established ones, such as political preferences and ideas about child development, to those probably adopted for the first time during the experiment itself, such as preferences between verdicts in mock murder trials or essay and multiple-choice examinations. The communications have been, most often, written articles offered in a way that clearly communicates their positions on the issue. However, the choice has sometimes been between oral presentations, and sometimes actual exposure, rather than stated preferences, has been measured. The appropriate dependent variable, in all cases, is a measure of interest in supportive information relative to interest in nonsupportive information. "Supportive" information is usually defined simply as the communicator's taking the same general position as the subject, and "nonsupportive" as his taking the opposite position.

Preference for Supportive Information. A clear preference for supportive information was obtained in two studies. In one, persons who had recently bought a car were shown eight envelopes allegedly containing advertisements for different brands of cars, and asked to indicate which two they would most like to read. Over 80 per cent of the respondents chose an envelope containing ads for their own car (presumably supportive of their purchase), as contrasted with the chance figure of 25 per cent. The difference is highly significant.[31]

Freedman and Sears gave California citizens a choice among several pamphlets on the two candidates in the 1962 gubernatorial contest. Considering only those subjects who selected a partisan pamphlet as their first choice, 58 per cent chose one favoring their candidate. This, too, was significantly greater than chance (50 per cent).[32]

In both these studies it was possible to control for any special attractiveness of one alternative, because subjects holding various positions were tested. In a third study this was not possible, so the results are equivocal. Adams gave mothers of young children a choice between two speeches to be given later at a local university—one supporting the hereditary theory of child development, the other supporting an environmental position. The speech conforming to their own initial opinions was selected by 75.9 per cent of the mothers, significantly greater than chance.[33] Unfortunately, 94 per cent of the mothers expressed a pro-environmental view, and the few pro-heredity mothers were not considered in the analysis, thus confounding preference with initial position. A pro-environment speech would seem to be more useful and intrinsically interesting, regardless of whether or not one agreed with it: information on how environment shapes behavior in often useful to the mother of a young child, while information on the genes' impact may not be quite so timely. So, in the absence of pro-heredity subjects, it is not possible to assess whether the obtained preference for the environmental talk was due to its universal attractiveness or to its supportiveness.

The results of two other studies are even more difficult to interpret. Mills, Aronson, and Robinson gave students a choice between taking a multiple-choice exam or an essay exam, and then asked them to rank their interest in various articles favorable or unfavorable to the two kinds of exams. Some subjects were given a choice among positively oriented articles, and these subjects significantly preferred those favorable to the chosen exam. Others chose among negatively oriented articles, and these subjects slightly (not

[31] Ehrlich *et al., op. cit.*

[32] J. L. Freedman and D. O. Sears, "Voters' Preferences among Types of Information," *American Psychologist,* Vol. 18, 1963, p. 375 (abstract).

[33] J. S. Adams, "Reduction of Cognitive Dissonance by Seeking Consonant Information," *Journal of Abnormal and Social Psychology,* Vol. 62, 1961, pp. 74–78.

significantly) preferred articles unfavorable to the chosen exam.[34] In other words, supportive information was preferred among the former subjects, nonsupportive slightly preferred among the latter.

Rosen's attempt at replication of this study raises an important question about even these rather equivocal results. One would think that the most relevant belief to the student's choice of exam is his estimate of which one will give him the better grade. Thus, to support this belief, an article should argue that the chosen exam will give him the better mark, and, to challenge it, an article should take the position that he would have done better on the kind of test he did not choose. In fact, the article titles used by Mills *et al.* dealt with matters such as the difficulty of the tests and how much anxiety they usually aroused, and not on how well the subject would do relative to the rest of the class. It is therefore doubtful that any of the articles were supportive or nonsupportive in any meaningful sense. Rosen therefore improved the design by including two such articles. These suggested that the subject had made the wrong choice, e.g., "These authors present some evidence that students who prefer essay exams generally do a lot better on objective tests." Clearly, this title is nonsupportive for those who chose essay exams.

Rosen's findings are both striking and odd. Considering all article titles, the subjects significantly preferred information favorable to the chosen exam. But 67 per cent of the subjects preferred the clearly nonsupportive new title to the other new title![35] This certainly conflicts with the over-all result of the study. And the two studies, considered together, provide evidence of about every kind: with positive articles, subjects prefer supportive information; with negative articles, they have no preference; and with titles advocating reversal of choice (and thus clearly differing in supportiveness), they strongly prefer nonsupportive information.

No Preference.   A series of experiments show no preference between supportive and nonsupportive information. In two separate studies, Feather found that neither smokers nor nonsmokers had any significant preference between an article suggesting that smoking causes lung cancer and one arguing that smoking does not cause lung cancer. Similarly, Mills and Ross obtained opinions on the use of television as an educational tool, and then asked the subjects to indicate their interest in reading articles for and against their position. In none of a variety of experimental conditions was there any significant preference for either supportive or nonsupportive articles. And Jecker told subjects they would play a competitive game in cooperation with a partner, and then measured the time devoted to reading favorable and unfavorable information about the partner. Exposure times for the two kinds of information

[34] J. Mills, E. Aronson, and H. Robinson, "Selectivity in Exposure to Information," *Journal of Abnormal and Social Psychology*, Vol. 59, 1959, pp. 250–253.

[35] S. Rosen, "Post-decision Affinity for Incompatible Information," *Journal of Abnormal and Social Psychology*, Vol. 63, 1961, pp. 188–190.

did not differ, regardless of whether the subject had already chosen the partner, was about to choose the partner, or was only given limited choice in the matter.[36]

In three other studies, each subject read excerpts from a (fictitious) murder-trial transcript, and gave his verdict. He then indicated his preferences among several articles dealing with the case, two of which were pro-acquittal and two pro-conviction. Considering only these four articles, Sears found that exactly 50 per cent of the subjects preferred an article supporting their votes; Sears and Freedman found that 45.4 per cent preferred a supportive article; and the figure for the third study was 43.1 per cent. In the three studies combined, 46.1 per cent ($N = 317$) ranked a supportive article first. This slight preference for nonsupportive information is not significant, nor do the percentages for the individual studies differ significantly from chance (50 per cent in each case). Furthermore, actual exposure was measured in the last two of these studies. Each subject was given either a supportive or a nonsupportive communication to read, and the length of time he spent reading it was recorded. In the first study, subjects spent more time reading nonsupportive articles than supportive, but in the second study there was no difference between the two types of articles.[37]

Thus, several studies demonstrate no preference between supportive and nonsupportive information. It might be argued, however, that the jury situation, in particular, is not ideal for obtaining selective exposure effects, owing to natural pressures on jurors toward impartiality and fairness. Although it would be pleasant to believe that people suddenly become impartial, fair, and objective when they become jurors, it seems quite implausible. Other data collected in these experiments indicated that the subjects reacted in a highly partisan manner to the communications they actually read: they evaluated the supportive communication much more favorably than its nonsupportive counterpart in each experiment, regardless of which verdict they had supported. So partisanship was not absent, but it operated on information evaluation rather than on information selection.

[36] N. T. Feather, "Cigarette Smoking and Lung Cancer: A Study of Cognitive Dissonance," *Australian Journal of Psychology*, Vol. 14, 1962, pp. 55–64; N. T. Feather, "Cognitive Dissonance, Sensitivity, and Evaluation," *Journal of Abnormal and Social Psychology*, Vol. 66, 1963, pp. 157–163; J. Mills and A. Ross, "Effects of Commitment and Certainty upon Interest in Supporting Information," *Journal of Abnormal and Social Psychology*, Vol. 68, 1964, pp. 552–555; J. D. Jecker, "Selective Exposure to New Information," in L. Festinger, *Conflict, Decision and Dissonance*, Stanford, Calif., Stanford University Press, 1964.

[37] D. O. Sears, "Opinion Formation and Information Preferences in an Adversary Situation," *Journal of Experimental Social Psychology*, Vol. 2, 1966, pp. 130–142; D. O. Sears and J. L. Freedman, "Commitment, Information Utility, and Selective Exposure," *USN Technical Reports, ONR*, Nonr-233(54) NR 171–350, No. 12, August 1963; D. O. Sears and J. L. Freedman, "The Effects of Expected Familiarity with Arguments upon Opinion Change and Selective Exposure," *Journal of Personality and Social Psychology*, Vol. 2, 1965, pp. 420–426.

Preference for Nonsupportive Information.   In one of the studies described above there was actually some indication of a preference for *nonsupportive* information: Rosen obtained a general preference for the nonsupportive choice-reversal article. Several other studies have produced quite convincing evidence of a preference for nonsupportive information.

In Brodbeck's study, subjects in groups of eight were led to believe that the group as a whole was evenly divided on the issue of wire tapping. Then each subject chose the group member whose opinions on wire tapping she would most like to hear. By chance 42.9 per cent of the subjects would have been expected to choose someone they agreed with, but only 20.2 per cent did so. That is, they strongly tended to choose someone with whom they disagreed; presumably they preferred to hear nonsupportive information.[38]

Feather's results were described above only for smokers as a group and for nonsmokers as a group, without considering the most relevant belief involved: Is there convincing evidence that smoking leads to lung cancer? In the first of these studies, Feather divided each group into those who believed there was convincing evidence for the relationship and those who believed the evidence was not very convincing. Smokers of both kinds preferred the article *contradicting* their beliefs, while nonsmokers showed no particular exposure preference, regardless of their position. Hence, this again is evidence of preference for nonsupportive information, in subjects who were presumably highly ego-involved about an important issue.[39]

In two final studies, the subjects' opinions were experimentally manipulated. Sears gave subjects brief synopses of the testimony at murder trials. The content of the evidence was varied only slightly, but crucially, so that all subjects read very similar cases, but generally emerged with different verdict preferences. They then were offered either the defense or the prosecution summation. Of those given "guilty" cases, 31.2 per cent preferred the supportive summation; of those given "innocent" cases, 27.3 per cent preferred the supportive summation. Both differ significantly from chance (50 per cent), so this study, too, records a clear preference for nonsupportive information.[40]

Even more dramatic is Freedman's study. Subjects listened to a (fictitious) interview between a candidate for an overseas conference and the person in charge of the conference. For some subjects, the candidate was made to sound very good; for others, very bad. After each subject evaluated the candidate, he was offered a choice between two additional evaluations of the candidate by people who supposedly knew him well, one of which was described as very favorable, and the other as very unfavorable. Only 18 subjects

[38] May Brodbeck, "The Role of Small Groups in Mediating the Effects of Propaganda," *Journal of Abnormal and Social Psychology*, Vol. 52, 1956, pp. 166–170.

[39] Feather, 1962, *op. cit.*

[40] D. O. Sears, "Biased Indoctrination and Selectivity of Exposure to New Information," *Sociometry*, Vol. 28, 1965, pp. 363–376.

were run because the results were so consistent and striking. Only 1 subject chose the evaluation that agreed with his own, and 17 chose the nonsupportive evaluation.[41]

Conclusions. By now it must be clear that there is no consistent result in this research. Five studies showed some preference for supportive information: Ehrlich *et al.* (1957), Freedman and Sears (1963), Adams (1961), Mills *et al.* (positive articles) (1961), and Rosen (positive articles) (1961). Eight showed no preference: Mills *et al.* (negative articles) (1959), Feather (nonsmokers only) (1962), Feather (1963), Mills and Ross (1964), Jecker (1964), Sears (1966), and Sears and Freedman (1963 and 1965). And five showed a preference for nonsupportive information: Rosen (choice-reversal articles) (1961), Brodbeck (1956), Feather (smokers only) (1962), Sears (1965), and Freedman (1965a). The conclusion seems clear. The available evidence fails to indicate the presence of a general preference for supportive information.

COGNITIVE DISSONANCE AND SELECTIVE EXPOSURE

Even if there is no general preference one way or the other, there must be conditions under which supportive information will be preferred. The most concrete specification of what these conditions might be has been made within the context of cognitive dissonance theory. Two specific hypotheses have been offered, each based on the assumption that dissonance may be reduced or avoided by selectivity in information seeking. One is that selectivity increases following a decision or a commitment to do something, and the other is that selectivity increases following involuntary exposure to nonsupportive information. Several studies have been done to test these hypotheses, each based essentially on a comparison between a high-dissonance condition and a

---

[41] J. L. Freedman, "Preference for Dissonant Information," *Journal of Personality and Social Psychology*, Vol. 2, 1965a, pp. 287–289. Four additional articles have appeared since the completion of this paper. Brock found that smokers preferred supportive information on lung cancer more than did nonsmokers, but did not avoid nonsupportive information to any greater extent (T. C. Brock, "Commitment to Exposure as a Determinant of Information Receptivity," *Journal of Personality and Social Psychology*, Vol. 2, 1965, pp. 10–19). In only one of three experiments does Mills report respondents in a market research situation seeking supportive information, but in all three he reports avoidance of dissonant information (J. Mills, "Avoidance of Dissonant Information," *Journal of Personality and Social Psychology*, Vol. 2, 1965, pp. 589–593, and "Effect of Certainty about a Decision upon Postdecision Exposure to Consonant and Dissonant Information," *Journal of Personality and Social Psychology*, Vol. 2, 1965, pp. 749–752). Finally, in a study done in the 1964 presidential election, apparently supportive information was not significantly sought nor nonsupportive information significantly avoided (R. J. Rhine, "The 1964 Presidential Election and Curves of Information Seeking and Avoiding," *Journal of Personality and Social Psychology*, Vol. 5, 1967, pp. 416–423). So the evidence continues to be highly inconclusive.

low-dissonance condition. Since these studies have been reviewed intensively elsewhere, it is not necessary to go into detail about them here. It is enough to say that the results are again equivocal. Of the five studies specifically designed to test the first hypothesis, only one, a survey study, offers even a marginally significant difference in selectivity between high- and low-dissonance conditions. None of the three studies testing the second hypothesis provides a significant difference between two such conditions.[42]

A third hypothesis has been offered more recently, that selectivity is inversely related to the amount of confidence a person has in his initial opinion. Two studies are directly relevant to this hypothesis. The first supported it, while the second, an attempt at an exact replication of the first, yielded no favorable evidence.[43]

Thus the use of dissonance theory to specify particular circumstances under which selectivity would occur has not been a great success. Unfortunately, it remains the only systematic theoretical effort, as well as the only one that has generated a body of empirical research.

VOLUNTARY EXPOSURE TO INFORMATION

It is possible to take an entirely different approach to the lack of support for the selective exposure hypothesis. Rather than attempt to explain, or explain away, the negative results, it might be fruitful to accept them at face value (at least for the time being) and turn instead to the more general problem of the factors that *do* affect voluntary exposure to information. In this way, it might be possible to understand more about exposure in general, and thus to determine why *de facto* selectivity occurs.

Education and Social Class.   One class of factors is those individual differences or predispositions that are theoretically independent of partisan preferences. As indicated above, clearly the most powerful known predictor of voluntary exposure to mass communications of an informational or public affairs sort is the general factor of education and social class. Two representative studies indicate the magnitude of its predictive power. Star and Hughes report that 68 per cent of their college-educated respondents were exposed to the UN campaign in at least three media, while only 17 per cent of the grammar-school-educated respondents were, only one-fourth as many.[44] Key

---

[42] For a review of these studies, see J. L. Freedman and D. O. Sears, "Selective Exposure," in L. Berkowitz, ed., *Advances in Experimental Social Psychology*, Vol. 2, New York, Academic Press, 1965.

[43] L. K. Canon, "Self-confidence and Selective Exposure to Information," in Festinger, 1964, *op. cit.*; J. L. Freedman, "Confidence, Utility and Selective Exposure: A Partial Replication," *Journal of Personality and Social Psychology*, Vol. 2, 1965b, pp. 778–780.

[44] *Op. cit.*

presents Survey Research Center data indicating that college-educated persons comprised over four times as many of those who were exposed to the 1956 presidential campaign in at least four media as did grammar-school-educated respondents. And of those exposed to the campaign in no media, 3 per cent were college-educated and 58 per cent had only grade-school educations, almost twenty times as many.[45] So, in contrast to the rather pale and ephemeral effects of selectivity, de facto or otherwise, education yields enormous differences. Why it produces such differences is not known and remains a provocative question, and a subtler one than might appear at first glance.[46]

Utility of Information. The perceived utility of the information is another factor likely to have a major effect on exposure preferences. It is obvious that information varies greatly in the extent to which it will serve a useful, practical purpose, although this fact has often been ignored in previous research. It seems likely that the greater the perceived utility of the information, the greater will be the subject's desire to be exposed to it. Utility may have been an important variable in several exposure experiments. For example, in Adams's study mentioned earlier, in which he offered women a choice between a talk on environmental factors and one on hereditary factors in child behavior, the former was potentially of greater practical importance and was preferred by a 3-to-1 margin.[47] Similarly, Maccoby et al. offered housewives a pamphlet on toilet training and recorded how many requested the pamphlet; they sent the pamphlet to a different group of women and recorded how many actually read it. The subjects were divided into those who had an only child between the ages of three and twelve months (critical group), those who had an older child (post group), and those who had no children (pre group). Presumably the pamphlet was most useful to the critical group. This group expressed more interest in getting the pamphlet (71 vs. 36 per cent and 38 per cent for the other groups); and a greater percentage of them read it when it was sent to them (88 vs. 48 and 47 per cent).[48] And both Mills et al. and Rosen found that students were more interested in reading about the merits and demerits alike of the exam they had decided to take than about the exam they had decided not to take.[49] Finally, Canon and Freedman explicitly varied utility.

[45] V. O. Key, Jr., *Public Opinion and American Democracy*, New York, Knopf, 1961, p. 349.

[46] For example, see the discussion in R. E. Lane and D. O. Sears, *Public Opinion*, Englewood Cliffs, N. J., Prentice-Hall, 1964, pp. 62–63. Another possibility worth mentioning is that social class or education may be directly related to selectivity. Most of the experimental studies cited here were conducted with middle-class college students, and other types of subjects might have yielded greater support for selective exposure. However, there are no relevant data available, and, given the record to date, we would hesitate to bet on these being critical factors.

[47] *Op. cit.*

[48] N. Maccoby, A. K. Romney, J. S. Adams, and Eleanor E. Maccoby, "Critical Periods in Seeking and Accepting Information," in *Paris-Stanford Studies in Communications*, Stanford, Calif., Institute for Communications Research, 1962.

[49] *Op. cit.*

The subjects made a decision on what was supposedly a case study in business and were then offered a choice of articles supportive or nonsupportive of their choice. Before rating the articles, they were told either that they would have to present their reasons for deciding on the case as they did, or that they would engage in a written debate in which they would have to rebut arguments from the opposing side. It was assumed that in the former case supportive information would be more useful, since it would provide necessary reasons for their decision. In the latter case, nonsupportive information would presumably be more useful, since the subject could not prepare his rebuttal without knowing what the opposition believed. In both studies, the more useful information was significantly preferred to the less useful, regardless of which was supportive or nonsupportive of the subject's decision.[50]

Thus, the evidence strongly supports the contention that information that is expected to serve a practical purpose is preferred to less useful information. And, just as with education, the effects are large and highly significant.

Past History of Exposure on the Issue.   One would surely think that an individual's past history of exposure would influence his subsequent information preferences. Indeed, in several studies it has been shown that exposure to one side's arguments is likely to increase the chances of voluntary exposure to the other side's. As indicated above, Sears gave subjects testimony indicating, in some cases, the defendant's guilt, and in others, his innocence. After being introduced to the case in this one-sided manner, the subjects strongly preferred to see the summation given by the attorney favoring the opposite view.[51] In another study, Sears gave subjects neither, one, or both attorneys' summations from a court trial. In the no-summation and two-summation conditions, subsequent information preferences were unsystematic, and unrelated to the subject's opinions. When given a single summation, however, the subject strongly preferred information favoring the *other* side, regardless of whether or not they sympathized with it.[52] And when Freedman gave subjects material biased against a candidate for an overseas conference, subjects preferred material favorable to him; if the bias was in his favor, they preferred material unfavorable to him.[53]

These three studies give, therefore, a highly consistent picture: in each case, when subjects were exposed initially to biased or one-sided information, they later preferred information favoring the opposite position, regardless of whether it attacked or supported their own position. How far this generalization may be extended is, however, unclear at this time.

Education, information utility, and past history of exposure are but three of the many factors that no doubt influence exposure preferences and

[50] *Op. cit.*
[51] Sears, 1965, *op. cit.*
[52] Sears, 1966, *op. cit.*
[53] Freedman, 1965a, *op. cit.*

rates of exposure. These are important in the present context for two main reasons: first, they have been demonstrated to affect exposure in a powerful way, whereas demonstrations of selective exposure have been very weak. Hence, selectivity may at best be a rather trivial variable relative to other influences upon exposure. Second, they offer ways of explaining the occurrence of *de facto* selectivity without assuming the existence of underlying preferences for supportive information. As indicated earlier, propaganda may often reach mainly those sympathetic to it simply because it advocates positions generally shared by those who have high rates of exposure to *all* propaganda. And when supportive information is most useful, as in the case of Adams's pro-environment talk or articles describing the merits of an exam one must take, it may be preferred; but when nonsupportive information is more useful, as in the case of Rosen's choice-reversal article, it may be preferred. So *de facto* selectivity effects may occur as a result of particular combinations of variables that are themselves extraneous to the supportive-nonsupportive dimension.

CONCLUSIONS

This paper has been concerned primarily with evaluating the evidence for the existence of selectivity in voluntary exposure to information. There seems to be some evidence (although not as unequivocal as often claimed) for the existence of *de facto* selectivity. Most audiences for mass communications apparently tend to overrepresent persons already sympathetic to the views being propounded, and most persons seem to be exposed disproportionately to communications that support their opinions.

On the other hand, a considerable amount of experimental research has uncovered no general psychological preference for supportive information. Under some circumstances, people seem to prefer information that supports their opinions; under other circumstances, people seem to prefer information that contradicts their opinions. In no way can the available evidence be said to support the contention that people generally seek out supportive information and avoid nonsupportive information.

These two conclusions are paradoxical. How can it be that people are in fact selective, yet display no trace of a general preference for supportive information? A variety of answers have been provided above and need not be summarized here. Most generally, examples of *de facto* selectivity come from communication settings in which exposure is complexly determined by a great many factors that are incidental to the supportiveness of the information. We have reviewed research on only three of these factors, but many more are surely as important. Clearly, these factors can themselves on occasion produce *de facto* selectivity. One general possibility is that they do more often than they do not, presumably because in natural communication situations such variables are not randomly related to communicators' positions on various social, political, economic, religious, etc., issues. For example, those who find a particular kind of information most useful may also sympathize most with the particular editorial stance that happens, in most cases, to be paired with it. Financiers find the *Wall Street Journal's* financial news very helpful and also (probably incidentally) tend to agree with its politics. College professors and diplomats rely upon the *New York Times's* comprehensive news coverage and often agree with its editorials as well. These are not merely coincidences. Nor are they necessarily examples of selective exposure. However, it is beyond the scope of this paper to inquire into the reasons for such correlations.

Another possibility is that selectivity may be considerably more important on a long-term basis than at any given moment. Many people may be willing to take on the task of exposing themselves to nonsupportive information on any given occasion. Yet it may be quite tiring and aggravating, and thus something to be undertaken only at widely separated moments of particular intellectual fortitude. So dramatic selectivity in preferences may not appear at any given moment in time, but, over a long period, people may organize their surroundings in a way that ensures *de facto* selectivity. The data relevant to this point deal mostly with the acquisition of friends and spouses (rather than with information or exposure preferences), and so also lie beyond the scope of this paper. Nevertheless, the argument is intriguing and the data have been ingeniously gathered.[54]

Finally, this research suggests a change of emphasis in our thinking about how people deal with discrepant information. It has generally been assumed that selective exposure and other processes that bar information reception are prime mechanisms by which people resist influence.[55] Perhaps such processes are not very important after all. Feather reports that smokers do not avoid reading unpleasant information about smoking and lung cancer; rather, they subject it to careful and mercilessly unsympathetic scrutiny.[56] Perhaps resistance to influence is accomplished most often and most successfully at the level of information evaluation, rather than at the level of selective seeking and avoiding of information.

[54] T. M. Newcomb, "The Persistence and Regression of Changed Attitudes," *Journal of Social Issues*, Vol. 19, 1963, pp. 3–14; Berelson *et al., op. cit.*

[55] Cf. Klapper, *op. cit.*

[56] Feather, 1963, *op. cit.*

Demetrios Papageorgis*[1]

WARNING
AND PERSUASION

Studies dealing with the effects on audience opinions of
(a) advance information about the topics and the direction
of argument of forthcoming communications (warning) and
(b) instructions that describe the experiment as a study of
opinion change (persuasion context) are reviewed.
Conclusions include: (a) So far, warning and persuasion
context have not been viewed as separate manipulations;
(b) their effects on postcommunication opinion change are
not clear; (c) warning and persuasion context probably
cause precommunication opinion change. It is suggested
that neither warning nor persuasion context, by themselves,
are crucial variables in postcommunication opinion change.
On the other hand, in some instances persuasion may begin
prior to actual exposure to persuasive communications.

A disguised subject orientation or context is a notable characteristic of
most of the experimental research in opinion change. The experimenter
attempts to hide from his subjects the fact that he is investigating persuasion
by calling to their attention some other plausible interpretation of his objectives. Use of a persuasion orientation or context, where the subject is explicitly
informed that the experiment deals with persuasion or opinion change, has
been very limited. Moreover, in addition to the disguised context, experimenters
refrain from giving their subject specific advance information about the topics
and positions that the forthcoming persuasive communications advocate.

*The University of British Columbia, Canada.

[1] The author wishes to thank Paul C. Rosenblatt for his valuable comments on an
earlier version of this paper.

Reprinted from the *Psychological Bulletin,* 70 (1968), 271–82, with permission of the
author and the American Psychological Association.

Thus, the subject in a typical opinion-change experiment is deceived about its purpose and lacks concrete foreknowledge of the material he will be exposed to.

The term "forewarning" is used to describe the disproportionately small number of opinion-change studies that use persuasion contexts and/or provide the subjects with specific advance information about forthcoming communications. "Warning" appears to be just as sufficient and shorter. The inconsistency in the definition of the term, either as persuasion context or as specific advance information or both, is a more serious matter. There is no empirical evidence that the effects of these two possible manipulations are either the same or cumulative. Furthermore, the two definitions are clearly distinguishable both conceptually and in terms of research strategy. The argument, then, for a sharp, agreed-upon definition of warning can be made at the outset. It is also necessary to divest warning of its customarily negative lexical connotation.

The relative scarcity of opinion-change research within a persuasion context probably results from the usually implicit, infrequently (e.g., Lazarsfeld, Berelson, & Gaudet, 1948) explicit, assumption that awareness of persuasion reduces or eliminates the impact of persuasive communications. The saying "forewarned is forearmed" illustrates this assumption, but, as will be shown subsequently, its few empirical investigations have produced contradictory outcomes. Adherence to this assumption, however, is often justified: Opinion-change research has focused on effects of independent variables other than context (e.g., order of presentation, source of the communication, type of appeal), and it is understandable that experimenters chose contexts that, in their opinion, would maximize opinion change as well as reflect one type of real-life persuasion situation. One also suspects the occasional influence of a second factor related to what almost amounts to an unwritten rule of social psychological research, that experimenters should deceive their subjects about experimental objectives (Kelman, 1967).

The lack of persuasion research within the persuasion context may thus be attributed to both rational and irrational causes. The author contends that a strong argument for increased emphasis on opinion-change studies within the persuasion context can be built on the basis of three considerations.

First, there is the practical difficulty of disguising persuasion experiments in ways that are plausible and acceptable to *all* the subjects. Experimenters have been quite ingenious in this respect and, on the whole, successful. Still, the deceits can introduce confounding effects into the experimental design. Some studies include checks on the acceptance of the deceit, but these checks tend to be cursory and insensitive; unfortunately, if their sensitivity were increased, the percentage of false positives would probably also increase. At any rate, these minimal checks have indicated that a small percentage of the subjects recognizes the true purpose of the experiment. What remains unknown, however, is the proportion of the subjects who neither recognize the persuasive purpose of the experiment nor accept the disguise at face value: These individuals may formulate their own plausible interpretations of the proceedings and thus, in effect, nullify the single disguised context that the experimenter had intended. This lack of experimental control that may amount to an unavoidable feature of disguised contexts is complicated further by the very real likelihood that the "naive" subject may have become a rare phenomenon in the undergraduate samples that are used in most opinion-change studies (Kelman, 1967).

Second, the assumption that awareness of persuasion reduces its impact needs further study. It has been noted above that empirical support for this assumption is scarce and ambiguous. The persuasion context has been found to reduce opinion change (e.g., Kiesler & Kiesler, 1964) to have no effect on opinion change (e.g., McGuire & Papageorgis, 1962), and to enhance opinion change (Mills, 1966; Mills & Aronson, 1965). It appears likely that all three outcomes are real and predictable on the basis of other variables, such as the attractiveness of the communicator, the neutral or negative content of the warning, and so forth. Yet in the absence of relevant and systematic research conclusions are inappropriate. It is reasonable, however, to hypothesize that the effects of warning on subsequent persuasion will range all the way from substantial decrement to substantial enhancement depending on the values of other variables.[2] Elaboration and further suggestions are presented in the final section of this review.

Third, in addition to the effects of warning on subsequent persuasion, warning has been shown to produce immediate effects on opinions prior to any persuasive communication or even in the absence of any expected communication (McGuire & Millman, 1965; Papageorgis, 1967). These findings suggest that warning, in addition to its possible "immunizing" role in persuasion (e.g., McGuire & Papageorgis, 1962), may also serve as a persuasive communication. It is also possible that opinion change, previously attributed solely to the impact of the persuasive communication, may begin during the precommunication period that follows warning (Deaux, 1967; McGuire & Millman, 1965). The review that follows touches on both the direct effects of warning and on its effects on subsequent persuasion.

THE RELEVANT LITERATURE

Effects of Warning on
Subsequent Persuasion

Studies Using Explicit Persuasion Contexts.   Only four studies known to the author clearly belong in this category, and two of these are unpublished.[3] Their distinguishing feature is that the instructions given to the subjects *ex-*

---

[2] The author is indebted to Paul C. Rosenblatt (personal communication, February 1967) for lending further support to the possibility of persuasion enhancement with warning.

[3] A study by Kerrick and McMillan (1961) which reported significantly less com-

plicitly and unambiguously labeled the experiment and/or the communication as persuasive. There are several other studies that used instructions which suggest that the subject's most likely inference would be that the experiment had to do with persuasion, but, since persuasion or opinion change were not explicitly mentioned in the instructions, these studies will be discussed in the next section.

McGuire and Papageorgis (1962) investigated the persuasion context and its possible immunizing effects against subsequent persuasive attack. The experiment was described to the undergraduate subjects either as a test of analytic thinking or as an investigation of susceptibility to persuasion. The persuasive communications argued against public health truisms, such as the advisability of annual chest X-ray examinations. The subjects were told in advance that they would read passages dealing with health topics, but no other information about the exact topics and the position advocated in the communications was given. Thus, in terms of the earlier distinction, the warning consisted of a persuasion orientation but did not include specific information about the forthcoming communications. The results of the experimental conditions that are relevant to the present discussion showed that the persuasive communications induced significant opinion change regardless of the context; moreover, mean differences between the persuasion and disguised contexts were trivial. Thus the assumption that warning (persuasion context) reduces communication impact found no support. The role of warning in immunization against subsequent persuasion was indirect: The results showed that the persuasion context enhanced the immunizing effectiveness of belief-supporting messages that, in some conditions, had preceded the persuasive attack. This study was criticized by Rosenblatt and Hicks (1966) who pointed out that the impact of the warning may have been weakened by the within-subjects experimental design: No subject received a propaganda message without also having been exposed to belief-bolstering messages on other issues. It is possible that the *absence* of the immunizing message on one issue increased the vulnerability of the subject's belief on that issue. Thus, the warning may have lost its immunizing effectiveness because it was coupled with a weakened belief.

In their experiment, Rosenblatt and Hicks (1966) compared the effects of disguised and persuasion orientations on communication acceptance. In the disguised orientation the subjects were told that the experiment dealt with the readability and interest value of written articles; they were also told that the article contained factual information and was written to educate

---

munication impact when subjects were informed that the purpose of the experiment was to assess attitude change could also be included. It should be noted, however, that the persuasion context in this instance was created *after* the presentation of the messages and prior to the final attitude measurement. Thus, this study resembles and, if so, contradicts the effects of the "afterwarning" manipulation used by Kiesler and Kiesler (1964) in an experiment discussed in this section.

people about chest X-rays. In the persuasion orientation the undergraduates were told that the experimenters were trying to influence attitudes about chest X-rays; they were also told that the communication used the standard persuasive techniques, including deception, scare tactics, and biased statistics. Thus, the warning created a persuasion context and, in addition, supplied advance information about the issue; unfortunately, the instructions also introduced positive evaluative comments in the disguised orientation and negative comments in the persuasion orientation. Accordingly, the study may involve a comparison between a *negative* persuasion context and a *positive* disguised context. The results showed significantly greater communication acceptance within the disguised context; however, because of the introduction of the positive and negative communication descriptions, the results cannot be viewed as contradicting the McGuire and Papageorgis (1962) findings. Together the results of the two studies are consistent with the hypothesis that it is not the warning itself, but its specific content that determines the effect on communication acceptance. A relatively simple experiment where a persuasion and a disguised context are varied orthogonally with positive and negative information about the communication may help resolve the issue.

In a third study (Kiesler & Kiesler, 1964), undergraduates read a communication that was described as an "emotional" appeal to increase United States foreign aid. The persuasion context was created by means of an asterisk that directed attention to a footnote which stated that the communication was designed to produce opinion change and that it was taken from a book entitled *Technique of Persuasion*. It is possible that the emotional nature of the article and its attributed origin added a negative aura to the general communication context, but this must remain a matter for conjecture. The asterisk appeared at the beginning of the article (forewarning), or at the end (afterwarning), or not at all (no warning); a fourth group of control subjects read an irrelevant message. The nonwarned and the afterwarned subjects showed significant opinion change, while no significant changes in opinion were found for the forewarned and for the control subjects. The authors concluded that the warning nullified the impact of the communication provided that it preceded the communication. The temporal placement requirement was explained in terms of dissonance theory (Festinger, 1957). Apart from reservations arising from the possibility of a generally negative communication context, the reduction of communication impact in a persuasion context receives strong support from the Kiesler and Kiesler results, particularly since the warning was a relatively incidental feature of the communication context. The discrepancy between their findings and those by McGuire and Papageorgis (1962) may be the result of differences in the types of issues and messages that were used in the two studies. Kiesler and Kiesler used an emotional appeal on a controversial issue, while the McGuire and Papageorgis communications appeared factual and dealt with cultural truisms. Two hypotheses may be suggested: (*a*) Warning reduces the impact of emotional appeals but does not affect factual appeals;

(*b*) Warning reduces the impact of communications on controversial issues but does not affect communications arguing against truisms accepted by the public. In connection with Hypothesis *b*, there is recent evidence (McGuire & Millman, 1965) that communications on technical, matter-of-fact issues have greater impact on opinions than communications that deal with emotional, unverifiable issues. Rosenblatt[4] reported that he has replicated the Kiesler and Kiesler findings with forewarning but has also obtained an afterwarning effect.

Finally, in a recent unpublished study, the author presented to undergraduates written, belief-discrepant communications dealing with the American contribution to outer space exploration and with the likelihood that graduate academic degrees will become prerequisites for types of employment now requiring only undergraduate degrees. The communications were "factual" and were described to the subjects as designed to produce opinion change. The topics and the direction of argument of the communications were also stated to the subjects in advance. Thus the warning manipulation created a persuasion context and also provided specific information about the communications. No disguised context was used, but half of the subjects were also warned that they would be asked to read the two communications, while the remaining subjects were told that they were serving in a "control" condition and would not be exposed to the communications. All subjects were then asked to express their beliefs about the two issues (see section "Direct Effects of Warning on Opinions" for the relevant results) and afterward read the communications. Postcommunication opinions moved significantly closer to the viewpoints advocated in the messages; in addition, there were no significant differences between the two groups. This study does not provide a comparison between disguised and persuasion orientations; it does, however, show that significant opinion change can result from communications despite warning. The study also shows that, given warning, certainty of self-exposure does not serve to reduce subsequent communication impact. This last conclusion may be at variance with the findings of Freedman and Sears (1965b) to be reviewed below.

In summary, the effects of persuasion context on communication acceptance are not clear. There are too few studies that have used explicit persuasion contexts and their results conflict. The persuasion context alone may not be a critical variable in communication acceptance; what may be crucial is the *type* of persuasion context and its content. The idea of "persuasion" often carries a negative connotation, but it can be also viewed in a neutral or positive light.[5] This notion receives support from everyday observation. It would receive

[4] Personal communication, July 1967.

[5] For example, communication impact may be greater in an experiment that investigates "persuasion," uses messages that appear reasonable and factual and are described as "effective," and attributes these messages to reputable and congruent sources, than in a similar experiment that uses a disguised orientation.

further support if the persuasion contexts created by McGuire and Papageorgis and by Papageorgis could be viewed as nearly "neutral," and if the persuasion contexts in the Rosenblatt and Hicks and the Kiesler and Kiesler studies could be viewed as "negative."

Studies using relatively ambiguous persuasion contexts. The studies reviewed in this section used instructions that did not explicitly mention persuasion or opinion change: the instructions, nonetheless, created contexts that could lead the subjects to infer that persuasion was involved. Usually these experiments are also classified as studies of forewarning. This section also includes digressions into two closely related areas, the effects of distraction and those of overhearing the persuasive communication.

Allyn and Festinger (1961) presented a speech to high school students which argued that teen-age drivers are dangerous. Subjects served in either a disguised or a persuasion context. In the disguised context (personality orientation) they were told that an expert was going to speak to them and that they were to assess his personality; the topic of the speech was not announced in advance. In the persuasion context (opinion orientation) the subjects were told that they would listen to an expert who thought that teen-age drivers were a menace and that they would give their opinions after the speech. Thus the opinion orientation includes advance information about the communication and creates a persuasion context quite similar to the contexts of the studies reviewed earlier; the study was not reviewed in the previous section only because the instructions did not mention opinion change or persuasion. Also to be noted is that the speaker description that was used in the opinion orientation may have placed upon him a negative valence. The results showed that the two orientations did not differ significantly in terms of the average opinion change that they produced. Further analyses, however, revealed that for the 37% of the subjects who held extreme initial opinions and/or stated that the issue was important, the personality orientation resulted in significantly greater opinion change than did the opinion orientation. The remaining 63% of the subjects were not even affected by the communication. Sears and Freedman (1965) reported an experiment in which undergraduates participated in a simulated jury situation. After voting for acquittal or conviction, the subjects read a communication that either favored their decision or argued against it. The position of the communication was not announced in advance, but the same communication was described as containing either arguments already familiar to the subject or "new" arguments. The results showed greater opinion change following communications that were described as containing new arguments, especially for those subjects who had earlier indicated less certainty about their verdict. Sears and Freedman presented evidence that their findings did not result from differences in communication evaluation, source credibility, or attention; they suggested instead that the greater impact of the "new" communication was caused by the subject's recognition that his verdict had been based on only partial information and the consequent invalidation of his prior commitment. Another plausible hypothesis may be suggested: The "new" communication is more likely to be perceived as a persuasive attempt and thus result in greater opinion change. This latter possibility remains to be tested. In view of subsequent findings of pre-communication opinion change (Deaux, 1967; McGuire & Millman, 1965; Papageorgis, 1967), it is also possible that most of the impact of the "new" communication occurred prior to its receipt.[6]

The tentative findings of Allyn and Festinger (1961) were reinterpreted by Festinger and Maccoby (1964). Rather than attributing the drop in communication impact to the defense-stimulating nature of the opinion orientation, they suggested that the personality orientation introduced distraction and thus enhanced communication impact by preventing the subject from developing effective counter-arguments against the communication. To test this hypothesis, they presented an aural communication on college fraternities in place of the sound track of the irrelevant color film *Day of the Painter* that was viewed by the subjects serving in the distraction condition. As predicted, distraction enhanced the impact of the communication, but the effect, as in the Allyn and Festinger study, was limited to those subjects for whom the issue was salient. Subsequently, Freedman and Sears (1965b) repeated the Allyn and Festinger experiment, but called the personality orientation "distraction." In this case distraction effects were no different from the effects of a content orientation given immediately prior to the communication. McGuire (1966) pointed out that distraction, by interfering with message comprehension, should actually decrease, not enhance, communication impact. The curvilinear distraction effect was also tested by Rosenblatt (1966) who suggested that the distraction effect was mediated through decreased suspicion of persuasive intent. His results showed that a moderate amount of distraction enhanced communication impact relative to absence of distraction, while strong distraction reduced communication acceptance relative to moderate distraction but in only one of two replications. His subjects also expressed less suspicion when distracted, but, since no differences in suspiciousness between distraction conditions were found, Rosenblatt's alternative interpretation was not supported. These studies raise the possibility of confounding between disguised orientation and moderate distraction. Thus, when differences between the effects of disguised and persuasion contexts on communication acceptance are found, caution must be exercised before attributing the differences solely to the hypothesized adverse effects of warning on communication acceptance.

Rosenblatt's (1966) suggestion that moderate distraction enhances opinion change by decreasing the subject's suspicion of persuasive intent agrees with the general hypothesis that knowledge of persuasive intent increases resistance

---

[6] Sears and Freedman (1965) also examined the effect of expected familiarity on selective exposure and find it, in this instance, minimal. Warnings, generally, may affect selective exposure; on the other hand, the available evidence suggests that there is no general tendency to avoid information contrary to one's beliefs (Freedman & Sears, 1965a; Lowin, 1967).

to persuasion (Hovland, Janis, & Kelley, 1953). This hypothesis may be the main justification for the assumption that warning, whether explicit or implicit, decreases persuasion. It should be clear by now that knowledge of persuasion does not, by itself, invariably lead to decreased communication acceptance. A related line of investigation, where communications are attributed to biased or to unbiased sources, has also resulted in ambiguity (Hovland & Mandell, 1952; Kelman & Hovland, 1953). Recently, Walster and Festinger (1962) showed that communications on involving issues that advocated positions that the audience *favored* were more effective in inducing opinion change when the audience was made to feel that the communicator was unaware of their presence; no differential impact was found between "overheard" and regular communications on issues that were not ego-involving. Brock and Becker (1965) replicated this finding and also showed that communications which argued *against* the subject's initial position were equally effective in the overheard and regular conditions. Apparently, overheard communications are more effective than regular communications only if the audience is involved in the issue and then only if the communication advocates a viewpoint that the audience would like to accept. Mills and Jellison (1967) suggested that these findings result from suspicion of the communicator's sincerity. Their experiment supports this view. The studies that used the "overheard" manipulation suggest that suspicion of persuasive intent has limited and complex effects on communication acceptance. Other findings indicate that persuasive intent, under certain conditions, may actually enhance persuasion (Mills, 1966; Mills & Aronson, 1965). In the Mills and Aronson experiment a physically attractive communicator with an acknowledged desire to influence the audience tended to be more persuasive than either a physically unattractive communicator with a stated desire to influence or, regardless of attractiveness, a reluctant communicator who stated no persuasive intent. The findings, however, failed to reach conventional levels of statistical significance, and the published report failed to indicate if significant opinion change took place in any of the experimental conditions. In a similar design, Mills (1966) showed that communication impact was highest when the audience perceived that the communicator liked them *and* desired to influence them.

The Freedman and Sears (1965b) study, already mentioned in connection with the distraction controversy, also contains findings that are relevant to warning and communication impact. The subjects were high school students, they served with an opinion or a personality (distraction) orientation, and the communication was against teen-age drivers (all as in Allyn & Festinger, 1961). Warning was given 10 minutes, 2 minutes, or immediately before the communication. The results showed a significant main effect of warning, with subjects in the 10-minute group showing the least opinion change. The investigators were also interested in the cognitive activities of the subjects during the interval between warning and communication: They were only able to find some indirect evidence that the warning may have stimulated rehearsal of belief-supporting arguments. In a personal communication to the author (1966), Freedman has reported that he has been unable to find evidence of relevant cognitive activity in warned subjects other than opinion change in the direction of the anticipated communication and a reported loss of confidence about their initial opinion (see next section). The Freedman and Sears experiment demonstrates that warning, if it precedes the communication by a few minutes, does decrease communication impact, and that its effect is over and above that of (weak) distraction. The possibility remains, as in the Allyn and Festinger study, that the persuasion context that was used had a negative character. The cognitive mechanisms that mediate the warning effect also remain obscure.

Finally, mention will be made of the study by McGuire and Millman (1965) which was designed to assess the relative effects of warning and subsequent persuasive attack on opinions. The results are meaningful if both components are considered together, and, hence, detailed discussion of this study will be presented in the next section. At the risk of oversimplification, one finding of the McGuire and Millman experiment will be presented at this point: Overall, the warning (which, in this instance, amounted to specific advance information about the communications within a *disguised* context) did not result in significant differences in *final* communication acceptance.

Direct Effects of Warning on Opinions

The possibility that warning, regardless of its effect on subsequent communication acceptance, could have a direct and immediate effect on the subject's opinions was first revealed in an incidental finding by McGuire and Papageorgis (1962). Subjects who had been warned that the experiment dealt with persuasion, but who were not exposed to the persuasive message, indicated opinions that were closer to the position of the message than did subjects who had received no warning. This difference was not statistically significant but, because it was unexpected and because it was consistent with dissonance theory (Festinger, 1957), it was noted and interpreted as a preparatory change in belief in anticipation of the belief-attacking message. Whatever the theoretical interpretation, opinion change appeared as one possible consequence of warning.

Subsequent studies have confirmed that warning has a direct effect on opinions. Some conditions that facilitate or hinder the effect have been specified. Until recently it had been taken for granted that belief changes following warning were due to the subject's anticipation of the persuasive message. Thus, Sears, Freedman, and O'Connor (1964) presented evidence that anticipation of debate led to moderation of a previously established opinion if the opinion had not been made public; if the subject had publicly announced his opinion, polarization (i.e., a strengthening of the opinion, thus, the reverse of the anticipatory change) was more likely. As noted earlier, Freedman[7] found postwarning opinion change in his subjects which was accompanied by expressions of lower confidence in their initial beliefs. In a recent unpublished study, Wicklund, Cooper, and Linder reported significant belief changes in the direction of an anticipated communication if the beliefs were measured 15 minutes (rather than immediately) after the warning or if the subject had chosen to be exposed to the discrepant communication (the two variables of time and choice were confounded).

McGuire and Millman (1965) compared the effects of warning on precommunication and postcommunication beliefs. The warning consisted of advance information about the topics of the communications within a disguised persuasion context. The communications dealt either with emotional and unverifiable issues (e.g., the likelihood of a third world war) or with technical, matter-of-fact issues (e.g., the shortage of laboratory animals). The messages were attributed to sources of high or low reputability. Using self-esteem theory (e.g., Deutsch, Krauss, & Rosenau, 1962), the investigators reasoned that the opinions of the subjects would reflect their efforts to avoid appearing gullible to themselves. It was therefore predicted that the subjects would show greater precommunication belief change when they were anticipating communications on the emotional issues. The results confirmed this prediction: 66% of the total (i.e., combined pre- and postcommunication) belief change on the emotional issues appeared after the warning but before the communications, whereas the corresponding figure on the technical issues was only 6%. Predictions were also made on the basis of the reputability of the attributed sources of the communications. The source manipulation, however, did not yield significant differences in precommunication belief change. McGuire and Millman attributed this failure to lack of sufficient differentiation of the sources in terms of overall persuasive effectiveness.

Papageorgis (1967) designed an experiment in which the source manipulation was more carefully controlled. Source characteristics suggesting high or low reputability were combined orthogonally with characteristics suggesting high or low persuasive effectiveness. The experiment, which was limited to the direct effects of warning on beliefs, was presented to the subjects as an opinion change study. Each subject was led to anticipate exposure to a speech attributed to each of the four reputability/effectiveness source combinations. The speech topics, on issues similar to McGuire and Millman's "emotional" type, and their purported direction of argument (against the subject's initial belief) were announced in advance. The orthogonal source manipulation was included in order to test self-esteem theory predictions (McGuire & Millman, 1965). In addition, the topic and direction of argument of a fifth speech was announced to the subjects, but the subjects were also clearly informed

[7] J. L. Freedman, personal communication, March 1966.

that they would not hear this last speech. This condition was introduced in order to assess whether postwarning belief change required anticipation of exposure to the communications; conceivably, the change could result from awareness of defensible positions contrary to one's own, as would be suggested from cognitive consistency theories of attitude change (e.g., Abelson & Rosenberg, 1958). The results of the experiment confirmed two of the findings by McGuire and Millman: Warning (except in the case of source attributions described as low in both effectiveness *and* reputability) resulted in significant precommunication belief changes, and the source effects were negligible. In addition, however, it was found that anticipation of a communication was not necessary for belief change. The announcement of the topic and direction of argument of a speech that the subject did not expect to hear resulted in significant belief change; the amount of change was similar to the amount of change obtained when exposure was anticipated.

Because the anticipation in the Papageorgis (1967) experiment was manipulated within-subjects, it was possible that postwarning belief change without anticipation of exposure to a communication was a phenomenon limited to contexts characterized by anticipation of exposure to other communications. A later unpublished study by the author introduced the anticipation variable in a between-subjects experimental design. Two of the issues from Papageorgis (1967) were used. Some subjects were given the topics and direction of argument of communications and were warned of forthcoming exposure. Other subjects were given the topics and direction of argument of communications but were assured that they would not be exposed to them; they were only asked to provide what purported to be base-line opinions with which the opinions of fellow students who had been exposed to the communications, could be compared. Both groups showed virtually the same amount of postwarning opinion change; their opinions were significantly more in the direction of the communications than the opinions of a true control group. Thus, anticipation of exposure to persuasive communications does not appear to be a *necessary* condition for postwarning belief change. On the other hand, under certain circumstances, anticipation may, as suggested by self-esteem theory, account for at least part of the obtained effect. In short, both self-esteem and cognitive consistency interpretations may have applicability.

Further confirmation of precommunication belief change was obtained by Deaux (1967) within an anticipatory context and with a salient issue. Female college students were told that they would view a film advocating the drafting of women into the armed forces. Half the subjects were told that they would view this film in an attempt to convince them of the necessity of drafting women (persuasion condition); the remaining subjects were told that their reactions to the film would influence the final decision about the female draft (defense condition). In addition, half of the subjects in each condition were allowed to select and read arguments for or against the drafting of women (information condition), while the remaining subjects had no access to any arguments (no-information condition). Opinions were measured both before and after the film, but only the prefilm results are relevant to this discussion. Especially relevant are the results from the no-information conditions: The defense group showed a significantly greater shift in opinion in the direction of the anticipated film than did the persuasion group. Deaux interprets this finding as an unwillingness on the part of the subjects to defend at a later time an extreme position. This interpretation is supported by the smaller shift found in the information-defense condition. In addition, the opinion shift by the no-information-persuasion groups was small and probably was not statistically significant. The procedure followed by Deaux in the no-information-persuasion condition is similar to the procedures used in other experiments (McGuire & Millman, 1965; Papageorgis, 1967) that reported significant postwarning shifts in opinion. The discrepancy may be the result of the ego-involving issue used by Deaux.

In summary, a direct effect of warning on beliefs has been demonstrated, although it may be limited to noninvolving issues. Apparently, the effect may be obtained without actual anticipation of exposure to persuasive communications. Minimally, the effect may be attributed to awareness on the part of the subject that positions contrary to his own do exist and may be defensible. Whether under such circumstances the effect, which is small, represents "true" opinion change or a slight change in belief expression within a subject's "latitude of acceptance" (Papageorgis, 1967; Sherif & Hovland, 1961) remains a matter for conjecture and further research. Alternatively, postwarning belief change may be viewed as a preparatory "true" change in opinion in anticipation of expected exposure to persuasive attack (McGuire & Millman, 1965). As Deaux (1967) suggests, it is quite possible that effects heretofore attributed solely to a persuasive communication may, in fact, occur prior to the receipt of the communication. "Attitude change thus becomes a two-stage process, wherein an initial self-evaluation and possible self-persuasion stage is followed by persuasion directly attributable to the communication and speaker [Deaux, 1967, p. 66]."

SUMMARY AND IMPLICATIONS

To begin with, the main issues and findings to date about the role of warning in persuasive communications will be summarized. Following the summary, the discussion will become more speculative and will attempt to state a coherent position regarding warning and persuasion.

1. Warning (or forewarning) refers to either a more-or-less explicit prior announcement that persuasion will be attempted or to a prior announcement of the topics and positions of forthcoming communications. This wide range of operational meanings is unwarranted since it is questionable that they are pragmatically interchangeable. Unless empirically shown to be so, a specific,

neutral, and widely adopted definition of warning is highly desirable. The author suggests (*a*) that the term "warning" be used to denote the mere prior announcement of the topics and of the direction of argument of communications, without the intrusion of evaluative comments or information; (*b*) that the expression "persuasion context" be used to denote the prior announcement that the experiment deals with persuasion, again without the intrusion of evaluative comments; "persuasion context" is to be contrasted with "disguised context" where the experimenter does not mention "persuasion" and suggests to the subjects some other plausible experimental objective. Depending on the hypotheses, it may be necessary to specify further the nature of the warning or the persuasion context: Either may be characterized as "positive," "neutral," or "negative" in order to indicate the particular connotative meaning given to "persuasion," the motives of the communicator, the quality of the communication, and the like.

2. Warning and persuasion context have been investigated in terms of their effect on subsequent communication acceptance and also in terms of their direct, immediate, precommunication effect on beliefs.

3. In terms of immediate effects on beliefs, warning and persuasion context produce small but significant and replicable changes in the direction of the communications. The changes occur even in situations where the subject does not anticipate (at least immediate) exposure to the communications. The reasons for these changes in belief are still a matter of conjecture. Under certain circumstances, the changes may not occur, for example, public acknowledgement of initial belief may serve to "polarize" belief. It has been suggested that postwarning belief change may be a consequence of a defensive maneuver to protect one's self-esteem (McGuire & Millman, 1965) or that it may be a cognitive adjustment of one's position in the light of learning or being reminded that a discrepant (and defensible) position exists (Papageorgis, 1967). If the latter is the case, the implications are considerable, but also highly speculative, for instance, belief adjustment following "warning" may depend on a general personality disposition in addition to the specific belief involved; consequently, a moderate general tendency in this direction may be characteristic of people capable of effective behavior in other respects. It has also been suggested that in most instances persuasion may be viewed as a two-stage process, with the first stage occurring prior to the communication (Deaux, 1967).

4. In terms of effects on subsequent communication acceptance, warning, in the sense of Suggestion 1 above, neither reduces nor enhances communication impact. This conclusion, however, must be considered highly tentative, since it is based on the findings of the single relevant study (McGuire & Millman, 1965) published to date.

5. In terms of effects on subsequent communication acceptance, the persuasion context, by itself or coupled with warning, has been sometimes found to affect acceptance and in other instances to have no measurable effect. In the majority of instances where the persuasion context has affected

acceptance, its effect has been to reduce or to nullify communication impact; there are, however, instances (Mills, 1966; Mills & Aronson, 1965) where it may have enhanced communication impact. The author has suggested that the persuasion context itself is not the critical factor in communication accept-ance, and that increased or decreased communication impact depend on additional positive or negative characteristics that are introduced into the context. Other variables that may influence the effects of the persuasion context include saliency of issue, type of appeal, position of the subject relative to the communication, and attractiveness of the communicator.

6. The author has also suggested increased use of persuasion contexts in studies of opinion change. The main reasons for this suggestion include the relevance of such experiments to persuasion as it takes place under natural conditions, and the numerous difficulties created by disguised contexts, such as plausibility, ethics, and the possibility that these contexts may become con-founded with other variables (e.g., distraction).

To conclude, a consistent explanation of the role of warning and per-suasion context in attitude change will be presented. The explanation fits with empirical findings to date, and could provide guidelines for deriving further testable experimental hypotheses.

Both warning and persuasion context, as specified earlier, may be viewed as potentially containing two components: one *informational*, the other *persuasive*. The informational component consists of what the subject learns about the situation and then interprets as straightforward, factual information: Examples include the purpose of the research project, and learning about the existence of a communication. The persuasive component, on the other hand, informs the subjects of the intentions of the experimenter regarding their behavior or suggests to them what the experimenter expects them to do as a result of the experimental procedures: Specifically, it implies that the subjects could, willingly or unwillingly, change their opinions. It is now assumed that the persuasion context involves both informational and persuasive components, as do positive and negative warnings. Neutral warning involves, for most sub-jects, only the informational component.

A neutral warning, therefore, should, other things being equal, have no effect on communication acceptance (or, more properly, affect acceptance in the same way that a successfully disguised orientation will). Because, how-ever, of its informational value it will produce direct, precommunication opin-ion change, since the subject will be confronted with knowledge that a well-formulated argument against his position exists. As already noted, it is not clear whether such opinion change is the same kind of change as is found fol-lowing persuasive communication or represents a temporary shift within the subject's latitude of acceptance. The problem can be settled empirically.

Positive warnings and positive (and, sometimes, neutral) persuasion contexts are expected to enhance communication acceptance. The possibilities of subject acquiescence and experimenter bias (Rosenthal, 1964) are also present and should be guarded against. Similarly, the informational component, in conjunction with the positive context, should also produce precommunication belief change.

Finally, negative warnings and negative persuasion contexts should, other things being equal, decrease communication acceptance. The extent of decrement will, of course, depend on other factors surrounding the experiment, such as the type of appeal, the quality of the communication, the issue, and possibly, the source of the warning. Precommunication belief change is also expected, but, in this instance, it may depend more on self-esteem maintenance and less on the informational component.

REFERENCES

ABELSON, R. P., and ROSENBERG, M. J. Symbolic psycho-logic: A model of attitudinal cognition. *Behavioral Science*, 1958, 3, 1–13.

ALLYN, J., and FESTINGER, L. The effectiveness of unanticipated persuasive communications. *Journal of Abnormal and Social Psychology*, 1961, 62, 35–40.

BROCK, T. C., and BECKER, L. A. Ineffectiveness of "overheard" counterpropaganda. *Journal of Personality and Social Psychology*, 1965, 2, 654–660.

DEAUX, K. K. The effects of warning on information preference and attitude change. Unpublished doctoral dissertation, University of Texas, 1967.

DEUTSCH, M., KRAUSS, R. M., and ROSENAU, N. Dissonance or defensiveness? *Journal of Personality*, 1962, 30, 16–28.

FESTINGER, L. *A theory of cognitive dissonance*. Evanston, Ill.: Row, Peterson, 1957.

FESTINGER, L., and MACCOBY, N. On resistance to persuasive communications. *Journal of Abnormal and Social Psychology*, 1964, 68, 359–366.

FREEDMAN, J. L., and SEARS, D. O. Selective exposure. In L. Berkowitz (Ed.), *Advances in experimental social psychology*. Vol. 2. New York: Academic Press, 1965. (a)

———. Warning, distraction, and resistance to influence. *Journal of Personality and Social Psychology*, 1965, 1, 262–266. (b)

HOVLAND, C. I., JANIS, I. L., and KELLEY, H. H. *Communication and persuasion*. New Haven: Yale University Press, 1953.

HOVLAND, C. I., and MANDELL, W. An experimental comparison of conclusion drawing by the communicator and by the audience. *Journal of Abnormal and Social Psychology*, 1952, 47, 581–588.

KELMAN, H. C. Human use of human subjects: The problem of deception in social psychological experiments. *Psychological Bulletin*, 1967, 67, 1–11.

KELMAN, H. C., and HOVLAND, C. I. "Reinstatement" of the communicator in delayed measurement of opinion change. *Journal of Abnormal and Social Psychology*, 1953, 48, 327–335.

KERRICK, J. S., and McMILLAN, D. A., III. The effects of instructional set on the measurement of attitude change through communications. *Journal of Social Psychology*, 1961, 53, 113–120.

KIESLER, C. A., and KIESLER, S. B. Role of forewarning in persuasive communications. *Journal of Abnormal and Social Psychology*, 1964, 68, 547–549.

LAZARSFELD, P., BERELSON, B., and GAUDET, H. *The people's choice.* (2nd ed.) New York: Columbia University Press, 1948.

LOWIN, A. Approach and avoidance: Alternate modes of selective exposure to information. *Journal of Personality and Social Psychology,* 1967, 6, 1–9.

McGUIRE, W. J. Attitudes and opinions. *Annual review of psychology,* 1966, 17, 475–514.

McGUIRE, W. J., and MILLMAN, S. Anticipatory belief lowering following forewarning of a persuasive attack. *Journal of Personality and Social Psychology,* 1965, 2, 471–479.

McGUIRE, W. J., and PAPAGEORGIS, D. Effectiveness of forewarning in developing resistance to persuasion. *Public Opinion Quarterly,* 1962, 26, 24–34.

MILLS, J. Opinion change as a function of the communicator's desire to influence and liking for the audience. *Journal of Experimental Social Psychology,* 1966, 2, 152–159.

MILLS, J., and ARONSON, E. Opinion change as a function of the communicator's attractiveness and desire to influence. *Journal of Personality and Social Psychology,* 1965, 1, 173–177.

MILLS, J., and JELLISON, J. M. Effect on opinion change of how desirable the communication is to the audience the communicator addressed. *Journal of Personality and Social Psychology,* 1967, 6, 98–101.

PAPAGEORGIS, D. Anticipation of exposure to persuasive messages and belief change. *Journal of Personality and Social Psychology,* 1967, 5, 490–496.

ROSENBLATT, P. C. Persuasion as a function of varying amounts of distraction. *Psychonomic Science,* 1966, 5, 85–86.

ROSENBLATT, P. C., and HICKS, J. M. Pretesting, forewarning, and persuasion. Paper presented at the meeting of the Midwestern Psychological Association, Chicago, May 1966.

ROSENTHAL, R. The effect of the experimenter on the results of psychological research. In B. A. Maher (Ed.), *Progress in experimental personality research.* New York: Academic Press, 1964.

SEARS, D. O., and FREEDMAN, J. L. Effects of expected familiarity with arguments upon opinion change and selective exposure. *Journal of Personality and Social Psychology,* 1965, 2, 420–426.

SEARS, D. O., FREEDMAN, J. L., and O'CONNOR, E. F. The effects of anticipated debate and commitment on the polarization of audience opinion. *Public Opinion Quarterly,* 1964, 28, 617–627.

SHERIF, M., and HOVLAND, C. I. *Social judgment.* New Haven: Yale University Press, 1961.

WALSTER, E., and FESTINGER, L. The effectiveness of "overheard" persuasive communications. *Journal of Abnormal and Social Psychology,* 1962, 65, 395–402.

WICKLUND, R., COOPER J., and LINDER, D. E. Expected effort and attitude change prior to exposure, Durham, N. C.: Duke University, 1966. (Mimeo)

William J. McGuire

INDUCING RESISTANCE
TO PERSUASION:
SOME CONTEMPORARY
APPROACHES

III. THE INOCULATION APPROACH

A. Use of Cultural Truisms

McGuire's series of experiments on inducing resistance to persuasion stems from a biological analogy, whence the term "inoculation theory." In the biological situation, the person is typically made resistant to some attacking virus by pre-exposure to a weakened dose of the virus. This mild dose stimulates his defenses so that he will be better able to overcome any massive viral attack to which he is later exposed, but is not so strong that this pre-exposure will itself cause the disease. Alternatively, biological resistance can be augmented by supportive therapy such as adequate rest, good diet, and vitamin supplements. Inoculation is likely to be superior to supportive therapy to the extent that the person has previously been brought up in a germ-free environment. It is a seeming paradox that individuals raised aseptically tend to appear vigorously healthy (even without supportive therapy) but are highly vulnerable when suddenly exposed to massive doses of the disease virus.

Since the experimenter wished to make heuristic use of the inoculation analogy in deriving hypotheses about producing resistance to persuasion, he chose to deal as far as possible with beliefs that had been maintained in a

Excerpted from *Advances in Experimental Social Psychology*, I, pp. 191–229, with permission of the author and Academic Press, Inc.

"germ-free" ideological environment, that is, beliefs that the person has seldom, if ever, heard attacked. Nearly all beliefs should be of this sort, according to the selective-avoidance postulate, which implies that a person avoids dissonant information wherever possible. While this has been widely accepted (Festinger, 1957; Klapper, 1949, 1960), the empirical evidence for it is not clear-cut (Steiner, 1962). Hence, to be more certain that the beliefs used in these experiments met the conditions of inoculation theory, "cultural truisms" were used as the beliefs to be made resistant to persuasive attacks. "Cultural truisms" are beliefs that are so widely shared within the person's social milieu that he would not have heard them attacked, and indeed, would doubt that an attack were possible. Beliefs maintained in so monolithic an ideological environment would approximate, as regards inoculation theory, the health status of an organism raised in a germ-free environment.

After much pretesting (which showed that cultural truisms were rarer in our college samples than had been expected), one area was finally found that abounded in almost unanimously accepted propositions, namely, health beliefs. Upwards of 75% of the student samples checked "15" on a 15-point scale to indicate their agreement with propositions like: "It's a good idea to brush your teeth after every meal if at all possible"; "Mental illness is not contagious"; "The effects of penicillin have been, almost without exception, of great benefit to mankind"; "Everyone should get a yearly chest X-ray to detect any signs of TB at an early stage." These truisms (which, as shown below, proved quite vulnerable when exposed to massive attacks without any prior "immunizing" treatment) were used, in the experiments described below, as the beliefs to be made resistant to persuasion by procedures derived by analogy from biological inoculation.

B. Basic Assumptions and Relevant Variables

1. UNDERLYING ASSUMPTIONS

McGuire's version of the inoculation theory assumes that pretreatments designed to make truisms resistant to subsequent persuasive attacks will be effective to the extent that they overcome two basic difficulties: one, the believer is unpracticed in defending his belief; and two, he is unmotivated to undertake the necessary practice. He is unpracticed because he has never been called upon to defend the truism. He is unmotivated to start practicing because he regards the belief as unassailable.

It follows that any prior treatment designed to improve the believer's defenses must motivate him to develop a defense of a truism whose validity he regards as obvious. Motivation can be supplied by making him aware of the vulnerability of the truism. That is, to be effective the prior defense of a truism presumably should be threatening rather than reassuring about the belief. An obvious way of threatening him is by pre-exposure to weakened forms of the attacking arguments.

It also follows that supplying motivation alone is inadequate for an effective defense. Because of the believer's lack of prior practice, he may not be able to bolster his belief sufficiently unless he is given careful guidance in developing defensive material; or, if he is required to develop such material on his own initiative, he must at least be given considerable time to do so.

From this background of assumptions, we derive a number of predictions about the relative immunizing effectiveness of various kinds of prior defenses. The three basic variables which are involved in most of these predictions are described first. The derivation of the specific predictions involving them is taken up in the later sections of this chapter which present the separate experiments.

2. THE DEFENSIVE VARIABLES

The first of these three variables is the amount of threat contained in the defenses. Two basic types of defenses were used which differed in amount of threat: "supportive" and "refutational." The supportive defense was non-threatening; it consisted of giving the believer various arguments in support of the truism. The refutational defense was more threatening; instead of positively supporting the truism, it mentioned several arguments attacking the belief, and then proceeded to refute these attacking arguments. The experimenter reasoned that this pre-exposure would be threatening enough to be defense-stimulating, but not so strong as to overwhelm the truism.

These refutational defenses, considered in relation to the subsequent attacks, were one of two types. Either they mentioned and refuted the very arguments against the truism that were to be used in the subsequent attacks, or they mentioned and refuted arguments different from the ones to be used in the attacks. This refutational-same vs. refutational-different defensive variation is useful in determining whether any increased resistance to persuasion derives from the generalized motivational effect of the threatening mention of the arguments against the truism (as required by inoculation theory), or whether it stems from the useful defensive material provided directly by the refutations.

A second defensive variable that was manipulated in many of the experimenter's inoculation studies was the amount of unguided, active participation in the defense required of the believer. Two levels of this variable were generally used: a relatively passive condition, in which the believer read a defensive essay that had been prepared for him, and an active condition, in which the believer wrote such an essay. This variable was relevant to both of the assumed difficulties in immunizing cultural truisms: the believer's lack of practice and his lack of motivation.

A third variable manipulated in several of the experiments was the interval between the defense and attack. This time period ranged from a few minutes to a maximum of one week. Here the primary concern was the interaction between time and the other variables. The theoretical relevance of these three variables will be discussed later, along with the description of the experiments that tested the predictions in which they were involved.

A number of additional variables were manipulated to clarify certain theoretical ambiguities in one or another of the studies described below, but they are described later in the chapter with the experiment where they were employed.

IV. GENERAL EXPERIMENTAL PROCEDURE

The basic procedures were quite similar from experiment to experiment in the series reported below. Hence, for economy of exposition the general methodological paradigm will be described at the outset. Then, in describing each individual experiment, its method will need to be described only in so far as it departs in important ways from this general paradigm.

The experiments involved two sessions, the first devoted to the defenses; the second, to the strong attacks and to measuring the resultant belief levels. The interval between the two sessions varied from a few minutes to 7 days. The subjects were usually college students enrolled in introductory psychology courses at large state universities who were fulfilling a course requirement that they participate in a certain number of hours of psychological experiments. The present studies were usually represented to them as studies of verbal skills. The issues being defended and attacked were the health truisms described above.

A. First (Defensive) Session

The subjects were told the experimenter was studying the relation between reading and writing skills in the two-session experiments. In the first 50-minute session the subject actually participated in several defensive conditions, e.g., he might receive an active-refutational, passive-refutational, active-supportive, and passive-supportive defense, each defense dealing with a different truism.

An active refutational defense consisted of a sheet of paper on which was listed a truism—e.g., "Everyone should brush his teeth after every meal if at all possible." Then would come a one-sentence argument against this truism—e.g., "Too frequent brushing tends to damage the gums and expose the vulnerable parts of the teeth to decay"—and the instructions to use the white space below to write a paragraph refuting this argument against the truism. Halfway down the page came another argument against the truism and instructions to refute it in the space following. The passive-refutational defense stated the truism and the two arguments against it in an introductory paragraph; then followed two further paragraphs, each refuting one of these arguments. The active and passive supportive defenses were analogous to the refutational in format, except that instead of arguments against the truism, they cited two arguments supporting it, and then (in the active condition) asked the subject to write paragraphs defending these supportive arguments, or (in the passive condition) presented two such defensive paragraphs for him to read. In the passive defenses, to substantiate the subterfuge that we were studying reading skills, the subject was asked to pick out and underline the crucial clause in each paragraph.

In some of the experiments, the subject filled out an opinionnaire on the truisms after completing these defenses, so we could measure the direct strengthening effects of the defenses prior to the attacks. More typically, no opinionnaire was administered until the end of the second session, and the direct strengthening effect was determined by including defense-only, no-attack conditions in the design.

B. Second (Attacking) Session

Immediately after (or 2 or 7 days after this defensive session) followed a 50-minute second session devoted to attacks on the truisms and administration of an opinionnaire to determine final belief levels on the truisms. The attacks all had the form of a three-paragraph essay (similar in format to the passive defenses). The first paragraph stated the truism, remarked that some informed people were beginning to question its validity, and mentioned two attacking arguments. Each of the next two paragraphs developed in detail one of these attacking arguments. For those conditions in which a refutational defense had been given, half were followed by an attack using the same arguments against the truism as had been refuted in the prior defense (constituting it a "refutational-same" defense); the other half were followed by attacks using quite different arguments against the truism from those that had been refuted in the defense (constituting a "refutational-different" defense). The designs typically had each subject furnish control data on a "defense-only" and a "neither-defense-nor-attack" truism. The specific truisms were, of course, rotated around the conditions from subject to subject.

After reading (and underlining the crucial clause in) the attacking messages, the subject filled out some personality tests (introduced to substantiate the claim that the experiment was investigating personality correlates of verbal skills). He then filled out the opinionnaire on the truisms, purportedly to determine if the subject's feelings about the topics had any effect on his ability to utilize his verbal skills in the reading and writing "tests." The opinionnaire consisted of four statements dealing with each truism. The subject was called upon to check off his agreement with the statement on a scale from one to 15. The direction of the statement was varied, so that sometimes 15 represented complete acceptance of the truism, and sometimes complete rejection. However, in the results reported below, to make reading easier, the appropriate responses are reversed so that the 15 score always represents complete acceptance of the truism and a one score, complete rejection of it.

After completing the opinionnaire, the subject replied to standardized questions probing his actual perception of the experiment. Finally, the true purpose of the experiment was revealed to him, and the various deceits used and the reasons for employing them were explained. Approximately 3 months later a follow-up letter was sent to him, reminding him that the argumentative material he had dealt with had been selected solely for experimental purposes and that the arguments were not necessarily true. More detailed information on the materials, designs, etc., are given in the original published reports of the experiments cited in the paragraphs that follow.

V. SUPPORTIVE VS. REFUTATIONAL DEFENSES

A series of experiments were carried out to test the hypothesis that defenses of truisms are effective to the extent that they contain threatening mention of arguments against the truism. These studies, in which the experimenter manipulated the extent to which the defenses mentioned arguments supporting the truism vs. arguments attacking the truism, are described in the present section. The first study showed that defenses which present arguments supporting the truism are less effective in conferring resistance to subsequent strong attack than are refutational-same defenses (which ignore arguments positively supporting the truism but do mention and refute the same arguments against the belief as are to be used in the subsequent attack). The second experiment demonstrated that a refutational defense is almost as effective when it refutes arguments against the truism which are different from those to be used in the later attack as when it refutes the very same arguments used in the attack.

A third study illustrated that, when combined with the threatening refutational defense, the supportive defense gains an efficacy that it lacks when used alone. In the fourth study, it was demonstrated that an extrinsic threat (forewarning of the impending attack) prior to the defenses, enhances their immunizing effectiveness, especially that of the otherwise not-threatening supportive defense. Conversely, a fifth study showed that a prior reassurance (feedback that one's peers also agree with the truism) decreases the effectiveness of the defenses. A sixth study revealed that the immunizing efficacy of the refutational defense derives at least as much from the threatening prior mention of the attacking arguments as from the reassuring earlier refutations of the attacking arguments which had been mentioned. Each of these studies is described in more detail, together with additional findings of interest, in the paragraphs below.

A. Supportive vs. Refutational-Same Study

1. EXPERIMENTAL CONDITIONS

In a first experiment (McGuire and Papageorgis, 1961), each of 130 students read a defensive essay on one truism and wrote a defensive essay on another in a regular meeting of his freshman English course. Two days later, he read messages attacking these two truisms and also a third, nondefended truism. On a fourth truism he received neither defense nor attack (the four specific truisms being rotated around the four conditions from student to student). He then filled out an opinionnaire measuring his beliefs on all four truisms.

For 66 of the students, each defensive essay was supportive, mentioning four arguments supporting the truism and then presenting a paragraph substantiating each argument (in the reading, passive condition), or then asking the student to write a substantiating paragraph for each argument (in the writing, active condition). For the other 64 students, each defensive essay was refutational, ignoring supportive arguments and mentioning four arguments against the truism and then presenting a paragraph refuting each (in the passive condition), or then calling upon the student to write a refuting paragraph against each argument (in the active condition). The passive-condition subjects were allowed 5 minutes to read each of the 1000-word essays; the active-condition subjects were allowed 10 minutes to write each essay. The attacks 2 days later consisted of 1000-word essays to be read, each mentioning four arguments against the belief and then presenting a paragraph substantiating each argument.

2. IMMUNIZING EFFECTIVENESS

As Table I shows, the more threatening, refutational defense was clearly superior to the supportive defense in conferring resistance to the subsequent attacks. The attacks, when not preceded by a defense, reduced adherence to the truisms from 12.62 to 6.64 on the 15-point scale. When the refutational defense preceded the attacks, the mean belief score was reduced only to 10.33, which is significantly ($p < .001$) higher than in the attack-only condition. The supportive defenses were much less successful in inducing resistance. In the supportive defense conditions, the mean belief score after the attacks was 7.39, which is not only significantly ($p < .001$) lower than in the refutational-defense treatment, but is not even significantly higher than the no-defense,

TABLE I

MEAN BELIEF LEVELS AFTER ATTACKS[a] PRECEDED BY
REFUTATIONAL–SAME VS SUPPORTIVE DEFENSES[b,c]

Type of participation	Refutational defense then attack	Supportive defense then attack	Refute minus support
Passive reading	11.51 (35)[d]	7.47 (32)	+4.04
Reading and underlining	11.13 (31)	7.63 (32)	+3.50
Writing from outline	9.19 (31)	7.94 (32)	+1.25
Writing without guidance	9.46 (35)	6.53 (32)	+2.93
Weighted mean	10.33 (132)	7.39 (128)	+2.94

[a] Control levels: neither attack nor defense = 12.62 ($N = 130$); attack only (with no prior defense) = 6.64 ($N = 130$).

[b] 15.00 indicates complete adherence to the truism; 1.00 indicates complete disagreement.

[c] Data from McGuire and Papageorgis (1961).

[d] Numbers in parentheses give the number of cases on which cell means were based.

attack-only condition ($p = .16$). Hence the supportive defense is not only much less effective than the refutational in conferring resistance, but has not clearly been shown to be effective at all.

3. DIRECT STRENGTHENING EFFECT

In this experiment, the subjects completed the opinionnaire not only at the end of the second session, but also at the end of the first session. Comparing each subject's two responses provides a measure of the direct strengthening effects of the various defenses (as opposed to their conferred resistance to the later attacks). In terms of this criterion, the supportive defenses apparently were superior to the refutational. Immediately after the supportive defenses, the mean belief score was 14.34; immediately after the refutational, it was 13.91 ($p = .10$ for the difference). Furthermore, while the refutational defense was superior to the supportive one in all four participation conditions as regards resistance conferral (see Table I), the supportive defense was superior in producing a direct strengthening effect. This type of reversal was found repeatedly in the present series of experiments: the defenses which left the beliefs seemingly strongest tended to be the defenses which conferred the least resistance to subsequent attacks. This reversal, called the "paper tiger" phenomenon, shows the peril of assuming the immunizing effectiveness of a defense to be a direct function of its apparent strengthening effect, and is in accord with the inoculation theory.

B. Refutational-Same vs. -Different

1. HYPOTHESES

A later experiment by Papageorgis and McGuire (1961) compared the resistance-conferring efficacy of the refutational defense when the later attacks used arguments which differed from those mentioned and refuted in the defense, with their efficacy when the later attacks used the same arguments used in the defense. If, as implied by the inoculation theory, the refutational defense derives immunizing efficacy from the motivation-stimulating threatening mention of arguments against the truism, then its effectiveness should be general and manifested even against attacks using novel arguments. On the other hand, if the refutational defense gains its effectiveness solely from the refutation rather than the mention of the arguments, the resistance it confers should be more specific to attacks by the same arguments that had been refuted.

2. PROCEDURE

The study designed to distinguish between these two explanations employed only refutational defenses, since the hypotheses did not concern the supportive defenses. Also, only passive (reading) defenses were employed, since the relevance of the active defenses (even of the refutational type) to the predictions is less clear; the amount of refutational material received was more under the subject's control than the experimenter's in the active condition. Alternative forms of the passive refutational defense were made up for each truism. Each form employed a different pair of arguments against the truism, the defensive message first mentioning and then refuting this pair in a 600-word essay. Correspondingly, there were two forms of the message attacking each truism, each form mentioning and then corroborating one of these pairs of attacking arguments. A crossover design was used so that each given pair of arguments refuted in a defense was followed by an attack using the same arguments for half the subjects, and by one using the different pair of arguments for the other half. A total of 73 summer school students served in the two sessions, defensive and attacking, which were separated by a one-week interval.

3. RESULTS

Once again the attacks proved very damaging to the truisms when they were not preceded by a defense. In the attack-only condition, the mean belief level went down to 5.73 on the 15-point scale as compared to a mean of 13.23 in the neither-defense-nor-attack control condition, a drop significant at well above the .001 level. The refutational defenses did confer appreciable resistance to the attack: When the attack had been preceded by the refutational-same defense, the mean belief level was 9.25; after one preceded by the refutational-different defense, it was 8.70. Each of these means in the defense-and-attack conditions is significantly higher than the 5.73 mean in the attack-only condition, and they are not significantly different from one another. These outcomes tend to conform to inoculation theory, since the refutational defense confers resistance even to novel attacks. Indeed, the resistance to novel attacks that was produced is not significantly less than the resistance to attacks by the very same arguments that were refuted.

.   .   .   .

VI. EFFECTS OF ACTIVE PARTICIPATION IN THE DEFENSE

A. Theory

A second series of hypotheses derived from the inoculation notion dealt with the effects of requiring the believer to participate actively, without guidance, in the prior defense of the truisms. Our initial analysis of the resistance of cultural truisms to attack assumed that because these truisms had been maintained in an ideologically "germ-free" environment, there would be two deficits making it difficult to utilize prior defense to make them resistant to persuasion. First, there would be a practice deficit: since the believer would seldom if ever have been called upon to defend the truism, he would not find it easy to do so unless he was carefully guided in the defense. Second, there would be a motivational deficit: because the believer would be too confident of the validity of these supposedly obvious and unassailable truisms, he would be little motivated to assimilate defensive material that was presented to him.

It follows that this "active participation in the defense" variable is relevant in opposite ways to both the practice and the motivational deficits of the truisms. With regard to the deficit in prior practice, the active (writing) defensive condition is more disadvantageous than the passive (reading) condition, since it imposes more demands upon the believer to summon up bolstering material from his inadequate cognitive repertory. He will tend to perform the writing task poorly and, consequently, the active defensive session tends to be unproductive and wasted. In contrast, the passive defense makes relatively little demand on the believer's prior preparation; he has only to read the presented defensive material. Hence, his lack of practice is no great handicap. In the case of the motivational deficit, on the other hand, the active condition is at less of a disadvantage than the passive, since the very poorness of the believer's performance at the essay-writing task should bring home to him how inadequately based is his confidence in the truism. This should motivate him to correct this state of affairs.

Since the theoretical analysis indicates that the two processes touched off by this active-passive manipulation have opposite effects on the dependent variable (conferred resistance), the experimenter might seem to be left in a sorry state for making predictions. Such is not the case, however. Predictions can be made regarding interaction effects between this activity variable and other variables which tend to intensify the advantages or disadvantages of active participation with respect to conferring resistance.

B. *Effects of Requiring Participation*

1. THEORY AND METHOD

The first experiment designed to test the effect on conferred resistance of manipulating the amount of unguided, active participation in the defense varied this participation over four levels. The highest degree of unguided participation was called "unguided writing." It consisted of giving the subjects a sheet of paper headed by a statement of the truism and telling him that he had 20 minutes to write an essay defending the truism. Subjects were assigned either to a supportive-defense condition by being told that their essays should be restricted to presenting arguments positively supporting the truism, or to a refutational-defense condition by being told that their essays should mention and then refute possible arguments against the truism. They were told that their essays would be scored for argumentative skill and relevance, but were given no further guidance.

A slightly less demanding condition, called "guided writing" was the same as above, except that the sheets headed by the truisms also listed arguments that could be used in writing the essay. The people in the supportive-defense condition were given one-sentence synopses of each of four arguments supporting the truisms. Those in the refutational defense conditions were given four pairs of sentences, each pair consisting of a statement of an argument attacking the truism, and a statement suggesting a refutation of that argument.

Still less demanding was the "reading and underlining condition." Here each subject received a mimeographed, defensive essay about 1000 words long to read. In the supportive condition the first paragraph mentioned four arguments supporting the truism, and then followed four paragraphs, each developing more fully one of the supporting arguments. In the refutational condition the first paragraph mentioned four arguments attacking the beliefs, and then followed four paragraphs, each refuting one of these attacking arguments. The subjects in this reading condition were instructed that they would have 5 minutes to read and to underline in each paragraph the shortest clause that contained the gist of the whole paragraph. They were told they would be scored on the basis of their accuracy at this task and their ability to answer a later series of reading comprehension questions.

The least demanding participation condition, called "passive reading," was the same as the reading and underlining condition, except that the underlining task was omitted so that the subject had simply to read the paragraph passively during the 5 minutes and prepare for the later reading comprehension questions.

In this experiment (McGuire and Papageorgis, 1961), each of the 130 subjects served in two defensive conditions in the first session: a writing defense on one truism and a reading defense on another. All the refutational defenses were of the refutational-same type. In the second session 2 days later, each received attacks on the two defended truisms and also an attack on a third, undefended truism (to yield an attack-only control score), and no attack on still a fourth truism (to yield a neither-defense-nor-attack control score). The four specific truisms were rotated around these four conditions from subject to subject. Beliefs were measured at the ends of both the first and second sessions.

While there are, as described above, both beneficial and detrimental effects to be expected from requiring active participation in the defense, it is possible under the experimental conditions obtaining here to make a main order prediction: the detrimental effects are likely to be dominant so that the active-participation requirement will probably have the net effect of interfering with the immunizing effectiveness of the defense. The reason is that the relative disadvantage of the active conditions (their being too demanding for the unpracticed subject) is likely to be fully operative, while their relative advantage (supplying motivation to take part seriously in the defense) is somewhat obviated by the moderate degree of such motivation established by the present conditions, even in the passive group. As the previously described series of experiments showed, the refutational defense, even in the passive condition, contains a motivation-stimulating threat to the belief. In addition, the reading-comprehension instructions also motivate these college student subjects to address themselves seriously to assimilating these defensive essays, even though the essays seem to belabor the obvious.

The above reasoning enables the experimenter to make predictions regarding both main effects and interactions in this study. Forced-compliance studies (Kelman, 1953; King and Janis, 1956; Brehm and Cohen, 1962) usually find that active participation in the defense of a belief opposing one's own views generally augments the amount of internalized attitude change. However, in the present case of defending already accepted truisms, the opposite is predicted: namely, the greater the active participation requirement, the less the conferred resistance to subsequent attacks.

The above considerations also give rise to the interaction prediction: the superiority of the passive over the active defense will be more pronounced with the refutational defense than with the supportive. As pointed out in the analysis of the experimental conditions, whatever advantage the active condition might offer—its motivation-inducing threat—is lost in the case of the refutational defense because here even the passive condition offers two sources of motivation to assimilate the defense: the mention of the threatening, attacking arguments which are to be refuted, and the achievement motivation to do well, produced by the announcement of the reading comprehension test.

2. MAIN EFFECT RESULTS

The outcome of this experiment has already been presented in Table I, which shows the final belief scores in the eight defense-and-attack conditions (i.e., four levels of active participation for the supportive and for the refutational defenses) and in the attack-only and neither-defense-nor-attack control conditions. As Table I shows, the main effect prediction is confirmed; over the four levels of increasing participation there is a steady decline in immunizing effectiveness. With regard to the main manipulation of this variable, reading vs. writing, the superiority of the former is significant at the .001 level. (Also noteworthy is the finding of the same consistent trend over the four conditions in the direct strengthening effects of the defense, as shown by the mean belief levels at the end of the first session. The superiority of reading over writing in this regard reached the .05 level of significance, despite the low ceiling restraining any further increase in the pre-attack means.) This immunizing superiority of reading over writing is especially striking considering that the time allowed for the writing defense (20 minutes) was four times that allowed for the reading.

3. INTERACTION RESULT

The interaction prediction is also confirmed by the results. While the reading defense was superior to the writing for both supportive and refutational defenses, reading was only slightly superior to writing for the supportive defense (7.56 vs. 7.23) but considerably superior for the refutational defense (11.33 vs. 9.33). This interaction was significant at the .05 level. Several subsequent studies (McGuire, 1963 a,c) confirmed both the main and the interaction effects reported here. However, they showed in addition that the sizable superiority of reading over writing for the refutational-same defense, which was demonstrated in this study, does not hold also for the refutational-different defense. Indeed, the superiority of reading over writing tends to be even less for the refutational-different defense than for the supportive defense.

. . . .

VII. PERSISTENCE OF THE INDUCED RESISTANCE

A. Theory

1. UNDERLYING ASSUMPTIONS

The theoretical discussions in this chapter have continually assumed that the immunizing efficacy of the prior defenses derives from two mechanisms: from a threatening realization of the vulnerability of the belief, which, in the case of cultural truisms, supplies the much needed motivation to assimilate bolstering material; and from the actual presentation of such material. In the case of the active (essay-writing) defenses, the second mechanism is largely inoperative since little information is presented and the unpracticed believer is unable to summon up much defensive material from his own cognitive repertory. For the passive (essay-reading) defenses, however, the situation is more complex. The efficacy of the supportive defense derives primarily from the first mechanism; of the refutational-different, from the second; and of the refutational-same, from both.

Making additional assumptions about the different temporal trends of the two underlying mechanisms, this line of reasoning yields predictions about the persistence of the resistance conferred by the various kinds of defenses. The first of these assumed resistance-conferring mechanisms, the motivation-stimulating threat, may show a nonmonotonic time trend for the following reasons. Once the threat has motivated the previously over-confident believer to accumulate belief-bolstering material, he will still need time before he can act effectively on this motivation, since material relevant to these uncontroverted truisms is rather scarce in the ordinary, ideological environment. Hence, the believer will continue to accumulate additional material for a considerable time after being exposed to the threatening defense, resulting in a delayed-action effect as far as resistance to later attacks is concerned. On the other hand, as time passes and the threat recedes, the induced motivation to accumulate material will itself tend to decay. The result of these two tendencies is a nonmonotonic time trend (first rising, then falling) for induced resistance deriving from this first mechanism. Note that this time trend is the same as that for the typical biological inoculation; there too, a few days or weeks must pass after exposure to the weakened inoculation dose before the resistance builds up to its full strength, after which it tends to decay gradually. The parallel is not surprising since the analogy between the mechanisms in the two situations was our theoretical point of departure.

The second resistance-conferring mechanism, the actual communicating of belief-bolstering material in the defense, should show a much simpler relationship to time. Since the resistance conferred by this mechanism is a direct function of the retention of the bolstering material, we would expect its decay to follow the ordinary forgetting curve.

2. PREDICTION REGARDING ACTIVELY CONFERRED RESISTANCE

Since we hypothesize different persistence curves for the resistance conferred by the two underlying mechanisms, we can make distinctive predictions regarding the time trends of the resistance conferred by each type of defense, depending on the extent that each of the two mechanisms is assumed to be involved in that defense. The prediction is much the same for all types of active (essay-writing) defenses, whether supportive, refutational-same or -different. None of these variations presents appreciable amounts of useful belief-bolstering material in the active condition, and thus the second mechanism is inoperative from the start and does not contribute to the time trend. Such resistance as is conferred derives from the first (motivation-stimulating threat) mechanism, and hence the net time trend should be nonmonotonic. Most interesting, all three types of defense should show a delayed-action effect in the active condition, producing actually more resistance to attacks coming some time after the defense than to immediate attacks.

3. PREDICTIONS REGARDING PASSIVELY CONFERRED RESISTANCE

In the passive (essay-reading) condition, the predictions depend on the type of defense. What resistance is conferred by reading the supportive essay stems from the second mechanism (retention of the direct bolstering material it contains), so a simple decay function is predicted; the resistance conferred by the passive, supportive defense should decline progressively as the interval between the defense and attack increases. Since, as we have already seen, the passive refutational-different defense derives its efficacy almost entirely from the second (motivating-threat mechanism), we would expect its time trend to show the same nonmonotonic trend as would all three types of active defense. Since the efficacy of the passive refutational-same defense depends on both mechanisms we predict its time trend to be a composite of those of the two: namely, little decline at first, while the "forgetting" trend of the second mechanism is being largely offset by the delayed-action trend of the first mechanism, after which there is a much faster fall-off as both underlying trends are downward. Two studies that were designed to test these various time trend predictions are described in the sections following.

4. SELECTION OF TIME PARAMETERS

To test hypotheses about time trend differentials, especially when the functions are nonmonotonic or decay to a common asymtote (e.g., to zero in this case), it is necessary to set the time parameters at theoretically-strategic points in order that the predicted effects can be demonstrated. Selecting these strategic points presents a formidable methodological difficulty when, as in the present case, the theory is not well formed enough quantitatively to specify the exact time parameters. In anticipation of this problem, in the earlier studies reported above, the interval between defense and attack was deliberately set at different points from experiment to experiment. An examination (Mc-Guire, 1962) of how these different settings appeared to affect the outcomes suggested that the critical persistence predictions could be tested by varying the intervals between defense and attack over the range of a few minutes to one week. Hence, in the studies reported below, these settings were selected as the range over which time was to vary.

B. Persistence of Passively Conferred Resistance

1. METHOD

The experiment designed to test the predictions about the differential decay rates of the resistance conferred by the three types of defense (supportive, refutational-same and refutational-different) under the passive (reading) conditions involved a mixed design in which each of the 160 subjects served in four conditions. Each subject received the defense of one truism several days before the attack (for 80 subjects, it was 2 days before; and for the other 80, 7 days before), and all received another defense a few minutes before the attack, so that the design included three different intervals between defense and attack. Equal numbers of subjects received supportive, refutational-same, and refutational-different defenses at all three intervals. Further details of the design, analyses, and other aspects of the procedure can be found in an earlier publication (McGuire, 1962).

2. RESULTS

The persistence of the resistance conferred by the three types of passive defense is shown by the final belief scores contained in Table VI. As predicted, such small resistance as the supportive defense confers against immediate attacks has decayed ($p < .05$) almost completely within 2 days. At both the 2- and the 7-day intervals, the level to which the attack reduced the belief is approximately the same after a supportive defense as in the no-defense, attack-only condition.

For the refutational-same defense, however, the conferred resistance, as predicted, decays at a much slower rate. It is particularly in the early stages (again, as predicted) that the resistance produced by the refutational-same defense is more persistent. The interaction between the time (immediate vs. 2-day) variable and the supportive vs. refutational-same type of defense variable is significant at the .01 level. It can be seen that the direction of this interaction effect is in the opposite direction from that which would tend to result from a simple regression artifact.

The predicted nonmonotonic effect in the refutational-different condition is also confirmed. Resistance to attacks 2 days later is actually greater than to immediate attacks. This predicted delayed-action effect is significant at the .05 level. The predicted greater persistence during the first 2 days of the resistance conferred by the refutational-different over that conferred by the refutational-same defense is significant at the .05 level.

TABLE VI

MEAN BELIEF LEVELS AFTER DEFENSES AND ATTACKS[a] SEPARATED BY
VARIOUS TIME INTERVALS, SHOWING THE PERSISTENCE OF THE
RESISTANCE TO PERSUASION CONFERRED BY THREE TYPES OF
PRIOR, PASSIVE BELIEF DEFENSES[b,c]

Interval between defense and attack	Defense-and-attack conditions		
	Supportive defense	Refutational-same defense	Refutational-different defense
Immediate	9.71	11.36	10.41
	(80)[d]	(80)	(80)
2 Days	8.51	11.08	11.45
	(40)	(40)	(40)
7 Days	8.82	9.49	9.68
	(40)	(40)	(40)

[a] Control levels: neither defense nor attack = 11.74 ($N = 80$); attack-only = 8.49 ($N = 80$).

[b] 15.00 indicates complete adherence to the truism.

[c] Data from McGuire (1962).

[d] Numbers in parentheses give the numbers of cases on which cell means were based.

C. Persistence of Actively Conferred Resistance

1. METHOD

In a final experiment designed to test the relative persistence of actively and passively conferred resistance, the experimenter adopted the questionable economy of dropping out the 2-day interval condition. Each of the 72 subjects received an active and a passive defense (of two different truisms) one week prior to the attacks, and an active and passive defense of a third and fourth truism immediately prior to the attacks. The specific truisms were rotated around the defensive conditions from subject to subject. Then all four truisms were subjected to the usual attacks and the final belief levels were measured. Twenty-four of the subjects received supportive defenses, another 24, refutational-same, and a third 24, refutational-different defenses.

2. RESULTS

The primary interest in this study was in the active conditions and the comparison between the active and passive. Thus, the 2-day condition, which is a crucial interval for some of the passive-defense effects that were demonstrated in the previous experiment, was omitted in this study. Even under these conditions, however, the distinctive effect in the passive condition was still apparent (see Table VII) : the resistance conferred by the passive refutational-different defense showed significantly less of a decline over the week than that produced by the other two types of passive defenses, supportive and refutational-same. In fact, the slight increase in resistance conferred by the passive, refutational-different defense (not significant) suggests a delayed action effect even after one week, although, as the previous experiment showed (see Table VI) this effect is more apparent at the shorter, 2-day interval. For the active condition it was predicted that all three types of defense (supportive, refutational-same, and refutational-different) would show delayed action effects and, as seen in Table VII, just this was found. The greater resistance to attacks

TABLE VII

Mean Belief Levels after Defenses and Attacks Separated by Various Time Intervals, Showing the Persistence of Actively and Passively Conferred Resistance[a,b]

Type of defensive material	Active defense		Passive defense		All 4 combined
	Immediate attack	Attack one week later	Immediate attack	Attack one week later	
Supportive	8.30	9.89	9.72	9.47	9.34
	(24)[c]	(24)	(24)	(24)	(96)
Refutational-same	9.61	10.13	12.12	10.42	10.57
	(24)	(24)	(24)	(24)	(96)
Refutational-different	9.77	9.98	9.61	9.99	9.84
	(24)	(24)	(24)	(24)	(96)
All 3 Combined	9.22	10.00	10.48	9.96	9.91
	(72)	(72)	(72)	(72)	(288)

[a] 15.00 indicates complete adherence to the truism.

[b] Data from McGuire (1963b).

[c] Numbers in parentheses give the number of cases on which cell means were based.

one week later than to immediate attacks for the three active types combined is significant at the .05 level. The design (as described above) used four different truisms for each of the three types of active defenses, and in nine of the twelve resulting comparisons there was the predicted delayed-action effect as regards conferred resistance.

The greater persistence of the actively-conferred resistance as compared to that produced by the passive defenses can be seen by inspecting the Table VII means. The belief level in the active condition has generally increased over the week, while it has weakened in the passive groups. This predicted interaction between time and activity is significant at the .01 level. Furthermore this interaction effect derives, as predicted, almost entirely from the supportive and the refutational-same types of defenses. As required by the theory, the resistance stemming from refutational-different defense is about equally persistent whether conferred actively or passively.

VIII. GENERAL CONCLUSION

The strategy used in this research program involved starting with relatively few assumptions and deriving from them a wide range of predictions. These were tested under a standardized set of conditions in experiments designed to be highly sensitive. The accumulating knowledge derived from the successive experiments clarified some of the parameters left undefined in the theory and thus allowed the experimenter to test progressively more elegant and complex derivations from the theory as he proceeded.

Space has not allowed a discussion of all the predictions and findings in this program. The positive was slightly accentuated by the experimenter's passing off with brief mention and references the failure to confirm the predicted order effects. Also omitted were results regarding cross-issue generalizations, effects of forewarnings, and effects of various kinds of prior commitments which were included in some of the studies reported. These findings were not described here because they were only peripherally related to inoculation theory.

The reader will note that all the studies reported here dealt with conferring resistance on a special type of belief, cultural truisms. The same inoculation theory which yielded these largely confirmed predictions regarding immunizing cultural truisms against persuasion might yield different hypotheses regarding the effects of the same defensive variables on making controverted beliefs resistant to persuasion. Hence, generalization from the above studies to the latter type of belief is not warranted. Further experiments will have to determine if inoculation theory will predict the immunizing efficacy of various types of defenses in the case of controversial beliefs as successfully as it has for truisms.

REFERENCES

ABELSON, R. P., and ROSENBERG, M. J. (1958). *Behav. Sci.* 3, 1–13.
ALLPORT, F., and LEPKIN, M. (1945). *J. Abnorm. Soc. Psychol.* 40, 3–36.
ANDERSON, L. R. (1962). M A. Thesis. University of Illinois, Urbana, Illinois.
ANDERSON, N. H. (1959). *J. Abnorm. Soc. Psychol.* 59, 371–381.
BENNETT, E. B. (1955). *Human Relat.* 8, 251–273.
BERKOWITZ, L., and COTTINGHAM, D. R. (1960). *J. Abnorm. Soc. Psychol.* 60, 37–43.
BIDDLE, W. W. (1932). *Teach. Coll. Contrib Educ. No.* 531.
BREHM, J. W. (1960). *In* "Attitude Organization and Change" (C. I. Hovland and M. J. Rosenberg, eds.), pp. 164–197. Yale Univ. Press, New Haven, Connecticut.

BREHM, J. W., and COHEN, A. R. (1962). "Explorations in Cognitive Dissonance." Wiley, New York.

CANTRIL, H. (1958). In "Readings in Social Psychology" (E. Maccoby, T. M. Newcomb, and E. Hartley, eds.), 3rd ed., pp. 291–300. Holt, New York.

CARLSON, E. R. (1956). J. Abnorm. Soc. Psychol. 52, 256–61.

CHARTERS, W. W., and NEWCOMB, T. M. (1958). In "Readings in Social Psychology" (E. Maccoby, T. M. Newcomb, and E. Hartley, eds.), 3rd ed., 276–281. Holt, New York.

CITRON, A. F., and HARDING, J. (1950). J. Abnorm. Soc. Psychol. 45, 310–328.

COHEN, A. R., BREHM, J. W., and FLEMING, W. H. (1958). J. Abnorm. Soc. Psychol. 56, 276–278.

COHEN, A. R., BREHM, J. W., and LATANÉ, B. (1959). J. Pers. 27, 63–73.

COLLIER, R. M. (1944). J. Social Psychol. 20, 3–17.

COOPER, E., and DINERMAN, H. (1951). Public Opin. Quart. 15, 243–264.

CRUTCHFIELD, R. S. (1955). Am. Psychol. 10, 191–198.

DAS, J. P., RATH, R., and DAS, R. S. (1955). J. Abnorm. Soc. Psychol. 51, 624–628.

DEUTSCH, M., and GERARD, H. (1955). J. Abnorm. Soc. Psychol. 51, 629–636.

DITTES, J. E., and KELLEY, H. H. (1956). J. Abnorm Soc. Psychol. 53, 100–107.

FESTINGER, L. (1957). "A Theory of Cognitive Dissonance." Row, Peterson, Evanston, Illinois.

FISHER, S., RUBENSTEIN, I., and FREEMAN, R. W. (1956). J. Abnorm. Soc. Psychol. 52, 200–207.

HARARY, F. (1959). Behav. Sci. 4, 316–323.

HICKS, J. M., and SPANER, F. E. (1962). J. Abnorm. Soc. Psychol. 65, 112–120.

HOVLAND, C. I., and MANDELL, W. (1957). J. Abnorm. Soc. Psychol. 47, 581–588.

HOVLAND, C. I., LUMSDAINE, A. A., and SHEFFIELD, F. (1949). "Experiments on Mass Communication." Princeton Univ. Press, Princeton, New Jersey.

HOVLAND, C. I., CAMPBELL, F., and BROCK, T. (1957). In "Order of Presentation in Persuasion" (C. I. Hovland, ed.), pp. 23–32. Yale Univ. Press, New Haven, Connecticut.

JANIS, I. L., and FESHBACH, S. (1953). J. Abnorm. Soc. Psychol. 48, 78–92.

JANIS, I. L., and FIELD, P. B. (1959). In "Personality and Persuasibility" (I. L. Janis and C. I. Hovland, eds.), pp. 55–68. Yale Univ. Press, New Haven, Connecticut.

JANIS, I. L., and RIFE, D. (1959). In "Personality and Persuasibility" (I. L. Janis and C. I. Hovland, eds.), pp. 121–140. Yale Univ. Press, New Haven, Connecticut.

KELLEY, H. H. (1957). In "Emerging Problems in Social Psychology" (M. Sherif and M. O. Wilson, eds.), pp. 229–248. Univ. of Oklahoma, Norman, Oklahoma.

KELLEY, H. H., and VOLKHART, E. H. (1952). Am. Sociol. Rev. 17, 453–465.

KELLEY, H. H., and WOODRUFF, C. L. (1956). J. Abnorm. Soc. Psychol. 52, 67–74.

KELMAN, H. C. (1950). J. Abnorm. Soc. Psychol. 45, 267–285.

———. (1953). Human Relat. 6, 185–214.

KELMAN, H., and HOVLAND, C. I. (1953). J. Abnorm. Soc. Psychol. 48, 327–335.

KENDALL, P., and WOLF, K. M. (1949). In "Communications Research, 1948–1949" (P. F. Lazarsfeld and F. N. Stanton, eds.), pp. 152–179. Harpers, New York.

KING, B. T., and JANIS, I. L. (1956). *Human Relat.* 9, 177–186.

KLAPPER, J. T. (Aug., 1949) "Effects of the Mass Media." Bureau of Applied Social Research, Columbia Univ. (mimeo), New York.

———. (1960). "Effects of Mass Communication," Free Press, Glencoe, Illinois.

LANA, R. E. (1959). *Psychol. Bull.* 56, 293–300.

LEWIN, K. (1951). *In* "Field Theory in Social Science" (D. Cartwright, ed.), Harper, New York.

———. (1958). *In* "Readings in Social Psychology" (E. Maccoby, T. Newcomb, and E. Hartley, eds.), 3rd ed., pp. 197–211. Holt, New York.

LESSER, G. S., and ABELSON, R. P. (1959). *In* "Personality and Persuasibility" (I. L. Janis and C. I. Hovland, eds.), pp. 187–206. Yale Univ. Press, New Haven, Connecticut.

LINTON, H., and GRAHAM, E. (1959). *In* "Personality and Persuasibility" (I. L. Janis and C. I. Hovland, eds.), pp. 69–101. Yale Univ. Press, New Haven, Connecticut.

LUCHINS, A. S. (1957). *In* "The Order of Presentation in Persuasion" (C. I. Hovland ed.), pp. 33–61. Yale Univ. Press, New Haven, Connecticut.

McGUIRE, W. J. (1960a). *J. Abnorm. Soc. Psychol.* 60, 345–353.

———. (1960b). *J. Abnorm. Soc. Psychol.* 60, 354–358.

———. (1961a). *J. Abnorm. Soc. Psychol.* 63, 326–332.

———. (1961b). *Sociometry* 24, 184–197.

———. (1962). *J. Abnorm. Soc. Psychol.* 64, 241–248.

———. (1963a). Threat and reassurance as factors in conferring resistance to persuasion. (In preparation.)

———. (1963b). Comparative persistence of actively and passively conferred resistance to persuasion. Unpublished manuscript.

———. (1963c). Cross-issue generalization of conferred resistance to persuasion. Unpublished manuscript.

McGUIRE, W. J., and Papageorgis, D. (1961). *J. Abnorm. Soc. Psychol.* 62, 327–337.

———. (1962). *Public Opin. Quart.* 26, 24–34.

MAUSNER, B. (1954). *J. Abnorm. Soc. Psychol.* 49, 65–68.

NEWCOMB, T. M. (1961). "The Acquaintance Process." Holt, New York.

NUNNALLY, J., and BOBREN, H. (1959). *J. Pers.* 27, 38–46.

PAPAGEORGIS, D., and McGUIRE, W. J. (1961). *J. Abnorm. Soc. Psychol.* 62, 475–481.

RAVEN, B. H., and FISHBEIN, M. (1961). *J. Abnorm. Soc. Psychol.* 63, 411–416.

ROSENBAUM, M. E., and FRANC, D. E. (1960). *J. Abnorm. Soc. Psychol.* 61, 15–20.

ROSENBAUM, M. E., and ZIMMERMAN, I. M. (1959). *Public Opin. Quart.* 23, 247–254.

ROSENBERG, M. J. (1956). *J. Abnorm. Soc. Psychol.* 53, 367–372.

ROSENBERG, M. J., and HOVLAND, C. I., eds. (1960). "Attitude Organization and Change." Yale Univ. Press, New Haven, Connecticut.

SAMELSON, F. (1957). *J. Abnorm. Soc. Psychol.* 55, 181–187.

SCHACHTER, S., and HALL, R. (1952). *Human Relat.* 5, 397–406.

SMITH, E. E. (1961). *Public Opin. Quart.* 25, 626–639.

STEINER, I. D. (1962). *J. Abnorm. Soc. Psychol.* 65, 266–267.

STUKÁT, K. G. (1958). *Acta Psychol. Gothoburgensia* 2.

TANNENBAUM, P. H. (1955). *Public Opin. Quart.* 19, 292–302.

———. (1956). *Public Opin. Quart.* 20, 413–425.

218   William J. McGuire

U.S. SENATE, COMMITTEE ON GOVERNMENT OPERATIONS. (1956). "The Interrogation, Indoctrination and Exploitation of American Military and Civilian Prisoners." U.S. Government Printing Office, Washington, D.C.

WEISS, W., and FINE, B. J. (1956) *J. Abnorm. Soc. Psychol.* 52, 109–114.

WEITZENHOFFER, A. M. (1953). "Hypnotism." Wiley, New York.

ZAJONC, R. (1960). *J. Abnorm. Soc. Psychol.* 61, 159–167.

SECTION II

THE SOURCE: PROPERTIES OF SPEAKER CREDIBILITY

"You tell them. They'll believe *you.*"

Statements such as this reflect the belief that the source of a persuasive message influences what effect that message has on its receivers. Not only is the message content important—who produces it is critical as well. For example, if identical persuasive messages are attributed either to *Pravda* or the *New York Times*, American receivers are more likely to be influenced by the message attributed to the *Times*. We are more likely to favor leniency for juvenile delinquents if the appeal for leniency comes from a respected judge of a juvenile court than if it comes from a former juvenile delinquent who recently has been accused of a felony. Television commercials abound which employ well known and respected people to endorse products and causes, and the spokesmen for special interest groups are frequently chosen on the basis of their public reputation.

Recognition that the source of a persuasive message is an important factor in its total impact is hardly a recent phenomenon. In the *Rhetoric,* Aristotle commented: "It is not true, as some writers assume in their treatises on rhetoric, that the personal goodness revealed by the speaker contributes nothing to his power of persuasion; on the contrary, his character may almost be called the most effective means of persuasion he possesses" (1, 1356a lines 10–14).

The amount of credibility possessed by a speaker—often referred to as his "ethos"—results from the combination of several components. Aristotle identified three: the intelligence of the speaker, his character, and his good will toward the audience. Hovland concluded that two major factors were involved with speaker credibility: expertness and trustworthiness.

An individual's tendency to accept a conclusion advocated by a given communicator will depend in part upon how well informed and intelligent he believes the communicator to be. However, a recipient may believe that a communicator is capable

219

of transmitting valid statements, but still be inclined to reject the communication if he suspects the communicator is motivated to make nonvalid assertions. It seems necessary, therefore, to make a distinction between (1) the extent to which a communicator is perceived to be a source of valid assertions (his 'expertness'), and (2) the degree of confidence in the communicator's intent to communicate the assertions he considers most valid (his 'trustworthiness') (4, p. 21).

Recently, two attempts have been made to identify what criteria people use to assess speaker credibility. Bettinghaus (2, pp. 105–7) reported an investigation by Berlo, Lemert, and Mertz in which the investigators used a number of bi-polar adjective scales to rate several different concepts and then subjected their results to factor analysis procedures. These results indicated that speaker credibility involves three separate dimensions. They called the first factor "safety," a dimension somewhat analogous to Hovland's "trustworthiness" factor. The second dimension they labeled "qualification," a dimension similar to Hovland's "expertise" factor. The scales associated with this factor rated how competent or well trained the receiver perceived the speaker to be. The third dimension they identified as "dynamism." Individuals apparently judge a speaker to be more credible if he appears bold and aggressive than if he appears meek and timid.

Thus, a speaker's credibility is a composite of how well qualified, trustworthy, and dynamic he is perceived to be. If he apparently possesses all three of these attributes, then he is said to have high credibility (or high ethos). If he lacks one or more of these attributes, then his credibility, and hence his overall potential to influence others, is reduced.

The selection by Andersen and Clevenger provides a summary of the major areas of research interest relevant to speaker credibility. They divide their review into three sections by areas of research. The first pertains to how speaker credibility directly affects the persuasive impact of a message or interacts with other variables to produce changes in persuasive impact. The second focuses on "techniques for generating or changing ethos," and the third deals with the measurement of ethos and its components.

Several issues relating to the effect of speaker credibility have emerged since the Andersen and Clevenger review. One of these issues concerns the relative effectiveness of low credible sources. Although the general finding has been that high credible sources are more persuasive, this need not be true in every case. Zimbardo (10) has argued that a disliked source may produce greater attitude change than a liked source in situations where audience members voluntarily commit themselves to belief-discrepant behavior. This happens because a liked source enables an individual to reduce the dissonance created by his belief-discrepant behavior by viewing his actions as a favor to the message source. Such a dissonance-reducing technique is unavailable to the person exposed to a disliked source. Hence, he is more likely to reduce dissonance by changing his attitudes to conform with his actions.

This rather intriguing prediction has received some support from investigations by Smith (9) and Zimbardo *et al.* (10). In both of these investigations the researchers presented a persuasive message to subjects asserting the positive qualities of an extremely disliked food (fried grasshoppers). The source of the message was manipulated to make it either liked or disliked by the subjects. Following the persuasive message the subjects were asked to volunteer to eat fried grasshoppers. Of those subjects who volunteered, subjects who heard the message from the disliked source displayed a significantly more positive attitude toward eating fried grasshoppers than subjects who heard the message from the liked source.

Those experiments which found significant differences in favor of high credible over low credible sources usually had one factor in common: the significant differences were found immediately after the persuasive attempt. Studies which included posttests over an extended period of time noted changes in the patterns of source effect differences. Whereas the effect of messages attributed to high credible sources diminished, the effect of messages attributed to low credible sources remained constant and in some cases increased in size. This phenomenon has become known as the "sleeper effect."

The "sleeper effect" was first noted by Hovland, Lumsdaine, and Sheffield (5) while investigating the length of time opinions formed from high and low credible sources are maintained. Their finding that the opinion change produced by some low credible sources increased after a period of time prompted several follow-up studies. Hovland and Weiss (6) employed a delayed test (four weeks after the presentation) to find out if there was an increased tendency to accept material attributed to an untrustworthy source. While the number of subjects influenced by high credible sources had decreased, the number influenced by low credible sources showed a marked increase. These results provide additional evidence for a "sleeper effect."

Hovland, Lumsdaine, and Sheffield implied that the "sleeper effect" occurs because the source had been forgotten. However, there is little experimental evidence to support this inference. An alternate explanation has been provided by Kelman and Hovland (8). They argued that the "sleeper effect" occurs because individuals gradually dissociate the message from its source. To test this hypothesis, Kelman and Hovland presented messages attributed to a high, neutral, and low credible source. Three weeks later they administered posttests to all subjects. Half of the subjects completed the posttest questionnaire after having the message source reintroduced to them. The other half completed the questionnaire without an introduction. This reintroduction removed the "sleeper effect." Furthermore, those subjects who did not have the source reintroduced displayed the "sleeper effect"; and those who displayed it most strongly were those who best remembered the source. Thus these results provide evidence that dissociation rather than simple forgetting produces the "sleeper effect."

The "sleeper effect" is the product of two psychological processes—the forgetting of information contained in the persuasive message and the dissociating of the message content from its source. With a high credible source, these processes are reinforcing; gradually receivers forget the information presented and dissociate the high credible source from his message. With a low credible source, these processes are competing; the person forgets the message information, but fails to associate the low credible source with what he remembers.[1]

[1] Festinger (3) has argued that the appearance of the "sleeper effect" may be a product of Hovland's experimental procedures. He observed that Hovland's experimental design did not control for the possibility that subjects exposed to high credible messages might interact with those exposed to low credible messages. If such interaction were commonplace, it could account for the different regression rates for opinion change found. We should also note, however, that Watts and McGuire (see Section IV) found evidence of a "sleeper effect" using experimental procedures which minimized the probability of subject interaction between experimental conditions.

But even in situations where low credible sources have less persuasiveness than high credible sources, the effectiveness of the former can be enhanced by the appropriate timing of source introductions. Experimental results obtained by Husek (7), for example, indicate that the comparative effectiveness of a low credible source is enhanced by delaying his introduction. The selection by Greenberg and Miller focuses on this issue, suggesting that there exists an interaction effect between level of source credibility and time of introduction. High credible sources are more effective if identified prior to the persuasive message. Low credible sources are more effective if identified following the message.

Another factor investigated is the mediating effect stress has on the relative persuasiveness of speakers with differing amounts of credibility. Most investigations of speaker credibility have been conducted such that the message recipients respond under conditions of relatively unpressured choice—that is, low stress conditions. The selection by Sigall and Helmreich reports an investigation in which the effectiveness of high and low credible sources was tested under conditions of high and low stress. These authors found that differences in persuasive effects attributable to differences in source credibility were present under conditions of low stress only.

REFERENCES

1. ARISTOTLE. *Rhetoric.* Translated by W. Rhys Roberts, in *The Basic Works of Aristotle,* Richard McKeon, editor. New York: Random House, 1941.
2. BETTINGHAUS, E. P. *Persuasive Communication.* New York: Holt, Rinehart and Winston, 1968.
3. FESTINGER, L. "Social Psychology and Group Processes," *Annual Review of Psychology,* 6 (1955), 187–216.
4. HOVLAND, C. I., I. L. JANIS, and H. H. KELLEY. *Communication and Persuasion.* New Haven: Yale University Press, 1953.
5. HOVLAND, C. I., A. A. LUMSDAINE, and F. D. SHEFFIELD. *Experiments on Mass Communication.* Princeton: Princeton University Press, 1949.
6. HOVLAND, C. I., and W. WEISS. "The Influence of Source Credibility on Communication Effectiveness," *Public Opinion Quarterly,* 15 (1951), 635–50.
7. HUSEK, T. R. "Persuasive Impacts of Early, Late, or No Mention of a Negative Source," *Journal of Personality and Social Psychology,* 2 (1965), 125–28.
8. KELMAN, H. C., and C. I. HOVLAND. "'Reinstatement' of the Communicator in Delayed Measurement of Opinion Change," *Journal of Abnormal and Social Psychology,* 48 (1953), 327–35.
9. SMITH, E. E. "The Power of Dissonance Techniques to Change Attitudes," *Public Opinion Quarterly,* 25 (1961), 626–39.
10. ZIMBARDO, P. G., M. WEISENBERG, I. FIRESTONE, and B. LEVY. "Communicator Effectiveness in Producing Public Conformity and Private Attitude Change," *Journal of Personality,* 33 (1965), 233–55.

Kenneth Andersen / Theodore Clevenger, Jr*

A SUMMARY OF
EXPERIMENTAL
RESEARCH
IN ETHOS

Although the number of quantitative studies employing the term *ethos* in their titles is small, related rubrics such as *credibility* and *prestige* encompass such a quantity and variety of research clearly related to this classical concept that a summary should be valuable to those undertaking further studies. The primary purpose of this paper is to provide such a summary. In this study *ethos* is defined as the image held of a communicator at a given time by a receiver—either one person or a group. The use of the words *communicator* and *receiver* is deliberate, for the writers have chosen to include studies of written and nonverbal communication as well as those involving a speaker-auditor relationship.

The major sections of this paper are summaries of experimental findings pertaining to (1) the influence of ethos upon the effect of the communication, (2) techniques for generating or changing ethos, and (3) measurements of one or more aspects of ethos and attempts to assess the relative levels of ethos of individuals or groups.

*Dr. Andersen is Associate Professor in Speech at the University of Illinois. His doctoral thesis at the University of Wisconsin was an experimental study in ethos. Dr. Clevenger is Professor of Speech and Chairman of Department at Florida State University.

Reprinted from *Speech Monographs,* 30 (1963), 59–78, with permission of the authors and the Speech Association of America.

223

INFLUENCE OF ETHOS UPON
THE INTENDED EFFECT
OF THE COMMUNICATION

Experiments concerning ethos have dealt with many and varied topics: with the effects of differences in prestige, credibility, likeableness, and other variables upon attitudes toward political-social issues, upon evaluations of art and literature, and upon learning; with the relative effectiveness of majority and expert opinion and the relative susceptibility of the sexes, different age groups, and persons of various educational levels to *prestige* suggestion; and with the temporal effects and the permanency of the attitude change and the learning induced by different levels of ethos.

It is important to remember that these studies, which arise from such fields as psychology, speech, sociology, and education, are quite diverse in origin, that many of the experimenters did not use rhetorical terminology, and that many of them also did not perceive a relationship between their studies and ethos. Studies are included, however, if the independent variable is a difference in treatment which is basically related to ethos and if the dependent variable is some measurement which is basically a communication effect index.

Theoretical and Methodological Differences

Studies differ so much in the definition of ethos and in certain other theoretical and methodological features that an analysis of these distinctions is a necessary preliminary to reporting the experiments.

1. Fixed Ethos vs. Congruity Hypothesis. In most studies the ethical element is treated as relatively fixed in value during the communication act, and persuasion is construed as the linking of a proposition with an *approved* source for a positive effect or a *disapproved* source for a negative one.[1] However, in some recent studies, especially those using semantic differential measurement, ethos is regarded as flexible, because during the act of communication alterations in the image of the speaker may be caused either by the sender's propositions or by other situational factors.[2]

---

[1] Such as John Highlander, "Audience Analyzer Measurements and Informational Effects of Speaker Variables in Radio Talks," unpubl. diss. (Wisconsin, 1953); Franklyn Haiman, "An Experimental Study of the Effects of Ethos in Public Speaking," unpubl. diss. (Northwestern, 1948); also briefly reported in *SM*, XVI (Sept., 1949), 190–202.

[2] Such as Charles Osgood, George Suci and Percy Tannenbaum, *The Measurement of Meaning* (Urbana: University of Illinois Press, 1957); Erwin Bettinghaus, "The Operation of Congruity in an Oral Communication Situation," unpubl. diss. (Illinois, 1959).

2. *Ethos Assumed vs. Ethos Measured.* Early studies of ethical effects commonly followed the pattern of employing two sources (such as Franklin Roosevelt and Herbert Hoover) assumed to differ greatly in credibility, prestige, or some other ethical component and then comparing the attitude change for Group I, which received the message credited to the first source, with that for Group II, which received the same message except that it was ascribed to the second source.[3] This method assumes that for the group of subjects in question, the experimenter can determine intuitively the relative levels of ethos of the given sources. Recent studies, in contrast, have tended to measure ethos. Experimenters have either selected their sources on the basis of pretests of credibility or chosen them arbitrarily and then checked for credibility differences by direct measurement after the completion of the experiment.[4] The last of these techniques, of course, is valid only if one is willing to espouse the fixed ethos model; for if the image of the speaker may change during the speech, a measurement rendered after the address may be quite deceptive concerning ethos at the outset.

3. *Topic-Oriented vs. Topic-Irrelevant Ethos.* The assumption for the majority of the studies apparently is that the prestige, the credibility, or some other ethical characteristic of the speaker varies from one topic to another. Thus, in most of the studies of *expert* opinion the authorities were selected because they were reputed to be well informed on the topic of the experimental message.[5] Some studies, on the other hand, seem to be based on a concept of generalized credibility and to discount or ignore the possibility that the prestige varies from topic to topic.[6]

4. *Average vs. Individual Measure.* Although the assumption in most studies is that the experimental group as an entity places the communicator at a certain level of prestige,[7] in some studies ethos is regarded as differing from one subgroup to another, and data are treated separately for such variables as sex, occupation, educational status, and political affiliation.[8] A few studies even

[3] Such as Helen Lewis, "Studies in the Principles of Judgments and Attitudes: IV. The Operation of 'Prestige Suggestion,'" *Journal of Social Psychology*, XIV (1941), 229–256.

[4] Such as Muzafer Sherif, "An Experimental Study of Stereotypes," *Journal of Abnormal and Social Psychology*, XXIX (1935), 371–375; Herbert Kelman and Carl Hovland, "'Reinstatement' of the Communicator in Delayed Measurement of Opinion Change," *Journal of Abnormal and Social Psychology*, XLVIII (1953), 327–335.

[5] Such as Malcolm Moos and Bertram Koslin, "Prestige Suggestion and Political Leadership," *Public Opinion Quarterly*, XVI (1952), 77–93; Irving Lorge with Carl Curtis, "Prestige, Suggestion and Attitudes," *Journal of Social Psychology*, VII (1936), 386–402.

[6] Such as Clare Marple, "The Comparative Susceptibility of Three Age Levels to the Suggestion of Group Versus Expert Opinion," *Journal of Social Psychology*, IV (1933), 176–186.

[7] Such as Raymond Bernberg, "Prestige Suggestion in Art as Communication," *Journal of Social Psychology*, XXXVIII (1953), 23–30; William Michael, Bernard Rosenthal, and Michael DeCamp, "An Experimental Investigation of Prestige-Suggestion for Two Types of Literary Material," *Journal of Psychology*, XXVIII (1949), 303–323.

[8] Such as Helen Lewis, *loc. cit.*

consider the prestige of the source in respect to each individual auditor.[9] Whereas in the first two types of experiment the usual statistical test is for the significance of difference between means, in studies of the individual auditor the common method is correlation.

5. *Extent of Audience Analysis.* Finally, the studies differ in that some examine audience characteristics, whereas others do not. Both approaches have interpretative hazards as well as distinctive advantages. In studies which assess the effect upon attitude change of such audience properties as sex, age, and educational level it is also possible (although infrequently done) to investigate the interaction of ethos with each of the audience variables. Thus, a study in which two levels of prestige are employed with an audience of men and women can include data on the effect of prestige level upon attitude change (ignoring sex), the difference in the persuasibility of the sexes (ignoring prestige), and differences in the relative susceptibility of the two sexes to prestige and nonprestige communication (the interactions). Careful interpretation, however, is necessary: First, the experimenter must distinguish over-all persuasibility differences between the sexes (main effect of sex) from prestige-suggestibility (the interaction). Second, where prestige is taken with reference to the entire sample of subjects, he must note the possibility of confounding prestige level with sex—that is, a source may not have the same prestige for the two sexes, and this difference may result in a spurious sex-by-prestige level interaction if prestige level is measured as a group average. Thus, some of the results seeming to show greater prestige-persuasibility for women than for men may have been products of concealed differences in the prestige level of the source for the two sexes.

Within the limits of the five methodological distinctions described above, the studies of the effects of ethos present a reasonably harmonious body of findings. In the following pages those studies employing the conception of a fixed ethos model will be presented first, and the limited number employing the congruity model will follow.

Studies Assuming That Ethos is Fixed

A number of studies which employ the relatively common fixed ethos model indicate that certain ethical factors can produce changes in attitude toward political and social issues. Arnett, Davidson, and Lewis found that a group of graduate students shifted significantly toward agreement with graduate educators on Harper's test of liberalism.[10] The study was conducted without a

[9] Such as Herbert Birch, "The Effect of Socially Disapproved Labeling upon a Well-Structured Attitude," *Journal of Abnormal and Social Psychology*, XL (1945), 301–310: David Cole, "'Rational Argument' and 'Prestige-Suggestion' as Factors Influencing Judgment," *Sociometry*, XVII (1954), 350–354.

[10] Claude Arnett, Helen Davidson, and Hallett Lewis, "Prestige as a Factor in Attitude Changes," *Sociology and Social Research*, XVI (1931), 49–55.

control group, however, and during the lapse of four weeks between the two administrations of the test, factors other than prestige may have operated to produce the observed shifts.

Birch studied the effect of political labels of *Fascist* or *Communist* and *Reactionary* or *Liberal* on college students' judgments of two statements.[11] No significant differences in preference for the two statements were observed, but this conclusion may be misleading. The fact that ninety-nine per cent of all subjects favored one statement over the other may have masked any possible prestige effect.

While the preceding studies were concerned with the effect of referential group or class prestige upon attitude change, a number of studies have been directed toward an investigation of the prestige of individuals. Saadi and Farnsworth found greater acceptance for dogmatic statements which were attributed to well-liked persons than to the same assertions when attributed to disliked individuals.[12] Lorge and Curtis found a significant tendency for subjects to shift opinion toward the supposed position of a prestige source, but they found no significant negative shift when the proposition was linked with a disapproved source.[13]

In apparent conflict with these findings are the results obtained by Lewis. She reported that college students remained relatively unchanged in the evaluation of statements and that they tried to explain away the "prestige source" through rationalization.[14] Unhappily, the conclusions to the study show the bias of an author who quite evidently hoped to support an hypothesis: for example, she describes rank-order correlations of a magnitude of .50 as "high." This bias renders suspect the assertion that informal interviews with the subjects and free responses revealed that suggestion, when effective, usually redefined an ambiguous situation.

A more satisfactory design for testing a similar hypothesis was that employed by Moos and Koslin, who discovered that vague quotations were those which were the most likely to be influenced by attribution to differing sources.[15]

Hastorf and Piper, using a variety of problems, studied the effects of supposed ratings of businessmen and educators on the attitudes of subjects. They found that all groups, including one which was instructed to duplicate its pretest responses and ignore the supposed ratings, shifted significantly.[16]

Smith found that printed propaganda statements when labeled as fact

[11] *Loc. cit.*

[12] Mitchell Saadi and Paul Farnsworth, "The Degrees of Acceptance of Dogmatic Statements and Preferences for Their Supposed Makers," *Journal of Abnormal and Social Psychology*, XXIX (1934), 143–150.

[13] *Loc. cit.*

[14] *Loc. cit.*

[15] *Loc. cit.*

[16] A. H. Hastorf and G. W. Piper, "A Note on the Effect of Explicit Instructions on Prestige Suggestion," *Journal of Social Psychology*, XXXIII (1951), 289–293.

produced greater belief than when labeled as rumor. The success of the "fact" label, however, clearly varied with the prior attitude of the subject and with the relation of the alleged "fact" to truth.[17]

The objective of all of the above studies was to assess the effects of prestige upon judgment of political and social issues, and the method in all instances was to link a source with a proposition but to provide no message by which the source supported the proposition. A question of more immediate interest to students of speech is whether differences in the speaker's prestige significantly influence the persuasive outcome of a speech.

Haiman presented to three groups a tape recorded speech variously attributed to Thomas Parran, Surgeon General of the United States; to Eugene Dennis, Secretary of the Communist Party in America; and to a "Northwestern University Sophomore." Not only was Parran rated significantly more competent than the other two, but also, as measured by the Woodward Shift-of-Opinion Ballot, his speech was significantly more effective in changing attitude than was either of the other two. The "Dennis" and the "Sophomore" speeches did not differ significantly.[18]

Employing essentially the same techniques—a tape-recorded speech, differing introductions, and the Woodward ballot—Strother and Paulson in separate studies obtained results similar to Haiman's. Not only did Strother find significant differences in the persuasiveness of the "Parran" and the "Dennis" speeches, but also he noted that only those who thought they had been listening to Dennis wrote unfavorable comments concerning the speech techniques employed.[19] Paulson attributed a taped speech to a political science professor and to a student. For female auditors there was no significant difference in the effects of the "two" speeches, but among the male auditors the proportion of those shifting opinion was greater for the group which thought it had been addressed by the professor.[20]

The supposed differences in prestige level in the experiments cited above were assumed to be quite large, and the methods of establishing the prestige levels were straightforward and obvious. On the other hand, Hovland and Mandell, in an effort to assess subtler sources of the speaker's image, manipulated credibility through the *suggestion* of differing degrees of selfish interest and self-motivation. The nonsignificant difference in attitude change which the speakers produced was very small, but the audiences, apparently reacting to

[17] George Smith, "Belief in Statements Labeled Fact and Rumor," *Journal of Abnormal and Social Psychology*, XLII (1947), 80–90.

[18] *Loc. cit.*

[19] Edward Strother, "An Experimental Study of Ethos as Related to the Introduction in the Persuasive Speaking Situation," unpubl. diss. (Northwestern, 1951).

[20] Stanley Paulson, "Experimental Study of Spoken Communications; The Effects of Prestige of the Speaker and Acknowledgement of Opposing Arguments on Audience Retention and Shift of Opinion," unpubl. diss. (Minnesota, 1952); also briefly reported in *SM*, XXI (1954), 267–271.

their presumed prejudices, rated the "unbiased source" as the significantly fairer and more honest of the two.[21] Since these evaluations were rendered after the speech, the initial ethos of the two sources, the point at which the "biases" of one began to emerge, or the ways in which the images of the two speakers changed during the speech are unknown.

A study by Kraus likewise suggests the possibility of evaluating indirect, implicative sources of ethos. Using pairs which were racially homogeneous and others which were racially heterogeneous, he compared whites with Negroes in respect to their persuasiveness in filmed discussions of segregation issues. The results indicated that arguments favorable to integration were more persuasive when advanced by the heterogeneous pairs, and Kraus explained the results in terms of differing levels of credibility.[22]

All the studies mentioned thus far have dealt with ethos as determined by the position or reputation of the source. Messages, if used, have been standardized so that the only variable was the introduction given the speaker.

Other studies, in contrast, have been designed so that some internal message elements have been varied systematically. Gilkinson, Paulson, and Sikkink, who incorporated or excluded authority quotations in two versions of the same speech, found that both versions engendered a significant shift in attitude with only a trend to favor the inclusion of authorities.[23] In another study Sikkink similarly employed quotations, but neither attitude shift nor ratings of convincingness showed significant differences.[24] While the use of authorities certainly has persuasive implications beyond the ethical dimension (and indeed the authors of these experiments apparently did not consider ethos the critical variable), the fact that the speaker was not evaluated as significantly more convincing when he used authorities suggests that citing reputable sources does not necessarily enhance ethos—as some theorists have suggested.

The two studies above are included within the fixed ethos model because the prestige of the authorities seemingly served directly as the basis for the shift in opinion, if any. Other experimenters varied the procedure by apparently employing authorities for the purpose of altering the image of the speaker; this altered image, in turn, was to serve as the warrant for the persuasive effect.

[21] Carl Hovland and Wallace Mandell, "An Experimental Comparison of Conclusion Drawing by the Communicator and the Audience," *Journal of Abnormal and Social Psychology*, XLVII (1952), 581–588.

[22] Sidney Kraus, "An Experimental Study of the Relative Effectiveness of Negroes and Whites in Achieving Racial Attitude Change Via Kinescope Recordings," unpubl. diss. (Iowa, 1959); *SM*, XXVII (1960), 87–88.

[23] Howard Gilkinson, Stanley Paulson, and Donald Sikkink, "Effects of Order and Authority in an Argumentative Speech," *QJS*, XL (1954), 183–192.

[24] Donald Sikkink, "An Experimental Study of the Effects on the Listener of Anticlimax Order and Authority in an Argumentative Speech," *Southern Speech Journal*, XXII (1956), 73–78.

(Possibly both effects could occur.) Studies of attitude changes dependent upon such attempts at artistic ethos are reported in a subsequent section of this paper.[25]

Historically parallel to the study of the effects of ethos upon political and social attitudes has been the study of its effect upon judgments of literature, art, and matters of personal taste. In three experiments in Turkey and at Harvard Sherif found correlations of .45 to .53 between rankings of authors and subsequent rankings of passages to which authors' names were randomly attached. Sherif asserts that the name of the author exerts an influence upon ratings of passages.[26]

Michael, Rosenthal, and DeCamp matched authors with prose and poetry passages and found little evidence of the effect noted by Sherif.[27] Although they claimed methodological improvements over the Sherif study, their rank-of-summed-ranks technique actually produced a measure of dubious statistical reliability.[28] The entire study was conducted in such a manner that results confirming the Sherif finding were highly unlikely. The interpretation of their inconclusive results as evidence contrary to the Sherif hypothesis seems unjustified.

More recently, in India, Das, Rath, and Das studied the effect of author prestige upon evaluations of poetry. Working with quite small groups and crude statistical measures, they concluded that prestige influenced judgment greatly but that this effect was weakened when the factors of understanding and merit were stressed.[29]

Judgments of art seem to be similar. Data obtained by Farnsworth and Misumi displayed a trend indicating that recognition of the artist's name had some favorable effect on the evaluations of pictures.[30] In another experiment Bernberg found that positive and negative evaluations of alleged art critics significantly affected the judgments by artistically naive students with regard to seven of ten paintings.[31]

Cole presented abstract finger paintings for discussion in small groups. In situations in which the art teacher presented judgments in opposition to those of the group, significant shifts occurred only when the teacher was

[25] See p. 238. Still other implications for a theory of ethos stemming from the authority quotation problem will be discussed in a subsequent paper.

[26] *Loc. cit.*

[27] *Loc. cit.*

[28] The problems in the use of a rank-of-summed-ranks technique are discussed by Roger Nebergall, "Some Applications of Measurement Theory to the Judgment of Speech Contests," unpublished paper read at the Central States Speech Association Conference, April 8, 1960.

[29] J. P. Das, R. Rath, and Rhea Stagner Das, "Understanding Versus Suggestion in the Judgment of Literary Passages," *Journal of Abnormal and Social Psychology*, LI (1955), 624–628.

[30] Paul Farnsworth and Issei Misumi, "Further Data on Suggestion in Pictures," *American Journal of Psychology*, XLIII (1931), 632.

[31] *Loc. cit.*

present. A peer leader, to cite a second finding, secured significant shifts only when he also presented pseudo-rational arguments.[32]

Again, similar effects have been found in the area of personal taste and perceptions. Duncker presented a story to nursery school children in which a fictional hero endorses a food actually less desirable than an alternative selection. The after-effect was decidedly positive—a large percentage of the children selected the endorsed food when given a choice. Over a period of twelve days, however, the selection of the less satisfying food declined to the level of a control group. Some of the initial preference for the less desirable food was reinstated by recalling the story, but this effect degenerated very quickly.[33]

Donceel, Alimena, and Birch presented adults and high school and college students with personality descriptions of themselves. These supposedly came from tests and expert evaluations, but actually were determined by chance. Under mild suggestion a significant number of students accepted these statements as valid, and under strong suggestion all subjects yielded. They accepted as true the false descriptions of their personalities and reversed previous answers to questions in a personality test.[34]

Aveling and Hargreaves found *personal suggestion* capable of affecting performance in a variety of perceptual and psychomotor tasks, but they also secured evidence of strong negative suggestibility among some of their subjects.[35]

Although there is little reason to suppose that those elements of ethos which are designed to obtain attitude change are also capable of producing differences in learning, a small number of studies pertain to this possibility. Weiss taught responses to groups of students, one of which was told that the answers were untrue. No differences in learning occurred, but what was learned correlated with the attitude change which took place during the experiment.[36] Paulson found no significant differences in retention between high and low ethos sources, although certain audience variables did appear to be related to learning.[37] Sikkink's results were substantially the same.[38]

An experiment by Harms shows that cloze test scores are somewhat higher when the speakers are high in status than when they are low. The inferred reason for this result is that high-status speakers are more "comprehensible."

[32] *Loc. cit.*

[33] Karl Duncker, "Experimental Modification of Children's Food Preferences Through Social Suggestion," *Journal of Abnormal and Social Psychology,* XXXIII (1938), 489–507.

[34] Joseph Donceel, Benjamin Alimena, and Catherine Birch, "Influence of Prestige Suggestion on the Answers of a Personality Inventory," *Journal of Applied Psychology,* XXXIII (1949), 352–355.

[35] F. Aveling and H. L. Hargreaves, "Suggestibility with an Without Prestige in Children," *British Journal of Psychology,* XII (1921–1922), 53–75.

[36] Walter Weiss, "A 'Sleeper' Effect in Opinion Change," *Journal of Abnormal and Social Psychology,* XLVIII (1953), 173–180.

[37] *Loc. cit.*

[38] *Loc. cit.*

A further result, secured through a differential analysis of listener groups, is that listeners respond with greater comprehension to those from their own class than to speakers from either a higher or a lower class.[39]

The above studies were concerned with the effects of the ethos of individual communicators. A smaller number of investigations have attempted to compare the effects of expert opinions with those produced by majority opinion.

Using as a criterion the frequency with which the subjects reversed their preferences so as to conform to the prestige group, Moore measured the relative influence of majority and expert opinions upon judgments of grammar, ethics, and music. The two sources were about equally effective except with respect to grammar, where the majority opinion prevailed by a ratio of 10 to 7.[40] The primitive design of this experiment may have concealed other differences.

An experiment by Marple, who found that both the group and experts influenced opinions about solutions to seventy-five assorted problems, reinforced Moore's results. Majority opinion was roughly one-third more effective than expert opinion with students and roughly one-fifth more effective with adults.[41]

With respect to religious beliefs, Burtt and Falkenburg discovered that opinions of both the majority and experts influenced judgments significantly, that expert (clerical) opinions tended to have greater influence than majority views in some matters of religious belief, and that a contrary tendency existed in other areas.[42]

Incidental findings of a number of studies bear upon the question of the relative susceptibility of various audience types to prestige as a means of suggestion. Within the narrow range which an undergraduate psychology class affords, Hovland and Mandell found that personality and intelligence were not related to prestige-suggestibility.[43] Kersten reports a similar finding for intelligence;[44] but Wegrocki reports a tendency for intelligence to be negatively associated with prestige-suggestibility.[45] Strother discovered no shifts in opinion which correlated with either sex or the urban-versus-rural dimension, but he did find that members of the audience with initially neutral views on the

[39] Leroy Stanley Harms, "Social Judgments of Status Cues in Language," unpubl. diss. (Ohio State, 1959); *SM*, XXVII (1960), 87.

[40] Henry Moore, "The Comparative Influence of Majority and Expert Opinion," *American Journal of Psychology*, XXXII (1921), 16–20.

[41] *Loc. cit.*

[42] Harold Burtt and Don Falkenberg, Jr., "The Influence of Majority and Expert Opinion on Religious Attitudes," *Journal of Social Psychology*, XIV (1941), 269–278.

[43] *Loc. cit.*

[44] Barbara Kersten, "An Experimental Study to Determine the Effect of a Speech of Introduction upon the Persuasive Speech that Followed," unpubl. thesis (South Dakota State College, 1958).

[45] Henry Wegrocki, "The Effect of Prestige Suggestibility on Emotional Attitudes," *Journal of Social Psychology*, V (1934), 384–394.

speech topic were significantly more responsive to variations of ethos than were either the pro or the con groups.[46] Kersten,[47] Paulson,[48] and Pross[49] obtained results confirming those of Strother.

Sikkink found that women rated the persuasiveness of all speeches significantly higher than did men, but that women were neither easier nor harder to influence than men.[50] Cathcart also concluded that sex was not significantly related to persuasibility.[51] Pross reported some indication that women were the more suggestible, and Wegrocki also concluded that girls, as compared with boys, tended to be more suggestible and to react more strongly to sympathetic propaganda.[52] Paulson found that women reacted more but retained less information. Freshmen, also according to Paulson, tended to shift less in response to the high ethos source than did upperclassmen, but there was no guarantee that the freshmen and the upperclassmen perceived the high ethos source in the same light.[53] Cathcart found that education, speech training, and subject matter competence had no effect on persuasibility.[54] The discovery by Aveling and Hargreaves of great differences in suggestibility on a number of perceptual and psychomotor tasks leads to speculation that two sharply divided groups, the suggestible and the contrasuggestible, may exist. They found no tendency, however, for suggestibility to correlate with any of a number of psychometric variables.[55]

Marple found that high school and college students shift more than do adults.[56]

A single study has illustrated the possibility of investigating the effects of audience size upon the relationship between ethos and attitude change. Knower compared the effect of delivering a speech in an audience situation with giving the speech to one auditor at a time. The speech in the individual situation was somewhat more effective, women were more influenced than men, and women speakers obtained greater attitude shifts than did men. In the audience situation, however, male speakers obtained greater shifts than did women.[57]

[46] *Loc. cit.*

[47] *Loc. cit.*

[48] *Loc. cit.*

[49] Edward Pross, "A Critical Analysis of Certain Aspects of Ethical Proof," unpubl. diss. (Iowa, 1942).

[50] *Loc. cit.*

[51] Robert Cathcart, "An Experimental Study of the Relative Effectiveness of Four Methods of Presenting Evidence," *SM*, XXII (1955), 227–233.

[52] *Loc. cit.*

[53] *Loc. cit.*

[54] *Loc. cit.*

[55] *Loc. cit.*

[56] *Loc. cit.*

[57] Franklin Knower, "Experimental Studies of Changes in Attitudes: I. A Study of the Effect of Oral Argument on Changes in Attitude," *Journal of Social Psychology*, VI (1935), 315–347.

Most of the studies described above deal primarily with the immediate effects of prestige, credibility, and other ethical elements. Hovland and his associates, however, have investigated the temporal effects of the source upon persuasion. In one of these experiments Hovland and Weiss held all of the message elements constant except for factors which produced an impression of high credibility for one source and low credibility for another. The subjects exposed to the former stimulus shifted in significantly greater numbers on immediate post-tests of attitude than did those receiving the message with low credibility. Over a period of one month the favorable effect, however, decreased, and the subjects exposed to the "inferior" source moved toward agreement with the attitudes expressed in it. Hovland postulated a "sleeper effect"—that in the absence of further stimuli agreement with high credibility sources decays while agreement with low credibility sources grows. The possible explanation is that the subject forgets the source but retains the information and the essential arguments.[58] In a specific test of the sleeper hypothesis, Kelman and Hovland found that a high ethos source, who was rated significantly fairer, better qualified to speak, and of sounder judgment than a supposedly low ethos source, produced significantly greater attitude shifts. Over a three-week period, however, the extent to which subjects agreed with the positive source decreased significantly, and the extent to which they agreed with the negative source increased nonsignificantly. Reinforcing the recall of the sources by playing back the introductions of the tape-recorded messages produced greater agreement with the high prestige speaker and less agreement with the one of low ethos in an experimental group than occurred in a control group which received no repetition of the stimuli.[59]

In a variation of the above approach Weiss determined that a group exposed to a low credibility source showed less regression toward its original attitude than did a group exposed to a high credibility source.[60]

Also supporting the sleeper effect is the finding that over a period of time those who originally disliked a communicator became slightly more positive toward him while those who had originally liked him became slightly less favorable (nonsignificant).[61] The results of Duncker's study of the effect of prestige suggestion upon children's food preferences also confirm the Hovland sleeper effect findings in respect to both the decline of the effect over time and the renewal of strength following reinstatement.[62]

[58] Carl Hovland and Walter Weiss, "The Influence of Source Credibility on Communication Effectiveness," *Public Opinion Quarterly,* XVI (1951), 635–650.
    [59] *Loc. cit.*
    [60] *Loc. cit.*
    [61] Arthur Cohen, "Need for Cognition and Order of Communication as Determinants of Opinion Change" in *Order of Presentation,* eds. Carl I. Hovland et al. (New Haven: Yale University Press, 1957), pp. 79–97.
    [62] *Loc. cit.*

Studies Assuming That Ethos
Is Variable

Diverse as the studies discussed above appear to be, they share a common model of ethos—that is, they are all based on the assumption that the speaker's image is relatively fixed throughout the period of communication. In sharp contrast with this view is the ethical model based on a congruity principle enunciated by Osgood.[63] Intended to explain many psychological functions, the congruity principle holds that an image (or meaning) depends upon the other concepts with which it is associated and thus is subject to perpetual change. Among the factors causing these variations are the successive parts of the message.

Drawing upon this generalized congruity hypothesis, Tannenbaum formulated predictions of attitude change toward communication sources and then compared these estimates with the results obtained when college students were exposed to written messages. Since the correlation was .91, the conclusion is that attitude changes of the college students in this experiment conformed to the congruity hypothesis.[64]

A study of the same hypothesis applied to public speakers showed that the congruity model predicted changes in attitude somewhat better than chance alone.[65] This study, however, failed to produce the goodness of fit observed in the Tannenbaum experiment.[66]

Bettinghaus hypothesized that the difference between these results was caused by the presence of a greater number of elements in the cognitive structure for oral than for written messages. Extending the cogruity model to four elements—speaker, central proposition, speech composition, and delivery—he obtained results which fit his extended model significantly better than they do the two-element model (speaker and central proposition) employed in the earlier experiments.[67]

GENERATING OR CHANGING ETHOS

Unlike the studies discussed in the preceding section, which typically attempted to assess the utility of a presumed or measured ethos, the experi-

[63] Osgood, Suci, and Tannenbaum, *loc. cit.*; Charles Osgood and Percy Tannenbaum, "The Principle of Congruity in the Prediction of Attitude Change," *Psychological Review*, LXII (1955), 42–55.

[64] Percy Tannenbaum, "Initial Attitude Toward Source and Concept as Factors in Attitude Change Through Communication," *Public Opinion Quarterly*, XX (1956), 413–425.

[65] David Berlo and Halbert Gulley, "Some Determinants of the Effect of Oral Communication in Producing Attitude Change and Learning," *SM*, XXIV (1957), 10–20.

[66] Compare the results of Berlo and Gulley with those of Osgood, Suci, and Tannenbaum, p. 212.

[67] *Loc. cit.*

ments discussed below are concerned with the means of generating or altering a receiver's image of a communicator. These efforts, in general, fall into two categories: those which tried to establish extrinsic ethos by techniques employed before the message itself began, and those which attempted to create intrinsic ethos by techniques employed by the speaker during the presentation.[68]

Extrinsic Ethos

The following experiments deal with the generation or the modification of a communicator's image by stimuli which are not part of the actual presentation.

Since the ethos of the individual depends in part upon the reputation of the group to which he belongs, experiments concerning the alteration of group images are relevant to the concept of ethos. One such experiment showed that very short speeches produced immediate attitude changes in favor of either China or Japan but that over a five-month period significant regression occurred toward the original attitudes.[69] In a similar experiment Roman Catholic school children were found to be quite persuasible to some but not all items in propaganda covering a wide range of topics. Other conclusions were that attitudes toward well-known individuals seemed about as subject to change as other attitudes and that reactions toward groups outside the students' immediate experience seemed especially subject to the influence of propaganda.[70]

Closely related to the question of changing attitudes toward individuals is that of building an image. Annis and Meier set out to create an image of an unknown source through planted editorials which linked the source with certain opinions and actions. The experimenters assumed that they could predict whether the subjects of the experiment favored or opposed these opinions and actions. As few as seven planted editorials generated the desired image, and most of the effects persisted over a period of four months.[71]

Berlo and Kumata studied the effect of a dramatic allegory, "The Investigator," in modifying images. Attitudes toward Joseph McCarthy, the subject of the satire, tended to become more favorable, while attitudes toward the source (the Canadian Broadcasting Company) and toward Congressional committees became significantly less favorable. The experimenters felt that the extreme

---

[68] Extrinsic ethos is the image of the speaker as it exists prior to a given speech. Intrinsic ethos, comparable to Aristotle's artistic ethos, is the image derived from elements during the presentation of the speech, consciously or unconsciously provided by the speaker. In real life speech situations, the final ethos is a product of the interaction of extrinsic and intrinsic ethos.

[69] William Chen. "The Influence of Oral Propaganda Material upon Students' Attitudes," *Archives of Psychology*, XXIII (1933); "Retention of the Effect of Oral Propaganda," *Journal of Social Psychology*, VII (1936), 479–483.

[70] Wegrocki, *loc. cit.*

[71] Albert Annis and Norman Meier, "The Induction of Opinion Through Suggestion by Means of 'Planted Content,'" *Journal of Social Psychology*, V (1934), 65–81.

one-sidedness of the presentation may have caused these "boomerang" effects.[72]

Using a single tape-recorded speech, Kersten compared two introductions, one of which employed techniques estimated by experts to focus attention on the speaker and his subject and to build the speaker's prestige and the other of which did not. The persons hearing the speech with the favorable introduction changed opinion significantly more than did those who heard no introduction or the poor one.[73] The confounding involved in the simultaneous manipulation of prestige and attention-focussing elements makes it impossible to conclude that the enhanced prestige of the speaker was the source of the observed difference. Indeed, Pross found that an introduction stressing the character, the reputation, and the intelligence of the speaker added little to the persuasiveness of either "ethical" or "nonethical" forms of a speech.[74]

Neither Kersten nor Pross actually measured differences in ethos; they assumed that different introductions would affect the variable. The same is true of Highlander's experiment, which seems to show that variable levels of authoritativeness of the speakers do not affect either the likeableness of radio programs or the amount of information gained from them.[75] In all such studies it is possible that the experimental treatments failed to take effect in the supposed manner.

Andersen constructed three introductions designed to establish varying levels of prestige and authoritativeness for speakers dealing with the farm problem. His conclusions were these: (1) Students perceived significant differences between a college student and a Professor of Agriculture or a Farm Extension Agent on two scales: (*a*) the evaluative and the dynamism dimensions of a semantic differential designed to measure ethos; (*b*) authoritativeness as estimated by a Likert-type scale. (2) The expected differences between the professor and the extension agent did not result except on the authoritativeness scale. (3) The more rhetorically sophisticated students seemed to perceive differences in ethos that the rhetorically naive students did not. (4) There was no proof that the variations in ethos and authoritativeness affected persuasiveness.[76]

A speech of introduction, one should note, creates special theoretical problems; for if the audience image of the introducer is low, this attitude through transfer may affect the ethos of the speaker. For instance, at the time of this writing, a laudatory introduction of a political candidate in the United States performed by James Hoffa or Fidel Castro might prove a serious detriment to persuasiveness. Since less obvious factors may also affect the experi-

[72] David Berlo and Hideya Kumata, "The Investigator: The Impact of a Satirical Radio Drama," *Journalism Quarterly*, XXXIII (1956), 287–298.

[73] *Loc. cit.*

[74] *Loc. cit.*

[75] *Loc. cit.*

[76] Kenneth E. Andersen, "An Experimental Study of the Interaction of Artistic and Nonartistic Ethos in Persuasion," unpubl. diss. (Wisconsin, 1961).

mental situation, it is conceivable that ethos may be more sensitive to such un-foreseen and uncontrolled variables than it is to the verbal content of the introductions.

Intrinsic Ethos[77]

That changes in ethos result from hearing speeches seems clear from a study of the effect of a campaign speech by Thomas E. Dewey. Comparing ratings obtained before a speech with those recorded immediately afterwards, Thompson found that students raised their estimation of Dewey as a public speaker but did not change their opinions significantly concerning the sound-ness of his ideas and his acceptability as a candidate.[78]

Studies which have altered the presentational elements may be divided into those which have manipulated characteristics of the manuscript and those which have altered such nonmanuscript stimuli as the speaker's appearance or his style of delivery.

A common type of study is the comparison of the effect of presenting both sides with the effect of giving but one—a distinction which seems to the writers to be ethically significant.[79] In one such investigation Hovland, Lumsdaine, and Sheffield found (1) that the "both sides" presentation was significantly more effective for subjects with a high school education when the weight of evidence clearly supported one side; and (2) that a one-sided presentation was more effective with subjects initially favoring the advocated view and with subjects who had not completed high school.[80]

Similarly, Paulson's experiment involved two speeches, one of which omitted opposing arguments and the other of which made the barest mention of them. Opinion changes did not differ significantly, but the "both sides" speech was significantly superior in respect to the amount of information which was obtained.[81] Shanck and Goodman also tested reactions to propa-ganda which presented equal amounts of argument on both sides or one-sided pro or con arguments. That no significant difference was observed,[82] might be explained by the extreme subtlety of the propaganda.

[77] *Intrinsic ethos* is defined in this study as the image of the speaker which is generated during the presentation of the message.

[78] Wayne Thompson, "A Study of the Attitude of College Students Toward Thomas E. Dewey Before and after Hearing Him Speak," *SM*, XVI (1949), 125–134.

[79] The presentation of both sides of an issue is often treated as one aspect of ethical proof. The practice also has logical connotations. It is possible to consider the impact of the treatment of both sides on the image of the speaker and the impact of this image on persuasive-ness as distinct from the logical value of the treatment and the resultant persuasiveness.

[80] Carl Hovland, Arthur Lumsdaine, and Fred Sheffield, *Experiments on Mass Communi-cation:* Vol. III of *Studies in Social Psychology in World War II* (Princeton: Princeton University Press, 1949).

[81] *Loc. cit.*

[82] R. C. Shanck and Charles Goodman, "Reactions to Propaganda on Both Sides of a Controversial Issue," *Public Opinion Quarterly*, III (1939), 107–112.

Another rhetorical element which is sometimes held to carry ethical implications is the use of authority and citations of source. Three studies described earlier in this paper reported that the inclusion of authority did not increase persuasiveness.[83] Cathcart presented four versions of a speech with variations from form to form in respect to the amount of specific evidence and documentation. He found that the forms which supported but did not document contentions and which supported, documented, and specified that the sources cited were experts produced significantly greater shifts at the five per cent level than did the form which merely supplied generalizations. A fourth form which supported the assertions and documented fully but did not say that the cited sources were experts was not significantly more effective than the one which merely supplied generalizations.[84] That such differences as were observed were attributable to nonethical considerations is suggested by the finding that none of the speeches differed in terms of the audience's evaluations of the speaker's competence, enthusiasm, or clarity of ideas.[85]

Ludlum constructed a speech in which he incorporated several elements designed to increase the credibility of the source. His techniques include the acknowledgment of opposing arguments, "leading thoughts rather than forcing," showing alleged facts to be consistent with known facts, showing material to be recent, and manifesting a "high degree of credibility" by means of self-praising statements. Comparing the persuasiveness of this speech with that of a "straight argumentative" address, he found the latter to be more effective.[86] Since he did not measure received ethos, the effect of the variables in the nonargumentative speech is unknown. Moreover, since all of the variables were incorporated in a single speech, it is impossible to isolate the effect of any one of them. If some of the techniques produced positive effects and others acted negatively, the effects may have counterbalanced one another. Thirdly, some of the self-praising statements in the nonargumentative speech may have had an effect quite different from that intended. Finally, argumentative technique may have an ethical dimension for college students, such as those whom Ludlum employed, with the result that the argumentative talk may well have produced a more favorable speaker image than did the speech employing an assortment of "conciliatory" techniques.

The experiment by Ludlum points up the importance of specifying carefully any differences in content between speeches intended to produce high credibility and those against which their effects are to be compared. This same consideration applies to an early experiment by Pross, who constructed four

[83] See the studies previously cited by Sikkink, by Cole, and by Gilkinson, Paulson, and Sikkink.

[84] *Loc. cit.*

[85] The problem of separating the logical and the ethical effects of the same complex stimulus is again at issue. The writers believe that a complex stimulus may affect both logical and ethical proof and perhaps pathetic proof as well.

[86] Thomas Ludlum, "A Study of Techniques for Influencing the Credibility of a Communication," unpubl. diss. (Ohio State, 1956).

forms of a speech on a single topic. Two of these employed techniques of "ethical appeal" (as judged by speech experts) and the other two did not. Length was kept constant.[87] The interpretation of Pross' nonsignificant findings is difficult, for matching the lengths necessitated the removal of material in order to make room for the ethical elements. As a consequence the two ethical speeches had almost no logical structure.

This investigation and other studies indicate a confusion in the use of the terms *ethos* and *ethical*. On the one hand, these terms are used to refer to the audience's image of the speaker, as when it is said that Parran is more credible or higher in ethos than is Dennis; on the other hand, certain types of speech content are labeled *ethical appeals*. For example, a speech which employs many self-references and conciliatory elements is described as higher in ethos content than an address which follows a straightforward proposition-and-proof format. Usually, when rhetoricians classify a speech content element as "ethical," they seem to mean that the elements *seem to the classifier* to be calculated to gain the good will of the audience or to enhance the speaker's ethos. In our present state of knowledge concerning audience response, such a judgment is at best only an educated guess. Therefore, when the results of the Pross and the Ludlum studies are cited in support of the proposition that ethical speeches are no more effective in inducing attitude change than are logical speeches, it should be specified very carefully that the results are based upon analysis of speech content and not upon the image of the speaker which the audience holds. The present writers as rhetorical critics believe that some of the Pross and Ludlum "ethical" speech techniques probably had decidedly negative effects on the ethos of the speaker. The basis of this judgment, of course, is intuitive, not empirical.

The message which an audience receives during a speech obviously involves more than verbal (manuscript) stimuli. Several studies indicate that nonverbal factors produce audience judgments concerning the speaker. Haiman found (1) that an audience rated a graduate male speaker higher in competence than it did an undergraduate male and two females; (2) that with content held constant, graduate speakers obtained higher rates of fairmindedness, sincerity, and likeableness than did undergraduates; (3) that in two experiments shifts of opinion within the audience were correlated positively with the speakers' competence ratings and with nothing else; and (4) that although variations in ratings of likeableness and physical attractiveness could be produced through changes in appearance and demeanor, significant changes in attitude did not result.[88]

Many of the variables in the Haiman study are those associated with differences in social status. Harms has shown that, regardless of their own position, listeners in general assign high credibility to speakers of high social

[87] *Loc. cit.*
[88] *Loc. cit.*

status and low credibility to those of low status. Such judgments occur even though the stimulus is nothing more than a short tape-recorded sample of speech. The Harms study further shows that listeners can discriminate class differences with rough accuracy and that they identify the low status speakers somewhat more readily than they do those of superior background.[89]

Consistent with these results is the experimental finding that audiences may construct relatively complete assessments of a speaker's personality and physical characteristics on the basis of his voice. Other conclusions to this study were that personality, physical characteristics and occupation were likely to be perceived correctly, that consistency of response (right or wrong!) was a stronger tendency than accuracy of judgment, and that gross psychological characteristics were judged more accurately than physical features.[90]

These findings suggest the plausibility of the "truth-will-out" theory regarding the action of subliminal, nonverbal stimuli upon the ethos of the speaker. As the theory goes, an insincere speaker's sophistry will betray itself through unconscious behaviors which act subliminally upon the auditors. An experiment by Hildreth, however, offers no confirmation for this hypothesis. Defining sincerity in terms of the speaker's expressed preference for one side of a controversial issue and using a large number of speakers who filmed speeches on both their preferred and their nonpreferred sides, he discovered that audiences were unable to distinguish the sincere from the insincere speeches and that the ratings of the two types of speeches did not differ significantly in effectiveness. Rather, ratings of effectiveness and of *estimated* sincerity were positively correlated.[91] Unfortunately, methodological considerations render the results of the experiment inconclusive. Since the "sincere" speech was composed, practiced, and delivered first in all instances, the time allowed for composition was very brief, and the making of a film was presumably unfamiliar to a majority of the speakers, a number of factors were operating to enhance performance in the "insincere" presentation as contrasted with the "sincere" one.

Indeed, the role which subliminal perception may play in the establishment of ethos has been little clarified by experiments. Drawing upon the "hidden persuader" approach, Steiner found that placing visually superimposed words on a screen at subliminal intensity levels did not alter either the effectiveness of a filmed speech or the judgment of the sincerity of the speaker.[92]

[89] *Loc. cit.*

[90] Gordon Allport and Hadley Cantril, "Judging Personality from Voice," *Journal of Social Psychology*, V (1934), 37–55; also in Hadley Cantril and Gordon Allport, *The Psychology of Radio* (New York: Harper and Row, 1935).

[91] Richard Hildreth, "An Experimental Study of Audiences' Ability to Distinguish Between Sincere and Insincere Speakers," unpubl. diss. (Southern California, 1953).

[92] George Edward Steiner, "An Experimental Study of the Influence of Subliminal Cue Words on an Audience's Perception of a Filmed Speaker's Sincerity, Effectiveness, and Subject Matter," unpubl. diss. (Southern California, 1959); *SM*, XXVII (1960), 93–94.

Combining prior and intrinsic elements, Strother attempted to study a combination of factors. The addition of ethical techniques either singly or in combination did not significantly increase the persuasiveness of a low ethos source. However, as measured by a hostility scale, the combination of elements apparently surpassed a control speech in allaying hostility toward the low ethos source. In the control presentation neither conciliatory nor special introductory techniques were employed.[93]

In another investigation of combinations of variables Andersen used two tape-recorded speeches, both of which were attributed to three sources described in tape-recorded introductions. The principal results were these: (1) Despite great manuscript variations which speech experts predicted would produce different levels of ethos, the only significant differences between the two speeches were those measured on a dynamism scale. (2) The elements of artistic and inartistic ethos did interact significantly in producing the final image of the speaker. (3) The variations in ethos did not cause a significant difference in persuasiveness.[94]

MEASUREMENTS OF ETHOS AND ATTEMPTS TO ASSESS THE RELATIVE DEGREES OF ETHOS

In a few instances the development of a measure of ethos has been the main goal of a research project, but more often the measurement of prestige, credibility, or some other ethical component has been ancillary to the study of such presumed results of ethos as preferences, attitude change, and information gain. The methods of measurement in both types of investigation are the same: (1) rankings, (2) sociograms, (3) "prestige indexes" obtained from attitude change data, (4) linear rating scales, (5) Thurstone-type attitude scales, and (6) devices similar to Likert scaling techniques, including the semantic differential.

Perhaps the most elementary method of determining differences among sources in respect to prestige, credibility, likeableness, etc., is to require subjects to arrange the sources in rank order. Sherif, for example, presented a list of sixteen authors to a group of undergraduates and asked them to rank the authors according to personal preferences for their writings. A month later the subjects were told to rank sixteen passages in respect to literary merit. Since all of the passages had been written by a single author not included in the list and since literary experts had judged all of them to be of equal merit, the only variable was the false attachment of a different author's name to each excerpt. Correlations between the two sets of ranks were held to represent

[93] *Loc. cit.*
[94] *Loc. cit.*

the effects of "prestige." The replication of the study with similar results in three instances indicates the usefulness of the rank-order technique for simple experiments of this type.[95] The method was to determine the rank order for individuals, to compute rank correlations for individuals, and to draw conclusions from the average correlations. While this technique seems justified, the rank-order method employed by Michael, Rosenthal, and DeCamp was not. In an effort to discredit the "constant stimulus" theory of prestige, these authors worked with mean and median ranks—[96] statistics which are generally meaningless.

Cole demonstrated the possibility of using sociometric data for the determination of certain characteristics of ethos. Using a particular personal characteristic (judgment, personal appeal, etc.) as the basis for sociometric choices, he selected one or more members of a group as "stars" and then assumed that they were more highly regarded than their colleagues. Under some conditions, these preferred members were as persuasive as authorities from outside the group.[97]

Kulp apparently made the first attempt to develop an index of prestige based upon attitude change. In a classic design which was to be repeated with variations many times during the ensuing years, he first administered Harper's test of liberalism to more than three hundred graduate students at Columbia. Later, various subgroups were told that the responses supplied them had been written by social scientists, educators, and other learned persons. The relative amounts of attitude shift toward each of these sources was used as the basis for computing a prestige index for each of the several professional groups.[98] Bowden, Caldwell, and West replicated the essential features of Kulp's study in an experiment using junior high, high school, and college students as subjects and employing a variety of different prestige levels. Sample findings with respect to the economic problems considered were these: "Prestige of the educators seems to increase as progress is made up the educational ladder" and "Ministers received the lowest rank in every case."[99]

Underlying these measuring techniques is the assumption that the prestige of a source is directly proportional to the ability to produce attitude shift. In 1938 Lurie formalized this point of view when he defined prestige as "The change in scale value of certain items brought about by attaching the name of the symbol to these items." He obtained scale values for prestige by administering a test of attitude without attaching prestige labels to the items, by administering the same test two weeks later with prestige labels attached,

[95] *Loc. cit.*

[96] *Loc. cit.*

[97] *Loc. cit.*

[98] Daniel Kulp, II, "Prestige, as Measured by Single-Experience Changes and Their Permanency," *Journal of Educational Research*, XXVII (1934), 663–672.

[99] A. O. Bowden, Floyd Caldwell, and Guy West, "A Study in Prestige," *American Journal of Sociology*, XL (1934), 193–203.

and by then subtracting the scores on the first test from those on the second. The remainder was the index of prestige.[100]

Naturally, prestige measures obtained in this manner are not pure or independent measures of the variable. Moreover, to use any of these measures to test the hypothesis that prestige induces attitude change is impossible, for the measure of prestige *is* attitude change. In an effort to develop an independent index suitable for testing this hypothesis, Saadi and Farnsworth combined gross ratings of "like," "indifferent," and "dislike" by the formula $100 [(L + \frac{1}{2}I)(L + I + D)]$ to obtain a score for likeableness based on group data.[101]

The multiple-choice aspect of the Saadi-Farnsworth measure was an early precursor of an obvious means of measuring various aspects of ethos—the rating scale. An early experimenter with this type of measurement was Lorge, whose subjects rated seventy sources on a five-interval scale ranging from "those individuals whose opinions you respect most" to "those individuals for whose opinions you have least respect."[102] More recently, Hovland and Weiss employed a five-point linear scale of "trustworthiness" to evaluate the credibility of two sources.[103]

The well-known study by Haiman used a variety of scales. In one phase of his experiment two nationally prominent public figures were evaluated on nine-point scales of reputation and competence. In other parts of the investigation student speakers were rated on similar scales for the qualities of sincerity, fairmindedness, physical appearance, conceit, competence, and likeableness.[104]

In addition to being one of the first experimental research workers to recognize explicitly the multidimensionality of ethos, Walter made the earliest effort to apply recognized test construction methods to the problem of creating a measuring device. His specific project was the development of an instrument to measure a single factor, the evaluation of character. Beginning with nearly 400 character-describing statements and employing both the Thurstone sorting techniques and the Seashore rating methods, he developed two tests of twenty-two items each. When applied to such individuals as Franklin Roosevelt and "The person with the best character I have known," the two forms of the test were normally distributed, distinguished among intuitively perceived gross character levels, and correlated well (.86) with each other. Applied to two speakers in the classroom, the two forms correlated extremely well (.96).[105]

The Osgood and Stagner use of bipolar nouns in a set of scales to rate occupations and occupational groups was a forerunner of the semantic dif-

---

[100] Walter Lurie, "The Measurement of Prestige and Prestige-Suggestibility," *Journal of Social Psychology*, IX (1938), 219–225.

[101] *Loc. cit.*

[102] *Loc. cit.*

[103] *Loc. cit.*

[104] *Loc. cit.*

[105] Otis Walter, Jr., "The Measurement of Ethos," unpubl. diss. (Northwestern, 1948).

ferential technique. They found that the prestige of jobs and workers could be determined through the use of their scales.[106]

Although Walter asserted the multidimensionality of ethos and although Haiman's technique actually employed a polydimensional approach, until recently no practical way of employing multivariate measures of ethos in research seemed to exist. Now the semantic differential technique makes such research possible. Berlo and Gulley,[107] Berlo and Kumata,[108] and Bettinghaus[109] used the differential to measure attitude toward the communicator, but in each instance they reported only one dimension of the semantic space, the evaluative aspect of the image. "Although it does not tap much of the *content* of an attitude in a denotative sense . . . it does seem to provide an index to the location of the attitude object along a general evaluative continuum."[110]

Employed in this manner, the semantic differential is similar in many ways to a traditional Likert scale in which a number of judgments concerning the concept are rendered on a linear scale and the sum of the scale values recorded by the subjects is used as a more-or-less unidimensional measure of the single property with which the scale is concerned.

Andersen developed a semantic differential which was specifically designed to measure ethos. Employing terms garnered from theoretical and experimental literature and securing responses to famous living people from freshmen engineering and physical education students, he obtained two major dimensions (evaluative and dynamism) in the images.[111] Berlo carried out a similar study, but he used a greater number of concepts and more students than did Andersen. Berlo also employed an oblique solution, whereas Andersen's method was the orthogonal factor solution.[112] Inspection suggests that the two structures were not essentially dissimilar if allowance is made for the difference in the factor rotation methods.

SUMMARY

Despite the great number of experimental studies relevant to ethos, the scope of this concept is such that the findings are not yet sufficiently numerous and sophisticated to permit definitive conclusions about the operation of ethical proof.

[106] Charles Osgood and Ross Stagner, "Analysis of a Prestige Frame of Reference by a Gradient Technique," *Journal of Applied Psychology*, XXV (1941), 275–290.

[107] *Loc. cit.*

[108] *Loc. cit.*

[109] *Loc. cit.*

[110] Osgood, Suci, and Tannenbaum, p. 195.

[111] *Loc. cit.*

[112] David K. Berlo, "An Empirical Test of a General Construct of Credibility," unpubl. paper presented at the SAA convention, New York City, December 29, 1961.

The finding is almost universal that the ethos of the source is related in some way to the impact of the message. This generalization applies not only to political, social, religious, and economic issues but also to matters of aesthetic judgment and personal taste. Some evidence even shows that "prestige-suggestion" can affect the appetite for certain foods and can influence performances of perceptual and psychomotor tasks. On the other hand, there is not enough evidence to suggest that the amount of information gained from exposure to a message is related to the ethos of the source—at least this lack of relationship seems to be true of college populations. The effect of ethos, again according to many studies, has a temporal dimension. In other words, when the stimulus is not renewed, material presented by a high ethos source loses in persuasiveness and that given by a poor source gains. Recall of the source reestablishes some of the initial effect, but the improvement which renewal produces decays more rapidly than does the original increment.

Some auditors appear to be more susceptible to ethical appeal than others; some may be contrasuggestible. However, there is no evidence to show that suggestibility to prestige correlates well with intelligence, education, speech training, subject-matter competence, age, or sex. The only variable which seems clearly related to differences in suggestibility to prestige is the initial attitude toward the topic or the purpose: consistently, those who are neutral initially shift more often than do those who are at one extreme or the other.

Research shows that expert opinion may be about as influential as majority opinion in inducing attitude change.

While most experimentation has been conducted in a fixed ethos model, recent research shows that a congruity model can be used to predict attitude change toward both a communicator and his topic. Incorporating elements concerning speech composition and delivery increased the usefulness of the model.

Printed and oral propaganda can succeed in creating and altering images of groups or of individuals, but attempts to produce unfavorable reactions to individuals may backfire. When this response occurs, the prestige of the criticized person may increase and that of the attacker may decline.

Speeches of introduction probably influence the image of a speaker, but most of the evidence on this point is indirect.

Certain characteristics of a speech affect the ethos of the speaker. No evidence, however, supports the common beliefs (1) that giving "both sides" is a superior way to present controversial material, (2) that citing the sources of evidence increases persuasiveness, and (3) that including conciliatory remarks, statements of self-praise, and other conscious, obvious attempts at ethical appeal enhances the speaker's status.

Such noncontent stimuli as dress, voice, and manner apparently affect the attitude of the audience toward the speaker, but these factors may not be related to persuasiveness on a given occasion. There is no evidence that the audience can perceive lack of sincerity; rather, audiences appear to react to their evaluations of the competence of the speaker.

Many techniques of measurement have been applied to ethos: among these are ranking, sociograms, prestige indexes, linear rating scales, Thurstone scales, and the semantic differential. Each of these has proved useful in assessing one or more of the aspects of ethos.

This preceding body of findings suggests certain possibilities for future research:

1. The dimensions of ethos should be explored through multivariate analysis in terms of different auditors, different speakers, and different speech situations. New measurement techniques, and especially the semantic differential, make this type of research possible.

2. Ethos or ethical proof should be measured in experiments designed so that this variable is not confounded with persuasiveness.

3. The effect upon ethos of the interaction of prior reputation and the artistic elements in the message should be studied. Findings in this area would be of great importance to rhetorical theory.

4. Some research suggests that differences in ethos are not established as easily with some audiences as previous experimenters often assumed. More research dealing with the methods of establishing and modifying ethos is needed.

5. The effect of variations in auditors, situations, and topics upon the function of ethical proof in persuasion should receive renewed attention. The utilization of improved designs and measuring devices can create experimental conditions that may lead to more meaningful results than those obtained in the past.

Bradley S. Greenberg / Gerald R. Miller*

THE EFFECTS
OF
LOW-CREDIBLE SOURCES
ON
MESSAGE ACCEPTANCE

That sources of low credibility are not as persuasive as highly credible communicators is a firmly established empirical generalization.[1] Beyond this, however, little is known about the impact of low-credible sources on audiences' acceptance of persuasive messages. The present studies investigate several questions related to the effectiveness of low-credible sources. The investigators were particularly interested in the possibility that the effects of low credibility can be minimized by manipulating the time at which the source and the message are linked.

The assumption underlying the major problem of these studies may be stated as follows: *A message attributed to a low-credible source immediately before its presentation generates maximum resistance to the message; hence, favorable attitude change among audience members exposed to the message will be minimal.*

The bases for this assumption are found in the work of Lumsdaine and

---

Dr. Greenberg is Assistant Professor and Dr. Miller Associate Professor, Department of Communication, Michigan State University. The studies reported here were supported by a contract (OCD-TS-64–71) from the Office of Civil Defense, Department of Defense.

[1] For a review of much of this literature see K. Andersen and T. Clevenger, Jr., "A Summary of Experimental Research in Ethos," *Speech Monographs,* XXX (June 1963), 59–78.

Reprinted from *Speech Monographs,* 33 (1966), 127–36, with permission of the authors and the Speech Association of America.

Janis[2] dealing with innoculation, and in the research of McGuire and Papageorgis[3] on belief immunization. These investigators have demonstrated that certain antecedent factors function to make an individual's beliefs more resistant to change (i.e., to reduce the effectiveness of a subsequent persuasive attempt). For example, McGuire and Papageorgis[4] have found that when a communicator mentions arguments that are contrary to a respondent's beliefs and then explicitly refutes these arguments, that respondent's beliefs are more resistant to change when later attacked.

Low source credibility may be one antecedent condition that serves to immunize an individual's beliefs and thus make him more resistant to persuasion. When, prior to its presentation, a persuasive message is attributed to a low-credible source, the audience is forewarned that the information to follow may be unreliable. This forewarning is likely to cause audience members to ignore the message's persuasive appeals and to retain original attitudes toward the issue discussed.

By contrast, the effects of low credibility should be reduced by delaying identification of the source until after the message has been presented to an audience. This procedure would eliminate any forewarning about the possible unreliability of the message source. It also would increase the probability that the message's persuasive appeals would be more attentively received. When provided the opportunity to assimilate message content without predisposing prior information, one would suppose that audience members would be less influenced by the subsequent attribution of the message to a low-credible source. This should be so, especially if the message appeals had relatively high substantive and stylistic quality. Taken together, these considerations led to the following hypothesis:

> (1) When the source has low credibility, attribution of the message to the source after presentation of the message will result in more favorable audience attitudes toward the proposal than when the message is attributed to the source prior to presentation of the message.

A recent study by Husek[5] has provided some support for this hypothesis. His findings are difficult to interpret, however, primarily because the study is

[2] A. A. Lumsdaine and I. L. Janis, "Resistance to 'Counterpropaganda' Produced by One-Sided and Two-Sided 'Propaganda' Presentations," *Public Opinion Quarterly*, XVII (Fall 1953), 311–318.

[3] For an excellent review of this research see W. J. McGuire, "Inducing Resistance to Persuasion: Some Contemporary Approaches," in *Advances in Experimental Social Psychology*, ed. L. Berkowitz (New York, 1964), I, 191–229.

[4] W. J. McGuire and D. Papageorgis, "The Relative Efficacy of Various Types of Prior Belief-Defense in Producing Immunity to Persuasion," *Journal of Abnormal and Social Psychology*, LXII (March 1961), 327–337.

[5] T. R. Husek, "Persuasive Impacts of Early, Late, or No Mention of a Negative Source," *Journal of Personality and Social Psychology*, II (July 1965), 125–128.

methodologically ambiguous. There was no independent assessment of the source's credibility. Data relevant to the source's credibility (semantic differential ratings of the concept "ex-mental patient") were treated as part of the dependent variable and combined with similar ratings of such diverse concepts as "psychotherapy," "neurotic people," and "mental hospital" to arrive at one summated dependent measure. The probable multidimensionality of this measure makes it impossible to ascertain just what was being rated by the subjects; furthermore, the study offers no empirical evidence of the source's low credibility.

The present studies examine two additional aspects of the effectiveness of low-credible sources. The first of these concerns the relative effectiveness of a low-credible source and an unidentified source. Previous research by Greenberg and Tannenbaum[6] demonstrated that a message attributed to a high-credible source results in greater attitude change than a message in which the source remains unidentified. One purpose of the studies presented here was to determine whether the converse effect also holds—whether a message attributed to a low-credible source will result in less favorable attitudes toward the message topic than a message in which the source remains unidentified. We reasoned that, regardless of the point in time at which the message is attributed to the source, the source's low credibility should result in some detrimental audience effects. Thus, the following hypothesis was investigated:

> (2) A message from an unidentified source will result in more favorable audience attitudes toward the message proposal than will a message attributed to a low-credible source.

Second, the studies reported here investigated the possible interaction between level of source credibility and immediate or delayed attribution of the message to the source. If, as suggested above, attribution of the message to a low-credible source prior to its presentation results in maximal audience resistance to persuasion, it seems reasonable that highly credible sources should have the opposite effect: attribution of the message to the source before its presentation should enhance its persuasion. Audience members should believe that the information which follows is reliable and should subsequently respond more receptively to the message. As a result, an interaction between level of credibility and immediate or delayed source identification would be expected; specifically:

> (3) Immediate attribution of a message to a highly credible source will result in more favorable audience attitudes toward the proposal advocated than will delayed attribution to the same source, but delayed attribution

[6] B. S. Greenberg and P. H. Tannenbaum, "The Effects of Bylines on Attitude Change," *Journalism Quarterly*, XXXVIII (Autumn 1961), 535–537.

of a message to a low-credible source will result in more favorable audience attitudes toward the proposal advocated than will immediate attribution to that source.

METHOD AND RESULTS

Experiment I: The Effects of Low-Credible and Unidentified Sources

As mentioned above, earlier research on source effects has demonstrated that highly credible sources elicit more audience attitude change than unidentified sources. This first experiment tested whether a message attributed to a low-credible source resulted in more favorable attitudes than a message presented without identification of its source. The rationale presented above predicts that a low-credible source will increase resistance to persuasion; hence, as Hypothesis 2 stipulates, a message presented without identification of its source is expected to be more persuasive.

Procedures

Subjects were 45 adult members of a PTA organization in a small, semi-rural Michigan community. Subjects were told that a project dealing with the "dissemination of scientific information" was being conducted, and that as a part of that project, they were to evaluate some scientific messages written for laymen. All subjects were then randomly assigned to one of two treatment groups. An experimenter accompanied each group to its respective room, and the test materials were immediately distributed.

For the Low-Credibility group (n = 24) these materials consisted of a cover sheet describing the task, a description of the message source which aimed at inducing low credibility, and the experimental message. For the Unidentified-Source group (n = 21) the materials were identical, except that the sheet describing the source was omitted.

All subjects were asked to read the message once, then to return to the beginning and underline all the main points in the message. This latter procedure was employed to insure attention to the message content. Fifteen minutes were allotted for the task. The message described the benefits of building public schools underground in order to provide protection in case of nuclear war or natural disaster.

The credibility induction was based upon the following paragraph, included in the materials given to all subjects in the Low-Credibility group:

> *For your information.* The piece you are about to read was included in a sales brochure written and distributed in several American communities by a small

group of men recently indicted for unethical business practices. The men traveled across the country trying to persuade school systems to build schools which could be used as fallout shelters. The salesmen would then offer to be "advisors" to the school board about this possibility. They charged a sizeable fee for their services, and made up some kind of report without doing any work.

At the end of the allotted 15 minutes, subjects completed a test booklet which asked them to evaluate the message in terms of its content, style, and clarity, and to express their attitudes toward underground schools on a series of eight, Likert-type items with five response categories per item. These items were selected on the basis of a prior factor analysis which demonstrated their internal consistency and their high loading on the underground-school issue.[7]

Finally, all subjects rated the source's perceived competence and trust-worthiness on seven-point scales. Subjects in the Unidentified-Source condition also evaluated the source, even though the source was not identified. After the rating instruments were completed, the true purpose of the study was explained to the subjects.

Results

In order to obtain a measure of audience attitude the subjects' responses were summed across the eight items, yielding a range from 8 to 40. Also, the measures of credibility obtained for the Low-Credibility and Unidentified-Source conditions were compared in order to determine the success of the credibility induction.

The mean attitude score for subjects in the Unidentified-Source condition was 27.1; the mean score for subjects in the Low-Credibility condition was 23.9. The higher score is indicative of more favorable attitudes toward the construction of underground schools.

Analysis of the attitude score data, by use of the Mann-Whitney U-test,[8] indicated that subjects in the Unidentified-Source treatment expressed significantly more favorable attitudes toward the message topic than did subjects in the Low-Credibility condition ($z = 1.65$; $p < .05$, one-tailed test). In essence, then, having no source appended to the message proved more effective than using an unfavorably evaluated source.

What is not apparent from the attitude data is the extent to which the source induction was successful. Subjects in the Unidentified-Source condition were favorably inclined toward the source. These subjects' mean rating of the source's trustworthiness was 5.1, while their mean rating of competence was 5.4. The maximum score possible was 7. Although they received no prior

[7] G. R. Miller and M. A. Hewgill, "An Experimental Study of the Relationships of Fear Appeals, Source Credibility, and Attitude Change," Unpublished research report, Department of Communication, Michigan State University, June 1964.

[8] S. Siegel, *Non-parametric Statistics for the Behavioral Sciences* (New York, 1956), pp. 116–127.

source information, the quality of the message was apparently sufficient to induce subjects to create a somewhat favorable perception of the source. It would appear that these subjects reasoned that such a good message could only have come from a good source. This interpretation is supported by the fact that they rated positively both the content and style of the message.

For subjects in the Low-Credibility treatment, lower ratings were obtained on both source criteria. For trustworthiness the mean rating was 4.4, for competence, 4.7. These two means differ significantly from those obtained in the Unidentified-Source group ($t = 1.93$ and 1.70 respectively; $p < .05$, one-tailed tests). Even so, the ratings of the source by subjects in the Low-Credibility condition are at essentially the midpoint of the trustworthiness and qualification scales. Thus, although the study sought to investigate low-credible sources, the induction did not result in extremely low credibility. It appears, therefore, that for this situation it is empirically more meaningful to speak of a source that is relatively less credible than the unidentified source. Despite the negatively valenced induction, one-third of the subjects in the Low-Credibility group rated the source as "quite trustworthy." The investigators believe that attempts to induce perceptions of low credibility, while still maintaining situational credence for the source-message combination, are offset by a normative response that seeks positive source factors where, objectively, there are none. Had the credibility manipulation been more successful, it is probable that the differences in attitudes would have been even more extreme than those found in the present study.

Experiment II: The Effect of Immediate vs. Delayed Identification of a Low-Credible Source

In this experiment the investigators examined the effect of delaying identification of a low-credible source until the message had been presented. Hypothesis 1 stipulates that the effect of a message attributed to a low-credible source will be enhanced by delaying identification of the source until after the completion of the message.

Procedures

Subjects were 71 undergraduates enrolled in beginning speech courses at Western Michigan University. At regular class meetings subjects were told that a project was being conducted to test their aptitude in scientific areas, principally in the field of medical health.

Subjects were randomly assigned to two treatments. A test booklet was distributed in both treatments. The booklet contained a cover sheet describing the pseudo-project, a background data sheet, a sheet attributing the message to a low-credible source, the persuasive message, and a set of attitude items including a subset dealing with the message topic. The two booklets were identical except that for the Immediate-Identification group (n = 37) the sheet attributing the message to a low-credible source immediately preceded the message, while for the Delayed-Identification group (n = 34) this information immediately followed the message. Half the students in each class received the first version; the other half, the second.

The subject's task was identical to that assigned in the first experiment: to underline the key points in the message. Eight minutes were allotted for this task. The message dealt with the possible health hazards of constant tooth brushing,[9] and several sections emphasized that proper diet, especially natural health foods, was superior to tooth brushing as a means of preventing dental cavities.

The credibility induction was based upon the following paragraph, given to subjects in both treatments as described above:

> The article you will read (OR have just read) was written by the publicity director of a group which advocates natural foods as the means of maintaining proper health. It was written in the form of a publicity release designed to promote the sale and consumption of natural foods. The article is being used only because of its appropriateness for the assigned task. No endorsement is implied.

Three items were used to assess the subject's attitude toward the message topic (e.g., "Brushing one's teeth can become a harmful practice, if one does it too often"). Response categories ranged from "definitely disagree" to "definitely agree," with 15 scale units between the extremes. Since responses to the three items were summed, a subject's attitude score could range from 3 to 45. Subjects also rated the message source on a seven-point scale ranging from "very good" to "very bad." After the experiment was completed, subjects were told that the message was a bogus one, and that they should give no credence to the arguments it contained.

Results

The mean attitude score for subjects in the Delayed-Identification condition was 19.3; for subjects in the Immediate-Identification condition, it was 21.7. Since in this case the messages argue against rather than for a proposal, the lower score indicates a more favorable attitude toward the proposal advocated in the message.

These attitude measures were analyzed by use of the Mann-Whitney U-test. The analysis indicates that significantly more favorable attitudes toward

[9] This message was based on one of the "cultural truisms" utilized by McGuire in his research on belief immunization.

the message topic were expressed by the group who received information about the source after reading the message ($z = 2.57$; $p < .005$, one-tailed test). On the other hand, the attitudes of the group which received immediate information about the source are less favorable. Apparently, the message had already persuaded subjects in the Delayed-Identification group, and if the low-credible source inhibited persuasion, that effect was less marked than in the Immediate-Identification condition.

Again, the attempt to induce low credibility was not completely successful. Fourteen of the subjects in the Immediate-Identification treatment and 11 in the Delayed-Identification group rated the source "slightly," "quite," or "very good." Since this variance in source perception could only have deterred or limited the difference between groups, the significant difference between the treatments is all the more striking. It can be concluded that when a source is likely to be perceived somewhat unfavorably, delay of information about the source of a persuasive message is more effective than immediate identification of the source.

Experiment III: The Effect of Immediate vs. Delayed Identification of a Low-Credible Source: A Partial Replication

Given the positive results of the second experiment, the investigators next chose to replicate the test of Hypothesis 1. The replication was undertaken to establish higher-order generalizability across various message topics and for various audiences. Particular interest was directed at an audience composed of individuals with some professional training in communication. Since most prior research on source credibility has used essentially naïve audiences, we sought to determine whether effects similar to those found in Experiment II could be obtained with a more sophisticated audience.

Procedures

Subjects were 95 sophomores and juniors enrolled in journalistic editing classes at Michigan State University. At regular class meetings subjects were told that a series of studies on news editing was being conducted. They were then asked to edit a news story. Subjects received one of two versions of a test booklet. In one booklet (Immediate-Identification treatment) the source was identified before the subject read and edited the message. The other booklet contained no source information; rather, subjects in this Delayed-Identification treatment received their source information later in the test period. This procedure eliminated the possibility that subjects might look to the end of the message for source information and thus negate the function of the treatment.

Subjects were asked to underline the major points of the story in addition to editing the message. Fifteen minutes were allotted for the task. The message, which was identical to the one used in Experiment I, dealt with the benefits of constructing underground schools for use as shelters.

The credibility induction was based upon the following paragraph, given to subjects in both treatments:

> The story you will edit (OR have just edited) was actually submitted to a Michigan daily newspaper for publication. It was written by a man who was new to the area, and had just opened an office as a "business consultant." He was also attempting to borrow money to begin a construction company. The man was promoting the company as one which would build schools that could be used as fallout shelters. At the time he wrote the story, he was trying to interest the local school board in his own construction plans for a new school the board was planning. Then he offered to be an "advisor" to the local school board about this possibility and, for a sizeable fee, to analyze the local situation.

After 15 minutes, all subjects were given a second booklet. The booklet given to subjects in the Immediate-Identification condition contained the Likert-type items used to assess attitudes toward the message topic in Experiment I and two items concerned with the credibility of the source. Subjects in the Delayed-Identification condition received the same rating instruments; but, in addition, the first pages of their booklets contained the source description that subjects in the Immediate-Identification condition had read before editing the message. After subjects had completed the rating scales, they were told the true purpose of the experiment.

Results

The mean attitude score for subjects in the Delayed-Identification condition was 24.3, while the mean score for subjects in the Immediate-Identification condition was 21.4. A higher score reflects a more favorable attitude toward the message topic. The data for all subjects in both conditions were analyzed by use of the Mann-Whitney U-test. The result obtained fell barely short of significance ($z = 1.62$; $p < .10$, one-tailed test). Nevertheless, the direction and extent of the differences provide additional support for Hypothesis 1.

Examination of the credibility ratings revealed that the induction had been unsuccessful for a number of subjects. In order to gain further information relevant to Hypothesis 1, a secondary analysis was performed. Here, only those subjects in both treatments who rated the source as either "slightly," "quite," or "very negative" on either the trustworthiness or competency scales were compared. Since this procedure eliminated a number of subjects from both conditions, it should be emphasized that the population to which results may be generalized is difficult to specify. Even so, it was believed that this secondary analysis would be of some use in evaluating the hypothesis, especially since the same criterion was used for eliminating subjects from the two conditions.

Among subjects in both treatments who perceived the source as somewhat negative, the mean attitude in the Delayed-Identification condition was 23.2, while the mean attitude in the Immediate-Identification condition was 18.6. This difference was statistically significant ($z = 1.90$; $p < .03$, one-tailed test). Thus, both analyses yield results consistent with the earlier studies and with the principal hypothesis of the experiments. Among a group of subjects with training in professional communication, the location of information about a low-credible source significantly affected attitudes toward the message topic.

Experiment IV: A Tentative Test of the Effects of Immediate vs. Delayed Identification of High- and Low-Credible Sources

A fourth experiment was conducted which attempted to tie together the findings of two separate experiments. The data from our present studies strongly support the notion that delay of information about a low-credible source will be more effective than immediate information about the source; the earlier experiment by Greenberg and Tannenbaum[10] supported the parallel notion, implied by the same theoretic framework, that immediate information about a high-credible source is more advantageous than delaying information about the source. Therefore, an interaction was anticipated between level of credibility and immediate or delayed identification of the message source (Hypothesis 3).

Subjects were members of parent-teacher organizations in two elementary schools in a southern Michigan community. Testing was conducted at regular group meetings, held on the same evening at both schools. Subjects were randomly assigned to one of five treatments: (1) High Credibility-Immediate Identification; (2) High Credibility-Delayed Identification; (3) Low Credibility-Immediate Identification; (4) Low Credibility-Delayed Identification; and (5) a No-Exposure control group. Experimental procedures used in this study were comparable to those in the earlier experiments.

In this experiment, as in the others reported here, we were unable to induce low source ratings across entire subject groups. Our test of the interaction hypothesis must therefore be interpreted with caution, for this analysis included only those subjects who discriminated the source as high or low in the relevant source-induction treatment. The behavior of some 60 per cent of all subjects, who did not perceive the sources as either highly credible or of relatively low credibility, is not examined here. The same criteria were, of course, applied to all four experimental groups in excluding subjects who gave neutral or ambivalent source ratings. This selective analysis provided a signifi-

---

[10] Greenberg and Tannenbaum, *op. cit.*

TABLE 1

Mean Attitude Scores and Analysis of Variance Summary for
Subjects in Experimental Treatments*

		Source Identification	
		Immediate	Delayed
Source Credibility	High	30.4	27.7
	Low	21.3	28.0

Source of Variance	df	SS	MS	F	p
Identification	1	3	3	< 1	n.s.
Between Credibility	1	106	106	4.69	$< .05$
Credibility by Identification	1	109	109	4.82	$< .05$
Within	23	519	22.6		

*High attitude score indicates a more favorable attitude in direction advocated by the message.

cant Credibility by Identification interaction (Table 1) which was consistent with Hypothesis 3 and also with the more rigorous findings of the three other experiments reported here. In general, then, it appears reasonable to conclude that if the source is perceived as highly credible, immediate identification results in more favorable attitudes toward the topic; while, if the source is of relatively low credibility, more favorable attitudes are expressed by those individuals for whom identification of the source is delayed until after exposure to the message.

DISCUSSION

The most provocative result of the present studies is the thrice-replicated finding that the effects of low credibility can be largely obviated by delaying source identification until after a message has been presented. In each experiment in which time of identification was manipulated, delayed identification of the low-credible source enhanced the persuasiveness of the message.

This key finding is, of course, consistent with the position taken earlier in this paper. Individuals who heard a message following its attribution to a low-credible source seem to have been on their guard, to have been immunized against subsequent persuasion. In instances involving low-credible communicators, immediate identification appears to have served as a forewarning which alerted audience members to the fact that the message information might be unreliable. On the other hand, delayed identification of the source afforded an opportunity for audience members to evaluate and to respond to the message without the knowledge that its persuasive appeals came from a source whose competence and trustworthiness were questionable. It seems probable that peruasion occurred before these individuals were apprised of the source's low credibility.

The conclusion that the effects of low credibility can be minimized by delayed identification of a source must be tempered by at least two qualifications. First, as was previously stressed, the messages used in these studies met relatively high standards of literacy and cogency. In all instances in which ratings were obtained from subjects, the messages were evaluated positively in terms of informational content, clarity, and style. The most defensible generalization emerging from the present studies must therefore be stated as follows: Given a message of relatively high quality, delayed attribution of the message to a low-credible source will result in more favorable attitudes toward the message topic than will immediate attribution.

Theoretical considerations already presented suggest that message variability should be a significant factor in determining attitude change only if the message is of such poor quality that it, alone, has little or no persuasive impact. If more persuasion occurs in the delayed identification condition because the audience has not been forewarned and therefore attends more receptively to the message appeals, then any message possessing some persuasive impact should be more effective if linkage with a low-credible source is delayed until after presentation. If, on the other hand, the message is minimally effective, it is doubtful that any strategy based upon manipulation of the identification of low-credible sources will be sufficient to affect persuasion markedly. A future study in which both message quality and source credibility are systematically manipulated seems to be the most feasible method for assessing the relative impact of message and source on audience attitudes.

A second limiting factor of the present studies is the somewhat equivocal success of the low-credibility manipulation. Even though audience members were given information that should have prompted them to question severely the competency and trustworthiness of their sources, a number of respondents failed to rate the source's credibility low in any absolute sense. While this reluctance to respond negatively may have been partially due to the quality of the message, the investigators believe that some additional variable is involved. Specifically, as mentioned earlier, a normative standard may operate in such a manner that audience members give a source the benefit of a doubt (i.e., in the absence of personal experience with the source, audiences may respond to sources in a somewhat positive manner).

Had the credibility ratings been more positive in the Delayed-Identification condition, it would be possible to argue for some kind of impression-formation interpretation. One might hold that the positive characteristics of the message had a greater impact on source perception than did subsequent information about the source's dubious motives and questionable competence. Such an interpretation would be consistent with previous research demonstrating the importance of primacy in impression-formation.[11] But while the sources in the Delayed-Identification conditions were consistently rated somewhat more favorably than those in the Immediate-Identification conditions, differences never achieved acceptable levels of statistical significance. Therefore, the lack of differences between credibility ratings for individuals in the Immediate and Delayed conditions militates somewhat against this explanation.

That the credibility induction was sufficiently powerful to affect the persuasiveness of the message is confirmed by comparing the attitude scores for individuals exposed to a message presented by a low-credible source with like scores of persons exposed to a message presented by an unidentified source (Hypothesis 2). The fact that the latter group expressed significantly more favorable attitudes toward the message topic indicates that it may be advantageous to eliminate source attribution from the communication situation, if the only alternative available is linkage of the message with a low-credible source. This study suggests that it is desirable to omit identification of a source whose credibility is likely to be perceived as relatively low; on the other hand, the Greenberg-Tannenbaum study[12] demonstrates the wisdom of early identification of the source where he is likely to have high credibility with the audience.

Finally, these studies illustrate once again the conjunctive relationships between source and message variables, relationships which function to determine the outcome of any given communication event. The significant interaction obtained between level of credibility and immediate or delayed identification of the source, although only tentatively established in these studies, indicates that no simple generalizations can be made regarding optimum source-identification strategies. The success or failure of such strategies is dependent upon relevant source and message variables, many of which still remain uninvestigated.

[11] See for example, N. H. Anderson and A. A. Barrios, "Primacy Effects in Personality Impression Formation," *Journal of Abnormal and Social Psychology*, LXIII (September 1961), 346–350; A. S. Luchins, "Primacy-Recency in Impression Formation," in C. I. Hovland *et al.*, *The Order of Presentation in Persuasion* (New Haven, 1957), pp. 33–61.

[12] Greenberg and Tannenbaum, *op. cit.*

Harold Sigall / Robert Helmreich*[1]

OPINION CHANGE AS A FUNCTION OF STRESS AND COMMUNICATOR CREDIBILITY

An experiment investigating the effects of audience stress
and communicator credibility on opinion change was
conducted. High and low stress and high-relevant,
high-irrelevant, and low communicator credibility
comprised a 2 × 3 factorial design. The nature of the
stress was unrelated to the topic of the communication.
Sixty subjects were each randomly assigned to one of the six
experimental conditions. It was predicted that differences in
communicator credibility would lead to differences in
opinion change under low stress, and that under high stress
opinion change would not be affected significantly by
differences in communicator credibility. The results
supported these predictions.

The effect of perceived threat or stress on opinion change has received considerable attention from students of the persuasion process. Janis and Feshbach (1953) found that a fear-arousing communication was increasingly persuasive up to a moderate level of fear, but that persuasiveness decreased

*The University of Texas.
[1] This research was supported by Contract N00014-67-A-0126-0001 with the Office of Naval Research, Group Psychology Branch, Robert Helmreich, principal investigator. We thank James Zinn, who served as the first experimenter.

Reprinted from the *Journal of Experimental Social Psychology,* 5 (1969), 70–78, with permission of the authors and the Academic Press, Inc.

when high levels of fear were aroused. On the other hand, Leventhal and his associates (e.g., Leventhal and Niles, 1964; Dabbs and Leventhal, 1966; Leventhal and Singer, 1966) have generally found that persuasion attempts become more effective as fear level increases. Although the evidence, on the whole, seems to support the latter position better, the controversy remains unresolved. For example, the nature of the dependent measure seems to affect the results, with observed changes in *attitude* not always being reflected in accompanying *behavior* (see Dabbs and Leventhal, 1966).

One source of the confusion, as Dabbs and Leventhal (1966) have suggested, may lie in the nature of the recommendations made in the communication. The consequences of following proposed recommendations can be a crucial determinant of whether attitude or behavior change is effected. If, for example, stress is manipulated by pointing out dangers of smoking with respect to lung cancer, and recommendations include getting a chest X-ray, high fear subjects may employ defensive avoidance of the communication and may ignore its recommendations (dependent-variable related) because they fear learning that they have lung cancer.

In most of the experiments dealing with stress and opinion change, the fear manipulation affects more than the fear level of the subjects; the communication differs across stress conditions. The result is that subjects in different stress conditions are exposed to different communications as well as being subjected to various stress levels. It is difficult to conclude that differential attitude change between stress conditions is, in fact, due to differing stress levels, and not to differential communications.

One step toward eliminating this confounding can be taken by separating the situation in which stress is manipulated from the one in which the communication is presented. This, however, is not sufficient, because while it achieves the aim of maintaining constant information transmission *via the communication*, differential information about the issue is given to subjects in different stress conditions, as long as the stress is relevant to the communication. For example, varying stress by noting the horrors of a particular disease, changing the specific dreadful effects, or altering the emphasis on certain points, does not alter the fact that subjects in different stress conditions possess different amounts or kinds of information.

The relationship between persuasion and stress when the two are related is an extremely interesting one. But it includes peculiarities that distinguish it from a more general area of inquiry—the relationship between stress and persuasion, *regardless of the connection between stress and communication*. To investigate the relationship between stress, *per se*, and opinion change requires that the nature of the stress be *irrelevant* to the issue under consideration in the persuasive communication.

Irrelevant stress, in its own right, may very well affect opinion change. High stress seems to increase the need for social comparison (Schachter, 1959).

Therefore, increasing stress may produce increasing attitude change. But this relationship can change as other factors vary. For example, communicator credibility may interact with audience stress level. It may be that people under high stress are so in need of supports to grasp that they ignore the implications of the source of the communication. On the other hand, people under little or no stress may be better able to sift and weigh the information they receive, which could lead to greater salience of communicator credibility under such conditions. If, for example, a group of people are under high stress due to learning about an impending disaster in a radio news bulletin, does this make them more likely to buy a particular dog food which is advertised immediately following that bulletin? Moreover, in such a situation, would a veterinarian be more effective at persuasion than John Doe from Main Street? If not, would opinion change be affected as a function of such differences in credibility when high stress was absent?

One of the more consistent findings in the attitude change literature is that effective persuasion is a positive function of communicator credibility (see Hovland, Janis, and Kelley, 1953). Credibility may be defined in a number of different, but similar, ways. Differences in prestige, status, expertise, etc. each make for differences in credibility.

Expertise may be defined in terms of the knowledgeability a communicator possesses about the topic he is discussing. Status differences are more subtle: but if one conceives of status in terms of social position, it is not difficult to conceptualize a situation in which, due to the issue involved, communicators of relatively equal status have grossly *unequal* expertise. In one sense, a high-status communicator whose expertise is pertinent to the communication may be viewed as having high *relevant credibility*, while a communicator of similar status, but whose expertise is unrelated to the issue under question, may be said to have high *irrelevant credibility*.

How important is the relevance of the communicator's credibility as a determinant of effective persuasion? In an experiment that bears on this question, Aronson and Golden (1962) demonstrated that subjects who were prejudiced against Negroes were less likely to change their opinions for a Negro communicator than for a white communicator, even though the objective credibility of both was the same. The interpretation given to this finding is that irrelevant aspects (skin color) of the communicator's credibility affect opinion change. The nature of that irrelevance is quite unlike the irrelevance factor we want to consider. Our concern is with the relevance of the communicator's expertise to the topic, while in Aronson and Golden (1962) the relevance variable was independent of the persuasive communication. Our hypothesis is that, other things being equal, resultant opinion change will be greater when a persuasive communication is delivered by a highly credible communicator whose credibility is issue-relevant than one whose credibility is irrelevant. In addition, we expect that a high-credible-irrelevant communicator will be more effective at persuasion than a low-credible communicator.

The relationships predicted above hold for situations in which credibility (and relevance) are the only factors that vary. How is opinion change affected when, in addition to communicator credibility, audience stress level is manipulated? As noted above, high stress seems to be conducive to increasing needs for social comparison (Schachter, 1959). An increase in dependence on the social environment has strong implications for how stress can affect opinion change.

An hypothesis that immediately suggests itself is that high-stress subjects should be more easily persuaded, under all circumstances, than low-stress subjects. Close examination, however, indicates that although this is doubtless a possibility, viable alternatives exist.

We believe that stress both increases dependency and decreases (narrows) the field of attention at the same time. Thus, we predict that credibility and stress will interact; i.e., *under low stress* agreement with the position presented in a communication will be greatest when the communicator is high-credible-relevant, next when he is high-credible-irrelevant, and least when he is low-credible; under *high stress* we predict that the credibility effect will be greatly reduced, if at all present, and that the communication will produce approximately equal agreement, regardless of the credibility condition.

METHOD

As the concern of the study was with the effects of *irrelevant* stress on opinion change, the nature of the stress manipulation had to be unrelated to the nature of the communication. In addition, we considered it prudent to separate the situation in which stress was manipulated from that in which the communication was presented. Thus, subjects were led to believe that they were participating in two experiments rather than one. In the first "experiment" stress was varied; in the second, credibility was manipulated and the communication presented. There were two levels of stress and three levels of credibility, resulting in a 2×3 factorial design.

SUBJECTS

Subjects were 60[2] male undergraduates in introductory psychology classes at the University of Texas. Each subject was randomly assigned to one of six experimental conditions and tested individually.

[2] Sixty-four subjects were actually run. Four subjects' data were excluded from the analysis because they were unable to recall the occupation of the communicator, thereby indicating that the credibility variable had not been effectively manipulated for these subjects. Inclusion of the data obtained from these subjects does not alter the results of the analysis in any meaningful way; i.e., neither significance levels nor the relationship of any mean to any other mean was affected.

PROCEDURE

Each subject reported for an experiment entitled "Perception and Physiology," and was ushered into an experimental room. Then the experimenter (Experimenter 1) explained the "purpose" of the experiment. He said that he was interested in studying perception and how it was related to some physiological measures. At this point instructions branched according to the stress condition.

Low-stress subjects. Pointing out various pieces of electrical apparatus present in the room, the experimenter told the subject that he would be monitoring certain of the subject's physiological activities, such as galvanic skin response and blood pressure.

High-stress subjects. Subjects in the high-stress condition underwent a similar procedure, with the following addition: Blood sampling equipment (syringes, cotton, glass containers, and alcohol) was in full view of the subject. Experimenter 1 also said: "One of the physiological tests involves blood analysis. So, when you come back, I'm going to have to take a blood sample from you—it's not very painful, though."

In both stress conditions Experimenter 1 was dressed in a full-length laboratory coat and wore full beard—features which may have added impact to the high-stress manipulation.

After the stress induction, Experimenter 1 handed the subject a form, titled "General Perception." The form consisted of five different questions, each of which asked the subject about his present perceptions. This five-question set appeared twice on the same page. The first set was headed by "Part I: First Impressions." The second set of identical items by "Part II: Post-Physiological Testing." Experimenter 1 instructed the subject to fill out "Part I," explaining that he was interested in his subjects' first impressions, and wanted to know if their perceptions were at all altered after physiological testing. He told the subjects that they would fill out "Part II" after the physiological testing had taken place.

The two-part perception questionnaire was designed to increase the impact of the stress manipulation. We wanted subjects to expect to return to Experimenter 1, after listening to the communication. By allowing subjects to think that they had half of the questionnaire to complete, we hoped to increase the likelihood that they would expect to return.

When the subject had completed "Part I," Experimenter 1 told him that it would take a few minutes to ready the equipment for physiological testing. He then explained, "Someone from the Speech Department is doing some work and needs subjects for a few moments. I've told him that since the subjects in my experiment have to wait for me to get ready anyway, they would participate in his research." The experimenter then sent the subject to the "Speech Department Researcher" (Experimenter 2) in a nearby room, telling him to return as soon as he was finished.

Credibility and the communication. After greeting the subjects, Experimenter 2 told them that he was from the Speech Department, and that he was going to play a videotape of a speech given at an earlier date. The experimenter explained that, "Some time ago there was an open citizens' meeting in Oakland, California, at which people from all walks of life were invited to come and express their views on the drug and drug-legislation issue." Experimenter 2 told the subjects that the Speech Department at Stanford University had videotaped some of the speeches given at that meeting and was sending copies of those tapes to universities in various parts of the country, "because they are interested in how people from different parts of the country react to identical speeches." Experimenter 2 then explained that although Texas' Speech Department was anxious to help Stanford with their project, Texas was "really more interested in a more basic question: How good is this videotape machine as a device for presenting information and communications?" Experimenter 2 elaborated by telling the subject that the videotape machine was a device that the Speech Department had recently bought, that its effectiveness in presenting information was not yet known, and that the Speech Department was interested in learning about how people reacted to information presented on videotape, as opposed to other methods of administering standardized material. Subjects were instructed to listen carefully and were told that they would be expected to answer questions at the conclusion of the speech.

The speech, heard by all subjects, was a persuasive communication favoring the legalization of "non-habit forming drugs, like marijuana or LSD" for people over the age of twenty-one. It contained strong, rational arguments favoring such legalization, noting the problems associated with the prohibition of drugs.

All subjects were exposed to identical stimulus material; i.e., the speech and speaker remained constant in all conditions. Communicator credibility was manipulated by varying the manner in which the speaker was introduced. In the *High-Credible-Relevant* condition the speaker was introduced as a professor of biology and physiology at Stanford University, who had conducted a great deal of research on the effects of hallucinogenic drugs on human and animal behavior. The *High-Credible-Irrelevant* communicator was described as a professor of astronomy at Stanford. The *Low-Credible* communicator was presented as a postal clerk in Palo Alto, California. In each case the speaker was described as being "very much interested in the current drug question."

At the conclusion of the speech, the subject was instructed to fill out a questionnaire. One of the items asked subjects to indicate their agreement, on a 9-point scale extending from "strongly disagree" to "strongly agree," with the following statement: "Use of non-habit-forming drugs, like marijuana or LSD, should *not* be illegal for people who are over 21." This item was the dependent measure. To check on the credibility manipulation, subjects simply were asked: "What was the speaker's profession?" The remaining items on the questionnaire asked subjects to recall various aspects of the content of the communication.

After the questionnaire was completed, the subject was debriefed. The experimenter explained the need for the deception, and informed the subject of the nature of the hypothesis under investigation.

RESULTS AND DISCUSSION

Observation of subjects under high and low stress indicated that stress was effectively manipulated. Subjects under high stress appeared tense, verbally expressed apprehension over having to return to Experimenter 1, and seemed to be generally anxious.

Figure 1 presents the mean agreement on the part of subjects with the position advocated in the persuasive communication. These results support our hypothesis: Under high stress the agreement manifested by the subjects

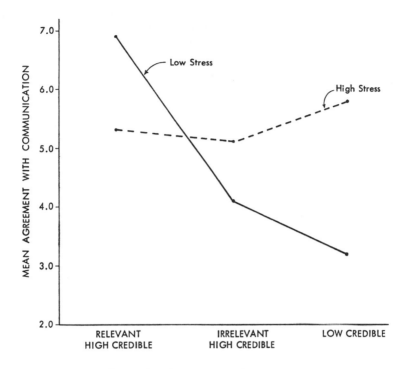

FIGURE 1.   *Agreement with the Communicator.*

was, by and large, unaffected by the credibility level of the communicator, the means being 5.3 when the communicator was high-credible-relevant, 5.1 when he was high-credible-irrelevant, and 5.8 when he was low-credible. Under low stress, communicator credibility greatly affected the extent of the resultant agreement: mean agreement obtained by the high-relevant communicator was 6.9, that by the high-irrelevant communicator 4.1, with a mean of 3.2 resulting when the communicator had low credibility.

Analysis of variance was used to assess the significance of the differences in mean agreement. Table 1 presents the results of the analysis. Although more persuasion was effected under high than under low stress, the stress main effect did not reach an acceptable level of statistical significance. The main effect for credibility demonstrated differences of borderline significance among communicator conditions ($p < .10$), despite the fact that these differences were attenuated by the similar means in the high-stress conditions. Our prediction, that stress level and credibility would interact, is borne out by the data ($p < .025$).

In one sense, the present report describes two experiments, or more precisely, an experiment within an experiment. The low-stress conditions, in and of themselves, provide a study of communicator credibility. Let us look at this "subexperiment" before discussing the primary problem. A separate

TABLE 1

<small>ANALYSIS OF VARIANCE OF AGREEMENT WITH THE COMMUNICATOR</small>

Source	df	Mean Square	F
A (Stress)	1	6.33	1.15
B (Credibility)	2	16.07	2.91*
A × B	2	22.64	4.10**
Error	54	5.52	
Total	59		

*$p < .10$.
**$p < .025$.

analysis of variance was used to examine credibility effects under low stress. This provided a more conservative test (larger error term and fewer degrees of freedom) than would have resulted from the use of the error term yielded by the analysis shown in Table 1. Even so, the credibility main effect was statistically significant at beyond the .01 level ($F = 6.23$, 2 and 27 df). The comparison of high-credible-relevant condition versus the high-credible-irrelevant and low-credible conditions yielded an $F = 11.78$ (1 and 27 df), demonstrating the differences between these means to be highly significant ($p < .005$). Although in the predicted direction, the difference between the high-irrelevant and low-credible conditions (under low stress) failed to reach statistical significance ($F < 1$). Thus, the relevance of the communicator's credibility to the topic of the persuasive communication seems to be an important factor in determining opinion change. We must point out that this finding seems less interesting if one views credibility as an arithmetical sum of, in addition to other factors, status and expertise. One can then argue that since our high-credible-relevant communicator possessed both status and expertise he simply is more credible than our high-credible-irrelevant communicator, and that relevance, *per se*, is not a crucial variable. However, this problem boils down to one of definition; i.e., how credibility is defined. At the very least, the present findings suggest that status may be a feature of communicator credibility that is not terribly important for effective persuasion. Whether one defines issue pertinent expertise as an aspect of credibility or irrelevant to credibility, a communicator who possesses such expertise is likely to be far more effective at persuasion than a communicator who lacks it, even when status is held constant.

The most important finding of the present experiment is that while differences in communicator credibility have a marked effect on opinion change when the audience is under little or no stress, such differences carry little impact with regard to opinion change when the audience is under high stress. It might be noted that in an earlier study (Helmreich, Kuiken, and Collins, 1968) subjects under high stress did not differentially respond to different levels of communicator credibility. We interpret this result in terms of social comparison concepts. A person under high stress seems to be so in need of social pillars that others, regardless of credibility, can affect his opinions. When stress, and therefore need for social comparison, diminishes, the level of the communicator's credibility becomes an important feature of the persuasion situation. The audience has less of a need to agree, and may make its decision more "rationally"; e.g., agreeing with a high-credible-relevant communicator is fairly rational—much more so, at any rate, than agreeing with a low-credible communicator.

Looking at differences in opinion change for the same communicator under both high and low stress reveals that stress was most salient when the communicator was low-credible. The low-credible communicator was significantly more effective ($F = 6.12$, 1 and 54 df, $p < .025$) when the subjects were under high stress. The high-credible-relevant communicator seemed to lose effectiveness when audience stress was high. This difference between means (5.3 in the high-relevant high-stress condition versus 6.9 in the high-relevant low-stress condition) did not reach an acceptable level of statistical significance ($F = 2.32$, 1 and 54 df).

Nevertheless, this finding seems to replicate the results of Janis and Feshbach (1953), if we assume that the communicator used in that study had high-relevant credibility. On the other hand the fact that the stress, in the present experiment, was irrelevant to the communication appears to rule out an explanation in terms of defensive avoidance—the concept invoked by Janis and Feshbach to explain their results.

REFERENCES

ARONSON, E., and GOLDEN, B. W. The effect of relevant and irrelevant aspects of communicator credibility on opinion change. *Journal of Personality*, 1962, 30, 135–146.

DABBS, J. M., JR., and LEVENTHAL, H. Effects of varying the recommendations in a fear-arousing communication. *Journal of Personality and Social Psychology*, 1966, 4, 525–531.

HELMREICH, R., KUIKEN, D., and COLLINS, B. Effects of stress and birth order on attitude change. *Journal of Personality*, 1968, 36, 466–473.

HOVLAND, C. I., JANIS, I. L., and KELLEY, H. H. *Communication and Persuasion.* New Haven: Yale University Press, 1953.

JANIS, I. L., and FESHBACH, S. Effects of fear-arousing communications. *Journal of Abnormal and Social Psychology*, 1953, 48, 78–92.

LEVENTHAL, H., and NILES, P. A field experiment on fear arousal with data on the validity of questionnaire measures. *Journal of Personality*, 1964, 32, 459–479.

LEVENTHAL, H., and SINGER, R. P. Affect arousal and positioning of recommendations in persuasive communications. *Journal of Personality and Social Psychology*, 1966, 4, 137–146.

SCHACHTER, S. *The Psychology of Affiliation.* Stanford: Stanford University Press, 1959.

SECTION III:

CHARACTERISTICS OF THE MESSAGE

OVERVIEW

Whenever a speaker develops a persuasive message he must make a number of choices about its content. For example, he must determine what evidence to include or exclude, what arguments to elaborate or truncate, what appeals to use and how intense they should be. In short, each persuasive message represents the product of a number of decisions about its form and content. Most of these decisions are not dictated by the persuasive goal of the message, but rather by characteristics of the audience, the skills of the speaker, and so forth.

The purpose of this section is to survey materials related to two major dimensions of message variation. The first dimension involves variations in message content characteristics. That is, it deals with the effects of varying the nature of material included in the message. The second dimension concerns variations in the organization of the single message and the sequence effects produced by two or more messages.

PART I: CHARACTERISTICS OF THE CONTENT

It is a time honored assumption that there is a clear distinction between logical and emotional proofs and that man, a rational animal, should be more persuaded by the logical argument. (Becker (1) has attributed this assumption to the influence of faculty psychologists who contended that the mind was divided into compartments which separated understanding and will.) An early investigation by Knower (11) produced limited support for this proposition. He found that although there was no overall difference in their effectiveness, under some conditions logical speeches produced greater attitude change than emotional speeches. However, an investigation by Hartmann (5) at about the same time (1936) produced contradictory evidence. He prepared and distributed "emotional" and "rational" political leaflets, concluding, "There seems to be no escape from the decision that emotional political appeal is a better vote-getting instrument than the rational approach" (5, p. 113). More recent research has not resolved this discrepancy.

There are at least two reasons for this. In the first place, experimental distinctions between emotional and logical proofs have usually been pragmatic rather than theoretical. For example, Hartmann distinguished between logical and emotional appeals by having his messages rated by six psychologists; Knower used ten speech teachers. As an outgrowth of such procedures, emotional and logical appeals have been treated as occupying the polar positions on some ill-defined continuum. Becker observed, "Thus as a message became more emotional, by definition, it was less rational; and as it became more rational, it had to become less emotional" (1, p. 198).

Unfortunately, the receivers of persuasive messages do not perceive this continuum. Rueschelle (14) had experienced public speakers prepare persuasive messages and then had audience members rate each message for the existence of emotional and intellectual appeals. He reasoned that if the rational-emotional continuum was perceived by receivers, those speeches rated high in intellectual appeals should be rated low in emotional appeals and vice versa. Thus, if the intellectual and emotional ratings were related, a strong negative correlation should result. His data, however, yielded non-significant correlations, suggesting the absence of any emotional-intellectual dichotomy in the minds of the receivers.

Second, few attempts have been made to distinguish types of emotional appeal to determine if people respond differently to various types. The possibility of differing response patterns seems quite likely if one accepts Katz's functional analysis of attitudes. But even if emotional appeals are considered as a single class, Becker (1) argues that any analysis of effects must specify at least three attributes of the appeal: its sign (whether it is designed to produce approach or avoidance behavior), its intensity (the power of the appeal to produce approach or avoidance behavior), and its duration (whether it produces a momentary motivation or one which endures over a longer period of time).

A.   Fear Appeals

A type of non-rational appeal which has received considerable experimental attention is the fear appeal. One might intuitively assume that as the intensity of fear appeals used in a persuasive message increases, the amount of attitude change produced by the message would also increase. Such, however, has not always been true. Janis and Feshbach (9) presented subjects with communications advocating improved dental hygiene which were constructed to vary the intensity of fear arousal produced. For example, under conditions of high fear arousal, extremely graphic language and photographs of severe mouth disease were employed. Under conditions of mild fear arousal, much less extreme language and artist illustrations were used.

Somewhat to their surprise, Janis and Feshbach found that the message with minimal fear appeals produced the greatest persuasive effect, while the message with high fear levels was least effective.

These results have not remained unchallenged. Cronkhite has commented, "It is important to point out that a good many experiments conducted since 1953 have either failed to replicate the findings of Janis and Feshbach, or have found strong fear appeals producing greater attitude change" (4, p. 181). For example, Berkowitz and Cottingham (2) found that high fear appeal messages dealing with the advisability of wearing seat belts were more effective in producing attitude change than messages with low fear appeals. Powell (13) reported similar results.

The pattern of inconsistent results suggests that although the level of fear arousal and the magnitude of attitude change are related, their relationship is not nearly as simple as initially envisioned. In his selection, Janis atttempts to account for these inconsistencies. He postulates that as the level of fear produced in an individual by a persuasive message increases, so does the individual's level of vigilance and his need for reassurance. Both of these factors can either facilitate or inhibit the amount of attitude change produced by a message. For example, increasing an individual's vigilance makes him more aware of the persuasive message and hence susceptible to its appeals. However, the more vigilant person will also be more cognizant of loopholes in suggestions made by the communicator.

Because both of these factors produce facilitating and inhibiting effects, Janis postulates a nonmonotonic relationship between level of fear arousal and amount of attitude change produced. This relationship appears quite similar to that postulated by McGuire in his essay, "Personality and Susceptibility to Social Influence" (See Section I). There are important conceptual distinctions, however. While McGuire postulates that raising the level of fear hinders an individual's ability to perceive a message and increases his tendency to yield to it, Janis argues that either of these factors can be enhanced or impeded by fear arousal, depending on the defenses employed by the individual.

B. Specificity of Conclusions

Another choice available to a speaker is whether to recommend specific actions to his audience or merely to suggest a general orientation. Hovland and Mandell (6) found that more than twice as many individuals modified their attitudes in the direction advocated when the speaker drew specific conclusions as compared with when the speaker left the conclusions to be drawn by the audience. Thistlethwaite, deHaan, and Kamenetzky (15), however, contended that Hovland and Mandell's results could be accounted for by differences in audience comprehension. Using different data and statistically controlling for the level of comprehension, they found no difference between the amount of attitude change produced when conclusions were drawn explicitly as opposed to when they were left implicit.

The selection by Leventhal, Singer, and Jones reports an investigation which considered the effects of conclusion-drawing in a larger context. The authors compare the effects of a message containing a specific solution with the effects of one containing no solution—both under conditions of high and low fear arousal. They measure the effects both in terms of attitude change and in changes in overt behavior.

Their results support the hypothesis that the level of fear arousal is directly related to the amount of attitude change produced; however, even more significant, the level of fear arousal is unrelated to changes in behavior. Finally, conclusion-drawing produces significantly greater changes in overt behavior.

C. The Role of Evidence

Most speakers attempt to bolster the persuasiveness of their messages by including evidence—that is, statements containing either factual material or opinions which are attributed to sources other than the speaker. This practice stems from the belief, widely supported by persuasion texts, that the speaker can legitimize his position by showing it to be consistent with the position of others, and this legitimization increases his persuasiveness. Bearing this in mind, the research findings reported by McCroskey are somewhat disconcerting. In the investigations surveyed, only two reported that including evidence in a message significantly enhanced its persuasiveness. Two other investigations found a trend in this direction, but the remainder reported no differences in persuasiveness between messages using evidence as opposed to those which did not.

Apparently the use of evidence does not inevitably increase the persuasiveness of a message. A number of factors are involved. One of these is the speaker's credibility. McCroskey reviews several investigations which found that the use of evidence improved the persuasiveness of low credible sources but did not affect the persuasiveness of high credible sources. A second factor is the credibility of the evidence source itself. Warren (16) found that when the message source possessed neutral credibility, including testimony attributed to high credible sources produced greater attitude change than did the same testimony attributed to low credible sources.

Third, factual evidence and opinion evidence may produce different effects. This possibility has remained uncontrolled in research on evidence effects. Most investigators have incorporated both types in messages, making it impossible to determine if only one type is affecting message acceptance, or, possibly, if the two types are counteracting each other. Kline (10) did attempt to compare the effectiveness of messages containing specific factual evidence, nonspecific factual evidence, or no factual evidence. He found that messages containing specific factual evidence were significantly more persuasive than messages containing either non-specific factual evidence or no factual evidence. Even in this investigation, however, the relation between factual and opinion evidence was not explored.

The selection by McCroskey summarizes much of the research pertinent to the effects of evidence. By doing so, McCroskey points out both what is presently known about the effects of evidence usage and that many issues remain unresolved.

PART II: THE STRUCTURE OF MESSAGES

The speaker also makes choices about the organization of his message, and occasionally he is able to choose his position in a series of messages. One choice he has is whether to acknowledge both sides of an issue or to focus exclusively on the position he advocates. His concern may result from two questions. First, which type of message produces the greater persuasive effect? Second, which type of message produces the more durable effect? The selection by Cohen discusses experimental evidence on these two questions and indicates the effects of topic familiarity and group affiliation.

Suppose you find yourself in a debate. Can you obtain a persuasive advantage by being either first or last to present your case? This question was first investigated by Lund (12). He presented two messages in a pro-con order to subjects and had them indicate their opinion change following each message. He found that, regardless of the topic, the "pro" communication produced greater attitude change. Since the "pro" communication was always first in sequence, he postulated the existence of a "law of primacy" in persuasion. More recently, however, Cromwell (3), presented a series of two persuasive messages to subjects, finding that the second message produced greater attitude change (a recency effect). And when Hovland and Mandell (7) attempted to replicate Lund's procedures they obtained primacy effects on only one of three issues employed. These results prompted Hovland and Mandell to comment, "It appears, then, that primacy is not an easily reproducible phenomenon but may occur only under a certain set of conditions. Hence it is probably premature to postulate a universal law of primacy" (7, pp. 21–22).

One condition which apparently affects the existence of a primacy effect is public commitment. Lund had his subjects respond to the opinion questionnaire after they had read the initial message. This response may have produced a feeling of commitment in the respondent which resulted in his being more resistant to the second message. Cromwell measured subjects' opinions only after they had been exposed to both messages, thus reducing the possibility of commitment effects. When Hovland and Mandell used Lund's topics without the intervening questionnaire, they found no primacy effects. Thus it appears that commitment increases the likelihood of primacy effects.

A number of other conditions may affect the appearance of primacy or recency effects. Among these are the topic familiarity, the time interval between the messages themselves, and the time interval between the messages and the measurement of attitude change. The article by Rosnow discusses the influence of these as well as other factors in some detail.

One further elaboration of the effects of message structure has been suggested by Insko (8). In his investigation he considered the relative effectiveness of one-sided versus two-sided messages when they appeared first or second in a sequence. He found that when both messages were one-sided, or when both were two-sided, neither primacy nor recency predominated. When a one-sided message was followed by a two-sided message, he found a recency effect. Finally, under conditions where subjects were familiar with the issue prior to the messages, a two-sided followed by a one-sided message yielded a primacy effect.

The selection by Koehler represents a more recent treatment of this problem. Koehler concerns himself with the sequence effects of one-sided and two-sided messages. In addition he investigates the effects of the time interval between messages and the time interval between message presentation and the measurement of attitude change.

REFERENCES

1. BECKER, S. T. "Research on Emotional and Logical Proofs," *Southern Speech Journal,* 28 (1962–63), 198–207.
2. BERKOWITZ, L., and D. R. COTTINGHAM. "The Interest Value and Relevance of Fear-Arousing Communications," *Journal of Abnormal and Social Psychology,* 60 (1960), 37–43.
3. CROMWELL, H. "The Relative Effects of Audience Attitude in the First Versus the Second Argumentative Speech of a Series," *Speech Monographs,* 17 (1950), 105–22.
4. CRONKHITE, G. *Persuasion: Speech and Behavioral Change.* New York: Bobbs-Merrill, 1969.
5. HARTMANN, G. W. "A Field Experiment on the Comparative Effectiveness of 'Emotional' and 'Rational' Political Leaflets in Determining Election Results," *Journal of Abnormal and Social Psychology,* 31 (1936), 99–114.
6. HOVLAND, C. I., and W. MANDELL. "An Experimental Comparison of Conclusion-Drawing by the Communicator and by the Audience," *Journal of Abnormal and Social Psychology,* 47 (1952), 581–88.
7. HOVLAND, C. I., W. MANDELL, E. H. CAMPBELL, T. BROCK, A. S. LUCHINS, A. R. COHEN, W. J. McGUIRE, I. L. JANIS, R. L. FEIERABEND, and N. H. ANDERSON. *The Order of Presentation in Persuasion.* New Haven: Yale University Press, 1957.
8. INSKO, C. A. "One-Sided versus Two-Sided Communications and Counter Communications," *Journal of Abnormal and Social Psychology,* 65 (1962), 203–6.
9. JANIS, I. L., and S. FESHBACH. "Effects of Fear-Arousing Communications," *Journal of Abnormal and Social Psychology,* 48 (1953), 78–92.
10. KLINE, J. A. "Interaction of Evidence and Readers' Intelligence on the Effects of Short Messages," *Quarterly Journal of Speech,* 55 (1969), 407–13.
11. KNOWER, F. H. "Experimental Studies of Changes in Attitudes: A Study of the Effect of Oral Argument on Changes of Attitude," *Journal of Social Psychology,* 6 (1935), 315–47.
12. LUND, F. H. "The Psychology of Belief: IV. The Law of Primacy in Persuasion," *Journal of Abnormal and Social Psychology,* 20 (1925), 183–91.
13. POWELL, F. A. "The Effects of Anxiety-Arousing Messages When Related to Personal, Familial, and Interpersonal Referents," *Speech Monographs,* 32 (1965), 102–6.
14. RUESCHELLE, R. C. "An Experimental Study of Audience Recognition of Emotional and Intellectual Appeals in Persuasion," *Speech Monographs,* 25 (1958), 49–58.
15. THISTLETHWAITE, D. L., H. DeHAAN, and J. KAMENETZKY. "The Effects of 'Directive' and 'Nondirective' Communication Procedures on Attitudes," *Journal of Abnormal and Social Psychology,* 51 (1955), 107–13.
16. WARREN, I. D. "The Effect of Credibility in Sources of Testimony on Audience Attitudes Toward Speaker and Message," *Speech Monographs,* 36 (1969), 456–58.

Irving L. Janis*

EFFECTS OF FEAR AROUSAL ON ATTITUDE CHANGE: RECENT DEVELOPMENTS IN THEORY AND EXPERIMENTAL RESEARCH [1]

I. INTRODUCTION

Key Issues

Is the average person more likely or less likely to accept a persuasive communication if it arouses a relatively high degree of fear, as compared with equivalent communications that arouse mild fear or no fear at all? This

*Department of Psychology, Yale University.

[1] This chapter presents a condensed and somewhat modified version of the material in several chapters of a forthcoming book. *The Contours of Fear* (John Wiley & Sons, 1968). The theoretical analysis of factors that influence the acceptance of precautionary recommendations in warning communications grew out of recent experimental studies on tolerance for self-imposed deprivations and was facilitated by Grant MH-08564 from the National Institute of Mental Health, United States Public Health Service.

During the fall of 1966, when this chapter was written, the author was a visiting research fellow at the Western Behavioral Sciences Institute, La Jolla, California, and professor of psychology in residence at the University of California at San Diego (while on leave of absence from Yale University).

Excerpted from *Advances in Experimental Social Psychology*, III, pp. 166–224, with permission of the author and Academic Press, Inc.

question is asked again and again in recent discussions of research on the effectiveness of fear-arousing appeals in inducing attitude change. But is it the right question to ask? Does not this question take too much for granted by assuming a simple monotonic relation between the intensity of fear arousal and communication effectiveness?

The questioning of assumptions is certainly our first task when we are confronted with the inconsistent outcomes of relevant experiments. One series of communication experiments shows a negative relation between fear arousal and attitude change (e.g., Janis and Feshbach, 1953; Haefner, 1956; Janis and Terwilliger, 1962), but another series shows a positive relation (e.g., Insko *et al.*, 1965; Leventhal *et al.*, 1965). A few other studies report no significant differences or a mixed outcome for essentially the same variables (Moltz and Thistlethwaite, 1955; Leventhal and Niles, 1965; Leventhal and Watts, 1966). As McGuire (1967) has pointed out, those psychologists whose views lead them to expect a monotonic function must acknowledge that the results from the relevant attitude-change experiments "constitute a remarkable show of impartiality on the part of Nature."

Nature's impartiality in this area of experimental social psychology, which often makes us feel that we are dealing with subtractive rather than additive research, creates a maximum of confusion when several different indicators of attitude change yield opposite outcomes within the same experiment. For example, Leventhal and Niles (1964) found that a strong fear-arousing version of an antismoking communication was less effective than milder fear-arousing versions in producing professed willingness to stop smoking, but was more effective in gaining acceptance for the belief that smoking causes cancer, and made no significant difference in verbal acceptance of the communicator's recommendation to obtain chest X-rays. A more recent experiment by Leventhal and Watts (1966) again reports a mixed outcome, but the specific findings are not the same as those from the earlier experiment. (See Section IV, A.)

Whenever we encounter such incompatible results from a series of experiments carried out by competent investigators, we must become highly skeptical about our way of conceptualizing the problem and start looking for hitherto neglected variables that might be interacting with those under investigation. Should we expect to find lawful cause-and-effect relations between emotional arousal and attitude change, or should we regard the observed positive, negative, and mixed relations as accidental outcomes that merely reflect the influence of other correlated variables? To what extent can the disparate outcomes be reconciled if we postulate a nonmonotonic relation between intensity of fear arousal and communication effectiveness? What new questions should we try to put to the test so that our experiments will yield more dependable outcomes? Are there any innovations in research strategy that might help us to obtain some additive findings about the conditions under which emotional arousal has a facilitating effect on attitude change and the conditions under which it has an interfering effect? These are the main questions on which the present chapter will be focused.

. . . .

II. THEORETICAL FRAMEWORK

Functional Properties of Anticipatory Emotions

The arousal of vigilance and of efforts to gain reassurance have received strong emphasis in recent theoretical analyses and experiments bearing on anticipatory emotions whose rise and fall depend on the person's cognitive appraisals of the threat (cf. Janis, 1962, 1968; Janis and Leventhal, 1967; Schachter, 1964; Lazarus, 1966). For example, one of Schachter's key assumptions, supported by some of his experimental findings, is that whenever any environmental cue arouses emotional excitement, the person will become motivated to obtain information about what is happening to him. Schachter assigns a steering function to cognitive factors and this seems to fit in especially well with certain communication effects, such as the extraordinary responsiveness to authoritative information observed among the residents of a threatened city during the initial phases of a hurricane or tornado disaster, when there is considerable ambiguity about the nature of the danger. If emotional excitement is highly aroused at a time when the external threat remains ambiguous, informative announcements can make the difference between a mass flight in terror and a vigorous, stoical effort to maintain business as usual (Janis, 1962).

Lazarus (1966), in reviewing the extensive research from laboratory experiments and field studies on the effects of fear, also emphasizes the heightened motivation to obtain relevant information. He concludes that whenever fear is aroused, the person will become alert to internal and external cues related to the threat and will start thinking about the resources available for coping with it. Lazarus assumes, however, that once vigilant apprehensiveness is induced, the person may resort to defensive avoidances that ward off full awareness of the threat if he fails to gain emotional relief by developing plans for coping with it. Similar behavioral consequences, as will be seen shortly, are emphasized in my analysis of the way in which fear influences cognitive functions, particularly with respect to inducing vigilance and motivating the person to seek reassurance.

Although differing in many essential details, there is at least one common assumption about the cognitive consequences of induced fear that the recent theoretical analyses share with earlier theoretical formulations by psychoanalysts (e.g., Freud, 1936; Sullivan, 1953) and by reinforcement-learning theorists (e.g., Dollard and Miller, 1950; Mowrer, 1950; Skinner, 1938). This common assumption is that whenever fear or any other unpleasant emotion is strongly aroused—whether by a verbal warning or by a direct encounter with signs of danger—the person becomes motivated to ward off the painful emotional state and his efforts in this direction will persist until the distressing cues are avoided in one way or another. Thus, if the distressing threat cues do not rapidly disappear as a result of environmental changes, the emotionally aroused person is expected to try to escape from them, either physically or psychologically (for example, by imagining himself as taking successful protective action or distracting himself by pleasant daydreams). The characteristic shifts in content of cognitions, which the emotionally aroused person directs toward warding off external signs and internal anticipations that give rise to his distressing affective state, have been described in similar ways by the adherents of diverse psychological theories, although they use different terms— such as "defenses," "coping mechanisms," "security devices," "aversive habits," and "avoidance efforts"—to designate them.

Reflective Fear

The implications of the foregoing theoretical assumptions for attitude changes have been discussed by Janis (1962) in an analysis of the concept of reflective fear. The term "reflective" was introduced in order to emphasize two distinctive features of fear reactions in normal adults—first, that the emotional state is based to some extent on thoughtful *reflection*; and second, that as a result of being mediated by higher mental processes, the intensity of the emotion tends to increase or decrease as the signs of external threat increase or decrease, *reflecting* like a mirror the presence or absence of environmental threat cues. More specifically, a key assumption is that a person's level of reflective fear is roughly proportional both to the perceived probability of the dangerous event materializing and to the anticipated magnitude of the damage, if it does materialize, that could be inflicted on himself, his family, and other significant persons or groups with whom he is identified. The person's level of reflective fear will increase or decrease depending on the information he receives concerning his personal vulnerability to danger or deprivation, whether it involves anticipations of physical pain, career failure, social rejection, economic deprivation, or any other potential loss. In contrast to the relatively unmodifiable character of neurotic anxiety, reflective fear will tend to be low, moderate, or high, depending on whether warning messages are presented that evoke anticipations of a low, moderate, or high degree of personal vulnerability to the predicted danger. Reflective fear can sometimes be temporarily aroused to such a high level that it seems indistinguishable from a neurotic type of panic state, but it will nevertheless subside in response to authoritative reassurances that the threat is no longer present or that adequate coping resources are available.

The anticipations of personal vulnerability evoked by any warning communication are presumably determined by cultural norms, socializing experiences, and other predisposing factors that shape the person's expectations as to where, when, and how much he might be affected by whatever source of danger is being called to his attention. Many idiosyncratic factors in each person's temperament and past training may influence the way he processes informational inputs about potential danger and thus determine the intensity of his reflective fear reactions. Despite these sources of individual differences, however, there may be a number of relatively invariant consequences of fear arousal that are shared by all human beings. Janis (1962) postulates three such behavioral consequences of reflective fear and presents a number of partially tested hypotheses concerning the conditions under which each is likely to become dominant.

1. One major consequence is that the aroused unpleasant emotional state gives rise to *heightened vigilance*, which takes the form of increased attention to threat-relevant events, scanning for new signs of danger, attending to information about the nature of threat, and thinking about alternative courses of action for dealing with emergency contingencies. The arousal of vigilance affects not only cognitive processes of perception, attention, and planning, but also actions: The individual becomes keyed up in a way that makes him more likely to execute precautionary actions in response to any cue indicating the onset of danger. More complicated forms of mental and physical activity may also result from a strong need for vigilance. During an epidemic, for example, apprehensive people not only learn about the danger signs and scan the newspaper for announcements by public health officials, but they also pay closer attention to internal stimuli from their own bodies. Sometimes they become hypervigilant, exaggerating the significance of their mild physical discomforts to the point where they become sleepless and demand prompt medical attention.

2. Another important consequence of reflective fear is that the person displays a strong need to *seek reassurances* in order to alleviate emotional tension. Again, the need for reassurance involves changes in both cognition and action. For example, some of the actions of moderately fearful surgery patients are oriented toward gaining verbal reassurances from the doctor and other staff members; on the cognitive side, such patients may focus their thoughts repeatedly on the reassuring instructions given them for dealing with post operative pain (Janis, 1958). Other manifestations of the heightened need for reassurance include selective attention to complacent assertions that alleviate fear by minimizing the danger, and acquisition of new attitudes that alleviate fear by bolstering the person's confidence in his ability to cope with the danger. Some of the attitude changes may lead to highly adaptive behavior, such as taking precautionary measures recommended by trustworthy authorities. But an endangered person will sometimes resort to a fatalistic outlook, superstitious rituals for warding off bad luck, and other unrealistic forms of reassurance that foster anticipations of total invulnerability. The person may end up firmly believing that the danger will not materialize ("It can't happen here!") or

that if it does, he will somehow be completely unscathed ("Others may suffer, but we shall be safe"). These complacent anticipations, referred to as "blanket reassurances," may lead to a maladaptive lack of vigilance when the external danger is actually approaching.

3. A third consequence is that the arousal of reflective fear increases the chances that the person will develop new attitudes involving a compromise between vigilance and reassurance tendencies. The two tendencies may give rise to manifestations of conflict, as when a combat soldier feels at one moment that he must watch out for ever-present danger and at the next moment that he ought to relax and forget about it because he is safe from harm. Sometimes one tendency dominates the other entirely, as in the case of blanket reassurances. But when the average person is repeatedly exposed to impressive warnings, he is likely to develop a *compromise attitude*, which combines discriminative vigilance (seking further information about the threat, remaining alert to signs of oncoming danger) with discriminative reassurances (expecting to be able to cope successfully, or to be helped by others, if the danger becomes extreme). Outstanding examples of compromise attitudes are seen among victims of heart disease who learn to live with their illness. Realizing they might be subject to another heart attack, they make specific plans for carrying out protective actions that will help them to survive if such an attack happens to materialize. For instance, after his first heart attack, a man will go about his business carrying a well-labeled bottle of digitalis in a prominent pocket and a legible note in his wallet stating the appropriate dosage to give in case he is found unconscious. Such an individual displays a mixed attitude, because he remains vigilant to possible signs of worsening of his illness and worries about being incapacitated or killed by it, and yet is able to gain some reassurance by adhering to a medical plan that could actually save his life in an emergency. Obviously, this type of attitude is likely to be much more adaptive than either blanket reassurance or indiscriminate vigilance.

Figure 1 shows diagrammatically the three alternative modes of adjustment to threat that are specified in the foregoing analysis; the three different outcomes are shown in the last column. A major task for research on fear-

FIGURE 1.   *Hypothetical consequences of the arousal of reflective fear (from Janis, 1962).*

arousing communications is to determine the conditions under which one or another of these three modes of adjustment to threat will become dominant.

One factor that is assumed to determine which of the three types of reaction will be evoked by a warning message is the magnitude of the threat. The influence of this factor is represented in Fig. 2, which shows the expected

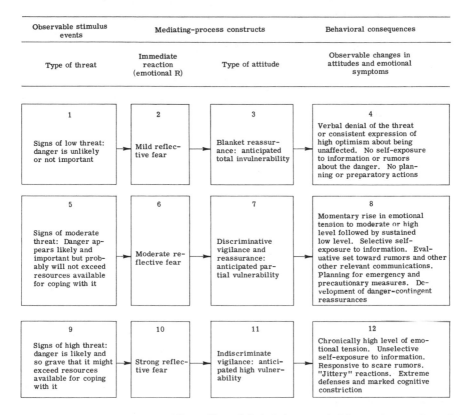

FIGURE 2. *Schematic summary of "normal" psychological changes evoked by warnings or signs of external danger (from Janis, 1962).*

reactions of normal persons to low, moderate, and high threats. At one extreme, when the threat cues make the danger appear unlikely to materialize or so mild as to be unimportant, the person's behavior remains essentially unchanged; an attitude of blanket reassurance is likely to be dominant. The behavioral effects of this type of complacency are described in box 4, in the upper right-hand corner of the figure. At the other extreme, when very strong warnings are given, reflective fear may mount to such a high level that indiscriminate vigilance tends to be the predominating reaction. The resulting changes in attitudes and emotional symptoms, as described in box 12 in the lower right-hand corner of the figure, are likely to be disruptive and maladaptive.

When a person is warned about an impending danger that he judges to be potentially serious but manageable, he is likely to experience a moderate degree of reflective fear, and the predominant attitude is most likely to be a combination of discriminative vigilance with reassurance. This sequence, depicted in the second row of Fig. 2, represents what happens when a person successfully carries out the "work of worrying" (cf. Janis, 1958, pp. 374–388). The compromise attitude, which develops as the person engages in the work of worrying at a relatively moderate level of arousal, is likely to be sufficiently tested by reality to help him maintain emotional control later on, if he finds himself confronted by actual danger or deprivation. Thus, the resulting changes in attitude and action described in box 8 in the figure are assumed to have a better chance of being adaptive than those resulting from either very mild or very strong arousal.

. . . .

Facilitating and Interfering Effects of Emotional Appeals

In this and the next section we shall examine the theoretical implications of the foregoing analysis of reflective emotions for the relation between attitude change and the intensity of emotional arousal. Whenever a negative type of emotional appeal is introduced for the purpose of motivating people to adopt a recommended policy or to take protective action—such as stopping smoking to avoid lung disease—its success requires the development of a compromise attitude. On the one hand, the communicatee must become sufficiently vigilant to be attentive to signs of potential danger and he must continue to take the threat seriously if he is to avoid backsliding to his former attitude of complacency and inaction. On the other hand, his decision to adhere to the policy recommended by the communicator must satisfy his need for reassurance sufficiently so that he is not left in a distressing emotional state that will motivate him to seek some other (nonrecommended) means of averting or ignoring the threat.

A number of specific assumptions about the facilitating and interfering effects of emotional arousal (Janis, 1968) highlight the potential deficiencies of emotional appeals that are either very weak or very strong when a communicator is attempting to persuade the audience to adopt his recommendations for coping with a realistic threat. Three main sources of failure to produce attitude change can be singled out, one resulting from insufficient stimulation and the other two from excessive stimulation:

1. *Insufficient vigilance*: A persuasive communication may fail to achieve any facilitating effects if it evokes little or no emotional arousal. Statements about the pertinent threat, especially when presented in a bland manner without any concrete or personalized images, may pose no challenge at all to the recipients' initial beliefs about the unimportance of the predicted danger

and may leave intact their anticipations of personal invulnerability. They will devote little attention or thought to the threat and will not be in the market for the proposed solution to the threat that the communicator is trying to promote. Thus, when vigilance is not stimulated, preexisting attitudes of blanket reassurance will remain dominant. (For example, an antismoking communication would be totally ineffective if it merely induced complacent thoughts in the recipient, such as "lung cancer hardly ever occurs in young people like us, so there is no reason to pay any attention to what is being said about it.")

2. *Cognitive impairment from hypervigilance*: At the opposite extreme, excessive arousal can induce a temporary state of hypervigilance that interferes with reception of the communicator's message. Members of the audience may become so preoccupied with the threat content of the communication and so disorganized in their thinking that they fail to attend to or comprehend the communicator's recommendations for averting the threat. Although the available evidence, which will be cited later on, indicates that this extremely high level of arousal is likely to be evoked only very rarely by mass communications containing strong emotional appeals, a temporary decrease in mental efficiency during exposure to a persuasive communication will interfere with attitude change insofar as it prevents the person from grasping crucial parts of the message.

3. *Unintended attitude changes resulting from residual emotional tension*: An optimal degree of emotional arousal that falls somewhere in the broad intermediate range between the extremes of insufficient vigilance and excessive vigilance is presumed to be a necessary but not a sufficient condition for acceptance of the communicator's recommendation. Emotional equanimity cannot always be restored merely by an authoritative recommendation and the audience may choose alternative means for satisfying the aroused need for reassurance. (For example, an antismoking communication that arouses fear of lung disease may lead some recipients to adopt a nonrecommended solution, such as switching to filtered cigarettes.)

The probability of selecting the particular means recommended by the communicator is a function of many independent variables that are unrelated to level of arousal—such as the degree of anticipated protection, the relative costs of adopting alternative means, and other considerations that enter into cognitive evaluation of any proposed solution to a serious problem. In addition to these independent variables, the level of arousal is assumed to be one of the determinants of degree of resistance. As the level of unpleasant emotional arousal increases, the audience will become increasingly motivated to examine the communicator's recommendation critically and to consider alternative means that might lend greater reassurance. Thus, as reflective fear, shame, or guilt mounts from a low to a moderate and then to a high level, the average person will become increasingly alert to aspects of the potential danger situation that might be overlooked by the communicator. In this more vigilant state, a person will consider more carefully than otherwise the possible loopholes in any proposed solution that purports to offer a high degree of safety. The higher the level of aroused vigilance, the greater the chances that any proposed solution will be critically evaluated to see if it offers sufficient protection, and hence the higher the probability that members of the audience will remain apprehensive about the riskiness of relying on the communicator's recommendations. Consequently, they will be motivated to seek a more reassuring solution to reduce the state of relatively high arousal that remains after they have critically evaluated the communicator's recommendation. The tendency to resist the communicator's influence and to refute his message may also be enhanced by the arousal of aggression in response to the frustration created by the unpleasant state of arousal.

Moreover, the more strongly reassurance needs are aroused by a fear-arousing appeal in a persuasive communication, the higher the likelihood that the person will try out various habitual forms of defensive avoidance that have been strongly rewarded by fear-reduction in the past. Among the effective forms of cognitive defenses that can function as powerful resistances to the communicator's message are the following: (1) doubts about the communicator's sincerity and suspicions that he may be an alarmist who is trying to manipulate the audience; (2) refutations of statements about the magnitude or personal relevance of the potential danger, which enable the person to deny that he could be affected by it; (3) selective attention to arguments and signs that the threat is not imminent, even if the potential danger is not minimized, which enables the person to set the problem aside while he passively awaits future developments before trying to work out a solution.

These cognitive defenses can operate as powerful resistances to the communicator's message during or after exposure to the communication, insofar as they succeed in enabling the person to avoid thinking about the threat. The greater the need for reassurance, the more likely the person is to make use of these and other types of defensive avoidance, such as fatalistic attitudes. Hence, the arousal of a strong need for reassurance by use of a strong emotional appeal runs the risk of inducing unintended attitude changes, since the audience becomes more inclined to dismiss the communicator as untrustworthy and to minimize the importance or imminence of the alleged threat. Later on, it will become apparent that these considerations do not lead to any simple formula for predicting the optimal level of arousal, but they do suggest some hypotheses concerning the interacting variables that will make a difference in the observable outcome.

.   .   .   .

Summary: Major Propositions

The following are the major propositions derived from the theoretical analysis of reflective fear, shame and guilt.

1. At very low levels of emotional arousal, the average person will remain relatively unaffected by very mild warnings that attempt to induce changes in attitude and actions as compared with warnings that arouse a moderate intensity of fear, shame, or guilt. When the warning is very mild, the average person will tend to dismiss all information about the threat as inconsequential by means of blanket reassurances, whereas when vigilance and reassurance tendencies are stimulated to a moderate degree, the chances are increased that he will develop a compromise attitude of the type required for sustained acceptance of whatever plausible safety measures are recommended by the communicator.

2. As emotional arousal increases toward the high end of the continuum, the heightened motivation to alleviate the unpleasant emotional state will generally lead to the mobilization of resistances—such as defensive detachment from the threat, minimization of the potential danger, and suspicion of the alarmist intentions of the communicator—which eventually reach a critical level where they begin to increase at a greater rate than the facilitating effects of emotional arousal; beyond this critical level, which varies as a function of stimulus variables and predispositional attributes, increases in arousal will bring diminishing returns in the degree of acceptance of the safety measures recommended by the communicator.

3. When a warning communication arouses an extremely high level of fear, shame, or guilt, the average person's state of intense emotional excitement will be characterized by hypervigilant speculations and fantasies as well involuntary constriction of cognitive processes, resulting in marked interference with attention, comprehension, and learning. Once the threshold for hypervigilant reactions is reached, the chances are reduced that the message will be correctly understood and assimilated into the person's system of beliefs and plans for action.

Since there are no established measures of emotion that form an absolute scale, these propositions are difficult to test. A very extensive experimental assessment is required in which behavioral and verbal indicators of degree of arousal and attitude change are obtained for a large series of points all along the entire arousal continuum, ranging from near-zero through a series of intermediate values up to very high emotional excitement at the upper limits of stress tolerance. No such experiments have ever been carried out. It must be acknowledged, therefore, that the evidence now at hand bears only a rough approximation to what is needed for testing the three propositions. Moreover, the propositions themselves are still in a somewhat crude state, since certain of the key terms are incompletely defined. But, as was stated earlier, it seems to me that when the conflicting experimental evidence is reexamined in the light of the analysis of reflective emotions, even though the theory is still in preliminary form, we can bring some order out of the confusing results that perplex us and pose some new questions that may reorient research on the effects of emotional arousal in a more productive direction.

III. EXPERIMENTAL FINDINGS

Effects of Arousal on Attention and Comprehension

A large number of experiments deal with cognitive performances of human subjects exposed to varying degrees of induced stress and many of them provide preliminary support for the notion that a nonmonotonic function might hold for the relation between cognitive efficiency and intensity of emotion arousal. Brown (1961, p. 350) points out that recent neurophysiological findings have led Hebb (1955), Malmo (1958), Schlosberg (1954), and other psychologists to consider just such a function on the presumption that the ascending reticular system may deliver insufficient stimulation to the cortex at low levels of emotional or motivational arousal and too intense bombardment of the cortex at high levels of arousal. Optimal efficiency would therefore always occur at intermediate levels, where the amount of arousal is neither too weak (as when the person remains unalert and lethargic) nor too strong (as when a person is frozen with terror). These neurophysiological considerations suggest that the relationship between emotional arousal and cognitive efficiency in attending to, comprehending, and learning the content of verbal messages might prove to be a special case of a more general relationship between the intensity of any form of motivation arousal and any type of cognitive performance (see Duffy, 1962). Nevertheless, it still remains an open question whether the inverted U-shape function does in fact accurately describe the way in which the average person's attention to and comprehension of an emotion-arousing communication will vary as a function of the intensity of his arousal.

.   .   .   .

In experimental studies, cognitive efficiency seems to be rarely impaired by fear-arousing messages, except when severe threats of pain or punishment are given. By and large, the results from experiments on persuasive communications indicate that variations in amount of arousal via emotional appeals have little or no demonstrable effect on comprehension or retention of the essential content of the message, even though acceptance of the communicator's recommendations may be significantly influenced by these same variations. For example, in the initial experiment on fear appeals, Janis and Feshbach (1953) found that a strong fear-arousing version of a dental hygiene communication produced less attitude change among high school students than versions containing milder appeals, which evoked less worry about decayed teeth and gum disease; but the decrement in effectiveness could not be accounted for by any decrements in attention, comprehension, or learning, since the subjects exposed to the strong arousal condition attained just as high scores as the others on a comprehensive information test covering the essential content of the communication. Moreover, a higher percentage of the subjects in the strong arousal condition than in the moderate or low arousal conditions reported that it was easy to pay attention to what the speaker was saying and that they experienced little "mind-wandering" during the communication. Thus the evidence does not support an interpretation of the attitude change findings that postulates decreased attentiveness, distraction, impaired comprehension, or any temporary cognitive loss that would interfere with learning efficiency.

Similar negative results on the learning and retention of the informational content of persuasive communications have been reported in other experiments that have compared different levels of arousal evoked by emotional appeals (e.g., Berkowitz and Cottingham, 1960; Haefner, 1956; Janis and Milholland, 1954; Janis and Terwilliger, 1962). A statistically significant difference in amount of information recalled following exposure to strong versus mild fear appeals was reported by Niles (1964), but the difference was of small magnitude and was unrelated to any changes in beliefs or attitudes.

Although a null hypothesis can never be proved, the scarcity of significant differences on this point in the existing literature is consistent with the expectation stated earlier, that when sufficient data become available for plotting the entire curve for cognitive efficiency, we might find a relatively level plateau (or random fluctuations) extending over a broad range of arousal values up to a relatively high level of arousal, where the decrement from hypervigilance sets in. This expectation, however, does not preclude the possibility that the arousal of vigilance may have some selective effects on attention, without affecting over-all cognitive efficiency. This possibility is suggested by the findings from an experiment by Janis and Milholland (1954) that compared the verbatim recall of two equated groups exposed to strong and mild fear-arousing versions of a dental hygiene communication. As in the other experiments, there was no significant difference in the mean number of items of information recalled by the two groups. But there were significant differences in the types of information acquired, indicating that the high arousal condition had a selective effect on what was learned. Information about the causes of the threat (such as how food particles adhering to unbrushed teeth after each meal generate acids and dissolve the enamel coat) was better recalled by the subjects exposed to the mild arousal condition; whereas information about the unfavorable consequences of the threat (such as necessity for painful dental treatments) was better recalled by those exposed to the strong arousal condition. Janis and Milholland conclude that under conditions where relatively minor threats are depicted, elaborations of the potential dangers have the effect of focusing attention on the threatening consequences, making them more vivid and therefore better learned; but the heightened learning of the consequences detracts from attention to and learning of other material contained in the communication—in this case, material on the causes of the threat.

In this experiment, both groups recalled equally well the main recommendations made by the communication. Nevertheless, the selective recall tendency noted in the strong versus mild arousal conditions suggests that threat appeals can exert an important effect on what is learned and retained from a communication. Under certain circumstances (notably where subsequent precautionary actions are contingent upon understanding the complicated causes of a threat) this selective tendency could conceivably reduce the ultimate effectiveness of a fear-arousing communication. This lead concerning the selective attention effects of arousing vigilance has not yet been adequately explored.

Effects of Arousal on Acceptance of Recommendations

We turn next to the first two propositions derived from the analysis of reflective emotions (Section II, F). According to these propositions, the average person will be most likely to accept precautionary recommendations when his level of reflective fear is aroused to an intermediate degree, rather than when it is either very low or very high. This prediction would apply to all plausible threat-reducing recommendations in all types of warning communications— the emergency evacuation requests by local authorities when an imminent natural disaster is predicted; the advice of leaders in large business or trade union organizations urging their followers to accept new policies to counteract anticipated financial losses; the admonitions of religious leaders urging their followers to perform an act of charity or self-sacrifice to expiate their past sins; the scare propaganda by political leaders urging the public to support new policies in order to prevent a national political catastrophe; the news releases by public health authorities that call attention to the harmful effects of cigarette smoking or to any other hazards requiring adaptive changes in attitudes and action.

If the two propositions are valid, we should find in every instance that the degree to which an audience will accept the main recommendations in a warning communication will vary in nonmonotonic fashion . . . . According to the first proposition, which refers to the positive motivating effects of arousing vigilance and reassurance needs, we should expect to find that when the level of reflective fear, shame, or guilt is increased by using increasingly more powerful emotional appeals, there will be a corresponding rise in audience acceptance of the communicator's recommendations up to a certain point. The second proposition in Section II, F, which pertains to resistances that give rise to unintended attitude changes, implies that the inflection point of the curve will generally be below the point of maximum stress tolerance. Thus, we should find that diminishing returns begin to set in somewhere in the inter-mediate range of fear arousal.

· ·

The most pertinent experimental findings indicate that under certain conditions a persuasive communication containing a strong threat appeal, as compared with parallel versions of the same communication containing milder appeals, can arouse psychological resistances that reduce the effectiveness of the communicator's message in the long run.

1. THE INITIAL EXPERIMENT ON DENTAL HYGIENE RECOMMENDATIONS (JANIS AND FESHBACH, 1953)

The diminishing returns from increasing the intensity of fear was first suggested in the experiment by Janis and Feshbach (1953) that compared the effectiveness of three different forms of an illustrated lecture on dental hygiene. Strong-, moderate-, and minimal-fear-arousing versions of the same persuasive message were presented to equivalent groups of high school students. As expected, immediately after the communication was over there were more signs of aroused vigilance among the subjects exposed to the strong-fear-arousing version than among those exposed to the milder versions. The former reported being more worried about the condition of their teeth, more interested in the information conveyed, and more impressed by the communication than the others. When attitude changes were assessed one week later, however, the strong-fear version proved to be less successful than the milder versions. The greatest amount of reported change in the direction of accepting the new dental hygiene practices recommended by the communicator was found in the group exposed to the mildest-fear-arousing version. Attitude changes were also assessed by observing the degree to which the subjects resisted the influence of counterpropaganda that contradicted the main theme of the original communication, and again the mildest-fear-arousing version proved to be most effective. Thus, a significantly smaller percentage of the group that had received the strong-fear-arousing version continued to accept the recommendations given by the original dental-hygiene communication. Moreover, when all subjects who rejected the counterpropaganda were asked to explain why they disagreed with it, the ones in the strong-fear group were less likely than those in the milder-fear groups to mention spontaneously any of the arguments from the illustrated talk to which they had been exposed one week earlier.

An analysis of individual differences in level of anxiety indicated that the unfavorable effects of strong-fear arousal occurred among those persons who were chronically most anxious—as manifested by high scores on a questionnaire (given a week before the communication) dealing with characteristic symptoms of anxiety (Janis and Feshbach, 1954). On the main measure of attitude change, a significant interaction effect was found ($p < .01$) between chronic level of anxiety and intensity of fear appeals: The strong-fear-arousing version evoked markedly less attitude change than the minimal version among

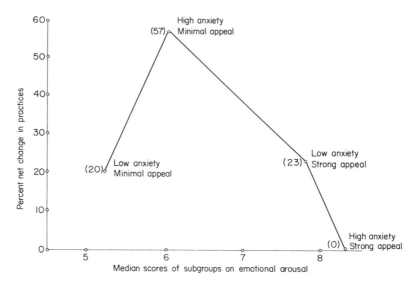

FIGURE 5.   *Observed relationship between level of fear arousal and acceptance of the communicator's recommendations (based on data from Janis and Feshbach, 1954).*

subjects with high scores on initial level of anxiety, but not among those with low scores.

The data can be nicely fitted to an inverted U-shaped curve, as shown in Fig. 5, if we assume that the obtained level of arousal is a joint product of anxiety predisposition (as assessed by high versus low scores on the personality scale) and strength of fear appeal material presented in the communication. The lowest level of arousal would be expected in the subgroup of low predisposed subjects exposed to the mild fear appeal and the highest level of arousal in the subgroup of high predisposed subjects exposed to the strong fear appeal; intermediate degrees of arousal would be expected in the other two subgroups. This set of expectations is borne out by the data from a five-item scale dealing with feelings of worry about tooth decay and gum disease that was administered immediately after exposure to the illustrated talk. The scores on this arousal scale for the four subgroups are shown on the X axis in Fig. 5 and were used as the basis for plotting the relation between degree of fear arousal and degree of acceptance of the communicator's recommendation. The latter indicator is the net percentage of change in conformity with the recommended dental hygiene practices, as assessed by comparing each subject's description of how and when he was brushing his teeth one week after exposure to the dental hygiene communication with his answers to the same questions before exposure to the communication.

On the basis of all the various findings from their experiment, Janis and Feshbach concluded that the diminishing returns from the use of a strong-fear-arousing appeal could be explained in terms of the following "defensive avoidance" hypothesis:

> When fear is strongly aroused but is not fully relieved by the reassurances contained in a persuasive communication, the audience will become motivated to ignore, minimize, or deny the importance of the threat.

. . . .

2. SUBSEQUENT EXPERIMENTS BEARING ON THE DEFENSIVE-AVOIDANCE HYPOTHESIS

Several subsequent experiments appear to support the defensive-avoidance hypothesis and indicate that the mobilization of resistances, which accompanies increased emotional arousal, can lead to diminishing returns in acceptance of the communicator's recommendations. An extensive experiment was carried out by Haefner (1956), using communications with varying intensities of guilt-arousing appeals as well as fear-arousing appeals to promote favorable attitudes among American college students concerning an international agreement to ban H-bomb tests. One guilt-arousing version, for example, emphasized the enormous number of people killed in the United States' A-bomb attacks on Hiroshima and Nagasaki, and the suffering unexpectedly inflicted upon Japanese fishermen exposed to radioactive fallout from the H-bomb tests in the Pacific. Haefner's results concerning the effects of the fear-arousing appeals were ambiguous (see the critique in Leventhal and Niles, 1965, p. 231), but his results were clear-cut in indicating that the high-guilt version produced more resistance and less attitude change than the low-guilt version.

The main propositions under discussion (as stated in Section II, F) pertain to the effects of arousing reflective guilt and shame, as well as fear; consequently, Haefner's findings on guilt arousal can be regarded as relevant supporting evidence. Additional supporting data that directly bear out the predicted nonmonotonic relation were obtained by Zemach (1966). Her study was essentially a field experiment, carried out under the auspices of a civil rights organization that was trying to recruit Yale students as volunteers. The research purpose was to examine the relation between three intensities of guilt-arousing themes in the organization's persuasive pamphlets and the degree of acceptance of the recommendations for action. In response to a strong guilt-arousing version of the communication, relatively few college students volunteered to participate in the civil rights activities and relatively few expressed favorable attitudes toward the movement. A version that used a medium level of guilt-arousing material and did not personalize the blame was found to be more effective in inducing students to sign up for civil rights activities and in modifying general attitudes than either the high-guilt version or the low-guilt version.

The prediction that strong fear appeals will evoke more resistance than milder appeals is suggested by three additional experiments that used public health communications. Nunnally and Bobren (1959) investigated public willingness to expose themselves to communications concerning the treatment of mental illness. In a survey of almost 300 residents representing varied strata of an urban community, these investigators found that when the subjects were given pamphlets containing a strong fear appeal, they reported less interest in reading about the problem than when given pamphlets containing a milder appeal.

Robbins (1962) used a health education broadcast dealing with the threat of cancer and found that exposing the audience to fear-arousing material without any preliminary build-up evoked more feelings of irritation and aggression toward the communication than milder versions. No significant differences were found, however, in the subjects' answers to a question that asked if they would like to continue listening to the broadcast.

Using a public health pamphlet on the link between smoking and lung cancer, Janis and Terwilliger (1962) carried out an experiment with adult smokers and nonsmokers to test the defensive-avoidance hypothesis. They sought to obtain measures of resistance to fear-arousing material during exposure to a pamphlet containing authentic quotations from medical authorities. Each subject was given a private interview during which he was asked to express his thoughts and feelings after reading each paragraph. In order to eliminate cues that might give a distorted picture of the subject's reactions, a special device (auditory feedback suppressor) was used which enabled the subject to give his spontaneous associations aloud without hearing the sound of his own voice. The verbalizations of an experimental group exposed to a strong-threat version that played up the painful body damage and fatalities produced by lung cancer were compared with those of an equated group exposed to a milder version that merely referred to lung cancer without elaborating on the threatening consequences of the disease. The subjects in the strong-fear condition reacted differently from the subjects in the mild-fear condition in the following three ways: (1) They were somewhat less likely to express antismoking attitudes after the communication was over ($p < .10$); (2) They expressed much more emotional tension and concern about the possibility of being stricken by the disease while they were reading the communication and afterwards ($p < .05$); (3) They showed more manifestations of resistance to the main message of the communication while they were being exposed to it, making significantly more rejection statements ($p < .02$), as well as fewer favorable comments about the style and objectivity of the communication ($p < .06$) and fewer paraphrasing responses of the type that indicate implicit acceptance of what is being said ($p < .05$).

The Janis and Terwilliger experiment supplements the earlier experiments by providing more direct evidence of the interfering responses mobilized during the period when the subject is exposed to the communication. The findings indicate that the recipients of a warning communication tend to become more strongly motivated to develop psychological resistances to the communicator's arguments and recommendations if fear-arousing information is added that elaborates on the dire consequences in store for people who fail to accept the recommended precautionary measures.

3. EVIDENCE OF FACILITATING EFFECTS

Next we turn to the findings from a series of experiments that point to the facilitating effects of emotional arousal. Most of the results fit in nicely with the nonmonotonic model, but a few do not.

In two replicating experiments, Berkowitz and Cottingham (1960) presented college students with illustrated talks urging the use of automobile safety belts and compared the effectiveness of a version that played up the risk of serious injury in an automobile accident with an equivalent one containing the same arguments with no threat material at all. The strong-threat version produced more reported emotional tension than the milder version but there were no significant differences in over-all attitude change. A breakdown of the audience into two "relevance" categories, however, showed that the strong-threat version produced more attitude change than the milder version among those students who infrequently rode in cars, for whom the warning communication was of relatively low relevance.

The authors conclude that one of the determinants of the effectiveness of a persuasive communication is its interest value, which can be augmented when a strong threat is presented in a provocative way. This conclusion implies that whenever a low threat version is regarded by members of the audience as boring, uninteresting, or of low relevance to them, the inclusion of a strong fear-arousing appeal can have a facilitating effect on attitude change; under these circumstances, the negative effects of defensive avoidance, if any, may be offset by an increase in interest value. Those for whom the threat was clearly relevant from the outset, however, would be less likely to benefit from the enhanced interest-value evoked by a fear appeal and more likely to become defensively resistant.

From the standpoint of the predicted nonmonotonic relation, the findings from the Berkowitz and Cottingham experiments appear to support the assumption that at the low end of the fear arousal continuum, increased stimulation of fear will facilitate acceptance of the recommendations. The percentage asserting that they felt uneasy when exposed to the fear-arousing communication was comparatively low (31% of an experimental group exposed to the strong-threat version and 5% of an equated group exposed to the no-threat version, which contrasts markedly with the corresponding percentages in the Janis and Feshbach experiment of 74% for the strong-fear-appeal group, 60% for the moderate-appeal group, and 48% for the minimal-appeal group). Although none of the percentages can be taken at face value, these comparative findings suggest that the so-called strong-threat condition in the Berkowitz and Cottingham experiments may have aroused only a very low degree of fear, comparable to that aroused by the minimal threat appeal in the Janis and Feshbach experiment. This inference appears particularly likely for the subjects for whom the threat was of low relevance; if so, the findings would support the conclusion that when information about a potential threat arouses a slight or moderate degree of fear, in contrast to the near-zero level of fear evoked by a no-threat version, it will tend to facilitate acceptance of the communicator's recommendation. In terms of the curvilinear functions shown in Fig. 4, this interpretation would assume that we are dealing with two points near the left end of the arousal continuum, with the higher level of fear still well within the moderate range. Thus the warning communication does not appear to have aroused fear to the level where we might expect a predominance of psychological resistances that interfere with acceptance.

In any case, it should be noted that Berkowitz and Cottingham's data actually yield a good approximation to an inverted U-shaped curve, as shown in Fig. 6, if we treat the low versus high relevant subgroups as equivalent to

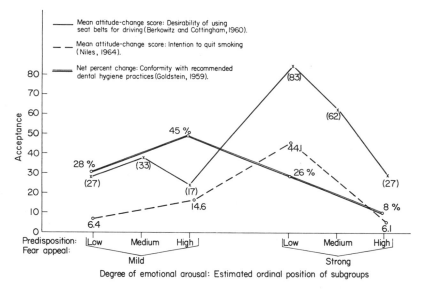

FIGURE 6. *Observations from three attitude-change experiments on acceptance of recommendations as a joint function of predisposition and strength of fear appeal.*

the low versus high predispositional groups in the Janis and Feshbach (1954) experiment. It can be seen that the peak of the acceptance curve occurs for a subgroup that is at an intermediate level of arousal (low-relevance subjects exposed to a strong-fear version); thereafter, the curve goes down sharply, since the subgroup with the highest level of arousal (high-relevance subjects exposed to the strong-fear version) shows markedly less attitude change. The data from the other two experiments included in Fig. 6, which will be discussed shortly, also show a nonmonotonic relation but the peak does not always occur at the same ordinal position on the arousal axis.

Several recent studies by Leventhal and his co-workers bear out the Berkowitz and Cottingham findings on the facilitating effects of fear arousal at the low end of the curve and indicate that this outcome can sometimes occur even among subjects for whom the threat is highly relevant. Using the same issue of automotive safety, Leventhal and Niles (1965) found that automobile drivers exposed to the greatest amount of threat material in technicolor movies focusing on the gory details of automobile accidents showed the highest arousal of fear and guilt and also the greatest amount of immediate acceptance of certain safety rules, such as "Never drive after drinking." These effects, however, tended to be dissipated by one week later.

Essentially the same facilitating type of outcome is reported by Leventhal and Singer (1966) and Singer (1965) from two experiments on the effectiveness of dental hygiene communications. But here again, just as in the Berkowitz and Cottingham (1960) experiment, there are indications suggesting that despite the efforts of the experimenters to use vivid threat material and gory film sequences to arouse strong fear, their findings nevertheless may pertain only to the low end of the arousal continuum. In other words, the findings can be plausibly interpreted as showing a slight increase in acceptance as we move from near-zero arousal to a mild degree of arousal that evokes a slight increase in vigilance and reassurance needs. In the Leventhal and Singer experiment, which was conducted with adults at a New York State Fair, the group exposed to the so-called high-fear-arousing film reported somewhat more fear than the group exposed to the so-called low-fear-arousing film, but contrary to the experimenters expectations, the low-fear group did not differ on any of the indicators of emotional arousal or concern about tooth decay and gum disease from a control group that had been exposed only to the recommendations with no references at all to threatening consequences. These findings imply that the so-called low-fear communication failed to arouse fear at all, while the so-called high-fear communication may have aroused a relatively slight degree of fear (perhaps comparable to the minimal appeal in the Janis and Feshbach experiment), which would be expected to have a predominantly facilitating effect on acceptance.

Two other experiments using dental hygiene lectures with young adults also ran into difficulties in eliciting expected differences in emotional arousal. One experiment (Moltz and Thistlethwaite, 1955) reported no significant difference in attitude changes; the other (Goldstein, 1959) found that the high fear-arousing communication was less effective than the milder versions, as in the Janis and Feshbach experiment. But in both experiments, the indicators of emotional arousal showed no significant differences between the so-called high- and low-fear conditions and hence the data are of dubious relevance for ascertaining the effects of strong versus mild intensities of fear arousal.

It should be noted, however, that a nonmonotonic relation clearly emerged when Goldstein compared high versus low predisposed subjects sorted on Mainord's (1956) personality measure of chronic avoidance tendencies. (Goldstein calls the high scorers "avoiders" and the low scorers "copers.") The curve obtained from Goldstein's data, which is shown in Fig. 6, is almost the same as the curve obtained for the Janis and Feshbach (1954) data in Fig. 5. In the case of Goldstein's data, however, the degree of arousal is based on estimated ordinal position of the four subgroups on the arousal continuum and there is no evidence that the "avoiders" were more highly predisposed to become emotionally aroused by threat material on tooth decay and gum disease than the "copers."

Evidence that strong fear arousal might under certain conditions be more effective than mild arousal in modifying attitudes, despite whatever resistances may be evoked, is provided by Niles' (1964) experiment, which compared different versions of a film on smoking and lung cancer. The strong-fear-arousing version, which included a technicolor sequence showing the surgical removal of a young man's cancerous lung, with all the gory details, proved to be more successful in inducing college students to resolve to give up smoking than a milder threat version that included the same case study of a lung cancer patient, leaving out the surgical sequence. But this outcome held only for a particular subgroup who initially reported feeling low vulnerability to the threat and not for the subgroup located at the highest level on the arousal continuum. Niles used two predispositional measures that proved to be significantly correlated. One was the neurotic anxiety scale developed by Janis and Feshbach (1954) for their study of high school students. For the college students in Niles' experiments, this measure did not yield statistically significant results. The second personality scale, however, which was developed by Niles for the purpose of assessing college students' feelings of vulnerability to illness, provided a significant interaction with degree of acceptance, like the interaction effect found by Janis and Feshbach (1954).

Using Niles' data from the feelings of vulnerability scale, we again obtain an inverse U-shaped function, as shown in Fig. 6. Verbal acceptance of the antismoking recommendations presented in both versions of the film shows a gradual but pronounced rise as we move from low to intermediate levels of arousal, followed by a sharp drop for the subgroup highest on the arousal continuum. This evidence, however, is not entirely compelling because the assumed ordinal position of the four subgroups on the fear continuum was only partially borne out by Niles' analysis of variance of arousal scores based on three questionnaire items dealing with feelings of fear; the only significant finding concerning reported feelings of fear was a main effect for the mild versus strong fear appeals. In view of this finding, the corresponding attitude change results showing a main effect for the mild versus strong fear appeal would appear to be a more dependable result than those showing an interaction effect between this stimulus variable and the predispositional variable. If we consider only the main effects, Niles' results imply that a very high level of arousal can have a markedly facilitating effect on attitude change.

Leventhal (1965) has culled a few findings from other experiments that he believes bear out the same tendency (e.g., Leventhal and Niles, 1964; Leventhal and Watts, 1966), but he acknowledges that this additional evidence comes from ambiguous studies, with both positive and negative effects showing up on different indicators of acceptance. The most impressive evidence he cites comes from a study by Leventhal *et al.* (1965) that shows the facilitating effects of a relatively low degree of fear arousal. In this experiment, a behavioral measure was obtained from the records of a university health center to ascertain the effectiveness of different versions of a warning communication that recommended antitetanus shots. A mild and strong fear-appeal version were found to be about equally effective in inducing students to obtain the shots, as compared with a control communication that gave the same recommendations without any fear-arousing material. Additional results also showed that the fear appeals were more effective when accompanied by specific information as to where, when, and how to get the shots. Those given a great deal of such information, as compared to those given relatively little, were more likely to obtain inoculations, irrespective of whether they had received the strong or mild fear-arousing version. But none of the subjects exposed to the specific information and the recommendation without the fear-arousing material went to the health center for the shots. In this instance, some minimum degree of fear-arousal apparently was necessary, along with the specific instructions, in order to instigate protective action in line with the communicator's recommendation. These findings provide additional empirical support for the first of the three main propositions derived from the analysis of reflective fear.

[Two final sections of this chapter are omitted: IV. Theoretical Model for Analyzing Determinants of the Optimal Level of Arousal and V. Discussion of the Model. The chapter concludes with a discussion of recent experiments on emotional role playing.]

Conclusion

Although a number of new substantive hypotheses have been suggested, it seems to me that the most important heuristic value of the theoretical model discussed in this paper is in the sphere of posing new types of questions for systematic research on emotional arousal and attitude change. Of particular importance for those of us who have become increasingly pessimistic about making progress in this research area, as we continue to encounter gross inconsistencies between the outcome of the latest experiment and the one before that, is the reformulation of the central problem. Instead of continuing to ask unproductive questions about how acceptance varies as a function of different intensities of emotional arousal, we can turn to a set of theoretically oriented questions that may be much more productive: What are the determinants of the optimal level of arousal?

ACKNOWLEDGMENTS

The author thanks Professors William McGill and William J. McGuire for their valuable criticisms of the first draft of this chapter, and Professor Leonard Berkowitz for his excellent criticisms and editorial recommendations.

REFERENCES

BEIER, E. G. (1951). The effect of induced anxiety on flexibility of intellectual functioning. *Psychol. Monogr.* 65, No. 9.

BERKOWITZ, L., and COTTINGHAM, D. R. (1960). The interest value and relevance of fear arousing communications. *J. abnorm. soc. Psychol.* 60, 37–43.

BERKUN, M., BIALEK, H., KERN, R., and YAGI, K. (1962). Experimental studies of psychological stress in man. *Psychol. Monogr.* 76, 1–39.

BROWN, J. S. (1961). *The motivation of behavior.* New York: McGraw-Hill.

DEWOLFE, A., and GOVERNALE, CATHERINE. (1964). Fear and attitude change. *J. abnorm. soc. Psychol.* 69, 119–123.

DOLLARD, J., and MILLER, N. (1950). *Personality and psychotherapy.* New York: McGraw-Hill.

DUFFY, ELIZABETH. (1962). *Activation and behavior.* New York: Wiley.

EASTERBOOK, J. A. (1959). The effect of emotion on cue utilization and the organization of behavior. *Psychol. Rev.* 66, 183–201.

FREUD, S. (1936). *The problem of anxiety.* (Translated by H. A. Bunker.) New York: Norton.

GOLDSTEIN, M. (1959). Relationship between coping and avoiding behavior and response to fear-arousing propaganda. *J. abnorm. soc. Psychol.* 58, 247–252.

HAEFNER, D. (1956). Some effects of guilt-arousing and fear-arousing persuasive communications on opinion change. Unpublished tech. rep. Aug. 15, 1956, Office of Naval Res., Contract No. N6 ONR 241. (Mimeo. abridgement of unpublished doctoral dissertation, Univ. of Rochester.)

HALL, J. F. (1961). *Psychology of motivation.* Philadelphia: Lippincott.

HEBB, D. O. (1955). Drives and the C. N. S. (conceptual nervous system) *Psychol. Rev.* 62, 243–254.

HOVLAND, C. I., JANIS, I. L., and KELLEY, H. H. (1953). *Communication and persuasion.* New Haven, Connecticut: Yale Univ. Press.

INSKO, C. A., ARKOFF, A., and INSKO, V. M. (1965). Effects of high and low fear-arousing communication upon opinions toward smoking. *J. exp. soc. Psychol.* 1, 256–266.

JANIS, I. L. (1958). *Psychological stress.* New York: Wiley.

———. (1962). Psychological effects of warnings. In C. W. Baker and D. W. Chapman (Eds.), *Man and society in disaster.* New York: Basic Books.

————. (1968). *The contours of fear: Psychological studies of war, disaster, illness, and experimental stress.* New York: Wiley.

JANIS, I. L., and FESHBACH, S. (1953). Effects of fear-arousing communications. *J. abnorm. soc. Psychol.* 48, 78–92.

————. (1954). Personality differences associated with responsiveness to fear-arousing communications. *J. Pers.* 23, 154–166.

JANIS, I. L., and LEVENTHAL, H. (1965). Psychological aspects of physical illness and hospital care. In B. Wollman (Ed.), *Handbook of clinical psychology.* New York: McGraw-Hill.

————. (1967). Human reactions to stress. In E. Borgatta and W. Lambert (Eds.), *Handbook of personality theory and research.* Chicago: Rand McNally.

JANIS, I. L., and MANN, L. (1965). Effectiveness of emotional role-playing in modifying smoking habits and attitudes. *J. exp. Res. Pers.* 1, 84–90.

JANIS, I. L., and MILHOLLAND, W. (1954). The influence of threat appeals on selective learning of the content of a persuasive communication. *J. Psychol.* 37, 75–80.

JANIS, I. L., and TERWILLIGER, R. (1962). An experimental study of psychological resistances to fear-arousing communications. *J. abnorm. soc. Psychol.* 65, 403–410.

KAUSLER, D., and TRAPP, E. (1960). Motivation and cue utilization in intentional and incidental learning. *Psychol. Rev.* 67, 373–379.

KORCHIN, S. (1965). Some psychological determinants of stress behavior. In Klausner, S. (Ed.) *The Quest for Self-Control.* New York: The Free Press, pp. 247–266.

LAZARUS, R. S. (1966). *Psychological stress and the coping process.* New York: McGraw-Hill.

LEVENTHAL, H. (1965). Fear communications in the acceptance of preventive health practices. *Bull. N. Y. Acad. Med.* 41, 1144–1168.

LEVENTHAL, H., and NILES, PATRICIA. (1964). A field experiment on fear arousal with data on the validity of questionnaire measures. *J. Pers.* 32, 459–479.

————. (1965). Persistence of influence for varying durations of exposure to threat stimuli. *Psychol. Rep.* 16, 223–233.

LEVENTHAL, H., and SINGER, R. P. (1966). Affect arousal and positioning of recommendations in persuasive communications. *J. Pers. soc. Psychol.* 4, 137–146.

LEVENTHAL, H., and WATTS, JEAN C. (1966). Sources of resistance to fear-arousing communications on smoking and lung cancer. *J. Pers.* 34, 155–175.

LEVENTHAL, H., SINGER, R. P., and JONES, SUSAN. (1965). The effects of fear and specificity of recommendation upon attitudes and behavior. *J. Pers. soc. Psychol.* 2, 20–29.

LEY, P. (1966). What the patient doesn't remember. *Med. Opin. Rev.* 1, 69–73.

LUCHINS, A. S., and LUCHINS, E. H. (1959). *Rigidity of behavior: A variational approach to the effect of Einstellung.* Eugene, Oregon: Univ. of Oregon Books.

McGUIRE, W. J. (1967). Personality and susceptibility to social influence. In E. Borgatta and W. Lambert (Eds.), *Handbook of personality theory and research.* Chicago: Rand McNally.

MAINORD, W. (1956). Experimental repression related to coping and avoidance behavior. Unpublished doctoral dissertation, Univ. of Washington.

MALMO, R. B. (1958). Measurement of drive: an unresolved problem in psychology. In M. Jones (Ed.), *Nebraska symposium on motivation, 1958.* Lincoln, Nebraska: Univ. of Nebraska Press.

MANN, L. (1968). The effects of emotional role playing on smoking attitudes and behavior. *J. exp. soc. Psychol.*

MANN, L., and JANIS, I. L. (1967). A follow-up study on the long-term effects of emotional role playing. Mimeo ms. (To be published.)

MOLTZ, H., and THISTLETHWAITE, D. L. (1955). Attitude modification and anxiety reduction. *J. abnorm. soc. Psychol.* 50, 231–237.

MOWRER, O. H. (1950). *Learning theory and personality dynamics.* New York: Ronald Press.

NILES (KAFES), PATRICIA. (1964). The relationship of susceptibility and anxiety to acceptance of fear-arousing communications. Unpublished doctoral dissertation. Yale Univ.

NOWLIS, G., and JANIS, I. L. (1967). Factors influencing the effectiveness of emotional role playing in modifying attitudes and actions. Mimeo ms. (To be published.)

NUNNALLY, J. D., and BOBREN, H. M. (1959). Variables governing the willingness to receive communications on mental health. *J. Pers.* 27, 38–46.

OSLER, S. F. (1954). Intellectual performance as a function of two types of psychological stress. *J. Exp. Psychol.* 47, 115–121.

ROBBINS, L. R. (1962). Self-reports of reactions to fear-arousing information. *Psychol. Rep.* 11, 761–764.

ROSENBLATT, P. C. (1962). Persuasive value of threat and amount of attitude change advocated. Unpublished doctoral dissertation, Northwestern Univ.

SCHACHTER, S. (1964). The interaction of cognitive and physiological determinants of emotional state. *Advance. exp. soc. Psychol.* 1, 49–80.

SCHLOSBERG, H. (1954). Three dimensions of emotion. *Psychol. Rev.* 61, 81–88.

SINGER, R. P. (1965). The effects of fear-arousing communications on attitude change and behavior. Unpublished doctoral dissertation, Univ. of Connecticut.

SKINNER, B. F. (1938). *The behavior of organisms.* New York: Appleton-Century-Crofts.

SULLIVAN, H. S. (1953). *The interpersonal theory of psychiatry.* New York: Norton.

ZEMACH, MINA. (1966). The effects of guilt-arousing communications on acceptance of recommendations. Unpublished doctoral dissertation, Yale Univ.

Howard Leventhal / Robert Singer / Susan Jones*

EFFECTS OF FEAR AND SPECIFICITY OF RECOMMENDATION UPON ATTITUDES AND BEHAVIOR[1]

The study dealt with the effects of (a) level of fear and (b) specific plans for action vs. general recommendations on attitudes toward tetanus inoculations and actually getting tetanus shots. The arousal of fear resulted in more favorable attitudes toward inoculation and the expression of stronger intentions to get shots. However, actually getting shots occurred significantly more often for Ss receiving a specific plan for action. Although action was unaffected by fear level some level of arousal was necessary for action to occur. A specific plan was not sufficient for action to appear. Although the 2 dependent measures were affected by different independent variables, those people getting shots were also more favorable toward doing so. The results are compared with other studies on fear arousal and actions, and speculations were presented on the role of specific action plans in the translation of attitudes into actions.

Information alone seldom provides sufficient impetus to change attitudes or actions toward a given object (Cohen, 1957; Klapper, 1960; Rosenberg, 1956). The information must not only instruct the audience but must create

[1] This study was conducted under United States Public Health Service Grant CH00077-02. We would like to thank John S. Hathaway and James S. Davie of the Department of University Health for the cooperation and help they gave to this study.

*Yale University.

Reprinted from the *Journal of Personality and Social Psychology*, 2 (1965), 20–29, with permission of the authors and the American Psychological Association.

motivating forces which induce attitude and behavioral change. Janis and Feshbach (1953, 1954) were among the first to explore the effects of information which arouses fear or avoidant motivation on the changing of attitudes. Their results indicated that high fear arousal produced less adherence to recommendations, presumably because high fear produced responses of defensive avoidance. Support for the finding of less persuasion with high- than with low-fear communications has also been presented by Goldstein (1959) and by Janis and Terwilliger (1962). However, in other recent studies evidence has accumulated which suggests the need to reevaluate the relationship between fear arousal and persuasion.

First, Berkowitz and Cottingham (1960) have demonstrated that, at relatively low levels, increments in fear may produce increased attitude change especially for subjects for whom the communication was less relevant. Leventhal and Niles (1964), and Niles (1964) have also found that fear arousal increases persuasion. They obtained a positive correlation between reported fear and intentions to act (Leventhal & Niles, 1964), and increases in intentions with increasingly powerful communications (Niles, 1964). These effects were found using stimuli considerably more vivid and frightening than those used in any of the earlier investigations. Thus, these experiments suggest that fear functions as a drive which promotes the acceptance of recommended actions, and, regardless of the absolute level of fear arousal used in any study, the communication which arouses more fear will be more persuasive.

There are a number of incidental factors that may account for the different results in these studies: for example, Janis and Feshbach's topic was dental health while lung cancer was the topic for Leventhal and Niles (1964) and Niles (1964); Janis and Feshbach (1953) used high-school students, Leventhal and Niles used people attending the New York City health exposition, and Niles used college students. However, while these factors could be responsible for the different outcomes, one variable which seems of particular importance is the availability of the recommended action. In their study, Janis and Feshbach (1953) suggested that fear arousal could lead to increased persuasion if the action was immediately available. In the Leventhal and Niles study, action was immediately available to all groups of subjects; that is, they could get an X-ray, and, while stopping smoking may require concerted effort over a long period of time, it can be initiated immediately. In the Niles experiment the arousal of fear increased desire to take action principally for subjects who do *not* see themselves as vulnerable to disease. Subjects who feel vulnerable to disease showed relatively small increases in willingness to take preventive action when made fearful. Their greater resistance to persuasion seemed to be related to their tendency to judge the recommendations to prevent lung cancer as ineffective. In addition, subjects high in vulnerability scored low on a scale of self-esteem that relates to seeing oneself as able to cope with the environment (Dabbs, 1962; Leventhal &

Perloe, 1962). The findings suggest that when environmental conditions or the subject's dispositional characteristics make action seem highly possible and effective, fear will promote action and attitude change.

The present study was designed to provide additional data on this question. Fear-arousing and non-fear-arousing communications were used recommending a clear action (taking a tetanus shot) which is for all intents and purposes 100% effective. Thus, in line with our earlier findings (Leventhal & Niles, 1964; Niles, 1964), it was predicted that more attitude change and more action would be produced by the high-fear conditions. Second, an attempt was made to experimentally manipulate the perceived availability of the recommended action by giving some subjects a *specific plan* to guide their action. It was hypothesized that adherence to the recommended act would be greater among subjects possessing a specific plan. Finally, an interaction was expected between fear and specificity: highly motivated subjects, that is, those exposed to the fear-arousing materials, were expected to show the greatest attitude and behavioral compliance when a clear plan for action was given to them.

Another question which was raised with regard to these divergent findings was the kind of emotion evoked by the stimulus. Careful attention has been given to discriminating levels of fear arousal, and to the possibility that fear-arousing communications arouse aggression as well as anxiety (Janis & Feshbach, 1953; Robbins, 1962). Other studies in the current program (Leventhal, Jacobs, & Trembly, 1963 unpublished[2]) suggest that fear may be experienced with many other emotions. Therefore, several items were used to assess emotional arousal with the hope that these would provide added information on the nature of the fear associated with persuasion.

METHOD

Design and Subjects

The experimental design incorporated two levels of fear and two levels of information on the availability of the recommended action. Additional control groups were run to clarify questions unanswered by the factorial design. These are described in the Results section. Booklets were used to present the fear-arousing stimuli and to deliver the recommendation for inoculation. A questionnaire was completed after reading the booklet.

All subjects were seniors at Yale University and were selected by taking every other name from the class list. Initial contacts were by mail, and specific appointments for the experimental session were made by phone. No inducements were offered for participating in the study and subjects only knew that they were to evaluate a public

[2] Unpublished study entitled "Negative Emotions and Persuasion."

health pamphlet. All contacts with the subjects were made by using the name of the John Slade Ely Center and the University Department of Health.

Subjects were run individually and in a building 2.5 blocks away from the University Health Service. Conducting the study in the University Health Building would have made it far too simple for subjects to get shots. When a student entered the experiment, he was given a pamphlet and told: "Would you please read this pamphlet carefully. When you are finished, please bring it back to me and I will give you a questionnaire to fill out about it." After reading the pamphlet and filling out the questionnaire the students departed. There was minimal conversation with the experimenters.

Experimental Manipulations

The booklets were composed of two sections: a "fear section," dealing with the causes of tetanus and including a case history of a tetanus patient; and a "recommendation section," dealing with the importance of shots in preventing the disease. There were two forms of each section: high fear and low fear, specific recommendation and nonspecific recommendation, making four pamphlets.

Fear manipulation. The same facts about the disease were present in both fear levels. Three devices were used to manipulate fear: coupling frightening or nonfrightening facts with basic information on tetanus; emotion-provoking or emotion-nonprovoking adjectives to describe the causes of tetanus, the tetanus case, and the treatment of tetanus; and including different kinds of photographs to illustrate the pamphlet. For example, in the high-fear booklet the incidence was described as being as high as that for polio, and the bacteria were described as "under your finger-nails, in your mouth" etc., and as literally surrounding the reader. The low treatment simply stated these facts in a nondramatic way. The aim of the high-fear booklet was to create a strong feeling of personal vulnerability.

A case history, constructed from reports in medical journals, was presented to make vivid the severity of the disease. In the high-fear condition, the wording was constructed to create a clear image of the patient's symptoms (convulsions, his back arched upwards, his head whipped back, mouth slammed shut, etc.). Photographs were also included which showed a child in a tetanic convulsion and bedridden patients. Three of the photographs were in color. One illustrated a gaping tracheotomy wound, the others depicted patients with urinary catheters, tracheotomy drainage, and nasal tubes. The treatments illustrated are actually used in the therapy of severe cases of tetanus. They proved to be quite startling to the subjects.

In the low-fear condition, colored photographs were omitted as were the pictures of the hospital patients and equipment. Two photographic copies of drawings of the facial expressions found in tetanus were included. The case history was described in unemotional terms and, whereas the patient died in the high-fear booklet, he survived in the low-fear case. Otherwise, the booklets were factually identical and were approximately of equal length (7 mimeographed pages).

Plan for action. After the presentation of the case history, all pamphlets contained identical paragraphs on the importance of controlling tetanus by inoculation. This point was illustrated by statistics which clearly demonstrated that shots are the only powerful and fully adequate protection against the disease. In addition, it was stated that the University was making shots available free of charge to all interested students.

For the high availability treatment additional material was included urging the students to take a shot and providing a detailed set of suggestions as to how he could do this within the context of his daily activities. The points made can be paraphrased as follows: The University Health Service expressed the hope that all students would take the necessary action to protect themselves, the location of the University Health Service was described and the times that shots were available were listed, precisely where to go and what to do to get a shot was indicated, a map was presented of the campus with the University Health Building clearly circled, and a request was made that each student review his weekly schedule to locate a time when he would pass by the University Health so that he could stop in to be inoculated. The specific recommendation, then, is essentially a detailed plan to make the subjects rehearse the various steps needed to take the suggested action. Thus, the low availability groups are told of the effectiveness of shots and that shots are available. The high availability groups have this information plus additional material helping them to plan and to review the specific steps needed to take shots. It should be made clear, however, that since the subjects were seniors, they *all* knew the location of student health, and it is extremely likely that they had all visited the building at some time in the past. The plan, therefore, would simply make salient that which is *already* known rather than providing new information.

Response Measures

Two types of responses were observed for all subjects participating in this experiment. Immediately after the communication all subjects completed a questionnaire on which they reported their attitudes, feelings, and reactions to the experimental setting. In addition, a record was obtained of all subjects taking a tetanus inoculation.

Questionnaire measures. The questionnaire included items on: prior inoculation against tetanus; intentions to be inoculated; attitude regarding the importance of inoculation; judgments of the likelihood of contracting tetanus and its severity *if* contracted; emotions experienced while reading the communications; and reactions to, and interest in, the communications. The items used will be reported in the Results section.

Behavioral measures. The records of all participants were checked by student health authorities and a count was made of the subjects in each condition who were inoculated. The dates for inoculation were also obtained. Those students who were inoculated at the close of the semester, more than 1 month *after* the study termination, were not included in the inoculation count. It is common practice for students taking trips abroad to receive inoculations at the end of the semester.

The questionnaire also included a variety of items on many diseases besides tetanus. The items were included principally to suggest to the subject that the investigation was on *health*, rather than an attempt to coerce him into taking an inoculation. Thus, items asked about prior shots for polio, typhoid, and flu, and feelings of susceptibility to and the severity of six other diseases.

RESULTS

Fear Arousal

As can be seen from Table 1, the fear manipulation was highly successful. Subjects report feeling greater fright, tension, nervousness, anxiety, discomfort, anger, and nausea in the high- than in the low-fear treatment.[3] All differences were significant at $p < .005$. Incidental observations indicated that the high-fear booklets were indeed distressing. All subjects were extremely intent and focused on the materials; some appeared pale, others shaken and many made other sounds and gestures indicating distress. These treatment effects were significant whether or not subjects had been inoculated against the disease. (Means are also presented for two control groups. One was not exposed to any communication and simply filled out the "Health Practices Questionnaire." The other received only the specific recommendation material prior to completing the questionnaire.)[4]

Attitudes. A general question ("How important do you think it is to get a tetanus shot?"—13-point scale) was used to assess the degree of importance which subjects attached to tetanus shots. Another question was used to assess his intentions to avail himself of inoculation ("Do you intend to get a tetanus shot?"—13-point scale). As can be seen in Table 2, regardless of prior inoculation, subjects in the high-fear conditions feel that shots are more important than do subjects in the low-fear conditions ($F = 8.45$, $df = 1/140$, $p < .01$).

For the intention question, there were two important trends. First, subjects who had had a shot within the last 2 years scored lower than those who had not had a shot ($F = 16.8$, $df = 1/136$, $p < .005$). In addition, there was a trend for subjects in the high-fear treatment, regardless of inoculation status, to express stronger intentions to get shots than did subjects in the low-fear condition ($F = 3.55$, $df = 1/136$, $p < .08$). Since the distributions were skewed downwards and the means in the high-fear cells were over 11, using a 13-point scale, it appeared that a ceiling effect was operating to minimize the differences. Therefore, a test of the effect of fear on intentions was performed by treating all scores of 13 as very strong intentions and scores of 12

---

[3] The self-reports of emotion were obtained by asking "While you were reading the pamphlet did you find that you had any of the following feelings?" A series of adjectives with 21-point scales followed this statement.

[4] The control subjects completed essentially the same questionnaire as the experimental subjects. However, all references to the communication were omitted for the questionnaire-only control. The relatively high mean for anger in the questionnaire-only groups reflects the irritation felt by some of these subjects upon having to answer questions (on emotion) which did not seem to have a clear referent. On the other hand, a few of the recommendation-only subjects felt upset by the suggestion to get shots. The detailed suggestion to act seemed unusual enough to convince a few that a threat must be imminent.

TABLE 1

Mean Reported Emotions by Treatment and
Prior Inoculation of Subject

Emotion[a]	High fear		Low fear		Significance data	
	No prior shot	Shot	No prior shot	Shot	F (high-low)	df
Fear	9.25	8.47	4.51	3.21	43.19*	1/139
Base line (n = 11)	2.61					
Recommendations only (n = 29)	3.00					
Tension	9.28	9.07	4.43	3.58	35.28*	1/139
Base line	1.35					
Recommendations only	2.83					
Nervousness	7.85	7.79	3.93	2.70	36.40*	1/139
Base line	1.53					
Recommendations only	3.10					
Anxiety	9.51	9.06	5.43	3.26	32.30*	1/139
Base line	2.97					
Recommendations only	4.03					
Discomfort	11.43	10.40	4.47	3.36	63.84*	1/139
Base line	3.87					
Recommendations only	3.52					
Anger	4.56	3.40	2.19	1.59	15.54*	1/140
Base line	5.94					
Recommendations only	3.41					
Nausea[b]	7.34	5.22	2.61	2.19	27.81*	1/140
Base line	3.87					
Recommendations only	1.59					
N[c]	30	44	29	44		

Note.—The means are *averages* of the means for specific-nonspecific for each fear level. This was done for ease in presentation. The analyses were conducted on the complete table using Walker and Lev's (1953) technique for unequal *n*'s. There were *no* significant interactions.

[a] Twenty-one points on scale. Higher numbers on all scales indicate higher reported affect.

[b] Nausea was also effected by specificity. This will be reported in a later table.

[c] Ns are the number of cases for the averaged pair of means. The N in the second column was actually higher than 44 for two figures.

*p = .005.

and below as weak intentions. Using only those subjects who *had not* had a shot within the last 2 years (relevant subjects), a significantly greater number of subjects expressed a strong intention to be inoculated in the high-fear treatment than in the low ($\chi^2 = 6.22$, $df = 1$, $p < .02$).

Action. During the 4—6 week period between the experimental sessions and the end of classes 9 of the 59 eligible subjects went for shots. Of the 9, 4 were in the high fear specific, 4 in the low fear specific, 1 in the low fear non-

TABLE 2

MEAN IMPORTANCE OF TETANUS SHOTS AND
INTENTIONS TO BE INOCULATED

	No prior shots		Prior shots		Control
	High fear	Low fear	High fear	Low fear	
Importance of shots (13-point scale)					
Specific	11.92	10.00	11.61	11.82	
N	13	16	23	22	
Nonspecific	11.29	10.54	11.93	10.32	
N	17	13	22	22	
Recommendations only					8.76
N					29
Base line					8.82
N					11
Intention to get shots (13-point scale)					
Specific	11.23	10.00	8.43	5.90	
N	13	15	23	22	
Nonspecific	11.29	9.69	7.52	7.55	
N	17	13	21	20	
Recommendations only					7.00
N					29
Base line					6.75
N					10
Strong intention (13)	18[a]	9			
Moderate intention (1–12)	12	20			

[a] $\chi^2 = 6.22$, $df = 1$, $p < .02$.

specific, and none in the high fear nonspecific. A comparison between the 27.6% of specific takers and the 3.3% of nonspecific takers is significant (CR = 2.65, $p < .01$). Subjects in the specific condition were more likely to get shots.[5] Thus, attitudes and actions appear to be affected by different factors. While a low fear nonspecific communication has little influence on either attitudes or actions, fear-arousing messages affect attitudes regardless of specificity of plan, and recommendations using specific plans affect actions regardless of the level of fear.[6]

[5] Seven additional eligible subjects took shots following the close of classes. These were distributed as follows: four specific (two high and two low) and three nonspecific (two high and one low). Adding in these cases gives 41% specific, 13% nonspecific taking shots (CR = 2.44, $p < .02$). Among the ineligible subjects two in the high fear nonspecific condition took shots. It appears that most of these subjects were receiving shots as part of a series in preparation for travel.

[6] One could argue that the specificity effect was obtained because subjects in the nonspecific condition missed the statement that shots could be obtained at University Health. However, when subjects were asked where they would get shots, 70% of those in the nonspecific treatment and 72% of those in the specific mentioned University Health.

Recommendations-only control. Because the specificity factor did not inter-act with arousal as predicted, it was unclear whether the arousal of fear was a necessary condition for action. The main effect suggests that specific infor-mation may be a sufficient condition for the occurrence of action. To test this possibility a control group was run of subjects exposed only to specific information. This group was run the following year and a time difference is involved which was absent in the other comparisons.

The procedures for contacting and dealing with subjects were identical to those used in the four experimental groups. Of the 30 eligible subjects in the group not one availed himself of the opportunity to obtain an inoculation. Thus, specific information alone does not seem to be sufficient to influence actions or attitudes (see Table 2).

Action base line. The date of tetanus inoculation for a sample of 60 students was also obtained to record the base rate of inoculation seeking during the experimental period. None of the students (eligibles or ineligibles) were inocu-lated during that period. Therefore, while the rate of shot taking was not high in the specific experimental treatments (27.6%), it is obviously greater than the base rate.[7]

Mediating Factors

Variables associated with attitude change. In addition to the fear measures, several other measures of reported feelings varied in the same manner as did attitudes toward tetanus inoculations. Subjects in the high-fear condition felt that tetanus was more serious than did subjects in the low-fear treatments ("How serious do you think it would be if you contracted tetanus?" $F = 22.94$, $df = 1/139$, $p < .005$). Subjects in the high-fear conditions also reported more concern about getting tetanus ("When you think about the possibility of getting tetanus, how concerned or worried do you feel about it?" Table 3, $F = 3.92$, $df = 1/140$, $p < .05$), more worry about the way they had treated cuts ("While you were reading the pamphlet, did you feel worried about the way you have treated abrasions, cuts, or bruises?" $F = 3.75$, $df = 1/136$, $p < .10$), and reported more irritation directed at the photographs than did subjects in the low-fear condition ("Did the illustrations irritate you or make you angry?" $F = 6.95$, $df = 1/136$, $p < .01$). High-fear subjects were also more certain than low-fear subjects that the pictures used enhanced the pamphlet ("Did the illustrations in the pamphlet enhance the message of the pamphlet?" $F = 11.62$, $df = 1/134$, $p < .001$). These effects were significant regardless of the subjects prior vaccination history. As with the prior measures of emo-

---

[7] Only one of the subjects included in the experimental groups had had a shot just prior to participating. He had received it as treatment for an injury. Thus, there is little reason to believe that students spontaneously take shots during the year to protect themselves against tetanus.

TABLE 3

MEAN OTHER DIFFERENCES BETWEEN HIGH AND LOW FEAR
CORRELATED WITH ATTITUDE CHANGE

	High fear		Low fear		F (high-low)	df
	No prior shot	Prior shot	No prior shot	Prior shot		
1. Seriousness of tetanus[a]	10.88[b]	10.68	8.16	8.02	22.94***	1/139
N	30	44	29	44		
Control ($N = 11$)	7.02					
Recommendations only						
($N = 30$)	8.90					
2. Concern over contracting						
tetanus	10.48	10.59	9.13	7.67	3.92*	1/140
N	30	45	29	44		
Control ($N = 11$)	5.58					
Recommendations only	7.53					
3. Worry over cuts and						
bruises	7.20	7.39	6.43	4.72	3.75	1/136
N	30	45	28	41		
Control ($N = 11$)	1.26					
Recommendations only	4.17					
4. Anger at illustrations	3.71	3.94	2.37	2.62	6.95**	1/136
N	30	45	28	41		
5. Pictures enhance pamphlet	7.06	7.13	5.69	5.55	11.62***	1/134
N	29	43	28	42		

[a] Item 1 used a 13-point scale, Items 2 and 3 used 21-point scales, and Items 4 and 5 used 9-point scales.

[b] Means reported are the average of the means for specific and nonspecific cells.

*$p = .05$.

**$p = .01$.

***$p = .005$.

tional arousal, being vaccinated is no protection against the distressing emotions which appear to be elicited by the pamphlet per se. It is also interesting to note that the arousal of aggression (anger and irritation) occurs in the same conditions as opinion change. Therefore, either the annoyance and irritation prompted by the communication and the illustrations does not minimize their effectiveness or was not of sufficient strength to arouse resistance to persuasion.

Variables associated with action. In examining data relating to action, we shall compare the means only for those subjects *eligible* for vaccination. Subjects receiving specific recommendations tended to report stronger feelings of susceptibility to tetanus. Though the difference is at the .10 level ("The chances are ——— in 100 that I will contract tetanus" Table 4, $F = 3.14$,

TABLE 4

<small>MEAN DIFFERENCES BETWEEN SPECIFIC AND NONSPECIFIC TREATMENTS</small>
(NO PRIOR SHOT SUBJECTS ONLY)

	Specific		Nonspecific		Control	
	High fear	Low fear	High fear	Low fear	Question-naire only	Recommen-dations only
Susceptibility						
(100-point scale)	7.089	13.569[a]	4.736	4.615	5.58	11.61[a]
N	13	16	17	13	11	28
Nausea (21-point scale)	5.61	1.75	9.06	3.46	3.87	1.59
N	13	16	17	13		
Interested in pamphlet	8.15	7.73	7.17	7.3	—	
(9-point scale)						
N	13	15	17	13		

[a] A few subjects had extremely high scores for these questions which caused an unduly inflated mean.

$df = 1/136$, $p < .10$), the scores are highly skewed and do not approach significance using an appropriate test.

Subjects receiving the specific recommendation reported feeling *less* nauseated than those getting the general recommendation ($F = 6.14$, $df = 1/140$, $p < .01$). Thus, while nausea was increased by the high-fear booklets, it was depressed by the specific recommendation and for the low fear specific was below the control mean. In addition, the specific subjects reported more interest in the communication ("Did you find the pamphlet interesting?" $F = 4.26$, $df = 1/137$, $p < .05$). It seems, therefore, that the correlates of action are a greater interest in the outer environment and a lessening of what may be potentially inhibiting visceral reactions, though fear itself is high.

Takers versus nontakers. The analyses to this point appear to indicate that fear arousal is sufficient to influence attitudes while both arousal stimuli and specific recommendations are needed for action. Since an increase in the level of fear does not increase the rate of action taking, it may appear that actions and attitudes are no longer related to one another. To obtain further evidence on this question a post hoc comparison was made of takers and nontakers on the questionnaire measures. In making the comparisons, a constant equal to the difference between the high- and low-fear means was added to all scores in the low-fear condition. This eliminated the main effects of arousal and allowed a comparison of shot takers and nontakers ignoring the effect of the fear treatment. The only values that approached significance were for anxiety, fright, importance of shots, and feelings that the illustrations enhanced the pamphlet. Thus, shot takers, who are mainly in the specific recom-

TABLE 5

Mean Comparison of Shot Takers with Nontakers

	Takers	Nontakers	t
Emotion			
Anxiety	11.90	9.07	1.55
N	9	50	
Fright	11.39	8.88	1.47
N	9	50	
Attitude			
Importance	11.96	10.49	1.89*
N	9	50	
Illustrations enhance	8.89	6.36	1.59
N	9	48	
Susceptibility[a]	19.16	10.32	1.28
N	8	21	

[a] Specific treatment subjects only.

*$p = .05$, one-tailed.

mendation condition, not only differ from nontakers in the *general* recommendation condition in the ways discussed before, but they *also* show higher scores on the above measures. Attitude and arousal are related, therefore, to action.

DISCUSSION

The data lend mixed support to the hypotheses. As in the earlier experiments (Leventhal & Niles, 1964; Niles, 1964) fear-arousing communications increased attitudinal acceptance of the recommendations, in this case, favoring tetanus inoculations. Supporting evidence for the facilitating effect of fear on attitude change can also be found in Weiss, Rawson, and Pasamanick (1963) where high scores on dispositional anxiety facilitated opinion change. However, these results are contradictory to the data reported in two studies of acceptance of recommendations for dental hygiene (Goldstein, 1959; Janis & Feshbach, 1953) where increases in fear level appeared to be associated with resistance to the recommendations.[8] As suggested earlier (Leventhal & Niles, 1964; Niles, 1964), the discrepancy between the experiments may relate to differences in the perceived effectiveness of the recommended actions. Thus, tetanus inoculations are far more effective as a preventive measure for tetanus than toothbrushing is for dental disease. No matter how one cares for his teeth, he is

[8] The Janis and Terwilliger (1962) experiment also tends to support the thesis that high fear increases resistance to persuasion. However, the experiment was not specifically designed to test this hypothesis and the results on this particular issue were borderline; the trend for high fear (6-2/11) versus low fear (11-0/16) on acceptance of a nonsmoking recommendation being only suggestive ($CR = 1.35$, $p < .18$, two-tailed).

still likely to have some caries. On the other hand, the incidence of tetanus is practically zero for protected people, and for lung cancer, the incidence is extremely low for nonsmokers. Therefore, when fear is aroused it may be critical to present an extremely effective (or effective-appearing) recommendation to minimize the possibility that subjects will leave the communication setting still in need of reassurance and thus open to counter-persuasion.

It has also been suggested (Weiss *et al.*, 1963) that fear will have opposite effects upon attitude change depending upon the subject's initial position. When subjects hold competing opinions, the increased drive level could be predicted to strengthen the incorrect responses more than the correct ones (e.g., Farber & Spence, 1953). In the present experiment, it is clear from the control-group data that subjects are initially favorable toward shots. It is possible, however, that subjects in the dental hygiene study (Janis & Feshbach, 1953, 1954) were negative toward some of the recommended practices and that fear strengthened the "incorrect" responses. However, this argument loses some strength as smokers in the lung cancer studies also showed more acceptance of recommendations with high levels of fear (Leventhal & Niles, 1964; Niles, 1964). Still, the actions recommended in the current setting are preventive, simple to take, and relatively painless.

Of greater interest, however, is that specific plans for action influence behavior while level of fear does not. But specific information alone is insufficient as action is influenced only when specific information is combined with one of the fear-arousing communications. The group exposed only to specific information is generally quite similar to an unexposed control for reported emotions and very similar to the unexposed control's attitudes concerning the importance of shots. Therefore, while emotional arousal is necessary for attitudinal and behavioral change, it seems to be sufficient for the former and only necessary for the latter. Does this mean that behavior and attitudes are entirely independent of one another? In our first study on lung cancer (Leventhal & Niles, 1964) a very high correspondence was found between intentions to get X-rays and actually having one taken. In addition, X-ray takers reported more fear than nontakers. In the present study, the comparisons of takers and nontakers revealed a similar effect, that is, the takers regarded shots as more important (though intentions were *not* stronger) than the nontakers, and the takers had higher scores on some of the fear indices. Neither of these experiments shows significant differences between fear treatments for the action measures. If one reexamines the setting for the lung cancer study, it soon becomes apparent that subjects in all conditions were given a highly specific plan for taking X-rays; that is, while delivering the recommendation for X-rays, "the experimenter pointed directly at the X-ray unit which was down the corridor from the 'theatre.' The unit was clearly visible to all Ss . . . [Leventhal & Niles, 1964, p. 462]." Therefore, the effects on action are extremely similar in both studies and both studies produced a relationship between attitude and actions, though the relationship is weaker in the present experiment.

Although there is a positive relationship between attitudes and behavior, the present data show that the independent variables have different effects upon attitudes and actions. Specific information for taking action does not in itself produce favorable attitudes but does establish a link between attitude and action. What is the nature of this link that permits the attitude to be translated into action? In certain situations, for example, those where the action is immediately possible, specificity may entail the elimination of barriers to action (Leventhal & Niles, 1964). However, in situations such as the present, where the actions were carried out several days subsequent to the communication, other aspects of the manipulations, for example, rehearsing the action, making a decision to act, as well as simple information on how to make the response, could be responsible for the link. An examination of questionnaire effects associated with the specificity manipulation tentatively suggests that specificity altered the subject's emotional state. Thus, subjects receiving the specific plan for action were somewhat more interested in the materials and reported significantly less nausea which can be interpreted to mean that the specific information eliminated various inward-turning inhibitory features of the fear state. Several authors have distinguished between inhibitory or depressive fear states and excitatory fear states (Bull, 1962; Kollar, 1961; Shands, 1955) and have associated striving and protective activity with the latter. However, while it is clear that these affective states can be distinguished in communication studies (Leventhal et al., 1963, unpublished) the study of their relationship to persuasion and action has just begun. The present data do suggest, however, that providing a clear possibility or plan for action can reduce the inhibitory properties of certain fear states.

Regardless of the exact process by which specific information links the evaluative and action components, it is still puzzling why more action did not occur in that condition where the attitude change was greatest. There is a very simple hypothesis that can be suggested to account for this. If the effects of fear dissipate rapidly with time, then it may be that the failure to find more action in the high-fear treatments reflects the fact that attitudes were measured *at* the time of exposure while action took place *after* the fear-induced attitude effects had been dissipated (Leventhal & Niles, 1965). If this is the case, no relationship between attitude change and behavior could possibly be expected.

REFERENCES

BERKOWITZ, L., and COTTINGHAM, D. R. The interest value and relevance of fear arousing communications. *Journal of Abnormal and Social Psychology*, 1960, 60, 37–43.

BULL, NINA. *The body and its mind: An introduction to attitude psychology.* New York: Las Americas, 1962.

COHEN, A. R. Need for cognition and order of communication as determinants of opinion change. In C. I. Hovland *et al.* (Eds.), *The order of presentation in persuasion.* New Haven: Yale Univer. Press, 1957. pp. 79–97.

DABBS, J. Self esteem, coping and influence. Unpublished doctoral dissertation, Yale University, 1962.

FARBER, I. E., and SPENCE, K. W. Complex learning and conditioning as a function of anxiety. *Journal of Experimental Psychology,* 1953, 45, 120–125.

GOLDSTEIN, M. J. The relationship between coping and avoiding behavior and response to fear-arousing propaganda. *Journal of Abnormal and Social Psychology,* 1959, 58, 247–252.

JANIS, I. L., and FESHBACH, S. Effects of fear-arousing communications. *Journal of Abnormal and Social Psychology,* 1953, 48, 78–92.

JANIS, I. L., and FESHBACH, S. Personality differences associated with responsiveness to fear-arousing communications. *Journal of Personality,* 1954, 23, 154–166.

JANIS, I. L., and TERWILLIGER, R. F. An experimental study of psychological resistances to fear arousing communications. *Journal of Abnormal and Social Psychology,* 1962, 65, 403–410.

KLAPPER, J. T. *The effects of mass communications.* New York: Free Press of Glencoe, 1960.

KOLLAR, E. J. Psychological stress: A re-evaluation. *Journal of Nervous and Mental Disease,* 1961, 132, 382–396.

LEVENTHAL., H., and NILES, P. A field experiment on fear-arousal with data on the validity of questionnaire measures. *Journal of Personality,* 1964, 32, 459–479.

LEVENTHAL, H., and NILES, P. Persistence of influence for varying durations of exposure to threat stimuli. *Psychological Reports,* 1965, 16, 223–233.

LEVENTHAL, H., and PERLOE, S. I. A relationship between self-esteem and persuasibility. *Journal of Abnormal and Social Psychology,* 1962, 64, 385–388.

NILES, P. Two personality measures associated with responsiveness to fear-arousing communications. Unpublished doctoral dissertation, Yale University, 1964.

ROBBINS, P. R. An application of the method of successive intervals to the study of fear-arousing information. *Psychological Reports,* 1962, 11, 757–760.

ROSENBERG, M. J. Cognitive structure and attitudinal effect. *Journal of Abnormal and Social Psychology,* 1956, 53, 367–372.

SHANDS, H. C. An outline of the process of recovery from severe trauma. *American Medical Association Archives of Neurology and Psychiatry,* 1955, 73, 403–409.

WALKER, HELEN M., & LEV, J. *Statistical inference.* New York: Holt, 1953.

WEISS, R. F., RAWSON, H. E., and PASAMANICK, B. Argument strength, delay of argument, and anxiety in the "conditioning" and "selective learning" of attitudes. *Journal of Abnormal and Social Psychology,* 1963, 67, 157–165.

James C. McCroskey*

A SUMMARY OF EXPERIMENTAL RESEARCH ON THE EFFECTS OF EVIDENCE IN PERSUASIVE COMMUNICATION

Traditional theories of rhetoric, person-to-group persuasive communication, stress the value of documented supporting materials, commonly called evidence, in the production of attitude change. Contemporary theorists for the most part concur with traditional theorists in this regard. However, because of the conflicting findings of the few reported experimental studies of the effect of evidence on attitude change, some writers have questioned whether evidence actually has much, if any, impact in persuasion. After reviewing some of these studies, for example, Gregg concluded that "the audience reaction to an argument may have little or nothing to do with whether the argument includes fully documented or completely undocumented evidence, relevant or irrelevant evidence, weak or strong evidence or any evidence at all."[1]

*Mr. McCroskey is Assistant Professor of Communication, Michigan State University. The early phases of the research discussed in this paper were the basis of Mr. McCroskey's doctoral dissertation at Pennsylvania State University (1966) under the direction of Dr. Robert E. Dunham.

[1] Richard E. Gregg, "Some Hypotheses for the Study of the Psychology of Evidence," paper read at the 1964 SAA Convention.

Reprinted from *Quarterly Journal of Speech,* 55 (1969), 169–76, with permission of the author and the Speech Association of America.

The purpose of this paper is to examine the results of several studies of the effects of evidence, most of which have been conducted by the present writer, and to suggest when and how evidence may function in persuasive communication. The studies conducted by the writer that underlie this paper are reported in detail elsewhere.[2]

STUDIES REPORTED BY OTHER RESEARCHERS

Nine studies have been reported by other investigators that involved research on the effect of evidence on attitude change in persuasive communication. Two of these found that inclusion of evidence increased the amount of attitude change produced by the message; two found a trend in this direction; and five observed no significant effect on attitude change attributable to evidence.

The two earliest reported studies, those reported by Cathcart[3] and Bettinghaus,[4] were the only ones to produce statistically significant results favoring inclusion of evidence in a speech designed to achieve attitude change. Studies reported by Gilkinson, Paulson, and Sikkink[5] and Ostermeier[6] demonstrated trends favoring inclusion of evidence that did not meet normal criterion levels for statistical significance. Anderson,[7] Costley,[8] Dresser,[9]

[2] An extensive report of these studies is available in James C. McCroskey, *Studies of the Effects of Evidence in Persuasive Communication*, Report SCRL, 4–67, Speech Communication Research Laboratory, Michigan State University, 1967. Copies of this report are available from the writer upon request.

[3] Robert S. Cathcart, "An Experimental Study of the Relative Effectiveness of Selected Means of Handling Evidence in Speeches of Advocacy" (unpublished Ph.D. dissertation, Northwestern University, 1953). See also "An Experimental Study of the Relative Effectiveness of Four Methods of Presenting Evidence," *Speech Monographs*, XXII (August 1955), 227–233.

[4] Erwin P. Bettinghaus, Jr., "The Relative Effect of the Use of Testimony in a Persuasive Speech upon the Attitudes on Listeners" (unpublished M.A. thesis, Bradley University, 1953).

[5] Howard Gilkinson, Stanley F. Paulson, and Donald E. Sikkink, "Effects of Order and Authority in an Argumentative Speech," *Q JS*, XL (April 1954), 183–192.

[6] Terry H. Ostermeier, "An Experimental Study on the Type and Frequency of Reference as Used by an Unfamiliar Source in a Message and Its Effect upon Perceived Credibility and Attitude Change" (unpublished Ph.D. dissertation, Michigan State University, 1966).

[7] Delmar C. Anderson, "The Effect of Various Uses of Authoritative Testimony in Persuasive Speaking" (unpublished M.A. thesis, Ohio State University, 1958).

[8] Dan L. Costley, "An Experimental Study of the Effectiveness of Quantitative Evidence in Speeches of Advocacy" (unpublished M.A. thesis, University of Oklahoma, 1958).

[9] William R. Dresser, "Studies of the Effects of Satisfactory and Unsatisfactory Evidence in a Speech of Advocacy" (unpublished Ph.D. dissertation, Northwestern University, 1962). See also "Studies of the Effects of Evidence: Implications for Forensics," *AFA Register*, X, No. 3 (1962), 14–19; "Effects of 'Satisfactory' and 'Unsatisfactory' Evidence in a Speech of Advocacy," *Speech Monographs*, XXX (August 1963), 302–306; and "The Impact of Evidence on Decision Making," paper read at the 1965 SAA Convention.

Gardner,[10] and Wagner[11] found no significant superiority in the production of attitude change for a speech including high quality evidence over a speech including either no evidence or low quality evidence.

In the only reported study of the effects of evidence on perceived source credibility conducted by an individual other than the writer, Ostermeier found that including a form of evidence significantly increased perceived credibility.[12]

From these studies no firm generalization can be drawn concerning the effect of evidence on attitude change and one can only tentatively conclude that evidence has an impact on source credibility.

In an attempt to provide data upon which meaningful generalizations concerning the effect of evidence in persuasive communication could be based, the writer has conducted twelve studies. The following discussion is organized around the variables that were suspected as interacting with evidence in producing either attitude change or perceived source credibility. In each section there is presented a theoretic rationale for the hypothesized relationship between evidence and the other variable and a discussion of studies investigating this relationship. Since all of these studies have been reported in considerable detail elsewhere, the discussion in the following sections will stress results rather than procedures. The reader may find information on procedural details in previous reports that are cited.

A consideration of relationships between evidence and other communication variables requires several operational definitions to avoid confusion in interpreting the material that follows.

The meaning of the term "evidence" as used by various authors of articles and books on persuasive communication is not always the same. The definition of "evidence" employed by the researchers involved in the studies discussed in this paper is compatible with that of the majority of writers. "Evidence" is taken to mean *factual statements originating from a source other than the speaker, objects not created by the speaker, and opinions of persons other than the speaker that are offered in support of the speaker's claims.* Only opinions and factual statements clearly identified with a source other than the speaker have been used in most of the studies; the use of audio-tape as the medium of transmission in most of the experiments precluded the use of tangible objects as evidence.

Source credibility or ethos was operationally defined in this series of studies as perceived "authoritativeness" and "character" as measured by either Likert or semantic differential instruments designed for this purpose.[13] Attitude change was operationally defined as the difference between attitude

[10] James C. Gardner, "An Experimental Study of the Use of Selected Forms of Evidence in Effecting Attitude Change" (unpublished M.A. thesis, University of Nebraska, 1966).

[11] Gerard A. Wagner, "An Experimental Study of the Relative Effectiveness of Varying Amounts of Evidence in a Persuasive Communication" (unpublished M.A. thesis, Mississippi Southern University, 1958).

[12] See note 6.

[13] James C. McCroskey, "Scales for the Measurement of Ethos," *Speech Monographs,* XXXIII (March 1966), 65–72.

prior to exposure to the experimental stimuli and attitude subsequent to exposure as measured by Likert or semantic differential instruments designed for this purpose.[14]

EVIDENCE AND SOURCE CREDIBILITY

The first variable suspected of interacting with evidence in the production of attitude change was source credibility. Specifically it was hypothesized that a speech including evidence would be more successful in producing attitude change than a speech not including evidence when the speech was presented by a moderate-to-low-credible source but that inclusion of evidence would have no effect when the speech was presented by a high-credible source. The rationale behind this hypothesis is twofold. First, the use of opinions or facts attested to by a source other than the speaker is a direct attempt to employ the credibility of the cited source as a persuasive tool. When the speaker's credibility is initially high, bringing even more credibility to bear on the case may be unnecessary. In short, there may be a point beyond which increasing credibility does not increase attitude change. Second, consistency theory suggests that, within limits, the greater the inconsistency between attitude toward source and attitude toward concept the greater the pressure to change attitude. When the speaker's credibility is initially high, the fact that other high-credible sources agree with him is consistent and thus unlikely to have much effect on the speaker's credibility. The initially low-credible source, on the other hand, has much to gain in credibility by demonstrating that high-credible sources agree with him. As his credibility increases the inconsistency between the audience's attitude toward him and toward the concept he favors is increased. Thus, while the initially high-credible source has little to gain from evidence, the low-credible source may increase his credibility by citing evidence and, in turn, increase the amount of attitude change produced in his audience.

The previously cited study by Ostermeier found that evidence did increase a source's credibility. For the most part, my studies have produced similar results, but only when the source was perceived by the audience initially as moderate-to-low-credible. My first study involved an unknown, unidentified, tape-recorded speaker. The subjects were college students participating in an experiment outside their normal classroom in the evening with only an unknown experimenter present. The results of this study indicated that inclusion of evidence increased both perceived credibility and attitude change.[15] A partial replication of this study employed subjects who were high school students participating in an experiment under classroom conditions with two known

[14] James C. McCroskey, "Experimental Studies of the Effects of Ethos and Evidence in Persuasive Communication" (unpublished D.Ed. dissertation, Pennsylvania State University, 1966).

[15] *Ibid.* See also "The Effects of Evidence in Persuasive Communication," *Western Speech*, XXXI (Summer 1967), 189–199.

and respected teacher-experimenters present.[16] The results of this study indicated no effect of evidence on either credibility or attitude change. These conflicting results led to the speculation that the initial credibility of the unknown, unidentified, tape-recorded speaker was artificially increased in the second study by the presence and tacit sponsorship of the known and respected teacher-experimenters.[17] This speculation was borne out by the results of a study reported by Holtzman that employed the same instruments included in the previous studies under more controlled conditions.[18]

The combined finding of these three studies provide support for the hypothesis that inclusion of evidence can increase the credibility of and the attitude change produced by an initially moderate-to-low-credible source but has no effect when the source is initially high-credible.

Six subsequent studies have provided additional support for this hypothesis.[19] In no case was evidence observed to increase the attitude change produced by an initially high-credible source while, in most cases, inclusion of evidence by an initially moderate-to-low-credible source was observed to increase attitude change. Similarly, inclusion of evidence rarely was observed to increase the perceived credibility of initially high-credible sources but, in most cases, was observed to increase perceived credibility of initially moderate-to-low-credible sources.

Taken as a whole, these nine studies provide substantial justification for the generalization that initial credibility and evidence usage interact to produce attitude change and perceived credibility. Briefly stated, the initially high-credible source gains little from including evidence but the initially moderate-to-low-credible source can substantially increase his perceived credibility and the attitude change he produces in his audience by including evidence to support his position. This generalization, however, will be somewhat tempered by the results concerning evidence and other communication variables discussed below.

CREDIBILITY OF SOURCES OF EVIDENCE

Traditional theory insists that for evidence to have a favorable impact on an audience it must come from sources the audience accepts as credible. Because of conflicting results across topics in two studies[20] it was suspected that

[16] McCroskey, *Studies of the Effects.* . . .
[17] James G. McCroskey and Robert E. Dunham, "Ethos: A Confounding Element in Communication Research," *Speech Monographs,* XXXIII (November 1966), 456–463.
[18] Paul D. Holtzman, "Confirmation of Ethos as a Confounding Element in Communication Research," *Speech Monographs,* XXXIII (November 1966), 464–466.
[19] McCroskey, *Studies of the Effects.* . . .
[20] *Ibid.*

evidence included in the experimental messages employed may not have been the "best" evidence. Most of the evidence included was of the "unbiased" type. Several writers have asserted that, while unbiased evidence is better than biased evidence, reluctant evidence (a biased source testifying against what appears to be his best interests) is the best of all. Two studies by Arnold and McCroskey[21] and two by McCroskey and Wenburg[22] found no support for this theory. In each study biased sources were perceived to be less credible than unbiased or relucant sources, but unbiased sources were found regularly to be more credible than reluctant sources. While these four studies do not provide definitive answers to questions concerning the credibility of sources of evidence, their results provide ample support for the contention that the evidence included in the other evidence studies was of sufficiently high quality so that the results of the studies were not contaminated by audiences perceiving the evidence as emanating from low-credible sources. Additional support for this contention was provided by ratings on evidence quality obtained from subjects in several of the studies. In each case where such ratings were requested, subjects rated speeches including evidence much higher on "evidence usage" than speeches not including evidence.

EVIDENCE, DELIVERY, AND MEDIA OF MESSAGE PRESENTATION

In two experiments results relating to the effects of evidence on attitude change and perceived credibility were conflicting across topics when the message was attributed to a moderate-to-low-credible source.[23] In both studies evidence had its predicted effect when the speech topic was federal control of education, but in neither study did evidence have its predicted effect when the speech topic was capital punishment. Post-experiment interviews with selected subjects indicated that they perceived the delivery of the speaker on federal control of education to be very good but the delivery of the speaker on capital punishment to be dull and monotonous. Therefore the quality of presentation of a message was suspected as a variable that could interact with evidence usage and, in turn, could produce the conflicting findings across topics.

Delivery long has been thought to be a significant variable in oral communication. Poor delivery theoretically distracts from the content of the message by drawing attention of the audience to poor delivery characteristics and by reducing the clarity of the verbal message. Because poor delivery might cause an audience to miss evidence as it is presented by causing them to attend to

[21] William E. Arnold and James C. McCroskey, "The Credibility of Reluctant Testimony," *Central States Speech Journal*, XVIII (May 1967), 97–103.
[22] McCroskey, *Studies of the Effects. . . .*
[23] *Ibid.*

something else and because it might prevent the audience from clearly under-standing evidence which they do hear, poor delivery could interact with evidence usage in persuasive communication.

Two studies were designed and conducted to test the following hypothesis: Inclusion of evidence in a persuasive speech increases attitude change and perceived credibility when the speech is well delivered but has no effect on either attitude change or credibility when the speech is poorly delivered. The results of both studies provided partial support for this hypothesis.

Arnold and McCroskey employed a live speaker to present an "evidence speech" and a "no-evidence speech" under conditions of both good delivery and very poor delivery.[24] Greater attitude change and higher perceived credibility were produced by the condition including evidence and good delivery than any of the other three conditions. The other three conditions did not differ in amount of attitude change produced. However, even in the poor delivery condition, the speech including evidence produced higher perceived credibility than the speech with no evidence, though not as high as in the condition including evidence and good delivery.

In a subsequent and much broader study, the results were consistent with those of the Arnold and McCroskey study. In this study four main variables were manipulated—evidence, delivery, initial credibility, and media of transmission.[25] The results indicated that inclusion of evidence increased immediate attitude change only under conditions of good delivery accompanied by initial low credibility. The results were consistent across transmission media—audio-tape and video-tape. Although poor delivery was found significantly to reduce perceived credibility, again, as in the Arnold and McCroskey study, the speech including evidence consistently produced higher perceived credibility than the speech not including evidence.

The results of these studies, taken together, support the conclusion that poor delivery can inhibit the effect of evidence on immediate attitude change but does not inhibit its effect on credibility. Because the results of these studies were consistent for live, audio-taped, and video-taped speakers, one has no reason to believe that media of presentation is related to the effect of evidence in persuasive communication.

EVIDENCE AND PRIOR KNOWLEDGE OF AUDIENCE

Although the findings discussed in the previous section indicate that evidence and delivery are related in the production of attitude change, this does not provide a full explanation of the conflicting results across topics in the two

[24] *Ibid.*
[25] *Ibid.*

studies previously noted. In those studies the results on credibility also con-flicted. As a result of post-experiment interviews with subjects involved in the studies in which conflicting results were obtained, another variable was sus-pected to be related to evidence in the production of attitude change and per-ceived source credibility. This is the variable of prior familiarity of the audience with evidence cited by a speaker.

In the post-experiment interviews the almost universal reaction from the subjects was that the evidence cited in the capital punishment speech was "old hat." On the federal control of education topic, on the other hand, the most frequent comment was one of interest and surprise at what was described by several subjects as the "shocking facts" presented.

If evidence must be "new" to have an effect, the inconsistent results become explainable. Such an assumption is highly consistent with some infor-mation theories. It is also consistent with dissonance theory. Old evidence has already entered the cognitive domain of the subject. If it created dissonance, that dissonance would have already been resolved or defense mechanisms constructed to avoid the recurrence of dissonance as a result of that evidence. Thus the presentation of that evidence to the subject would have no effect.

On the basis of this theory it was hypothesized that presenting evidence to people who previously have been exposed to that evidence will have no effect on either attitude change or credibility, but presenting the same evidence to people who are not familiar with it will significantly increase attitude change and credibility if the source of the message is initially moderate-to-low-credible.

The study designed to test this hypothesis involved the manipulation of three variables—evidence, initial credibility, and degree of prior familiarity with the evidence on the part of the subjects.[26] Evidence and credibility were manipulated as in previous studies. The speeches on the topic of federal control of education were selected as experimental stimuli because it was assumed that the subjects were not familiar with the evidence included in these speeches. Half of the subjects, therefore, were systematically exposed to this evidence under appropriate cover conditions prior to being exposed to the experimental speeches.

The results of this study were precisely predicted by the hypothesis. Evi-dence increased attitude change and credibility only in the condition including low initial credibility and no prior familiarization with the evidence. These results seem to provide an explanation of the conflicting results of the earlier studies. But more importantly, the results indicate that evidence must be "new" to the audience before it can have an impact on their immediate attitude change or their perception of the message source.

[26] *Ibid.*

THE EFFECTS OF EVIDENCE ON
SUSTAINED ATTITUDE CHANGE

The previous sections of this paper have been concerned only with the effects of evidence on credibility and attitude change measured *immediately* subsequent to exposure to persuasive messages. Evidence has an impact on these important variables only under relatively limited circumstances. In several of these studies the effects of evidence on sustained attitude change for periods up to seven weeks were measured.[27] In four of the five cases in which the effect of evidence on sustained attitude change was measured, inclusion of evidence was found significantly to increase the amount of attitude change retained over time. In the fifth case the difference was in the same direction although not statistically significant. Further, no interactions between evidence usage and other communication variables were found relating to sustained attitude change.

Precisely why evidence has an effect on sustained attitude change even when it has no effect on immediate attitude change is not at all clear. Since all speeches produced significant immediate attitude change, one possible explanation is that evidence may interfere with the process of selective recall. The evidence included in the experimental messages in the studies that measured sustained effect was, for the most part, quite vivid and memorable. Such material may have been more memorable than other elements of the messages. Whether less striking evidence would have a similar impact is unknown.

CONCLUSIONS

Some twenty-two studies concerned with the functioning of evidence in persuasive communication have now been reported in the literature. The purpose of this paper has been to examine these studies to determine what generalizations of value to the practicing communicator or communication researcher tentatively may be drawn at this point in time. The following are generalizations which seem appropriate:

(1) Including good evidence has little, if any, impact on immediate audience attitude change or source credibility if the source of the message is initially perceived to be high-credible.

(2) Including good evidence has little, if any, impact on immediate audience attitude change if the message is delivered poorly.

(3) Including good evidence has little, if any, impact on immediate audience attitude change or source credibility if the audience is familiar with the evidence prior to exposure to the source's message.

(4) Including good evidence may significantly increase immediate audi-

[27] *Ibid.*

ence attitude change and source credibility when the source is initially perceived to be moderate-to-low-credible, when the message is well delivered, and when the audience has little or no prior familiarity with the evidence included or similar evidence.

(5) Including good evidence may significantly increase sustained audience attitude change regardless of the source's initial credibility, the quality of the delivery of the message, or the medium by which the message is transmitted.

(6) The medium of transmission of a message has little, if any, effect on the functioning of evidence in persuasive communication.

NEED FOR FUTURE RESEARCH

Although the number of studies concerning the functioning of evidence in persuasive communication has increased sharply in recent years and several studies not discussed in this paper are in progress, there is a major need for more, and more imaginative, research in this area. Only a few very tentative generalizations about the place of evidence in persuasive communication are available. What are some of the questions that remain to be answered? The following are some that seem worthy of consideration: (1) What is the effect of evidence on overt behavior change? All the studies to date have been concerned with attitude. (2) Can evidence from non-credible sources serve as well as evidence from credible sources? Dresser's results suggest they can, but in his study credibility of the speaker was not manipulated.[28] (3) What type of evidence (opinion, statistics, examples) produces the most favorable impact? Some researchers have investigated this area, but too many uncontrolled factors were in their designs to make interpretation of the results possible. (4) Are there factors that interact with evidence in producing sustained attitude change? The studies to date have found none, but they have been very limited in scope. (5) What factors other than delivery, source credibility, and prior knowledge interact with or inhibit the effects of evidence? Some that might are structure of the message, intelligence of the audience, and salience of the topic. (6) Do non-students respond to evidence the same way as students? Most of the subjects in the studies to date have been college students. Have we merely contributed one more "tidbit" to the rhetoric of the college sophomore? (7) Does evidence function the same way in interpersonal or group communication as it does in person-to-group communication? This area has received no previous attention. (8) Does evidence function in the written media the same way it does with live, audio-taped, and video-taped speakers? There is no previous research here either. (9) Can evidence enhance a communicator's efforts to inoculate his audience against counterpersuasion? The consistent effects favoring evidence on sustaining attitude change suggest that it might. (10) Does evidence function

[28] Dresser, "Studies of the Effects of Satisfactory. . . ."

the same way in various cultures? The response may be very different if one studies evidence in something other than the U. S. middle-class culture in which the previous studies have been conducted.

The above questions are included in this paper to make clear that, while considerable information has accumulated upon which generalizations may be formed about the place of evidence in persuasive communication the surface of this problem area has barely been scratched. If we as communication researchers are to continue to focus our attention on message variables within the communication process, evidence should continue to be one of the major variables we study.

Arthur R. Cohen

ATTITUDE CHANGE
AND SOCIAL INFLUENCE

THE EFFECTS OF ONE-SIDED VERSUS
TWO-SIDED COMMUNICATIONS

What role does the organization of arguments play in the effectiveness of a persuasive appeal? In attempting to answer this question, writers have in the past dealt with methods of refutation, problems of emphasis, number of repetitions, and so forth. One of the central problems, however, is whether it is more effective to present only one side of an issue or to present both sides. Should a communicator concentrate only on the points supporting the position he advocates or should he also discuss opposing arguments? Which strategy is the more effective?

In *Experiments on Mass Communication*, the volume in which they report the results of their wartime studies, Hovland, Lumsdaine, and Sheffield (1949) investigate whether, when the weight of evidence supports the main thesis of a communication, it is more effective to present only the materials supporting the point at issue or to introduce opposing arguments as well.

These investigators presented to two experimental groups of 214 soldiers and to a control group of 197 soldiers communications on whether there would be an early end to the war with Japan after the surrender of Germany in 1945. All of the soldiers were tested some time before the communication on their beliefs about whether Japan would surrender. One experimental group was given a fifteen-minute talk that presented only the arguments supporting the idea that the war with Japan would be a long one; the talk included much factual material stressing Japan's strength. The other experimental group was given a communication which contained the same material plus an addi-

Pp. 2-5 of *Attitude Change and Social Influence* by Arthur R. Cohen, © 1964 by Basic Books, Inc., Publishers, New York.

tional four minutes of information, woven into the presentation, which stressed the United States' advantages and Japan's weaknesses.

The investigators' hypothesis was that those soldiers who were given only a one-sided argument would distrust a presentation that had failed to include opposing arguments and would be stimulated to rehearse their own position and to seek new ways of supporting it. After the presentation of the material, the soldiers were again measured on their beliefs about the probable length of the war with Japan, and a measure of change from before to after the presentation was computed. The effectiveness of the program was evaluated by comparing the average change in each of the expermental groups with the changes in a control group which had heard no communication but had merely been given the "before" and "after" attitude measures at the same time as the experimental groups.

Both experimental programs were found to be extremely effective in producing change in the men's opinions, but neither program had any advantage over the other for the audience as a whole. Depending upon the initial position of the listener, however, the net effects were different for the two ways of presenting the material. The program giving both sides was more effective for those men initially opposed to the position advocated (those who expected a short war), whereas the program giving the one-sided picture was more effective for men initially favoring the stand taken (those who expected a long war).

The investigators also expected that an obviously one-sided communication would be less effective with well-educated men and that these men would be more likely to take seriously arguments that seem to take all the factors into account. Less well-educated men, on the other hand, with undeveloped skill in critical thinking, might be more impressed with the strength of a one-sided argument, without thinking of objections. These expectations were borne out: The program which presented both sides was more effective with the better-educated men, and the program which presented one side was more effective with the less educated.

When initial position and amount of education are considered together, the two-sided communication turned out to be more effective with better-educated men, no matter what their initial position, and the one-sided presentation most effective with those less-educated men already convinced of the position advocated. Thus, to decide the most effective type of presentation requires information about the educational level of the audience and the beliefs that audience already holds.

Do these two types of communication reveal differences in resistance to counterinfluence? A further experiment (Lumsdaine & Janis, 1953) bears directly on this point. In this experiment, a week after having been exposed to either a one-sided or a two-sided communication on Russia's inability to produce atomic bombs for many years to come, half of the subjects in each experimental group were exposed to a counterargument before being asked to state their opinions again. The counterpropaganda consisted of a playing-up and an elaboration of the arguments in the two-sided communication, as well as some new material. When the scores for change were examined, it was found that while there was no difference for those not exposed to the counterpropaganda, those who had been exposed to the counterpropaganda and who had heard the two-sided program were more resistant to the counterpropaganda than those who had heard only the one-sided argument.

In summarizing the results of these two experiments, Hovland, Janis, and Kelley (1953, p. 110) conclude that a two-sided communication is more effective in the long run when, no matter what its initial opinion, the audience is exposed to subsequent counterpropaganda or when, regardless of subsequent exposure, the audience initially disagrees with the position advocated by the communicator. The two-sided communication is less effective if the audience agrees with the initial position and is not exposed to later counterpropaganda. With respect to the second experiment, the two-sided argument apparently prepares the listener to meet counterarguments; it would thus seem especially effective in "inoculating" the listener against subsequent counterinfluence. "Inoculation" relates also to the problem of building up resistance to pressures toward attitude change.

The concept of inoculation also raises questions about the way in which two-sided communications present opposing arguments. Although the investigators are most interested in resolving the issue of which type of communication is the more effective, their results make it clear that further work should take account of the manner in which opposing arguments are introduced, the character of the arguments, and the extent to which they are explicitly refuted. Some of these questions are considered in Chapter 8, and their investigation increases our understanding of the conditions under which two-sided communications are most effective as well as those under which refutation can be successful.

The foregoing conclusions about the relative effectiveness of one-sided and two-sided communications have been extended by other investigators (Thistlethwaite & Kamenetsky, 1955). Attitude change tends to be greater for those subjects whose comprehension of the communicator's conclusion is greater or who show fewer and less intense discounting reactions to the communication. Introducing facts in support of the "other side" leads to less change of attitude when the facts are unfamiliar to the subjects, but failure to include well-known facts on the "other side" also weakens the appeal. Thus, to the degree that the facts included in the different communications are comprehensible and familiar, the appeals will be differentially effective in producing changes in attitude.

The experiments cited take little account of the fact that the persons subjected to attempts at influence are not merely members of an audience but also persons with active social lives within their social groups. Festinger (1955) has commented on the fact that knowledge about the effect of interpersonal and group processes implies that such processes may be modifying the effects obtained by one-sided versus two-sided arguments. It is possible that the two-sided presentation, by stressing the controversial aspect of the problem, may set off considerable discussion among the listeners in the week-long interval after hearing it. Thus, rather than showing the effectiveness of a one-sided versus a two-sided presentation, the results may show the resistance to counter-influence under one set of conditions, where opinions are not anchored in a membership group, as compared to the resistance under conditions where they are firmly anchored in a membership group. . . .

Ralph L. Rosnow*

WHATEVER HAPPENED TO THE "LAW OF PRIMACY"?

The Law of Primacy in Persuasion refers to Lund's [49] assertion of a principle in answer to the question, "When an audience is presented with both sides of an issue, which has the advantage—the side presented first (primacy) or the side presented last (recency)?" Lund's principle was based upon research which consisted of presenting mimeographed, counterbalanced pairs of arguments to groups of college students—the first argument advocating one side of a controversial issue, the second, diametrically the opposite.[1] His results consistently showed that the first presented arguments were significantly more effective than the second for influencing opinions concerning the issues involved.

Subsequent investigations appeared first to confirm but then to refute the primacy principle.[2] But it was not until the middle 1950's, when the late

*Ralph L. Rosnow is an Assistant Professor in the Division of Communication Research and Fellow in the Communication Research Center at Boston University.

This study was supported in part by grant MH 11972-01 from the National Institute of Mental Health, United States Public Health Service. The author is indebted to R. E. Lana and E. J. Robinson for their valuable criticisms of an earlier version of this paper.

[1] The issues involved in the arguments were "whether all men should have equal political rights," "whether the protective tariff is a wise policy for the United States," and "whether monogamous marriage will continue to be the only socially accepted relation between the sexes." The students completed an opinion questionnaire two days before the communications and again immediately after each communication.

[2] On the one hand, Knower, [34] using communications pro- and anti-prohibition, observed that ". . . primacy in the order of reading influenced the amount and possibly the direction of change in attitude which occurred in the group." On the other hand, the possibility that Lund's Law might have been overstated was suggested by the opposite results obtained by Cromwell. [13] Instead of primacy, Cromwell found that recency was the greater influencing factor.

Reprinted from the *Journal of Communication,* 16 (1966), 10–31, with permission of the author and the Journal of Communication.

Carl Hovland and his associates published the now well-known *The Order of Presentation in Persuasion*, [28] that systematic study of the primacy-recency problem began.

In a paper first presented in 1952 at an Eastern Psychological Association meeting, but receiving wider attention when it was reprinted in *Order of Presentation*, Hovland and Mandell [27] pointed out the prematurity of stating either a "law of primacy" or a "law of recency." Suspecting that primacy-recency might be associated with, and confounded by, several other variables, they both directly and systematically replicated the Lund study. Presenting, as Lund had done, posttest questionnaires after each communication, Hovland and Mandell were unable to produce consistent order effects with the Lund arguments. However, when topics of current interest were substituted, three of four treatment groups exhibited recency. Those findings, in apparent contradiction to Lund's, led Hovland to conclude that "when two sides of an issue are presented successively by different communicators, the side presented first does not necessarily have the advantage." [28, p. 130]

Since that time, a variety of primacy-recency variables have been probed. The influence of the order of presentation of communications has been studied in such diverse contexts as persuasion [e.g., 22, 30, 37, 53] and personality impression-formation. [3, 4, 5, 7, 8, 45, 46, 47, 50, 71] In persuasion alone, the influence of variables such as "controversiality of the topic," [38] "familiarity of the audience with the issues involved," [37, 40, 60] "forgetting," [30, 53] and others have since been studied.

Although several preliminary attempts have been made to account for the various findings within such theoretical contexts as Sensory-Variation, [62, 64] *Einstellung*, [42, 47] and Conditioning, [51] it has been pointed out [42, 52] that there has been no success to date in embracing all of the different findings within any one explanatory system.

For that reason, in this paper we shall examine some of the major empirical findings related to primacy-recency without speculating about their apparent interrelationships from a "grand" theoretical point of view. Our objectives are threefold: (a) to review the major experimental findings which either directly or indirectly bear upon the type and intensity of order effects yielded in persuasive communications research, (b) to introduce a system for classifying the independent variables associated with those findings and thereby pointing out commonalities where they may exist, and (c) to suggest several promising paths for future research to follow.

Although placing those findings in one category and not in another in some cases admittedly required an entirely arbitrary decision, for the purpose of presenting them in a systematic fashion and in order to view them in proper perspective they were categorized, and will be discussed, following the conventional Smith, Lasswell, and Casey [67] formula "*who* (communicator) says *what* (communication) to *whom* (audience) through which *medium* with what *effect*."

EMPIRICAL FINDINGS

The Communicator

One of the many principles regarding the manipulation of human behavior that has been gleaned from communications research is that one-sided arguments consisting of passages consonant with recipients' beliefs are more effective than two-sided arguments for strengthening, or reinforcing, opinions, while two-sided persuasive communication is more effective for changing their direction. [26] Since arguments counter to the communicator's position (that is, "negative" arguments) may be used to advantage to "inoculate" an audience against subsequent counterpropaganda, [48] the two-sided presentation may not only influence the direction of change, but resistance to counter-stimuli as well.

A study by Janis and Feierabend [32] sought to determine the conditions under which the introduction of opposing arguments could be used to best advantage. Specifically, the investigators were concerned with comparing the relative effectiveness as persuasive appeals of positive-first and negative-first orders of presentation when (a) the source of the communication was a high-prestige communicator (under this condition, they refer to the messages as "authoritative communications") and (b) the negative information was non-salient for the recipients.

The investigators made the following assumptions: [31] first, assuming that there is strong pressure on the recipient to take a new position on a controversial issue, an approach-avoidance conflict should be generated. Second, the strength of the subject's motivation to *reject* a communication is assumed to increase when a nonsalient con argument is presented; but, third, the strength of the subject's motivation to *accept* a communication is assumed to increase whenever pro arguments supporting the communicator's conclusion are presented.

Since the source of the communication was highly respected, it further was assumed that the recipient would at the outset be favorably disposed toward the source and motivated to accept his conclusions. However, when negative arguments were stated first, an avoidance tendency was presumed to be established—a tendency which the later positive arguments would be unable to reverse. On the other hand, hearing positive arguments first, and provided that the negative arguments were nonsalient, was presumed to establish an approach tendency which, now, the later (negative) arguments would be unable to reverse. The results of the Janis and Feierabend study confirmed the implied primacy hypothesis. When positive and nonsalient negative arguments were attributed to an authoritative communicator, the positive-first order of presentation was superior to the negative-first order of presentation for inducing the behavioral compliance desired by the source.

It is convenient to think of this variable isolated by Janis and Feierabend as a "primacy-bound variable"—primacy-bound in that it is tied only to the primacy effect. For the purpose of classifying further the miscellaneous findings discussed in this paper, pertinent independent variables shall be categorized on the basis of their "bound" or "free" effects. "Primacy-bound variables" will refer to those which lead only to primacy. "Recency-bound variables" will refer to those which lead only to recency. "Free variables" will refer to those which lead *both* to primacy and to recency—the particular effect determined by the utilization or temporal placement of the variable; in that sense, the variables are not *bound* to a particular order effect but are *free* to differentially facilitate one or the other effect. Primacy-bound, recency-bound, and free variables are summarized in Table 1.

TABLE 1

VARIABLES LEADING TO PRIMACY AND RECENCY
IN PERSUASIVE COMMUNICATIONS RESEARCH

Primacy-Bound Variables	*Recency-Bound Variables*	*Free Variables*
Positive and nonsalient negative authoritative communications [31, 32]		
Controversial topic [38, 44]		
Interesting subject matter [39]	Uninteresting subject matter [39]	
		Strong arguments [2, 56, 59]
Familiar topic [37, 60]	Unfamiliar topic [37, 60]	
Delayed "punishment" [58]	Delayed "reward" [61]	
	Increased time interval between communications [30, 53]	

The Communication

Research on communication-related factors in primacy-recency has focused on such variables as the "controversialism of the topic," whether the topic deals with "interesting or dull subject matter," the "relative strength of the communications," and probably most perplexing, the "familiarity of the topic."

Controversial Topic. Along with the finding by Janis and Feierabend, [31, 32] another example of a primacy-bound variable is "controversialism." In two experiments carried out by Lana, [38] the first—using high school students as subjects—yielded no significant order effects, while the second—using college students—yielded primacy under conditions of high controversialism. Another study [44]—also using college students—yielded three out of four insignificant effects, but the one effect that was significant ($p < 0.05$) was consistent with Lana's [38] finding of primacy for topics perceived as relatively controversial in nature. Additional indirect support for that relation was the recent finding by Holz [22] of a primacy effect when Lana [38] controversially perceived "use of nuclear weapons" topic and arguments were used in a study comparing one- with two-sided communications under conditions of awareness and unawareness of the communicator's manipulatory intent. Although none of the results are as definitive as one would like them to be, they do imply a controversialism/primacy relation in persuasive communication.

Interesting Subject Matter. In another study carried out by Lana [39] both the medium of presentation of the communications as well as the interestingness of the subject matter were varied. A significant primacy effect was obtained when either moderately or highly interesting subject matter was used. Recency was obtained when communications on a topic rated uninteresting by judges were read by the communicator to the audience. However, when an impersonal mode of presentation (tape-recorded messages) was used, neither significant primacy nor significant recency was produced. One possible commonality between the present variable and the preceding one may lie in the finding that interest-evoking topics (that is, highly controversial issues and interesting subject matter) tend to yield primacy effects in opinion change, while less interesting topics tend toward recency. However, with extremely dull subject matter the audience's attention probably will be completely lost, with the result that instead of recency there will be no significant opinion change.

Assuming, then, uninteresting (but not extremely dull) subject matter, "uninterestingness" can be classified as a recency-bound variable, and "interestingness" as a primacy-bound variable.

Strong Arguments. Anderson and Hovland [6] assert that, all things being equal, opposing communications on the same issue potentially should induce an equal amount of opinion change. That is, if two communications, although they be opposite in direction, are otherwise equivalent, then a person who is subjected to both communications should in the end exhibit no significant opinion change. Since the change advocated in the first communication is in the opposite direction to the change advocated in the second one, the second effect should counteract the first. Thus, the recipient's opinions first should be moved a given amount in one direction, and then an equal amount in the opposite direction. The result should be that his opinions return to his initially stated position.

If, however, the communications are successive, then a slight recency effect is predicted. On the premise that the more opinion change asked for, the more obtained, Anderson and Hovland suggest that the first communication will move opinions a given amount, thus increasing the distance between the recipient and the second communication. If the second communication is proportionally as effective as the first, then, because more opinion change is asked for, it will have the effect of producing greater change. Hence, recency.

It was on this premise that Anderson and Hovland [6] designed a mathematical model to represent order effects induced by opposed communications. That the model has predictive validity was demonstrated by Anderson, who reported two experiments [2] to test hypotheses derived from it. Of particular interest to us in this paper is Anderson's experimental finding of a relation between the amount of opinion change and the strength of the persuasive communication.

Anderson's "strength of argument" finding is consistent with the general finding by Fisher and Lubin, [16] Fisher, Rubinstein, and Freeman, [17] Goldberg, [20] and Hovland and Pritzker [29] that the greater the amount of opinion change advocated, the greater is the amount produced.

More recently, Rosnow, Holz, and Levin [59] carried out an exploratory study to determine the effects of several interacting variables. One of them was the "strength" variable. Primarily based on the work by Anderson [2] and Hovland and Pritzker, [29] the study tested Rosnow's [56] contention that the stronger a communication is perceived, the more striking seems to be the change advocated; hence, the greater the change produced. Using a summarized law case on bigamy for the pro and con arguments, results of the study tended to support the strength hypothesis.

However, when one recalls the results obtained in the assimilation-contrast studies carried out by the Sherifs, Hovland, and their associates [65, 66] it becomes apparent that the strength/opinion change relation must be further qualified. An important finding in those studies was that under conditions of low involvement and wide discrepancy,[3] the greater was the latitude of acceptance of persuasive communication, and hence the greater tended to be the amount of opinion change produced. [18, 65] Such conditions were satisfied in the Rosnow, Holz, and Levin [59] study. Had there been greater involvement, the obtained effects might have been considerably weaker. [18, 23, 25]

Thus, at this point we are able to note several more important findings. First, "strength" can be considered a free variable. Depending upon the order

[3] This refers to the discrepancy between the recipient's own opinion and the information communicated to him.

of presentation of strong and weak arguments, a primacy *or* a recency effect can be predicted. Second, an interaction between involvement and discrepancy may sometimes serve to decrease and sometimes serve to increase opinion change. When involvement is low, and when there is wide discrepancy, opinion change will tend to be increased. [18, 65] When involvement is high, and when there is wide discrepancy, opinion change will tend to be decreased. [18, 23, 25, 65] Factors which tend to increase opinion change (by facilitating or enhancing it) and factors which tend to decrease opinion change (by weakening or suppressing it) in two-sided persuasive communication are summarized in Table 2.

TABLE 2

FACTORS WHICH RESULT IN AN INCREASE OR A DECREASE IN
OPINION CHANGE IN TWO-SIDED PERSUASIVE COMMUNICATION

Factors Associated with Incremental Changes in Opinion	*Factors Associated with Decremental Changes in Opinion*
Low involvement, wide discrepancy [65]	High involvement, wide discrepancy [65]
Need arousal followed by need-satisfying communication [12]	
Desirable message content first [51]	
	Delayed posttest opinion measurement [30, 53]
	Impersonal mode of presentation; reduced attention and/or reduced comprehension [39]
	Awareness of manipulatory intent [22, 63]
	Pretest sensitization resulting in pretest–treatment interaction [41, 44]

Familiar Topic. "Familiarity" presents us with two more examples of "bound" variables. Both Lana [37] and Rosnow and Lana [60] have found that increased familiarity with the topic (and presumably the issues) of a communication is directly related to an increased primacy effect, while decreased familiarity is related to an increased recency effect. That the familiarity relationship is perplexing, however, is evident when we consider the fact that a consistent primacy effect has been obtained in a series of personality impression-formation studies [3, 4, 5, 8, 45, 46, 47] where the topic of a pair of opposing communications dealt with the personality of a fictitious individual and, most important, where a condition of total unfamiliarity thus may be assumed.

Besides the fact that Lana and Rosnow have found a recency/unfamiliarity relation in persuasive communication and that Anderson, Barrios, Asch, and Luchins imply a primacy/unfamiliarity relation in their studies of personality impression-formation, probably the principal difference between those two groups of studies lies in the stimuli used to produce those different order effects. The former studies [37, 60] used two-sided persuasive messages, while the latter [3, 4, 5, 8, 45, 46, 47] used two-sided descriptive messages (consisting either of short passages describing the personality of an anonymous individual, or paired lists of adjectives descriptive of positive and negative personality characteristics).

Several other persuasion studies [40, 70] have found no significant relation between order effects in opinion change and familiarity with the topic. However, since neither of these latter studies [40, 70] provide any indication that the effectiveness of their communications as persuasive appeals was separately pretested, there is the possibility that their negative results were simply a function of impotent stimuli.

Moreover, since the instances of recency in impression-formation that have been reported are directly associated with variables other than "unfamiliarity," they do not provide support for either side.[4] An experiment which certainly seems to be called for is one which varies the degree of prior familiarity, but under conditions of personality impression-formation.[5]

Need Satisfying Communication.   Cohen [12] found that if a communication containing information relevant to the satisfaction of a need was presented

---

[4] For example, Weiss and Lieberman [71] reported finding "a kind of recency effect" in an impression-formation study in which they examined the possible differential effectiveness of an emotional and a nonemotional communication for inducing opinion change. Also, Anderson and Hubert [7] found that the introduction of recall tends to reduce the usual primacy effect in impression-formation, and in one study they actually were able to produce a recency effect by introducing concomitant verbal recall of adjectives and thus causing subjects to concentrate more on later presented stimuli. Similarly, Stewart [69] found a recency effect when a continuous mode of responding was utilized (but primacy, when impressions were formed after completion of all communication). Another indication of recency derives from a study by Mayo and Crockett [50] which uncovered a significant relationship for "cognitive complexity."

[5] Jeffrey Goldstein and I have just completed a pair of experiments designed to explore this very possibility, and to test a "U-curve hypothesis" intended to reconcile the apparent inconsistency between the unfamiliarity/recency finding in persuasion and the usual unfamiliarity/primacy finding implied in impression formation. The U-curve hypothesis posits a nonmonotonic curvilinear relation between the probability of occurrence of primacy–recency and the degree of familiarity with the topic. Specifically, it predicts that the probability of occurrence of primacy will be greatest when familiarity with the topic is either very high or very low, but that the probability of occurrence of recency will be greatest under conditions of moderate familiarity. Although a trend analysis failed to corroborate the hypothesis, several of our findings seem to be able to be predicted purely on the basis of the U-curve hypothesis. The decision to accept or reject the hypothesis has been deferred until more definitive experimental evidence can be gathered.

after the need had been aroused, there tended to be greater acceptance of the position advocated than in the case where need arousal followed presentation of the communication. If we consider this finding from the viewpoint of Contiguity-Reinforcement, and if we may assume (a) that the reaction that is being "strengthened" is one in response to the communications, and (b) that "reinforcement" in this situation is synonymous with need-satisfaction, then what we have is the classic finding that reinforcement is more effective for strengthening a response which has just occured (or is occurring) than one which will occur after the reinforcement.

Initial results obtained in a series of studies by Rosnow [55, 58, 61] also are consistent with that interpretation. For example, in one study Rosnow and Russell [61] found that by reading opposed persuasive communications to subjects immediately prior to the initiation of a rewarding incident, opinion was changed in the direction advocated by the one communication closer in time to the reward (recency). Also, [58] when communications were read to subjects just prior to initiation of a punishing incident, reaction to the second communication was depressed and opinion was changed in the direction of the communication farther in time from the punishment (primacy). Consistent with Cohen's [12] finding vis-a-vis Contiguity-Reinforcement, in neither one of Rosnow's studies was positive or negative reinforcement effective for influencing the direction of change when it preceded the communications.[6] Thus, we have two more examples of "bound" variables in "delayed reward" [61] and "delayed punishment." [58]

An investigation by McGuire [51] fits more within the framework of Conditioning but also provides another example of a communication-related variable. This widely known study showed that greater opinion change tends to be induced by placing highly desirable message content first, followed by less desirable message content, than using the reverse order of presentation. Both the McGuire [51] finding along with Cohen's [12] "need-arousal" may be considered examples of factors which serve to increase opinion change in two-sided persuasion, and they are listed as such in Table 2.

The Audience

Forgetting. By extending Ebbinghaus's classic forgetting curves to situations where (a) opposing arguments were presented in varied orders, (b) with

---

[6] In a more recently completed study, Rosnow [57] used an "active participation technique" (where subjects extemporaneously argued aloud in defense of both sides of a controversial issue, and where reinforcement—in the form of approval or disapproval—was interpolated among the arguments) to demonstrate both the "forward" and the "backward" effects of reinforcement on opinions to contiguous communications. Results showed that (a) when opposed communications preceded and followed "reward," opinions changed in the direction of the arguments closer in time to the reward, but (b) when opposed communications preceded and followed "punishment," opinions changed in the direction of the arguments farther in time from the punishment.

varied time intervals between the arguments, and (c) with varied times for the presentation of a criterion measurement, Miller and Campbell [53] derived and were able to test empirically a relation between order effects in attitude formation and incremental forgetting of the content of persuasive communications. One general finding in their research was that the temporal arrangement of communications and of the measurements of their effects may, in themselves, markedly alter retention, and thus affect acceptance of the message and subsequent opinion change.

Although the Ebbinghaus curves suggested to the investigators several additional findings, at least two empirical relationships emerge from the Miller and Campbell experiment, both of which subsequently were replicated by Insko. [30] The first relationship identifies another recency-bound variable (see Table 1) in persuasive communication: the longer the time interval between two communications the greater the recency effect after the second communications. The second relationship identifies a factor which can result in a weakened recency (see Table 2): the longer the time elapsed from the second communication until measurement the less the recency effect.[7]

Commitment. An assumption made by Miller and Campbell [53] was that a first communication is differentially more potent than a second (either successive or delayed) communication because of factors associated with prior entry. Mindful of that assumption and accepting, therefore, their idea that a higher asymptote will be associated with the primary communication, then their prediction of primacy for a delayed criterion measurement can be derived from Jost's [33] Second Law.[8] Though Insko's [30] attempt to produce the implied primacy was unsuccessful, there is common sense support for the notion of greater potency for primary communication. This is especially true when we consider the possibility that once having been presented with the initial persuasive appeal the audience may make commitments to the position advocated, and thereby "freeze" their own position and lead them to reject any subsequent counterappeal.

Tentative experimental support for the hypothesis that commitment may effectively strengthen an attitude can be derived from the results of an experiment by Bennett [10] (where commitment was in the form of a decision regarding a future action), and, in the primacy-recency situation, indirect evidence is the Hovland, Campbell, and Brock [24] finding that if after hearing only one side of a controversial issue the recipient indicates his own position, then the impact of the second-presented side will be reduced. However, the

---

[7] A third relationship receives tentative support from an earlier study by Bateman and Remmers [9] but is contradicted by Insko's [30] findings: the greater the delay in measurement after the second of two successive communications the greater the chance of primacy (because of a reduced rate of decay due to the higher asymptote associated with prior entry of the first communication).

[8] Jost's Second Law states that of two associations equally strong at the moment, the newer will decay more rapidly than the older.

mere act of stating one's opinions on an anonymous questionnaire will not necessarily cause such a primacy effect to occur. [27]

The Medium of Presentation

There has been a conspicuous dearth of experimental research in primacy-recency on factors related to the medium of presentation of persuasive communications. That the medium of presentation is an important factor, and one which needs to be systematically probed, is apparent when we consider the possibility that the medium may in part, or even altogether, influence the general effectiveness of the communication as a persuasive appeal.

If one may assume that variables such as "attention" (to the communicator) and "comprehension" (of the message) are "necessary conditions"[9] to be satisfied for there to be opinion-attitude change in persuasive communication, then one may conclude that the role played by the medium is an important one in determining whether or not those conditions will be satisfied. An impersonal mode of presentation may produce conditions unsatisfactory for eliciting attention or (in the absence of feedback) facilitating comprehension. In that case an otherwise perfectly effective communication may prove completely impotent.

Evidence tentatively in support of such a hypothesis is the recent finding by Lana [39] cited earlier in this paper. When subjects listened to a communicator read aloud a pair of opposed persuasive communications, Lana found significant order effects associated with the factor of interest. However, when opposed communications were delivered through a more impersonal medium (a taped recording), primacy in opinion change was found for a moderate interest topic, but neither primacy nor recency was found for a high interset one. There are at least two alternative interpretations that can be offered: (a) either the personal mode of presentation facilitated opinion change by enhancing attention, or (and probably more plausible) (b) the impersonal mode of presentation artificially reduced opinion change by depressing attention. Obviously further experimentation using varied modes of presentation is needed.

Miscellaneous Effects Associated with Primacy-Recency

When an audience is confronted with a communicator whose intention it is to persuade its members to modify their attitudes about a particular controversial issue, the reactions will depend to a considerable extent not only on

[9] "Necessary conditions" are those which are absolutely required in order for there to be opinion–attitude change in persuasive communication. "Sufficient conditions" would be those which, if given, and assuming that necessary conditions were satisfied, would lead to the effect in question; for example, "familiarity" is "sufficient" to produce primacy *if* the subject attends to and comprehends the communication ("attention" and "comprehension" are "necessary conditions").

what the communicator has to say but also on the conditions under which he says it. We already have noted how the mere order of presentation of strong and weak arguments, [59] of pro and nonsalient con communications, [31, 32] and of desirable and undesirable message content [51] can affect both the direction as well as the amount of change or compliance desired.

Awareness of Manipulatory Intent.   Theoretically, innumerable extrinsic variables may influence the effectiveness of two-sided persuasive communication. We know from research on one-sided communication that when members of the audience are cognizant of the fact that someone intends to influence them, the communicator's persuasive efforts may tend to make them suspicious and hostile. This will usually lead to increased resistance, with the result that the effectiveness of the communicator's persuasive appeal will be reduced. [1, 19] It is also possible that an awareness of the manipulatory intent of the communicator may result in an overreaction to the communication, particularly when the communicator is attractive and when he states frankly his desire to influence the audience. [54]

In two-sided communication, however, the effect of awareness of manipulatory intent seems to work differently. Instead of facilitating opinion change, awareness appears to depress it. [22, 63] Unlike one-sided communication, where the audience may quite simply conclude that the side which is presented is the one held by the communicator himself, in two-sided communication it is unlikely that the audience will be able to associate a particular side with the communicator's personal beliefs. Moreover, since the communicator presents opposing sides, not only is there an absence of implicit endorsement of one or the other side by him, but the presentation of both points of view may imply to the audience that he holds neither side to be representative of his own attitude on the topic. Thus the benefits derived from having an attractive, credible communicator deliver a persuasive appeal may be altogether lost in two-sided communication, except under the conditions used by Janis and Feierabend [31, 32] in their study cited earlier.

At least two hypotheses are suggested, and although there is some tentative support for them in the findings by Holz [22] and Schultz, [63] more definitive support would be highly desirable: (a) One-sided persuasive communication is more effective than two-sided persuasive communication when the audience is aware of the manipulatory intent of the communicator. (b) Two-sided persuasive communication is more effective than one-sided persuasive communication when the audience is unaware of the manipulatory intent of the communicator.

Pretest Sensitization.   A more basic methodological problem is the one associated with pretest sensitization and the contaminating effects resulting from pretest-treatment interaction.

In a series of studies on one-sided communication by Lana, based on the conceptualization and analysis of the problem by Solomon [68] and Campbell,

[11] no interaction effect was found between pretest and treatment when the pretest was an opinion questionnaire, [35, 36] although pretest sensitization was indicated when the posttest responses were a direct result of learning. [43][10] More recently, however, in research on two-sided communication, Lana and Rosnow [44] found that the act of responding to the pretest may markedly influence responses to a posttest. When a disguised pretest, in the form of opinion items embedded in a regularly scheduled classroom examination, was used prior to the presentation of opposed communications, a strong primacy effect occurred. When the more customary exposed pretest was used, no order effect occurred.

Lana [41] suggests that the pretest may be considered a set-producing task which renders ineffective in changing opinions the presentation of succeeding material. Thus, he concludes that the first communication in a set of two should be more influential in changing opinion in the direction of its argument than should a communication which was preceded by a pretest relevant to the same topic. In an experiment specifically designed to test that particular hypothesis, Lana [41] again found that the pretest tends to have a depressive effect on opinion change in the usual primacy-recency type design (see Table 2). The pretest interaction problem is an intriguing and important one, and findings could weigh heavily as design considerations for future research in primacy-recency.

CONCLUSIONS

We have noted some of the more perplexing problems associated with the primacy-recency phenomenon in persuasion. Variables such as "commitment," "familiarity," "pretest sensitization," and "audience awareness" involve subtle relationships, and it will be a difficult task to delineate their effects conclusively in one or even a few studies. Patient, systematic research will be required.

There are other variables where relationships seem clear-cut perhaps only because of the absence of systematic probing of their effects. For example, although communication-related variables in general have been the subject of many fascinating and widely quoted experiments, in primacy-recency the only relevant study that could be found is the one by Janis and Feierabend. [32] Even though the Janis and Feierabend experiment is an interesting and an important one, it leaves us with many more questions than it is able to answer. This is similarly true of Lana's [39] experiment varying the medium of presentation. One can only speculate at this point about the role of the me-

---

[10] Other indications of pretest sensitization or pretest–treatment interaction outside the context of primacy–recency are reported in the work by Entwisle [14, 15] and Hicks and Spaner. [21]

dium in primacy-recency. More empirical data is needed, and further experimental investigation is clearly called for.

But it also probably would prove worthwhile to systematically replicate almost all of the other studies discussed in this paper. The findings from those replications would in some instances extend the principles already identified, in other instances qualify their generalizations, but in all instances—whether or not the findings confirm or contradict the earlier results—they would aid prediction immeasurably.

It is important to probe further the effects associated with each of those independent variables, but it is equally important to determine the effects of interactions.[11] We often hear the warning that it is hazardous to generalize the results obtained in experimental research (where one independent variable at a time is manipulated) to the field persuasion situation (where a variety of observable and nonobservable independent variables and countless extraneous factors may all be interacting). The research that is suggested would be designed to determine the effects of interactions of primacy-bound, recency-bound, and free variables as well as interactions between and among factors associated with incremental or decremental changes in opinion. The findings should make it easier to translate laboratory results into field experiences, and perhaps even vice versa.

REFERENCES

1. ALLYN, JANE and LEON FESTINGER. "The effectiveness of unanticipated persuasive communications." *Journal of Abnormal and Social Psychology* 62 (1961) 35–40.
2. ANDERSON, NORMAN H. "Test of a model for opinion change." *Journal of Abnormal and Social Psychology* 59 (1959) 371–381.
3. ———. "Application of an additive model to impression formation." *Science* 138 (1962) 817–818.
4. ———. "Primacy effects in personality impression formation using a generalized order effect paradigm." *Journal of Personality and Social Psychology* 2 (1965) 1–9.

[11] An example of such an investigation is one reported recently by Rosnow and Lana. [60] The study, designed to determine the effects of interactions between the variables "familiarity" and "reinforcement," varied (a) the order of presentation of opposed communications, (b) the familiarity of the audience with the topic, and (c) the temporal placement of the reinforcement. Results indicated that when complementary variables interacted, the expected order effects were consistently obtained. For example, when "reward" immediately *followed* presentation of opposed communications on an *unfamiliar* topic, recency was obtained. Similarly, when reward immediately *preceded* presentation of opposed communications on a *familiar* topic, primacy was obtained. In the first case, the complementary recency-bound variables "unfamiliarity" and "delayed reward" yielded recency; in the second, the complementary primacy-bound variables yielded primacy. Moreover, it was found that when competing variables interacted (i.e., when a primacy-bound variable interacted with a recency-bound variable), no significant opinion change was produced.

5. ANDERSON, NORMAN H. and ALFRED A. BARRIOS. "Primacy effects in personality impression formation." *Journal of Abnormal and Social Psychology* 63 (1961) 346–350.

6. ANDERSON, NORMAN H. and CARL I. HOVLAND. "The representation of order effects in communication research." *The Order of Presentation in Persuasion*, Carl I. Hovland *et al.* New Haven: Yale University Press, 1957, pp. 158–169.

7. ANDERSON, NORMAN H. and STEPHEN HUBERT. "Effects of concomitant verbal recall on order effects in personality impression formation." *Journal of Verbal Learning and Verbal Behavior* 2 (1963) 379–391.

8. ASCH, SOLOMON E. "Forming impressions of personality." *Journal of Abnormal and Social Psychology* 41 (1946) 258–290.

9. BATEMAN, RICHARD M. and H. H. REMMERS. "A study of the shifting attitude of high school students when subjected to favorable and unfavorable propaganda." *Journal of Social Psychology* 13 (1941) 395–406.

10. BENNETT, EDITH BECKER. "Discussion, decision, commitment, and consensus in group decision." *Human Relations* 8 (1955) 251–274.

11. CAMPBELL, DONALD T. "Factors relative to the validity of experiments in social settings." *Psychological Bulletin* 54 (1957) 297–312.

12. COHEN, ARTHUR R. "Need for cognition and order of communication as determinants of opinion change." *The Order of Presentation in Persuasion*, Carl I. Hovland *et al.* New Haven: Yale University Press, 1957, pp. 79–97.

13. CROMWELL, HARVEY. "The relative effect on audience attitude of the first versus the second argumentative speech of a series." *Speech Monographs* 17 (1950) 105–122.

14. ENTWISLE, DORIS R. "Attensity: factors of specific set in school learning." *Harvard Educational Review* 31 (1961) 84–101.

15. ———. "Interaction effects of pretesting." *Educational and Psychological Measurement* 21 (1961) 607–620.

16. FISHER, SEYMOUR and ARDIE LUBIN. "Distance as a determinant of influence in a two-person serial interaction situation." *Journal of Abnormal and Social Psychology* 56 (1958) 230–238.

17. FISHER, SEYMOUR, IRVIN RUBINSTEIN, and ROBERT W. FREEMAN. "Intertrial effects of immediate self-committal in a continuous social influence situation." *Journal of Abnormal and Social Pscychology* 52 (1956) 200–207.

18. FREEDMAN, JONATHAN. "Involvement, distraction, and change." *Journal of Abnormal and Social Psychology* 69 (1964) 290–295.

19. FREEDMAN, JONATHAN L. and DAVID O. SEARS. "Warning, distraction, and resistance to influence." *Journal of Personality and Social Psychology* 1 (1965) 262–266.

20. GOLDBERG, SOLOMON C. "Three situational determinants of conformity to social norms." *Journal of Abnormal and Social Psychology* 49 (1954) 325–329.

21. HICKS, JACK M. and FRED E. SPANER. "Attitude change and hospital experience." *Journal of Abnormal and Social Psychology* 65 (1962) 112–120.

22. HOLZ, ROBERT F. "An experimental investigation of the influence of awareness of manipulatory intent on reactions to persuasive communications." Unpublished Master's thesis, Boston University School of Public Communication, 1965.

23. HOVLAND, CARL I. "Reconciling conflicting results derived from experimental and survey studies of attitude change." *American Psychologist* 14 (1959) 8–17.

24. HOVLAND, CARL I., ENID H. CAMPBELL, and TIMOTHY BROCK. "The effects of commitment on opinion change following communication." *The Order of Presentation in Persuasion*, Carl I. Hovland *et al*. New Haven: Yale University Press, 1957, pp. 23–32.

25. HOVLAND, CARL I., O. J. HARVEY, and MUZAFER SHERIF. "Assimilation and contrast effects in reactions to communication and attitude change." *Journal of Abnormal and Social Psychology* 55 (1957) 244–252.

26. HOVLAND, CARL I., ARTHUR A. LUMSDAINE, and FRED D. SHEFFIELD. "Experiments on mass communication." *Studies in Social Psychology in World War II*, Volume 2. Princeton: Princeton University Press, 1949, pp. 201–227.

27. HOVLAND, CARL I. and WALLACE MANDELL. "Is there a law of primacy in persuasion?" *The Order of Presentation in Persuasion*, Carl I. Hovland *et al*. New Haven: Yale University Press, 1957, pp. 13–22.

28. HOVLAND, CARL I., WALLACE MANDELL, ENID H. CAMPBELL, TIMOTHY BROCK, ABRAHAM S. LUCHINS, ARTHUR R. COHEN, WILLIAM J. MCGUIRE, IRVING L. JANIS, ROSALIND L. FEIERABEND, and NORMAN H. ANDERSON. *The Order of Presentation in Persuasion*. New Haven: Yale University Press, 1957.

29. HOVLAND, CARL I. and HENRY A. PRITZKER. "Extent of opinion change as a function of amount of change advocated." *Journal of Abnormal and Social Psychology* 54 (1957) 257–261.

30. INSKO, CHESTER A. "Primacy versus recency in persuasion as a function of the timing of arguments and measures." *Journal of Abnormal and Social Psychology* 69 (1964) 381–391.

31. JANIS, IRVING L. "Motivational effects of different sequential arrangements of conflicting arguments: a theoretical analysis." *The Order of Presentation in Persuasion*, Carl I. Hovland *et al*. New Haven: Yale University Press, 1957, pp. 170–186.

32. JANIS, IRVING L. and ROSALIND L. FEIERABEND. "Effects of alternative ways of ordering pro and con arguments in persuasive communications." *The Order of Presentation in Persuasion*, Carl I. Hovland *et al*. New Haven: Yale University Press, 1957, pp. 115–128.

33. JOST, ADOLPH. "Die Assoziationsfestigkeit in ihrer Abhangigkeit von der Verteilung der Wiederholungen." *Zeitschrift für Psychologie und Physiologie der Sinnesorgane* 14 (1897) 436–472.

34. KNOWER, F. H. "Experimental studies of changes in attitudes. II. a study of the effect of printed argument on changes in attitude." *Journal of Abnormal and Social Psychology* 30 (1936) 522–532.

35. LANA, ROBERT E. "A further investigation of the pretest-treatment interaction effect." *Journal of Applied Psychology* 43 (1959) 421–422.

36. ———. "Pretest-treatment interaction effects in attitudinal studies." *Psychological Bulletin* 56 (1959) 293–300.

37. ———. "Familiarity and the order of presentation of persuasive communications." *Journal of Abnormal and Social Psychology* 62 (1961) 573–577.

38. ———. "Controversy of the topic and the order of presentation in persuasive communications." *Psychological Reports* 12 (1963) 163–170.

39. ———. "Interest, media, and order effects in persuasive communications." *Journal of Psychology* 56 (1963) 9–13.

40. ————. "Existing familiarity and order of presentation of persuasive communications." *Psychological Reports* 15 (1964) 607–610.

41. ————. "The influence of the pretest on order effects in persuasive communications." *Journal of Abnormal and Social Psychology* 69 (1964) 337–341.

42. ————. "Three theoretical interpretations of order effects in persuasive communications." *Psychological Bulletin* 61 (1964) 314–320.

43. LANA, ROBERT E. and DAVID J. KING. "Learning factors as determiners of pretest sensitization." *Journal of Applied Psychology* 44 (1960) 189–191.

44. LANA, ROBERT E. and RALPH L. ROSNOW. "Subject awareness and order effects in persuasive communications." *Psychological Reports* 12 (1963) 523–529.

45. LUCHINS, ABRAHAM S. "Experimental attempts to minimize the impact of first impressions." *The Order of Presentation in Persuasion*, Carl I. Hovland *et al.* New Haven: Yale University Press, 1957, pp. 62–75.

46. ————. "Primacy–recency in impression formation." *The Order of Presentation in Persuasion*, Carl I. Hovland *et al.* New Haven: Yale University Press, 1957, pp. 33–61.

47. ————. "Definitiveness of impression and primacy–recency in communications." *Journal of Social Psychology* 48 (1958) 275–290.

48. LUMSDAINE, ARTHUR A. and IRVING L. JANIS. "Resistance to 'counterpropaganda' produced by one-sided and two-sided 'propaganda' presentations." *Public Opinion Quarterly* 17 (1953) 311–318.

49. LUND, F. H. "The psychology of belief: a study of its emotional and volitional determinants." *Journal of Abnormal and Social Psychology* 20 (1925) 174–196.

50. MAYO, CLARA W. and WALTER H. CROCKETT. "Cognitive complexity and primacy–recency effects in impression formation." *Journal of Abnormal and Social Psychology* 68 (1964) 335–338.

51. McGUIRE, WILLIAM J. "Order of presentation as a factor in 'conditioning' persuasiveness." *The Order of Presentation in Persuasion*, Carl I. Hovland *et al.* New Haven: Yale University Press, 1957, pp. 98–114.

52. ————. "Attitudes and opinions." *Annual Review of Psychology* Volume 17. Palo Alto: Annual Reviews Incorporated, 1966, pp. 475–514.

53. MILLER, NORMAN and DONALD T. CAMPBELL. "Recency and primacy in persuasion as a function of the timing of speeches and measurements." *Journal of Abnormal and Social Psychology* 59 (1959) 1–9.

54. MILLS, JUDSON and ELLIOT ARONSON. "Opinion change as a function of the communicator's attractiveness and desire to influence." *Journal of Personality and Social Psychology* 1 (1965) 173–177.

55. ROSNOW, RALPH L. "A spread-of-effect in persuasive communication?" Paper read at the Eastern Psychological Association, Philadelphia, April, 1964.

56. ————. "An 'order effect hierarchy' in attitude formation?" Paper read at the Eastern Psychological Association, Atlantic City, April, 1965.

57. ————. " 'Conditioning' the direction of opinion change in persuasive communication." *Journal of Social Psychology*. (In press.)

58. ————. "A delay-of-reinforcement effect in persuasive communication?" *Journal of Social Psychology* 67 (1965) 39–43.

59. ROSNOW, RALPH L., ROBERT F. HOLZ, and JACK LEVIN. "Differential effects of complementary and competing variables in primacy–recency." *Journal of Social Psychology*. (In press.)

60. Rosnow, Ralph L. and Robert E. Lana. "Complementary and competing-order effects in opinion change." *Journal of Social Psychology* 66 (1965) 201–207.

61. Rosnow, Ralph L. and Gordon Russell. "Spread of effect of reinforcement in persuasive communication." *Psychological Reports* 12 (1963) 731–735.

62. Schultz, Duane P. "Primacy–recency within a sensory variation framework." *Psychological Record* 13 (1963) 129–139.

63. ———. "Time, awareness, and order of presentation in opinion change." *Journal of Applied Psychology* 47 (1963) 280–283.

64. ———. "Spontaneous alternation behavior in humans: implications for psychological research." *Psychological Bulletin* 62 (1964) 394–400.

65. Sherif, Carolyn, Muzafer Sherif, and Roger E. Nebergall. *Attitude and Attitude Change*. Philadelphia: Saunders Company, 1965.

66. Sherif, Muzafer and Carl I. Hovland. *Social Judgment*. New Haven: Yale University Press, 1961.

67. Smith, Bruce Lannes, Harold D. Lasswell, and Ralph D. Casey. *Propaganda, Communication, and Public Opinion*. Princeton: Princeton University Press, 1946.

68. Solomon, Richard L. "An extension of control group design." *Psychological Bulletin* 46 (1949) 137–150.

69. Stewart, Ralph H. "Effect of continuous responding on the order effect in personality impression formation." *Journal of Personality and Social Psychology* 1 (1965) 161–165.

70. Thomas, Edwin J., Susan Webb, and Jean Tweedie. "Effects of familiarity with a controversial issue on acceptance of successive persuasive communications." *Journal of Abnormal and Social Psychology* 63 (1961) 656–659.

71. Weiss, Walter and Bernhardt Lieberman. "The effects of 'emotional' language on the induction and change of opinions." *Journal of Social Psychology* 50 (1959) 129–141.

J. W. Koehler

EFFECTS ON AUDIENCE OPINION OF ONE-SIDED AND TWO-SIDED SPEECHES SUPPORTING AND OPPOSING A PROPOSITION[1]

INTRODUCTION

In 1945, Hovland, Lumsdaine and Sheffield (1949) set forth to explore the following question:

> When the weight of evidence supports the main thesis being presented, is it more effective to present only the material supporting the point being made, or is it better to introduce also the arguments of those opposed to the point being made? (p. 201)

This question, almost as old as rhetorical inquiry itself, is important because it probes into the way a speaker deals with audience viewpoints which are contrary to what he advocates. Aristotle, over two thousand years ago, advised speakers to meet the opposing arguments by direct refutation or by "pulling

[1] A paper presented to the Behavioral Sciences Interest Group of the Speech Association of America, December 29, 1968, by Dr. J. W. Koehler, California State College, Fullerton.

Reprinted with permission of the author.

them to pieces in advance." (Cooper, 1932, p. 235) Rhetoricians have continued to take that view. Winans (1915, p. 259), for example, suggested that "when objections are certainly in your hearers' mind recognize them and answer them directly..." Contemporary theorists such as Bettinghaus (1968), relying on experimental testing of such an hypothesis, have begun to qualify the conditions under which both sides of an issue should be presented by a communicator.

In their research, Hovland, Lumsdaine and Sheffield found that a presentation including only the material supporting the point being made (one-sided speech) was more effective in changing opinions when (a) the audience initially agrees with the position advocated by the speaker, and when (b) the audience consisted of people with less than a high school education. A presentation which included material supporting the point being made and also a discussion of opposing arguments (two-sided speech) was more effective in changing opinions when (a) the audience initially opposed the position advocated by the speaker, and when (b) the audience consisted of people with more than a high school education.

Lumsdaine and Janis (1953) extended the preceding study by comparing the effects of a one-sided and a two-sided presentation when followed by a "later" opposing communication. Their results revealed that when the audience was subsequently exposed to a communication advocating a point of view opposing that taken by a previous speaker, the previous speaker was more effective in changing opinions when he presented a two-sided rather than a one-sided speech.

The above findings, although tentative, present some insight into the effects of an initial speaker employing a one-sided or a two-sided communication. Lumsdaine and Janis (1953), one of the studies cited above, employed a subsequent opposing speaker. However, their study was mainly concerned with the effects of a later countercommunication on listeners who had previously heard a one-sided speech compared to those who heard a two-sided speech. They were not concerned with the differential effects of a subsequent opposing speaker employing a one-sided or a two-sided speech.

The present study investigated the effects of a one-sided and a two-sided speech employed by an opposing speaker. The problem is similar to the one which interested Hovland and others (1949) during World War II. Whereas Hovland and his associates focused on the effects of an *initial speaker* employing a one-sided or a two-sided communication, this study focuses on the effects of an *opposing speaker* employing a one-sided or a two-sided speech. That is, if a speaker presents a speech which is followed by another speaker advocating an opposite point of view, would the second speaker be more effective in changing audience opinions in the desired direction if he employed a one-sided or a two-sided speech?

Another problem examined in this study is source credibility, or ethos. Aristotle averred that the character of the speaker (ethos) is, under some circumstances, the most potent of all the means of persuasion. His statement as to the persuasiveness of the communicator himself (ethos) has been cited often.

> The character of the speaker is a cause of persuasion when the speech is so uttered as to make him worthy of belief; for as a rule we trust men of probity more, and more quickly, about things in general, while on points outside the realm of exact knowledge, where opinion is divided, we trust them absolutely. (Cooper, 1932, p. 8)

Modern writers in persuasion have found little reason to disagree. It is reasonably well established, for example, that a communicator can move an audience further in the direction he advocates if he is positively perceived by members of the audience. The study of Hovland and Weiss (1951) in which they attributed identical communications to both "high" and "low" credibility sources is a case in point. For the most part, high credibility sources were positively correlated with significantly greater opinion change.

Since ethos is a factor making for success in a persuasive communication, research to find those variables which may increase or decrease the ethos of the speaker has been carried out. For example, Bettinghaus (1961) investigated five variables believed responsible for attitude change, one of which was the speaker's delivery. The researcher stated that:

> The experiment tends to confirm what rhetorical theorists have said for centuries: that effectiveness in delivery contributes not only to credibility of the speaker but also to the persuasiveness of the speaker in achieving acceptance of his message. (p. 141)

McCroskey (1966) in his study on ethos and evidence concluded the following:

> . . . that good use of evidence can be an important asset to a speaker who wishes to produce favorable immediate post-communication audience attitudes toward his propositions. This will likely be the case for speeches on some topics which the speaker is a moderate-to-low-ethos communicator. (p. 124)

These studies indicate that ethos interacts with other variables involved within the actual speech. Therefore, it seems plausible that the one-sided versus the two-sided variable is factor which may increase or decrease the ethos of a speaker. It seems reasonable that audience members would perceive a speaker as having higher ethos if he included a discussion of opposing arguments rather than simply presenting arguments which exclusively support his position.

HYPOTHESES INVESTIGATED

Primary Hypotheses:

OPINION CHANGE

1. A two-sided initial speech is more effective in changing opinions of listeners in the direction advocated than a one-sided initial speech.
2. A two-sided initial speech is more effective in changing opinions of listeners in the direction advocated than a one-sided initial speech when listeners are exposed to an immediate opposing speech.
3. A two-sided initial speech is more effective in changing opinions of listeners in the direction advocated than a one-sided initial speech when listeners are exposed to a delayed opposing speech.
4. A two-sided initial speech is more effective in changing opinions of listeners in the direction advocated than a one-sided initial speech when opinions are tested two and one-half weeks after listeners are exposed to an opposing speech.
5. A two-sided immediate opposing speech is more effective in changing opinions of listeners in the direction advocated than a one-sided immediate opposing speech.
6. A two-sided delayed opposing speech is more effective in changing opinions of listeners in the direction advocated than a one-sided delayed opposing speech.

ETHOS HYPOTHESES

7. A speaker employing a two-sided initial speech is perceived by listeners as having higher ethos than a speaker employing a one-sided initial speech.
8. A speaker employing a two-sided opposing speech is perceived by listeners as having higher ethos than a speaker employing a one-sided opposing speech.

RESEARCH DESIGN

The present study was designed to investigate the differential effects of a speaker employing a one-sided or a two-sided speech opposing a point of view advocated by a previous speaker. The basic procedure was to present a persuasive one-sided or a two-sided speech, followed by a one-sided or two-sided opposing speech. Students enrolled in the basic speech course at The Pennsylvania State University served as experimental subjects. Opinions towards the topic and the speakers were measured by the semantic differential.

Ten audiences were chosen by randomly assigning forty-four sections of Speech 200 students to groups. Two of the audiences, plus three additional sections constituted control groups. The two control group audiences were exposed only to the initial one-sided or two-sided speech. The three additional sections heard no speech. Each audience assigned to the experimental treatments heard two speeches, an initial speech and an opposing speech.

The initial speech advocated the proposition, that is, that all citizens should be guaranteed an annual minimum cash income. The opposing speech advocated the rejection of the proposition. In treatments I and II, the initial speaker presented a one-sided speech. In treatments III and IV, the initial speakcr prcsented a two-sided speech. The opposing speaker presented a one-sided speech in treatments I and III, and a two-sided speech in treatments II and IV. In treatments I, II, III, and IV, the time interval between the initial speech and the opposing speech was approximately ten minutes. The type of treatment administered in each of these groups is shown in the following table:

TABLE 1

TYPE OF TREATMENT ADMINISTERED
TO GROUPS I, II, III, AND IV

Group I	*Group II*
Initial Speaker—One-Sided (For)	Initial Speaker—One-Sided (For)
Opposing Speaker—One-Sided (Against)	Opposing Speaker—Two-Sided (Against)

Group III	*Group IV*
Initial Speaker—Two-Sided (For)	Initial Speaker—Two-Sided (For)
Opposing Speaker—One-Sided (Against)	Opposing Speaker—Two-Sided (Against)

Four more audiences were exposed to the treatments as shown in Table 1, except the time interval between the initial speaker and the opposing speaker was one week. This is shown in the following table:

TABLE 2

TYPE OF TREATMENT ADMINISTERED
TO GROUPS V, VI, VII, and VIII

Group V	*Group VI*
Initial Speaker—One-Sided (For)	Initial Speaker—One-Sided (For)
Time Interval: One Week	Time Interval: One Week
Opposing Speaker—One-Sided (Against)	Opposing Speaker—Two-Sided (Against)

Group VII	*Group VIII*
Initial Speaker—Two-Sided (For)	Initial Speaker—Two-Sided (For)
Time Interval: One Week	Time Interval: One Week
Opposing Speaker—One-Sided (Against)	Opposing Speaker—Two-Sided (Against)

Two audiences were exposed to only the initial speaker. These audiences served as one of the control groups. One audience heard the initial one-sided speech, and the other audience heard the initial two-sided speech. This is shown in Table 3.

TABLE 3

TYPE OF TREATMENT ADMINISTERED
TO CONTROL GROUP AUDIENCES

Audience I	*Audience II*
Initial Speaker—One-Sided	Initial Speaker—Two-Sided
(For)	(For)

Subjects in forty-seven Speech 200 sections, including control groups, were administered semantic differential pretests on the topic employed in the experiment. Subjects who were exposed to the various experimental treatments were given opinion and ethos scales immediately following the initial speech (first posttest), immediately following the opposing speech (second posttest), and two and one half weeks later (delayed posttest). The administration of opinion and ethos scales is shown in Table 4.

Two control groups were employed. In one control group, subjects did not hear any speech. They were given opinion scales at approximately the same times as the scales were given to subjects receiving experimental treat-

TABLE 4

ADMINISTRATION OF OPINION SCALES AND ETHOS SCALES

Groups	1	2	3	4	5	6	7	8	9	10	11
Pretest OS	X	X	X	X	X	X	X	X	X	X	X
Initial Speech	S	S	S	S	S	S	S	S	S	S	
First Posttest OS, ES	X	X	X	X	X	X	X	X	X	X	X
Opposing Speech (Immediate)	S	S	S	S							
Second Posttest OS, ES	X	X	X	X					X	X	
Opposing Speech (Week Later)					S	S	S	S			
Second Posttest OS, ES					X	X	X	X			
Delayed Posttest ($2\frac{1}{2}$ weeks after Opposing Speech) OS	X	X	X	X	X	X	X	X			X

OS: Semantic Differential Opinion Scale
ES: Semantic Differential Ethos Scale

ments. The other control group consisted of two audiences. One audience was exposed to the initial one-sided speech, while the other was exposed to the initial two-sided speech. They were given opinion and ethos scales at the conclusion of the speech and one week later.

DEVELOPMENT OF EXPERIMENTAL SPEECHES

The experimental speeches were developed with the following taken into account: (1) topic; (2) speakers; (3) introductions; (4) mode of communication; and (5) arrangement of arguments.

1. Topic. "Guarantee all Citizens a Minimum Annual Cash Income" was selected as the proposition to be discussed by both speakers. A preliminary study conducted by the writer revealed that very few of the students surveyed either strongly agreed or strongly disagreed with the proposition.

2. Speakers. Two speakers were selected to record the experimental speeches. One speaker was selected to record both the one-sided and two-sided initial speeches. The other speaker recorded both the one-sided and two-sided opposing speeches. Five graduate students in the Speech Department of The Pennsylvania State University were asked to record approximately three minutes of text from an issue of New York Times Magazine. These recordings were played in random order to two sections of students in Speech 200. After listening to the tapes, the students were asked to evaluate the presentation of each speaker. The two speakers rated most similar in effectiveness were selected to record the experimental speeches.

3. Introductions. The initial and opposing speakers were introduced as graduate students in Sociology at The Pennsylvania State University and presently writing dissertations for their Ph.D.'s. The only difference between their introductions was in their "names" and the title of the dissertation they were writing.

4. Mode of Communication. In order to control extraneous variables and to provide identical one-sided and two-sided speeches for the experimental conditions, the communications were tape recorded. The initial one-sided speech was approximately nineteen minutes in length, while the two-sided initial speech was twenty-two minutes. The opposing one-sided speech was approximately eighteen minutes in length, while the two-sided opposing speech was twenty-two minutes in length.

5. Arrangement of Arguments. A study conducted by Jaksa (1964) revealed that the two-sided climactic and the two-sided interwoven orders of counter-arguments were significantly superior in changing opinions to one-sided or two-sided speeches with an anti-climactic order of counter-arguments. Based on these results, the two-sided interwoven order of presenting counter-arguments was used in the speeches composed for this study.

RESULTS: OPINION CHANGE
HYPOTHESES

Hypothesis one was not confirmed. Table 5 shows the mean opinion scores obtained from subjects who heard a one-sided initial speech and subjects who heard a two-sided initial speech. In this instance, the higher the score, the more the opinion is in the direction advocated by the initial speech. This analysis indicates that, in terms of opinion change measured immediately after the speech, a two-sided initial speech was *not* significantly more effective than a one-sided initial speech, although the trend in the data was in that direction.

Hypothesis two was partially confirmed. Results of three factor analysis of covariance produced a significant interaction between the type of speeches and the order in which subjects heard them.[1]

TABLE 5

MEAN OPINION SCORES FOR SUBJECTS
WHO HEARD A ONE-SIDED INITIAL SPEECH VERSUS
SUBJECTS WHO HEARD A TWO-SIDED INITIAL SPEECH

Mean Opinion Scores After Initial Speech					
One-Sided Initial Speech		Two-Sided Initial Speech			
N	Mean	N	Mean	$\bar{D}$	t	P
180	26.7	180	27.5	.8	1.19	< .23

Pretest Mean Scores Before Initial Speech
Equalized by Covariance

Note—The higher the score, the greater opinion change in the direction advocated by the initial speech. The hypothetical neutral point on the scale is 24.0.

[1] Three factor analysis of covariance, with opinion scores obtained after the initial speech equalized by covariance, produced a significant interaction (F = 4.85) between the type of initial speech, type of opposing speech, and the time separating the initial and opposing speeches. Results of the interaction disclosed that it made a significant difference in the opinion response of subjects depending on the *type of initial speech*, one-sided or two-sided, the *type of opposing speech*, one-sided or two-sided, and *when* they heard the opposing speech, immediately after the initial speech, or one week later. To demonstrate the significance of these differences, t-tests comparing mean opinion scores obtained in each group are computed. The F score cited above also indicated the interaction involved in testing hypotheses three, five, and six, and therefore, were investigated accordingly.

Table 6 illustrates the four sequences to which four groups of subjects were exposed and the mean opinion scores that resulted. The table shows that the group who heard an initial one-sided speech on the topic shifted away from that opinion after subsequently hearing an opposing speech that was two-sided. The mean score of 16.8 indicates the largest vulnerability to opposing persuasion. The group who heard a one-sided initial speech and a one-sided opposing speech showed less change at 20.9. Among the two groups who heard a two-sided initial speech advocating a minimum annual cash income, there was a general change away from that position after hearing a one-sided or a two-sided opposing speech, but no significant difference between them.

Hypothesis three was partially confirmed. Table 7 shows that subjects who heard a one-sided initial speech changed their opinions in the direction supported in the delayed one-sided opposing speech to a mean score of 15.5 while subjects who heard a two-sided initial speech changed their opinions in the direction supported by the same type of opposing speech to a mean score of 17.3. The mean difference between the two scores yielded 1.8 units which is statistically significant within the .05 level. The two-sided initial speech was significantly more effective in changing opinions of listeners in the direction advocated than a one-sided initial speech *when followed a week later* by a one-sided opposing speech.

Table 7 also illustrates that neither the two-sided nor the one-sided initial speech was significantly more effective in maintaining opinion change when followed by a delayed two-sided speech.

Hypothesis four was confirmed. Results of a three factor analysis of covariance, with mean opinion scores obtained prior to the initial speech equalized by covariance, revealed that the effect produced by the initial speech was still significant two and a half weeks after subjects heard an opposing speech ($F = 5.28$). Subsequent *t*-tests revealed that a two-sided initial speech was significantly more effective than a one-sided initial speech in changing opinions in the direction advocated when tested after that interval. This includes all types of opposing speeches.

Table 8 shows that subjects who heard a one-sided initial speech changed their opinions in the direction urged by the opposing speech when tested two and a half weeks after hearing the opposing speech to a mean score of 19.8; subjects who heard a two-sided initial speech, on the other hand, changed their opinions to a mean score of 21.7. The mean difference was statistically significant within the .01 level. These results indicate that in terms of opinion change, the two-sided initial speech was significantly more effective in changing opinions and sustaining the change than a one-sided initial speech when subjects heard an opposing speech and opinions were tested two and a half weeks later.

Hypothesis five was partially confirmed. Table 6 shows that subjects who heard a one-sided initial speech changed their opinions in the direction advocated by the immediate one-sided opposing speech to a mean score of

TABLE 6

MEAN OPINION SCORES FOR SUBJECTS WHO HEARD A ONE-SIDED OR A TWO-SIDED INITIAL SPEECH, FOLLOWED IMMEDIATELY BY A ONE-SIDED OR TWO-SIDED OPPOSING SPEECH

Mean Opinion Scores After Hearing Opposing Speeches

Sequence	N	Mean	$\bar{D}$	t	P
One-Sided Initial Speech					
One-Sided Opposing Speech	50	20.9			
Two-Sided Opposing Speech	50	16.8	4.1	2.73	< .001*
$\bar{D}$			1.2		
t				.80	
P					< .50
Two-Sided Initial Speech					
One-Sided Opposing Speech	50	19.7			
Two-Sided Opposing Speech	50	19.8	.1	.03	< .99
$\bar{D}$		3.0			
t		2.0			
P		< .05*			

Mean Scores Before Opposing Speeches Equalized by Covariance

*Statistically Significant

Note—The lower the score, the greater the opinion change in the direction advocated by the opposing speech. The hypothetical neutral point on the scale is 24.0.

TABLE 7

MEAN OPINION SCORES FOR SUBJECTS WHO HEARD A ONE-SIDED OR A TWO-SIDED INITIAL SPEECH, FOLLOWED BY A DELAYED ONE-SIDED OR TWO-SIDED SPEECH A WEEK LATER

Mean Opinion Scores After Hearing Opposing Speeches

Sequence	Delayed One-Sided Opposing Speech N	Mean	Delayed Two-Sided Opposing Speech N	Mean	$\bar{D}$	t	P
One-Sided Initial Speech	40	15.5	40	17.9	2.4	2.26	< .05*
Two-Sided Initial Speech	40	17.3	40	18.5	1.2	.76	< .50

Comparison between initial speeches (Delayed One-Sided Opposing Speech): $\bar{D}$ 1.8, t 1.79, P < .05* (one-tailed)

Comparison between initial speeches (Delayed Two-Sided Opposing Speech): $\bar{D}$ .6, t .36, P < .80

Mean Scores Before Opposing Speeches Equalized by Covariance

*Statistically Significant

Note.—The lower the score, the greater the opinion change in the direction advocated by the opposing speech. The hypothetical neutral point on the scale is 24.0.

TABLE 8

MEAN OPINION SCORES FOR SUBJECTS TWO AND
A HALF WEEKS AFTER HEARING OPPOSING SPEECHES

Sequence	Delayed Posttest Mean Scores	
One-Sided Initial Speech		
Opposing Speech		
(One-Sided or Two-Sided	N	Mean
Immediate, or Delayed)	180	19.8
Two-Sided Initial Speech		
Opposing Speech		
(One-Sided or Two-Sided	N	Mean
Immediate, or Delayed)	180	21.7
	$\overline{D}$	1.9
	t	2.30
	P	< .01*
		(one-tailed)
Pretest Mean Scores Equalized by Covariance		

*Statistically Significant

Note—The lower the score, the greater the opinion change in the direction advocated by the opposing speech.

20.9, while subjects who heard a one-sided initial speech changed their opinions in the direction supported by the immediate two-sided opposing speech to a mean score of 16.8. The mean difference between the two scores yielded 4.1 units which is statistically significant within the .001 level of confidence. These results reveal that a two-sided opposing speech presented immediately after listeners heard a one-sided speech was significantly more effective in changing opinions in the direction advocated than a one-sided opposing speech.

Table 6 also illustrates that neither the two-sided nor the one-sided immediate opposing speech was significantly more effective in modifying opinions when listeners previously heard a two-sided speech.

Hypothesis six was not confirmed. Table 7 shows that subjects who heard a one-sided initial speech, changed their opinions in the direction supported by the delayed one-sided opposing speech to a mean score of 15.5, while subjects who heard a one-sided initial speech, changed their opinions in the direction supported by the delayed two-sided opposing speech to a mean score of 17.9. The mean difference between the two scores was statistically significant within the .05 level. This result was, indeed, surprising. Not only was the hypothesis not confirmed, but there was a significant finding in the opposite direction. It indicates that a one-sided opposing speech presented one week after listeners heard a one-sided speech was significantly more effective than a two-sided opposing speech presented at the same time.

Table 7 shows, on the other hand, that a delayed one-sided opposing speech was not significantly more effective in changing opinions in the direction advocated than a two-sided delayed opposing speech when subjects heard a two-sided initial speech, although the trend in the data was in that direction.

A question of interest in the present study, beyond the hypotheses tested, is whether it is more effective to present an opposing speech immediately after the audience hears a speech advocating a different view, or delay one week before presenting an opposing point of view? Table 9 shows that subjects

TABLE 9

OPINION SCORES FOR EXPERIMENTAL SUBJECTS WHO
HEARD AN IMMEDIATE OPPOSING SPEECH AND A DELAYED
OPPOSING SPEECH VERSUS CONTROL GROUP SUBJECTS
WHO WERE TESTED IMMEDIATELY AFTER HEARING AN
INITIAL ONE-SIDED OR TWO-SIDED SPEECH AND TESTED
AGAIN ONE WEEK LATER (REGRESSION EFFECT)

Experimental Subjects			*Control Group Subjects*		
Immediate Opposing Speech	N	Mean	Initial Speech (One-Sided or Two-Sided)	N	Mean
	200	19.3		80	30.3
Delayed Opposing Speech	N	Mean	Delayed Posttest (One Week Later)		
	160	17.7		N	Mean
				80	28.5
	$\overline{D}$	1.6		$\overline{D}$	1.8
	t	1.96		t	1.79
	P	$< .05^*$		P	$< .10$

*Statistically Significant

who heard the initial speeches, and subsequently heard the immediate opposing speeches, changed their opinions in the direction advocated to a mean score of 19.3. Subjects who heard the initial speeches, but did not hear the opposing speeches until one week later, changed their opinions more in the direction of the opposing speech to a mean score of 17.7. The mean difference was statistically significant within the .05 level of confidence.

It would appear from these results that a delayed opposing speech is more effective than an immediate opposing speech. However, an analysis of mean opinion scores obtained from subjects in the control group who heard only the initial speech, one-sided or two-sided, and tested one week later, revealed that the significant difference obtained between the immediate and opposing speech is only a regression effect and is not produced by the opposing speech.

Table 9 illustrates that subjects in the control groups also changed their opinions away from the direction advocated by the initial speeches, when tested a week later. They regressed 1.8 units back towards their opinion of guaranteed annual cash income prior to hearing the initial speeches. Thus, the significant 1.6 units difference obtained from subjects in the experimental groups, is attributed to regression, rather than to the time the opposing speech was presented. Further, when opinions were obtained two and a half weeks after subjects in the experimental groups heard an opposing speech, the time factor, immediate or a week later, was not statistically significant.

These results, then, reveal that it made no significant difference in changing opinions if an opposing speech was presented immediately or one week after the first speech.

RESULTS: ETHOS HYPOTHESES

Hypothesis seven was not confirmed. Table 10 shows the mean authoritativeness and character scores obtained from subjects who heard a one-sided or two-sided initial speech. It indicates no significant difference on perceived authoritativeness and character for a speaker employing either type of speech.

TABLE 10

COMPARISON OF MEAN AUTHORITATIVENESS AND CHARACTER
SCORES FOR SUBJECTS WHO HEARD A ONE-SIDED INITIAL SPEECH
VERSUS SUBJECTS' SCORES WHO HEARD A TWO-SIDED INITIAL SPEECH

Ethos Measure	N	Initial One-Sided Mean	N	Initial Two-Sided Mean	$\overline{D}$	t	P
Authoritativeness	180	32.6	180	32.9	.3	.56	< .58
Character	180	30.2	180	30.5	.3	.53	< .61

Note—The higher the score, the higher the perceived authoritativeness and character. The hypothetical neutral point on each scale is 24.0.

Hypothesis eight was not confirmed. Table 1 shows the results of t-tests computed on mean authoritativeness scores to demonstrate the significance of the interaction disclosed by analysis of covariance (F = 11.61). The only finding in Table 10 to reach statistical significance was for subjects who heard a one-sided initial speech who perceived the opposing speaker employing a delayed one-sided speech as having significantly higher authoritativeness than an opposing speaker employing a delayed two-sided opposing speech. The mean authoritativeness scores of 34.1 for subjects who heard a delayed one-sided opposing speech was significantly higher than the mean of 29.8 obtained by subjects who heard a delayed two-sided opposing speech.

Table 12 shows the comparison of mean character scores obtained after subjects heard a one-sided immediate or delayed opposing speech. It indicates

TABLE 11

Comparison of Authoritativeness Scores for Subjects Who Heard a One-Sided Initial Speech Versus Scores of Subjects Who Heard a Two-Sided Initial Speech, Followed by an Immediate or Delayed One-Sided or Two-Sided Opposing Speech

Sequence	N	Mean		N	Mean	$\bar{D}$	t	P
One-Sided Initial Speech Immediate One-Sided Opposing Speech	50	33.5	Immediate Two-Sided Opposing Speech	50	33.6	.1	.06	< .99
Two-Sided Initial Speech Immediate One-Sided Opposing Speech	50	33.0	Immediate Two-Sided Opposing Speech	50	31.4	1.6	1.05	< .30
One-Sided Initial Speech Delayed One-Sided Opposing Speech	40	34.1	Delayed Two-Sided Opposing Speech	40	29.8	4.3	2.57	< .02*
One-Sided Initial Speech Delayed One-Sided Opposing Speech	40	33.0	Delayed Two-Sided Opposing Speech	40	32.2	.8	.48	< .70

*Statistically Significant

Note—The higher the score the higher the perceived authoritativeness. The hypothetical neutral point on the scale is 24.0.

TABLE 12

COMPARISON OF CHARACTER SCORES FOR SUBJECTS
WHO HEARD A ONE-SIDED OPPOSING SPEECH VERSUS
SUBJECTS WHO HEARD A TWO-SIDED OPPOSING SPEECH

Ethos Measure	N	Opposing One-Sided Mean	N	Opposing Two-Sided Mean	$\overline{D}$	t	P
Character	180	28.4	180	28.0	.4	.54	< .89

Note—The higher the score, the higher the perceived character. The hypothetical neutral point on the scale is 24.0.

that the opposing speaker was not perceived as having significantly higher character whether he used the one-sided or two-sided speech.

SUMMARY OF RESULTS

1. A two-sided initial speech was not significantly more effective in changing opinions of listeners in the direction advocated than a one-sided initial speech when opinions were tested immediately after listeners heard the initial speech.

2. A two-sided initial speech was significantly more effective in changing opinions in the direction advocated than a one-sided initial speech when listeners were tested after hearing a two-sided opposing speech presented immediately after the initial speech. It was not more effective for listeners who heard a one-sided opposing speech presented immediately after the initial speech.

3. A two-sided initial speech was significantly more effective in changing opinions in the direction advocated than a one-sided initial speech for listeners who heard a one-sided opposing speech presented one week after the initial speech, but not for listeners who heard a two-sided opposing speech presented after the same interval.

4. A two-sided initial speech was significantly more effective in changing opinions in the direction advocated than a one-sided initial speech when listeners were tested two and one half weeks after they heard an opposing speech.

5. A two-sided opposing speech presented immediately after listeners heard a one-sided initial speech was significantly more effective in changing opinions in the direction advocated than a one-sided immediate opposing speech. However, when listeners heard a two-sided speech first, there was no significant difference in opinion scores after hearing a one-sided and a two-sided opposing speech.

6. A one-sided opposing speech presented one week after listeners heard a one-sided initial speech was significantly more effective in changing opinions

in the direction advocated than a two-sided delayed opposing speech. However, when listeners heard a two-sided initial speech, there was no significant difference in opinion scores between a delayed one-sided and two-sided opposing speech.

7. A speaker employing a two-sided initial speech was not significantly perceived by listeners as having higher ethos than a speaker employing a one-sided initial speech.

8. A speaker employing a two-sided opposing speech was not significantly perceived by listeners as having higher ethos than a speaker employing a one-sided opposing speech. The only significant finding regarding ethos revealed that a speaker employing a one-sided opposing speech one week after listeners heard a one-sided initial speech was perceived as having higher authoritativeness than a speaker employing a two-sided opposing speech presented at the same time.

CONCLUSIONS

In general, the study was designed to test the superiority of the two-sided speech over the one-sided speech under conditions more varied and extended than in previous studies. The hypotheses were framed to require a statistically significant difference in favor of the two-sided speech in order to be confirmed. It may now be useful to look at the relative effectiveness of the two types of speeches in the various situations set up for the experiment—to ask under what circumstances the two-sided speech was just as effective as the one-sided speech as well as when it was significantly more effective. The following summary emerges:

A two-sided speech was *more* effective (measured by opinion change) than a one-sided speech as:

(1) an initial speech followed immediately by a two-sided opposing speech.

(2) an initial speech followed one week later by a one-sided opposing speech.

(3) an initial speech tested two and a half weeks after listeners heard an opposing speech.

(4) an opposing speech heard immediately after a one-sided initial speech.

A two-sided speech was *equally* effective (measured by both opinion change and ratings of the speaker's authoritativeness and character) as a one-sided speech as:

(1) an initial speech tested immediately after the speech before listeners heard an opposing speech.

(2) an initial speech followed immediately by a one-sided opposing speech.

(3) an initial speech followed one week later by a two-sided opposing speech.

(4) an opposing speech heard immediately after a two-sided initial speech.

(5) an opposing speech heard one week after a two-sided initial speech.

A one-sided speech was *more* effective (measured by both opinion change and ratings of the speaker's authoritativeness) than a two-sided speech as:

(1) an opposing speech heard one week after a one-sided initial speech.

Under the varying conditions in the experiment, the two-sided speech was either just as effective or more effective in every instance except one: where listeners heard a one-sided speech of opposition a week after having heard a one-sided speech advocating a change in public policy. The superiority of the two-sided speech in certain conditions found by earlier investigators did not reach statistical significance in some instances (e.g., when tested immediately after an initial speech), but in no case did the one-sided speech show greater effectiveness under conditions similar to those tested by these researchers. Overall the study further supported the desirability of treating both sides of a question in discussing a matter of public policy.

With regard to the specific question raised earlier as to whether a speaker who opposed a position taken by a previous speaker should use a one-sided or a two-sided speech, the study indicates: A two-sided speech if the audience heard a one-sided speech immediately before he speaks; a one-sided speech if the audience heard a one-sided speech one week before he speaks. The two types of speeches are equally effective if the audience heard a two-sided speech immediately before, or one week before he speaks.

This study failed to confirm the rationale presented earlier that a two-sided speech would be perceived as "more fair," thereby increasing the ethos of a speaker employing it. Whatever advantage the two-sided speech may have in persuading an audience is not a result of according the speaker greater personal attributes for his decision to discuss both sides of a proposal.

REFERENCES

BETTINGHAUS, E. *Persuasive Communication.* New York: Holt, Rinehart and Winston, Inc., 1968.

———. "The Operation of Congruity in an Oral Communication Situation," *Speech Monographs.* 1961, 28, 131–141.

COHEN, A. R. *Attitude Change and Social Influence.* New York: Basic Books, Inc., 1964.

COOPER, L. *The Rhetoric of Aristotle.* New York: Appleton-Century-Crofts, Inc., 1932.

HOVLAND, C. I., JANIS, I. L. and KELLEY, H. H. *Communication and Persuasion.* New Haven: Yale University Press, 1953.

HOVLAND, C. I., LUMSDAINE, A. A. and SHEFFIELD, F. D. *Experiments on Mass Communication.* New Jersey: Princeton University Press, 1949.

HOVLAND, C. I. and MANDELL, W. "An Experimental Comparison of Conclusion

Drawing by the Communicator and by the Audience," *Journal of Abnormal and Social Psychology.* 1952, 47, 581–588.

HOVLAND, C. I. and WEISS, W. "The Influence of Source Credibility on Communication Effectiveness," *Public Opinion Quarterly.* 1951, 15, 635–650.

JAKSA, J. A. "An Experimental Study of One-Sided and Two-Sided Argument, with Emphasis on Three Two-Sided Speeches," *Speech Monographs.* 1964, 31, 234.

KELMAN, H. C. and HOVLAND, C. I. "Reinstatement of the Communicator in Delayed Measurement of Opinion Change," *Journal of Abnormal and Social Psychology.* 1953, 48, 327–335.

LINTON, H. and GRAHAM, E. "Personality Correlates of Persuasibility," in Janis, I. L. and Hovland, C. I., eds. *Personality and Persuasibility.* New Haven, Conn.: Yale University Press, 1959, 69–101.

LUMSDAINE, A. A. and JANIS, I. L. "Resistance to 'counter-propaganda' Produced by One-Sided and Two-Sided 'Propaganda' Presentation," *Public Opinion Quarterly.* 1953, 17, 311–318.

McGUIRE, W. J. "Persistence of the Resistance to Persuasion Induced by Various Types of Prior Defenses," *Journal of Abnormal and Social Psychology.* 1962, 64, 241–248.

———. "The Relative Efficacy of Various Types of Prior Belief-Defense in Producing Immunity Against Persuasion," *Journal of Abnormal and Social Psychology.* 1961, 62, 327–337.

McCROSKEY, J. C. "Experimental Studies of the Effects of Ethos and Evidence in Persuasive Communication." Unpublished doctoral dissertation, The Pennsylvania State University, 1966.

———. "Scales for the Measurement of Ethos," *Speech Monographs.* 1966, 30, 65–72.

PAPAGEORGIS, D. and McGUIRE, W. J. "The Generality of Immunity to Persuasion Produced by Pre-exposure to Weakened Counter Arguments," *Journal of Abnormal and Social Psychology.* 1961, 62, 475–481.

PAULSON, S. F. "The Effects of the Prestige of the Speaker and Acknowledgment of Opposing Arguments on Audience Retention and Shift of Opinion," *Speech Monographs.* 1954, 21, 267–271.

WINANS, J. A. *Public Speaking.* New York: The Century Co., 1915.

SECTION IV

THE EFFECTS
OF PERSUASION

To say that attitude change occurs as the result of a persuasive message is to make a broad generalization. In order to describe fully the process that takes place, we need to consider several additional dimensions: the magnitude of attitude change produced; the extent to which attitude change persists and what conditions enhance or retard its persistence; the extent to which the attitude change produced is translated into behavioral change; and the effect that producing the persuasive message has on the source himself.

A. The Amount of Change Produced

Which is more persuasive, a message which confronts its receiver with a position contradictory to his own or one which presents a position only somewhat discrepant from his own? One answer to this question was provided by Hovland and Pritzker (4). They presented communications advocating positions which differed from those of the receivers; the magnitude of discrepancies ranged from slightly to markedly different. Hovland and Pritzker found that the more opinion change they advocated, the more they obtained. That is, the communications which presented positions markedly different from those of the receivers produced greater attitude change than those which presented positions somewhat or slightly different. At least two factors combined to produce these results. The sources used were high credible ones, and the issues evoked low audience involvement.

Aronson, Turner, and Carlsmith (1) investigated the effect of source credibility on the relationship between the amount of change advocated and that produced. They attributed messages (about poetry) to high and low credible sources. They found that for high credible sources the amount of change produced was an ever increasing function of the amount requested. For low credible sources, the amount of change produced was a curvilinear function with the greatest change produced by communications having a moderate discrepancy. They argued that as the size of the discrepancy increases so does the magnitude of dissonance produced. Further, individuals possess at least two methods for dissonance reduction—changing one's attitude in the direction advocated by the source or discrediting that source. If the source has high credibility, then source derogation is difficult and the magnitude of attitude change should increase with increasing discrepancies. Since the low credible source is more easily rejected, increasingly large discrepancies will eventually lead to source rejection rather than to attitude change.

The role of ego-involvement has also received attention. Freedman (2), for example, found that under conditions of low involvement the amount of attitude change produced increased with the size of the discrepancy. Under conditions of high ego-involvement, the amount of change produced first increased and then diminished as the discrepancy size increased. In the article included here, Whittaker interprets the results of this study and others from the social judgment-involvement approach. This orientation predicts a curvilinear relationship between the amount of change requested and that produced. The parameters of the curve are determined by an individual's latitudes of acceptance and rejection, and these in turn are functions of his ego-involvement.

B. The Stability of Change Produced

One problem plaguing political candidates is how to translate the enthusiasm of March or July into votes in November. This problem suggests two basic questions: (1) How long will a persuasive effect last? and (2) What social and psychological factors contribute to its retention?

The effect of a persuasive message is hardly, if ever, permanent. Nearly all experimental evidence to date indicates that persuasive effects tend to dissipate or decay, and subjects move toward their previously held positions. The rate of decay, however, may vary widely. Hovland and Janis accounted for this variation in the following manner:

> If one remembers none of the arguments from the communication, one's opinion about the issue may revert to its initial level. Or if one is no longer motivated to accept what was said, the opinion change following exposure to a communication depends on retention both of the informational content and of the incentives for acceptance (3, p. 244).

The selection included by Watts and McGuire centers on the first requirement mentioned by Hovland and Janis—retaining the informational content of the message. These authors found that although the overall retention of opinion change was related to initial message comprehension, as the time interval increased the amount of opinion change retained "became functionally autonomous" of some aspects of message recall.

The selection by Newcomb focuses on the second requirement—retaining the incentive for accepting the message. According to Newcomb, one primary incentive for retaining specific attitudes is provided by the individual's social context. An individual will tend to retain attitudes which are reinforced by his social environment and will eliminate those which are not. Thus, when an individual modifies an attitude he must seek out social contexts which are supportive of it if the newly modified attitude is to be retained. Otherwise the attitude change will decay and his position will revert to that reinforced by his current social contexts.

C. Attitude Change and Behavioral Change

Throughout this book we have continually discussed attitudes, attitude change, persuasion, the persuader and the persuasive message. Less frequently have we discussed behavior and behavioral change. Yet quite obviously our concern with attitudes and attitude change stems from a presumption that the attitudes an individual holds and the behavior he exhibits are related. This is an interesting presumption, but one that has not always proven to be true. For example, La Piere (8) compared the attitudes and behavior of American motel and restaurant owners. Although over 90% of those businessmen responding to a questionnaire indicated that they would refuse service to Chinese (the stated attitude), when La Piere and a Chinese couple appeared in person at the same establishments, they were refused service only once (the overt behavior). In a more recent investigation by Kutner, Wilkins, and Yarrow (7), a similar lack of correspondence between attitudes and behavior was found. In this study two white women and one black woman entered a number of restaurants in a fashionable suburb and were never refused service. Later each establishment received a written inquiry about reservations for a social party. The letter included the statement, "Since some of them are colored, I wonder whether you'd object to their coming." Seventeen days after the letters were sent no replies had been received. When the investigators then called the restaurant managers, eight out of the eleven denied having received the letters.

Thus it seems rather naive to assume that attitudes and behavior are inevitably related. The implications of this potential lack of correspondence are explored in the article by Miller. He concludes that many of the relationships found between attitude change and other variables apply only to "paper and pencil, verbal responses" and suggests that behavioral measures of attitude must be developed.

In the second selection, Rokeach attempts to develop a theoretical framework to account for discrepancies between attitudes and behavior. He postulates that two types of attitude need to be considered in any context—the individual's attitude toward an object and his attitude toward the situation. According to Rokeach, part of the inability of previous research to correlate attitudes and behavior can be attributed to the investigators' focus on attitudes toward objects at the expense of attitudes toward situations.

What Rokeach suggests is that the nature of the situation acts as an intervening variable between an individual's attitudes and his behavior. Warner and DeFleur identify two aspects of the situation which may operate as intervening variables—social constraint and social distance. If these aspects operate such that they reinforce an individual's initial attitude, his behavior becomes more predictable. If these two factors operate in such a way to discourage his initially held attitude, then his behavior becomes less predictable.

D. Self-Persuasion

It has long been accepted that one way to increase an individual's commitment to a position is to involve him in some public activity. For this reason, evangelists call forth sinners to be saved, and politicians create rallies which maximize the active participation of those attending. One of the first experimental attempts to investigate the effects of active versus passive participation was by Janis and King (5). They found that subjects who silently read or listened to a message were less influenced by that position than were subjects who played the role of sincere advocates for the same position. King and Janis (6) extended their previous study by differentiating between subjects who were asked to read a message aloud and those who were asked to improvise a statement after reading the message silently. They found that the subjects who improvised the message were more affected by it than were those who merely read it aloud.

Several theoretical interpretations have been advanced to account for these results. Dissonance theorists contend that since the active participant expends more energy, he experiences greater dissonance which can be resolved through increased attitude change. Learning theorists argue that the active participant pays closer attention to the stimulus than the passive observer and hence has a greater probability of comprehending the message content—the main appeals and their support. He is thus more likely to be influenced by the message.

Regardless of which interpretation is accepted, the conclusion still holds that one of the most influenced recipients of a persuasive message is the source himself. The selection by Jones focuses on the persuasive impact a message has on its source. It also attempts to differentiate between influence occurring during the investigative and expressive states of advocacy.

REFERENCES

1. ARONSON, E., J. TURNER, and M. CARLSMITH. "Communicator Credibility and Communicator Discrepancy as Determinants of Opinion Change," *Journal of Abnormal and Social Psychology,* 67 (1963), 31–36.
2. FREEDMAN, J. L. "Involvement, Discrepancy, and Opinion Change," *Journal of Abnormal and Social Psychology,* 69 (1964), 290–95.
3. HOVLAND, C. I., I. L. JANIS, and H. H. KELLEY. *Communication and Persuasion.* New Haven: Yale University Press, 1953.
4. HOVLAND, C. I., and H. A. PRITZKER. "Extent of Opinion Change as a Function of Amount of Change Advocated," *Journal of Abnormal and Social Psychology,* 54 (1957), 257–61.
5. JANIS, I. L., and B. T. KING. "The Influence of Role-Playing on Opinion Change," *Journal of Abnormal and Social Psychology,* 49 (1954), 211–18.

6. KING, B. T., and I. L. JANIS. "Comparison of the Effectiveness of Improvised Role Playing in Producing Opinion Changes," *Human Relations,* 9 (1956), 177–86.
7. KUTNER, B., C. WILKINS, and P. YARROW. "Verbal Attitude and Overt Behavior Involving Racial Prejudice," *Journal of Abnormal and Social Psychology,* 47 (1952), 649–52.

James O. Whittaker

RESOLUTION OF THE COMMUNICATION DISCREPANCY ISSUE IN ATTITUDE CHANGE*

Few issues in the area of attitude change are of such importance or have aroused greater controversy and confusion than that relating to the effects of communication discrepancy. The problem fundamentally involves the question of whether presentation of an extremely divergent stand generates more change than one close to the position of the subject. For example, if we wish to modify the attitude of a staunchly conservative Republican, should we present a communication advocating an extremely liberal view, or should the position presented be only slightly different from that of the subject?

Common sense tells us that if we take a position substantially different from that of our listener, he will reject our position completely. Perhaps he will become even more entrenched or more extreme in his position. He may become more convinced that he is right and we are wrong. There is substantial evidence from psychological warfare efforts to substantiate this common sense notion. For example, many propaganda leaflets were prepared in England during the Second World War as part of a continuing effort to change opinions about the conditions that prevailed in allied POW camps, the treatment prisoners received, and so on. The hope, of course, was that if the attitudes of German soldiers toward probable treament could be changed, more of them would surrender.

*Part of the research reported here was supported by a grant from the U.S. Air Force Office of Scientific Research (AF-AFOSR 62-188).

Reprinted from *Attitude, Ego-Involvement, and Change,* pp. 159–77, with permission of the author and John Wiley and Sons, Inc.

One particular leaflet contained photographs of conditions in a POW camp in Canada. These photographs showed prisoners engaged in playing cards, ping pong, and other activities. The accompanying message included, among other things, a description of meals in the camp—for example, coffee, eggs, and toast for breakfast. An important fact relevant to this particular leaflet is that it represented the unadulterated truth. The photographs were actually taken in the Canadian camp, and the meals described were those actually provided for prisoners.

Before dropping the leaflet behind enemy lines, however, Army personnel decided to "pretest" it with German prisoners already in camps in Italy. These prisoners, it should be emphasized, were already captives and knew something of conditions in allied POW camps. They had discovered that actual conditions and treatment differed considerably from what they had been led to expect. Yet almost without exception, they could not accept the leaflet as truthful. It was too divergent from their own opinions concerning general conditions in allied prison camps, and consequently they regarded it as "propagandistic" (Daugherty and Janowitz, 1958).

Of course we know that common sense notions are often incorrect. Further, it is quite apparent that most psychological warfare activities hardly qualify as scientific experiments, including the one just described. Still, it is surprising that when we look to the psychological literature for an answer to the discrepancy problem, we find a mass of contradictory evidence. Several studies have reported results indicating that more opinion change occurs with *greater* rather than with less discrepancy (Hovland and Pritzker, 1957; French, 1956; Ewing, 1942; Goldberg, 1954; Fisher and Lubin, 1958; Zimbardo, 1960; Fisher, Rubinstein, and Freeman, 1956; Harvey, Kelley and Shapiro, 1957). Festinger (1957) has provided a theoretical interpretation of these findings. He suggests that when individuals are presented with a communication taking an extremely divergent stand, they experience "cognitive dissonance," defined as a tension state with motivational properties.

According to Festinger, a person in such a situation experiencing dissonance may react in one of several ways. He may seek social support for his position, he may derogate the communicator, or he may change his attitude in line with the stand presented in the communication. In several recent publications, Sherif (1965) has taken issue with Festinger's contention. He has pointed out that "the highly committed person exposed to an extremely discrepant communication will *never* react to it by changing his attitude toward the communication. He will feel irritated, derogate the communicator, speak to his friends about it; but he will *never* resort to the alternative of changing toward the communication in order to reduce his irritation, tension, or dissonance." Sherif's contention has been that extremely discrepant communications yield less attitude change than those taking a stand closer to that upheld by the subject. In 1961, for example, Sherif and Hovland presented results showing less frequent change with greater discrepancies between the individual's initial stand on the issue and the position of the communication.

Just as there is evidence supporting the hypothesis that greater discrepancy results in greater change, there is also considerable evidence to support the hypothesis of *smaller* discrepancy, that is, greater change. Hovland, Harvey, and Sherif (1957), Sherif and Hovland (1961), and Whittaker (1957) have all presented such results. In addition, Sherif has provided a theoretical interpretation of these findings, just as Festinger provided a theory to interpret the opposite results.

Sherif's theory is based in part on results of psychophysical studies of judgment in which the discrepancy between the subject's internal anchor and stimulus presented determines either an assimilation or a contrast effect. Applying these observations to communication situations, Sherif has pointed out that the subject's own position serves as an anchor in his perception of other positions. Thus, if the position presented to him is close to his own, he tends to perceive it as being even closer than it objectively is. Conversely, if a substantial discrepancy exists, the subject perceives the position presented as being even more discrepant. The former, of course, is the assimilation effect, and the latter is the contrast effect (Sherif and Hovland, 1961).

There is no question that assimilation-contrast effects do occur in the perception of presented stands. In one of our own experiments, for example, we had farmers holding various attitudes toward government controls in agriculture estimate the position or stand of a procontrol communication (Whittaker, 1965a). These results are presented in Figure 1. It will be noted that farmers favoring controls (positions A and B) perceived the position of the

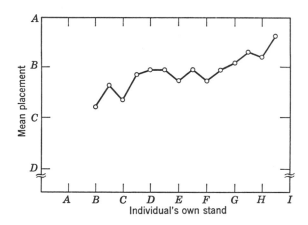

FIGURE 1.   *Placement of communication favoring farm policy by individuals whose most acceptable positions differed from A (favorable) to I (opposed). Higher location on figure represents placement as more favorable to policy (Whittaker, 1965a).*

communication as much closer to their own than farmers opposed to controls (positions *H* and *I*) ($p < .05$).

Furthermore, as one might expect, subjects tend to perceive positions close to their own more favorably than those that are considerably divergent. When we asked the farmers in the experiment mentioned above to evaluate the communication in terms of fairness and lack of bias, we obtained the results shown in Figure 2. Those whose own positions were essentially in line with the

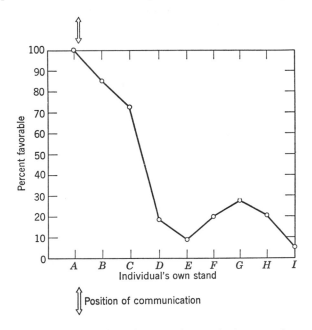

FIGURE 2. *Favorable evaluations of communication supporting farm policy (A) by persons upholding stands from extremely favorable (A) to extremely opposed (I) to the policy. Each location represents percentage of persons choosing that position as most acceptable who appraised communication as "fair, unbiased," and so forth (Whittaker, 1965a).*

communication (positions *A* an *B*) judged the communication as fair and unbiased, whereas those opposed tended to judge it as "propagandistic" (Whittaker, 1965a).

These results suggest that when a person is presented with a divergent position, he perceives it as being more in line with his own than it actually is *if* the discrepancy is small. Furthermore, he judges it as essentially fair and unbiased. On the other hand, he perceives extremely divergent positions as even *more* divergent than they are objectively, and he tends to regard such positions as biased and unfair.

If we accept Festinger's formulation, we are forced to conclude that in some cases individuals are more likely to change their opinions when faced with a position that they judge as even more extreme than objectivity dictates and at the same time one they perceive as biased and propagandistic. In other words, Festinger's theory would lead us to predict that under some circumstances the more biased and propagandistic we perceive a communication to be, the more likely we are to be influenced by it. However unreasonable this may sound, in order to resolve our original problem, we still need evidence from studies of the degree of opinion change as a function of the extent of communication discrepancy. Before going into this, however, let me mention one additional aspect of Sherif's theory that is highly relevant to this issue.

LATITUDES OF ACCEPTANCE
AND REJECTION

Traditionally, social psychologists have tended to regard attitudes in terms of the stand or position the individual upholds. Sherif, however, prefers to specify the *range* of positions acceptable (latitude of acceptance), the range of positions rejected (latitude of rejection), and the range of positions toward which the individual feels no commitment (latitude of noncommitment): In terms of predictions about probable reactions to other stands, he has observed that by specifying latitudes of acceptance and rejection we should be able to make more accurate predictions than if we know only the position which the individual chooses as most acceptable. This is because two individuals specifying the same position as their own may differ in the extent to which they tolerate other positions.

In general, it has been demonstrated in several experiments that as the individual's "own position" becomes more extreme, his tolerance for other positions diminishes. In our experiment involving farmers, for example, we asked subjects to choose from among nine statements concerning government controls in agriculture those that were objectionable, those they found unobjectionable, and, in addition, the one statement most closely representing their own stand. The statements ranged from extremely *pro-* to extremely *anti*-control positions.

The data from this part of the experiment is shown in Table 1. Note that tolerance for other positions tends to diminish as the subject's own position becomes more extreme. Those subjects either strongly for or strongly against controls rejected almost twice as many items as they accepted. We found one Farm Bureau member, for example, who complained to the experimenter that the most extreme statement he presented was not *extreme* enough. She had checked the most extreme statement as acceptable and had crossed out every other statement on the sheet.

With subjects holding less extreme positions, on the other hand, tolerance

TABLE 1

ACCEPTABILITY OF STATEMENTS IN RELATION TO SUBJECTS' POSITION
ON ISSUE (WHITTAKER, 1964A)

Subjects' Positions	(N)	Mean Number of Items Acceptable	Mean Number of Items Not Checked	Mean Number of Items Rejected
Extreme (1,2,8,9)	(37)	1.97	3.05	3.97
Intermediate (3,4,5,6,7)	(141)	2.86	2.74	3.40
	$t = 3.65$	$p < .01$		

for other positions is much greater. They clearly do not tend to see issues in black and white terms, as do those with extreme stands. The extremist, whether on political or other issues, tends to dichotomize in his thinking. He does not discriminate the shades of gray, and more often than not his feeling is that "you're either for us or against us."

We mentioned previously that knowledge of a subject's latitudes of acceptance and rejection should enable us to make accurate predictions about his probable reaction to a communication. In a paper published in 1963, I pointed out that communications taking positions within the subject's latitude of acceptance (which we define as "small" discrepancies), yield smaller shifts than do communications taking positions at the end of or adjacent to the latitude of acceptance (defined as "moderate" discrepancies). We suspect that communications taking positions within the latitude of acceptance and closest to the person's actual stand yield the smallest shifts and that greater shifts occur as the position of the communication is moved progressively further away from the subject's position but still within the latitude of acceptance. Furthermore, it appears warranted to conclude that positive opinion shift diminishes as the position of the communication is moved progressively into the latitude of rejection (defined as "large" discrepancies). Finally, it is apparent that when the communication position is moved far into the latitudes of rejection, increasingly larger negative shifts occur. These points were reiterated in a *Public Opinion Quarterly* paper published the following year (Whittaker, 1964a).

Thus, as I pointed out first in 1963, there is a *curvilinear* relationship between opinion change and the degree of discrepancy between the position of the communication and the stand of the subject. Small discrepancies yield small change, moderate discrepancies yield greater change, and large discrepancies yield either negligible positive change, or negative change that becomes more pronounced as the discrepancy increases. This relationship is shown in Figure 3.

If the latitude of acceptance is small, as it is for those holding extreme positions, and the latitude of rejection is large, then the optimal position pre-

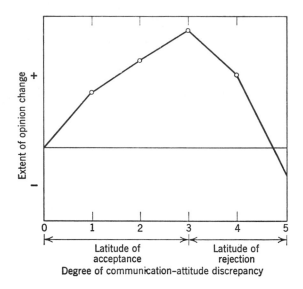

FIGURE 3. *Hypothetical curve showing relationship between opinion change and communication-attitude discrepancy (Whittaker, 1963).*

sented must be very close to the position of the subject. On the other hand, when the latitude of acceptance is large, as it is for those holding moderate positions, the optimal position of the communication is much further away.

There is, as we noted previously, a considerable body of evidence in support of these generalizations. But before presenting it, let us turn our attention to evidence that appears to support the opposite view, namely, greater discrepancy equals greater change.

EVIDENCE SHOWING THAT GREATER DISCREPANCY EQUALS GREATER CHANGE

In my opinion, investigators have reached the conclusion that greater discrepancy equals greater change either because they were: (1) working with issues about which subjects did not feel strongly, that is, subjects were not ego-involved, or (2) they neglected to employ adequate parameters in their experimental designs, or (3) a combination of these factors was involved.

Sherif has put it very nicely, I think, when he points out that the first question we must consider is

What is it that is to be changed when a person is exposed to a communication or some other attempt at attitude change? What is it that is resistant to change?

Is it his guesses about the number of beans in a jar, or leaves on a tree, or sand pebbles on a square yard of beach? Or, is it his views on his family, on how he stacks up relative to his contemporaries, on the worth of his religion, his politics, his profession, his country, or his way of life?

It is one thing to change from one brand of soap to another. It is quite another thing to change the person's stand toward persons, objects, groups, and institutions that he accepts or rejects as related to himself (Sherif, 1965).

Far too often, in my opinion, psychologists working in the area of attitude change have tended to use issues about which subjects have little concern. In an experiment designed by Hovland and Pritzker (1957), for example, some of the issues with college students were: Was Washington or Lincoln the greater President? Will a cure for cancer be discovered in the next five years? Should the executive branch of government be given greater control? They had the students check a position from "agree strongly" to "disagree strongly" in connection with a statement relative to each of the issues employed, that is, "Washington was a greater President than Lincoln." Then they asked the students to check an authority group whose opinion they would most respect on each issue.

Some time later, other questionnaires were returned to the students with a position marked on each issue, and the position checked was attributed to a particular "authority" group. Check marks and authority groups for each issue were determined by the responses of individual students on the first questionnaire. Hence if a student checked "agree strongly" in connection with the statement "Washington was a greater President than Lincoln" and indicated he would most respect the opinions of historians on this issue, he later received a questionnaire with "agree *slightly*" or some other position checked, and this was indicated as the response of historians.

In some cases the fictitious check marks were close to those originally marked by subjects, whereas in other cases they were further away. At any rate, subjects were again asked to indicate their opinions. When the opinions on the second administration were compared with those on the first, the authors noted that greater discrepancy yielded greater change.

There are three factors in this study that appear to account for the results observed by the investigators. *First*, there is little reason to believe that college students are generally ego-involved in issues such as those employed in this study. Consequently, such opinions are easily changed. *Second*, the "communication" presented was attributed to sources marked as highly authoritative by the subjects involved. Hence credibility was maximal. *Third*, the discrepancies employed were relatively small. No check mark was ever more than three positions away from the original position, and no subjects were faced with communications in absolute disagreement with their original positions. In other words, acceptance of the "communication" never required a complete about-face on the part of the subject.

A MODIFICATION OF THE
HOVLAND-PRITZKER STUDY

We repeated this experiment in 1963 using the same procedure that Hovland and Pritzker employed. In this case, however, we also utilized issues more likely to arouse involvement in college students, that is, "No athletic scholarships should be awarded"; "There should be curfews for male students"; "Sororities and fraternities should be abolished." We also expanded Hovland and Pritzker's response scale, that is, from "agree strongly, disagree strongly" to "agree absolutely, disagree absolutely." And in addition, when the second questionnaire was given, check marks were as much as eight positions away from those originally marked. Thus we employed greater discrepancies than they had used. Finally, the check mark on the second questionnaire was attributed to "other college students," rather than to highly credible groups of experts.

When the above changes were incorporated into this study, we did not find the linear relationship of greater discrepancy (greater change) as observed by the original authors. Rather, as shown in Table 2, the relationship was

TABLE 2

MEAN CHANGE SCORE WITH EIGHT STRENGTHS OF COMMUNICATION
(WHITTAKER, 1965B)

			Degree of Change Advocated				
1	2	3	4	5	6	7	8
0.36	1.09	1.21	1.64	1.88	2.36	2.00	1.50

curvilinear. Small discrepancies yielded small change, moderate discrepancies yielded the maximum change, and the degree of change tended to diminish as the discrepancies became even larger.

The breakdown of change on each individual issue in the study is shown in Table 3. It is interesting to note that in this table, on those issues originally included in the Hovland and Pritzker study, greater discrepancy still yielded greater change. Increasing the discrepancy and decreasing the credibility of the source, as we did in our study, was clearly not enough to alter the results. We suspect that on issues that are low in involvement, the discrepancies would need to be much greater than those we employed before decreasing change would result. This is undoubtedly because the latitudes of acceptance on such issues are so large relative to the latitudes of rejection.

On the other hand, with issues about which subjects feel strongly and where the latitude of acceptance is small and latitude of rejection large, communication discrepancies that appear to be objectively small often result in negli-

TABLE 3

CHANGES IN OPINION WITH EIGHT DEGREES OF COMMUNICATION
DISCREPANCY FOR EACH ISSUE (WHITTAKER, 1963)

	1	2	3	4	5	6	7	8
1. President should have power to reduce tariffs	0.50	0.86	1.31	1.05	2.30	3.33	2.50	1.00
2. No athletic scholarships should be awarded	0.13	1.04	0.95	2.11	2.20	2.72	3.25	—
3. Executive branch should have greater control*	0.23	1.08	1.47	2.21	2.50	2.22	2.75	—
4. We should continue supporting the United Nations	0.60	1.05	0.88	1.35	1.42	1.76	1.42	2.42
5. We should purchase $100 million U.N. bonds	1.22	1.72	1.70	1.88	2.71	2.85	2.50	—
6. Sororities and fraternities should be abolished	0.00	1.06	1.05	1.18	1.40	2.90	1.42	0.50
7. Federal aid should be provided to schools	0.52	1.11	1.62	1.33	1.75	1.66	1.50	1.50
8. Medical care for aged under Social Security	0.25	0.94	1.17	1.85	1.38	2.50	2.00	2.00
9. There should be curfews for male students	0.07	1.05	0.76	0.90	0.92	1.10	1.00	0.00
10. No foreign aid should be given to Communist governments	0.65	1.47	1.20	1.57	2.21	3.85	3.00	5.00
11. Likelihood of cancer cure within 5 years*	0.42	0.95	1.27	1.85	2.22	3.00	4.00	—
12. Washington or Lincoln greater President*	0.58	0.73	1.12	0.81	1.66	1.75	2.00	—
Median change	0.46	1.05	1.19	1.46	1.98	2.61	2.25	1.50

*These issues included in the Hovland and Pritzker study.

gible positive change or in negative change. This latter effect, often referred
to as the "boomerang effect," was revealed in our 1963 study of farmers' attitudes toward increased government controls in agriculture.

THE FARM STUDY

In our 1963 farm study we presented a strong argument for increasing
government controls in agriculture to members of the Farmer's Union,
Farm Bureau, and unselected adults and college students. The Farm Bureau,
it should be pointed out, has long taken a public position of strong opposition
to what it calls "government meddling in the farmer's business."

Table 4 presents the results of this study.

TABLE 4

Opinion Change for Subjects with Differing Initial Stands
(Whittaker, 1964a)

Group	(N)	Before Communication	Perceived Position of Communication	After Communication	Change in Direction of Communication
Farm group A	(17)	2.60	2.50	2.62	−0.02
Unselected student	(18)	5.50	2.00	4.37	+1.13
Unselected adult	(50)	6.41	2.00	6.43	−0.02
Farm group B	(22)	7.31	1.75	8.00	−0.69

Note that Farm Bureau members (farm group B) moved in the opposite direction from that proposed in the communication. This is the "boomerang effect" so often noted in studies of attitude change. We believe this effect results when communications are presented that take positions well within the subject's latitude of rejection.

ADDITIONAL EVIDENCE SUPPORTING THE HYPOTHESIS OF A CURVILINEAR RELATIONSHIP

In 1964 Freedman tested the hypothesis that more change would occur with greater discrepancy under conditions of *low* involvement but that with high involvement maximum change would occur at the moderate level of discrepancy.

In this experiment a concept formation task was employed as the "issue." A number of concept instances were presented, and the subjects were required to decide what the correct concept was. The first description of the concept was considered as their initial position. Additional concept instances were then presented that essentially constituted discrepant information. Following this information, subjects were asked to give a final description of the concept. Position change was the difference between the subject's initial and final concepts.

Involvement was manipulated before the experiment began by telling members of the high involvement group that the first response was an indication of intelligence and perceptiveness. Members of the low involvement group were told that the first response was relatively unimportant as a personality indicator.

Results of the experiment are shown in Table 5 and Figure 4. Under conditions of high involvement, the greatest shift occurred with an intermediate

TABLE 5

AMOUNT OF CHANGE FROM INITIAL TO FINAL POSITION
(FREEDMAN, 1964)

	Discrepancy		
Condition	Low	Moderate	High
Low involvement	1.85	2.16	3.15
High involvement	1.14	2.12	0.94

discrepancy. But with low involvement, the greatest shift occurred with maximum discrepancy.

Here is another example of a study that yields misleading results because the author neglected to employ adequate parameters, at least under the condition of low involvement. Had he increased the discrepancy still more under this condition, decreased change would doubtless have been the result. Then the monotonic relationship for the low involvement condition (Figure 4) would have become curvilinear.

Under conditions of high involvement and when the latitude of acceptance is very narrow, the optimal position yielding maximum change is very close to the subject's own position. Under conditions of low involvement, on the other hand, the optimal position is much further away. Regardless of involvement, however, the relationship between discrepancy and change is nonmonotonic provided that sufficiently large discrepancies are employed. That is, a curvilinear relationship is found between the degree of communi-

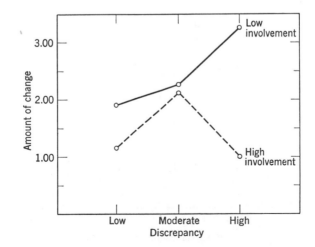

FIGURE 4.   *Mean amount of change from initial to final response (Freedman, 1964).*

cation discrepancy and amount of attitude change when the conditions of research are adequate to test the relationship.

Like the blind men attempting to describe an elephant by feeling of its various parts, social psychologists have been confused by the failure on the part of many investigators to employ adequate parameters in their studies of this issue. We ourselves, I should hasten to add, contributed to the confusion in 1957 when we presented results of a study of this problem at the Fifteenth International Congress of Psychology in Belgium (Whittaker, 1957).

In the study we evaluated the effects of various discrepancies upon judgments in the autokinetic situation. It should be noted that this situation is not ordinarily highly ego-involving for subjects.

We first had subjects serve in one session alone, during which they made a series of forty judgments concerning autokinetic movement. Then, in a second session, each subject served with a "plant" or "confederate" who had been instructed to make judgments in accordance with a prearranged scheme. With some subjects the "plant" made judgments centered around a median one inch higher than the subject's largest judgment in the first session. The "plant" always used the same *range* of judgments as that used by the subjects in the first session, but his median differed in the various conditions. With other subjects, the "plant" distributed his judgments about a median and within a range much further away from those originally made by the subject. In fact, in the most extreme conditions, the "plant" made judgments ranging upward from a value twelve times the subject's largest judgment in session one.

Our results in this experiment are shown in Figure 5. Note that these

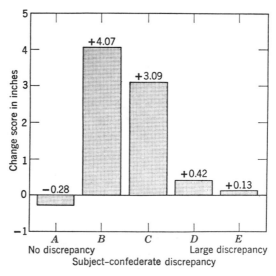

FIGURE 5.   *Mean change scores as a function of subject-confederate discrepancy in judgments (Whittaker, 1964b).*

data show a monotonic relationship between discrepancy and change. Smaller discrepancy equals greater change in this case, which is the reverse of Freedman's findings under conditions of low involvement as shown in Figure 4.

As we did additional work on this problem, we became increasingly convinced that the earlier results were not entirely accurate because the smallest discrepancy employed was considerable. In 1962 we again utilized the autokinetic situation and a procedure very similar to that employed earlier. In this later study, however, we included one experimental condition in which the discrepancy employed was *smaller* than the smallest we had utilized in the previous study. In other words, in Figure 5, this condition would be located between *A* (control group) and *B* (the smallest discrepancy employed in the earlier study). In this condition the lowest the judgment of the "plant" was set only one inch above the *lowest* judgment of the subject in session one. Hence the range of judgments of the subject and "plant" overlapped considerably.

With this new condition added to the experiment, we found an average change of only +1.06 inches, whereas subjects in group *B* (smallest discrepancy condition in the 1957 study) showed an average change of +4.07 inches in the direction of the "plant." Thus the monotonic relationship we originally observed was a function of neglecting to include *very small* discrepancies. Conversely, we may conclude now that the monotonic relationship observed by Freedman was a function of his failure to include *very* large descrepancies.

It is clear that investigators have been describing the whole elephant

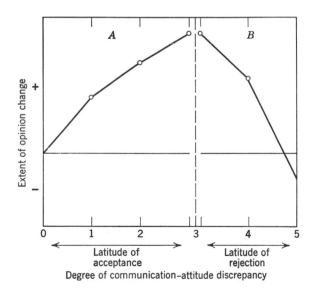

FIGURE 6.   *Hypothetical curve showing relationship between opinion change and communication-attitude discrepancy. Looking at the A part of the curve yields one conclusion, whereas looking only at the B part yields the opposite conclusion.*

of the discrepancy problem on the basis of examination of its different parts. If, for example, one set of limited discrepancies is employed, the investigator can easily be drawn to the conclusion that greater discrepancy equals greater change. This is illustrated in Figure 6. If we look only at the "A" part of the figure at the left, very obviously the curve shows that greater discrepancy equals greater change. On the other hand, if we look only at the "B" part of this figure (as we ourselves did in our 1957 study), we are forced to conclude that *smaller* discrepancy equals greater change.

As mentioned earlier, involvement is important insofar as it determines the relative sizes of the latitudes of acceptance and rejection. Under conditions of higher involvement, the optimal discrepancy (that yielding maximum change) is close to the subject's own position. Under conditions of low involvement, the discrepancy yielding maximum change is much further away. Thus, regardless of degree of involvement on the part of the subject, there is a curvilinear relationship between communication discrepancy and attitude change.

CONCLUSION

In conclusion, let me summarize the main points illustrated in the research results reported here. We have seen that tolerance for various positions on an issue is related to the subject's own stand on the issue and his degree of involvement in that stand. His perception of other positions is influenced by his own stand, causing him to perceive some positions as closer to his own than they actually are and other positions as farther away. His own stand also influences his judgment of other positions: some positions are judged as biased and propagandistic and others as fair and impartial.

The probability that a subject will judge a communication as biased and the probability of assimilation or contrast can be predicted from knowledge of a subject's latitudes of acceptance and rejection.

Regardless of the sizes of the latitudes of acceptance and rejection, however, or degree of involvement in the issue, there is a curvilinear or nonmonotonic relationship between attitude change and communication discrepancy. As discrepancy increases, positive attitude change increases up to a maximum point and then diminishes until, finally, increasingly larger negative changes occur. With narrow latitudes of acceptance, the point of maximum positive change is very close to the subject's own position, whereas with wider latitudes it is further away. If we know the latitudes of acceptance and rejection appropriate to a particular subject or the mean latitudes of acceptance and rejection appropriate to a particular audience, we can predict the optimal discrepancy with considerable accuracy.

Now for those who may think this is an esoteric issue having little to do with the realities of everyday life, let me point out some of the important implications.

First, this research shows that communicators *must* know the positions or stands of individuals with whom they are communicating, at least if they are at all interested in changing attitudes. It is not enough to simply present one's own position. In fact, presentation of one's own position without regard for that of the listener may result in convincing the listener that he is right and the communicator is wrong.

Second, this research shows that the position of the communication must be determined on the basis of latitudes of acceptance and rejection in the audience or at least the principal positions of the individuals who make up the audience. If it is not, the "truth" in many situations may result in "boomerang effects" because it is so discrepant from what the individual already believes. Conversely, it may yield less change than could otherwise be obtained because it is too close to what the individual believes. Clearly then, in many communication situations, presentation of the "truth" is not a guarantee of effectiveness, from the point of view of changing attitudes.

The major implication in these results, it seems to me, is that communicators must know what people believe before they attempt to present any communication. Furthermore, there must be a continuous feedback of information about audience positions or stands. This initial assessment of positions and feedback becomes particularly crucial when the communicator and audience are from very different cultures or social organizations, as is the case today in much international communication. Those responsible for the content of communications must learn to take this information into account. If they desire to be effective, the stands they present should be based on knowledge of the optimal discrepancy existing for specific audiences on specific issues. In addition, when circumstances dictate, they must learn to say nothing. If the truth is damaging, in other words, they need not lie but at least they must keep quiet.

REFERENCES

DAUGHERTY, W., and JANOWITZ, M. (Eds.), 1958. *A psychological warfare casebook.* Baltimore: Johns Hopkins Univ. Press.

EWING, T. N., 1942. A study of certain factors involved in changes of opinion. *J. soc. Psychol.*, 16, 63–88.

FESTINGER, L., 1957. *A theory of cognitive dissonance.* Evanston, Ill.: Row, Peterson.

FISHER, S., and LUBIN, A., 1958. Distance as a determinant of influence in a two-person serial interaction situation. *J. abnorm. soc. Psychol.*, 56, 230–238.

FISHER, S., RUBINSTEIN, I., and FREEMAN, R., 1956. Intertrial effects of immediate self-committal in a continuous social influence situation. *J. abnorm. soc. Psychol.*, 52, 200–207.

FREEDMAN, J., 1964. Involvement discrepancy and change. *J. abnorm. soc. Psychol.*, 69, 290–295.

FRENCH, J. R. P., JR., 1956. A formal theory of social power. *Psychol. Rev.*, 63, 181–194.

GOLDBERG, S. C., 1954. Three situational determinants of conformity to social norms. *J. abnorm. soc. Psychol.*, 49, 325–329.

HARVEY, O. J., KELLEY, H., and SHAPIRO, M., 1957. Reactions to unfavorable evaluations of the self made by other persons. *J. Pers.*, 25, 393–411.

HOVLAND, C. I., HARVEY, O. J., and SHERIF, M., 1957. Assimilation and contrast effects in reactions to communication and attitude change. *J. abnorm. soc. Psychol.*, 55, 244–252.

HOVLAND, C. I., and PRITZKER, H. A., 1957. Extent of opinion change as a function of amount of change advocated. *J. abnorm. soc. Psychol.*, 54, 257–261.

SHERIF, M., 1965. The social judgment-involvement approach vs. the cognitive dissonance approach. Paper presented at the meetings of the Amer. Psychological Ass., Chicago.

SHERIF, M., and HOVLAND, C. I., 1961. *Social judgment.* New Haven: Yale Univ. Press.

WHITTAKER, J., 1957. The effects of experimentally introduced anchorages upon judgment in the autokinetic situation. Paper presented before the Fifteenth Int. Congr. of Psychol., Brussels, Belgium.

———, 1963. Opinion change as a function of communication—attitude discrepancy. *Psychol. Rep.*, 13, 763–772.

———, 1964a. Cognitive dissonance and the effectiveness of persuasive communications. *Publ. Opin. Quart.*, 28, 547–555.

———, 1964b. Parameters of social influence in the autokinetic situation. *Sociometry*, 27, 88–95.

———, 1965a. In Sherif, C., Sherif, M., and Nebergall, R., *Attitude and attitude change: The social judgment-involvement approach.* Philadelphia: Saunders, p. 155.

———, 1965b. Attitude change and communication—attitude discrepancy. *J. soc. Psychol.*, 65, 141–147.

ZIMBARDO, P. G., 1960. Involvement and communication discrepancy as determinants of opinion change. *J. abnorm. soc. Psychol.*, 60, 86–94.

William A. Watts / William J. McGuire*

PERSISTENCE
OF INDUCED
OPINION CHANGE
AND RETENTION
OF THE INDUCING
MESSAGE CONTENTS[1]

Induced opinion change shows a strong positive relationship to recall of the
contents of the persuasive message 1 week after receipt of the communication
but tends, over time, to become functionally autonomous of recall of at least
some aspects of the contents of the inducing message. Induced opinion change
was found to decay rectilinearly over a 6-week period, while recall of contents
showed a negatively accelerated decay trend. Opinion change and recall of
the message topic were positively related 1 week after the communication,
but negatively related 6 weeks later. Recall of the side taken and of the
specific arguments used were positively related to opinion change both
1 week and 6 weeks after the communication. Recall of source was
complexly related to opinion change.

The present study was designed to investigate the persistence over time
of the opinion change induced by a persuasive message, and to relate this

*University of California, Berkeley, and Columbia University.
[1] This study was supported by a grant from the Division of Social Sciences, National
Science Foundation.

Reprinted from the *Journal of Abnormal and Social Psychology*, 68 (1964), 233–41, with
permission of the authors and the American Psychological Association.

persistence to memory for various aspects of the content of the message that induced the change. Three separate issues are involved in this question: the persistence of induced opinion change, the retention of message content, and the relation between opinion change and recall of contents. We shall review briefly the research on each of these issues.

Research on the persistence of induced opinion change yields abundant evidence that there is no such thing as *the* decay function of persuasion. Rather, there is a wide variety of such functions reflecting variations in the communication situations that induced the changes. In their classical study on the influence of commercial films on social attitudes of children, Peterson and Thurstone (1933) found that the opinion change induced by some films decayed completely within 8 months, while the persuasive effects of other films were higher after 6 months than immediately after the showing. Others who report almost complete decay within 6 months include Chen (1936) and Sims (1938). Those finding some decay but a still significant residual change after considerable periods include Cherrington and Miller (1933), Dietrich (1946), Janis, Lumsdaine, and Gladstone (1951), and McGuire (1960a). Almost complete persistence of the initially induced change was found by Annis and Meier (1934) and Smith (1943). Thus, the findings range from complete loss to complete persistence of induced opinion change over comparable periods of time.

Actually, the full range of findings indicate more diversity still, since a number of studies showed a delayed action persuasive effect; that is, an increase in opinion change with time since message. Lewin (1958) reported that the amount of compliance induced by group discussion was greater 3 weeks later than it was immediately after the discussion. In the World War II studies, Hovland, Lumsdaine, and Sheffield (1949) tested soldiers either 5 days or 9 weeks after they saw the *Battle of Britain* film and found that opinion change showed a net increase over that time. The experimenters named this phenomenon the "sleeper effect" and proposed various theories to account for it. One of these, the "discounting cue" theory, has been much studied subsequently (for example, Kelman & Hovland, 1953) and will be discussed below in connection with our source recall results. Delayed action effects have also been found when the persuasive message is complex or indirect (Cohen, 1957; McGuire, 1960b; Stotland, Katz, & Patchen, 1959), possibly because complex material can be fully assimilated into the cognitive system only with the passage of considerable time.

The second general question involved in the present investigation deals with retention of the content of the persuasive message. Research on this verbal learning topic has been voluminous, and competent reviews are so readily available (for example, McGeogh & Irion, 1952) that discussion is hardly needed here.

It is on the third question that the present research focuses; namely, to the extent to which the persistence of the induced opinion change is related to retention in memory of the various aspects of the persuasive content that induced it. We have found no previous study undertaken primarily to investigate this relationship directly, but a number of earlier investigators have reported incidental findings on the overall relationship. Hovland *et al.* (1949) found a slight negative relation between content recall and persistence of opinion change, but suggest a confounding due to postcommunication interactions among subjects of different predispositions. McGuire (1957) found a biserial r of $+ .53$ ($p < .01$) between content recall and opinion change immediately after the communication. Janis and Rife (1959), studying persuasibility in mental patients, found the correlation between content recall and opinion change to be $+ .21$ ($p = .06$) immediately after the message and $+ .24$ ($p < .05$) after 1 week. Miller and Campbell (1959) found attitude and recall complexly related. When measured immediately after the message, they were positively related ($r = .49$ and $r = .27$), and when a week intervened, the correlation was negative ($- .51$ and $- .40$).

The present study goes beyond these previous ones by attempting to relate opinion change to recall for the separate aspects of the communcation content. These aspects include the following: recall that a message on the given issue had even been received; recall of whether the pro or con side had been taken in the message; recall of the specific arguments that had been employed to support this side; and recall of the source of the message.

It is almost tautological (ignoring without trepidation any possibility of inducing opinion change through "subliminal perception") that for the opinion change to have been induced by the message, there must have been some initial learning of the inducing content. But granting this assumption of positive relationship between initial learning and opinion change, two alternative hypotheses regarding their concurrent decay rates are a priori plausible. One hypothesis we can call the "functional dependence" view. It would say that recall of the inducing content is necessary not only to induce the opinion change, but also to maintain it so that as inducing content is forgotten, the opinion falls back to its initial position. The alternative hypothesis, which we call the "functional autonomy" view (after Allport, 1937), holds that initial learning of the inducing content is necessary for producing the opinion change; but once the change is made, it is as if a switch were thrown and the new opinion persists, regardless of the retention of the content, unless subsequently some countercontent is received, thus throwing the opinion "switch" back again. As will be discussed in detail in connection with our findings, there is reason to expect induced opinion change to be functionally dependent on recall of some aspects of the communication and functionally autonomous of the retention of other aspects.

METHOD

Since we wished to measure persistence of induced opinion change and retention for learned message content, each experimental subject took part in four sessions spaced over a 6-week interval and in each session read a persuasive message on a different issue. Then, after the fourth session, for the only time in the experiment, we measured opinion change on all four issues and retention of the contents of all four messages.

Material

Since the design required persuasive messages on four different issues, a prestudy was carried out to select appropriate issues. A group of undergraduate education students were asked to indicate, on a 15-point scale, their degree of agreement with each item in an initial pool of opinion statements. On the basis of their responses, four items were selected as the experimental issues. These four best met the criteria of homogeneous initial opinions (the four mean agreement scores ranged from 5.38 to 5.91 on the 15-point scale) and high homogeneity among subjects as regards initial opinion on each issue. The four issues selected were the following: "Puerto Rico should be admitted to the Union as the 51st State"; "Courts should deal more leniently with juvenile delinquents"; "The Secretary of State should be elected by the people, not appointed by the President"; "The State Sales tax should be abolished."

The final opinion questionnaire used in this study consisted of these four statements. Each statement was followed by a 15-point graphic scale with the left end labeled "Definitely Disagree" and the right end, "Definitely Agree." The subject was instructed to mark an "X" in whichever of the 15 categories best indicated his own stand on the statement.

Four persuasive messages were prepared, one on each issue. Each argued in favor of one of the above statements so as to push the mean agreement from the 5.00- to 6.00-point initial level toward the high agreement, 15.00-point end of the scale. Each message consisted of a title, an attributed source, and about 600 words of text divided into four paragraphs. The introductory paragraph stated that the communicator favored the statement and mentioned three arguments supporting it. Each of the following paragraphs developed in detail one of these three arguments. The messages were written in a calm, authoritative fashion with frequent citation of (purported) facts and figures bearing on the point being made.[2]

Alternate forms of each of the four messages were prepared, the pair of messages on any one issue being identical except that on one form the attribution was to

[2] The four persuasive messages used in this study have been deposited with the American Documentation Institute. Order Document No. 7783 from ADI Auxiliary Publications Project. Photoduplication Service, Library of Congress, Washington, D. C. 20540. Remit in advance $1.25 for microfilm or $1.25 for photocopies and make checks payable to: Chief, Photoduplication Service, Library of Congress.

a positively valenced source and on the other form to a negatively valenced source.[3] For example, on the "Sales Tax" issue, the positively valenced source was the report of a "Presidential Council for the study of the sales tax," while the corresponding negatively valenced source was "a defense argument by a man convicted of sales-tax fraud."

Recall for the various aspects of the communications was measured by a series of recall and recognition tests of increasing demandingness. The first asked the subject to recall and state, in his own words, the general topic discussed in each of the four messages he had received over the past 2 months. The second test reinstated these four topics and called upon the subject to state whether a pro or a con stand had been taken in the message on each topic. The third test reinstated each topic and stand and listed four possible sources of each message, the subject being required to select the source to whom the message had actually been attributed. The fourth test consisted of three multiple-choice questions on each message designed to measure the subject's recall of the three specific arguments used in that message.

Opinion change was measured by the 15-point scales described above. Since we employed an after-only design, the opinion change scores were actually based on the final mean belief levels with the scales calibrated so that the messages were always pushing the person's opinion toward the 15-point end. The opinion change score in a given cell in Tables 1 through 5 is the final mean opinion level for subjects in that cell minus the final mean opinion level of the control (no message) subjects.

Subjects and Design

The subjects were 191 students enrolled in an introductory education course at the University of Illinois. Almost all of these subjects were women. They took part in all the sessions of the experiment during their usual section meeting. All 10 sections of the course were used. Four sections received the four messages from positively valenced sources; another 4 sections received them from negatively valenced sources; and a final 2 sections served as no message controls. The section size averaged 19 and ranged from 12 to 26. The precise numbers of cases serving in each condition are shown in each cell of the tables in the Results section below. The four topics were rotated around the four time intervals from section to section.

Procedure

The study was represented to the subjects as an attempt to develop instruments for measuring reading comprehension and analytic thinking ability in future teachers. The subjects were told they would be asked to read standardized passages dealing with controversial issues and that their task was to select and underline in each paragraph the shortest clause which epitomized the whole point being made in that paragraph. They were then allowed 6 minutes for reading and underlining in the prescribed manner one of the four persuasive messages.

Each subject (except those in the no message control condition) served in four experimental sessions. Each of the first three sessions was brief (lasting about 10

[3] The document referred to in Footnote 2 lists the positive and negative sources used with each of the four messages.

398   William A. Watts / William J. McGuire

minutes) and consisted of receiving the general instructions and then reading and underlining one of the four persuasive messages. The fourth session was much longer, lasting about 60 minutes. It began, like the others, with the general instructions and then reading and underlining the message on a fourth issue. Immediately afterward the subjects filled out (for the only time in the experiment) the opinion questionnaire on all four issues and took the tests of retention of the various aspects of the communications as described above.

Since the opinion change and recall for all four topics were measured at the same time, namely, immediately after receipt of the message on the fourth topic, the retention interval was determined by how long prior to this last session the message on a given topic had been received. For all subjects the message on the first topic preceded the final opinion and memory measurement session by 6 weeks; the second, by 2 weeks; the third, by 1 week; and the fourth, by a few minutes. The present design was employed to achieve the statistical sensitivity obtained by using the subject as his own control while avoiding the ambiguity of using repeated measurements. But while this design allowed us to avoid repeated measurement of the same subjects at successive time intervals, there does remain the problem that the subjects were exposed to repeated messages (on different issues) which could conceivably have resulted in some kind of a progressive wariness. Such a possible effect would be troublesome since the irrelevant wariness variation would be perfectly correlated with our experimental variable of recency. However, the wariness effect would go in the opposite direction to the recency effect, and the data reported below show that there was an overwhelming recency effect in these results. Hence, this possible wariness contamination is not a major worry in interpreting the present results.

RESULTS AND DISCUSSION

Overall Decay Rates

The persuasive impact of the messages and also the recall of each of the various aspects of the message contents decayed fairly steadily over the 6-week postcommunication interval. Table 1 and Figure 1 show the shapes of these time trends when the data on the four issues and two source credibility conditions are combined.

Induced opinion change can be seen to decay progressively over time. The 69% drop from immediately after to 6 weeks after is significant at the .01 level. (Unless otherwise specified, all p values given in this Results section for time trends and their interactions are based on analyses of variance in which the error terms consist of the residual within-subjects' variance, that is, the interactions between subjects and the treatments whose effects are being evaluated.) It would seem logical to expect this decay function to be negatively accelerated approaching an asymptote at about the 5.95-point control level. However, it can be seen in Figure 1 that the decay curve resembles very closely a straight line. An analysis using the F ratio of the deviations of means from the regression line to the within arrays shows that the obtained data do not

TABLE 1

Temporal Decay of Induced Opinion Change and of Recall
for Aspects of the Communication

Variable measured	Interval between message receipt and opinion measurement			
	Immediately after	1 week	2 weeks	6 weeks
Opinion change (on a 15-point scale) in the induced direction from 5.95-point no-message control level	2.53	2.12	2.09	0.78
Percentage of subjects recalling message topic	94	60	63	61
Percentage of subjects recalling the side taken in the message (after reinstatement of topic)	93	65	65	60
Percentage of subjects recognizing message source (after reinstatement of topic)	85	44	50	34
Percentage of subjects recognizing all three arguments in the message (after reinstatement of topic and side)	72	29	24	11

Note.—Each cell score is based on 151 subjects.

depart significantly $(F = .09)$ from the best-fitting straight line which has a slope of $-.287$. This slope is significantly different from zero $(F = 5.35,$ $df = 3/575, p < .01)$.

Recall of each of the three aspects of the communication can likewise be seen to fall over time as did the decay of induced opinion change. However, in contrast to the rectilinear decay of induced opinion change, all three of these retention curves show the negative acceleration characteristic of the forgetting curves usually reported in verbal learning studies. The fact that the function for opinion change decay has the same direction, but a different rate from the functions for retention of content, suggests that the persistence of the induced change is only partly dependent on the retention of the persuasive content of the message, a point which is brought out more clearly by analyses discussed below.

Relation between Persistence of Opinion Change and Recall of the Topic Discussed

In order to determine how the persistence of the induced opinion change is related to the retention of the most basic aspect of the content of the inducing message, namely, recall of topic, we compared the opinion change on the issue in question of those who could and those who could not recall this aspect of the

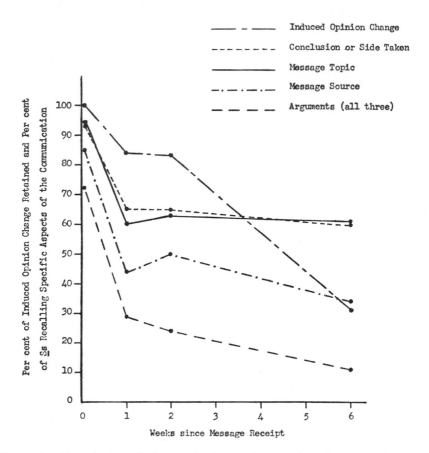

FIGURE 1.   *Temporal decay of induced opinion change and of recall for various aspects of the persuasive communication. (Points are based on percentages in Table 1.)*

message received 1 week earlier with the opinion change of those who could and could not recall the topic of the message received 6 weeks earlier.[4] It can be seen from the results in Table 2 that the two resulting decay functions for opinion change cross, indicating an interaction effect. One week after receipt of the message, those who remember the message topic are more influenced

---

[4] It might seem strange we did not compare decay trends for the immediately-before versus 6-weeks-before issue, rather than the 1- versus 6-weeks. The reason is that the immediately-before condition yielded too asymmetrical a split, only 9 of the 151 subjects being unable to recall the topic of the message that had come immediately before the test. This vanishing cell N made a sensitive statistical test impossible so we selected the less extreme time interval (even though this tended to weaken the magnitude of this trend difference) in order to obtain a nearer-the-median split on the basis of recall. For the sake of consistency, the same procedure was followed with respect to recall of each of the other aspects of the message. In any case, for each of the effects reported, the same trend is evident whether we compare the immediately-before or the 1-week-before condition with the 6-weeks-before condition.

TABLE 2

OPINION CHANGE AS RELATED TO ABILITY TO RECALL
THE TOPIC DISCUSSED IN THE MESSAGE

Recall of topic	Interval between message receipt and opinion measurement		
	1 week	*6 weeks*	*M*
Yes	2.57	0.38	1.39
	(80)	(92)	(172)
No	1.45	1.41	1.43
	(53)	(59)	(112)
M	2.12	0.78	1.41
	(133)	(151)	(284)

Note.—Number in parentheses indicates number of scores on which cell mean is based.

than those who do not remember it; while 6 weeks after the message, those remembering the topic are *less* influenced than those forgetting it. This interaction is significant above the .05 level ($F = 4.42$).[5]

While this inverse relationship after 6 weeks might seem paradoxical, it is neither unprecedented nor without a ready interpretation. Miller and Campbell (1959) found somewhat similar results: the overall relationship between attitude and recall was negligible ($r = -.10$); but when the opinion measure was taken immediately after the messages, the relationship was substantially positive ($r = .49$ and $r = .27$); while when the messages and opinion measurement were spread over a 2-week interval, substantial negative correlations ($-.51$ and $-.40$) were found.

Hence, both studies show that soon after message receipt, those subjects who recall having heard a message on the topic show more opinion change on it; while, after more time passes, more opinion change is shown by those not recalling having heard the message. (The time parameters were different in the two studies: 0 versus 2 weeks in the Miller-Campbell study and 1 versus 6 weeks in ours. However, the same trend shows up in our study also when we compare the 0—rather than 1—week interval with the 6 weeks. We did the significance test on the 1- versus 6-weeks comparison only to avoid the "vanishing cell N" problem discussed in Footnote 4.)

Our explanation for this rather unexpected, but highly significant and

[5] Partitioning the subjects on the basis of recall of the various aspects of the message contents frequently resulted in very disproportional cell *N*s, as can be seen in Table 2 and the following tables. Hence, in estimating the significance of the interaction effects shown in the tables we used an approximation for unequal frequencies in subclasses in analysis of variance (Walker & Lev, 1953, pp. 381–382).

replicated, interaction effect is as follows: Inability to recall so basic a point as the topic of a message soon after that message was presented indicates a high likelihood that, for some reason (such as inattention or misunderstanding), the person did not effectively receive the message in the first place and, hence, was unaffected by it. However, as time passes, there is increasing likelihood that the inability to recall the topic is due rather to forgetting of a message whose content was initially received. For the group whose inability to recall the topic after the prolonged interval due to forgetting of the specific communication situation, we would expect a sleeper effect to occur; that is, these subjects would tend to discount partially the arguments at first, while they still recalled that they heard them during a "propaganda" session. As time passed, however, and they forgot this discounting cue regarding the context in which they heard the argumentative material, the full persuasive impact of this material would tend to emerge undampened. As can be seen in Table 2, the interaction effect is due to such a delayed action effect in the no recall condition. This interpretation of the present finding is in close accord with Hovland's original interpretation of the "sleeper effect" (Hovland et al., 1949).

Regardless of the interpretation, however, the results indicate clearly that the persistence of induced opinion change tends to become, not only autonomous of recalling ever having heard a persuasive message on the issue, but actually negatively related to such recall. The significant interaction effect between persistence of induced opinion change and recall of topics has the result of canceling any first-order effect of the recall-of-topics variable. The trivial difference in opinion change between those recalling and not recalling the topic over both intervals (1 week and 6 weeks) yields an F of only .04.

Relation between Persistence of Opinion Change and Recall of the Side Taken on the Topic

The persistence of the induced opinion change was found to be related to retention of the conclusions drawn in the message. That is, when the topic was reinstated for the subject, his ability to recall which side of the topic had been supported in the message was positively related to the amount of opinion change, as can be seen in Table 3. Both of the marginals in this table are significant. The significant ($p < .01$) vertical margin indicates the overall decay of the induced opinion change which has already been discussed. The significant ($F = 5.65$, $p < .05$) horizontal margin indicates that, over both time intervals, those better able to recall the side taken in the message when the topic is reinstated are also more influenced. While there is some tendency for this positive relationship between recall of what side had been taken and amount of opinion change to lessen as time passes (see Table 3), the interaction

TABLE 3

OPINION CHANGE AS RELATED TO RECALL OF THE SIDE
WHICH HAD BEEN TAKEN IN THE MESSAGE
ON THE GIVEN TOPIC

Recall of side after message topic is reinstated	Interval between message receipt and opinion measurement		
	1 week	6 weeks	M
Yes	2.83	0.94	1.86
	(86)	(91)	(177)
No	0.81	0.53	0.66
	(47)	(60)	(107)

Note.—Number in parentheses indicates number of scores on which cell mean is based.

falls short of the conventional level of significance ($F = 2.49$, $p = .12$); and, hence, we cannot conclude that persistence of opinion change becomes functionally autonomous of recognition of which side had been taken in a prior persuasive message when its topic is reinstated.

Relation between Persistence of Opinion Change and Recognizing the Specific Arguments Used

After the topics and the sides taken on them in the messages were reinstated for the subject, he was asked three multiple-choice questions designed to measure his ability to recognize the three arguments that had been used in each message. On the basis of their responses to these questions, the subjects were partitioned into those who answered correctly three or two of the questions on a given issue versus those who answered only one or none correctly (this point of partition coming closest to yielding a median split for the 1- and 6-week intervals). The opinion scores of the resulting subsets of subjects are shown in Table 4. The main effect is significant ($F = 9.65$, $p < .01$), indicating that with the topics and the sides taken reinstated, the recall of the specific arguments contributes to the amount of opinion change. Those recalling two or more arguments show more change both 1 week after the message ($t = 2.26$, $p < .05$) and 6 weeks later, although the difference is trivial ($t = .98$) at the longer interval. The interaction effect is trivial ($F = .20$). Hence, there is evidence that opinion change is functionally dependent on the recall of the arguments originally inducing it, given that the topics and sides taken in the messages are reinstated.

TABLE 4

OPINION CHANGE AS RELATED TO RECALL OF THE
SPECIFIC ARGUMENTS USED IN A MESSAGE AFTER THE TOPIC
AND THE SIDE TAKEN ARE REINSTATED

Number of arguments recognized	Interval between message receipt and opinion measurement		
	1 week	*6 weeks*	*M*
3 or 2	2.75	1.52	2.21
	(86)	(68)	(154)
1 or 0	0.96	0.17	0.46
	(47)	(83)	(130)

Note.—Number in parentheses indicates number of scores on which cell mean is based.

Effect of Source without Regard to Recall

As shown in Figure 2, there is some evidence of a main-order source effect and of the "sleeper effect" interaction between source valence and time since communication. As regards the main effect of source valence, the mean change produced by the messages over the four intervals was 2.10 when they were attributed to the positively valenced sources and 1.54 when attributed to the negatively valenced sources ($F = 2.77$, $p = .10$). As regards the sleeper interaction effect, it can be seen that the induced change decays fairly steadily

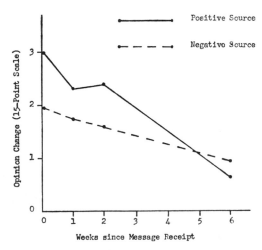

FIGURE 2. *Persistence of opinion change induced by positively and negatively valenced sources.*

over time in both source conditions, but more rapidly in the positively valenced source condition, even to the extent that the two curves cross (see Figure 2). This sleeper-effect interaction between the source-valence variable and the immediate versus 6-week interval variable is of only borderline significance ($F = 3.71$, $p < .10$) and could be due, at least in part, to a regression effect.

Effects of Recall of Source

After the topics and sides taken in the message were reinstated, the subjects' ability to recognize the source of the message on each issue was measured by a multiple-choice question that allowed him to select either the correct source or one of the incorrect sources of positive or negative valence. Hence, the subjects in the positive and those in the negative source-valence conditions could be further partitioned into those who could and those who could not recall the source. The mean opinion change of each of these four subsets is shown in Table 5 for each of the four time intervals. Insofar as recall of source contributes to opinion change, there should be an interaction effect between source valence and source recall such that those in the positive source condition should show more opinion change when they can recognize the source, and those in the negative source condition should show less change if they can recognize the source. As can be seen in Table 5, the data for all four intervals combined show no such trend. Rather, there is a main-order effect such that those who recall better the source show more opinion change ($F = 4.09$, $p < .05$) even when the source was a negative one. An inspection of the means shows that this effect was confined almost entirely to the positive source condition. With the negative source, those recalling and not recalling the source show about

TABLE 5

<small>Opinion Change as Related to Source Valence and Recall of Source after the Topics and Sides Taken in the Messages Are Reinstated</small>

Source condition	Interval between message receipt and opinion measurement				
	Immediate	1 week	2 weeks	6 weeks	M
Positive valence	3.17	2.59	2.78	1.16	2.54
Source recalled	(76)	(48)	(56)	(46)	(226)
	1.49	1.99	1.71	0.05	1.22
Source not recalled	(9)	(37)	(29)	(39)	(114)
Negative valence	1.75	2.05	1.35	0.72	1.62
Source recalled	(53)	(10)	(20)	(6)	(89)
	2.67	1.65	1.70	0.97	1.49
Source not recalled	(13)	(38)	(46)	(60)	(157)

Note.—Number in parentheses indicates number of scores on which cell mean is based.

equal change; while with positive sources, those recalling the source show far greater change ($t = 2.74$, $p < .01$).

The second-order interaction effect (involving source valence, source recall, and interval since message) is practically nil (see Table 5). Hence, the discounting cue theory receives no support if the theory is stated in terms of the subject's ability to recall the source. Hovland and Weiss (1951) and Kelman and Hovland (1953) have, however, already reformulated the theory in terms, not of the subject's ability to recall the source, but of his spontaneous tendency to do so.

An interesting incidental finding is that the positive sources were much better recalled than the negative. As shown in Table 6, the positive sources

TABLE 6

NUMBER OF SUBJECTS WHO RECALL HIGH VALENCED
AND LOW VALENCED SOURCES

Source condition	Interval between message receipt and opinion measurement			
	Immediately after	1 week	2 weeks	6 weeks
Positive valence				
Recalled	76	48	56	46
Not recalled	9	37	29	39
Negative valence				
Recalled	53	10	20	6
Not recalled	13	38	46	60
χ^2 (High versus Low)	1.80	14.43*	17.42*	31.40*

*$p < .001$

are better recalled than the negative at all four time intervals and the superiority increases with the length of the interval, attaining the .001 level of significance at each of the three longer intervals (1-, 2-, and 6-weeks). This differential can be explained in terms of the more rapid forgetting of dissonant material (Festinger, 1957). The messages used in the study were designed to be reasonable and logical. The incongruous attribution of so impressive a message to a negatively valenced source may account for the more rapid forgetting of the negatively valenced sources. Alternatively, the differential recall could be attributed to some systematic difference between the sets of negative and of positive sources used here such that the positive sources were systematically more familiar, more interesting, etc., than the negative and, hence, better recalled. However, the instances used within the sets are varied enough so that this interpretation is not compelling.

REFERENCES

ALLPORT, G. W. *Personality: A psychological interpretation*. New York: Holt, 1937.

ANNIS, A. D., and MEIER, N. C. The induction of opinion change through suggestion by means of "planted content." *J. soc. Psychol.*, 1934, 5, 65–81.

CHEN, W. K. C. Retention of the effect of oral propaganda. *J. soc. Psychol.*, 1936, 7, 479–483.

CHERRINGTON, B. M., and MILLER, L. W. Changes in attitude as a result of a lecture and of reading similar materials. *J. soc. Psychol.*, 1933, 4, 479–484.

COHEN, A. R. Need for cognition and order of communication as determinants of opinion change. In C. I. Hovland et al. (Eds.), *The order of presentation in persuasion*. New Haven: Yale Univer. Press, 1957. pp. 79–97.

DIETRICH, J. E. The relative effectiveness of two modes of radio delivery in influencing attitudes. *Speech Monogr.*, 1946, 13, 58–65.

FESTINGER, L. *A theory of cognitive dissonance*. Evanston, Ill.: Row, Peterson, 1957.

HOVLAND, C. I., LUMSDAINE, A. A., and SHEFFIELD, F. D. *Experiments on mass communication*. Princeton: Princeton Univer. Press, 1949.

HOVLAND, C. I., and WEISS, W. The influence of source credibility on communication effectiveness. *Publ. Opin. Quart.*, 1951, 15, 635–650.

JANIS, I. L., LUMSDAINE, A. A., and GLADSTONE, A. I. Effects of preparatory communications on reactions to a subsequent news event. *Publ. Opin. Quart.*, 1951, 15, 487–518.

JANIS, I. L., and RIFE, D. Persuasibility and emotional disorder. In C. I. Hovland and I. L. Janis (Eds.), *Personality and persuasibility*. New Haven: Yale Univer. Press, 1959. pp. 121–140.

KELMAN, H. C., and HOVLAND, C. I. "Reinstatement" of the communicator in delayed measurement of opinion change. *J. abnorm. soc. Psychol.*, 1953, 48, 327–335.

LEWIN, K. Group decision and social change. In Eleanor E. Maccoby, T. M. Newcomb, and E. L. Hartley (Eds.), *Readings in social psychology*. (3rd ed.) New York: Holt, 1958. pp. 197–211.

McGEOGH, J. A., and IRION, A. L. *The psychology of human learning*. New York: Longmans, 1952.

McGUIRE, W. J. Order of presentation as a factor in "conditioning" persuasiveness. In C. I. Hovland et al. (Eds.), *The order of presentation in persuasion*. New Haven: Yale Univer. Press, 1957. pp. 98–114.

———. Cognitive consistency and attitude change. *J. abnorm. soc. Psychol.*, 1960, 60, 345–353. (a)

———. A syllogistic analysis of cognitive relationships. In C. I. Hovland and M. I. Rosenberg (Eds.), *Attitude organization and change*. New Haven: Yale Univer. Press, 1960. pp. 65–111. (b)

MILLER, N., and CAMPBELL, D. T. Recency and primacy in persuasion as a function of the timing of speeches and measurements. *J. abnorm. soc. Psychol.*, 1959, 59, 1–9.

PETERSON, RUTH C., and THURSTONE, L. L. *Motion pictures and the social attitudes of children*. New York: Macmillan, 1933.

SIMS, V. M. Factors influencing attitude toward the TVA. *J. abnorm. soc. Psychol.*, 1938, 33, 34–56.

Smith, F. T. An experiment in modifying attitudes toward the Negro. *Teachers Coll. Columbia U. Contr. Educ.*, 1943, No. 887.

Stotland, E., Katz, D., and Patchen, M. Reduction of prejudice through the arousal of self insight. *J. Pers.*, 1959, 27, 507–531.

Walker, Helen M., and Lev, J. *Statistical inference.* New York: Holt, Rinehart, & Winston, 1953.

Theodore M. Newcomb

PERSISTENCE AND REGRESSION OF CHANGED ATTITUDES: LONG-RANGE STUDIES

One's attitude toward something is not only a resultant of one's previous traffic with one's environment but also a determinant of selective response to present and future environments. Viewed in the latter way, existing attitudes may determine one's selection among alternative environmental settings, and these in turn may serve to preserve or undermine the very attitudes that had been initially responsible for one's selection among the alternatives. Insofar as attitudes are self-preserving, such tendencies to select a supportive environment would, if empirically supported, provide an important explanation of their persistence. In its most general form, the hypothesis would run somewhat as follows: Existing attitudes are most likely to persist, other things equal, when one's environment provides most rewards for their behavioral expression. But this platitudinous proposition ("things persist when conditions are favorable to their persistence") is not very interesting, and is probably not even testable. A more interesting and more testable form of the proposition would take account of both change and persistence, both of attitudes and of environmental suppor- tiveness. In particular, it would say something about a changed selection of environments following attitude change, about the ways in which the recently formed attitude is or is not reinforced by the new environment, and about the

Excerpted from the *Journal of Social Issues,* 19, #4 (1963), 3–13, with permission of the author and the Journal of Social Issues.

persistence of the attitude in both supportive and hostile environments. Such a proposition, in its simplest form, would run somewhat as follows: A recently changed attitude is likely to persist—insofar as it leads to the selection of subsequent environments that provide reinforcements for the behavioral expression of the changed attitude.

Among the many possible forms of environmental reinforcements of behavioral expressions of attitudes, I shall consider a single class: behavior on the part of other people that one perceives as supportive of one's own attitudes. With few exceptions, such support comes from persons or groups toward whom one is positively attracted, according to the principles of what is perhaps most frequently known as balance theory (Cf. Heider, 1958; Brown, 1962; Newcomb, 1963). I am, in short, about to defend the limited proposition that a recently changed attitude is most likely to persist if one of its behavioral expressions is the selection of a social enviornment which one finds supportive of the changed attitude. This proposition differs from the one about autistic hostility primarily in that persistence of a recently acquired attitude depends upon continuing rather than cutting off sources of information about the attitude-object.

II.

There are various ways in which such a proposition might be tested in the laboratory. But insofar as one is interested, as I have been, in long-range effects, one will make use of "natural" settings. I shall therefore cite a few findings from two of my own studies, mentioning only briefly the less immediately relevant one (1961), which involved the daily observation of two populations of 17 male students, all initial strangers to one another, who lived intimately together for four-month periods. The only attitudes of these subjects that showed much change, from first to last, were their attractions toward each other—attitudes which had not even existed, of course, before their initial encounters in this research setting. Expressions of interpersonal attraction during the first week or two were highly unstable, but after about the fifth week they showed only slow and slight changes (Cf. Newcomb, 1963).

Under the conditions of this research, imposed environments (in the form of arbitrarily assigned rooms, roommates, and floors) had no consistent effects beyond the first week or two in interpersonal preferences. That is, one could predict little or nothing about interpersonal attraction from the fact of being roommates or floormates. Self-selected interpersonal environment, however, was closely associated with interpersonal attraction. At all times later than the first week or two, pairs of subjects who were reported by others to belong to the same voluntary subgroups were almost invariably pairs whose members chose each other at very high levels of attraction. If this seems to be a commonplace observation (as indeed it is), let me remind you of my reason for reporting it; interpersonal environments are not only consequences of existing attraction but also sources of future attraction. It is an everyday phenomenon that, having developed differential attitudes toward one's several acquaintances, one manipulates one's interpersonal environment, insofar as one can, to correspond with one's interpersonal preferences. And insofar as one is successful, chances are that the preferences will be further reinforced. My data, showing stability both of preferences and of voluntarily associating subgroups following the first month or so, indicate that exactly this was occurring. The fact that it is an everyday occurrence enhances rather than negates the importance of the principle involved, namely, that a recently acquired attitude will persist insofar as it results in the selection of an environment that is supportive of that attitude.

III.

I now turn to a totally different set of data, or rather to two sets of data from the same subjects, obtained over an interval of more than 20 years. The earlier responses were obtained between 1935 and 1939 at Bennington College (Newcomb, 1943); the later ones, obtained in 1960 and 1961, were from almost all of the subjects who had been studied for three or more consecutive years during the 1930's. To be specific, out of 141 former students in this category who in 1960 were alive, resident in continental United States, and not hopelessly invalided, 130 (scattered in 28 states) were interviewed, and 9 of the remaining 11 completed more or less parallel questionnaires. The interview dealt primarily with their present attitudes toward a wide range of public-affairs issues, with attitudes of their husbands and other contemporary associates, and with their histories and careers since leaving the College.

Before telling you some of the follow-up findings, I ought to report a few of the original ones. During each of four consecutive years (1935-36 through 1938-39), juniors and seniors were on the average markedly less conservative than freshmen in attitude toward many public issues of the day. Studies of the same individuals over three- and four-year intervals showed the same trend, which was not attributable to selective withdrawal from the College. Comparisons with other colleges showed almost no intercollege differences in freshmen attitudes, but much less conservatism at Bennington than at the other institutions on the part of seniors. Individual studies showed that at Bennington nonconservatism was rather closely associated with being respected by other students, with participation in college activities, and with personal involvement in the College as an institution. The relatively few malcontents were, with surprisingly few exceptions, those who held conservative attitudes toward public issues.

Given these initial findings, one of my concerns in planning the follow-up study was the following: Under what conditions would individuals who had become less conservative during their college years remain relatively nonconservative 20-odd years later, and under what conditions would they "regress" to relatively conservative positions? (As to the problem of comparing attitudes toward one set of issues in the 1930's with those toward quite different issues in the 1960's, I shall for present purposes note only that at both times we used indices of relative, not absolute standing: each subject is compared with the same set of peers.)

By way of noting the general pattern of persistence vs. regression on the part of the total population, I shall first compare one early with one later datum. In the 1940 presidential election, 51% of our interview sample who reported a preference for either major candidate chose the Democrat, F. D. Roosevelt, and 49% the Republican, W. Willkie. Twenty years later, the comparable figures were 60% for J. F. Kennedy and 40% for R. M. Nixon. No single election, of course, provides a very good test of what might be termed "general conservatism concerning public affairs," but at any rate this particular comparison does not suggest any conspicuous regression toward freshman conservatism. This conclusion is also supported by the following finding: In six consecutive presidential elections (1940 through 1960), an outright majority of our interviewees (51%) reported that they had preferred the Republican candidate either once or never, whereas only 27% of them had preferred that candidate as many as five times out of the six times.

The problem of regressive effects can also be approached by comparing relative conservatism on the part of the same individuals over the interval of 20-odd years. In terms of party or candidate preference in 1960, the degree of individual stability is startling. As shown in Table 1, individuals who were in the least conservative quartile of the total population, on graduating, preferred Kennedy by frequencies of 30 to 3, and those in the next quartile by 25 to 8; 83% of this half of the population preferred Kennedy 20 years later, while 37% of the initially more conservative half preferred Kennedy after 20 years. Political party preferences, and also an index of general political

TABLE 1

PRESIDENTIAL PREFERENCES IN 1960, ACCORDING TO QUARTILES
OF PEP SCORES ON LEAVING COLLEGE IN THE LATE 1930s

PEP quartile	Nixon preferred	Kennedy preferred	Total
1 (least conservative)	3	30	33
2	8	25	33
3	18	13	31
4 (most conservative)	22	11	33
TOTAL	51	79	130

conservatism, showed about the same relationship to political conservatism more than two decades earlier. These data provide no support for a prediction of general regression—either toward previous conservatism or in the statistical sense of regression toward the mean.

Other evidence concerning the general nonconservatism in this population in the early 1960's includes the following:

77% of them considered themselves "liberal" or "somewhat liberal," as compared with 17% who were "conservative" or "somewhat conservative";

76% "approved" or "strongly approved" of "Medicare" for the aged under Social Security;

61% "approved" or "strongly approved" of admitting Red China into the United Nations.

These and other data suggest that the population as a whole is now far less conservative than is to be expected in view of its demographic characteristics. Its socio-economic level may be judged from these facts: (1) 77% of the 117 respondents who were or had been married were judged by the interviewer to be at least "fairly well-to-do," with annual incomes of not less than $20,000; and (2) of 113 mothers in the population, 65% had sent at least one of their children to a private school. In religious background, about three-quarters of them were Protestants (more than half of whom were Episcopalian), and less than 10% were either Catholic or Jewish. According to information assembled for me by the Survey Research Center of the University of Michigan,* the proportion of Protestant women college graduates at the income level of this population who in 1960 expressed a preference for Kennedy over Nixon was less than 25—as compared with 60% of this alumnae population.

I shall now revert to my earlier theme: If this population is now less conservative than one might expect, to what extent is this explainable in terms of its members' selection of post-college environments that were supportive of nonconservative attitudes? It proves to be very difficult to categorize total environments from this point of view, and so for the present I shall limit myself to a single aspect of post-college environments: husbands. I am making no assumptions here except that (1) husbands were indeed a part of their wives' environments; (2) wives had had something to do with selecting this part of their environments; and (3) husbands, as environmental objects, were capable of being either supportive or nonsupportive of their wives' attitudes.

Nearly 80% of our respondents both had a husband and were able to report on his attitudes toward most of the issues with which we were concerned, during all or most of the past 20 years; one reason for placing a good deal of confidence in their reports is that they seem highly discriminating, as indicated by such responses as these: "I don't think I know how he'd feel on that par-

*By my colleague Philip Converse, to whom I am most grateful.

ticular issue," or "Now on *that* one he doesn't agree with me at all." Here are some summaries concerning all husbands whose wives were willing to attribute attitudes toward them (nearly all wives on most issues):

54% of the husbands in 1960 favored Kennedy over Nixon;

64% of them either "approved" or "strongly approved" of "Medicare" for the aged under Social Security;

57% of them either "approved" or "strongly approved" of admitting Red China into the United Nations.

And so it is almost as true of husbands as of wives that they are less conservative than is to be expected in view of their demographic characteristics: husbands' and wives' demographic characteristics are taken to be identical except for a very few couples differing in religious background, and their present attitudes are highly similar (90% of 1960 presidential preferences by pairs of spouses, for example, being reported as the same in 1960). It would hardly seem to be a matter of sheer chance that a set of men who are less conservative than is to be expected are married to a set of women of whom just the same thing is true. It seems necessary, therefore, to assume that attitudes toward public affairs had something to do with husbands' and wives' reciprocal selection of one another, or with post-marital influence upon one another, or with both. Here is one statistical support for this assumption: the correlation between wives' scores on an instrument labeled Political and Economic Progressivism, as of their graduating from college in the late 1930's, with the number of Republican candidates that their subsequent husbands voted for between 1940 and 1960 was .32; this does not account for much of the variance, but its p value is $< .0005$.

Another interesting finding has to do with the number of women in our interview sample whose husbands had attended Ivy League colleges; one would expect this proportion to be high, since so many of the women's fathers and brothers had attended these colleges. The actual frequency turned out to be just 50%. These Ivy League husbands' voting preferences in 1960, however, turned out to be much more like their wives' preferences than like their classmates' preferences: 52% of husbands whose wives were able to state a preference were for Kennedy—which is to say that they did not differ at all in voting preferences from all non-Ivy League husbands. This total set of facts best be interpreted as follows: Our Bennington graduates of the late 1930's found their husbands in the kinds of places where their families expected them to be found, but they selected somewhat atypical members of these "proper" populations of eligibles; they tended not to have conservative attitudes that were then typical of these populations.

One evidence of this atypical selection is to be seen in the occupational distribution of these women's husbands. Only 38% of all husbands are classifiable as "in management or business," the remaining 62% representing for the most part a wide range of professions (especially college teaching, entertainment, and the arts) and public employment (especially in goverment). Husbands in these two general categories (management and business vs. all others) differed sharply in their voting preferences in 1960; of the 113 husbands whose wives attributed preferences to them, 26% of those in management and business preferred Kennedy, and 68% of all other husbands preferred Kennedy. In sum, these women's husbands had typically come from "the right" places but a majority of them did not have "the right" attitudes or occupational interests.

If, therefore, I were to select a single factor that contributed most to these women's maintenance of nonconservative attitudes between the late 1930's and early 1960's, I think it would be the fact of selecting husbands of generally nonconservative stripe who helped to maintain for them an environment that was supportive of their existing attributes.

IV.

Now I shall turn from the total population of interviewees to some comparisons of subpopulations. The most crucial of these, from the point of view of my proposition about supportive environments, are to be found within the population of nonconservatives on leaving college in the late 1930's: What seem to be the differences between those who do and those who do not remain nonconservative in the early 1960's? Such comparisons will have to be impressionistic, since numbers of cases are small.

Among 22 individuals previously labeled as clearly nonconservative in their third or fourth year of attendance at the College, just half belong in the same category now. Only three of them are clearly conservative today, the remaining eight being classified as intermediate. Here are these wives' descriptions of their husbands' political positions over the years:

3 presently conservative wives: 3 Republican husbands (100%)

7 presently intermediate wives: 3 Republican husbands (42%)

8 presently nonconservative wives: 2 Republican husbands (25%)

Of the three presently conservative women, none mentions having engaged in activities related to political or other public issues; of the eight who are intermediate, six mention some activity of this kind, but they identify their activity only in such general terms as "liberal" or "Democratic Party"; of the 11 still nonconservative women, eight mention such activities, more than half of them specifying such "causes" or organizations as labor unions, civil liberties, the ADA, or the NAACP.

Each interviewee was also asked about the general orientation of "most of your friends" toward political and other public affairs. More than half (12) of the 22 women originally labeled as clearly nonconservative described their environment of friends as "liberal," in spite of the fact that most of them lived in suburbs or other geographical areas not generally renowned for liberalism. Interestingly enough, those who are now relatively conservative answered this question in just about the same way as did those who are still relatively nonconservative. The 16 women originally labeled as clearly conservative, on leaving college, answered this question somewhat differently; more than half of them (9) described their environment of friends as predominantly "conservative," but answers differed with the present attitudes of the respondents. That is, those who are now, in fact, relatively conservative with near-unanimity describe their friends as conservative, whereas those who are now relatively nonconservative consider a substantial proportion or even most of their friends to be "liberal." Thus only those who were quite conservative in the late 1930's and who still remain so see themselves surrounded by friends who are primarily conservative.

In sum, nearly all of the still nonconservative women mention either husbands or public activities (most commonly both) that have served to support and maintain previously nonconservative attitudes, while none of the three formerly nonconservative but presently conservative women mentions either husbands or public activities which have served to maintain earlier attitudes.

What about attitude persistence on the part of those who, after three or four years in college, were still relatively conservative? Sixteen of those who were then labeled conservative were interviewed in the early 1960's, ten of them being categorized as still conservative and three as now nonconservative. Only one of the nonchangers reported having a husband who was a Democrat, and in this lone case he turned out to have voted for Nixon in 1960. Two of the three changers, on the other hand, report husbands who were Democrats and Kennedy voters in 1960. Only two of the persistent conservatives mentioned public activities presumably supportive of their attitudes (in behalf of the Republican Party, in both cases); eight of the ten described most of their friends either as conservative or as Republicans. The conditions that favor the persistence of conservatism over the 20-odd years are thus about the same as those that favor the persistence of nonconservatism: supportive environments in the form of husbands, local friends, and (for the nonconservatives but not the conservatives) in the form of associates in activities related to public issues.

There is a special sub-population of students who, as of graduating in the late 1930's were, candidates for regression; that is, they became much less conservative during their college years. Of these, about one-third (9 of 28) were among the most conservative half of the same population in the early 1960's, and may be regarded as regressors, in some degree at least. Eight of these potential regressors were, for various reasons, unable to report on husbands' preferences. Among the remaining 19 respondents, five were actual regressors, four of whom reported their husbands to be Republicans or "conservative Republicans." Among 14 actual non-regressors reporting, ten described their husbands as Democrats or "liberal Democrats," two referred to them as "Republicans who have been voting Democratic," and only two call their husbands Republicans. These are highly significant differences: the actual regressors can pretty well be differentiated from the nonregressors merely by knowing their husbands' present attitudes. By this procedure only 3 of 19, or 16% of all predictions would not have been correct.

This total set of data suggests that either regression and persistence of attitudes as of leaving college are, over the years, influenced by husbands' attitudes, or early post-college attitudes had something to do with the selection of husbands, or both. In either case, both regression and persistence are facilitated by the supportiveness of husbands.

V.

If there is any very general principle that helps to account for this whole range of phenomena (both my 1946 and my 1963 versions), I believe that it is to be found in an extended version of "balance theory," as originally outlined by Heider (1946, 1958). Heider's formulations are formulated in individual and phcnomenological terms; a balanced state is a strictly intrapersonal, psychological state. But it is also possible to conceptualize an objective, multi-person state of balance, referring to the actual relationships among different persons' attitudes, regardless of the persons' awareness of each other. Such a concept is psychologically useful not only because it describes an actual, existing situation—an environment of which each person is himself a part, as suggested by Asch (1952)—but also because it describes a relationship which, given reasonably full and accurate communication, comes to be accurately perceived. My own recent work on the acquaintance process has been interesting to me primarily because it inquires into the processes by which and the conditions under which *intra*personal states of balance come to correspond with *inter*personal ones. As outlined by Heider, and subsequently by many others (Cf. Brown *et al.*, 1962), the processes by which imbalanced states serve as goals toward the attainment of balanced ones include both internal, psychological changes and external modifications of the environment. Thus, one may achieve a balanced state with the important figures in one's social environment—whether by selecting those figures, by modifying one's own attitudes, or by influencing others' attitudes—and at the same time continue to perceive that environment accurately.

According to such an extended, *inter*personal concept of balance, an imbalanced state under conditions of continued interaction is likely to be an unstable one, simply because when it is discovered it arouses *intra*personal imbalance on the part of one or more of the interactors, and this state arouses forces toward change. Given marked attitude change on the part of one but not the other member of a dyad actually in balance with respect to that attitude, imbalance results. This was what typically happened to students at Bennington College vis-à-vis their parents, in the 1930's. A common way in which they attempted to reduce imbalance was by avoidance—not necessarily of parents but of the divisive issues as related to parents. As Heider might say, unit formation between issue and parents was broken up, and psychological imbalance thus reduced. Such a "solution" resembles autistic hostility in that it involves a marked restriction of communication.

But this solution, as many of my subjects testified, was not a particularly comfortable one. Hence, it would hardly be surprising if many of them, during early post-college years, were in search of environments that would provide less uncomfortable solutions—or, better yet, more positively rewarding ones. An ideal one, of course, would be a husband who was rewarding as a supporter of one's own attitudes as well as in other ways.

And so, vis-à-vis parents and fellow-students at first, and later vis-à-vis husbands (or perhaps working associates), forces toward balance were at work. Specifically, support from important people concerning important issues came to be the rule, and its absence the exception. Support sometimes came about by changing one's own attitudes toward those of needed supporters, or, more commonly, by selecting supporters for existing attitudes. The latter stratagem represented not merely an automatic tendency for attitudes to perpetuate themselves. More significantly, I believe, it represents an adaptation to a world that includes *both* persons and issues. Such a dual adaptation can be made, of course, by sacrificing one's stand on the issues (regression). But if the dual adaptation is to be made without this sacrifice, then an interpersonal world must be selected (or created) that is supportive—in which case we can say that the attitude has been expressed by finding a supportive environment.

According to my two themes (of 1946 and 1963) an existing attitude may be maintained by creating environments in which *either* new information can be avoided *or* in which other persons support one's own information. In either case, the fate of an attitude is mediated by the social environment in which the individual attempts to maintain or to restore balance regarding that same attitude. Insofar as that environment excludes disturbing information or provides reinforcing information, the attitude persists. And insofar as the selection or the acceptance of that environment is a consequence of holding the attitude, we have a steady-state, self-maintaining system.

REFERENCES

Asch, S. E. *Social Psychology*. New York: Prentice-Hall, 1952.
Brown, R. Models of attitude change. In Brown, R., Galanter, E., Hess, E. H., and Mandler, G. *New Directions in Psychology*. New York: Holt, Rinehart & Winston, 1962.
Heider, F. Attitudes and cognitive organization. *J. Psychol*, 1946, *21*, 107–112.

————. *The Psychology of Interpersonal Relations.* New York: Wiley, 1958.

NEWCOMB, T. M. *Personality and Social Change.* New York: Holt, Rinehart & Winston, 1943.

————. Autistic hostility and social reality. *Human Relations,* 1947, *1,* 69–86.

————. *The Acquaintance Process.* New York: Holt, Rinehart & Winston, 1961.

Gerald R. Miller*

A CRUCIAL PROBLEM
IN
ATTITUDE RESEARCH

While research dealing with attitude formation and change has provided much valuable information for students of speech and communication, numerous important problems remain unsolved. This paper deals with one of these problems. In particular, it attempts to identify reasons for the existence of the problem and to point up some implications of the problem for attitude research.

The problem can perhaps best be identified by briefly describing a classic study by R. T. La Piere.[1] A number of hotel owners and managers were asked if they would be willing to house Chinese guests. The great majority of respondents stated that they would not. A short time later, La Piere and a well-dressed Chinese couple appeared in person at each of the hotels and requested lodging. Almost without exception, accommodations were provided for all three of the travelers.

Obviously, the La Piere study reveals a marked discrepancy between the hotel owners' stated unwillingness to accept Chinese guests and their subsequent housing of the Chinese couple. This discrepancy is probably not surprising. That people's actions are not always consistent with their utterances is reflected by such societal commonplaces as "Actions speak louder than

*Mr. Miller is Associate Professor of Communication, Michigan State University. Portions of this manuscript are based on a lecture delivered at Cornell University in May, 1966.

[1] R. T. La Piere, "Attitudes versus Actions," Social Forces, XIII (December 1934), 230–237.

Reprinted from the Quarterly Journal of Speech, 53 (1967), 235–40, with permission of the author and the Speech Association of America.

words" and "Put up or shut up." But while La Piere's finding is not startling, it illustrates an issue of central importance to attitude research. This problem is commonly—and somewhat misleadingly—labeled as the relationship between attitudes and behavior. More precisely, it can be labeled as the relationship between verbal indicators of an attitude and other classes of attitudinally related behaviors. Phrased as a question, it can be stated as follows: To what extent does knowledge of the verbal attitudinal responses of individuals allow for accurate prediction of other kinds of attitudinal behaviors?

To be sure, it is of considerable value and interest to study verbal behavior apart from any consideration of its relationship with other behaviors. Often, however, one seeks to make inferences about other behaviors from knowledge of an individual's verbal responses. If these other attitudinal behaviors are of primary importance, knowledge of verbal responses is valuable to the extent that it enables accurate prediction. Because of this fact, a crucial task for attitude change researchers is the development of measurement techniques that result in substantial correlations between verbal attitude measures and other categories of attitudinal responses.

Several active researchers have recognized the centrality of this task. Himmelstrand states that improvement of the predictive power of verbal attitude scales is of major import, and he further suggests that two of the frontiers that should be extended are "improvement of the methods of observing attitudinal verbal activity and of the methods for verbal attitude scale construction," as well as "assessment of the anchoring of verbal attitudes in the personality, or in other than verbal attitude components."[2] The late Arthur Cohen places even greater emphasis on the importance of the relationship of verbal attitude measures to other attitudinally related behaviors, stating:

> Probably the most important and long-range research problem in the sphere of attitude theory has to do with the implications of attitude change for subsequent behavior. In general, most . . . researchers . . . make the widespread psychological assumption that since attitudes are evaluative predispositions, they have consequences for the way people act toward others, for the programs they actually carry out and the manner in which they perform these programs. Thus attitudes are always seen to be a precursor to behavior, a determinant of what behaviors the individual will actually go about doing in his daily affairs. However, though most psychologists assume such a state of affairs, very little work on attitude change has explicitly dealt with the behavior that may follow upon a change in attitudes. Most researchers in this field are content to demonstrate that there are factors which affect attitude change and that these factors are open to orderly exploration, without actually carrying through to the point where they examine links between changed attitudes and changes in learning, performance, perception, and interaction. Until a good deal more experimental investigation demonstrates that attitude change has implications for subsequent behavior, we cannot

[2] U. Himmelstrand, "Verbal Attitudes and Behavior," *Public Opinion Quarterly*, XXIV (Summer 1960), 224–251.

be certain that our change procedures do anything more than cause cognitive realignments, or even, perhaps that the attitude concept has any critical significance for psychology.[3]

But what of other research which has sought to link verbal indicators of attitude with other behaviors? Recently, Festinger has analyzed the results of three studies dealing with the relationship between verbal attitude measures and other behaviors.[4] In general, his findings provide little cause for optimism. In one study, Maccoby, *et al.* found that a persuasive message produced changes in a group of mothers' verbal responses concerning the age at which toilet training should begin, but that these verbal indicators of attitude did not correlate positively with the time at which they actually commenced their own children's toilet training.[5] In a second study, industry foremen completed a two-week workshop stressing the importance of good human relations in superior—subordinate activities.[6] Although almost all of the foremen indicated a much stronger verbal acceptance of the importance of good human relations at the close of the workshop, subsequent on-the-job checks revealed that there was little change in the pattern of their supervisory behaviors. Finally, a study by Janis and Feshbach found an inverse relationship between the extent of verbal concern expressed by people about proper toothbrushing practices and subsequent actions aimed at improving their own oral hygiene programs.[7] After examining the evidence of all three studies, Festinger concludes:

> What I want to stress is that we have been quietly and placidly ignoring a very vital problem. We have essentially persuaded ourselves that we can simply assume that there is, of course, a relationship between attitude change and subsequent behavior and, since this relationship is obvious, why should we labor to overcome the considerable technical difficulties of investigating it? But the few relevant studies certainly show that this 'obvious' relationship probably does not exist and that, indeed, some nonobvious relationships may exist. The problem needs concerted investigation.[8]

Research of my own reinforces Festinger's pessimism. In a number of studies, we have found that certain types of persuasive messages produce more favorable verbal attitudes toward civil defense, that individuals say they would like to be better informed about the steps to follow in case of nuclear attack

---

[3] A. R. Cohen, *Attitude Change and Social Influence* (New York, 1965), pp. 137–138.

[4] L. Festinger, "Behavioral Support for Opinion Change," *Public Opinion Quarterly,* XXVIII (Fall 1964), 404–418. It should be noted that these were the only studies which Festinger found directly relevant to the question.

[5] *Ibid.,* 407–410.

[6] *Ibid.,* 410–411.

[7] *Ibid.,* 411–414.

[8] *Ibid.,* 417.

or natural disaster.⁹ In several instances, we have distributed an addressed envelope and a form letter to assist people in requesting further information about civil defense. To obtain this information, the person has only to write his name and address on the bottom of the envelope, put a stamp on the envelope, and post the letter.

A small percentage of people have expended the energy required to request further information. In addition, the data reveal no apparent relationship between the amount of attitude change resulting from the persuasive messages and subsequent information-seeking behavior. In other words, persons who reported little change in their verbal attitudinal responses toward civil defense following exposure to persuasive messages were just as likely to post letters as individuals for whom change in verbal response was marked. While our sample is small, this finding again illustrates the frequent discrepancy between verbally operationalized measures of attitude and other behaviors.

Why does this discrepancy exist? Several explanations have been advanced. Festinger attributes the discrepancy to the temporal brevity of any change resulting from a single exposure to a persuasive message.¹⁰ Briefly, his argument may be stated as follows: at any given moment in time, a person's attitude toward some concept or issue is probably a function of numerous prior learning experiences. If that individual is exposed to a persuasive message, the message may be sufficiently powerful to produce momentary attitude shift. If, however, this message represents an isolated incident and if further social reinforcement is not provided for the attitude change, the response should regress rapidly to its original level.

For example, assume that an individual's experiences with intercollegiate football have been generally unfavorable: that one of his good friends was permanently injured in a college football game, that a college football player tried once to start a fight with him, that a person whom he regards highly has repeatedly told him that college football is antithetical to academic values. Suddenly this individual is exposed to a persuasive message detailing all of the reasons why he should think that college football is desirable and good. Immediately following the message, his attitudes toward college football are measured. It is possible that the message stimulus will be of sufficient intensity to elicit a momentary change. But if he returns home and finds a newspaper headlining an athletic scholarship scandal, that change will be short lived.

Certainly, Festinger's explanation accounts for some of the discrepancy between verbal indicators of attitude and other attitudinally related behaviors. It is doubtful, however, that his explanation alone is sufficient to account for all of the instances in which discrepancies are observed. For example, in the above mentioned study of industrial foremen, an extensive series of

⁹ See *e.g.*, G. R. Miller and M. A. Hewgill, "Some Recent Research in Fear-Arousing Message Appeals," *SM*, XXXIII (November 1966), 377–391.
¹⁰ Festinger, 414–415.

persuasive messages aimed at changing the foremen's attitudes toward human relations was utilized.[11] But even though two weeks of intensive social reinforcement of these attitudes occurred, there was little subsequent change in the behavior of the foremen in their work situations. It would seem, then, that factors other than momentary exposure are also involved.

In a classic article dealing with attitudes, Campbell posits different response thresholds for various kinds of attitudinal responses.[12] Basically, he holds that the variables affecting verbal indicators of an attitude (e.g., "I am strongly in favor of school integration") may result in a different threshold for verbal responses than for other responses that are affected by different sets of variables (e.g., the contribution of ten dollars to a pro-integration organization [money-giving response] or the willingness to go from door to door seeking signatures on a pro-integration petition [doorbell-ringing response]). Thus, for Campbell, this so-called inconsistency between response categories becomes a pseudo-inconsistency, a pseudo-inconsistency resulting from failure to recognize that different responses are governed by different sets and different values of relevant antecedent variables.

In a sense, Campbell argues that in terms of psychological effort the cliché, "Talk is cheap," applies directly to the problem. Consider again our hypothetical individual's attitudes toward intercollegiate football. For this individual, the verbal responses, "I don't like college football," or "Intercollegiate football should be de-emphasized," require relatively little psychological effort. To use Campbell's language, the hurdle that must be cleared for performance of these responses is comparatively low. On the other hand, sacrificing numerous social rewards to boycott the big game of the season is another matter, as is foregoing a comfortable evening in front of the fireplace in order to circulate a petition calling for de-emphasis of college football. These latter responses require greater psychological effort; the hurdle that must be cleared is a high one. While a person with a middling attitude might be willing to say that he dislikes college football, only a person with a strong negative attitude will consent to sacrifice social and physical rewards in order to implement his opposition.

Both Festinger's and Campbell's notions help to explain the reasons that discrepancies are often observed between verbal indicants of attitude and other behaviors. To be sure, other explanations might be offered. Even so, the preceding remarks should serve to identify the problem of interest and to illustrate its relevance to attitude research. The following is a brief recapitulation: *frequently, there is a minimal positive relationship between verbal indicators of attitude and other attitudinally related behaviors. Given this minimal relationship, the results of attitude research utilizing such verbally operationalized measures, while perhaps interesting in their own right, afford extremely limited opportunities for gener-*

[11] *Ibid.*, 410.

[12] D. C. Campbell, "Social Attitudes and Other Acquired Behavioral Dispositions." In S. Koch (ed.), *Psychology: A Study of a Science*, Vol. XI (New York, 1963), pp. 94–172.

alizability. Or, to put it another way, the variables that have been found to influence attitude formation and change, as well as the laws into which these variables enter, may often apply only to paper and pencil, verbal responses. As a result, the theoretic and social utility of such attitude research is severely limited.

What steps could be taken to eliminate, or at least to reduce the shortcomings of attitude research using paper and pencil, verbal measures of attitude? In some cases, researchers may be able to use alternative behavioral measures of attitude. For example, assume that a speech or communication researcher wishes to assess public attitudes toward the NAACP. If he chooses to use the methodological approach discussed above, the researcher might present the following statement to his respondents: "People should be willing to make financial contributions to NAACP programs." This statement would be followed by the five alternatives: Strongly Agree, Agree, No Opinion, Disagree, and Strongly Disagree. The alternative checked by each respondent would constitute an operational measure of his attitude toward the NAACP.

Instead of employing this procedure, the researcher might use as a criterion each respondent's willingness to contribute money to the NAACP. Contributing respondents would be categorized as having favorable attitudes toward the NAACP, while non-contributors would be classified as having unfavorable, or at least less favorable attitudes toward the organization. Such a "put up or shut up approach" seeks to measure attitudes at a response level which, to use Campbell's language, would require the clearance of a rather high response hurdle.

While this kind of approach could be useful under certain circumstances, it presents several practical and methodological difficulties. First, it may often be difficult to establish uniform and consistent schedules for measurement. Assume, for example, that a number of respondents have just heard a persuasive speech seeking to engender more favorable attitudes toward the NAACP and that the researcher now wishes to gauge the effectiveness of the speech. While it is a relatively simple matter to obtain paper and pencil measures of each person's attitude toward the NAACP, the collection of money raises numerous questions. Suppose that some audience members assert that they have insufficient funds with them, but that they will be pleased to contribute at some later date. Others indicate that they have already made a substantial financial contribution to the organization, while a few state that they are ideologically opposed to, or financially incapable of making monetary contributions to organizations, but that they would be willing to do some work for the NAACP. Just how is the researcher to evaluate and code these various responses?

As an alternative, the researcher might specify a particular time period—say one week—during which monetary contributions could be submitted to the NAACP. Such an extended time period introduces inherent problems of data interpretation. For as the time between the speech and the actual monetary donation increases, it becomes increasingly more difficult to ascertain that the variable of interest—in this case, the speech—was the crucial determinant of behavior. Perhaps the individual read a magazine article that caused him to contribute to the NAACP, perhaps a discussion with his wife tipped the psychological scales, or perhaps during the time interim he filed his income tax return and decided that larger charitable deductions would be helpful when filing next year's returns. To be sure, intelligent use of control groups can reduce these kinds of ambiguities, but even so, the researcher may still face the dilemma of determining just *why* attitudes toward the NAACP have changed, even if such changes can be observed.

Finally, many of the alternative behavioral measures that could be employed in attitude research are "either-or" measures. Either an individual signs a petition, or he refuses; either he pulls the "Yes" lever at a school bond election, or he votes "No." A researcher is severely limited in the kinds of analyses that can be performed on such data; in fact, with all of their limitations, one of the major advantages of paper and pencil scales is the fact that the variable being measured can be treated as a continuous one. Such an assumption allows for more sophisticated statistical treatment, and most researchers would be exceedingly reluctant to sacrifice this analytical advantage.

Thus, while other behavioral indices of attitude may sometimes prove useful, the use of such alternative measures is only one possible step available to attitude researchers. A second alternative lies in the development of new methods of measuring attitudinal responses to verbal stimuli. Several of us are presently engaged in the preliminary phases of this kind of methodological research, but it is too early to evaluate our probable success. One method being tested allows the subject to construct his own scale, rather than responding to a prepared scale with established intervals. A second approach requires that the subject respond by pressing a particular button, instead of marking a scale with a pencil. Hopefully, this approach will tap certain potentially relevant dimensions of the response not usually indexed by paper and pencil measurements; *e.g.*, the vigor of the button-press (a drive-producing dimension) and the amount of time between stimulus exposure and actual response (a latency dimension).

The eventual fruitfulness of these two particular methods is not the crucial question. Rather, the major issue involves the willingness of attitude researchers to experiment with a wide variety of measurement techniques, so that methods which will yield higher relationships between verbal responses and other classes of attitudinal behaviors may be discovered. Certainly, no sudden or effortless panacea for this problem exists. It is safe to say, however, that the social and theoretical significance of attitude research is directly linked to the development of such methods.

Milton Rokeach

ATTITUDE CHANGE
AND
BEHAVIORAL CHANGE

Since World War II many experimental studies of opinion change, carried out within a variety of conceptual frameworks, have been designed to increase our theoretical understanding of the conditions under which men's minds and behavior may change. While the main *empirical* focus of these studies is on behavioral changes in the expression of opinion, their main *theoretical* concern is with the conditions facilitating and inhibiting change in underlying beliefs and attitudes. To what extent have these experimental studies actually advanced our theoretical understanding of processes leading to attitude and behavior change? And to what extent have they improved our understanding of the fundamental structure of underlying attitudes, the way attitudes are organized with respect to one another, and the way attitude and attitude change may affect behavior?

To discuss these questions I should like to begin with certain considerations, not about attitude change, but about the nature of attitude, and about the relationship between attitude and behavior. In contemporary approaches to "attitude change" the accent seems to be on the understanding of "change" rather than on the understanding of "attitude"; that is, one may note an interest in attitude theory as such only insofar as that interest is necessary to formulate testable hypotheses about attitude change. This would be roughly equivalent to a physicist telling us he is interested in theories of "nuclear change" rather than "nuclear structure" in order to understand better how to change nuclear structures.

The point of view to be developed here will therefore differ somewhat

Reprinted from Milton Rokeach, *Beliefs, Attitudes, and Values.* San Francisco: Jossey-Bass, 1968, pp. 133–55, Chapter 6, "Attitude Change and Behavioral Change."

from that expressed by Arthur R. Cohen who, in the preface to his book, *Attitude Change and Social Influence*, wrote: "This book does not take up the definition and conceptualization of attitude, but instead assumes that there is a commonly accepted core of meaning for the term 'attitude change' " (1964, p. xi). I shall show that the concept of "attitude change" can have no "commonly accepted core of meaning" apart from the concept of attitude—that, indeed, theory and research on the nature, determinants, and consequents of attitude formation and maintenance are prerequisite to and inseparable from theory and research on attitude change. "Before tackling the important problem of attitude change," Sherif, Sherif, and Nebergall have remarked, "we must have a clear notion of *what* it is that changes and *what* it is that is resistant to change" (1965, p. vi). I contend that any consideration of the relation between attitude change and behavioral change necessarily rests on a prior consideration of the relation between attitude and behavior.

ATTITUDE AND BEHAVIOR

For the purposes of this discussion let me offer the following coordinated definitions of attitude and attitude change. An *attitude*, as defined in the preceding chapter, is a relatively enduring organization of beliefs about an object or situation predisposing one to respond in some preferential manner. *Attitude change* would then be a change in predisposition,[1] the change being either a change in the organization or structure of beliefs or a change in the content of one or more of the beliefs entering into the attitude organization.[2]

Especially important for the major thesis to be developed in this chapter is that an attitude may be focused on either an object or a situation, and that behavior is always a function of at least these two types of attitudes (to be called A_o and A_s). These assumptions have at least two implications worth noting. First, a given attitude-toward-object, whenever activated, need not always be behaviorally manifested or expressed in the same way or to the same degree.

---

[1] A *predisposition* would be defined as a hypothetical state of the organism which, when activated by a stimulus, causes a person to respond selectively, affectively, or preferentially to the stimulus.

[2] With *attitude change* defined as a change in structure as well as in content it becomes immediately evident that virtually all contemporary theories of attitude change are typically concerned with changes in content (with changes in for-ness or against-ness on a posttest as compared with a pretest) and that they have virtually ignored the structural kinds of attitude change that might come about as a result of development, education, or therapy, which need not necessarily involve a change in content. For example, a person may change with respect to degree of differentiation, integration, and breadth of an attitude without changing the strength of his positive or negative feelings toward the object of attitude. Similarly, when a person changes from a literal to a figurative interpretation of the Bible a structural rather than a substantive change is implied—that is, he may not have changed in his positive feelings about the sacredness of the Bible.

Its expression will vary adaptively as the attitude activated by the situation varies, with attitude-toward-situation facilitating or inhibiting the expression of attitude-toward-object, and vice versa. Any attitude-toward-object has the inherent property of being differentially manifested *along a range of values*[3] rather than as a single value, depending on the situation within which the attitude object is encountered.[4] This same property is inherent in any attitude-toward-situation. Consequently, a significant change of opinion toward an object may indicate nothing more than that a given attitude-toward-object was activated, and thus behaviorally expressed, in two different situations, S_1 and S_2, activating, respectively, two different attitudes-toward-situation, A_{s_1} and A_{s_2}.

Second, in principle there is no difference between the verbal and the nonverbal expression of a given attitude. Every expression in behavior, verbal or nonverbal, must be a confounding and a compounding function of at least two underlying attitudes—A_o and A_s. Thus, any verbal expression of opinion, like any nonverbal behavior, is also a function of at least two attitudes— attitude-toward-object and attitude-toward-situation—and ascertaining the extent to which the opinion is a manifestation of one attitude or the other, or both, requires careful inference rather than careless assumption.

COGNITIVE INTERACTION BETWEEN TWO ATTITUDES

It is not enough merely to assert that social behavior is a function of two attitudes. To predict behavioral outcome requires a model about the manner in which the two attitudes will cognitively interact with one another. Such a model, the belief-congruence model, is described in Chapter Four. While this model was originally formulated to deal with various issues raised by the Osgood and Tannenbaum congruity model (1955), with only minor modification it can be more generally employed to predict the behavioral outcome of cognitive interaction between the two attitudes A_o and A_s.

By applying this model to the present context, we can conjecture that whenever a person encounters an attitude object within some situation, two

---

[3] The notion of an attitude-toward-object being manifested along a range of values is not the same idea as that expressed by Sherif and his co-workers (1965) when they speak of latitudes of acceptance, noncommitment, and rejection.

[4] H. C. Kelman expresses a similar view: "The attitudes expressed by an individual may vary from situation to situation, depending on the requirements of the situation in which he finds himself and the motivations which he brings into this situation. What the individual says will be determined at least in part by what he considers to be proper in this situation and consonant with group norms, and also by what he considers to be most conducive to the achievement of his personal goals . . . . The amount of discrepancy depends on the situational requirements, on the person's goals, on his relation to the group, and on some of his personal characteristics" (1958b, pp. 25–26).

attitudes, A_o and A_s, are activated; further, a comparison of the relative importance of these two attitudes is also activated. The two attitudes are assumed
to affect behavior in direct proportion to their perceived importance with
respect to one another. The more important A_o is perceived to be with respect
to A_s, the more will the behavioral outcome be a function of A_o; conversely,
the more important A_s is perceived to be with respect to A_o, the more will the
behavioral outcome be a function of A_s.

By substituting A_o and A_s for *characterization* (C) and *subject* (S) in Formula
[1] in Chapter Four we obtain:

$$B_{os} = (w)A_o + (1 - w)A_s \qquad [3]$$

where B_{os} refers to the behavior toward an object-within-a-situation and where
(w) and $(1 - w)$ refer to the perceived importance of A_o and A_s relative to one
another in the context of encountering a given object in a specified situation.[5]

How can the relative importance of two attitudes be determined? One
way is by strictly empirical means—for example, by the method of paired
comparison or by a rating procedure which would enable us to determine
(w) and $(1 - w)$. In this instance we would not be able to predict on purely
theoretical grounds the behavioral outcome of cognitive interaction between
two attitudes of varying importance because we would have no way of knowing
in advance their importance relative to one another or the absolute degree of
that importance. Fortunately, however, the comparison of relative importance
of the two attitudes does not occur in a vacuum; it takes place within the general
framework of one's total belief system, wherein all beliefs and attitudes are
arranged along a central-peripheral dimension of importance (Chapters One
and Two) and wherein, furthermore, the beliefs and attitudes activate values
varying in position along one's value hierarchy (Chapter Seven). Thus the
two attitudes, A_o and A_s, can be compared as if to determine their relative
position along this central-peripheral dimension or as if to determine which
values in the value hierarchy are activated by the two attitudes. Such concep-
tualizations enable us to make at least some educated guesses about which
of two attitudes is the more important.

The question may now be raised whether it is ever possible to obtain a
behavioral measure of a given attitude-toward-object that is uncontaminated
by interaction with attitude-toward-situation. The extent to which this is possible is a function of the extent to which the situation is a "neutral" one—that is,
a situation carefully structured by the experimenter to activate a relatively
unimportant attitude-toward-situation that is of relatively little influence in
the context of its interaction with attitude-toward-object. Learning how to

---

[5] To express the above as deviations from a zero-point Formula [3] then becomes:

$$d_{os} = w\,(d_{A_o}) + (1 - w)\,d_{A_o} \qquad [3a]$$

Formula [2] in Chapter Four, which is designed to handle overassimilation, can similarly be
transformed by substituting A_o and A_s for C and S.

structure the test or interview situation so that it is neutral is, of course, a major objective of attitude and survey research methodology, but this is only a methodological ideal to strive for and probably is rarely achieved in practice.

ATTITUDE CHANGE AND
BEHAVIORAL CHANGE

The proposition that behavior is always a function of two interacting attitudes has important and disturbing implications for theory and research on attitude change and behavioral change. If expressing an opinion is a form of behavior, then expressing a changed opinion is also a form of behavior; a changed opinion must also be a function of the two attitudes previously discussed—attitude-toward-object and attitude-toward-situation. Similarly, any change in nonverbal behavior is also a form of behavior, and hence must also be a function of the same two attitudes. The question therefore arises: When there is a change in opinion or behavior, how can we tell whether or not there has also been a change in attitude and, if so, *which* attitude?

Although a reasonably clear distinction can be made between an underlying attitude and an expression of opinion (or, if you will, between a covert and overt attitude, or between a private and public attitude), and between an underlying attitude change and an expressed opinion change, one may nevertheless observe in the experimental and theoretical literature a general tendency to use these concepts interchangeably and thereby to shift the discussion back and forth between "attitude" and "opinion," and between "opinion change" and "attitude change." It becomes difficult to tell whether one is dealing with phenomena involving attitude change, expressed opinion change, or both. Many writers have ridden roughshod over the distinction between attitude and expressed opinion by using the phrases "attitude change," "opinion change," "attitude *and* opinion change" and "attitude *or* opinion change" more or less arbitrarily and interchangeably in the context of a single discussion. In this way the impression is created that a significant change in the expression of an opinion also represents a change in underlying attitude. For example, Hovland opens his paper, "Reconciling Conflicting Results Derived from Experimental and Survey Studies of Attitude [sic] Change":

> Two quite different types of research design are characteristically used to study the modification of attitudes [sic] through communication. In the first type, the *experiment*, individuals are given a controlled exposure to a communication and the effects evaluated in terms of the amount of change in attitude or opinion [sic] produced (1959, p. 8).

Festinger opens his article entitled, "Behavioral Support for Opinion [sic] Change": "The last three decades have seen a steady and impressive growth in our knowledge concerning attitudes and opinions [sic]" (1964, p. 404). Both of these writers, like many others, then employ the concepts of "attitude" and "opinion" indiscriminately in carrying forward their discussions, which are usually discussions about how some empirical data involving a change in *expressed* opinion bear on some hypothesis or theory regarding a change in attitude.

As one tries to assimilate the growing experimental literature on opinion change, he becomes increasingly aware that this literature concerns primarily the conditions affecting change in the expression of opinion. But this literature, considered as a whole, does not seem to have much to say about the conditions leading to a change in the content or structure of underlying predispositions (or, as Doob [1947] would have it, of implicit responses) toward objects or toward situations.[6]

Theories of attitude change, with certain exceptions (for example, Kelman's work on processes of social influence [1958a], related work on the public-private variable and work on the "sleeper" effect, Cohen [1964]), seem to be generally unconcerned with whether an expressed opinion change does or does not represent an underlying attitude change. Indeed, the classical paradigm employed in experimental studies of opinion change—pretest, treatment, posttest—is not capable of telling us whether an expressed opinion change indicates an attitude change; it can only tell us whether an expression of opinion has or has not changed as a result of a particular experimental treatment. If the main theoretical concern of experimental studies on expressed opinion change is with the conditions leading to attitude change, then the classical paradigm is basically faulty and should be replaced with other or modified experimental designs (to be discussed later) more suited to deal with this issue. It is not possible to ascertain whether the posttest response is a manifestation of a change in original predispositions or a manifestation of an altogether different predisposition activated by the posttest situation per se.

A closely related point concerns the relationship among attitude change, expressed opinion change, and behavioral change. In his presidential address to Division 8 of the American Psychological Association, Leon Festinger (1964) expressed astonishment over the "absence of research, and of theoretical thinking, about the effect of attitude change on subsequent behavior" (p. 405). He could find only three empirical studies relevant to this problem and they all showed "the *absence* of a relationship between opinion change . . . and resulting behavior" (p. 416). Festinger stressed in his closing remarks that we ought not to ignore this problem or simply assume "a relationship between attitude change and subsequent behavior. . . ." He concluded that "The problem

---

[6] Brewster Smith expresses a similar view in the following: ". . . investigators and theorists alike have been entirely too cavalier in referring to 'attitude change' without specifying the *aspect* of attitude—belief, feeling, or action tendency—in which change is predicted and measured. It often seems as though any stray feature of opinion in which change can readily be produced will do for experimentation" (1968, in press).

needs concerted investigation" (p. 417). And Cohen (1964), in a similar vein, wrote: "Until experimental research demonstrates that attitude change has consequences for subsequent behavior, we cannot be certain that our procedures . . . do anything more than cause cognitive realignments" (p. 138). It should be noted, first, that we cannot even be certain whether the experimental procedures employed "cause cognitive realignments" and, second, that the absence of relationship noted by Festinger and Cohen is not between attitude change and subsequent behavior but between two forms of behavior—expressed opinion change and subsequent nonverbal behavioral change. My main point is that there would seem to be not one but two problems requiring "theoretical thinking" and "concerted investigation." First: Why is it so difficult to demonstrate a relationship between attitude change and behavioral change? And, second: Why is it so difficult to demonstrate a relationship between one form of behavioral change and another?

I propose that expressed opinion or behavioral change is always a function of at least two attitudes. This proposition only complicates our attempts to determine whether or not a particular change in expressed opinion or behavior represents a change in attitude. Because we have to contend with two types of underlying attitudes, we now have four possible determinants of a change in expressed opinion or behavior: (1) interaction between attitude-toward-object and attitude-toward-situation, neither of which has changed; (2) a change in only the attitude-toward-object; (3) a change in only the attitude-toward-situation; (4) a change in both attitude-toward-object and attitude-toward-situation.

Changes in expressed opinion or behavior as a result of (2), (3), and (4) are more or less self-evident, but the first determinant of expressed opinion or behavioral change—the interaction between A_o and A_s, neither of which has changed—merits further consideration because it goes against the widely held assumption that behavioral and expressed opinion changes cannot take place without a preceding change in attitude; it has implications for experimentally oriented and personality oriented studies of attitude and behavioral change; and it may open up fresh possibilities for bringing about changes in expressed opinion and behavior that do not depend on antecedent attitude change.

Let us consider a variety of instances in which a change of expressed opinion or behavior may be observed and understood without positing a change in underlying attitude. First, there are those actions that represent public conformity or compliance without private acceptance. Kelman (1958a) has shown that a subject exposed to an authority who is in a position to reward and punish will display a change of opinion in the direction of authority's opinion, but this change of opinion is manifested only under conditions of surveillance by authority and not under conditions of nonsurveillance. The surveillance condition represents a situation, S_1, activating the attitude A_{s_1}. The nonsurveillance condition represents another situation, S_2, activating another

attitude, A_{s_2}. A change in expression of opinion from conditions of nonsurveillance to surveillance can readily be accounted for without assuming a change
in underlying attitude-toward-object. The first measure of opinion toward
a specified object is the behavioral result of the interaction between A_o and
A_{s_1}; the second measure is a result of the interaction of the same A_o but another
attitude, A_{s_2}. The change of expressed opinion toward the specified attitude
object can be best understood as a reflection of the two different situations,
each activating a different attitude-toward-situation. There is no need to assume
that any one of the activated attitudes—A_o or A_{s_1} or A_{s_2}—has undergone any
change.

Not all instances of expressed opinion change unaccompanied by attitude
change necessarily represent acts of public compliance or conformity. Consider, for example, expressed opinion changes brought about as a result of what
Orne (1962) has called the "demand characteristics" of the experimental
situation or what Rosenberg (1965) has called "evaluation apprehension."
Both terms refer to methodologically unwanted situational variables that may
or may not motivate compliant behavior, variables that exist during the posttest
period and not during the pretest period, and that activate some attitude-
toward-situation persisting beyond that activated by the experimental treatment as such. Changes in expressed opinion toward an object from pre- to
posttest thus result because two different situations activated two different
attitudes, A_{s_1}, and A_{s_2}; we can therefore account for such changes without
adding further assumptions regarding underlying attitude change.

Incidentally, changes in expressed opinion thus obtained are difficult
to interpret because they violate a basic principle of measurement theory,
namely, that repeated measurements designed to assess the effects of some
experimental variable should be obtained under constant test conditions.
Unlike survey research methodology, experimental studies of opinion change
employing the pretest, treatment, and posttest paradigm cannot by their very
nature guarantee the required constancy of testing conditions. The posttest
situation is bound to be psychologically different from the pretest situation,
the former activating different attitudes from the latter. Moreover, a posttest
situation following one experimental treatment is not necessarily comparable
with another posttest situation following a different experimental treatment.
Orne expresses a similar view when he writes: "It should be clear that demand
characteristics cannot be eliminated from experiments; all experiments will
have demand characteristics and these will always have some effect" (1962,
p. 779). Nevertheless, the proposition that behavior is a function of A_o and
A_s would, if valid, require us to assess the relative effects of A_o and A_s in the
pretest and posttest situations separately, in order to determine the meaning
of a given change in expressed opinion.

Not only do social-psychological experiments have demand characteristics, but all social situations have them. Demand characteristics "cannot be
eliminated from experiments" because they cannot be eliminated from any

situation. Our two-attitude theory of behavior recognizes the inevitability of demand characteristics inherent in all social situations and tries to take them into systematic account in formulating the relationship between attitudes and behavior and between attitude change and behavioral change.

Let me turn now to another illustration, this time not of an opinion change but of a change in behavior, real-life behavior that is different from what we would ordinarily expect, that does not necessarily involve an attitude change, and that does not necessarily represent an act of public compliance or conformity. This experiment was described in Chapter Three. Recall that it took place in the natural setting of the personnel offices of two state mental hospitals near Detroit, Michigan. Recall also that the subjects, 50 applicants for low-status jobs, had to select as work partners two out of four other "job applicants"—two whites and two Negroes, one white and one Negro agreeing and one white and one Negro disagreeing with the subject on job-related issues.

One might reasonably expect that of 50 persons applying for low-status jobs a substantial number would, under the conditions described, choose two partners of their own race, given the salience of racial attitudes in our culture. But the results (shown in Table 8 in Chapter Three) do not confirm the expectation that attitude-toward-race is at all important.

Only two subjects of the 50—4 per cent—chose attitude objects of the same race (Pattern 3, $S + S -$), considerably less than would be expected even on a purely chance basis. That similarity of race is not an important criterion of choice of work partners, either for the white or for the Negro subjects, is indicated further in that three more subjects—6 per cent—chose two work partners of the other race (Pattern 4, $O + O -$). It is clear that the most frequent basis of choice is not similarity of race but similarity of belief. Thirty of the 50 subjects—60 per cent—chose two work partners, one white and one Negro, both of whom agreed with the subject, as compared with only two subjects who chose on the basis of similarity of race.

Even though we have no direct pretest and posttest data showing that there had been an actual change of behavior in the particular individuals studied, I would nevertheless regard these data as illustrating an instance of behavioral change that is not preceded by attitude change. The choice of work partners is not what we would ordinarily expect from 50 lower-class persons looking for a job, given the harsh facts of social discrimination in contemporary American culture. The data suggest that the observed absence of racial discrimination is a function of the subject's knowing the stand taken by a Negro or white on an important issue. Assuming that for at least some of these subjects there had been a change in behavior from discrimination on the basis of race to discrimination on the basis of belief, we are again not required to posit any changes in attitudes underlying that behavior (although such changes can come about subsequently, as dissonance theory suggests). We can more simply understand such behavior as arising from an interaction between two attitudes that are activated by an object encountered within a situation in which the activated attitude-toward-situation far outweighs in importance the activated attitude-toward-object.

As a final example of behavioral change occurring without underlying attitude change, let me discuss an as yet unpublished study by Jamias and Troldahl (1965). These investigators were studying differences in willingness to adopt new agricultural practices recommended by agricultural extension agents as a function of personality and social system. The frequency of adoption of recommended agricultural practices—the dependent variable—was measured by a series of questions, each designed to determine which of several alternative procedures the dairy farmer followed in the day-to-day management of his farm. On each question, one of the alternatives was the one recommended by agricultural extension agents. Personality differences in receptivity to new information were measured by the Dogmatism Scale, and social system differences in receptivity were determined by identifying two types of rural townships in Michigan, one type identified as high and the other as low in their "value for innovativeness." The two types of social systems were readily identified by agricultural extension agents on the basis of the generally positive or negative attitude of the people in the townships toward extension activities, size of attendance at extension meetings, and similar factors. The results are shown in Table 1.

Statistical analyses show a highly significant interaction between receptivity in the personality system and receptivity in the social system. In the social system having a low value for innovativeness, the correlation between scores on the Dogmatism Scale and adoption rate is $-.40$; in the social system having a high value for innovativeness, the correlation is $-.09$. Highly dogmatic persons (scoring above the median on a modified form of the Dogmatism scale constructed by Troldahl and Powell [1965]) living in social systems having a high value for innovativeness more frequently adopt recommendations of agricultural extension agents than highly dogmatic persons living in social systems having a low value for innovativeness. Conversely, low dogmatic subjects, regardless of the social system in which they live, have a relatively high adoption rate for new practices recommended by agricultural experts.

Table 1 shows that behavioral changes in highly dogmatic persons are the result of compliance or identification with social norms, and behavioral changes in low dogmatic persons are the result of a generalized receptivity to new information, which is routinely internalized according to its intrinsic correctness and usefulness. Again, no change of underlying attitude need be postulated to account for behavioral change, either in the unreceptive highly dogmatic subjects or in the more receptive low dogmatic subjects. Thus, the results suggest that we can produce changes in the behavior of different individuals through knowledge of personality organization, that is, a knowledge of how a particular situation will activate different beliefs and attitudes in persons who vary in the structure of their belief systems.

TABLE 1

MEAN ADOPTION RATE BY HIGH AND LOW DOGMATIC GROUPS LIVING
IN SOCIAL SYSTEMS HIGH AND LOW IN "VALUE FOR INNOVATIVENESS"

| | Social system in which value for innovativeness is | |
	Low	High
Low dogmatism group	7.3	6.2
High dogmatism group	4.9	6.8
Correlation between dogmatism and adoption rate	−.40	−.09

In summary, I have tried to suggest that a behavioral change (and this includes an expressed opinion change) may be determined by a change in attitude-toward-object, or in attitude-toward-situation, or both, or neither. I have concentrated mainly on behavioral changes that do not involve any kind of underlying attitude change, and have cited various instances of behavioral change in real life and in the laboratory that are attributable to compliance, demand characteristics, evaluation apprehension, the activation of salient beliefs and attitudes within the context of ongoing activity, or the activation of different beliefs and attitudes in persons with differing personality structures. All the illustrations cited have, I believe, a common thread. They all involve expressed opinion or behavioral changes that can be analyzed and reduced to two component attitudes, A_o and A_s, interacting within a figure-ground relationship, carrying differential weights, and affecting a behavioral outcome in proportion to their relative importance with respect to one another. These examples suggest that many kinds of behavioral change can be brought about by learning which attitude object to combine with which situation, which attitudes are activated by attitude object and situation in different personalities, and which outcome to expect from such interactions in different personalities.

Before terminating this portion of the discussion, however, let me mention one other relevant consideration that has thus far been altogether overlooked in contemporary theory and research on attitude change. If expressed opinion changes may be observed when there has been no underlying attitude change, then the converse is also true: an absence of expressed opinion change may be observed even after a change in underlying attitude has already taken place. For example, a dutiful son may continue to express proreligious sentiments even after he has changed his underlying attitudes toward religion, in order not to hurt his parents; a disillusioned Communist may continue to engage in Party activities because he is afraid of social ostracism; a person may continue to say "I love you" even after he has stopped loving. All these examples suggest a possible constancy in expressing an opinion despite a change in attitude. The conditions under which such phenomena will occur deserve more study than they have received so far.

METHODS FOR
ASSESSING ATTITUDE CHANGE

Thus far, I have tried merely to suggest that a change in behavior or expressed opinion may arise in different ways, and may or may not involve a change in underlying attitude-toward-object or attitude-toward-situation. I have also tried to suggest that the classical paradigm employed in experimental studies of opinion change cannot yield information about attitude change as such. The question is, then, how should we proceed if we wish to ascertain whether a given attitude has undergone change, or if we wish to increase the probability of correctly inferring that a given expressed opinion change represents an attitude change? I should like to discuss three methods, illustrating each with relevant research studies.

Test for Opinion Change across
Different Situations

If verbal or nonverbal behavior toward an object is observed in only one situation following an experimental treatment, we hardly have a basis for inferring a change of attitude. Orne (1962, p. 779) has pointed out: "If a test is given twice with some intervening treatment, even the dullest college student is aware that some change is expected, particularly if the test is in some obvious way related to the treatment." But the more posttest situations in which a changed opinion is manifested, the more confident we may be that a change in attitude has actually taken place. Any experimental study of expressed opinion change, if it is to qualify as a study in attitude change, should demonstrate the existence of change in at least two reasonably different situations.

One research design in which there are several posttests of opinion change is Kelman's study of three processes of social influence. Opinion change was assessed in three different posttest situations, under conditions of surveillance and salience, nonsurveillance and salience, and nonsurveillance and nonsalience. In the last condition, the posttest was administered "one or two weeks after the communication session, in a different place, under different auspices, and by a different experimenter" (1958a, p. 56). Kelman has shown that subjects who were given the experimental treatment designed to favor compliance manifested an opinion change only under conditions of surveillance and salience, thereby suggesting that there was no change in underlying attitude. Subjects who were given the internalization treatment, however, manifested opinion changes in all three posttest situations.

Another illustration of repeated posttest is my study on *The Three Christs of Ypsilanti*, which is concerned with underlying changes in delusional attitudes and beliefs among three paranoid schizophrenic patients who believed they were Jesus Christ. After several months of confrontation with each other over who was the real Christ, the youngest of the three, Leon Gabor, announced one day that he was no longer married to the Virgin Mary. Our problem was to determine whether or not this change in expressed opinion represented an underlying change in delusional belief. Our confidence that it did indeed represent such a delusional change increased as Leon Gabor repeatedly told us during the next few weeks and months in various contexts that he was about to get divorced, then that he was divorced, then that he had a new brother, then that his brother had married the Virgin Mary, then that he himself was about to remarry, then that he had remarried another woman, and so forth. Had we relied only on one "posttest" expression of a changed opinion about whom Leon was married to, our claim of a change in delusion would have been extremely weak.

A final illustration of repeated posttest is described in Chapter Seven. The experimental treatment described therein was designed to arouse inconsistent relations between two values, and between a value and an attitude. To find out if the experimental groups had changed their underlying values and attitudes as a result of the experimental treatment, the subjects were retested three weeks later and three to five months later. Three weeks later they were retested in the same classroom; three to five months later they were retested in their residence halls, no longer under the watchful eye of the experimenters, mailing the questionnaires back when finished. The fact that value and attitude changes were observed on both occasions and the fact that the changes observed on the second posttest were often larger than those observed on the first posttest increase our confidence that the significant changes obtained do indeed represent changes in underlying values and attitudes.

In the experimental literature on opinion change, one may find an occasional study in which two or more posttest situations are employed, but, unless I am mistaken, such studies are the exception rather than the rule. In the typical experiment the posttest is given only once, usually within a short time after the experimental treatment; thus the meaning of the expressed opinion changes in relation to attitude change is highly equivocal.

The preceding remarks concern the assessment of change in underlying attitudes-toward-object in several posttest situations. I have not said anything about assessing change in underlying attitude-toward-situation because this type of attitude is typically not employed in experimental studies of attitude change. The principle would seem to be the same: instead of testing for change in opinion toward an attitude object across situations, a change in attitude-toward-situation would be tested by substituting various attitude objects that might be encountered within that situation.

Test for Changes of Several Opinions in One Situation

In the classical paradigm only one opinion is pretested, experimentally treated, and then posttested. Evaluation of the nature of the opinion change is difficult because the expressed opinion is compared only with itself. But suppose several opinions that are thought to be systematically related to one another in some way were pretested, experimentally treated, and then assessed for change all in one posttest situation? Suppose, further, that we find differential opinion changes and that these differential changes are systematically related to one another in the same way as the original opinions are related to one another?

A good illustration of differential opinion changes observed in one situation is the Rokeach, Reyher, and Wiseman experiment described in Chapter Two, wherein 55 beliefs ranging from central beliefs about self-identity to inconsequential beliefs were subjected to change through hypnotic induction. This experimental situation, it will be recalled, was designed to determine whether different kinds of beliefs ranging systematically along a theoretically postulated central-peripheral dimension can be changed through hypnosis and, if so, which kinds of beliefs will be the easiest to change and which the most difficult. In other words, we were interested in determining whether differential changes in several beliefs will occur as a result of a single experimental treatment.

The various results described in Chapter Two show that the hypothesized differential changes in expressed opinions were indeed obtained as a result of one experimental treatment. As expected, the amount of change varied in inverse proportion to centrality of belief, the primitive beliefs changing least as a result of hypnotic suggestion, authority beliefs changing more, peripheral beliefs changing still more, and inconsequential beliefs changing the most. I might add that these differential results were obtained on three occasions: immediately after the hypnotic suggestion, a short time later while the subject was still under hypnosis, and immediately after he was awakened. It would be difficult to attribute such differential changes to compliance or to the operation of any other posttest situational variable, because the posttest situation, and the attitude activated by that situation, was a constant. Yet opinion changes varied systematically in the same way the original opinions varied, namely, as a function of centrality-peripherality. To account for such differential changes we would have to infer that they are manifestations of differential changes in underlying attitudes.

Another illustration from our own research program where several opinion changes are obtained in one posttest situation may again be taken from *The Three Christs* study. As a result of experimental confrontation with others over the issue of who was the real Chirst, Leon Gabor reported that he had changed his name from *Dr. Domino Dominorum et Rex Rexarum, Simplis Christianus Pueris Mentalis Doktor, the renicarnation of Jesus Christ of Nazareth* to Dr. R. I. Dung. Again the problem was whether this expressed opinion change regarding a new identity represented a true underlying change. And, again, our confidence increased that it did indeed represent a true change when he expressed a network of additional differential changes in opinion that were wholly consistent with the expressed change of name.

The value change study described in Chapter Seven provides us with a final illustration of differential change. The experimental manipulation of two target values—*freedom* and *equality*—led to differential increases and decreases in yet other values and attitudes within the subjects' value-attitude systems.

Test for Other Behavioral Changes Accompanying a Given Opinion Change

If a single expressed opinion change truly represents a change in underlying attitude, it is reasonable to expect that such a change will be accompanied by other changes—cognitive, affective, or behavioral—that theoretically should be related to the change in attitude. It is difficult to believe that a change in expressed opinion representing a true change in attitude would have no other behavioral manifestations. That Festinger and Cohen find virtually no studies in the experimental literature showing behavioral change following an attitude change only serves to reinforce my suspicion that most current experimental studies on opinion change do not deal with true attitude change, but with superficial opinion changes.

I should like to draw attention to some data, again from our own research program, which illustrate that behavioral changes following or accompanying opinion changes can indeed be obtained. In *The Three Christs* study, one may note many changes in Leon Gabor's behavior following changes in expressed opinion. After he verbally claimed to have a new wife, Madame Yeti Woman, his behavior with respect to money changed. He accepted, handled, and spent money when it allegedly came from Madame Yeti; these were actions we had never before observed. Furthermore, Leon Gabor, following suggestions allegedly coming from his new wife, changed the song with which he always opened the meetings on days he was chairman from *America* to *Onward Christian Soldiers*, a permanent behavioral change. Again, these behavioral changes serve to increase our confidence in the inference that Leon's expressed opinion change represented a true change in underlying delusion.

Perhaps more impressive in this respect is a study of changes in expressed values by Kemp (1960). His subjects were all religiously minded persons enrolled in a special training curriculum designed to prepare them for positions as Boy Scout executives or YMCA or YWCA secretaries. Kemp was interested in determining whether changes in values and in behavior were a function of personality. The subjects were given the Allport-Vernon Scale of Values while still in college in 1950. Six years later they were contacted again, given the Dogmatism Scale, and retested with the Allport-Vernon Scale. As shown in Table 2 closed, middle, and open-minded subjects all expressed identical value patterns in 1950, but in 1956, the rank order of values remained the same only for the middle group, and had changed for the closed and open groups:

> Although *religious* values were still predominant in all groups, the closed group increased in *political* and *economic* values and decreased markedly in *social* values. The open group remained unchanged in its *religious* and *social* values but increased in *theoretical* values and decreased in *economic* and *political* values. ... The vocational choices ... follow closely these changes or non-changes in value patterns. Roughly 70 per cent of the middle group became Boy Scout executives as planned, or entered closely related professions. But most of the open and closed subjects changed their vocational choice after leaving college; the open subjects more frequently entered vocations requiring more advanced professional training in careers involving social welfare, and the closed subjects more frequently entered military and commercial careers of an administrative nature (pp. 345–346).

That vocational changes accompanied changes in scores on the Allport-Vernon Scale of Value strengthens the likelihood that the changes in expressed values represent real changes in underlying values.

CONCLUSION

In closing, I should like to concede that the point of view I have presented will probably not appeal to those who, disliking to think in terms of genotypes and phenotypes, would insist on equating an attitude with its operational measurement by some opinion questionnaire. But, starting with a conception of attitude as a hypothetical construct, I have proposed that the literature on opinion change does indeed tell us a good deal about the social influence variables and cognitive processes affecting changes in expressed opinion. However, this is a literature concerning changes which, in the main, seem to be localized in the region of the lips and do not seem to affect the mind and heart, nor the hands and feet. It is a literature which, in the main, concerns phenotypic changes in opinion that cannot necessarily be taken as indications of, or be equated with, genotypic changes in attitude. It is a literature which, in the main, seems concerned with momentary modifications in the expression of opinions and not with enduring changes of beliefs, attitudes, or values.

TABLE 2

RANK ORDER OF IMPORTANCE OF SIX VALUES FOR THE TOTAL GROUP AND FOR OPEN, MIDDLE, AND CLOSED SUBGROUPS IN 1950 AND 1956

	(N)	Religious	Social	Political	Economic	Theoretical	Aesthetic
Test 1950:							
Open	(25)	1	2	3	4	5	6
Middle	(54)	1	2	3	4	5	6
Closed	(25)	1	2	3	4	5	6
Total group	(104)	1	2	3	4	5	6
Retest 1956:							
Open	(25)	1	2	4	6	3	5
Middle	(54)	1	2	3	4	5	6
Closed	(25)	1	5	2	3	4	6
Total group	(104)	1	2.5	2.5	5	4	6

Source: M. Rokeach, *The Open and Closed Mind*, New York, Basic Books, 1960, p. 339.

The view developed here on the relations existing among attitude, attitude change, and behavioral change is incomplete, however. It has neglected other kinds of change that must sooner or later be considered if there is to be a truly systematic consideration of antecedents and consequents of attitude and behavioral change, namely, the problem of changes in values, in ideology, in total belief systems, in therapy, and in personality. It seems to me that contemporary theory and research on opinion change, dealing as they typically do with changes in single and isolated expressions of opinion, and selecting as they typically do opinions that are, as Hovland (1959) points out, "relatively uninvolving" and thus easily capable of manipulation within the context of a relatively brief experimental session, have somehow lost touch with broader issues. I hope that the analysis presented in this chapter will serve as a contribution toward our regaining contact with these broader and more significant kinds of change, which may affect and be affected by our everyday life in local, national, and international affairs.

REFERENCES

COHEN, A. R. *Attitude Change and Social Influence.* New York: Basic Books, 1964.

DOOB, L. W. "The Behavior of Attitudes," *Psychological Review*, 1947, *54*, 135–56.

FESTINGER, L. "Behavioral Support for Opinion Change," *Public Opinion Quarterly*, 1964, 28, 404–17.

HOVLAND, C. I. "Reconciling Conflicting Results Derived from Experimental and Survey Studies of Attitude Change," *American Psychologist*, 1959, *14*, 8–17.

JAMIAS, J. F., and TROLDAHL, V. C. "Dogmatism, Tradition and General Innovativeness." Unpublished manuscript, 1965.

KELMAN, H. C. "Compliance, Identification, and Internalization: Three Processes of Attitude Change," *Journal of Conflict Resolution*, 1958, *2*, 51–60. (a)

———. "Social Influence and Personal Belief: A Theoretical and Experimental Approach to the Study of Behavior Change." Unpublished manuscript, 1958. (b)

KEMP, C. G. "Change in Values in Relation to Open-Closed Systems," in *The Open and Closed Mind*, M. Rokeach. New York: Basic Books, 1960.

ORNE, M. T. "On the Social Psychology of the Psychological Experiment: With Particular Reference to Demand Characteristics and Their Implications," *American Psychologist*, 1962, *17*, 776–83.

OSGOOD, C. E., and TANNENBAUM, P. H. "The Principle of Congruity in the Prediction of Attitude Change," *Psychological Review*, 1955, *62*, 42–55.

ROKEACH, M. *The Open and Closed Mind: Investigations into the Nature of Belief Systems and Personality Systems.* New York: Basic Books, 1960.

ROSENBERG, M. J. "When Dissonance Fails: On Eliminating Evaluation Apprehension from Attitude Measurement," *Journal of Personality and Social Psychology*, 1965, *1*, 28–42.

SHERIF, CAROLYN W., M. SHERIF, and R. E. NEBERGALL. *Attitude and Atttitude Change.* Philadelphia: Saunders, 1965.

SMITH, M. B. "Attitude Change." In *International Encyclopedia of the Social Sciences.* New York: Macmillan, 1968.

TROLDAHL, V. C., and F. A. POWELL. "A Short-Form Dogmatism Scale for Use in Field Studies," *Social Forces*, 1965, *44*, 211–14.

Lyle G. Warner / Melvin L. DeFleur*

ATTITUDE AS AN INTERACTIONAL CONCEPT: SOCIAL CONSTRAINT AND SOCIAL DISTANCE AS INTERVENING VARIABLES BETWEEN ATTITUDES AND ACTION

The present paper investigates the effect of selected situational variables on the relationship between a verbal attitude and overt behavior toward the object of that attitude. It provides data which suggest reformulation of two theoretical schemes describing the relationship between prejudice, discrimination and the situation of action. In a relatively large-scale field experiment in a university setting, two multidimensional factors, "social constraint" and "social distance," were systematically introduced as intervening conditions in order to assess the degree to which they reduced correspondence between verbal attitudes toward Negroes and overt acts of acceptance or rejection of Negroes. Generally, these intervening factors had different mediating influences on different types of subjects.

The issue of how much correspondence exists between attitudes and action has been widely debated. At present, there appear to be three rather

*Washington State University.

Reprinted from the *American Sociological Review*, 34 (1969), 153–69, with permission of the authors and the American Sociological Association.

446

distinct views. For convenience, these can be called (1) the postulate of consistency, (2) the postulate of independent variation, and (3) the postulate of contingent consistency. The principal ideas represented in each of these views are summarized below:

The Postulate of Consistency: Each year numerous studies are designed to probe attitudes through the use of standardized scales. Such research is frequently premised upon the supposition that verbal attitude assessments provide reasonably valid guides for predicting what action people would take if they were confronted with the object of their attitude.[1] Turner has recently summarized critically the attitude-action relationship as seen within this perspective:

> "The commonsense meaning of attitude is some psychic unit which corresponds exactly with a category of behavior. Given opportunity, the absence of countervailing attitudes, and an appropriate situation, one predicts behavior from attitude on the basis that behavior is a direct reproduction of attitude." (Turner, 1968:3).

The Postulate of Independent Variation: Perhaps the best-known challenge to the postulate of consistency in the area of racial attitudes was that of Robert K. Merton (1949). In a theoretical analysis of the relationship between prejudice and discrimination, he noted the gap between creed and conduct which Myrdal called the "American Dilemma." Merton maintained that this gap was a function of three variables: (1) the cultural creed honored in cultural tradition and party enacted in law; (2) the beliefs and attitudes of individuals regarding the principles of the creed; and (3) the actual practices of individuals with reference to it. Within this system of variables, he stated that there was no reason to assume that attitudes and behavior would be consistently related: "Stated in formal sociological terms, this asserts that attitudes and overt behavior vary independently. Prejudicial attitudes need not coincide with discriminatory behavior." (Merton, 1949: 102–103). Merton did note that in different regions of the country where distinctive normative climates prevailed, one might expect different probabilities of discrimination, depending upon initial attitude. Thus, he also suggested that attitudinal variables could be important.

The Postulate of Contingent Consistency: An impressive number of studies have accumulated which seriously challenge both the postulate of consistency and the postulate of independent variation. A clear cut conclusion from the data which have emerged from all of these studies seems inescapable: neither

---

[1] The reader is directed to a recent article by Deutscher (1966) for a detailed discussion of this issue.

postulate adequately describes the ways in which attitudes and actions are linked. Fortunately, much of the research which has led to this conclusion has also been aimed at exploring various "situational" concepts and their influence on attitude-related behavior. The results strongly suggest that such interactional concepts as norms, roles, group memberships, reference groups, subcultures, etc., pose *contingent* conditions which can modify the relationship between attitudes and action.

The nature and extent of consistency and inconsistency between attitudes and action have been explored in empirical studies of differing degrees of sophistication. Perhaps the best known early work is the classic study by LaPiere (1934). During the early 1950's, papers such as those by Minard (1952), Lohman and Reitzes (1954) and Kutner *et al.* (1952), reported on a variety of social settings in which behavior presumed to be related to attitudes was observed. It was not possible to predict the directions of these actions from the information used as indicators of the participants' attitudes. Although these studies lacked precision and control (Campbell, 1963:159–162 and Rokeach, 1967), they raised serious doubts about the correspondence between attitudes and action.

The experimental approach of DeFleur and Westie (1958), Linn (1965), and Fendrich (1967) placed subjects, whose attitudes had been carefully assessed, into more rigorously controlled situations where they were afforded "behavioral opportunities" to act in accord with their known attitudes. It was clear from these studies that there was no simple way in which actions toward an object could be accurately predicted from knowledge of relevant attitudes alone.

Clearly, an adequate theory of attitude must take into account the intervening situational variables which modify the relationship between attitudes and action. As a step toward this in the area of ethnic relations, Yinger (1965) has developed a theoretical model of the relationship between prejudicial attitudes and overt discrimination which is based in part upon the earlier analysis by Merton (1949). In Yinger's view, discriminatory behavior for both the prejudiced and the nonprejudiced is contingent upon the surrounding subcultural system within which action takes place. This model is illustrated in Figure 1.

Although, like Merton, Yinger did not provide data to support his model, it appears to clarify the issues which Merton pointed to earlier; and it also appears to be consistent with the findings of most of the research which has accumulated during the intervening years.[2]

In summary, we may assume that the weight of evidence indicates that neither the postulate of consistency nor that of independent variation is tenable. A number of intervening variables operate to alter the contingencies of action

[2] The study by Lohman and Reitzes (1954) provides a good empirical example of structural supports which support discrimination and those which do not.

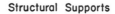

Structural Supports

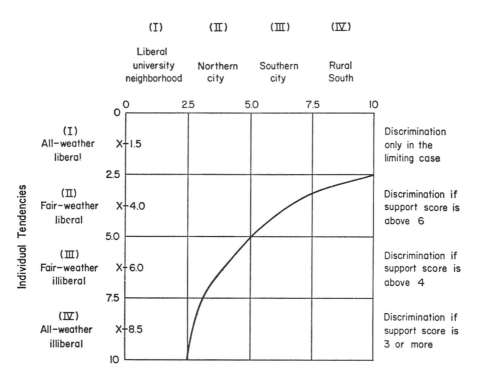

FIGURE 1.   *Yinger's Model of the Relationship Between Prejudice, Discrimination and "Structural Supports"*

for persons with given attitudes. Thus far, this set of situational variables and their influence on action has not been fully identified.

Social Constraint and Social Distance as Situational Variables

It is toward a better understanding of the influence of two specific types of situational variables on the relationship between attitudes and behavior that the present paper is addressed—namely, "social constraint" and "social distance." The ways in which these two terms are actually being used are clarified below.

Social Constraint refers to potential influences on behavior which are introduced into a situation of action because the nature of that behavior is likely to be known to others whose opinions and reactions are important to the actor. The term "constraint" was used by Durkheim (1950) to indicate that "ways of acting, thinking and feeling," collectively shared by others, have a "power of coercion" over an individual as he behaves in social situations. As Durkheim notes, "These ways of thinking and acting therefore constitute the proper domain of sociology." (1950:3–4). The concept of social constraint is a fundamental one. Sociologists hold it be to axiomatic that a person acting in relation to others is directly and indirectly compelled to *behave as others expect*. In other words, the presence of others, either in the immediate sense or in the actor's psychological definition of the situation, exerts pressure to act in accordance with what those others are perceived to feel as appropriate and desirable conduct.

We may use the probability of exposing one's acts to significant others as an index of the degree of social constraint which is present in a situation. Thus, as defined in the present study, a situation of high social constraint is one in which the individual's behavior takes place under conditions where it is likely that his reference groups (or others significant to him) will become aware of it. A situation of low social constraint would be one of relative anonymity, in which the individual's actions would be unlikely to be subjected to such potential surveillance.

Social Distance is based upon sociological considerations of status-position and role expectations in a social relationship.[3] Park (1924:339) noted that interaction can be cordial and informal between the lady of the house and her cook because each occupies a *well-defined position* in the structure of the group, with clearly understood role expectations. As long as these role expectations are fulfilled, the relationship can be permitted to be personal and intimate. Beneath their pleasant exchanges, however, lie the realities of differential status positions. Even the most intimate type of relationship can be entered into while social distance is maintained.

If underlying considerations of ascribed positions are ignored by an actor in entering into a social relationship with another from a lower status category, he *reduces* social distance between himself and the other. A denial of social distance considerations which others hold to be important may result in the application of sanctions. It is for this reason that, in a situation which requires a decision concerning acceptance or rejection of a person in a lower status category as a partner in interaction, social distance, social constraint and attitude form a single system of interactional considerations, a *gestalt*, confronting the actor. That is, they are experienced by a subject as a single system of variables impinging upon his decisions concerning acceptance or rejection of the attitude object.

The importance of these variables in mediating attitude-linked behavior became apparent in prior research. Subjects have reported these considerations as meaningful gestalts at the moment of contemplation of an act of acceptance or rejection of Negroes within the framework of sociological experiments and

[3] For a discussion of social distance as a cultural factor in prejudice, see Simpson and Yinger (1958: 150–164).

studies (DeFleur and Westie, 1958; Linn, 1965; DeFriese and Ford, 1968). In spite of their complexity from a conceptual point of view, therefore, both social distance and social constraint are meaningful considerations within the perspectives of an ordinary person who must decide how to behave in an attitude-action situation.

Overview of the Procedures

Verbal attitude data and information for controlled assignment of subjects to experimental conditions were collected from several hundred college students (mostly freshmen) in a border state university at the beginning of their spring semester 1967. The overt behavior data were collected toward the end of the same semester. The factors of social distance and social constraint were varied within a simple experimental design in such a way that several kinds of action situations were provided. Finally, fifty follow-up interviews were conducted by telephone with a sample of subjects in order to check on their perceptions of the "realism" of the study.

In the present field experiment, the attitude under study is prejudice toward Negroes.[4] Using this attitude topic permits the present research to build upon a tradition of prior studies in which this particular issue has been used in the investigation of attitude-action relationships (cf. Fendrich, 1967 for a discussion of these studies). The overt behavior under observation consists of responses to a *letter* which was received by each subject. This letter, which came in several different versions, requested the recipient to *sign a pledge* and to *mail this pledge* back to the sender. These pledges committed the subject to engage in one of several varieties of behavior involving Negroes. These behaviors ranged from dating a Negro to making an anonymous contribution to a Negro educational charity. The use of signatures as a form of overt behavior builds upon earlier studies of attitude-action correspondence (DeFleur and Westie, 1958; Linn, 1965; DeFriese and Ford, 1968). The details of these techniques, the instruments used, and the methods of control employed are discussed more fully in the sections which follow.

Measuring the Verbal Attitude

The verbal attitude data were collected by means of a standard Likert scale. This scale was constructed from items which had been used in previous research (Middleton, 1960; Westie, 1965; DeFriese and Ford, 1968). Data for a pretest of these items were collected from 60 students during the semester

---

[4] A basic assumption underlying the present research is that the normative environment is hostile toward integration. For a summary of evidence to support this assumption see Westie (1964: 581–603)

preceding the larger study. An item analysis was performed on the original 34 items in order to select those 16 items which best distinguished subjects who had prejudiced attitudes from subjects who had nonprejudiced attitudes (cf. Edwards, 1957; chap. 6).[5] A split-half reliability coefficient was then calculated (r = .84). Application of the Spearman-Brown Prophecy formula as a correction factor yielded a coefficient of .97.

The refined items were placed in an elaborate "Public Information Questionnaire," which was presented to 731 students enrolled in sections of Introductory Sociology during the first week of the spring semester. This questionnaire was portrayed as part of a routine study of public opinion concerning "topics which have been found to be of interest to college students like yourself." The topics covered in the twelve-page questionnaire ranged from the war in Viet Nam to questions about education, civil rights, the war on poverty, the draft, politics, and the American Negro. This device provided a context wherein the attitude scale "made sense" within the framework of opinion topics being probed.

After completion of the gathering of questionnaire data, the subjects were divided into four quartile groupings on the basis of their attitude scores. The first two quartiles constituted the "least-prejudiced" group, while the third and fourth quartiles constituted the "most-prejudiced" group. Further details will be presented in the section on the experimental design.

Measuring Overt Behavior and Controlling Situational Variables

A unique method was used for collecting data on overt behavior toward the attitude object. As has been indicated, a letter was sent through the mail to subjects who had filled out the "Public Information Questionnaire" earlier

[5] *Verbal Attitude Scale:*
1. Negroes ought to have the same access to swimming pools as whites.
2. The reason so many Negroes are on "relief" is that they do not want to work.
3. I would be willing to invite a Negro into my home for lunch.
4. White candidates can do a better job than Negroes in political office.
5. I would be willing to sit in public (for example, the Student Union) with a Negro.
6. Negroes seem to learn a little slower than whites.
7. I would be willing to have a Negro family live next door to me.
8. Negroes do not make good workers because they are lazy.
9. If I had children, I would not mind if they were taught by a Negro school teacher.
10. Negroes cannot be trusted in positions of responsibility.
11. There is nothing wrong with both races attending the same church.
12. Most Negroes would become overbearing and disagreeable if not kept in their place.
13. It is unimportant to me if an elected official is Negro or white, as long as he is capable and honest.
14. I would not be willing to invite Negroes to a dinner party at my home.
15. I would be willing to have a Negro as my supervisor in my place of work.
16. I prefer to see white and Negro children attend different schools.

in the semester. There were eight different letters. These letters were designed to elicit behavioral responses under varying social distance considerations. While each subject received only one version, every letter requested the recipient to participate in some form of action involving Negroes. The subject was to sign a pledge that he would engage in the action at a later date. Or, if he chose, he could sign indicating that he disapproved of the action being solicited. In either case, he was to return the signed document to the sender in an enclosed, stamped and self-addressed envelope.

In order to establish some outside criteria for the selection of the social distance considerations to be used in the letters, preliminary testing was done on 83 students during the semester preceding the major study. Eight items which posed various kinds of acts that the subject could indicate he would or would not perform were selected for inclusion in the "Public Information Questionnaire."[6] The data collected in the questionnaire were used to obtain ratings on the items in order to evaluate their potential use in the letters. The intent was to obtain a set of items which would provide implications of either reducing or maintaining social distance for a person *perfoming the acts* described in the items.

After the collection of the study data, the responses of the main body of subjects were analyzed to determine if the items met the criteria established for a Guttman scale (Edwards, 1957: chap. 7). A good ranking was obtained with respect to the level of social distance implied in the items.[7] For simplicity, however, this ranking was dichotomized. In the items listed in Footnote 6,

[6] *Behavioral items:*

1. If you were asked for a date by an attractive Negro college student, in order to participate in an evening of dancing, good music and good fellowship, what would you do?

2. If you were asked to contribute a very small sum of money (like 25¢) to a Negro civil rights organization, what would you do?

3. If a campus organization asked you to endorse an appeal to both political parties to seek out qualified Negro candidates for public office, what would you do?

4. Even today some local restaurants and hotels discriminate against Negro clients. If you were asked to sign a petition urging a local hotel or restaurant to serve Negroes, what would you do?

5. If you were invited to a dinner being held to welcome new Negro students to campus, what would you do?

6. The State Board of Education is considering a new policy of giving more complete treatment to the contributions of Negroes to American History and our society. If you were asked to endorse such a policy, what would you do?

7. If you were asked to volunteer to go into the home of a Negro family of potential college students and tell them about your experiences as a college student, what would you do?

8. There are several outstanding charitable groups organized to give aid to Negro college students who otherwise could never attend college. If you were asked to donate a very small sum of money (like 25¢) to such a charity, what would you do?

[7] The Guttman analysis was used to obtain information concerning social distance implications, as explained above, and data on the ordering of the items as forms of overt behavior for use in the letters. The coefficient of reproducibility was .89; the minimal marginal reproducibility was .70; the coefficient of scalability was .72 (Menzel, 1953).

Items 1 through 4 represent forms of action in which lowering of social distance is implied. That is, they all require a dropping of informal barriers which are culturally established by admitting Negroes to equalities of status which are not widely accepted by whites. These items, in other words, pose situations of action in which a *reduction* of social distance is implied.

Items 5 through 8, on the other hand, portray situations of action in which a reduction of social distance is not implied to the same degree as that of the first four items. That is, these forms of action can be engaged in by whites without a lowering of informal barriers, or the abandonment of established status distinctions. Thus, these items pose situations of action in which social distance can be *maintained*.[8] It should be noted that all these latter items involve acting with respect to Negroes within an educational framework. Apparently, these subjects defined participating in actions involving Negroes as "acceptable" as long as the framework of action pertained to educational matters. This interpretation is consistent with the findings of Westie, who in a recent study noted that " . . . people tend to go along with intergroup arrangements that are *faits accomplis*." (Westie, 1965:538).

In addition to the inclusion of social distance considerations, each letter was prepared in two forms: (1) a "private" form, which assured the subject of anonymity in the later action (and in the signed statement) and (2) a "public" form, which advised the subject that his pledged actions would be disclosed to others via the campus newspaper and other media. These two forms of the letters provided the high and low conditions of *social constraint*.

The letters were sent under the auspices of a fictitious campus student organization, the "Henry Clay Club," and signed by one of the authors as "President." The return envelope was addressed to a cooperating faculty member identified as "Faculty Advisor." There was, of course, no such club; it was strictly a creation of the research plan. The name of the club in our judgment has no significance concerning race relations. The name was widely known locally and provided a simple neutral cover. In spite of the elaborate prearrangements with the student newspaper, the campus office governing student organizations, and others, none of the subjects who received a letter questioned the club's authenticity or inquired about the nature and purposes of this fictitious organization.

Application of Controls in the Selections of Subjects

The initial "Public Information Questionnaire" included both the attitude scale described and information pertaining to social distance implications

---

[8] One could conclude that any noted attitude-behavior discrepancy would occur because of the difference between measuring a general orientation toward Negroes (the attitude scale)

of various kinds of behavior, plus a number of background variables to be used as controls. The subjects were assigned to attitude quartiles, depending upon their score on the verbal attitude scale. The subjects in each quartile were then matched on the following control variables, using the technique of frequency distribution control:[9] age, sex, education of father, education of mother, education of subject, marital status, social class (based upon father's occupation), residential history and group membership. Residential history was composed of two indices: a regional index and a mobility index. The regional index was based upon the area of the country (Southeast, Northwest, Southwest, etc.) in which the subject had spent the greater part of his life. The mobility index was based upon the degree to which the subject had moved from one region to another. Group membership refers to an index based upon the number and type of campus groups to which the subject belonged.[10]

The application of these controls resulted in reducing the number of subjects participating in the experiment. The availability sample for the study was originally composed of 731 students. After the application of the controls, a total of 537 subjects remained. However, the procedure yielded reasonably homogeneous groupings of subjects for the purpose of experimental design.

The Experimental Design

The experimental design used in the present study brings together the several factors and variables which have been discussed in previous sections. These include: (1) the subject's verbal attitude, (2) the control variables,[11] (3) the implications of social distance reduction or maintenance in the behaviors requested of the subjects, and (4) the level of social constraint pertaining to the requested behaviors.

A schematic representation of the experimental design is shown in

---

and measuring specific actions toward Negroes (responses to the letters). However, a separate analysis using responses to the eight social distance items included in the questionnaire as a more specific scale did not yield results significantly different from those found using the more general scale. It should also be noted that, because of the multiple correlation features of Guttman scales, one should not expect to find a closer correspondence between attitudes and behavior by relating the questionnaire response on a given action to actual willingness to engage in that same action.

[9] For a discussion of this technique, its advantages and disadvantages, see Selltiz *et al.*, (1965: 107–109).

[10] The controls are obviously elaborate. It was felt that every effort should be made to minimize influences of variables which could potentially disturb the dependent-independent relationship under study. It is recognized, however, that in a complex field experiment there still remain many variables that are not under rigorous control.

[11] The only control variable found to be significantly related to the subject's initial attitude was the sex of the subject. Females were generally less prejudiced.

VERBAL ATTITUDE QUARTILE	SOCIAL CONSTRAINT			
	High (public condition)		Low (private condition)	
	SOCIAL DISTANCE IMPLICATIONS		SOCIAL DISTANCE IMPLICATIONS	
	Reducing	Maintaining	Reducing	Maintaining
Least Prejudiced Subjects				
Most Prejudiced Subjects				

FIGURE 2.   *General Design for the Collection of Overt Behavior Data*

Figure 2. On the left side of the diagram it can be noted that the subjects were stratified into quartile groupings based upon their initial attitude. Once this step was completed, the subjects in each quartile were *randomly* assigned to one of the two social constraint conditions (high or low). The resulting groupings within a given quartile received the different forms of the letter (public or private), according to their assigned cell. The factor of social distance was handled in a similar manner. Within each social constraint condition, and for every quartile, the reducing and maintaining implications of social distance were appropriately represented.

Each cell in the design was balanced by assigning to it a proportionate number of males and females. Equal numbers of those who had indicated on the initial questionnaire that they would or would not engage in the behaviors under study (see Footnote 6) were also assigned to each cell.

Obviously, a number of hypotheses could be generated from Figure 2, which has the general form of a factorial design. However, the data were organized around several general propositions rather than around a large number of specific hypotheses. There is, after all, no tightly articulated theory underlying the present research in the sense of an interrelated set of generalizations from which theorems can be derived with the aid of a logical calculus. The research is inductive rather than deductive. Therefore, the following three broad propositions can be stated as a framework within which to discuss the results.

First of all, our interest centers on the relationship between attitudes and action. A general proposition can be stated in the following terms:

Proposition 1: There will be a significant relationship between initial attitude and overt behavior. However, the proportion of explained variance will be low because of the impact of situational variables.

Secondly, the factor of social constraint should have a substantial influence on attitude-action consistency. There is no reason to assume, however, that this influence will be uniform under all conditions indicated within the experimental design. We may state the following general proposition:

Proposition 2: There will be a significant relationship between social constraint and overt behavior. The proportion of explained variance will be low because of the impact of attitudes.

Finally, the factor of social distance should influence attitude-behavior relationships. The following proposition can be used as a guide in interpreting the data.

Proposition 3: There will be a significant relationship between social distance considerations and overt behavior. The proportion of explained variance will be low because of the impact of attitudes.

In addition to these general propositions, each cell of the experimental design places several variables in interactive conjunction with each other. Hypotheses could be formulated for each of these. Since there is no rigorous basis for predicting the direction of these influences, these combinations will be discussed in an *ad hoc* manner.

Results:

The results of the experiment are summarized in Tables 1, 2, and 3. Table 1 shows the percent of subjects in each of the major conditions who elected to *comply* with the request posed by the letter they received. That is, they signed the letter pledging that they would engage in the requested attitude-related act and they returned the letter to the sender. The rates of compliance differed greatly under the various experimental conditions. For example, for the most-prejudiced subjects under the combined conditions of "high" social constraint and an act requiring a "reducing" of social distance, the rate of return for a signed pledge of compliance was only 1.5% of the letters originally sent out to subjects in this experimental condition.

Table 2, on the other hand, shows the percent of subjects who refused to comply with the request in the letter they received. These subjects signed the letter indicating refusal and returned it to the experimenters. Examination of Table 2 indicates that refusal rates also varied substantially among the several conditions of the experiment. For example, the cell which corresponds to the illustration above, with the "most-prejudiced" subjects under the com-

TABLE 1

NUMBERS OF LETTERS SENT UNDER EACH EXPERIMENTAL CONDITION
AND PERCENT WHICH WERE SIGNED AND RETURNED TO COMPLY
WITH REQUESTED BEHAVIOR

	Social Constraint									
	High Social Distance Implications				Low Social Distance Implications				Total	
	Reducing		Maintaining		Reducing		Maintaining			
Verbal Attitude Quartile	n sent	percent compiled	n sent	percent compiled	n sent	percent compiled	n sent	percent compiled	n sent	percent compiled
Least Prejudiced $(Q_1 + Q_2)$	67	9.0	77	15.6	64	17.2	75	12.0	283	13.4
High social constraint:	.. (n sent = 144; 12.5%)									
Low social constraint:	.... (n sent = 139; 14.4%)									
Social distance reducing:	.... (n sent = 131; 13.0%)									
Social distance maintaining:	.... (n sent = 152; 13.8%)									
Most Prejudiced $(Q_3 + Q_4)$	67	1.5	59	6.8	69	13.0	59	6.8	254	7.1
High social constraint:	.. (n sent = 126; 4.0%)									
Low social constraint:	.... (n sent = 128; 10.2%)									
Social distance reducing:	.... (n sent = 136; 7.4%)									
Social distance maintaining:	.... (n sent − 118; 6.8%)									
Combined Quartiles	134	5.2	136	11.8	133	15.0	134	9.7		
High social constraint:	.. (n sent = 270; 8.5%)									
Low social constraint:	.... (n sent = 267; 12.4%)									
Social distance reducing:	.... (n sent = 267; 10.1%)									
Social distance maintaining:	.... (n sent = 270; 10.7%)									

TABLE 2

NUMBERS OF LETTERS SENT UNDER EACH EXPERIMENTAL CONDITION
AND PERCENT WHICH WERE SIGNED AND RETURNED REFUSING
TO COMPLY WITH REQUESTED BEHAVIOR

	Social Constraint								Total	
	High Social Distance Implications				Low Social Distance Implications					
	Reducing		Maintaining		Reducing		Maintaining			
Verbal Attitude Quartile	*n sent*	*percent refused*	*n sent*	*percent refused*	*n sent*	*percent refused*	*n sent*	*percent refused*	*n sent*	*percent refused*
Least Prejudiced ($Q_1 + Q_2$)	67	17.9	77	3.9	64	14.1	75	5.3	283	9.9
High social constraint:	.. (n sent = 144; 10.4%)									
Low social constraint:	.... (n sent = 139; 9.4%)									
Social distance reducing:	.... (n sent = 131; 16.0%)									
Social distance maintaining:	.... (n sent = 152; 4.6%)									
Most Prejudiced ($Q_3 + Q_4$)	67	22.4	59	20.3	69	10.1	59	8.5	254	15.4
High social constraint:	.. (n sent = 126; 21.4%)									
Low social constraint:	.... (n sent = 128; 9.4%)									
Social distance reducing:	.... (n sent = 136; 16.2%)									
Social distance maintaining:	.... (n sent = 118; 14.4%)									
Combined Quartiles	134	20.1	136	11.0	133	12.0	134	6.7		
High social constraint:	.. (n sent = 270; 15.6%)									
Low social constraint:	.... (n sent = 267; 9.4%)									
Social distance reducing:	.... (n sent = 267; 16.1%)									
Social distance maintaining:	.... (n sent = 270; 8.9%)									

TABLE 3

PERCENT COMPLYING MINUS PERCENT REFUSING, CONSIDERING
ONLY THOSE WHO RETURNED THEIR LETTER

| | Social Constraint | | | | |
| | High Social Distance Implications | | Low Social Distance Implications | | |
Verbal Attitude Quartile	Reducing	Maintaining	Reducing	Maintaining	Total
Least Prejudiced					
(Q₁ + Q₂)	−33.3	+60.0*	+10.0	+38.5	+15.2*
High social constraint:	(+9.1)				
Low social constraint:			(+21.2)*		
Social distance reducing:		(−10.5)			
Social distance maintaining:		(+50.0)*			
Most Prejudiced					
(Q₃ + Q₄)	−87.5*	−50.0	+12.5	−11.1	−36.8*
High social constraint:	(−68.8)*				
Low social constraint:			(+4.0)		
Social distance reducing:		(−37.5)*			
Social distance maintaining:		(−36.0)*			
Combined Quartiles	−58.8*	+3.2	+11.1	+18.2	
High social constraint:	(−29.2)*				
Low social constraint:			(+13.8)*		
Social distance reducing:		(−22.9)*			
Social distance maintaining:		(+9.4)			

*Indicates p less than .05.

bined conditions of "high" social constraint and an act requiring a "reducing" of social distance, the rate of signed refusal was 22.4% of the letters originally sent out within these conditions.

To interpret these findings within a probability framework, a third table was constructed. Table 3 is based upon only those who returned a signed letter, either agreeing to comply or refusing to comply. These letters were classified into the percent complying and the percent refusing. It must be noted that correspondence between attitude and action is indicated by compliance for the nonprejudiced and by refusal to comply for the prejudiced. If only chance factors were operating in a situation of this type, 50% of the returned letters should indicate compliance and the other 50%, refusal. Therefore, where the conditions imposed by the experiment had no influence on the results, subtracting the number of letters indicating refusal from those indicating compliance (in any given cell of the table) should yield results not significantly different from *zero*. On the other hand, if the conditions used in the experiment had some influence on the relative proportion of compliance and refusal, subtracting the percent who refused from the percent who complied should yield difference in percents which are significantly different from zero. Thus, the cells of Table 3 show plus and minus percentage values which were obtained by this procedure. A plus value indicates an excess of compliance over refusal. A minus value indicates the reverse, an excess of refusal over compliance. The probabilities for these differences were obtained by applying the (two-tailed) t-test for the significance of differences between proportions, where n's were greater than 20, or the (two-tailed) binomial distribution where n's were smaller than or equal to 20.

This analysis provides no interpretation of the impact of the experimental conditions for those subjects who did not return a letter. We may note that there was no expectation that the majority would return a letter. The interest was the relative predictability for those who complied versus those who refused. The technique used should not be confused with the usual "mail-back" procedure for data-gathering, where the objective is to infer population parameters from mailed returns. The present research aims at inferences concerning the comparative importance of conditions within a specific experimental design. It does not attempt to estimate population parameters. In this respect, it is quite similar to a laboratory experiment. A separate study of those who did not return a letter would be important and would undoubtedly produce interesting results. Because of limitations of space, the present report does not pursue this task.[12]

Proposition 1 stated that there would be a significant relationship between initial attitude and the direction of overt behavior, but that it would be weak because of the influence of intervening situational conditions. From Table 3, the influence of attitude on behavior is apparent. For the least prejudiced subjects, taken as a whole, the value in the right hand margin is $+15.2$ percentage points, indicating a significant excess of compliance over refusal. For the most prejudiced subjects, the marginal value of -36.8 indicates a significant excess of refusals over compliance. These findings lend some support to the idea that

---

[12] A typical way of dealing with the problem of non-response is to compare the characteristics of those who fail to respond with those of the respondents. If no systematic differences between these appear, then one concludes that the effects on the dependent variable are negligible. Since the present study commenced with a rather homogeneous sample of subjects, this problem is not of the same magnitude as it is for the survey researcher who has very little initial information concerning the characteristics of specific respondents. Nevertheless, attempts were made in the present study to investigate this problem. The control variables were cross-tabulated with the subject's overt behavior response to determine if the composition of the groups was affected by differential response rates. There was no relationship between any of the nine control variables and overt behavior responses for the total group. The overt behavior responses for the subjects in each of the four groups were then cross-tabulated with the control variables. One relationship out of thirty-six was significant at the .05 level. Since one would expect at least one out of twenty relationships to be significant on a chance basis, this occurrence is considered to be due to random fluctuation. In addition, a stratified random sample of those who returned the letter and those who did not was interviewed; data indicated that the subjects viewed the letter as a realistic request.

a person with a positive attitude will tend to act favorably toward the objects of that attitude while a person with a negative attitude will tend to refuse to engage in an act which is inconsistent with that attitude. These data may appear to support the postulate of consistency between attitudes and action. However, if this postulate were completely tenable, values of plus and minus 100 percent would be required in these marginal cells (assuming valid assessments of both attitudes and behavior). They are considerably less than that. Therefore a large amount of consistency is not present.

Since the postulates of consistency and of independent variation are not tenable, we may turn to the intervening variables of social constraint and social distance to assess their importance in the attitude-action relationship. Proposition 2 stated that there would be a significant relationship between social constraint and behavior. The impact of social constraint can be seen by examining the marginal values in the bottom of Table 3. The value of −29.2 percentage points, associated with high social constraint, indicates a significant excess of refusals over compliance. Thus, regardless of whether the subject was among the most or least prejudiced, the factor of high social constraint (disclosing his actions to others) tended to inhibit his willingness to comply with the requested behavior. For the condition of low social constraint, and regardless of initial attitude, the corresponding marginal in the table is +13.8. This indicates a significant excess of compliance over refusal. A condition of anonymity, in other words, led to increased probabilities of compliance with the attitude-related act. Subjects were more willing to pledge themselves to engage in the requested behaviors when they were assured their actions were not visible to others.

Finally, Proposition 3 stated that there would be a significant relationship between social distance considerations and overt behavior. The impact of social distance implications can be seen by examining the bottom marginals of Table 3. In situations which required a reduction of social distance, there was a significant excess of refusals over compliance. The difference is −22.9 percentage points. Thus, regardless of initial attitude, subjects tended to refuse to engage in the requested behavior in situations in which a reduction of social distances was implied; where social distance could be maintained, however, no clear relationship to behavior was noticed. That is, the +9.4 excess of compliance over refusal is not significantly different from zero. Thus Propositions 1, 2, and 3 were generally supported.

Propositon 2, however, suggests that the direction of one's attitude is an important factor. To assemble evidence on this issue, we may examine Table 4 (derived from Table 3) which shows the relevant data in convenient form.

As can be seen, high social constraint had a substantial inhibiting effect upon the least prejudiced subjects. Since the requested act was one generally disapproved within relevant norms, the exposure to potential surveillance provided by the condition of high social constraint produced inconsistency between attitudes and action for the least prejudiced subjects. In fact, there

TABLE 4

PERCENT COMPLYING MINUS PERCENT REFUSING,
HIGH AND LOW SOCIAL CONSTRAINT ONLY

Verbal Attitude	Social Constraint	
	High	Low
Least Prejudiced	+9.1	+21.2*
Most Prejudiced	−68.8*	+4.0

*Indicates p less than .05.

was no clear relationship under these conditions between attitude and action as indicated by a nonsignificant value of +9.1 percentage points. For the most prejudiced subjects, on the other hand, a condition of high social constraint tended to produce substantial consistency between attitudes and action. The general norms surrounding the act, the potential surveillance resulting from high social constraint and the initial attitude all combined to produce a very high level of refusal over compliance (−68.8). This indicates consistency between the negative attitude and rejection of the attitude object.

Low social constraint had a somewhat opposite influence. Here, the protections of anonymity permitted the least-prejudiced subjects to act more favorably toward the attitude object. They tended toward consistency in their attitudes and actions, under the conditions provided by low social constraint. The most prejudiced subjects, on the other hand, showed no significant relationship between their attitude and actions, under the conditions provided by low social constraint. Thus, in a relatively constraint-free environment, the most prejudiced subjects did not uniformly reject the attitude-object.

Overall, Proposition 2 appears to be tenable. High and low social constraint did indeed have differential effects upon the most and least prejudiced. These were, however, rather complex. The direction of initial attitude was clearly important, but the social constraint factor operated rather differently under specific interactional conditions.

The third general proposition, concerning the influence of social distance implications, also suggests that the direction of one's attitude will modify the relationship between social distance consideration and behavior. Evidence on this broad hypothesis can be derived from Table 3. The relevant data are summarized in Table 5.

For the least-prejudiced subjects, under the condition where the act implied a reduction of social distance, only a change-like relationship is observed between attitudes and action (a −10.5 percentage points excess of refusal over compliance). Where social distance could be maintained while performing the requested act, however, there was a significant excess of compliance over refusal (+50.0), indicating substantial correspondence between attitude and

TABLE 5

PERCENT COMPLYING MINUS PERCENT REFUSING,
SOCIAL DISTANCE IMPLICATIONS ONLY

| | Social Distance Implications | |
Verbal Attitude	Reducing	Maintaining
Least Prejudiced:	−10.5	+50.0*
Most Prejudiced:	−37.5*	−36.0*

*Indicates p less than .05.

behavior. For the most prejudiced subjects, where the act implied a reduction of social distance, the excess of refusal over compliance was −37.5. Under conditions in which the act did not imply a reduction of social distance, the most-prejudiced subjects still exhibited a significant excess of refusal over compliance (−36.0). This may be attributable to the confounding influence of high social constraint. Thus, social distance implications would seem to have substantial effects among both the least-prejudiced subjects and the most-prejudiced subjects. In particular, consistency between attitudes and action was sharply reduced for the least-prejudiced subjects when the act implied a reduction of social distance. Thus, the general idea expressed in Proposition 3 appears tenable.

The three-way interactions between social constraint, social distance and initial attitude are presented in Table 6. We may first observe the relationship between situational variables and behavior for the least prejudiced subjects. Under conditions of high social constraint in which a reduction of social distance is implied, there is an excess of refusal over compliance (−33.3 percentage points). However, because of small n's, this relationship is not significantly different from zero (indicating no relationship between attitudes and behavior). Under conditions of high social constraint in which social distance can be

TABLE 6

PERCENT COMPLYING MINUS PERCENT REFUSING, SOCIAL DISTANCE
AND SOCIAL CONSTRAINT CONSIDERED JOINTLY

| | Social Constraint | | | |
| | High Social Distance Implications | | Low Social Distance Implications | |
Verbal Attitude	Reducing	Maintaining	Reducing	Maintaining
Least Prejudiced:	−33.3	+60.0*	+10.0	+38.5
Most Prejudiced:	−87.5*	−50.0	+12.5	−11.1

*Indicates p less than .05.

maintained, there is a significant excess of compliance over refusal (+60.0), indicating a high degree of correspondence between attitudes and action. Under conditions of low social constraint, there is little or no relationship between attitudes and behavior (possibly due to the small n's in these cells). However, the trend appears to be in the same direction as that observed under conditions of high social constraint.

These interactional situations seem to have had a somewhat different effect for the most prejudiced subjects. Under conditions of high social constraint, where the act implied a reduction of social distance, there is a significant excess of refusal over compliance. Thus, the figure -87.5 percentage points indicates a high degree of consistency between a negative attitude and rejection of the attitude object. Under the conditions of low social constraint, the relationship between attitudes and behavior does not appear to be significant.

In summary of the foregoing examination of the results of the experiment, the following empirical regularities were observed:

1. For the *most-prejudiced* subjects, taken as a whole, there is a significant relationship between attitudes and behavior (Table 3).

2. For the *least-prejudiced* subjects, taken as a whole, there is a significant relationship between attitudes and behavior (Table 3).

3. Regardless of initial attitude, the factor of *high social constraint* tends to inhibit the subjects' willingness to comply with the requested behavior (Table 3).

4. Regardless of initial attitude, the factor of *low social constraint* tends to promote the subjects' willingness to comply with the requested behavior (Table 3).

5. Regardless of initial attitude, a situation which implies reduction of social distance tends to inhibit the subjects' willingness to comply with the requested behavior (Table 3).

6. Under conditions of *low social constraint*, there is a significant correspondence between attitudes and behavior for the least-prejudiced subjects (Table 4).

7. Under conditions of *high social constraint*, there is a significant correspondence between attitudes and behavior for the most-prejudiced subjects (Table 4).

8. Under conditions which imply either a *reduction of social distance* or *maintenance of social distance*, there is a significant correspondence between attitudes and behavior for the most-prejudiced subjects (Table 5).

9. Under conditions which imply *maintenance of social distance* there is a significant correspondence between attitudes and behavior for the least-prejudiced subjects (Table 5).

10. Under conditions of *high social constraint* in which *social distance* can be *maintained*, there is a significant correspondence between attitudes and behavior for the least-prejudiced subjects (Table 6).

11. Under conditions of *high social constraint* in which *social distance* is *reduced*,

there is a significant correspondence between attitudes and behavior for the most-prejudiced subjects (Table 6).

Discussion:

The experimental conditions used in the present study are composed of various combinations of the social constraint and social distance dichotomies discussed previously. Both of these rather complex factors relate directly to norms in the following manner. First, disclosure of an act (high social constraint situation) makes it possible for others to administer external sanctions upon one's behavior. Presumably, when one's behavior is open to surveillance by others, the individual is subject to possible negative sanctions if his behavior deviates from the expectations that others hold or the norms to which they give approval.[13] Secondly, social distance considerations have implications for interaction. If one denies social distance considerations which others define as normative, he risks potential sanctions—provided these others discover the nature of his act. It is therefore necessary to make assertions as to whether norms are favorable or unfavorable toward certain types of interaction. As was pointed out earlier, an underlying assumption of the present study is that the normative environment is hostile toward integration (see Footnote 4). In view of these statements, the findings of the present research are reasonably consistent with what one might expect. Thus, the least-prejudiced subjects tend to be most consistent when they are not exposed to potential sanctions which support norms that are unfavorable toward integration. That is, their attitudes and actions tend to correspond under low social constraint (anonymity protected) and social distance maintaining situations. When, however, they are asked to behave favorably toward the attitude object in situations in which they would be violating norms (social distance reduction) and directly disclosing their acts to others (high social constraint), a great deal of inconsistency can be noted between their attitudes and behavior.

For the most-prejudiced subjects, on the other hand, norms which are hostile toward integration are *supportive* of their attitudes. Thus, for the most-prejudiced subjects, one would expect the greatest correspondence between attitudes and behavior under conditions of surveillance (high social constraint) and for those acts which are normatively prohibited (reduction of social distance and hence lowering of barriers to interaction). The results of the present study seem to support these interpretations quite clearly.

In general, the present data and the interpretations are consistent with a "field view of prejudice and discrimination." (Yinger, 1965:244–266). This viewpoint specifies the joint implications of individual tendencies (atti-

---

[13] The early study by Schanck (1932) offers a demonstration of compliance to norms when one is under surveillance by others and violation of norms when the individual is not under direct surveillance. Kelman (1958) also discusses three processes which influence conformity to norms.

tudes) and structural supports (norms) for behavior. Or, stated differently, these data support the postulate of contingent consistency.

In spite of this general support for the point of view represented by Yinger, it can be suggested that a more adequate formulation of the way in which behavior is linked with attitude in the area of ethnic relations would combine: (1) Merton's original types of discriminators, (2) Yinger's model of the differential probability of discriminatory acts which are contingent upon varying socio-cultural environments, and (3) the theoretical implications of the data assembled in the present paper.

Merton's categories, of course, are little more than locations of individuals on a dichotomous measurement of attitude, combined with a two-fold classification of conformity or non-conformity to official creeds (of non-discrimination). Although Merton maintained, as we noted earlier, that attitude and action vary independently, his verbal discussion did little to clarify the issue.

The strength of Yinger's formulation is that he attempted to specify for each of Merton's types the kind of socio-cultural system within which discrimination was or was not likely to occur. This clarified the relationship between attitudes and action by subsuming it under the postulate of contingent consistency rather than that of independent variation.

Unfortunately, Yinger's model is not satisfactory in all respects. For one thing, it was generated (as was Merton's original work) on the basis of hypothetical data. Furthermore, it makes certain logically inconsistent predictions. (For example, it provides a cell representing the "all-weather illiberal" who does *not* discriminate in a "liberal environment." Such a person would scarcely be an "all-weather" discriminator.) Finally, the model depicts rather specific socio-cultural environments which may not be in tune with the contemporary climate of ethnic relations. (For example, a "northern city" may now be a highly prejudiced cultural environment.)

For these reasons, a modified and somewhat more general model, suggested in part by our present data, has been formulated to describe ideal-typical relationships prevailing between types of discriminators (following Merton) and the situational variables within which discrimination is to be predicted. This formulation is portrayed graphically in Figure 3.

The relationships suggested in Figure 3 constitute an oversimplified representation of the general shape which a more adequate theory of discrimination will eventually take. The Merton typology is still a simple two-fold system which should be replaced with more sophisticated continua. There may be a number of "individual tendencies" in addition to attitudes which can be identified. Rokeach, for example, suggests that beliefs and values play an important part in the attitudinal behavior of the individual (Rokeach 1967). Numerous other individual variables can be suggested (inner and other directedness, need for approval, alienation, status anxiety, etc.). The situational variables, which are lumped together into a simple four-fold system, can obviously be broken down into a multiplicity of interactional and cultural concepts. These may alter the probabilities that a person with given individual tendencies will engage in an act of discrimination. The present research has indicated in empirical terms the way in which two such variables can be important (social distance and social constraint, as defined). Numerous other potential situational variables have been or can be suggested (reference groups, significant others, voluntary organizations, peers, roles, subcultures, etc.). As research accumulates, these factors can be placed in multivariate systems

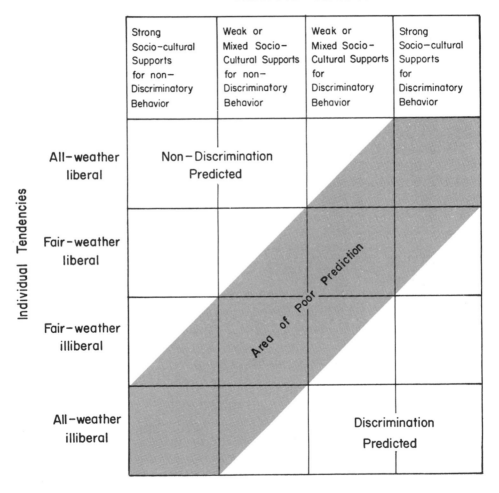

FIGURE 3.   *Schematic Representation of Hypothesized Relationship Between Attitudes, Situational Variables, and Overt Behavior.*

which should provide causal models explaining and predicting the probability of discrimination under a wide variety of personal, social and cultural situations. Hopefully, the oversimplified scheme suggested in Figure 3 will soon become obsolete.

Perhaps more than anything else, the implications of the present research pose a warning for sociological researchers who are interested in the problems of ethnic relations. There is a danger that *fundamental* research on minority relations will turn away from the sources, nature and consequences of prejudice to focus on the more dramatic riots, social movements and other collective behavior issues of the moment. Although these dramatic events are significant, the basic task of theory building concerning the manifestations of prejudice remains far from completion. Providing explanations of why one human being holds antipathies toward another in such a way that he commits acts of discrimination in a society deeply devoted to democratic principles is still the heart of the research task.

REFERENCES

BOGARDUS, EMORY, S. 1959 Social Distance. Yellow Springs, Ohio: The Antioch Press.

CAMPBELL, DONALD T. 1963 "Social Attitudes and Other Acquired Behavioral Dispositions." pp. 94–172 in Sigmund Koch (ed.), Psychology: A Study of a Science, Volume 6. New York: McGraw-Hill.

DEFLEUR, MELVIN L. and FRANK R. WESTIE. 1958 "Verbal attitudes and overt acts." American Sociological Review 23 (December): 667–673.

DEFRIESE, GORDON and W. SCOTT FORD. 1968 "Open occupancy—what whites say, what they do." Transaction (April): 53–56.

DEUTSCHER, IRWIN. 1966 "Words and deeds: social science and social policy." Social Problems 13 (Winter): 235–254.

DURKHEIM, EMILE. 1950 The Rules of Sociological Method. G. Catlin (ed.). New York: The Free Press.

EDWARDS, ALLEN L. 1957 Techniques of Attitude Scale Construction. New York: Appleton-Century-Crofts, Inc.

FENDRICH, JAMES M. 1967 "A study of the association among verbal attitudes, commitment, and overt behavior in different experimental situations." Social Forces 45 (March): 347–355.

KELMAN, HERBERT C. 1958 "Compliance, identification and internalization: three processes of attitude change." Journal of Conflict Resolution 2: 51–60.

KUTNER, BERNARD, CAROL WILKINS and PENNY YARROW. 1952 "Verbal attitudes and overt behavior involving racial prejudice." Journal of Abnormal and Social Psychology 47 (October): 649–652.

LAPIERE, R. T. 1934 "Attitudes vs action." Social Forces 13 (December): 230–237.

LOHMAN, JOSEPH D. and DIETRICH C. REITZES. 1954 "Deliberately organized groups and racial behavior." American Sociological Review 19 (June): 342–344.

LINN, LAWRENCE S. 1965 "Verbal attitudes and overt behavior: a study of racial discrimination." Social Forces 43 (March): 353–364.

MENZEL, HERBERT. 1953 "A new coefficient for scalogram analysis." Public Opinion
    Quarterly 17 (Summer): 268–280.
MERTON, ROBERT K. 1949 "Discrimination and the American creed." pp. 99–126 in
    Robert M. MacIver (ed.), Discrimination and National Welfare. New
    York: Institute for Religious and Social Studies.
MIDDLETON, RUSSELL. 1960 "Ethnic prejudice and susceptibility to persuasion." Ameri-
    can Sociological Review 25 (October): 679–686.
MINARD, R. D. 1952 "Race relations in the Pocahontas Coal Fields." Journal of Social
    Issues 8:29–44.
PARK, ROBERT E. 1924 "The concept of social distance." Journal of Applied Sociology 8
    (July–August): 339–344.
ROKEACH, MILTON. 1967 "Attitude change and behavioral change." Public Opinion
    Quarterly 30:529–550.
SCHANCK, R. L. 1932 "A study of a community and its groups and institutions con-
    ceived of as behavior of individuals." Psychological Monographs 430.
SELLTIZ, CLAIRE, MARIE JAHODA, MORTON DEUTSCH and STUART W. COOK. 1965
    Research Methods in Social Relations. New York: Holt, Rinehart and
    Winston.
SIMPSON, GEORGE E. and J. MILTON YINGER. 1958 Racial and Cultural Minorities.
    New York: Harper and Brothers.
TURNER, RALPH H. 1968 "Is the concept of attitude obsolete?" Paper read at the
    Pacific Sociological Association Meetings (March): San Francisco.
WESTIE, FRANK R. 1964 "Race and ethnic relations." pp. 576–619 in Robert E. L.
    Faris (ed.), Handbook of Modern Sociology. Chicago: Rand McNally
    and Company.
———. 1965 "The American dilemma: an empirical test." American Sociological
    Review 30 (August): 527–538.
YINGER, J. MILTON. 1965 Toward a Field Theory of Behavior. New York: McGraw-Hill.

Stanley E. Jones*

ATTITUDE CHANGES OF PUBLIC SPEAKERS DURING THE INVESTIGATIVE AND EXPRESSIVE STAGES OF ADVOCACY

It is not uncommon for speakers and writers to testify that while preparing and delivering speeches or writing essays they were persuaded as their work advanced. Antonius, in Cicero's *De Oratore*, is made to observe, "I never yet, upon my honor, tried to excite sorrow, or compassion, or envy, or hatred when speaking before a court of judicature, but I myself, in rousing the judges, was affected with the very same sensations I wished to produce in others."[1] Recent experimental studies, notably those by Janis and King on improvisation[2] and those based on Festinger's theory of cognitive dissonance,[3] have verified

*Dr. Jones is Assistant Professor, Department of Speech and Theatre and the Division of General Studies, University of Illinois. This paper is based on his doctoral dissertation completed at Northwestern University in 1964 under the direction of Professor Franklyn S. Haiman.

[1] *Cicero on Oratory and Orators*, trans. John S. Watson (Philadelphia, 1897), p. 149.

[2] Irving L. Janis and Bert T. King, "The Influence of Role Playing on Opinion Change," *Journal of Abnormal and Social Psychology*, IL (1954), 211–218. Also, King and Janis, "Comparison of the Effectiveness of Improvised Versus Non-improvised Role-playing in Producing Opinion Changes," *Human Relations*, IX (1956), 177–178.

[3] Leon Festinger, *A Theory of Cognitive Dissonance* (Stanford, Calif., 1957). See also Jack W. Brehm and Arthur R. Cohen, *Explorations in Cognitive Dissonance* (New York, 1962).

Reprinted from the *Speech Monographs,* 33 (1966), 137–46, with permission of the author and the Speech Association of America.

the general observation that communicative activity influences the belief of the communicator. The process, which might be called "self-persuasion," may be defined for theoretical purposes as "alteration of belief by speakers in anticipation of or during the act of attempting to persuade others."

The precise nature of self-influence during preparation or presentation of discourse has been little explored, yet how we shall resolve certain theoretical and pedagogical problems depends upon our understanding of the process itself. How speakers develop firm convictions, the rhetorical critic must know or hypothesize. The legitimacy of two-sided debating depends in part upon how the acts of communicating affect the speaker's thinking. Whether "consecrating oneself to a cause" or "being sincere" can contribute to self-confidence and persuasiveness in speaking depends at least partially on how self-persuasion occurs.

The purpose of the present study was to discover how the attitudes of speakers toward their advocated stands are changed by the "investigative" stage (evidence selection) and the "expressive" stage (writing and delivery) of the speech-making process.[4] An experiment and its replication were designed to overcome several limitations of past research. (1) Past studies have employed brief impromptu speeches or essays; they have not shown how belief changes occur during the investigative and expressive stages of the speech-making process. (2) No study has combined the conditions of "low choice" and "high justification." Recent research based on dissonance theory indicates that belief change is small or nonexistent under conditions of "low choice" or "high justification." In other words, this research suggests that a person will not be likely to change belief when defending a position in a speech if he feels he had little or no choice about speaking. Further, a person who is given numerous reasons (justifications) for defending a certain thesis in a speech would not be expected to experience commitment to his task or to change his attitude. Dissonance theory predicts attitude change under conditions of "high choice" and "low justification,"[5] but these conditions are seldom found in speaking situations of "real life." One does not often comply with a request to defend a position opposed to his private opinion if he feels little obligation to comply and can readily decline to speak. Thus, in order to test realistic conditions the present study investigates whether change in the direction of an advocated

---

[4] The terms "investigative" and "expressive" correspond roughly to the communication theory terms "decoding" and "encoding." When a speaker "investigates" a topic (reads materials and selects ideas and evidence to be used in a speech) he engages primarily in decoding rather than encoding activity, although he may also encode modes of organizing the materials and wording ideas. When he "expresses" his ideas by outlining, writing, rehearsing, and actually delivering the final product, he is principally encoding, although he may also decode information while re-reading the evidence he has selected and examining the outline and other notes he has written.

[5] See Jacob M. Rabbie, Jack W. Brehm, and Arthur R. Cohen, "Verbalization and Reaction to Cognitive Dissonance," *Journal of Personality*, XXVII, No. 3 (1959), 407–417.

stand can occur under the combined conditions of "no choice" and "adequate justification."[6] Some critics of the research on self-persuasion have suggested that subjects may have changed easily simply because they did not care one way or the other. To overcome this objection, a salient topic was employed in the present study. (4) No research indicates whether advocating a change in the *status quo* (a "pro" stand) is more or less self-persuasive than defending the *status quo* (a "con" stand). Past research has also been concerned almost exclusively with subjects who advocated discrepant stands (those favorable to a thesis argued against it and vice versa). In this study some speakers were assigned to defend pro stands, and others were assigned to take con stands. Among these subjects were some discrepant speakers arguing against their private beliefs. Others were "off-neutrals," initially undecided subjects advocating either a pro or con thesis. The rest were "consonant" speakers —those assigned to defend a thesis with which they were in initial agreement. (5) Past studies suggest that highly active participation in communication (writing or speaking) affects belief more than less active participation (reading or listening), but no studies have compared these activities in their normal sequence: reading followed by speaking. (6) Although research has shown that a person will seek information consonant with a choice and will tend to confirm his choice by this selection of information,[7] no studies have investigated whether a person changes his attitude as a result of completing an *assigned* task of information selection.

HYPOTHESES

The major predictions of the present study and the rationale for each were as follows.

> *Directional Hypothesis One:* Belief will shift toward an assigned thesis as a result of investigation for, outlining, and delivery of a speech of advocacy.

The expectation that a communicator will persuade himself as a result of completing an assigned task of advocacy is based on the findings of a number of descriptive and experimental studies. For example, G. C. Myers observed that "chronic kickers" in the Army noticeably changed their attitudes toward

---

[6] In the context of the present study, as in cognitive dissonance research, the term "no choice" (sometimes called "low choice") means that the subject is not allowed to select his topic or the stand he will take and is not given the alternative of withdrawing from the experiment. "Justifications" are reasons given the subject why he *should* participate and speak as directed. Giving numerous reasons constitutes "high justification"; giving few or no reasons is "low justification." In the present study "adequate justification" means giving sufficient reasons to convince the subject that the project is worthy of his participation.

[7] See Festinger, *op. cit.*

Army life as a result of extolling its virtues in classroom speeches.[8] Janis and King found that speakers who were forced to "improvise"—add their own ideas to arguments presented in an outline—changed more in the direction of an assigned discrepant thesis than non-improvisers, listeners and manuscript readers.

> *Directional Hypothesis Two:* Belief will shift toward an assigned thesis as a result of investigation which precedes expression.

Although this hypothesis has not been tested, it is derived from dissonance theory. Making many choices among evidential materials should arouse dissonance and bring belief change. When a speaker *needs* evidence, he is presumably gratified by its discovery and is likely, therefore, to be persuaded by its content. This tendency to self-persuasion should be heightened when the speaker chooses what he regards as *best* from among various materials favoring a given proposition.

> *Directional Hypothesis Three:* Belief will shift toward an assigned thesis as a result of expression which follows investigation.

Although there has been no research on the effects of expression which follows investigation, studies do show that expression can facilitate self-persuasion. Essay writing, outline construction, and impromptu speaking have been shown to cause belief change in the direction of an advocated thesis.[9]

> *Directional Hypothesis Four:* Investigation preceding expression will change belief in the direction of an assigned thesis more than expression which follows investigation.

Underlying this prediction is the notion that when people engage in tension-arousing behavior which tends to change their attitudes in a given direction, they will prefer to change their minds at the earliest possible time in order to reduce the ambiguity of the situation; they will prefer "preparatory" to "cumulative" change. If the preparation of a speech to be presented to an audience tends to arouse tension within a speaker, the experience would presumably be unpleasant. We would then expect the speaker to reduce tension *as soon as he can* by the means most readily available to him. In situations where he cannot refuse to prepare and to speak, the speaker would be expected to

---

[8] Gary C. Myers, "Control of Conduct by Suggestion: An Experiment in Americanization," *Journal of Applied Psychology,* V (1921), 26–31.

[9] See Mervin D. Lynch, "Modes of Resolution of Cognitive Inconsistency and Mood-Stress Through Communication Activity" unpubl. diss. (Wisconsin, 1963); also Janis and King and King and Janis, *op. cit.*

find changing his attitude in the direction of his advocated thesis the easiest way of reducing his anxiety.

No previous research deals specifically with the above hypothesis, but the results of various experiments are consistent with its prediction. Bostrom, Vlandis, and Rosenbaum found that subjects who wrote essays (engaged in expressive activity) changed their beliefs in the direction of an assigned thesis when they had no choice about whether or not to write.[10] On the other hand, when Rabbie, Brehm, and Cohen gave subjects choice about writing an essay, they found that writing did not influence belief beyond the change induced by the prior act of making the choice.[11] In both of these experiments it seems that subjects changed at their first opportunity, whether the first act was writing or choosing to write. Following this interpretation, we would expect the speakers in the present experiment to change their attitudes most during investigation, the first stage of their communicative activity.

In addition to the four directional hypotheses just discussed, the experiment attempted to test a methodological hypothesis. The object was to ascertain the effects of an "in-between" test, inserted between a pretest and a final posttest. The hypothesis tested was:

> *Methodological Hypothesis:* An attitude measure inserted between the first and second stages of a time series will depress belief change in the second stage.

DESIGN

In order to avoid the "testing effect" or tendency of subjects to be consistent from one questionnaire to another as a result of remembering answers and to avoid the "interaction of testing and the experimental variable" or tendency of subjects to be influenced in reactions to the experimental variable by having previously completed a questionnaire, a quasi-after-only design similar in principle to Campbell and Stanley's post-test-only or after-only design was employed.[12] While the Campbell and Stanley design prescribes only one measurement for each experimental and control group, the quasi-after-only design permits each subject to be tested twice, thus producing change

---

[10] Robert N. Bostrom, John W. Vlandis, and Milton E. Rosenbaum, "Grades as Reinforcing Contingencies and Attitude Change," *Journal of Educational Psychology,* LII (1961), 112–115.

[11] Rabbie, Brehm, and Cohen, *op. cit.*

[12] D. T. Campbell and Julian C. Stanley, "Experimental and Quasi-experimental Designs for Research on Teaching," in *Handbook of Research on Teaching,* ed. N. L. Gage (Chicago, 1963), pp. 195–196.

scores.[13] The attitudes of all subjects toward the relevant topic were pretested several weeks in advance of the experiment. At the time of the experiment, control-group subjects received a post-test with no exposure to communicative activity, one experimental group received a post-test after exposure to investigation, and another experimental group was post-tested after exposure to both investigation and expression.

Subjects were identified as initially pro, neutral, or con, according to their locations in the upper, middle, or lower third of the pretest score distribution. By random assignment, half the subjects in each of these groupings were assigned to take a pro stand and the other half to take a con stand. Finally, equal numbers of subjects from each of the six groups thus produced were randomly assigned to Group A (no exposure to the experimental variables), Group B (exposure to investigation), and Group C (exposure to investigation and expression).

PROCEDURES

The first experiment was conducted during the fall quarter of 1963 at Northwestern University. Fifty-four undergraduate students from several classes of the first course in public speaking were required by their instructors to participate. Approximately three weeks before the experiment, a person other than the experimenter administered to each class a pretest booklet of eight questionnaires, each on a different concept. Each questionnaire consisted of eight Likert-type items.[14] From among these concepts "Northwestern's

---

[13] In the typical design involving stages of activity, e.g., a series of trials in a learning experiment, all subjects are given a pretest before the first stage and subsequent tests after *each* stage. In the "quasi-after-only" design of the present study, only one post-test was given to each group. One group was post-tested without exposure to communication activity, another after one stage (investigation), and a third after two stages (investigation and expression). The after-only principle was employed to avoid more than one post-test. The rationale for this design was that there is little danger of testing effects and interaction between testing and the experimental variable when the pretest is given several weeks in advance of the single post-test. If a post-test were given after the investigation stage and followed by another test after the expression stage less than an hour later, a distortion in the responses obtained on the final test would be expected.

[14] Each questionnaire was composed of eight bi-polar, multi-level items. The rationale and evidence for this type of scale was discussed originally in an unpublished manuscript, "History of Attitude Testing" by D. T. Campbell, Northwestern University. A discussion of the scale may be found in the author's dissertation, "Attitude Changes of Public Speakers During the Investigative and Expressive Stages of Advocacy" (Northwestern, 1964), pp. 132–142. The Kuder-Richardson test of average inter-item correlation was employed to assess the reliability of the scale items. An inferred average inter-item correlation for each scale was then calculated to test the homogeneity of the test items independently of test length. For a discussion of the Kuder-Richardson and the inferred inter-item reliability formulas, see J. P. Guilford, *Psychometric Methods* (New York, 1954), pp. 385–387. A centroid rotation method of

Grading System" was chosen as the topic for the speeches subjects were to give. This topic had several advantages: it was highly salient; the scale was reliable and single-factored;[15] and the distribution of pretest scores was spread, allowing division of subjects into three initial positions. The experimenter prepared evidence cards from magazine and journal articles and the school newspaper. Judges rated each card on its degree of evidential value, strength of assertion, and persuasiveness. Forty-five cards were selected for the experiments. These were approximately equally distributed between pro and con sidedness and approximately equal, for each side, in force as rated by the judges.

Upon arriving to participate in the experiment each subject received certain instructions. The experimenter read aloud an article from the school newspaper, asserting that the Student Senate's polling commission was surveying student opinion on important issues by asking students to listen to pro and con presentations before giving their opinions and that tape-recorded speeches were being collected for this purpose. Control-group subjects were told some opinions were needed from people who heard no preliminary presentations, and these subjects were given the post-test immediately. Each subject in experimental groups heard directions telling him he would give one of the speeches described in the newspaper article, that he would have forty-five minutes to select six evidence cards to be kept with him during a second forty-five-minute period during which he would prepare an outline, rehearse, and deliver a speech to a tape recorder. The experimenter then left the room and each subject in the experimental groups examined the evidence cards given him, discovering the topic for speaking and whether he was to advocate the existing grading system or a pass-fail system. He selected six cards to use in defending his assigned thesis.

Subjects in the investigation group (Group B) took a post-test immediately after selecting their evidence cards; they then completed preparation, spoke, and were given another post-test. Subjects in the investigation-expression group (Group C) took the post-test only after they had delivered their speeches. As each subject was to speak, the experimenter re-entered the room, gave instructions on use of the tape recorder, turned it on, announced the speaker's name, and again left the room.

Experiment II, conducted during the winter quarter following the first

---

factor analysis described by Guilford (pp. 487–489) was employed to draw out the first factor. Then, a Lawley approximation for a chi-square test of the significance of the magnitude of the residuals remaining after extraction of the first factor was used to test whether each scale was single-factored. For a discussion of the Lawley test, see H. Harmon, *Modern Factor Analysis* (Chicago, 1960), p. 371.

[15] The inferred average, inter-item correlation for the eight items in the questionnaire concerning "Northwestern's Grading System" was .402; this correlation was significant at the .005 level. The hypothesis that there was more than one factor in the questionnaire was rejected since the Lawley test revealed a nonsignificant residual chi-square of 24.38.

experiment, was essentially a replication of Experiment I. The total number of subjects assigned to experimental conditions was one hundred and eight, double the number in the first experiment. There were no mortalities in Experiment I, but fourteen subjects were dropped from Experiment II principally because they failed to appear at scheduled times.[16] A successful revision of the scale on "Northwestern's Grading System" was employed in Experiment II.[17] Since many subjects in Experiment I said they had too little time for preparation in the expression stage, the time allowed for outlining, rehearsing, and delivering the speech in Experiment II was increased by ten minutes.

In both experiments the data satisfied assumptions necessary for analysis. A rating scale given to subjects at the time of the pretests revealed that "Northwestern's Grading System" was more salient for the subjects participating in Experiments I and II than any of the other pretested topics, including such topics as "The Function of a University Education," "Administration Policy on Student Life," and "Drug Addiction." Scales administered after each of the two experiments showed, as the experimenter had intended, that subjects perceived little or no choice about participating, that most felt the project was "worthwhile," and that their being assigned a stand was justified. As expected, subjects did not appear to differ in amounts of attitude change according to initial position, advocated stand, or the discrepancy of the advocated stand. These findings justified lumping together the change scores of all subjects within each group (A, B, and C) for purposes of comparing the groups statistically.

RESULTS AND INTERPRETATION

A change score was recorded for each subject by finding the difference between his pretest and post-test responses on the attitude questionnaire. Differences in the direction of assigned, advocated theses were given a plus sign, and changes opposite to the assigned position were given a minus sign. A constant score was then added to each number to eliminate negative values.

Examination of Table 1 shows that, as predicted, the only significant difference in Experiment I was among the three stages (the control, investigation, and investigation-expression conditions).

Table 2 reveals that the main effect of stages was significant in Experi-

---

[16] Tsao's technique of equating categories with unequal numbers of subjects was employed for the purposes of analysis of variance. See Palmer O. Johnson, *Statistical Methods in Research* (New York, 1949), pp. 260–266.

[17] In Experiment II, the levels of choice for each item were increased from five to seven, thus increasing the scale range by sixteen points and allowing more room for movement at the ends of the scale. The inferred average inter-item correlation of .400 was significant at the .005 level. The hypothesis that there was more than one factor in the questionnaire was rejected (chi-square = 23.53).

TABLE 1

ANALYSIS OF VARIANCE SUMMARY TABLE EXPERIMENT I

Source of Variance	Sum of Sqs.	d.f.	Mean Sq.	F-ratio
Stages (S)	536.33	2	268.17	7.40*
Initial Position (I)	192.11	2	96.06	2.65
Advocated Stand (A)	71.19	1	71.19	1.96
S × I	289.23	4	72.31	1.99
S × A	104.48	2	52.24	1.44
I × A	231.59	2	115.80	3.19**
S × I × A	141.74	4	35.44	< 1.00
Within groups	1,305.33	36	36.26	
Totals	2,872.00	53		

*p < .005.

**F-ratio nears significance at .05 level.

TABLE 2

ANALYSIS OF VARIANCE SUMMARY TABLE EXPERIMENT II

Source of Variance	Sum of Sqs.	d.f.	Mean Sq.	F-ratio
Stages (S)	960.23	2	480.12	8.29*
Initial Position (I)	273.26	2	136.63	2.36
Advocated Stand (A)	144.35	1	144.35	2.49
S × I	301.09	4	75.27	1.30
S × A	20.47	2	10.24	< 1.00
I × A	855.93	2	427.97	7.39**
S × I × A	84.49	4	21.12	< 1.00
Within groups	4,402.45	76	57.93	
Totals	7,042.27	93		

*p < .001.

**p < .005.

ment II, as in Experiment I; however, there was also a significant interaction effect of initial position and advocated stand in Experiment II. Subjects appear to have differed in attitude change according to the discrepancy between their advocated stands and their initial positions. For example, subjects who were initially pro, but who argued con, seemed to change more than initial pros who argued pro. But this apparent difference is deceptive, for examination of the control-group means for discrepant subjects (+4.54), off-neutrals (+.88), and consonant subjects (−4.00) suggests that the interaction was produced spuriously by addition of regression effects to the scores of discrepant subjects and subtraction of these effects from the scores of consonant subjects. Therefore, the significant interaction in Experiment II may be ignored because

TABLE 3

MEAN CHANGE SCORES FOR STAGES

Stages	Experiment I	Experiment II
Group A (Post-test without communicative activity)	− .28	+ .18
Group B (Post-test after investigation)	+5.06	+7.71
Group C (Post-test after expression)	+7.22	+2.09

+ = change in the direction of an assigned thesis from the pretest to the post-test.
− = change in the direction opposite to the assigned thesis.

it is a statistical artifact which does not seem to represent real differences among subjects in amounts of attitude change.[18]

Table 3 shows the mean change scores for each of the stages in Experiments I and II. The reader should keep in mind that the change scores recorded for each group in Table 3 are the means for the *total* attitude change occurring from the pretest (given several weeks in advance of the experiment) to the post-test. Thus, in Experiment I our best guess as to the amount of change occurring from the end of the investigation stage (Group B, mean = +5.06) to the end of the expression stage (Group C, mean = +7.22) is the difference between the means, +2.16. The expression stage appears to have produced a "boomerang" effect in Experiment II, since the difference between Group B (mean = +7.71) and Group C (mean = +2.09) is −5.62.

Evaluation of Substantive Hypotheses

A. *Directional Hypothesis One*, that "belief will shift toward an assigned thesis as a result of investigation for, outlining, and delivery of a speech of advocacy," is *accepted* in Experiment I, but *rejected* in Experiment II although the results were in the expected direction.

1. Experiment I:

a. The linear trend is significant at the .005 level.[19]

b. The gap between the control-group mean (−.28) and the investigation-expression group mean (+7.22) is significant at the .01 level according to Tukey's gap test.[20]

---

[18] For a discussion of regression, see Campbell and Stanley, pp. 180–182.

[19] For a discussion of trend analysis, see Allen L. Edwards, *Experimental Design in Psychological Research* (New York, 1950), pp. 224–250.

[20] For an explanation of Tukey's gap test, see Allen L. Edwards, *Statistical Methods for the Behavioral Sciences* (New York, 1954), pp. 330–332.

    c. The difference between the means is significant at the .001 level according to a one-tailed t test ($t = 3.52$, d.f. $= 34$).

2. Experiment II:

    a. The linear trend does not approach significance.

    b. The gap between the mean for the control group ($+.18$) and the mean for the investigation-expression group ($+2.09$) does not approach significance.

    c. The differences between the means does not approach significance according to a one-tailed t test ($t = .93$, d.f. $= 60$, $p > .15$).

      B. *Directional Hypothesis Two*, that "belief will shift toward an assigned thesis as a result of investigation which precedes expression," is *accepted* in both experiments.

1. Experiment I:

    a. The gap between the mean for the control group ($+.28$) and the mean for the investigation group ($+5.06$) is significant at the .05 level according to Tukey's gap test.

    b. The difference between the means is significant at the .01 level according to a one-tailed t test ($t = 2.56$, d.f. $= 34$).

2. Experiment II:

    a. The gap between the mean for the control group ($+.18$) and the mean for the investigation group ($+7.71$) is significant at the .01 level.

    b. The difference between the means is significant at the .001 level according to a one-tailed t test ($t = 3.86$, d.f. $= 60$).

      C. *Directional Hypothesis Three*, that "belief will shift toward an assigned thesis as a result of expression which follows investigation," is *rejected* in both experiments. In Experiment I the results were in the expected direction but were nonsignificant. In Experiment II the results were *opposite* to the expected direction.

1. Experiment I: Neither Tukey's gap test nor a one-tailed t test ($t = .87$, d.f. $= 34$, $.15 < p < .20$) reveals a significant difference between the investigation-group mean ($+5.06$) and the investigation-expression group mean ($+7.22$).

2. Experiment II:

    a. Tukey's gap test reveals that the gap between the mean for the investigation group ($+7.71$) and the mean for the investigation-expression group ($+2.09$) is significant at the .01 level.

    b. A one-tailed t test was not justified because the direction of the results was opposite to the prediction. A two-tailed t test reveals a significant boomerang response ($t = 2.57$, d.f. $= 60$, $p < .02$).

D. *Directional Hypothesis Four*, that "investigation preceding expression will change belief in the direction of an advocated thesis more than expression which follows investigation," is *rejected* in Experiment I although the results were in the expected direction and *accepted* in Experiment II.

1. Experiment I: The quadratic trend (deviation from linearity) of the results does not approach significance at the .05 level.
2. Experiment II: The quadratic trend is significant beyond the .001 level (indicating that the "bend" in the trend of the results was not a chance occurrence).

The prediction that investigation will facilitate belief change is the most consistently supported finding of the study, being affirmed with statistical significance in both experiments. In contrast, the prediction that expression will facilitate belief change in the direction of the advocated thesis was supported by the findings of the first experiment, although not at a level sufficient for statistical significance, and challenged by the results of the second study where expression brought a boomerang response. Rabbie, Brehm, and Cohen have suggested that improvisation may depress or have no effect on belief after an initial arousal of dissonance and change of attitude. In line with this reasoning a possible explanation of the apparent inconsistency between results of the two experiments of the present study is that the ten minutes of extra time allowed for outlining and rehearsal of the speech in Experiment II depressed belief built up in the investigation period.

Evaluation of Methodological Hypothesis

There was support in Experiment II for the notion that "an attitude measure inserted between the first and second stages of a time series will depress belief change in the second stage." The boomerang effect produced by the expression stage was significantly reduced in the group which received a post-test immediately before the expression stage.[21]

CONCLUSIONS

Judging from the results of this study, it does not seem necessary that an advocate have a choice of whether to speak or of the side which he will defend in order for self-persuasion to take place. The act of investigation (evi-

---

[21] A *t* test showed a significant difference between the final post-test scores for Groups B and C ($t = 2.48$, d.f. $= 59$, $p < .02$, two-tailed test). Although the changes in the expression stage were not in the expected direction in Experiment II, the fact that the second post-test mean of the group measured after investigation ($+7.49$) was a greater value than the mean of the group with only one post-test ($+2.09$) confirms the prediction that an intervening post-

dence selection) is sufficient in itself to bring attitude change in the direction of an advocated position. By logical extension, it may be that a debater, salesman, or politician will persuade himself while finding evidence for a given proposition even when he does not feel he has free choice about speaking. Furthermore, to the degree that we can generalize from the present study, it appears that a speaker will tend to convince himself even though he is given reasons why he *ought* to defend an assigned position. That is, if someone justifies his participation to him, he will not necessarily feel so obliged to comply as to preclude self-persuasion. On the other hand, there is no evidence in the present study that the act of utterance is crucial to self-persuasion where investigation precedes expression; the speaker need not "talk himself into belief."

SUMMARY

An experiment and its replication were designed to explore how speakers change their attitudes toward an assigned stand during the investigation stage (evidence selection) and the expression stage (outlining and delivery) of the speech-making process. Subjects' attitudes toward a highly salient topic were pretested and separate, randomized groups were given a post-test either (1) without engaging in speaking activity, (2) after selecting evidence cards, or (3) after selecting cards and preparing and delivering a speech.

The results revealed that under conditions of "no choice" and "adequate justification for participation," a task of selecting information for use in a speech of advocacy was sufficient in itself to bring attitude change in the direction of an assigned thesis. In the situation where investigation precedes expression, the findings of the study challenge the expectation of some theorists that highly active, expressive participation will be more influential in changing belief than less active participation (reading and choosing from among evidence materials). The results also provide evidence favorable to the post-test-only type of design by showing that a private questionnaire will influence subsequent responses.

---

test will inhibit belief change, for the "in-between" test *reduced* the boomerang effect. Experiment I did not provide an adequate test of the methodological hypothesis because there was not a statistically significant difference between Groups B and C; therefore, "depression" of belief change was not possible.

SUBJECT INDEX

AUTHOR INDEX

HM...
Bele...
The probl...   060101 000

0 1135 0042490 5

Emerson College Library